SWITZERLAND

Franziska Pfenniger/Switzerland Tourism

| **Executive Editorial Director** | David Brabis |
| **Chief Editor** | Cynthia Clayton Ochterbeck |

THE GREEN GUIDE SWITZERLAND

Editor	Gwen Cannon
Principal Writer	Evelyn Kanter
Production Coordinators	Allison Simpson, Anna Wilson
Cartography	Alain Baldet, Michele Cana, Peter Wrenn
Photo Editor	Lydia Strong, Cecile Koroleff
Proofreader	Gaven Watkins
Layout & Design	Tim Schulz
Cover Design	Ute Weber

Contact Us:

The Green Guide
Michelin Maps and Guides
One Parkway South
Greenville, SC 29615
USA
☎ 1-800-423-0485
www.michelintravel.com
michelin.guides@us.michelin.com

Michelin Maps and Guides
Hannay House
39 Clarendon Road
Watford, Herts WD17 1JA
UK
☎ (01923) 205 240
www.ViaMichelin.com
travelpubsales@uk.michelin.com

Special Sales:

For information regarding bulk sales,
customized editions and premium sales,
please contact our Customer Service
Departments:
USA   1-800-423-0485
UK   (01923) 205 240
Canada 1-800-361-8236

Note to the reader

While every effort is made to ensure that all information printed in this guide is correct and up-to-date, Michelin Maps and Guides (Michelin Tyre PLC; Michelin North America, Inc.) accepts no liability for any direct, indirect or consequential losses howsoever caused so far as such can be excluded by law.

One Team …
A Commitment to Quality

There's just one reason our team is dedicated to producing quality travel publications—you, our reader. We want you to get the maximum benefit from your trip—and from your money. In today's multiple-choice world of travel, the options are many, perhaps overwhelming.

In our guidebooks, we try to minimize the guesswork involved with travel. We scout out the attractions, prioritize them with star ratings, and describe what you'll discover when you visit them.

To help you orient yourself, we provide colorful and detailed, but easy-to-follow maps. Floor plans of some of the cathedrals and museums help you plan your tour.

Throughout the guides, we offer practical information, touring tips and suggestions for finding the best views, good places for a break and the most interesting shops.

Lodging and dining are always a big part of travel, so we compile a selection of hotels and restaurants that we think convey the feel of the destination, and organize them by geographic area and price. We also highlight shopping, recreational and entertainment venues, especially the popular spots.

If you're short on time, driving tours are included so you can hit the highlights and quickly absorb the best of the region.

For those who love to experience a destination on foot, we add walking tours, often with a map. And we list other companies who offer boat, bus or guided walking tours of the area, some with culinary, historical or other themes.

In short, we test and retest, check and recheck to make sure that our guidebooks are truly just that: a personalized guide to help you make the most of your visit. After all, we want you to enjoy traveling as much as we do.

The Michelin Green Guide Team

PLANNING YOUR TRIP

INTRODUCTION TO SWITZERLAND

SYMBOLS

- 😊 **Tips to help improve your experience**
- 😐 **Details to consider**
- ⊚ **Entry Fees**
- 🚶 **Walking tours**
- 🔑 **Closed to the public**
- 🕐 **Hours of operation**
- 🕐 **Periods of closure**

CONTENTS

DISCOVERING SWITZERLAND

HOW TO USE THIS GUIDE

Orientation

To help you grasp the "lay of the land" quickly and easily, so you'll feel confident and comfortable finding your way around the region, we offer the following tools in this guide:

- Detailed table of contents for an overview of what you'll find in the guide, and how it is organized.
- Map of Switzerland at the front to the guide, with the principal sights highlighted for easy reference.
- Detailed maps for major cities and villages, including driving tour maps and larger-scale maps for walking tours.
- Map of Switzerland Regional Driving Tours, each one numbered and color coded.
- Map showing the local resorts and places to stay for each area.

Practicalities

At the front of the guide, you'll see a section called "Planning Your Trip" that contains information about planning your trip, the best time to go, different ways of getting to the region and getting around, basic facts and tips for making the most of your visit. You'll find driving and themed tours, and suggestions for outdoor fun. There's also a calendar of popular annual events for the country. Information on shopping, sightseeing, kids' activities and sports and recreational opportunities is also included.

LODGINGS

We've made a selection of hotels and arranged them within the cities, categorized by price to fit all budgets (see the Legend at the back of the guide for an explanation of the price categories). For the most part, we selected accommodations based on their unique regional quality, their Swiss feel, as it were. So, unless the individual hotel embodies local ambience, it's rare that we include chain properties, which typically have their own imprint. If you want a more comprehensive selection of accommodations, see the red-cover *Michelin Guide Suisse*.

RESTAURANTS

We thought you'd like to know the popular eating spots in the country. So we selected restaurants that have a unique regional flavor and local atmosphere. We're not rating the quality of the food per se. As we did with the hotels, we selected restaurants for many towns and villages, categorized by price to appeal to all wallets. If you want a more comprehensive selection of dining recommendations in the region, see the red-cover *Michelin Guide Suisse*.

Attractions

Principal Sights are arranged alphabetically. Within each Principal Sight, attractions for each town, village, or geographical area are divided into local Sights or Walking Tours, nearby Excursions to sights outside the town, or detailed Driving Tours—suggested itineraries for seeing several attractions around a major town. Contact information, admission charges and hours of operation are given for the majority of attractions. Unless otherwise noted, admission prices shown are for a single adult only. Discounts for seniors, students, teachers, etc. may be available; be sure to ask. If no admission charge is shown, entrance to the attraction is free.

If you're pressed for time, we recommend you visit the three- and two-star sights first: the stars are your guide.

STAR RATINGS

Michelin has used stars as a rating tool for more than 100 years:

★★★	Highly recommended
★★	Recommended
★	Interesting

SYMBOLS IN THE TEXT

Besides the stars, other symbols in the text indicate tourist information 🖪; wheelchair access 🕭; on-site eating facilities 🍴; camping facilities △; on-site parking 🅿; sights of interest to children 🧒; and beaches ⛱.

See the box appearing on the Contents page for other symbols used in the text. See the Maps explanation below for symbols appearing on the maps.

Throughout the guide you will find peach-coloured text boxes or sidebars containing anecdotal or background information. Green-coloured boxes contain information to help you save time or money.

Maps

All maps in this guide are oriented north, unless otherwise indicated by a directional arrow. See the map Legend at the back of the guide for an explanation of other map symbols. A complete list of the maps found in the guide appears at the back of this book.

Addresses, phone numbers, opening hours and prices published in this guide are accurate at press time. We welcome corrections and suggestions that may assist us in preparing the next edition. Please send your comments to:

Michelin Maps and Guides
Hannay House
39 Clarendon Road
Watford, Herts WD17 1JA
UK
travelpubsales@uk.michelin.com
www.michelin.co.uk

Michelin Maps and Guides
Editorial Department
P.O. Box 19001
Greenville, SC   29602-9001
USA
michelin.guides@us.michelin.com
www.michelintravel.com

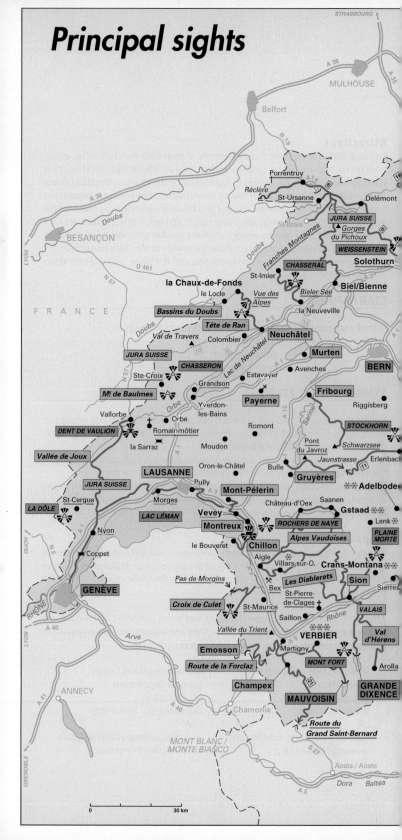

Principal sights

Driving tours

Jura Suisse and Lac Léman (Lake Geneva)
(650 km - 400 miles)

The Valais and Berner Oberland
(950 km - 590 miles)

Graubünden (700 km - 435 miles)

The Lakes and Appenzellerland
(600 km - 375 miles)

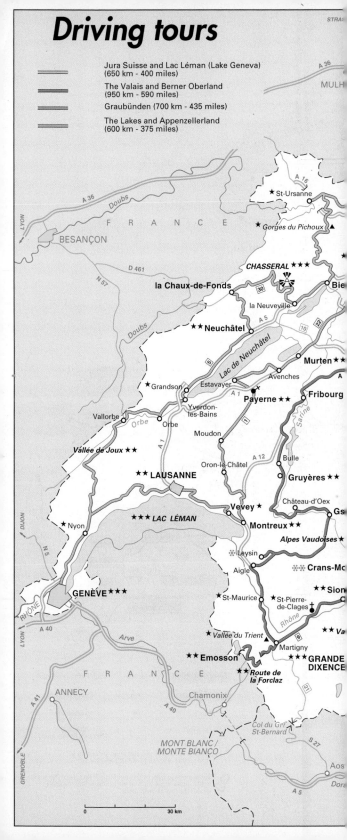

STRAS

A 36

MULH

A 16

★ St-Ursanne

★ *Gorges du Pichoux* ▲

LYON

Doubs

F R A N C E

BESANÇON

D 461

CHASSERAL ★★★

la Chaux-de-Fonds

30

Bie

N 57

la Neuveville

A 5

10

★★ **Neuchâtel**

Murten ★★

Doubs

Lac de Neuchâtel

Avenches

A

★ Grandson

Estavayer

★ **Payerne** ★★

Fribourg

Vallorbe

Orbe

Yverdon-les-Bains

Orbe

Moudon

Sarine

Vállée de Joux ★★

A 1

Oron-le-Châtel

A 12

Bulle

★★ **LAUSANNE**

Gruyères ★★

Vevey ★

Château-d'Oex

Gs

★★★ *LAC LÉMAN*

Montreux ★★

Alpes Vaudoises ★

★ Nyon

☀ Leysin

☀☀ **Crans-Mo**

Aigle

GENÈVE ★★★

★ St-Maurice

★ St-Pierre-de-Clages ♱

★★ **Sion**

RHÔNE

Rhône

LYON

A 40

Arve

★ *Vallée du Trient* ▲

★★ Va

Martigny

★★ **Emosson**

★★★ **GRANDE DIXENCE**

F R A N C E

★★ *Route de la Forclaz*

9

ANNECY

Chamonix

A 41

A 40

Col du Gra St-Bernard

S 27

GRENOBLE

MONT BLANC / MONTE BIANCO

Aos

Dor

A 5

0   30 km

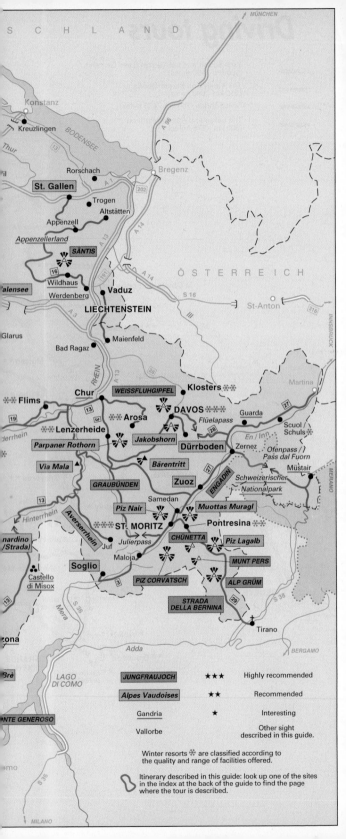

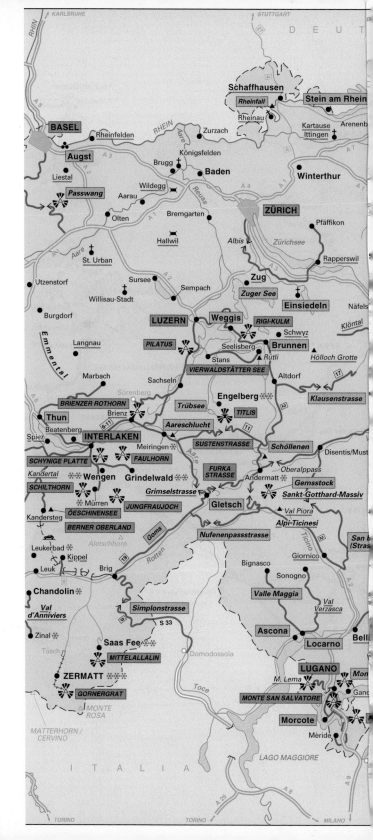

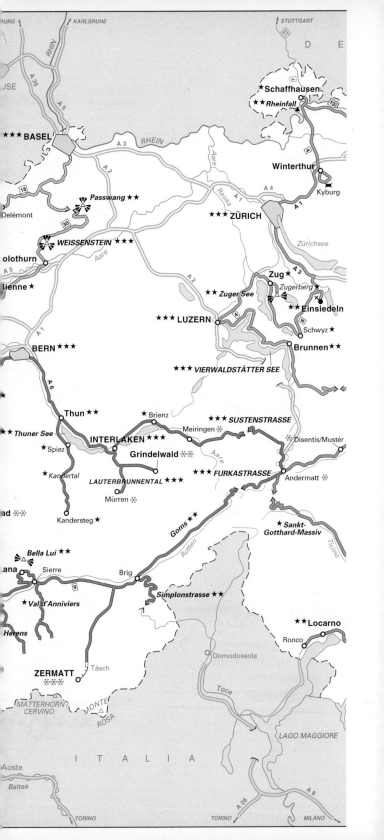

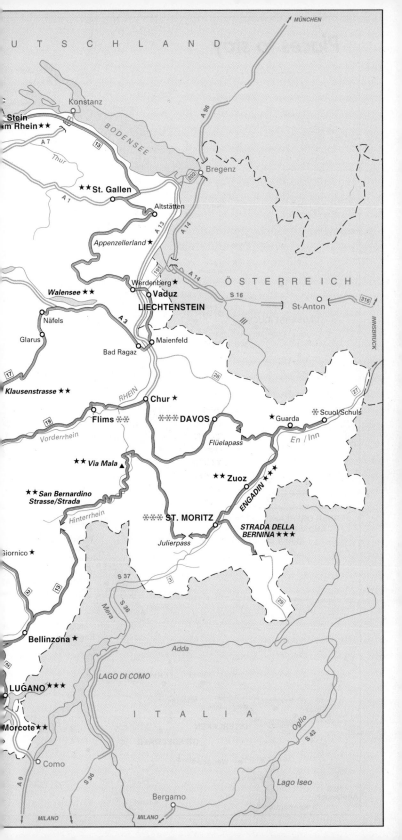

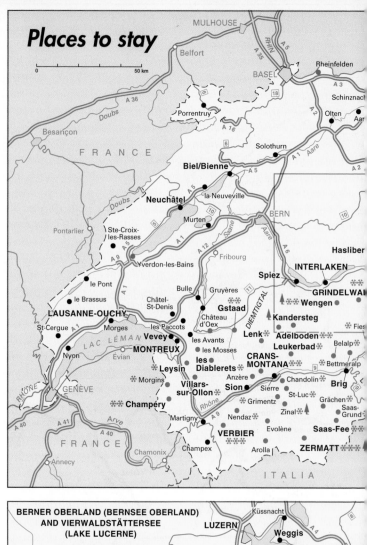

Places to stay

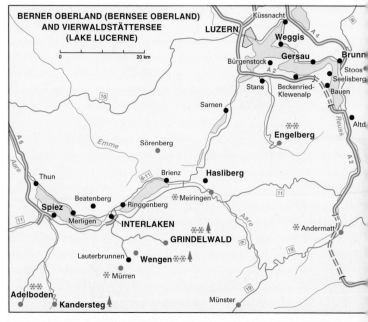

BERNER OBERLAND (BERNSEE OBERLAND)
AND VIERWALDSTÄTTERSEE
(LAKE LUCERNE)

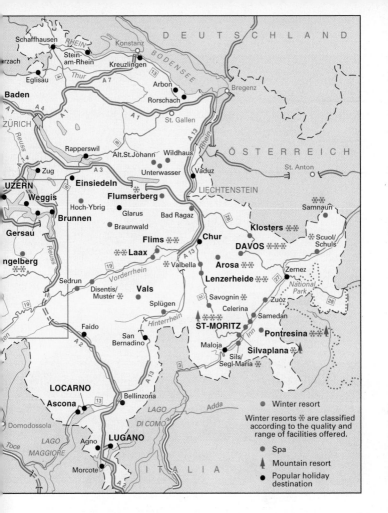

WINTER RESORTS

	Canton	Altitude
Arosa	Grisons	1742 m
Crans-Montana	Valais	1500 m
Davos	Grisons	1563 m
Gstaad	Berne	1080 m
Saas Fee	Valais	1790 m
St-Moritz	Grisons	1856 m
Wengen	Berne	1275 m
Zermatt	Valais	1620 m

*Hikers on a summer meadow near
Saas-Fee in Canton Valais*
Franziska Pfenniger/Switzerland Tourism

WHEN AND WHERE TO GO

Driving Tours

⟲ *See the Driving Tours map on pp 11–13.*

When to Go

Switzerland is remarkably beautiful any time of year. Dramatic Alpine peaks, rolling meadows and sparkling lakes change with each season, while cosmopolitan cities pulse with culture and nightlife, and quaint villages that follow a timeless, traditional culture that does not seem to change at all.

In **winter**, the snow-covered Alps are a playground for skiers and snowboarders, at world-famous resorts such as Zermatt, at the foot of the iconic Matterhorn; St. Moritz, which has hosted the winter Olympics twice, in 1928 and 1948, and celebrity-studded Gstaad to the less famous, but more challenging slopes of Titlis and the glacier plateau of Les Diablerets. Or, go dog-sledding, or try ice skating or curling. Winter is a magical time to visit Ticino, where a downhill *piste* can end at palm trees and flowering bushes in this surprisingly temperate Alpine micro-climate. Here, Italian *brio* is flavored with Swiss efficiency.

In **spring**, **summer** and **autumn**, there are hiking and biking on a network of well-marked trails and routes, including along monumental glaciers; whitewater rafting on rivers churning with snowmelt; and boating and fishing on lakes that polka-dot the countryside. And let's not forget golf; one of the highest courses in the world is in Arosa, where the 18-hole course is often shared with cows. Warmer weather is ideal, too, for a relaxing lake cruise, especially at sunset. Or, take a cable car or cog railway to the top of a mountain such as Rigi or Pilatus, and marvel at the panorama of peaks.

Festivals abound year-round, celebrating Switzerland's own culture and history, and the world's. The Montreaux Jazz Festival each July attracts the world's top musicans; while Christmas markets in numerous cities and villages focus on traditional crafts.

Any season is the right time to travel back in time to medieval castles and the historic parts of major cities such as Basel, Zurich, Lucerne and Bern, whose sandstone arcades house modern shops and boutiques. Tour the turrets of the Castle of Chillon, immortalized in a poem by Lord Byron, on Lake Geneva, and the 13C mountaintop fortress Tourbillon in Sion, surrounded by vineyards.

CLIMATE

The climate is more temperate than might be expected, with temperatures rarely higher than 86F/30C in summer, and rarely colder than 41F/-5C in winter, except high in the mountains. The warmest regions are Ticino (Lucarno and Lugano claim 298 sunny days a year), and Valais, south of Lake Geneva. Even so, capricious wind patterns can turn a bright, sunny day into a rainy or snowy one in minutes. There is no excessive heat or humidity, so the air is always crisp. Southern Switzerland has subtropical vegetation and enjoys year-round mild temperatures. Call ☎162 within Switzerland for daily weather reports.

WHAT TO PACK

As little as possible! Cleaning and laundry services are available almost everywhere, and most personal items can be replaced at reasonable cost. Porter help may be in short supply on some locations, so it is always better to travel with less than more. ☺ Be sure to take a lightweight tote bag for shopping at open-air markets.

KNOW BEFORE YOU GO

Useful Web Sites

www.myswitzerland.com
The Swiss National Tourist Office (SNTO) Web site is full of practical information on destinations, accommodations, weather, events and festivals, etc. Another section provides suggestions for specific types of vacation experiences, including family, golf, wellness spas and, of course, skiing.
There are links to each region, within which there are links to individual cities, towns and villages.

www.alpseurope.com
The Alpine Tourist Commission is a marketing organization for the five Alpine countries of Austria, France, Germany, Italy and Switzerland, with links to tour operators, airlines and special travel package offers.

www.visiteurope.com
The European Travel Commission provides useful travel information for 27 countries, plus links to rail schedules, car rental agencies, weather reports and more.

www.swissinfo.org
This Web site has comprehensive information about Swiss business, industry, education and politics. There also are links to developments in the arts, science and techology that involve Switzerland.

www.switzerland.tv
A guide to Swiss products and services, including chocolate, watches, cheese, private medical clinics and spas, plus banks and business centres. There also are links to shopping by city or category of product.

www.swisstravelsystem.ch
Comprehensive information about the various Swiss Pass options for train, bus, boat, cable car and other public transit.

Tourist Offices

Swiss National Tourist Offices (SNTO)
For information, brochures, maps and assistance in planning your trip, contact the relevant national office, or info@myswitzerland.com.

Swiss National Tourist Office Headquarters (Schweizerische Verkehrszentrale – SVZ)
Bellariastrasse 38, Postfach 695, CH-8027 Zürich, ☎ 01 288 11 11; Fax 01 288 12 05.

Canada
926 The East Mall, Etobpoke, Toronto, Ontario M9B6K1, ☎ 416 695 2090; Fax 416 695 2605.

United Kingdom
Swiss Centre, 10 Wardour St, London W1D 6QF, ☎ 0800 100 200 30 (toll free); Fax 0800 100 200 31 (toll free); info.uk@switzerland.com

United States
♦ Swiss Center, 608 Fifth Avenue, New York City, NY 10020, ☎ 011 800 100 200 30 (international toll free); 1 800 704 7795 (from within the USA) or 212 757 5914.
♦ 150 North Michigan Avenue, Chicago, IL 60601, ☎ 312 630 5840.
♦ 222 Sepulveda Boulevard, El Segundo, Los Angeles, CA 90245, ☎ 310 335 5980.

There are also SNTO locations in the following cities: Amsterdam, Brussels, Frankfurt, Madrid, Milan, Paris, Rome, Stockholm, Tokyo and Vienna.

Tourist Information Centres 🛈
Tourist Information Centres (*Verkehrsbüro; office de tourisme; ente turistico*) can be found in most large towns and

tourist resorts. Their contact details are shown after the introduction to each sight, where applicable. ⓘ on town maps.

Swiss Hotel Association **(Schweizer Hotelier-Verein)** – Monbijoustrasse 130, CH 3007 Bern, ☎ 031 370 41 11; Fax 031 370 44 44; info@swisshotels. ch; www.swisshotels.ch

Tourist Association
A total of 23 towns from several different cantons have joined to form an organisation providing information to visitors. The towns involved are Appenzell, Baden, Basel, Bellinzona, Berne, Biel, Chur, Fribourg, La Chaux-de-Fonds, Geneva, Lausanne, Lugano, Montreux, Neuchâtel, Sankt-Gallen, Schaffhausen, Sierre, Sion, Solothurn, Winterthur, Thun, Zug and Zurich. For further information, contact the **information and reservation centre** at Chur Tourismus, Grabenstrasse 5, CH-7002 Chur; ☎ 081 252 18 18; Fax 081 252 90 76.

International Visitors

SWISS EMBASSIES AND CONSULATES

United Kingdom
Swiss Embassy, 16-18 Montagu Place, London W1H 2BQ, ☎ 020 7616 6000; Fax 020 7724 7001; swissembassy@ lon.rep.admin.ch; www.swissembassy. org.uk.

Republic of Ireland
Swiss Embassy, 6 Ailesbury Road, Ballsbridge, Dublin 4, ☎01 218 63 82.

United States
Swiss Embassy, 2900 Cathedral Avenue NW, Washington DC 20008, ☎ 202 745 7900; Fax 202 387 2564; with consulates in Atlanta, Chicago, Houston, Los Angeles, New York and San Francisco.

Canada
Swiss Embassy, 5 Marlborough Avenue, Ottawa ON K1N 8E6, ☎ 613 235 1837; Fax 613 563 1394.

FOREIGN EMBASSIES AND CONSULATES IN SWITZERLAND

United Kingdom
♦ **Embassy**, Thunstrasse 50, CH-3000 Bern 15, ☎ 031 359 77 00; Fax 031 359 77 01; info@britain-in-switzerland.ch; www.britain-in-switzerland.ch;
♦ **Consulate General**, rue de Vermont 37-39, Geneva; ☎ 022 918 2400; Fax 022 918 23 22;
♦ **Vice-Consulate**, Minervastrasse 117, CH-8032 Zürich, ☎ 01 383 65 60; Fax 01 383 65 61.

Republic of Ireland
♦ **Embassy**, Kirchenfeldstrasse 68, CH-3005 Bern, ☎ 031 352 14 42; Fax 031 352 14 55; irlemb@bluewin.ch;
♦ **Consulate General**, Claridenstrasse 25, Postfach 562, 8027 Zurich; ☎ 01 289 25 15; Fax 01 289 25 50.

United States
♦ **Embassy**, Jubiläumstrasse 93, 3001 Bern, ☎ 031 357 70 11; Fax 031 357 73 44; www.usembassy.ch;
♦ **Consulate General**, 7 rue Versonnex, 1207 Geneva; ☎ 022 840 51 60; Fax 022 840 51 62;
♦ **Consulate**, Dufourstrasse 101, c/o Zurich America Center, 8008 Zürich; ☎ 01 422 25 66; Fax 01 383 98 14.

Canada
♦ **Embassy**, Kirchenfeldstrasse 88, 3000 Bern 6, ☎ 031 357 32 00; Fax 031 357 32 10; www.canada-ambassade.ch;
♦ **Consulate**, 5 avenue de l'Ariana, 1202 Geneva; ☎ 022 919 92 00; Fax 022 919 92 71.

DOCUMENTS

Visitors travelling to Switzerland must possess a valid national passport. Citizens of European Union countries need only a national identity card; British visitors need a valid passport. In case of loss or theft, report to the embassy or consulate and the local police. Entry visas are required by Australian, New Zealand, Canadian and US citizens if the intended stay exceeds 90 days. The nearest Swiss consulate or embassy will help if there is any doubt. US citizens may find the booklet **Your Trip Abroad** useful for information on visa requirements, customs regulations, medical care, etc. when travelling in Europe. Contact the Superintendent of Documents, PO Box 371954, Pittsburgh, PA 15250-7954, ☎ (202) 512 1800; Fax (202) 512 2104; www.access.gpo.gov

CUSTOMS

There are no restrictions concerning the import, export and exchange of Swiss francs. As Switzerland is not a member of the European Union, stricter conditions apply to the import and export of goods; contact the Swiss Tourist Office for further information. Tourists under the age of 17 are not allowed to import or export alcohol or tobacco.

Pets brought into Switzerland require a veterinary certificate stating that the animal has been vaccinated against rabies; they will be placed in quarantine, except for puppies and kittens aged under five months which simply require a health certificate issued by a veterinary surgeon. For further information, contact the Bundesamt für Veterinärwesen (BVET), Schwarzenburgstrasse 161, CH-3097 Liebefeld-Bern, ☎ 031 323 85 02.

HEALTH

Visitors are strongly advised to have medical or travel insurance to cover personal accident and sickness. There is no state health service in Switzerland and patients are required to pay for all medical treatment (keep any receipts). Special winter sports policies are also available for avalanche rescue.

Accessibility

Many of the sights described in ths guide are accessible to those with special needs. Sights marked with the symbol ♿ offer wheelchair access. However, it is advisable to check beforehand by telephone.

More than 150 Swiss railway stations have wheelchair ramps; in smaller locales, station employees may lift wheelchair passengers on and off the train by hand. Some cog railways and mountain cable cars also are wheelchair accessible. It is best to check with the local tourist office for specific information.

Larger lake steamers are wheelchair-accessible, and it is best to avoid purchasing a first-class ticket, which requires climbing steep stairs.

An international Wheelchair Badge on the dashboard of your vehicle is required to park in designated spots. Large modern and renovated hotels and vacation apartments usually have special handicap facilities such as wide-door bathrooms and roll-in showers; inns and *pensions* may have only cramped elevators.

Larger cities and towns have wheelchair-accessible public restrooms, most often unisex facilities, marked with the ♿ wheelchair symbol.

Mobility International Switzerland (MIS) publishes a guide for wheelchair users. Contact them at Froburgstrasse 4, CH-4600 Olten, ☎ 62 206 88 35 or www.mis.ch.

Federazione Ticinese Integrazione Andicap (FTIA) publishes accessibility guides for Lugano and Locarno and their surrounding areas. Contact them at Via Benda 28, ch 6512 Guibiasco, ☎ 91 850 90 90, www.ftia.ch.

GETTING THERE

By Air

Its location at the heart of Europe makes Switzerland a hub for international air traffic. The world's top airlines operate scheduled flights to Basel, Geneva and Zurich, plus such budget airlines as EasyJet (www.easyjet.com). There also is domestic service to Lugano.

CONNECTIONS WITH AIRPORTS

The Geneva and Zurich airports have rail stations with regular services to all major cities and to their own city centers (Geneva, 6min, Zurich, between 10min and 15min). Shuttle buses also operate from Basel, Berne and Lugano airports (between 15min and 20min). And, of course, there are taxis available at each airport.

FLY-RAIL LUGGAGE SERVICE

This service allows visitors flying into Zurich, Basel or Geneva to have their luggage transported directly to the railway station nearest to their destination. It also operates for outgoing flights from 50 railway stations in Switzerland to the passenger's final destination. Contact the Swiss Federal Railways at ☎ 0900 300 300 (from within Switzerland); www.rail.ch

By Train

Eurostar (☎ 08705 186 186; www.eurostar.com) operates high-speed passenger trains to Paris; from there, **TGV** high-speed trains run to a number of cities in Switzerland, including Geneva, Lausanne (with some trains calling at Montreux, Aigle, Bex, Martigny, Sion, Sierre, Visp and Brigue) and Zurich (with stops at Neuchâtel and Berne). All trains leave from the Gare de Lyon, with the exception of the train to Basel which operates from the Gare de l'Est. Direct TGV trains also run from to Neuchâtel and Berne from Dijon. Inside the country, the extensive Swiss railway system operates a frequent and efficient service.

For tickets, prices and discounts apply to:

◆ **Rail Europe**, 178 Piccadilly, London W1; ☎ 08708 08 371 371; www.raileurope.co.uk
◆ **Swiss Federal Railways** (SBB/CFF), ☎ 0900 300 300 (within Switzerland); www.rail.ch.

By Car

MAIN ROUTES

Visitors travelling by road from one of the Channel ports can choose one of two main routes: via **Calais** and the French motorway system through **France** (A 26 to Troyes, A 5 to Langres, A 31 to Beaune, A 6 to Mâcon and A 40 to Geneva – about 800km/500mi); or via **Ostende** and then through **Belgium, Luxembourg, France** and **Germany** (along E 40 to Liège, E 25 to Luxembourg, A 31 to just north of Metz, and the A 4 to Strasbourg, where you cross the Rhine and the German border to pick up the E 35 (A 5) to Basel – about 700km/450mi).

PLANNING YOUR ROUTE

Michelin offers a computerised route-finding system integrating information about roads, tourist sights, hotels and restaurants available on the **Internet** at www.ViaMichelin.com. For route planning, specify your point of departure and destination, stipulate your preference for motorways or local roads and it will do the rest. The Web site also gives information on campsites and interesting sights en route.

GETTING AROUND

By Train

The Swiss rail network covers about 4 989km/3 100mi, offering a practical and comfortable alternative to driving. Swiss trains are famous worldwide for running on time! All major cities and large towns have excellent connections and regular services. The variety of trains includes fast intercity trains (IC); regular direct trains; regional trains serving destinations normally considered to be off the beaten track; rack railways in the mountains; scenic railways and steam railways; not forgetting funicular railways, cable-cars, chairlifts and underground trains. Motorail services also operate between Kandersteg and Goppenstein (Lötschberg), Brig and Iselle di Trasquera in Italy (Simplon), Thusis and Samedan (Albula), Oberwald and Realp (Furka) and Andermatt and Sedrun (Oberalp).

Contact the Swiss Federal Railways at ☎ 0900 300 300 (within Switzerland) or go on-line to www.rail.ch

RAIL PASSES

The **Swiss Travel System** (STS) offers several different 1st and 2nd class passes. These can be purchased from Swiss National Tourist Offices, local travel agents or railway stations upon presenting a passport or identity card. The **Swiss Pass** allows visitors unlimited travel on a network of 16 000km/12 000mi of trains, boats, postal buses, tramways and urban bus services in 35 Swiss cities and towns. Discounts are also offered on most mountain and panoramic railways and a 15% reduction is available for two people or more. The Swiss pass is valid for 4, 8, 15, 22 days or one month. The **Swiss Flexipass** allows three days unlimited travel in a one month period, with a 15% discount for two people or more.

The **Swiss Youth Pass** gives young people under 26 years of age a 25% discount; children up to the age of 16 traveling with at least one parent with a valid STS ticket travel free of charge on the entire network.

The **Swiss Card** entitles visitors to unlimited train travel around one area, plus a 50% discount on trains, postal buses and mountain railways. **SaverPass** provides similar discounts for two people traveling together. Passes are valid for one month and can be purchased at airports and some border stations.

The **Swiss Transfer Ticket** offers transfers from any Swiss airport to any destination and back and is valid for one month, and a 50% discount on all further train, bus or boat travel in between.

From 2006 onwards, STS passes can be used as a **Swiss Museum Pass**, providing free entry to more than 400 museums and exhibits. Also, the passes now provide for a 50% discount on all mountain-top rides.

POSTAL BUSES

These famous postal buses (postauto), easily identifiable by their bright yellow colour and distinctive three-note horn, are a common feature on country roads. They usually leave from train stations or post offices and for many visitors provide a leisurely, inexpensive and scenic way to visit remote villages. **Swiss PostBus Lt. Tours & Travel,** Aareckstrasse 6, CH-3800 Interlaken, tel. 033 828 88 77, www.postbus.ch

By Boat

It is possible to explore the main Swiss lakes and parts of some major rivers on the large white boats that can be seen cruising up and down. A few of these boats still feature the original paddle wheels. *See Lake Boats in What to Do and See.*

By Public Transportation

The Swiss public transport system is second to none, especially in large cities where buses, trams and trolleycars operate a highly efficient service. Automatic **ticket machines** are available at each stop (exact change often required); daily or weekly passes can be bought in many towns. **Swiss Pass** holders are entitled to free, unlimited travel (& *see Discovering Switzerland*).

Driving in Switzerland

DOCUMENTS

A valid driving licence or international driving permit, car registration papers (log-book) and a nationality licence plate are required. An International Insurance Certificate (Green Card) is the most effective proof of insurance coverage, recognised by all Swiss police and other officials.

ROAD TAX

Instead of tolls, an annual road tax called a **vignette** is levied on cars and motorbikes using Swiss motorways. The *vignette* is valid from 1 December until 31 January of the following year; it must be displayed on the windscreen. The *vignette* costs 40CHF (trailers cost an additional 40CHF) and is available at border posts, post offices, petrol stations, garages and cantonal car registration offices. To avoid delays at the border, purchase the *vignette* in advance from the Swiss National Tourist Office.

ROAD REGULATIONS

Laws are strictly enforced and police are authorised to collect on-the-spot fines. Drivers must be at least 18 years old. **Seat belts** are compulsory; children under 12 are required to sit in the back. **Dipped headlights** are compulsory in tunnels. A red **warning triangle** or **hazard warning lights** are obligatory in case of a breakdown.

Use of the **horn** is discouraged except on mountain roads with blind turns. **Studded tires** are forbidden on motorways; on other roads, they are permitted only between 1 November and 30 April. "**STOP**" **signs** at crossings should be strictly obeyed. **Tram and light railway systems** are modern and run at high speed. Take great care at unguarded crossings, where the warning is generally three red blinking lights, arranged in a triangle and connected with a bell. **Pedestrians** getting on or off buses and trams have priority over motorists. It is strictly prohibited to overtake on the right, even on motorways. On **mountain roads**, if you want to pass another vehicle and meet an on-coming vehicle, it is the responsibility of the car coming down to pull over and if necessary reverse back to a suitable stopping place. **Post buses** – easy to recognised by their yellow colour and distinctive three-note horn (the first notes of Rossini's overture to *William Tell*) – always have priority. **Trailers** are restricted to 2.50m/8.20ft in width and 12m/39.36ft in length. Owners of larger trailers registered outside the country can apply to the Customs Office for authorisation to drive them in the country (20CHF tax). The speed limit for cars towing trailers is 80kph/50mph (up to 1t) or 60kph/37mph (over 1t) on all roads, including motorways. The Klausen, Nufenen, Schelten and Weissenstein Passes are closed to these cars; access is permitted to Bürgenstock and Diemtigtal.

SPEED LIMITS

Maximum speed on motorways is 120kph/75mph; on other roads 80kph/50mph and in towns and villages 50kph/31mph. Police radar speed trap detectors are forbiidden. At some traffic lights, signs ask motorists to reduce pollution by turning off their engine.

PARKING

There is a charge for most city-centre parking; some areas (marked by a blue sign) permit parking up to 1hr 30min. Visitors should buy a **parking disc** from the local police station or tourist office.

ROAD SIGNS

Motorways are indicated by signs in white on a green background. There are priority roads, numbered and marked by arrows in white on a blue ground. Secondary roads are marked and numbered in black on a white ground. These green signs are not to be mistaken for those used for indicating diversions, known as *itinéraires bis*.

CAR RENTAL

There are car rental agencies at airports, railway stations and downtown locations in most larger cities. Except at airports, rental agencies are closed Sundays; most non-airport locations close before 6pm weekdays and Saturdays. Smaller vehicles have manual transmissions; automatics require advance reservations. Drivers must be over 21 years of age (SIXT-Eurorent will rent mini-cars to drivers 18 to 21); drivers must be at least 25 for some luxury vehicles and large SUVs. Avis does not charge for an additional driver. Fly-drive packages are generally less expensive than renting separately. For longer stays, 17 days to six months, Renault EuroDrive offers a short-term lease that can be less costly than renting. Contact ☎ 1-800-221-1052 (in USA), www.renaultusa.com.

☺ Car Rentals ☺	
Avis	www.avis.ch
Kemwel	www.kemwel.com
AutoEurope	www.autoeurope.com
SIXT-Eurorent	www.esixt.com

PETROL

Most petrol stations are closed at night, even on motorways; self-service petrol pumps remain open (10CHF or 20CHF notes). Four-star and unleaded petrol are cheaper than the European average, whereas diesel is more expensive. Unleaded petrol is widely available.

EMERGENCIES

Emergency telephones are available on motorways, larger roads and in the mountains; emergency calls can also be made from any telephone 24hr a day by dialling ☎ 140. Automobile associations include the **Touring Club of Switzerland** (TCS), 4 chemin de Blandonnet, 1214 Vernier, ☎ 022 417 27 27; www.tcs.ch; and the **Swiss Automobile Club** (ACS) Wasserwerkgasse 39, CH-3000 Bern 13, ☎ 031 328 31 11; www.acs.ch.

ROUTE PLANNING

The Michelin map 729 covers all of Switzerland, including a list of towns and enlarged maps of the main cities. More detailed orange maps covering the North (551), South-West (552) and South-East (553) indicate very narrow roads (single track, where overtaking is difficult or impossible), gradients, difficult or dangerous roads, tunnels and the altitudes of passes.
The itineraries described in this guide often follow local roads which may intimidate drivers unfamiliar with mountain driving. All of these roads are accessible, at least in summer. The Michelin maps mentioned above highlight **snowbound roads** (with their opening and closing dates) as well as the location of emergency telephones.

Switzerland's Longest Road Tunnels
Sankt Gotthard (Uri, Ticino): 16.3km/10.2mi (1980)
Seelisberg (Nidwalden, Uri): 9.3km/5.8mi (1981)
San Bernardino: 6.6km/4mi (1967)
Gr Sankt Bernhard (Graubünden): 5.9km/3.6mi (1964)
Belchen (Solothurn, Berne): 3.2km/1.9mi
Landwasser (Graubünden): 2.8km/1.7mi
Isla Bella (Ticino): 2.4km/1.4mi
Binn (Valais): 1.9km/1.1mi
Grancia (Ticino): 1.7km/1mi

WHERE TO STAY AND EAT

Hotels and Restaurants are described-within the Address Books in *Discovering Switzerland*. See the Legend on the cover flap for coin ranges.

Where to Stay

See map of Places to Stay pp 14-15.

FINDING A HOTEL

For an exhaustive list of hotels consult the *Michelin Guide Switzerland*. The **Swiss Guide to Hotels** (Guide Suisse des Hôtels), published by the Swiss National Board of Hotel Owners, classifies hotels by region or canton and is available from Schweizer Hotelier-Verein Hotel-Boutique, Monbijoustrasse 130 Postfach CH-3001 Bern; www.swisshotels.ch.

E&G SWISS BUDGET HOTELS

These simple, convivial establishments offer dormitory accommodations, as well as rooms with washbasin, shower or bath, with breakfast included in the price. Make reservations from abroad directly to Case postale 160, 1884 Villars; ☎ 0848 805 508; Fax 024 495 75 14; www.rooms.ch; info@rooms.ch

VELOTELS, APARTMENTS, BED AND BREAKFAST

Velohotlels, distinguishable by their sign, cater specifically to cyclists. Contact ☎ 01 680 22 23; Fax 01 780 65 64 (*see also Outdoor Fun*). The publication **Vacances à la Campagne** lists furnished flats, bed and breakfasts, lodgings with full- or half-board, communal accommodation, mainly for German-speaking Switzerland; it is available from **Caisse Suisse de Voyage Reka**, Neuengasse 15, 3001 Bern, ☎ 031 329 66 33; Fax 031 329 66 01; www.reka.ch. Charming bed and breakfast accommodations throughout Switzerland can be recognised by

signs along the road (*B&B; Zimmer Frei; Chambre à Louer; Affitasi Camere*).

STAYING ON A FARM

Bauernhof Ferien (Holiday Farms) provides information on stays at over 250 farms. Participating farms must meet criteria, including quality of rooms and a range of animals; some offer extra facilities such as horse riding. Contact Swiss Holiday Farms, Reka, Neuengasse 15, 3000 Bern, ☎ 071 695 23 72 ; www.holiday-farms.ch.

SWISS FAMILY EXPERIMENT

This organisation was established to provide accommodations for visitors aged 18 to 40. Guest rooms are in Swiss homes; average stay is one to three weeks. Apply to The Experiment in International Living, Dufourstrasse 32, 8702 Zollikon, ☎ 01 262 47 77; www.experiment.org.

YOUTH HOSTELS

Switzerland has 67 youth hostels, open to visitors of all ages who belong to a youth hostel association. Hostels are popular with families, especially during school holidays. To join, contact the **Youth Hostels Association**, Trevelyan House, Dimple Road, Matlock, Derbyshire DE4 3YH, U.K. ☎ 0870 770 8868 or 01629 592 600; Fax 01629 592 702; www.yha.org.uk; or **Hostelling International-American Youth Hostels**, 8401 Colesville Road, Suite 600, Silver Spring, MD, ☎ (301) 495-1240; Fax (301) 495-6697; www.hiayh.org. A full list of Swiss youth hostels is available at www.youth-hostel.ch.

CAMPING AND CARAVANNING

Camping is only permitted on authorised sites. Maps and lists of sites with prices and facilities are published by the **Swiss Camping and**

Caravanning Federation (Schweizer Camping und Caravaning Verband) and the Swiss Touring Club (CP 820, CH-1214-Vernier, ☎ 022 417 25 20).

MOUNTAIN HUTS

The **Swiss Alpine Club** (Club Alpin Suisse) manages numerous mountain huts. Contact SNTO or the Swiss Alpine Club (Schweizer Alpenclub – SAC), Monbijoustrasse 61, CH-3000 Bern 23, ☎ 031 370 18 18; Fax 031 370 18 00; www.sac-cas.ch. SAC members have priority over other applicants.

Where to Eat

Address Books in the sight descriptions have dining suggestions and their prices (*see the Legend on the cover flap for coin ranges*). An extensive list is in the *Michelin Guide Switzerland*. For reasonably priced meals, look for the **Bib Gourmand symbol** 🍴.
Also, **station cafés** (buffets de gare), offer adequate and budget-priced meals in attractive or unusual settings. Some **restaurants** levy a cover charge, which may include bread (*pain et couvert*). At lunch, the *plat du jour*, or dish of the day, usually represents good value. Washed down with a glass of wine followed by coffee, this meal is both popular and affordable.

REGIONAL SPECIALITIES

Be sure to try **perch fillet** caught in Lake Geneva, eaten on the terrace of a charming lakeside restaurant with a glass of Fendant or Perlan; a cheese *fondue* with Gruyère or Vacherin or a combination of two cheeses, with a dry white wine; a tasty *raclette*, cheese melted in a wood oven or on a special grill, and served with potatoes; or *tripe à la neuchâteloise* with an Œil de Perdrix rosé. Meat specialities include **game** from the Valais, with a strong-bodied Cornalin wine; dried and smoked **beef** from the Grisons enhanced by a velvety Pinot Noir; or Zurich-style **veal slices** (geschnetzeltes Kalbfleisch) with a Pinot Noir. Other specialities worth sampling include the Bernese dish of **assorted cold meats**; spicy meat balls (*polpettone*) from the Ticino region, with a full-bodied Merlot; *papet vaudois*, a popular winter dish of sausages with cabbage, leeks and potatoes; *Rösti* (delicious diced potatoes, fried then baked); and traditional **veal sausage**, a nationwide speciality.
Desserts favor cream pastries, popular throughout Switzerland, as are the mouth-watering chocolates for which the country is world famous.

DRINKS

Wine - Switzerland produces some 200 million bottles of wine a year; nearly all of it consumed within the country. Popular grape varieties are:

- 🍷 **Whites**: Fendant (Valais), Perlan (Geneva), Chasselas (Neuchâtel, Vaud) and Johannisberg (Valais).

- 🍷 **Reds**: Gamay (Geneva), Pinot Noir (Grisons, Neuchâtel), Dôle (Pinot Noir and Gamay; blend, Valais).

- 🍷 **Rosé**: Oeil de Perdrix (Neuchâtel), Merlot Rosato (Ticino).

Most often, wines are served in two- to five-decilitre carafes. In German-speaking Switzerland, the **weinstub** (wine bar) offers a friendly, casual and pleasant setting for sampling the best wines by the glass.

Beer – Draught and bottled beer (Adler, Cardinal, Egger, Eichhof, Feldschlösschen etc) are popular. In German-speaking areas, the **bierstub** is similar in atmosphere to a *weinstub*.

Mineral water – Most Swiss order bottled water in restaurants, either still or sparkling mineral water. Swiss brands are Henniez and Passuger.

Coffee – This is often served with a small pot of cream (*Kaffeesahne*). In the afternoon, head for a Swiss café (tea room), usually offering an impressive choice of cakes and pastries (*kuchen*).

WHAT TO DO AND SEE

Outdoor Fun

HIKING AND WALKING

Switzerland's network of public footpaths is one of the world's longest with 68 000km/42 500mi of marked paths. Signs give the length and duration to various stops on the walk; the same markings are used throughout the country. Some footpaths are suitable for children and for wheelchairs. The most attractive of these include the walk around the Tomlishorn on Mount Pilatus, the "cheese circuit" (Käserstatt) on the Halisberg, and the panoramic walk around Aletsch Glacier. Further suggestions can be found at www.seilbahnen.org.

Trail Markings

Signposts with **black on a yellow background** and a yellow lozenge indicate footpaths suitable for children and inexperienced walkers. Mountain hikes for experienced walkers in good physical condition are marked by **yellow signs with a white arrow and red line** and a red lozenge. Difficult footpaths across glaciers, scree or snowfields, which require experience in rock-climbing, are indicated by **blue signs with a white arrow and a thin blue line**. Tricky sections are specifically marked; safety rails and ropes are provided along these sections. Signs with **white text on a brown background** highlight cultural sights of interest.

The Swiss Path

Built to celebrate the 700th anniversary of the Swiss Confederation in 1991, this 35km/25mi trail edges the fjord-like Lake Uri, the southernmost end of Lake Lucerne. Marble markers bearing the coats of arms of each canton and other information mark different sections of the route, with boat, bus or train connections at each destination. Additional information at: www.weg-der-schweiz.ch.

Information

The **Swiss National Hiking Association** publishes maps and guides, many of which can be bought at bookshops in the country. Or, contact the Swiss National Hiking Association (ASTP), Im Hirshalm 49, 4125 Riehen, ☎ 061 601 15 35. A selection of walks is listed at www.myswitzerland.com.

CYCLING

Swiss Federal Railways (SBB/CFF) and most private railway companies accept bicycles as **accompanied baggage**. Bicycles can be rented in over 100 railway stations and returned to a different station. The **train + bike** formula includes transport, bicycle hire, and civil liability insurance in case of an accident. Contact the Rail Service ☎ 0900 300; www.rail.ch.

Cycle Routes and Paths

There are nine marked cycle routes (3 300km/2 062mi) through magnificent scenery. These routes always start near a railway station and are clearly marked with a symbol of a bike, distances, destinations and altitude differentials. One of the most

Lucia Degonda / Switzerland Tourism

Bikers in the Lake Geneva Alps

challenging is the "Alpine Panorama" (480km/300mi); it crosses a dozen mountain passes and finishes at the Klausenpass (alt 1 948m/6 390ft). Switzerland also has over 3,000km/ 1,875mi of cycle paths. **La Suisse à vélo** publishes detailed guides and a list of hotels specifically recommended for cyclists, with covered bike shelters and repair kits. Consult: www. suisse-a-velo.ch.

MOUNTAINEERING

There are **climbing routes** throughout Switzerland. The largest is the Via Ferrata Tälli in the Bernese Oberland, open to all experience levels, including beginners: the route has 78m/256ft of ladders and 550 steel pitons embedded into the wall of the imposing Gadmerflue, at the Susten Pass. In Liechtenstein, the steep walls of the Eggstöcke, above Braunwald, are also suitable for serious climbing enthusiasts. The www.myswitzerland. com Web site lists suggested climbs. Most major resorts have their own **climbing school** plus expeditions with trained guides and instructors.

BEACHES

There are many fine lakeside beaches. Some of the most attractive are at Lenzerheide on the Heidsee; on Lake Cauma, whose waters are heated by underground streams running through the forest at Flims; and Estavayer-le-Lac, the country's largest natural sandy beach..

Sailing, windsurfing and water-skiing – Most larger lakes have their own sailing school. Visit www.myswitzerland.com for further information.

WATER SPORTS

Switzerland's wild Alpine rivers provide some of the best stretches of water for white-water **rafting.** Contact Swissraft ☎ 081 911 5250, www. swissraft.ch.
The Rotsee near Lucerne is a particular favourite for **rowing. Canoeing and kayaking** are available on many lakes and rivers. **Water parks** are extremely popular with their wave machines, huge water slides and different types of swimming pools. Two of the largest are the Säntispark at Abwill, near Sankt Gallen, and the Alpamare at Pfäffikon, near Zurich.

FISHING

Switzerland's 32 000km/20 000mi of rivers and 135 000ha/333 585 acres of lakes are a paradise for anglers. For further information on regulations and licences, apply to local Tourist Information Centres or **Schweizerischer Fischerei-Verband** (Swiss Fishing

The Swiss Army Knife

The genuine Swiss penknife, an essential part of any Boy Scout's kit, is recognisable by its red colour, white cross and rounded corners. This gem of the miniature cutlery industry was originally created to equip the Swiss army more than a century ago. Within a short time, the **"Schweizer Militärmesser"**, or Swiss Army Knife, became world famous and was adopted by all outdoor and do-it-yourself enthusiasts worldwide.

Today there are over 400 different models, ranging from the most basic to extremely sophisticated. There's even a model specifically for left-handed users! Newest designs are equipped with an altimeter and barometer, even a computer USB memory card, and available in a range of fashionable colors. It deserves its nickname as the world's smallest toolbox, one which can cut, slice, file, carve, sharpen, remove bottle tops, tighten, loosen, measure and more.

The two leading manufacturers are Wenger, in Delémont, in the Swiss Jura, and Victorinox, whose factories are in Schwyz.

Federation), Seilestrasse 27, Postfach 8218, CH-3001 Bern, ☎ 031 381 32 52, www.sfv-fsp.ch.

SPAS

Switzerland has a wealth of thermal spas fed by natural hot springs, offering swimming pools, jacuzzis and saunas. Spas are open to visitors of all ages and are particularly suitable for families. The baths at Saillon and Leukerbad, in the Valais mountains, are popular in summer; those at Vals were designed by the renowned contemporary architect Peter Zumthor. For further information, contact Schweizer Heilbäder, Avenue des Bains 22, 1400 Yverdon-les-Bains, ☎ 024 420 15 21; www.heilbad.org.

HANG-GLIDING AND PARAGLIDING

Switzerland offers the perfect landscape for the exciting sports of hang-gliding and paragliding. Competitions are frequently held in Villeneuve in the Lake Geneva region. For further information, contact the Office de Tourisme, 15 Grand-Rue, 1844 Villeneuve, ☎ 021 960 22 86; www.redbull-vertigo.com.

Activities for Children 🧒

In this guide, sights of particular interest to children are indicated with a 🧒 symbol. Some attractions may offer discount fees for children.

Calendar of Events

THE NATIONAL FESTIVAL

All Switzerland commemorates the anniversary of the alliance sworn on 1 August 1291 by the representatives of Uri, Schwyz and Unterwalden, with patriotic demonstrations and fireworks displays and spectacular mountaintop bonfires. The historic sites of Lake Uri, especially the Rütli Field and the Axenstrasse, are floodlit.

JANUARY

Solothurn — Swiss Film Festival
Davos - World Economic Forum

FIRST MONDAY IN LENT

Basel — Carnival (3 days)

MARCH

Geneva — International Motor Show

Delta Gliders in the Bernese Oberland

Robert Schoenbaechler / Switzerland Tourism

FEBRUARY OR EARLY MARCH

Ticino — Travelling carnival with risotto served outdoors

FIRST WEEK IN MARCH

Fribourg — International Film Festival

MARCH OR APRIL

Basel — European Watch, Clock and Jewelry Fair

MID-APRIL

Geneva — Chocolate Festival

Zurich — Sechseläuten: a spring festival to mark the end of winter; including burning of "Böögg" (Old Man Winter)

LAST WEEKEND IN APRIL

Aarberg — Second-hand Marke

Appenzell — Landsgemeinde: open-air assembly

MID-APRIL TO MID-MAY

Morges — Tulip Festival

FIRST SUNDAY IN MAY

Glarus — Landsgemeinde

LATE APRIL TO EARLY MAY

Montreux — International "Golden Rose" Television Festival

ONE WEEK IN MAY

Berne — International Jazz Festival

LATE MAY TO EARLY JUNE

Sierre — International Comic Book Festival

ASCENSION DAY

Beromünster — Over 100 horsemen bearing banners accompany the cross with music and psalm singing on a morning ride out, returning to the church in the afternoon for the blessing ceremony.

CORPUS CHRISTI THURSDAY

Appenzell, Fribourg, Saas-Fee Lötschental: Kippel, Ferden, Wiler, Blatten — Processions with traditional local costumes.

JUNE

Basel — International Art Fair (modern and contemporary art)

LAST WEEKEND IN JUNE TO FIRST WEEKEND IN JULY

Ascona — New Orleans Jazz Festival

LATE JUNE TO EARLY SEPTEMBER

Interlaken — Open-air performances of Schiller's *William Tell* in German

JULY

Fribourg (even years) — International Jazz Festival
Lausanne — Athlétissima: International Athletics Meeting
Lugano — Jazz Festival
Montreux — International Jazz Festival
Nyon — Paléo Festival: International Open-Air Rock and Folk Music
Vevey — Festival Images (photography, cinema, multimedia)

LATE JULY TO EARLY AUGUST

Montreux, Vevey, La Tour-de-Peilz — Léman Tradition Festival: exhibition of old boats, lake cruises, regattas etc

LATE JULY TO EARLY SEPTEMBER

Gstaad/Saanen — Classical Music Festival under the auspices of Yehudi Menuhin

FIRST TWO WEEKS IN AUGUST

Geneva — Genevese festivities; floral floats and fireworks
Locarno — International Film Festival

SECOND WEEKEND IN AUGUST

Saignelégier — National horse show, fair and horse racing

SECOND TWO WEEKS IN AUGUST

Montreux — Comedy Festival

MID-AUGUST TO EARLY SEPTEMBER

Lucerne — International Music Weeks: concerts, recitals, theatrical productions

LAST WEEK IN AUGUST

Fribourg — International Folk Festival
Vevey — Street Theatre Festival

LATE AUGUST

Aarberg — Second-hand Antique Market

EARLY SEPTEMBER

Saas-Fee — Pilgrimage to the Hohen Stiege Chapel (local costumes

Zurich (Albisgütli) — Knabenschiessen (Shooting Contest): a competition for Zurich schoolchildren, ending in the election of a "Shooting King" or "Shooting Queen", a procession and a prize-giving ceremony

MID-SEPTEMBER

Lausanne — Swiss Trade Fair

LAST WEEKEND IN SEPTEMBER

Neuchâtel — Grape Harvest Festival: great procession and Battle of the Flowers

LAST SATURDAY IN SEPTEMBER

Charmey — Fête de la Désalpe

Philipp Giegel / Switzerland Tourism

Illuminated Santa Clauses in Kuessnacht at Rigi

LATE AUGUST TO LATE OCTOBER

Ascona — International Classical
Music Festival

LATE SEPTEMBER OR EARLY OCTOBER

Martigny — Cow competitions during the Valais Fair

OCTOBER

Sankt Gallen — National Show for
the Dairy and Farming Industry

FIRST WEEKEND IN OCTOBER

Lugano — Autumn Festival

SECOND WEEKEND IN OCTOBER

Charmey — Race of special moun-
tain-type hay carts

THIRD SUNDAY IN OCTOBER

Châtel-St-Denis — Bénichon (Bene-
diction or harvest) festival to mark
the end of heavy summer work;
folklore procession, traditional
Bénichon meals

FOURTH MONDAY IN NOVEMBER

Berne — Zibelemärit: traditional
onion market to mark the beginning of winter; battle of confetti

DECEMBER (DATE CHANGES)

Geneva — Feast of the Escalade:
commemoration of the defeat of
the Savoyards in 1602; historical
procession and dancing

FIRST SATURDAY IN DECEMBER

Fribourg — St Nicholas parade and
fair

DECEMBER

Basel, Berne, Zurich— Christmas
Market

Sightseeing

ALPINE TRAINS

Swiss Pre-Alps

The **Voralpen-Express** running
between Romanshorn and Lucerne
provides a link between Lake
Constance and Lake Lucerne. This
2hr 30min trip affords delightful views
of the pre-Alpine ranges and lakeside
country; www.voralpen-express.ch
The **Train du Chocolat** runs between
Montreux, on the Swiss Riviera, and
Gruyères, home of the famous cheese
and milk chocolate. The trip includes
coffee and croissants, entrance to the
château and cheese factory at Gruyères, and a visit to the Cailler-Nestlé
chocolate factory, including a tasting.
The train runs every Wednesday from
June to October; www.mob.ch.
The **GoldenPass Line** offers panoramic views between Lucerne and
Montreux via the Brünig Pass, Lake
Brienz to Interlaken, the prestigious
resort of Gstaad and Lake Geneva.
(6hr). You can stop at Interlaken
for the excursion to Jungfraujoch
(3 454m/11 329ft), on the highest railway in Europe; www.goldenpass.ch.
The **Train du Vignoble** (13km/8mi)
operates between Vevey, Chexbres
and Puidoux in the Lavaux, along
the shores of Lake Geneva, passing
through wine-growing countryside
and picturesque villages, and offering
pretty views of the lake and the Swiss
and Savoy Alps, with several stops to
visit vineyards, cellars and museums.

Switzerland's Longest Railway Tunnels
Simplon (Valais): 19.8km/12mi (1906)
Furka (Valais, Uri): 15.4km/9.5mi (1982)
Sankt Gotthard (Uri, Ticino): 15km/9.3mi (1882)
Lötschberg (Berne, Valais): 14.6km/9mi (1913)
Ricken (Sankt Gallen): 8.6km/5.4mi
Grenchenberg (Solothurn, Berne): 8.6km/5.4mi
Hauenstein (Solothurn, Basel): 8.1km/5mi

Graubünden (Grisons)

The impressive **Bernina-Express** links Chur to Sankt Moritz and the Bernina Pass (2 253m/7 390ft) in 4hr, with an onward bus connection to Tirano (Italy) and Lugano.

The **Heidi-Express** travels between Landquart and Tirano (Italy) via Davos and the Bernina Pass. This 4hr tour crosses spectacular viaducts amid magnificent scenery and vertiginous slopes. In summer, a bus runs from Tirano to Lugano.

The famous **Glacier-Express** links Zermatt and Chur to Sankt Moritz or Davos. This unforgettable 7hr 30min journey passes through the majestic Alps, with drops in altitude of 1 400m/4 592ft, crossing 291 bridges and negotiating 91 tunnels. The trip crosses the Oberalp Pass (2 033m/6 668ft) by rack railway from Andermatt; www.glacierexpress.ch

The **Engadin Star** links Landquart to Sankt Moritz. This 9hr trip passes through the new Vereinatunnel and crosses the magnificent scenery of the Engadine; www.rhb.ch

Valais

The **Saint Bernard Express** runs from Martigny to Orsières (30min) through the Vallée de la Dranse. In summer (June to late Sept), there is a bus connection to Champex-Lac, La Fouly and the Great Saint Bernard hospice (55min); www.momc.ch

The **Mont Blanc Express** runs through the green landscapes of the Trient and Vallorcine valleys, linking France and Switzerland between Mar-tigny and Le Fayet, stopping at Argentière, Chamonix and Les Houches.

The **Allalin-Express** leaves from Berne or Interlaken to Brigue; continue by bus to Saas Fee, a charming village closed to road traffic. You then have the option of taking the **Alpin-Express** (45min) to a huge glacial cave hollowed out of the landscape at an altitude of 3 500m/11 482ft.

Ticino

The **William Tell Express** links central Switzerland to the Ticino area, taking passengers by paddle boat from Lucerne to Lugano or Locarno on Lake Maggiore. The journey (6hr) then continues by train. The trip only runs from north to south from May to October.

The **Lötschberg-Centovalli Express** connects Berne to Locarno. The route (4hr) is extremely spectacular as far as the Lötschberg Tunnel, before steeply descending towards Brig and the Rhône Valley. The journey continues through the Simplon Tunnel to Domodossola in Italy; www.centovalli.ch.

STEAM TRAINS

With their nostalgic plume of smoke, these trains are a charming countryside feature. Lovingly restored by volunteers, they operate during the summer, especially weekends.

- Vaud canton: **Blonay-Chamby** ☎ 021 943 21 21, **Le Pont-Le Brassus** ☎ 021 845 55 15, **Lausanne-Échallens-Berger**, nicknamed "La Brouette" (The Wheelbarrow) ☎ 021 886 20 00, **Montreux-Caux-Naye Rocks** ☎ 021 963 65 31.

- Neuchâtel canton: **St Sulplice-Travers** ☎ 032 861 36 78.

- Bernese Mittelland: **Bern Weissenbühl-Interlaken Ost-Brienz** ☎ 031 327 28 23, **Flamatt-Laupen-Gümmenen** ☎ 031 740 62 62, **Huttwil-Ram-sei-Huttwil** ☎ 034 422 31 51, **Worblaufen-Worb Dorf/Solothurn** ☎ 031 925 55 55.

Switzerland's Main Railway Bridges
Sitterviadukt (Sankt Gallen): 97m/319ft
Wiesenviadukt (Graubünden): 92m/302ft
Solisbrücke (Graubünden): 85m/278ft
Viaduc de Grandfey (Fribourg): 82m/269ft
Reussbrücke (Uri): 77m/252ft
Meienreussbrücke (Uri): 71m/232ft
Langwiesviadukt (Graubünden): 66m/216ft
Landwasserviadukt (Graubünden): 65m/214ft

- Solothurn canton: **Solothurn-Burgdorf-Thun-Solothurn** ☎ 034 422 31 51.

- Ticino canton: **Capolago-Generoso Velta** ☎ 091 648 11 05.

BUS TOURS

The **Palm-Express** links Sankt Moritz with Lugano by post bus, crossing the Upper Engadine region before heading to Val Bregaglia and Lake Como. The **Romantic Route Express** leaves Andermatt by the Furka Pass (2 431m/7 973ft) and follows the Rhône Glacier as far as Gletsch, which can also be reached by the charming Furka steam train. The tour wends its way through pastureland and stunning Alpine scenery, passing over the Grimsel Pass (2 165m/7 101ft), through the Hasli Valley, to Meiringen and Grindelwald, at the foot of the north face of the Eiger; www.post.ch.

LAKE BOATS

The steamer is another familiar feature of the landscape. Proudly sporting a red flag with a white cross on the stern, these boats are a wonderful way to tour the Swiss lakes during summer; many offer delicious meals in luxurious dining rooms.
On Greifensee, Lake Brienz, Lake Constance, Lake Geneva, Lake Lucerne, Lake Maggiore, Lake Thun, and Lake Zurich, traditional steamboats also provide regular ferry services.
The **Swiss Boat Pass** gives unlimited 50% discount travel for one or two weeks; sold at harbour ticket offices.

MUSEUM PASS

The **Swiss Museum Pass** provides entry to 400 museums, including temporary exhibitions. The Adult Pass (111CHF allows bearers to take up to five children free of charge. Museum passes can be purchased at major tourist offices or participating museums. Contact Hornbachstrasse 50, Zurich ☎ 01 389 84 56; www.museums.ch/pass.

Books and Films

BOOKS ABOUT SWITZERLAND

- **The Early Mountaineers** by Francis Gribble
- **The Swiss Army** by John McPhee
- **Switzerland's Amazing Railways** by CJ Allen
- **Turner in the Alps** by David Hill
- **The Swiss and the British** by John Wraight
- **Switzerland, her Topographical, Historical and Literary Landmarks** by Arnold Lunn
- **Scrambles among the Alps in the Years 1860-1869** by Edward Whymper
- **The Man in the Ice** by Konrad Spindler, translated by Ewald Osers

Written or Set in Switzerland

- **The Garden Party and Other Stories; The Doll's House** by Katherine Mansfield

Children's Favourites

- **Swiss Family Robinson** by Johann David Wyss, edited by his son Johann Rudolf Wyss
- **Heidi** by Johanna Spyri

About Famous Swiss

- **François de Bonivard and his Captivity – The Prisoner of Chillon** by Byron
- **The Le Corbusier Guide** by Deborah Gans (Butterworth Architecture)

FILMED IN SWITZERLAND

- **Star Wars III: Revenge of the Sith (2005)**
- **Syriana (2005)**
- **Goldfinger (1994)**
- **GoldenEye (1995)**
- **On Her Majesty's Secret Service (1969)**
- **Heidi (1954)**
- **Frankenstein (1994)**

USEFUL WORDS & PHRASES

German/English

Bahnhof	Railway station	Münster	Important church (cathedral)
Brücke	Bridge		
Burg	Feudal castle	Ober...	High, upper
Denkmal	Monument or memorial	Rathaus	Town hall
Fähre	Ferry	Schloss	Castle, château
Fall	Waterfall, cascade	Schlucht	Gorge
Garten	Garden	Schwimmbad	Swimming pool
Gasse	Street, alley	See	Lake
Gletscher	Glacier	Spielplatz	Sports ground
Hafen	Port, harbour	Strandbad	Bathing beach
Haupt...	As a prefix: main, chief, head	Strasse	Street
		Tal	Valley
Kirche	Church	Talsperre	Dam
Kleintaxi	Small taxi	Tobel	Ravine
Kloster	Monastery, convent, abbey	Tor	Gate (of a town)
		Unter...	Under, lower
Kursaal	Casino	Verboten	Forbidden, prohibited
Markt	Market	Wald	Forest, wood
		Zeughaus	Arsenal

Vocabulary for Skiers

German	French	English
Skischule	École de ski	Ski school
Skilehrer	Moniteur de ski	Ski instructor
Abfahrt	Départ, piste	Ski run
Schi, Ski (Bergski, Talski)	Ski (amont, aval)	Top ski, bottom ski
Kanten	Carres	Ski edges
Bindung	Fixation	Ski bindings
Skistock	Bâton	Ski stick
Skistock	Bâton	Ski stick
Skiwachs	Fart	Ski wax
Schussfahrt	Descente directe	Straight run
Querfahrt	Traversée	Traversing
Schneepflug, Stemmen	Position de chasse-neige	Snow-plough position
Abrutschen	Dérapage	Side slipping
Kurvenschwung, Bogen	Virage	Curve, swing, turn
Wedeln	"Godille"	Wedling
Riesenslalom	Slalom géant	Giant slalom
Abfahrtslauf	Descente libre	Clear run
Kombination	Combiné	All-round test
Langstreckenlauf	Course de fond	Long-distance race
Sprungschanze	Tremplin de saut	Ski jumping
Skilift	Téléski, remonte-pente	Ski lift
Sessellift	Télésiège	Chairlift
Kabinenbahn	Télécabine	Cable car
Schwebebahn	Téléphérique	Cable car
Drahtseilbahn	Funiculaire	Funicular
Lawine	Avalanche	Avalanche
Schutzhütte	Refuge	Refuge
Skiwerkstatt	Atelier de réparation de skis	Ski-repair shop
Rodelbahn	Piste de luge	Sledge run
Eisbahn	Patinoire	Skating rink

BASIC INFORMATION

Business Hours

Shops are usually open Mon-Fri, 8am-6.30pm; Sat, 8am-4pm or 5pm. Banks are open Mon-Fri, 8.30am-4.30pm. Shops generally close at 4pm on Saturday afternoons. In large towns, department stores are closed on Monday mornings, but have late-night shopping until 9pm once a week.

Electricity

220 volts (AC) is the usual voltage and most power sockets are designed for three-pin round plugs. Adaptors for two pin plugs are available in most hotels.

Language

Switzerland is a multilingual country. German is spoken in the centre and east, French in the west, Italian in the south and Romansh in the southeast.
For further details see the map and tables in the Introduction.

National Holidays

These general holidays are observed throughout the country:
- 1 and 2 January
- Good Friday
- Easter Sunday and Monday
- Ascension Day
- Whit Sunday and Monday
- Swiss National Day (1 August)
- Christmas Day (25 December)
- Boxing Day (26 December)

Other holidays tend to vary from canton to canton. Thanksgiving (*Jeûne Fédéral* in French; *Buß- und Bettag* in German), not to be confused with the American holiday, is observed in all the cantons, except Geneva, on the third Sunday in September. The Geneva canton observes Thanksgiving on the second Thursday in September.

Mail

All letters to Switzerland should have the international abbreviation CH and the post code number before the name of the town, eg CH-3000 Bern. In the cities, post offices often have a café serving sandwiches and pastries, and a stationery store selling anything from paper clips to DVDs. Offices are closed on Saturdays from noon onwards. Stamps are sold at two rates: priority mailing and standard (usually arriving within three days). Airmail postcards and letters to the USA and Canada: 1.80CHF. Airmail postcards and letters to the UK (up to 20g): 1.40F. Postcards and letters within Switzerland: 0.90F. Additional information is available on-line at www.post.ch

Money

CURRENCY

The currency is the Swiss Franc (abbreviation CHF). Denominations in circulation are: 5, 10, 20 and 50 *centimes* (*rappen* in German-speaking areas) and 1, 2 and 5 francs (coins), 10, 20, 50, 100, 200, 500 and 1 000 francs (notes).

BANKS

Travellers cheques and foreign currency can be exchanged in banks and official exchange offices. Your passport is necessary as identification when cashing cheques.Commission charges vary, with hotels charging more than banks. Generally, banks are open from 8am to 4.30pm (Mon-Fri). Money also can be withdrawn from cash dispensers by using your credit or debit card.

CREDIT CARDS

Major **credit cards** (American Express, Diners Club, Eurocard/Mastercard,

Visa, EC-Maestro, EC-Cirrus, Japan Card Bank etc) are accepted in shops, hotels and restaurants, although perhaps not in the smallest villages where cash is preferred.

The **euro** is accepted by some establishments on the borders of Germany, France, Italy and Austria. Geneva and Basel in particular have been keen to accommodate the European single currency.

Taxes and Tipping

TAXES

A 7.5% VAT is included in the retail price of most goods. Foreign tourists who shop in stores with the sign "Tax Free" and whose purchases equal or exceed 500CHF can claim back the VAT payment on their purchase. Ask the store for the relevant form.

TIPPING

Tips are included on all restaurant and hotel bills, for hairdressers, and on most taxi fares, so you are not usually expected to leave an extra tip.

Telephone

Credit cards are accepted in many phone boxes. Telephone cards, called **Taxcards**, are available from post offices, railway kiosks and hotel reception desks for 10 or 20 CHF. The minimum cost of a call is 0.60CHF. Prices are 50% cheaper from 5-8am, 5-7pm, 9-11pm and at the weekend, and 25% cheaper from 11pm-6am.

For calls within Switzerland, the number is formed by a three-figure code starting with 0, given in brackets, followed by another group of five, six or seven figures. When calling within in the same telephone district do not dial the area code.

For **international calls** dial 00 plus the following country codes:
- 61 for Australia
- 44 for the UK
- 1 for Canada
- 1 for the USA
- 64 for New Zealand

Useful telephone numbers	
111:	Directory enquiries for Switzerland
117:	Police in case of an emergency
118:	Fire brigade
120:	In winter, snow reports and avalanche bulletins; in summer, tourist information provided by the Swiss National Tourist Office
140:	Car breakdown service (open 24 hours)
144:	Emergency doctor; ambulance
161:	Talking clock
162:	Weather forecast
163:	Information on snow-bound roads, traffic conditions
187:	Avalanche bulletin
191:	International numbers and information on calling abroad

If calling from outside the country, the international code for **Switzerland** is 41. Dial the international access code, followed by 41, then the area code without the first 0, followed by the correspondent's number; for example, when calling Bern from the UK, dial 00 41 31, followed by the correspondent's number.

The international dialling code for the **Principality of Liechtenstein** is 423. There is a 24-hour **English-speaking** information and helpline called Anglo-Phone: ☎ 157-5014, which costs 2.13CHF per minute. The operators speak French, German and Italian depending on the region, English in main cities and major resorts. The Swisscom Mobile network covers 99% of Switzerland; for additional information contact www.swisscom-mobile.ch.

Time

Switzerland is 1hr ahead of GMT. In summer, the country operates a daylight-saving scheme when clocks are advanced by an hour. The actual dates are announced annually but always occur over weekends in March and October.

Personalized gifts are an important part of any relationship.

Your company's
name here

Viewing Gornergrat Glacier

Jerry Dennis / APA Publications

NATURE

Switzerland consists of a lowland area (the Mittelland or Middle Country) between the mountain barriers of the Alps and the Jura, both of which arose in the Tertiary Era.

The Swiss Alps

The Alps cover three-fifths of Helvetian territory, making Switzerland the second most Alpine country in Europe after Austria. Setting aside that part of the Grisons to the east of the Hinterrhein Valley—a high valley like the Engadine, which, with its extra—continental climate, is more typical of central Europe

– the Swiss Alps, like the French ones, belong to the western Alpine group, the steepest and most contorted chain, and therefore, most affected by erosion. The culminating point of this world of lakes and glaciers is Mount Rosa (at the Dufour Peak, 4 634m/15 203ft), although the Sankt Gotthard Massif (Pizzo Rotondo: 3 192m/10 473ft), which may be called the water tower of Europe, represents the keystone of the whole structure.

A motorist crossing a pass like the Sankt Gotthard is made aware of the sharp contrast between the relatively gentle slopes of the north face and the sudden descent which occurs on the south.

In the longitudinal direction, the remarkable depression which slashes through the mountains from Martigny to Chur and is drained in opposite directions by the Rhône and the Vorderrhein, forms a great strategic and tourist highway.

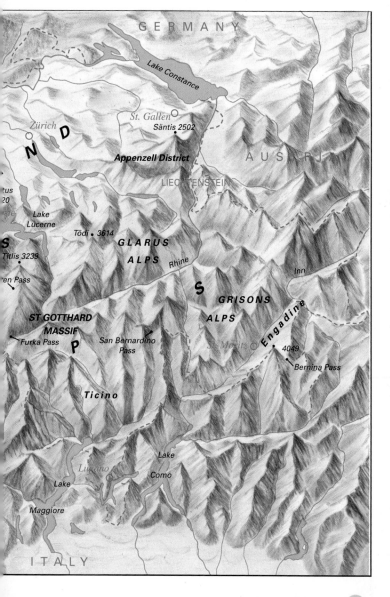

GLACIERS

The Swiss Alps comprise about 2 000km²/772sq mi of glaciers. Most typical are the valley glaciers, of which the Aletsch Glacier (🕯 see GOMS) is the most extensive in Europe (169km²/65sq mi).

Moving downstream, a **névé** (*Firn* in German), or snowfield, in which snow accumulates and is compacted into ice, is succeeded by a slowly moving **tongue of ice** (*Gletscher* in German) or glacier traversed by a close network of crevasses. Breaks or "steps" in the downward slope, which in the case of a torrent would form cascades or rapids, are marked by unstable masses of ice (*séracs*). On the Rhône Glacier, these look like a petrified cataract.

Moraines are accumulations of rocky debris brought down by the glacier. They often soil the whiteness of its tongue of ice and sometimes mask it completely as at the Steingletscher. Once they halt they form characteristic embankments, known as lateral moraines.

About 100 centuries ago the predecessors of present glaciers completely filled in the depression between the Jura and the Alps, reaching gigantic proportions. The Rhône Glacier, in what is now the Valais, was at least 1 500m/5 000ft thick. As glaciers withdrew, they created the rocky bars or **bolts** obstructing certain valley floors, as well as tributary **hanging valleys** described as **scoops** because of their U-shaped cross-sections. When the ice disappeared, the new river flow began to soften these contrasts. **Connecting gorges** then made deeper cuts through the bolts as in the Aareschlucht, or connected valleys, as in the Trient Gorges.

Alpine torrents were not only destructive. They also built up obstacles in the form of **cones of rubble**. The largest example in Switzerland is the cone of Illgraben as seen from Leuk.

ALPINE VEGETATION

Vegetation is closely bound to climatic and soil conditions as well as altitude and the degree of exposure to prevailing winds and sun. South-facing slopes, free from forests, favour settlement and cultivation, while sparsely populated north-facing slopes, with thick shade and humidity, favour the growth of thick forests, a contrast accentuated in valleys running west to east.

Above the agricultural land, which extends to about 1 500m/4 921ft, is the zone dominated by coniferous forest. At 2 200m/7 218ft this makes way for mountain pasture (*alpe*) where sturdy, short-stemmed species, bilberry and Alpine flowers grow. At 3 000m/9 842ft, the mineral zone, moss and lichen cling to the rock faces of an otherwise desolate landscape.

Forests

These are the most familiar types of conifers in the Swiss Alps:.

Norway spruce

In French: *épicéa*; in German: *Fichte*; in Italian: *abete rosso*. Found on north-facing slopes, it has a slim, pointed crest and a generally "hairy" appearance, with branches curled like a spaniel's tail. The reddish bark becomes very wrinkled as it grows old, and it bears prickly needles. The cones hang down and, when ripe, fall in one piece to the ground.

Spruce or fir

In French: *sapin*; in German: *Tanne*; in Italian: *abete bianco*. The tree has a broad head, flat on the top, like a stork's nest, in older specimens. The bark covers various shades of grey. Cones stand up like candles and, when ripe, disintegrate on the branch, dropping their scales. The needles are soft and grow in rows like the teeth of a comb. They have a double white line on their inside surface.

Larch

In French: *mélèze*; in German: *Lärche*; in Italian: *larice*. This is the only conifer in the Swiss Alps that sheds its needles in winter. The tree is found on sunny slopes in the high mountains, especially in the Valais and the Grisons. Cones are very small. The light shade of the thin, pale green needles does not prevent grass from growing, and this makes the shelter of larch-woods pleasant for tourists.

Alpine columbine   J. Blanc/ JACANA

Bear's ears   E. Soler/ JACANA

Edelweiss   M. Zahnd/ JACANA

Blue gentian   M. Viard/ JACANA

Martagon lily   P. Nief/ JACANA

Orange lily   F. Lieutier/ JACANA

Alpine aster   Egers/ JACANA

45

MICHELIN

Larch

Arolla pine

In French: *pin arolle*; in German: *Arve*; in Italian: *pino cembro*. A characteristic feature of the many species of pine is the arrangement of their needles in tufts of two to five, held together by a scaly sheath. Their cones have hard, tough scales. The arolla pine can be recognised by the shape of its branches, deeply curved like those of a candelabrum. The tree is often damaged by the wind.

Flora

The term "Alpine plants" is reserved for those which grow above the upper limits of the forests. The early flowering of these species, which are usually small and strong, reflects the brevity of the growing season (June to August). Disproportionately large blossoms, compared with the plants as a whole, and bright colouring are directly related to the high ultraviolet content of the light at high altitude. The most common Alpine species are:

Protection of Alpine flora

The picking of certain Alpine flowers that are particularly threatened, including cyclamen, Alpine aster, primrose and edelweiss, is strictly prohibited.

ALPINE CLIMATE

Differences of altitude, mountain formation and exposure create many variables. During the warm season, daily temperature variations cause different levels in a mountain valley to grow warmer or cooler, and produce winds called *brises*, similar to sea and land breezes elsewhere. Towards noon the warm, expanding air rises and causes clouds to form around the mountain tops, a sign of steady, fine weather. Walkers should head for viewpoints early, since the valley breeze dies away at about 5pm, and the air suddenly turns cold, especially in the shade.

The Föhn – This relatively warm wind, most keenly felt on the north side of the Alps in the upper Aare and Reuss valleys, unleashes torrential rainstorms, churns the water of the great lakes into fury, and causes thundering avalanches. The arrival of the springlike *Föhn* (called the *Chinook* in North America) first sheds its moisture on the Italian side of the Alps, then pours violently over the crest-line, finally growing warmer and becoming dry. Increased risk of disastrous forest fires prompts some communities to apply strict rules, often posted in cafés. Some go so far as to forbid smoking completely. But the *Föhn* also melts the snow, so animals can be put out to pasture early, and in some southern valleys, it enables such vegetation as maize, vines and chestnut trees to flourish beyond their normal geographical limits.

The Swiss Jura

The Jura end at the Crête de la Neige (alt 1 723m/5 653ft) in France. In Switzerland, they are a sheaf of strongly folded, mountains curving for 200km/125mi between the Dôle (alt 1 677m/5 502ft) and the Lägern (alt 859m/2 819ft above Baden). In France the Jura drop towards the plain of the Saône in a gigantic staircase of plateaux; in Switzerland the last ridges of the massif form above the Mittelland (☣ *see below*), a continuous rampart, rising in one bound to more than 1 000m/3 000ft to face the Bernese Alps and the Mont-Blanc Massif.

The green countryside of the Jura system reveals a regularly folded structure from the movements of the earth's crust, which built up the Alpine chain in the Tertiary Era. Beside this "fixed swell" of valleys and

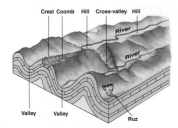

Crest Coomb   Hill   Cross-valley   Hill

River

River

Valley   Valley

Ruz

hills there are high, almost level plateaux such as the Franches Montagnes (👣 *see Les FRANCHES MONTAGNES*). Erosion has developed lush valleys and laid bare dramatic rock escarpments.

Parallel **valleys** are separated by the hills. The slashes made by erosion on the flanks of the hills form the **ruz** (a term derived from the name Val de Ruz). The **cross-valley** cuts across the hill, connecting two valleys. The **coomb** runs longitudinally along the top of a hill; its escarped edges are called **crests**.

Mittelland or Middle Country

From Lac Léman to the Bodensee, between the Alps and the Jura, stretches a gently sloping *glacis* on the surface of which lies the mass of debris torn from the Alps. The water network of the River

Aare shows that all the drainage here feeds the Rhine through a furrow running along the foot of the last ridge of the Jura. Before the Ice Age the Rhône itself flowed through this depression, in which a string of lakes (those of Biel and Neuchâtel) and marshy areas now lie.

In fact, the Mittelland is a region of hills deeply divided by clefts – ravines and winding, steep-walled valleys. The vital centres of the Swiss farming industry are and the largest cities of the Confederation tend to be concentrated there.

Conquest of the Heights

The victories of the 19C over the supposedly inaccessible peaks gradually destroyed the superstitious dread with which they were regarded (👣 *see PILATUS*).

Switzerland, with many of its summits exceeding 4 000m/13 123ft, is a paradise for climbers. One of the first climbs recorded was that of Titlis in 1744, by four peasants from Engelberg. In 1792, Spescha, a monk from Disentis, conquered Oberalpstock. In 1811, the **Meyer brothers**, rich merchants from Aarau, reached the Valais via Grimsel and, starting from Lötschental, climbed the **Jungfrau** (4 158m/13 642ft).

At the same time, Frenchmen and Austrians were attacking their highest peaks. In 1786 French guide **Jacques Balmat** reached the **Mont Blanc** summit and repeated his expedition in 1787 with the Swiss physicist De Saussure (👣 *see Michelin Green Guide French Alps*). Austrians summited Grossglockner (3 797m/12 457ft) in 1800. Breithorn (4 165m/13 665ft) was conquered in 1813, Tödi in 1824 and Piz Bernina (4 049m/13 284ft) in 1850. The British also recorded some famous first ascents, including **Stockhorn** in 1842 and **Wasenhorn** in 1844, by **JD Forbes**; **Pic Dufour** (4 634m/15 204ft) in 1855 by the three **Smyth brothers**; **Eiger** in 1858 by **Charles Barrington**; and above all, in 1865, **Matterhorn** (Mont Cervin 4 478m/14 692ft) by **Edward Whymper**. These achievements, with those of the French and Italians, make the 19C the golden age of mountaineering.

HISTORY

Time Line

EARLY HELVETIA

BC — Cro-Magnon man is believed to have lived about 12000 BC, an estimate reinforced by a Cro-Magnon skull discovered in the Jura.

200 BC — The **Helvetii** cross the Rhine. This powerful Celtic, semi-nomadic tribe settles on a territory stretching from Lake Constance to Geneva, from the Alps to the Jura.

100 BC — The Helvetii are driven out by the Alamans. Their exodus into Gaul is hindered by the Romans, led by Julius Caesar: the battle of Bibracte (Autun) takes place in 58 BC. The long period of colonisation that follows leads to the foundation of several settlements extending into the heart of the Alps, including those of Nyon and Augusta Raurica.

AD 1C — Helvetia becomes a province of the Roman Empire, with Vindonissa as its capital.

2C — Helvetia's geographical location, hemmed in between its possessions, compels the Romans into large-scale construction of roads and fortifications. The golden age of Aventicum (Avenches), founded by Augustus.

3C-5C — The **Burgundians**, originally a northern tribe, settle in the western part of Helvetia. The Germanic **Alamans** occupy Aventicum and colonise central and eastern Helvetia.

6C-9C — In 530 Franks invade the country. Their supremacy over the Merovingians and Carolingians extends to western Helvetia until 888. Irish monks led by Columba arrive in Helvetia to preach to the population and help build several monasteries. Sankt Gallen, founded by Gallus, becomes a major seat of learning in Europe.

Doris Brawand / Switzerland Tourism

Rütli Oath Mural at the Bundesbriefmuseum in Schwyz

THE MIDDLE AGES

1032 — Death of Rudolph II. The country passes to the rulers of Germany.

11C-13C —Feudal lords and their free cities are given the power to rule over Helvetia, although they are officially accountable to the kings and subsequently the emperors of Germany.

1191 — The city of Berne is founded.

1291 — **Rudolph of Habsburg** bequeaths Helvetia to his sons, the dukes of Austria.

1 August 1291 — In the valleys near Lake Lucerne, the three original forest cantons (Waldstätten) of Uri, Schwyz and Unterwalden, refusing to submit to the Habsburgs and the bailiffs whose authority has been imposed upon them, conclude a pact of mutual assistance and take the oath of the Everlasting League at Rütli. This pact is the founding document of the **Helvetic Confederation** (named Switzerland in 1350). The archer **William Tell**, who plays a highly symbolic role in this episode, becomes a national hero.

1315 — The Confederates defeat Duke Leopold at **Morgarten**.

1386 — The cantons (8 altogether) are victorious at **Sempach** but the Romands achieve autonomy at the expense of the Comte de Savoie.

15C — The **St Gotthard issue**: in order to gain possession of this strategic route, the Swiss occupy part of the Ticino, Aargau, Thurgau, Sankt Gallen and Graubünden regions. Encouraged by the King of France, Louis XI, they invade the Pays de Vaud.

BURGUNDIAN WARS AND ITALIAN WARS

1476 — The troops placed under the command of the **Duke of Burgundy**, Charles the Bold, are defeated at **Grandson**, then at **Murten**.

1513 — The number of cantons is extended to 13.

1515 — Allied with the Pope and the Milanese, the Swiss are defeated at Marignan by the King of France, **François I**, with whom they then sign a treaty of alliance.

1525 — The crushing Franco-Swiss defeat at Pavia, where the Swiss are wiped out by Charles V, marks the end of Switzerland's political and military history outside its borders.

REFORMATION TO THE 18C

16C — The **Reformation** preached by Zwingli and Calvin finds fruitful soil for expansion in Switzerland, thanks to Humanists like Erasmus. It is spread throughout Romansh Switzerland and heavily influences the 13 cantons.

1536 — Berne, which spearheaded the Protestant cause, regains possession of the Pays de Vaud from the Duke of Savoy.

1648 — Swiss neutrality, which avoided the Thirty Years War, is officially acknowledged at the Münster Conference.

18C — A united country where several languages and religions coexist, Switzerland is influenced by theories that blossom during the Age of Enlightenment, supported by such philosophers as **Jean-Jacques Rousseau;** revolutionary ideas spread.

1798 — Responding to an appeal from the Vaud population, the French Republican army marches into Berne and occupies the city. A Helvetic Republic is founded; its nature seems unsuitable for the Swiss national spirit.

19TH CENTURY

1803 — Disputes between conservative and progressive forces lead Bonaparte to introduce a new constitution and annex Geneva and the Valais.

1804-15 - Switzerland becomes a battlefield and acts of aggression are carried out against Napoleon's troops.

1815 — The Congress of Vienna reaffirms Switzerland's neutrality. The number of cantons is extended to 22. Part of the French Jura is annexed to the Berne canton.

1846 — Deep religious divisions lead to a separatist League of Roman Catholic cantons known as the **Sonderbund**. It is soon disbanded by the Diet, reunited in Berne. General Dufour, Commander of the Confederate Army, ends hostilities and paves the way for a general reconciliation.

1848 — A new constitution introduces centralised, secular rule.

1863 — **Henri Dunant** from Geneva founds the Red Cross .

THE 20TH CENTURY

1914-18 — Switzerland guards its frontiers and extends hospitality to those exiled by war.

1919 — Tribute is paid to Swiss neutrality by making Geneva seat of the **League of Nations**.

1939-45 — During the Second World War, Swiss troops are sent to their frontiers under the command of **General Guisan**. In the post-war years, Geneva, site of European UN headquarters, undertakes diplomatic commissions and conferences, including trade, human rights and disarmament. The first disarmament talks, in 1954, bring together Eisenhower, Dulles, Eden and Faure from the West and Bulganin and Molotov from Russia.

1971 — The World Economic Forum is held for the first time in Davos, where it will become an annual summit of the world's political and economic leaders.

1978 — The Jura canton is created. Cantons now number 23.

1986 — 76% of the electorate votes not to become a member of the United Nations. However, the country continues to be active in UN specialised agencies and programmes.

1989 — The Swiss vote to maintain their federal army.

1991 — Voting age drops to 18.

1992 — Switzerland decides not to join the European Community but becomes a member of the International Monetary Fund and the World Bank.

1995 — The International Trade Organisation (ITO), replaces the GATT (General Agreement on Tariffs and Trade). Headquarters are in Geneva.

1999 — Ruth Dreifuss becomes the first woman elected President of the Swiss Confederation.

1999 — Swiss scientist Bertrand Piccard and British co-pilot Brian Jones befome the first

The National Flag

All the boats gliding along Swiss lakes and rivers can be seen proudly sporting their national banner – a white cross on a red background. It was on 21 July 1840 that the Diet officially adopted this national emblem. Formerly, each contingent serving in the federal army fought under the colours of their own canton. As early as 1815, General Dufour, who was colonel at the time, had advocated the creation of a single flag in order to reinforce national unity and foster feelings of patriotism and comradeship.

The flag draws inspiration from the arms featured on the banner which belonged to the mercenaries of the Schwyz canton, which Frederick II gave to his loyal supporters.

balloonists to circumnavigate the globe with a non-stop, non-refueled flight. It takes 19 days, 21 hours.

THE NEW MILLENNIUM

2000 — 67% of the electorate votes for bilateral agreements to strengthen economic ties with the European Union.

2002 — 54.6% of the electorate votes to join the United Nations. Switzerland becomes its 190th member state.

2008 — UEFA (Union of European Football Associations) Championships in Bern, Basel, Geneva and Zurich.

Famous Swiss

A country as small as Switzerland boasts many world-famous citizens.

14C
William **Tell**; Arnold von **Winkelried**.

15C to 17C
St Nicholas of **Flüe,** Cardinal Matthew **Schiner**; Ulrich **Zwingli**; Joachim von Watt, known as **Vadian**; Theophrastus Bombastus von Hohenheim, known as **Paracelsus**, natural scientist and alchemist; François de **Bonivard**; Domenico **Fontana**, architect, and his student Carlo **Maderno**; Kaspar Jodok von **Stockalper**.

18C
Jakob and Johann **Bernoulli**, mathematicians; Daniel **Bernoulli**, mathematician; Jean-Étienne **Liotard**, painter; Leonhard **Euler**, mathematician; Jean-Jacques **Rousseau**; Salomon **Gessner**, poet and painter; Horace Bénédict de **Saussure**, physicist.

19C
Jacques **Necker**, financier and statesman; Johann Caspar **Lavater**, philosopher; Johann David **Wyss**, writer; Johann Heinrich **Pestalozzi**, educator; General Frédéric de **Laharpe**, politician; Guillaume-Henri **Dufour**, Swiss army general; Léopold **Robert**, painter; Albert Bitzius, known as Jeremias **Gotthelf**, writer; artist Rodolphe **Toepffer;** Louis **Agassiz**, geologist; Nikolaus **Riggenbach**, engineer; Jacob **Burckhardt**, philosopher; Gottfried **Keller**, poet; Henri Frédéric **Amiel**, writer; Conrad Ferdinand **Meyer**, author, poet.

20C
Arnold **Böcklin**, painter; Henri **Dunant**, founder of the Red Cross; César **Ritz**, hotelier; Carl **Spitteler**, poet; Ferdinand **Hodler**, painter; Ferdinand de **Saussure**, linguist; Félix **Vallotton**, painter; Carl Gustav **Jung**, psychoanalyst; Charles Ferdinand **Ramuz**, writer; clown Adrien Wettach, better known as **Grock**; Ernest **Ansermet**, orchestra conductor; Frédéric Sauser, known as Blaise **Cendrars**, writer; Édouard Jeanneret-Gris, known as **Le Corbusier**, architect; Frank Martin and Arthur **Honegger**, musicians; Michel **Simon**, actor; Alberto **Giacometti**, painter and sculptor; Mario **Botta**, architect; Hans **Erni**, painter; Jean **Tinguely**, sculptor; Max **Frisch**, writer; Friedrich **Dürrenmatt**, writer.

Famous Swiss Residents

Other famous Swiss are foreigners who settled in Swiss territory include painters Conrad **Witz**, **Holbein** the Younger, artists Paul **Klee** and Daniel **Spoerri**, author Hermann **Hesse**, film director/actor Charlie **Chaplin**, writer Georges **Simenon**, father of artist Commissaire Maigret, singer/composer Charles **Aznavour**, cigar importer Zino **Davidoff**, actress Audrey **Hepburn,** fashion designer Coco **Chanel**, the prolific author Frédéric **Dard**, who created the ribald Commissaire San Antonio, and Albert **Einstein,** who did much of his work on the Theory of Relativity while living in Bern.

Currently, entertainers Tina **Turner** and country music star Shania **Twain** make their homes in Switzerland.

ART AND CULTURE

Its position at the crossroads of three important civilizations – French, Italian and German – has made Switzerland a melting pot combining the cultural characteristics of its neighbors, drawing on their artistic and cultural heritage and adapting them to suit its own traditions. Swiss art did not acquire its own identity until the late 19C, and rapidly it influenced the Continent's cultural history, carving a niche on the international avant-garde art scene.

Art and Architecture

UNDER ROMAN RULE

Roman customs and traditions exerted a strong influence over early Swiss cultural heritage. Vestiges of the Roman period bear the signs of Imperial art but with strong regional and popular characteristics. Some sites contain many remains dating back to this period. One of the most famous, the site of **Augst** near Basel, provides a fascinating insight into daily life under the Romans and the remarkable technological achievements, such as villas fitted with sewers and central heating.

Mosaics and mural frescoes also reflect the high degree of sophistication and taste for refinement of this civilisation. The **Villa Rustica at Orbe** features magnificent mosaics depicting mythological scenes; the **Villa Commugny near Nyon** boasts mural paintings with *trompe-l'œil* façades and narrative scenes.

EARLY MIDDLE AGES

The collapse of the Roman Empire in the 5C led to a slackening of artistic activity. The mosaics and frescoes which had flourished under the Greco-Latin era became much rarer and a new aesthetic inspired by Christianity revived artistic life as the Church played a key role in art throughout Europe, including Switzerland. The early Middle Ages were characterised by development of religious mural paintings. The only remaining example, the **ceiling of Zillis Church**, has scenes illustrating the Life of Christ, featuring angels, allegorical figures and mythological beasts, depicted with startling realism and remarkable freedom of expression. Evangelisation

spread throughout the country from the 7C, evidenced by the construction of many convents, which became bastions of artistic activity and were seen as temples of cultural life. The **Convent of Sankt Gallen** exerted considerable influence within Europe between the 8C and 10C. This flourishing of the arts was reflected in the superb illuminations and manuscripts from the 7C that have been carefully preserved in the library.

ROMANESQUE AND CLUNY

Switzerland underwent a variety of influences, illustrated by its churches, which imbibed the artistic movements of surrounding countries and then moulded them to suit the Swiss national character.

The stamp of Lombard art can be observed in most churches in the Ticino area, such as the **Chiesa San Nicolao in Giornico** (doorway columns resting on crouching beasts, the crypt with three naves and three bays crowned

Chiesa San Nicolao in Giornico

Jerry Dennis / APA Publications

by groined vaulting, and the highly expressive sculptures). Likewise, in the **Chiesa Santi Pietro e Paolo in Biasca**, the basilica, displaying three naves and a single apse closing off the chancel, is typical of Lombard architecture. Lastly, in Zurich, the north doorway of the cathedral is shaped as a triumphal arch, a common occurence in Italy.

Burgundian influence is best observed in **Basel Cathedral**, one of the last great Romanesque monuments, marking the transition between Romanesque and Gothic art, with a three-tier elevation, lancet arches and the polygonal chancel. Another instance is the carved tympanum on the famous "**Sankt-Gallen Doorway**," a masterpiece of Romanesque sculpture: figures portraying Christ between St Peter and St Paul and the parable of the Wise Virgins and the Foolish Virgins display astonishing grace and fluidity, features generally associated with Burgundian art.

The influence of Provence is especially evident in sculpture. The four statue-columns depicting the Apostles in **Coire Cathedral** bear a strong resemblance to earlier sculptures in Saint-Trophime at Arles; with the tight folds of their robes falling stiffly over their legs, there is more than a touch of Antiquity about their style. However, the capitals in **Geneva Cathedral**, characterised by their sober simplicity, are more reminiscent of those found in Lyon or Vienne.

Lastly, Germanic Romanesque art is illustrated by the **Münster zu Allerheiligen in Schaffhausen.** distinguished by stark geometry surrounding a square and pure architectural lines, illustrated by the flat east end and basilica-style plan with columns.

The foundation of **Cluny Abbey Church** in 910 paved the way for an unprecedented revival of religious architecture, leading to the creation of several hundred convents in the span of two centuries. Cluny left its mark on many of these buildings, which featured the same tall, slender proportions. The abbey churches in Romainmôtiers and Payerne in the Vaud canton were early examples of Romanesque architecture influenced by Cluny Abbey. Romainmôtiers is a replica of the abbey church; the heavy columns on square bases suggest both sturdiness and stability, Payerne, a more recent edifice, is a wonderful architectural achievement. With its double elevation, chapels, apsidioles and its narthex at the entrance, it represents pure Cluniac tradition.

The 12C saw the golden age of Romanesque art with the emergence of a new Christian community, the Cistercian Order. Simplicity, austerity and formal perfection were its dominant traits. **Bonmont Abbey** near Nyon is a fine example of Cistercian architecture, with its plan designed after a Roman cross.

Heinz Schwab / Switzerland Tourism

Carolingian frescoes in Müstair in Graubünden

Sculpture

The various figures and motifs represented in sculpture tended to reflect their architectural environment; they did not seek to depict reality but to express the supernatural. Imagery was extremely rich and punctuated by references to the Old and New Testaments. The capitals of the **Église St-Jean-Baptiste in Grandson** are among the most minutely executed in Switzerland. "Eagle with Spread Wings" and "St Michael Slaying the Dragon" reflect remarkable craftsmanship and expertise on the part of the sculptor.

GOTHIC PERIOD

Gothic art and the ribbed arch were introduced into Switzerland in the 13C by Cistercian monks. In architecture, the Gothic style was conveyed by systematic use of lancet arches and flying buttresses to support the imposing nave and high clerestory windows enhanced by stained glass. In sculpture, it led to the creation of statues carved out of the same block of stone as the column. This new movement paved the way for many great construction projects, including **Geneva Cathedral**. In the 13C and the 14C, the Franciscan and Dominican religious orders developed an unadorned style of their own. The **abbey at Königsfelden**, founded in 1308 by the Franciscans, reflects such austerity, with its flat wooden ceiling crowning the bare nave.

Sculpture

Gothic sculpture displays a far freer approach, shedding Romanesque aesthetics for a more humane, graceful representation. Burgundian, Germanic and Lombard influences were still felt in projects involving artists working elsewhere, such as the German sculptor **Peter Parler**, who executed the chancels in the cathedrals of Fribourg and Basel around 1350. In the late 14C, an international style spread to all of Europe. Works of art became smaller so they could be transported more easily and foster cultural exchanges among countries. The Marian cult and the worshipping of saints became widespread and many sumptuous altarpieces were commissioned; the one designed for **Coire Cathedral** is an outstanding example.

Sculpted doorways also drew inspiration from Gothic art; the celebrated **painted doorway in Lausanne Cathedral** is a telling example. Remarkably well-preserved, the polychrome panel illustrates the Dormition of the Blessed Virgin and is clearly based on the one in Senlis Cathedral. This religious imagery was exceptional for the Gothic period. Such works were seen as decorative as well as intended to enlighten the faithful. The ultimate expression of Flamboyant Gothic is the doorway of **Berne Cathedral** portraying the Last Judgement. The graphics are said to be the most detailed in Europe and every episode is conveyed by a sculpture.

Sculpted furniture also was key to the development of Gothic art and exemplified the artistic changes occurring between the 13C and the Reformation.

Painting

Economic recovery was instrumental in allowing art to expand throughout Europe. From the 14C onwards, foreign artists were often called upon for projects in Switzerland, bringing with them many styles and techniques. Byzantine influence was evident in paintings such as the frescoes adorning the narthex of the 13C **Payerne Abbey Church**, devoted to the theme of the Apocalypse. Paintings often associated religious and secular elements: in Romainmôtiers, episodes from Genesis were depicted alongside scenes of musicians. In Gothic art, paintings were often replaced by stained glass and this coexistence of the religious and the non-religious was to be found in the rose window of **Lausanne Cathedral**, offering a profane vision of the world with a calendar of seasons and months.

Gothic painting flourished under such artists as **Conrad Witz** (1400-46), who worked in Basel and Geneva. His most famous canvas, *The Miraculous Draught of Fishes* (1444), represents Lake Geneva and its shores and displays both astounding realism and minute attention to detail. The religious subject is presented, perhaps for the first time, in a recognisable rather than an idealised landscape. However, in this he appears to have been an exception, since most of his contemporaries remained closer to the symbolic, more iconic representation associated with the Gothic tradition. Up to 1536, painting prospered with a fair amount of creativity. On the eve of the Reformation, fewer works were commissioned as reformers turned against visual imagery, and ended the last remaining vestiges of medieval art.

THE RENAISSANCE

The late 15C and the early 16C were characterised by flourishing arts and political upheavals. Large altarpieces were replaced by painted panels and canvases. The Renaissance also added a touch of humanism. Yet, in some regions, Gothic influence was still felt until the 15C even as Renaissance art occasionally bore signs of the Gothic style.

Architecture

Arcades, considered to be typically Renaissance, were becoming more widespread in Switzerland; the **Hôtel de Ville de Palud** in Lausanne is the most representative building of this period. Its outstanding façade, with subtle alignment of the windows, reveals genuine architectural genius. Architects from Berne, including Abraham **Düntz** and Samuel **Jenner**, displayed a novel approach to their art from 1667, advocating a plain, sober style devoid of Baroque embellishments. It was in this spirit that the oval became a popular feature of many buildings. This simple geometrical figure allowed the faithful to be reunited together in an area that was both simple and aesthetically pleasing, as is evidenced by the **Temple de Chêne-Paquer** (1667) in the Vaud canton.

Although the Reformation gave a new lease of life to civil architecture, the building of religious sanctuaries slowed down during the 16C, with reformers appropriating those Catholic churches which already existed.

Lausanne Cathedral

Bill Wassman / APA Publications

In German-speaking Switzerland, Late Gothic architecture, influenced by Germanic art, coexisted with Renaissance tradition in good harmony. The city of **Schaffhausen** is a perfect example of this trend with its richly sculpted "olliers". These Gothic towers, originally placed at the corners of houses, were subsequently moved to the centre of the façade above the main entrance. Italian influence gradually spread to the Ticino canton, adding a touch of mannerism which already heralded the Baroque style. This was reflected in the frescoes adorning **Santa Maria degli Angioli** in Lugano or those displayed in the former town hall of Lucerne. These two different manifestations of Renaissance art, associated with the north and the south respectively, are indicative of distinct cultural traditions.

Painting and Engraving

Artists such as the Berne painter **Niklaus Manuel Deutsch** (1484-1530) successfully negotiated the transition between Gothic and the more modern approach of the Renaissance. **Hans Holbein the Younger**, a German who settled in Basel, not only produced the portrait of his patron Erasmus (displayed in the city's Museum of Fine Arts), but undertook many influential façades and frescoes. His works are a fine combination of Italian Renaissance and styles from northern Europe, conveyed by a pleasing sense of harmony and masterful attention to detail. The Reformation seriously jeopardised his career and painting at large. Although reformers objected to religious images, they tolerated decoration with foliated scrolls, such as those in the **Temple of Lutry** (1577).

This period was marked by the invention of printing, which spread the views advocated by the Reformation. Printing was first introduced into Basel in 1468, and from then onwards, books replaced manuscripts. The new medium made it possible to popularize ideas more quickly and effectively. **Urs Graf** (1485-1527), a famous engraver, depicted macabre, erotic and military scenes, which carried strong dramatic impact.

Sculpture

The stiffness that characterised this period was to replace the ornamental profusion of Late Gothic. The decline in commissions from the clergy led to the sudden construction of fountains to enhance urban landscapes, a feature typical of Renaissance art in Switzerland. The centre of the basin was taken up by a tall sculpted and gilded column, frequently surmounted by an allegorical figure such as Justice. A monument of this type can be found in Lausanne: it portrays a young woman with her eyes blindfolded holding a pair of scales and a sword, assuming victory over the powers which govern the world.

18C

Society became more refined, elegant and sophisticated. Literary salons and musical societies flourished. Geneva and Lausanne dazzled the rest of Europe and attracted foreign artists and intellectuals. The period was symbolised by a taste for the extravagant and a strong spirit of imagination, fantasy and freedom.

Architecture

Up to 1770, Switzerland was mainly dominated by Baroque architecture, sculpture, painting and applied arts. To serve the views of the Counter-Reformation, Baroque was applied to religious buildings, becoming Rococo. The **abbey church in Einsiedeln** built by **Kasper Moosbrugger** (1656-1723) between 1674 and 1745 is a perfect example, as is the **abbey church** and **library of Sankt-Gallen** designed by **Peter Thumb** (1681-1766) and **Johann Michael Beer**. Jesuits and Franciscans encouraged construction of Baroque chuches in Lucerne, Fribourg and Solothurn. This grand era produced sumptuous creations featuring scrolls, painted ceilings and lavish ornamentation. The **abbey church in Disentis/Mustér** (1695-1712) shows the influence of Austrian Baroque.

The association of painting and sculpture with architecture is a typical feature of Baroque art. *Trompe-l'œil* motifs extended architectural plans, as do the paintings in Sankt-Gallen by **Johann Christian Wentzinger** (1710-97).

In the 18C, French architects such as Saussure came to work in Switzerland and exerted a strong influence over local artists. In Berne, the Swiss adapted Mansard's principles to their own country's traditions. However, the most outstanding architectural achievements derived from the French model are to be found in Geneva – **Hôtel Buisson, Hôtel de Saussure** – and in Solothurn – **Hôtel de la Couronne**.

Painting

The art of the portrait, much in vogue during the 18C, marked the revival of painting with the Geneva-born artist **Jean-Étienne Liotard** (1702-89), whose realistic style and a light, confident hand feature bold colour contrasts and finely observed details. At the end of the 18C, it became fashionable to give free rein to one's feelings; in his portraits **Anton Graff** (1736-1813) depicts his subjects with a modish Romantic sensibility.

After 1750, historical painting returned to fashion with the emergence of neo-Classical style. Events of national importance were commemorated and the country began to develop a patriotic consciousness and sense of national identity; the Geneva artist **Jean-Pierre Saint-Ours** (1752-1809) worked on the allegory of the Republic of Geneva in 1794. These portrayals of Swiss history remained popular until the mid-20C.

At the end of the 18C, a new genre appeared: landscape painting. Celebrating Mother Nature in lush landscapes became a feature of Swiss painting and, for the rest of Europe, defined Switzerland in the popular imagination: mountains and lakes, peaceful, dramatic and sublime. The two forerunners of this movement were **Wolf** (1735-83) and **Johann Heinrich Wüest** (1741-1821). The most famous English exponent was **JMW Turner**, whose views of Lake Geneva, Lucerne and Montreux fired a growing British enthusiasm for the Alps and helped launch the Swiss tourism industry.

Around this period, many Swiss artists travelled abroad (Rome, Paris or Munich) to complete their training, and some settled in those countries. **Heinrich Füssli** (1741-1825), anglicised as Henry Fuseli, became well-known in London. His tortured, obsessive visions often draw on literary works and are thought, in turn, to have been one source of inspiration for Mary Shelley's *Frankenstein*. Dismissed as a sensationalist by some critics, his weird, nightmarish canvases exerted considerable influence on his peers and on following generations.

19C

Republican ideals and nationalistic values found natural expression in the neo-Classicism that permeated official art and academic works. With this return to themes taken from Antiquity, new genres emerged, characterised by strong emphasis on emotion and feelings.

Architecture

The gradual fading of Baroque led to sober neo-Classicism, which embodied the republican ideal. In Lausanne, the edifice housing the Great Council, is a perfect example. Designed by the architect **Alexandre Perregaux** in 1803 -06, it became a symbol for the Vaud canton. In Avenches, the Casino, a private club, was conceived as a small temple of antiquity. The masterpiece of Palladian architecture remains the **Gordanne in Féchy**: with its cupola and its portico flanked by Ionic columns, it seems to date back to Antiquity.

After 1840, the trend turned toward classical landscaped gardens and mock ruins. The **Château de l'Aile in Vevey**, conceived by **Philippe Framel** and **Jean-Louis Brocher** in 1840-42, is an excellent representative of this lighter, neo-Gothic current.

The abbey church in Einsiedeln

Heinz Schwab / Switzerland Tourism

Bill Wassman / APA Publications

Abbey church interior in Disentis/Mustér

Painting

Alongside academic neo-Classicism, new genres caused a revival of the pictorial art form. They were Romanticism, Symbolism, poster art and satire. Nostalgia and sentimentality reflected the romantic spirit of the century, aptly conveyed by the works of **Charles Gleyre,** whose tender, graceful characters are bathed in a soft light. **Landscape painting** also took a sentimental dimension, with light playing an essential part of the composition. **Alexandre Calame** (1810-64) paid tribute to Alpine landscapes by revealing their grandiose, mysterious nature. **Arnold Böcklin** (1827-1901) adopted a similar approach; his *Isle of the Dead* (1880-86) is an eerie landscape shrouded in silence and mystery, said to have inspired the famous symphonic poem by Rachmaninoff.

At the end of the 19C, painting explored a new form of expression under the influence of Symbolism, which offered a spiritual or even mystical explanation for reality. Böcklin and his fantasy world peopled with human fears belonged to this movement. **Ferdinand Hodler** (1853-1918) is also seen as a Symbolist

for his new formal principles, which centre on the symmetry that reveals a sense of unity which is inherent in the world (*Truth*, 1903). The works painted towards the end of his life, however, display a lack of formalism and a spontaneous approach which were already the hallmarks of Impressionism. **Félix Vallotton**, a member of the Nabis movement who was greatly impressed by Gauguin's work, contributed to Symbolism by describing the social mores of his time in accordance with the theoretical principles of a pure and symbolic art form.

Lastly, **poster art** and **satire** developed considerably throughout the 19C thanks to Vallotton, **Théophile-Alexandre Steinlen** (1859-1923) and **Eugène Grasset** (1845-1917). Their role was to expose injustice, to defend the oppressed and to describe daily life in a simple manner, making art accessible to a wide cross-section of the population.

Sculpture

Sculpture saw a tremendous revival during the 19C. Salons in particular were instrumental in popularising small sculptures among private collectors, especially those belonging to the bourgeoisie. In the public sector, this art form was expressed through the decoration of theatres, casinos, banks and railway stations. It accompanied the other changes affecting Swiss urban landscapes and fostered deep feelings of patriotism and national identity.

The exuberance of Rococo was replaced by the grandiose dignity of neo-Classicism. **Trippel**, the first neo-Classical sculptor, advocated Englightenment ideas and his work is imbued with strong patriotic undertones.

The early 19C was also marked by a return to the styles and qualities of the Middle Ages, as was the case in painting and architecture. Nostalgia for the past and for bygone feudal traditions can be felt in the creations dating from this period, resulting in a neo-Gothic trend which affected mainly funerary monuments commissioned by the Church.

To counter this neo-Classical movement, **Vincenzo Vela** (1820-91) produced naturalistic sculptures and developed the concept of *Vérisme*. He was much appreciated in France, where, in 1866, he painted *The Last Days of Napoleon I*, which portrays the emperor as an ageing, disillusioned man. Vela was known for speaking out in favour of the oppressed and his political commitment took shape in *Memorial to the Victims of Work* in 1883.

In the latter part of the 19C, sculpture flourished with a new freedom of expression. Most of these works were intended for private collectors thanks to the creation of the Mario Pastori Foundry in Geneva, which made the latest casting techniques available to artists. The Symbolist movement and Art Nouveau both gave a new lease of life to sculpture. **Auguste de Niederhäusern**, known as Rodo, drew on Rodin's Symbolist theories and produced sculptures from which matter projected, like his *Jet of Water* from 1910-11. The different arts were skilfully combined under the influence of Art Nouveau. This approach was successfully explored by **Hermann Obrist**, who strove to achieve the merging of art, spirit and nature through his utopian reflexion on the spiral, the ultimate expression of vital energy.

20C AND EARLY 21C

Switzerland was part of the cultural wave that swept through Europe, in particular after 1930. The country was the recipient of artistic trends from abroad and began playing an active role in the international art scene.

Architecture

During the 1920s Swiss architecture was heavily influenced by the Bauhaus movement of Walter Gropius. Artistic creation was seen as a means of associating all art forms to create a new architectural identity. The notion of "order" was abandoned and buildings were stripped of their ornamentation. **Robert Maillard** (1872-1940) specialised in designing bridges with "aesthetic perfection". **Charles Édouard Jeanneret** (1887-1965), alias **Le Corbusier**, opted for functional architecture and became known as the "builder of radiant cities". Most of his work was carried out abroad, as his unusual views on architecture were not always well received at home. **Karl Moser** developed a new art form using modern materials such as reinforced concrete to design huge areas where light played an essential role. **Sankt Antonius Kirche** in Basel is his most typical work. In Lucerne, his work was continued by his pupils Fritz Metzger (St Charles' Church) and Otto Dreyer (St Joseph's Church).

Post-war architecture developed mainly in the Ticino area, Basel, Baden and French-speaking Switzerland, as economic growth required building up areas which, until then, had remained unexploited. Switzerland's national road network was the main achievement of this period.

In this utilitarian atmosphere, **Christian Menn** and **Rino Tami** produced outstanding creations such as the south entrance to the Sankt Gotthard tunnel at Airolo (Ticino), designed by Tami. Railway stations prompted new architectural research in order to make them more friendly and convivial.

With the decline of industry,disused warehouses and factories were converted into arts centres, a trend which became a distinguishing feature of the period. Contemporary architecture became linked to the prestigious image of firms which offered their patronage and for which it acted as a showcase.

Since the mid-1970s, environmental concern has spurred an ecological approach in architecture. In the 1960s, **Aldo Rossi** reacted against the "radiant cities" of Le Corbusier and advocated a universal vision of townscapes. Each building is designed for a particular purpose but nonetheless remains open to change if the situation requires it. His example was followed by architects **Luigi Snozzi**, **Aurelio Galfetti** and **Mario Botta**, known for his pure, geometrical proportions. Botta conceived the **Tinguely Museum** in Basel and the **Chiesa Santa Maria degli Angioli** on Monte Tamaro. In the case of the museum, the light, airy design forms a sharp contrast with Tinguely's heavy, overpowering machinery; as for the church, it offers a harmonious blend between architecture and mountain landscapes.

Post-Modernism explored the history of architecture, focusing on its structure, materials and motifs. **Bruno Reichlin** and **Fabio Reinhart** drew inspiration from past masters such as Andrea Palladio in the 16C and Francesco Borromini in the 17C. **Jacques Herzog** and **Pierre de Meuron** developed an aesthetic of based on surprising and unexpected juxtapositions.of materials.

In the second half of the 20C, modern architecture returned to fashion as buildings originally designed in the 1920s and 1930s needed restoration and the designs of **Karl Moser**, **Rudolf Gaberel** and **Maurice Braillard** were updated. The talent of Swiss architects did not pass unnoticed abroad. **Bernard Tschumi** took part in the Parc de la Villette project in Paris and Mario Botta, Switzerland's most celebrated architect, was commissioned to design buildings in Tokyo, San Francisco and Paris.

Painting and Sculpture

The Modernist movements which spread to Europe at the end of the First World War were represented in Switzerland only through temporary exhibitions. Swiss painting became isolated as ideas from abroad were perceived as a threat. Themes of isolation and escape became common in the work of Alberto Giacometti and **Meret Oppenheim**. However, from 1915-20, Zurich and Geneva became the center of opposition to conventional art.

This was Dadaism, which abolished logic, concentrating on absurd and irrational aspects of everyday life. In this period of war, the barbaric products of civilisation were denounced through collages, photomontages and poetry. Although Switzerland was seized with a feeling of doubt questioning centuries of art, it was abroad that avant-garde Swiss sculpture truly blossomed, with **Hans Arp, Sophie Taeuber-Arp** and **Alberto Giacometti**. In the 1920s, **Hermann Scherer** and his highly Expressionist wooden sculptures introduced a touch of novelty, which distinguished him from his contemporaries.

The inter-war period saw a revival of Swiss sculpture. **Alberto Giacometti** (1901-66) renewed the representation of human figures with his symbolic creations inspired by tribal art. His spindly, elongated sculptures present a rough texture bearing the imprint of his thumbs and the blade of a knife and convey the fleeting, elusive nature of man. **Max Bill** was a staunch defender of Concrete Art, which advocated order and rationality. Both his paintings and smooth, aesthetic sculptures (*Endless Ribbon*, 1935) are governed by rigorous mathematical considerations.

Simultaneously, a form of national art emerged, with many public buildings commissioned by the State. The regime wanted to maintain calm and order and encouraged art aimed at achieving a state of well-being. Any doctrine which strayed from this vision of happiness and which sought to combine different art forms was deemed degenerate and was systematically rejected (Meret Oppenheim, Sophie Taeuber-Arp).

During the Second World War, Switzerland became a refuge for many European artists, namely **Germaine Richier**, who expressed the war's traumas through highly imaginative sculptures, with strange mutilated surfaces featuring human, vegetable and animal motifs. Some Swiss artists returned to their home

Jean Tinguely Fountain in Basel

Heinz Schwab /Switzerland Tourism

country, such as **Paul Klee** (1879-1940), who explored the inner world of dreams and imagination, creating a new style halfway between Abstract and Figurative art, based on colour and perspective. Sculpture returned to vogue after WWII, and Zurich artist **Hans Äschbacher** (1906-80) created precariously superimposed blocks of marble or granite that seem to defy the laws of gravity. **Walter M Förderer** (b 1928), designed St Nicholas Church in Hérémence as a huge concrete sculpture. **Walter Bodmer**, a forerunner with his experimental wire paintings, undertook research in monumental iron works, focusing on lightness and transparency. The iron sculptures of **Bernard Luginbühl** (b 1929) and **Jean Tinguely** (1925-91) were far more imposing, overpowering and excessive: the former showed nostalgia for the bygone era of the Industrial Revolution while the latter expressed his contempt for history and the art trade through ephemeral, self-destructive machines. His sculpture *Eureka*, exhibited at the 1988 World Fair in Brisbane (Australia) was crafted with the precision which has earned the Swiss their worldwide reputation.

During the 1960s **André Thomkins**, **Daniel Spoerri**, **Dieter Roth** and **Karl Gerstner** spearheaded the Fluxus movement. Thomkins worked on the notion of changing identity and function while Spoerri paid tribute to objects with his ironical booby-paintings.

Since the 1980s, **Samuel Buri** and **Markus Raetz** have worked on the concept of metamorphosis. Buri is perhaps best known for his garish, life-size polyester cows which he exhibits at shows and fairs. Markus Raetz studies the changes occurring in the human body and head, as well as the effect of shade and movement. He also designs large pieces which are displayed in outdoor settings.

Art lovers will enjoy admiring works typifying the following famous painters and artistic movements:

♦ **Paul Klee** at Zentrum Paul Klee in Bern *(opened in 2005)*

♦ **Jean Tinguely** at the Musée Jean-Tinguely in Basel

♦ **Arnold Böcklin** and Konrad Witz at the Musée des Beaux-Arts in Basel

♦ **Félix Vallotton** at the Musée des Beaux-Arts in Lausanne

♦ **Impressionism** at the Fondation Collection EG Bührie in Zurich and the Stiftung "Langmatt" Sidney und Jenny Brown in Baden

♦ **Post-Impressionism** at the Villa Flora in Winterthur and the Fondation Beyeler in Riehen

♦ **Contemporary art** at the Museum für Gegenwartskunst in Basel

Language and Religion

One of the successes of the Swiss Confederation is the coexistence of four languages and several religions in a single community.

LANGUAGES

German-speaking Swiss represent 64% of the Helvetian people. **Schwyzerdütsch** (Swiss German) is a dialect of the Swabian group, with many local variations, and can be difficult to follow at first, even for native Germans and Austrians. It is used in daily conversation, while classical German (*Hochdeutsch*) is reserved for official business and correspondence. On the other hand, the French-speaking group (18%) have seen their dialect fall more and more into disuse. Italian (11%) is spoken almost entirely throughout the Ticino and in part of the Grisons (Graubünden). **Romansh** was recognised as a fourth national language in 1938. The Romansh League has done all it can to preserve and even spread its use in schools and in the press. Of Latin origin, Romansch is used by just 7% of the Swiss in the Grisons canton, especially in the Engadine and Grisons Oberland.

German, French and Italian are the official languages of the Confederation and are used as such by the authorities and the federal civil service. At least two languages are taught compulsorily in schools.

RELIGION

Until the middle of the 19C the religious question seemed an obstacle to unity in the Confederation. This was proved by the Sonderbund War (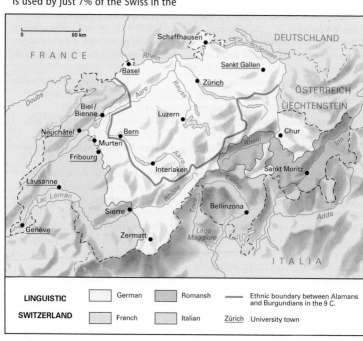 see History: Timeline), but since 1848 complete tolerance is the rule. Today Protestants represent 44% of the population, and Roman Catholics 47%.

The Swiss Protestant temperament, in its fundamentally democratic and patriotic aspects, owes more to the forceful personality of a man like Zwingli than to the strict doctrine of Calvin, whose influence was felt chiefly in Geneva. The flexible organisation of Protestant churches reflects the federalist structure of the country and allows subsidised state churches to exist alongside free churches supported by donations.

LINGUISTIC SWITZERLAND	German	Romansh	Ethnic boundary between Alamans and Burgundians in the 9 C.
	French	Italian	Zürich University town

Roman Catholics are attached to their dioceses: Basel (See of Solothurn), Lausanne-Geneva-Fribourg (See of Fribourg), Sion, Chur, Sankt Gallen and Lugano. Clergy are distributed among some large abbeys like those of St-Maurice, Einsiedeln and Engelberg.

The small Jewish population lives mostly in large cities such as Basel and Zurich.

Traditions and Folklore

Swiss folklore can always point to a rich collection of local costumes, and it is in the mountains that visitors have the best chance to see people who wear their traditional costumes every day, especially in the Gruyères and the Valais.

The *armailli* (herdsman) of Gruyères still wears the *bredzon*, a short cloth or canvas jacket with puffed sleeves which dates back to the Empire period, embroidered with thorn-points and with edelweiss on the lapels. The straw toque edged with velvet is called a *capette*. Similar costumes are found in the pastoral districts of the Bernese Oberland, although less often, but the man's jacket from this area is often made of velvet.

At Evolène the women's working dress includes a simple frock, with a red and white kerchief for the neck, and a straw hat with a brim edged with velvet and turned down over the ears; the crown is encircled by crochet-work ribbons arranged in bands. On high feast days the women of Évolène put on a rustling silk apron and the *mandzon* (a sort of jacket with long sleeves) and a very flat, round felt hat on top of a white lace bonnet.

Pastoral traditions are still very much alive in mountain districts like the Val d'Anniviers, where life is governed by the movements of cattle from the villages to the *mayens* and the high Alpine pasture *(alpe)*. The trek to summer pastures creates joyful and picturesque parades (late May, early June). Scores of beasts with beribboned and flower-decked horns move along the roads with cowbells tolling, escorted by herdsmen carrying necessities for living in the chalets, including a huge cheese-boiler on a

yoke. In the Valais the end of the journey is marked by **cow competitions**, after which the "queen" of the herd may wear the giant bell reserved for her.

Midsummer festivals lessen the loneliness of the *armaillis* by bringing a crowd of friends and relatives up from the valleys. The return from the alp, referred to as the *désalpe*, is equally spectacular and lively. The open-air performances of *William Tell* at Interlaken begin with a procession of this kind.

Urban traditions – These are generally patriotic and civic, like the commemoration of the Escalade at Geneva or the *Knabenschiessen* at Zurich (*see Calendar of events*). In quite a different spirit, more like the Rhenish customs, Basel Carnival, in which there are masked dances and processions preceding Lent, brings a touch of frivolity to the city of Erasmus. From behind the mask of some grotesque figure the merrymaker is free to taunt and tease friends and acquaintances.

Traditional rustic sports survive only at certain village fêtes in German Switzerland, where you might see games like wrestling on the grass, stone throwing, flag throwing and, most inscrutable of all, *Hornuss,* a team sport in which defenders with paddles try to deflect a puck which is hit, like a golf tee shot, as far as possible up the field. A summer festival in the Emmental is also the place to hear the cavernous tones of the great trumpet, the Alpenhorn, and the voices of yodellers may also be heard.

After a document by Ed. Kalt-Zehunder

Traditional costumes from the Appenzell

THE COUNTRY TODAY

Switzerland remains a fascinating mix of traditional and modern, pastoral and cosmopolitan. No other nation has a greater density of museums, a more efficient transportation network, or a citizenry more skilled in welcoming tourists. Its well-educated population enjoys one of the best standards of living in the world, with a strong currency driven in part by the country's political stability and international neutrality. Beyond Alpine panoramas, chocolate and trains that run on time, the country is a scenic, gastronomic and cultural delight.

Government

The Constitution of 1848, revised in 1874 and 1978, set up a modern federal state in place of the former Confederation of Cantons, in which each canton had its own coinage, postal services and customs.

THE COMMUNITIES

Liberty of the individual, liberty of faith and conscience, liberty of the press and of association are recognised by the Constitution, which gives every Swiss citizen over age 18 the right to vote and to be elected. Women, at last, obtained the vote in federal elections in 1971 but still do not always have a say in cantonal and community affairs. The whole regime, however, rests upon the principle of the sovereignty of citizens living in 3 000 free communities and forming the basis of the national will.

In all matters the community is competent to decide in the first instance. The canton intervenes only on appeal. So powerful is the citizenry that foreigners must first be admitted to the "corps of citizens" of a given community in order to acquire Swiss nationality.

CANTONAL AUTHORITY

Each canton has political sovereignty, with its own constitution and legislative body. In each of the 23 cantons (26 including the half-cantons) (⏾ *see below*) executive power belongs to the State Council and legislative power to the Grand Council.

The practice of direct democracy survives in a few mountain cantons like Appenzell, Glarus and Unterwalden. Here, each spring, citizens vote by a show of hands on questions affecting the community. These highly ceremonial meetings are called the **Landsgemeinden** (⏾ *see Calendar of events*).

THE FEDERAL AUTHORITIES

Legislative power is exercised by two assemblies, the National Council and

A Landsgemeinde in Glarus

Suisse Tourisme

the Council of States; executive power by a college of seven members, the Federal Council. The two assemblies, when sitting jointly, form the Federal Assembly. The National Council represents the people, with one deputy being elected for more than 30 000 inhabitants (200 members); each canton or half-canton is represented by at least one seat. The Council of States, which represents the cantons, has 46 members, or 2 per canton regardless of the size of the population.

This bicameral system, similar to American parliamentary institutions, protects as far as possible the interests of the small communities.

Executive power resides in the Federal Council. Its seven members are elected for a four-year term by the Federal Assembly, and each administers a department, or ministry. The annual election of the President—whose official title is President of the Confederation—and of the Vice-President appears to be a mere formality: the Vice-President invariably succeeds the President and his successor is chosen from a roster drawn up by agreement.

THE SOVEREIGN PEOPLE

Decisions by the Federal Assembly can be taken only after a favourable vote by both chambers. Here again, however, popular sovereignty has a role to play. If within 90 days after a decision by the Assembly, signatures can be obtained from 50 000 citizens, the entire population is then called upon to decide whether a law should finally be accepted or rejected. This is the **right of referendum**, which in practice has a conservative influence. Citizens of Vaud, according to tradition, are fond of saying: "The referendum is our right to say No when Berne has said Yes". During a referendum in December 1992, the Swiss nation answered no to joining the EEE *(Espace Économique Européen)*.

The Swiss also have the right to **initiate legislation**. Thus, 100 000 citizens may demand an amendment of the articles of the Constitution or the adoption of new articles. Thus, the popular will finds expression at every level of political activity and exercises permanent control over the country's institutions.

NATIONAL SERVICE

Although Switzerland is known to be a neutral country, military service plays a prominent part in the life of its citizens. The **Swiss Army** is a militia without "regular" units. "Active" service begins only at general mobilisation. There is no provision for performing civilian service instead of military service. The Army has a general only in time of war or general mobilisation (General Guisan, 1939-1945).

In 2003, voters approved a major military reform, *Army XXI*, reducing the size of the army by half to 220,000 conscripts and reducing mandatory service to 260 days. Service is required for able-bodied men; for women, it is voluntary.

The Swiss soldier keeps all his equipment at home: uniform, rifle, ammunition, gas mask against nuclear, biological or chemical weapons.

While landlocked Switzerland does not have a navy, **military boats** patrol Swiss border lakes Lake Geneva, Lake Maggiore and Lake Constance. There also is a Swiss **Air Force,** which defended national air space from Allied and Axis incursion in the Second World War.

Electoral Duty

Communal, cantonal and federal elections occur with a frequency that may seem surprising to outsiders.

In cantons like Berne and Zurich, which are very much attached to strict control of their budgets, it is a common joke that voting is as frequent as *Jass*, the Swiss game of poker. Voting may take place about the building of a bus shelter (communal) or the diversion of a mountain torrent (cantonal), as often as about the fixing of prices (federal). So many elections, which usually are scheduled on a Sunday, may account for low turn-outs (35-50% participation); in the case of cantonal voting attendance can be as low as 30%.

THE SWISS CANTONS

Under the shield: the name of the canton and its official abbreviation (used for car registration).

On the map: the boundaries of the cantons and their capitals. Cantons are listed alphabetically by their local names with their English version and/or alternative name. Area, population, language and religious majorities follow.

Abbreviations:

F: *French,* **G**: *German,* **I**: *Italian,* **P**: *Protestant,* **RC**: *Roman Catholic.*

Appenzell

Inner-Rhoden (AI):
172km²/66sq mi
population 15 000 (**G-RC**).

Ausser-Rhoden (AR):
243km²/94sq mi
population 53 200 (**G-P**).

The bear, which represents the Abbey of Sankt Gallen, adorns the shield of the canton.

Aargau (Argovia)
1 404km²/542sq mi
population 550 900 (**G-P**).

APPENZELL (AR/AI)

AARGAU (AG)

BASEL-LAND (BL)

BASEL-STADT (BS)

BERN (BE)

FRIBOURG (FR)   GENÈVE (GE)   GLARUS (GL)   GRAUBÜNDEN (GR)   JURA (JU)   LUZERN (LU)   NEUCHÂTEL

FRANCE

FRANCE

ITALIA

BASEL **BS**
BASEL (BÂLE)
Liestal
BL
Delémont   **SO**
JU   SOLOTHURN
JURA   (SOLEURE)
Aarau

AG
AARGAU
(ARGOV

LU
LUZERN
(LUCERNE)

NE
NEUCHÂTEL   Neuchâtel
(NEUENBURG)
Bern

Solothurn

Luze

Sar

UNTERWAL
OV

Fribourg

FR
FRIBOURG
(FREIBURG)

BE
BERN (BERNE)

VD
VAUD (WAADT)

Lausanne

LAC LÉMAN

Sion   ROTTEN

Genève   **GE**   GENÈVE
(GENF)

VS
VALAIS   (WALLIS)

Doubs

Aare

Lac de Neuchâtel

RHONE

RHEIN

The name means "the country of the Aare" and the river is represented by wavy lines. The three stars represent the three districts which together form the canton.

Basel (Bâle, Basel)
Basel District (BL):
482km²/165sq mi
population 261 400 (**G-P**).
Basel Town (BS):
37km²/14sq mi
population 186 700 (**G-P**).

The town was the seat of a prince-bishop. Its arms include a bishop's crosier (red for Basel District, black for Basel Town).

Bern (Berne)
6 050km²/2 659sq mi
population 947 100 (**G-P**).
🕭 *For the origin of the coat of arms see BERN.*

Fribourg
1 670km²/645sq mi
population 239 100 (**F-RC**).

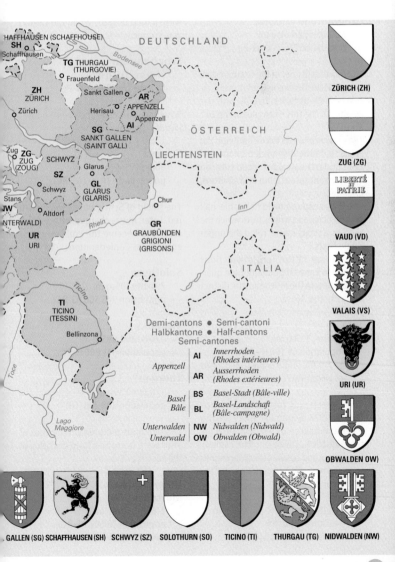

The shield of Fribourg is black and white, the colours of the dukes of Zähringen.

Genève (Geneva, Genf)
282km²/109sq mi
population 414 300 (**F-P**).
🕯 *For the origin of the coat of arms see* GENÈVE.

Glarus
684km²/2 654sq mi
population 38 300 (**G-P**).

Its coat of arms represents St Fridolin, the patron saint of the district.

Graubünden (Grisons)
7 106km²/2 744sq mi
population 185 700 (**G-P**).

The modern history of the Graubünden, known as the Grisons in English and Rhaetia in ancient times, begins with the alliance of the three Leagues in the 14C and 15C.
The League of God's House gathered the subjects of the Bishop and Chapter of Chur under the shield charged with "an ibex passant sable" (chur and environs, Engadin).
The Grey League (shield half sable, half argent, black and white), from which the Grisons gets its name, ruled the upper Rhine Basin.
The banner of the Ten Jurisdictions League (a cross of gold and blue quartering) flew in the Prättigau, the district of Davos and Arosa.

Jura
837km²/323sq mi
population 69 100 (**F-RC**).
🕯 *For the origin of the coat of arms see* DELÉMONT.

The canton was formed on 24 September 1978 by popular vote ratifying a Federal decree of 9 March 1978. Its three districts, Delémont (the capital), Porrentruy and Les Franches Montagnes were formerly the northern part of the canton of Berne.

Luzern (Lucerne)
1 492km²/576sq mi
population 350 600 (**G-RC**).

Neuchâtel
797km²/308sq mi
population 166 500 (**F-P**).

The present coat of arms dates from the proclamation (1848) of the Republic of Neuchâtel. The white cross on a red ground commemorates its adhesion to the Confederation.

Sankt Gallen
2 014km²/778sq mi
population 452 600 (**G-RC**).

The fascine on the shield recalls the union of the various districts which were joined in 1803, when the canton was formed.

Schaffhausen
298km²/115sq mi
population 73 400 (**G-P**).

Schaffhausen means "the sheep's house" (*Schaf* = sheep).

Schwyz
908km²/350sq mi
population 131 400 (**G-RC**).

The shield of Schwyz used to be plain red. Later, it was charged with a white cross and became the emblem of the entire Swiss Confederation.

Solothurn
791km²/305sq mi
population 245 500 (**G-RC**).

Ticino
2 811km²/1 085sq mi
population 311 800 (**I-RC**).

Thurgau
1 013km²/391sq mi
population 228 200 (**GP**).

The two lions pictured on the coat of arms were borrowed from the arms of the counts of Kyburg.

Unterwalden
Nidwalden (NW):
276km²/107sq mi
population 38 600 (**G-RC**).
– **Obwalden (OW);**

491km²/190sq mi
population 32 700 (**G-RC**).

The arms bear the keys of St Peter:
those of Nidwalden are on a red ground;
those of Obwalden on a red and white
ground.

Uri
1 076km²/415sq mi
population 35 000 (**G-RC**).

Valais (Wallis)
5 226km²/2 018sq mi
population 278 200 (**F-RC**).

The shield is red and white to commemorate the episcopal banner of
Sion. It bears 13 stars representing the
13 *dizains* (districts) of the canton.

Vaud (Waadt)
3 219km²/1 243sq mi
population 626 200 (**F-P**).

The green flag was adopted when the
Lemanic Republic was founded in 1798.
The white flag with the motto "Liberté
et Patrie", or "Freedom and Homeland",
was adopted when Vaud joined the Confederation in 1803.

Zug
239km²/92sq mi
population 100 900 (**G-RC**).

Zürich (Zurich)
1 729km²/667sq mi
population 1 228 600 (**G-P**).

Economy

Switzerland enjoys one of the highest standards of living in the world. Its
economic success relies on a thriving
services sector, a highly skilled and
motivated workforce, strong currency
and stable political situation. Swiss
industry, known to be both traditional
and innovative, is efficient but depends
heavily on exporting its goods. A mountainous country where only 10% of the
land is arable, it is also highly dependent
on the import of raw materials to meet
the needs of its population. Even so, the

overall mentality remains protectionist;
while foreigners account for some 25%
of the workforce, immigration is subject
to strict regulation.

Swiss voters decided in 1992 not to join
the European Community (now the
European Union), but in 1995, Switzerland became a member of the International Trade Organisation (ITO). The
country remains a **"haven of peace"**
and a refuge for many foreigners.
Geneva is the seat of many international organisations, including GATT
and specialised agencies of the United
Nations, including the High Commission
for Refugees.

WORLD FINANCE

Zurich is the country's economic capital,
where most banks have their headquarters. Swiss neutrality has done much
to attract foreign capital, thanks to a
strong, steady currency and bank con-
fidentiality (recently being made more
flexible to combat money laundering):
40% of the world's personal savings are
concentrated in Switzerland. Moreover,
foreign investments, in particular from
the United States, have increased considerably since the liberalisation of the
Swiss economy.

The banking system also supports important insurance and shipping industries;
vasts amounts of international financial
trade passes through Switzerland. Life
insurance is a prosperous sector, and it
is said that Swiss citizens enjoy the best
and most comprehensive insurance in
the world. Rentenanstalt/Swiss Life,
Winterthur and Zurich dominate.

AGRICULTURE

Agriculture enjoys a privileged status.
Strongly protected, heavily subsidised
by the state, and closely integrated into
rural life and the Swiss landscape, it is
simultaneously an integral part of Swiss
culture and a major tourist attraction.
Livestock farming accounts for 75% of
the agricultural production.

Since the Swiss farming industry can
grow only enough to satisfy 60% of
the country's needs, everything grown

is consumed in the home country; the remainder is imported.

Cereals, heavily subsidised by the government, remain expensive, although the use of chemical fertilisers has increased yield. Such farming methods, thought to damage the environment, are not well accepted by the population. Organic farming is very much in vogue but is still too costly to be applied on a large scale.

Half the cheese made in Switzerland (25% of dairy production) is exported. The country is famous worldwide for its Gruyère (from the Gruyères region) and Emmental (from the Lemme area).

Forestry has been carefully regulated since 1993. Forests cover about one-third of the land and contribute to the prevention of natural disasters such as avalanches and landslides. For these reasons, deforestation is strictly forbidden.

INDUSTRY AND TRADE

Swiss industry is characterised by extremely high standards of quality, an attitude which has earned it a worldwide reputation of excellence. The most prosperous sectors are those of machinery (machine tools, farming and printing equipment) and electromechanics, representing 45% of Swiss exports. Zurich, Baden and Winterthur are the major industrial centres.

The chemical and pharmaceutical industries, largely concentrated in the Basel area, are flourishing; research and development are extremely active. Swiss pharmaceutical groups are among the world's most powerful: Roche and Novartis (resulting from the merger of Ciba and Sandoz), two of the world's largest, are headquartered here; others have major offices here.

Watchmaking also has come to symbolise Switzerland. Renowned as the "international custodian of time," Switzerland boasts artisans that specialise in luxury timepieces (medium and low ranges have been left to Asian manufacturers), producing high-quality products that utilize classic hand-crafting and modern techniques. Swiss clocks and watches are universally appreciated and the "Made in Switzerland" label enjoys worldwide esteem: 95% of the national production is exported.

The **food-processing industry** is booming. Nestlé, established in Vevey, is Switzerland's leading group and is ranked first in the world.

Swiss **chocolate** enjoys an excellent reputation abroad; just over half the annual production is exported. The rest is consumed by the Swiss, whose sweet tooth consumes an estimated 107 bars per person per year. The designation "Swiss chocolate" is carefully controlled; it must be made entirely in Switzerland out of cocoa beans, cocoa paste, cocoa butter, sugar, and sometimes milk. Swiss chocolate pioneers include Francois-Louis Cailler, Philippe Suchard, Rodolphe Sprungli, Rudolf Lindt and Henri Nestle.

The Swiss **textile industry** has had the same problems as other nations with comparably high labour costs against the onslaught of low-cost Asian products. While many silk factories in the east and centre of Switzerland have shut down, the manufacture of synthetic fabric, particularly around Lucerne, has expanded.

Protecting the Environment

Preserving nature is equally important to private firms, public authorities and the population. Modern farming techniques are required to respect the environment, and the relatively new industry of recycling waste is faring well. The Swiss show great awareness of ecological issues and are careful to recycle their rubbish individually (sorting glass, paper and metal). A moratorium on new construction of nuclear plants was voted and enforced up to the year 2000. No nuclear plant projects have been undertaken since then.

FINANCIAL

Services are the backbone of the Swiss economy. They employ 70% of the working population and account for 70% of the GDP. The Swiss are known to have a natural penchant for saving money and the national currency attracts many foreign investments.

TOURISM

Picturesque chalets, beautiful landscapes and a tradition of hospitality have made Switzerland an ideal holiday destination for generations. Switzerland also benefits from its reputation as one of the safest destinations in Europe.

After metalworking and pharmaceuticals, tourism is is the country's main industry, attracting an international clientele, usually families, many of which return to the same resort every year. German tourists account for the highest number of visitors, followed by the British and the Dutch. Destinations such as Zermatt and Grindelwald also attract Japanese and American visitors. Of course, Swiss locals are as likely to vacation within the country as beyond.

Where winter and summer seasons were once distinct, increasing tourism has created a year-round season as visitors take advantage of special discounts and offers in non-peak times, especially for wellness retreats at Swiss spas and resorts and for discount airfare.

Switzerland is renowned for the excellence of its hotel industry. Some establishments are over 100 years old and are owned by families eager to welcome guests with attentive service.

Many multi-national companies are headquartered or have subsidiaries here, boosting business-related tourism (banking in Zurich, pharmaceuticals around Basel), as do international organizations (United Nations in Geneva, International Olympic Committee in Lausanne).

Even so, Swiss tourism remains susceptible to the same economic and global pressures as other nations.

The Urban Scene

Many Swiss villages and cities offer admirable examples of town planning. There is hardly a city or village which does not jealously guard some fragment of its Roman or medieval character.

Fountains

Fountains, always charmingly decked with flowers, are a welcoming note to

Oriel window in Stein am Rhein

the lively squares and streets of many Swiss towns and cities.

Arcades

Originating beyond the Alps, arcades (*Laufen* in German) became popular from the 14C onwards, when they were adopted by Berne: the arcaded streets in many towns of the Mittelland is evidence of a period of Bernese influence.

Painted Facades

Such painting (not to be confused with *sgraffito*—see below, "*The Engadine house*") has been popular since the Renaissance, especially in German Switzerland, where façades are proudly decorated with vast allegorical or historical compositions inspired by classical mythology and the Bible.

Throughout Switzerland, the shutters of historic monuments and public buildings are painted with chevrons in the colours of the canton's coat of arms.

Covered Bridges

These are especially popular in German Switzerland. In addition to providing towns like Lucerne with pleasant sheltered walks, the roof protects the walkway, reducing maintenance on a structure made wholly of timber. The latest covered bridge built in Switzerland was in 1943 (Hohe Brücke, on the road from Flüeli to Kerns – see SACHSELN). Some hillside villages have covered public staircases, also built entirely of wood.

Rural Architecture

Valais house
(Évolène)

Central Switzerland house
(Lucerne area)

Appenzell house
(Trogen area)

Bernese Country house
(Évolène)

Bernese Oberland house
(Jungfrau region)

R. Corbel/Michelin

Oriel Windows

These corbelled loggias (*Erker* in German), sometimes built over two storeys, are to be seen in northeastern towns where they are often elaborate works of art decorated with carving and painting. Oriel windows also can be seen adorning more modest houses throughout the Engadine region.

Official Buildings

The word "comfortable" well describes the impression of middle-class ease conveyed by Swiss public buildings such as the town hall (Rathaus) of which even the smallest city is so proud. These buildings testify to the quality of civil architecture in the Gothic, Renaissance and Classical periods. Their internal arrangements – rooms richly ornamented and furnished with stucco, woodwork, glazed cabinets and magnificent porcelain stoves – show a sophisticated way of life.

The old guild or corporation headquarters (Zunfthaus) vie with this luxury. One in Zurich houses the collection of pottery of the Swiss National Museum. Important buildings, like the great Gothic cathedrals, which dominate their surroundings, are Swiss specimens of foreign styles. The Helvetian genius is exhibited less by single monumental works than in the design of a group of buildings or a simple country church.

RURAL ARCHITECTURE

Carefully adorned with flowers, the Swiss peasant house shows, especially in German Switzerland, a remarkable care for comfort and propriety as well as a highly developed practical sense.

The Bernese Oberland House

It features a low-pitched roof, with wide eaves on all sides; in the high valleys, it is still covered with shingles weighted down by large stones. The ornamentation is profuse: the beams are carved with facets and the props of the roof are elaborately finished. This is the type of house that has made the Swiss chalet popular all over the world.

The Central Switzerland House

A highly distinctive style of building, recognisable by its steep roof and separate weatherboards sheltering the row of windows on each storey. The ground floor is high above the ground and can be reached only from the side, up an outdoor staircase.

The Appenzell House

In this rainy district, farm buildings are grouped together to form a single block and wooden shingles are arranged like the scales of a fish to cover the roof and sometimes part of the façade. The gable of the dwelling house invariably faces the valley. The windows of the cellar are located at ground level, where women working at fine embroidery find an even temperature. The shutters can be folded back vertically and made to fit into a groove at the top of the window.

The Bernese Country House

A huge roof, extending down to the first floor at the sides, also covers a large barn. The wealthier country dwellers, imitating townspeople, often choose to remove the triangular roof surmounting the gable and replace it with an imposing timber arch with wood panelling.

The Ticino house – A stone building of a somewhat primitive design: communication between the different parts of the house is by outdoor stairs and wooden galleries. Because of the uneven shape and size of the stones used in its construction, the Ticino house has very thick walls (up to 0.90m/3ft). The roof covering is made with stone slabs. The upper part of the gable is left open to the winds or enclosed with a rough partition of superimposed planks.

The Valais House

In the villages of the French-speaking Valais, wooden houses are often quite high. Living quarters (wooden section) are joined by open-side galleries to the kitchen area (masonry section), Nearby stands a **raccard** (⊚ *for illustration see Le VALAIS)*, a small wooden barn perched on piles and used as a granary or storehouse. This type of small chalet can also be found in the Ticino area, where it is known as a *torba*.

The Engadine house

The typical Engadine house, a massive grey structure, has plenty of room for two families under a broad gable crowning a façade sometimes interrupted by a break in its line. Floral, geometrical or heraldic designs frequently adorn the white walls. These may be painted, as the dry climate preserves paintwork, or they may be decorated by a technique known as **sgraffito**. To obtain this process the mason first applies a layer of rough grey plaster which is then covered with a coat of limewash. Finally, by scraping the surface with tremendous skill, the designs required (rosettes, foliated scrolls, etc. in the Renaissance style) are brought out again in grey.

Ornate wrought-iron grilles, sometimes curving out at the bottom, indicate reception rooms from which charming little oriel windows project. When not too elaborate, the *Bündnerstube* of hotels and inns gives a first glimpse of the local style of furnishing, which resembles that of the Tyrol. In hotels of the Graubünden region, the *Bündnerstube* is a friendly room, furnished and decorated according to regional tradition.

Wonderful examples of local furnishings are at the Engadine Museum at Sankt Moritz. The most typical room is the **sulèr**, a covered court common to the barn and living quarters, which serves both as a study and a meeting room. This cool, dark room, featuring carefully kept stone flags, a low, whitewashed vault and coffered ceiling, is lit only by an opening in the carriage gate.

Winter Sports

Thanks to its mountainous landscape, Switzerland has always been *the* ideal place for a winter holiday. It is, in fact, the first country where winter sports were developed on a large scale. Villages such as Sankt Moritz started to welcome British tourists for the winter season from the early 19C.

In most Swiss resorts, the winter season is from just before Christmas through early April with the best conditions usually between mid-January and mid-March, depending on the altitude.

The latter part of the season offers the advantages of longer days, mild temperatures and far fewer people. In the higher resorts (Zermatt, Saas Fee, Sankt Moritz), snow coverage is generally satisfactory until Easter, even early May in locations above 2 500m/8 202ft. Spring snow is ideal for off-piste skiing.

Winter offers a range of breathtaking landscapes, from medium-height mountains – wooded areas with gentle, rolling massifs – to the awe-inspiring high altitude peaks. Nature lovers will succumb to the charm of Grindelwald, Zermatt, Saas Fee, Crans-Montana, Sankt Moritz or Pontresina, whose rare beauty is world-renowned. Most Swiss ski resorts are above the tree line, giving even inexperienced skiers access to summits reaching some 4 000m/11 313ft and their inspiring, often panoramic views. Many resorts have winter hiking trails for long treks along gentle slopes, where packed snow crunches underfoot.

If you would rather just bask in the winter sun, you can pull up a chair as a spectator at any of the numerous competitions and events which take place throughout the winter season.

ALPINE SKIING

Switzerland simply has some of the world's best skiing and the world's best known resorts. The largest are the duo of **Davos** (248km/154mi of prepared pistes) and **Klosters** (170km/105mi), the ensemble formed by the 4 Vallées, with **Verbier** as the main resort, with 400km/250mi of pistes and the Jungfrau region (**Interlaken, Wengen, Murren**) with (220km/137mi of pistes). Some individual resorts are equally as expansive, such as **Sankt Moritz** (230km/143mi of pistes in the Engadine Valley) and **Zermatt** (313km/246mi of pistes, including on the Klein Matterhorn glacier).

Each has a massive modern networks of mountain railways, funiculars, cable cars and surface lifts (t-bars on the glaciers) and terrain for all levels of skers and snowboarders, from the timid beginner who favors gentle groomed slopes to the powderhound who glories in long stretches of virgin snowfields. Even resorts that are smaller by comparison,

Skiing in the Vaud Alps

Franziska Pfenniger / Switzerland Tourism

such as **Engelberg-Titlis** (82km/51mi of pistes) and **Aletsch** glacier (99km/61mi of pistes) have enough terrain to satisfy a ski holiday. Because of their proximity, it is possible to stay in one resort and visit another by train or bus for a day, such as Pontressina from Sankt Moritz. Some border resorts have teamed with their French, Italian or Austrian counterparts, such as the Franco-Swiss resort of Les Portes du Soleil, offering 600km/380mi of pistes lying mainly in the French resorts Avoriaz and Morzine Châtel. Zermatt's partnership with Breuil-Cervinia In Italy requires purchase of a separate ski pass for each country. Lastly, there is Samnaun, linked to the Austrian resort of Ischgl.

Many Swiss resorts are sought for their charming architecture, inspired by local tradition. Some developed from existing villages (Klosters, Arosa, Saas Fee, Zermatt, Adelboden). The chalet style has been preserved in larger resorts like Verbier, which can provide accommodation for up to 25 000 visitors. However, a boom in the popularity of winter holidays spurred the construction of vast, impersonal developments lacking traditional Swiss charm. This is the case with Davos, Sankt Moritz-Bad, Thyon and even Crans-Montana.

SNOWBOARDING

Switzerland has welcomed this popular snowsport by introducing snowparks with facilities such as half-pipes, boardercross and high jumps and by staging competitive events. While all resorts welcome snowboarders, the best equipped are Les Diablerets, Saas Fee and Laax, where World Cup events are held every year. Snowboarding was introduced as an official skiing event at the 1998 Olympic Winter Games in Nagano.

CROSS-COUNTRY SKIING

Cross-country skiing is one of the most popular sports after downhill skiing. It enables tourists to discover the mountains in a different way: treks through the calm, peaceful forests, at a leisurely or energetic pace, depending on the skier. The prettiest sites are in the Graubünden (150km/94mi of pistes near Sankt Moritz, 75km/47mi in Davos), at Laax-Flims and in the Gstaad region.

OTHER SNOWSPORTS

Ski touring is a combination of cross-country and alpine skiing. The boots are fastened to the heel for downhill skiing but left free for upward walking. The Swiss Alps offer countless opportunities for this sport, especially between

Chamonix and Zermatt and at Engadine. Always use the trails in the company of an experienced mountain guide.

Skijoring, in which one is towed behind a galloping horse, requires the skier to be of moderate skill or better. Originally a military competition held in Scandinavian countries. Sankt Moritz is one of the resorts which regularly organises skijoring races on the snow.

Walking: Perhaps the most pleasurable way to explore the countryside is on foot. All resorts feature signposted packed snow trails near the villages and much higher up *(access by chairlifts)*. Some of these trails are more suitable to walking with **snowshoes.** If you are going off the beaten track, it is advisable to go with a guide, to avoid areas prone to avalanches and also to learn more about local fauna and flora.

Many resorts set aside gentle slopes for **snow-tubing,** in which you sit in an inflated donut-like tube. It is a delightful diversion not limited to children. Also, many villages offer **dogsledding**, dashing through the snow in a sleigh drawn by a pack of dogs.

Sports practised on ice are also a popular feature of Swiss resorts, with many natural or artificial **skating rinks,** both indoors and outdoors. The Swiss are also fond of **ice hockey** and **curling**.

Switzerland is a great place if you love to fly downhill on a *luge,* a sled or a sleigh by any other name. Many resorts offer kilometres of signposted trails where the snow has been carefully packed. Grindelwald and Saas Fee boast outstanding facilities, with reserved hillsides. Bobsled runs are available for those in search of high-speed excitement , such as descent with a pilot at Sankt Moritz.

Food and Wine

SWISS SPECIALITIES

Combining the culinary traditions of France, Germany and Italy, Swiss cuisine offers memorable dining experiences, where meals in restaurants usually include soup, an entree (often fish), a meat dish with vegetables, potatoes or rice, and dessert.

Cheese Dishes -The great hard cheeses, Gruyère and Emmental, which carry the fame of the Swiss dairy industry abroad, are the basis of **fondue**, which is a national institution among the French Swiss. Every canton, especially Vaud, Neuchâtel and Fribourg, claims the perfect mix of Gruyère, Emmental, Vacherin and other ingredients.

Raclette, a Valais speciality, is prepared by toasting one side of a slice of Valais cheese (the soft cheese of Bagnes or Conches – Goms) at a fire. The melted cheese is scraped directly onto the plate

Franziska Pfenniger / Switzerland Tourism

Vintage in Sion

with a knife or a wooden blade. *Raclette* is eaten with gherkins and bread or potatoes cooked in their jackets.

Beef, Pork and Fish -The most original Swiss speciality is the dried meat of the Grisons, **Bündnerfleisch**. This is raw beef smoked and air-dried, served in thin slices. The most frequent meat dishes are fillet of veal *(Schnitzel)* and pork chop. A popular Zurich dish is minced veal or calf's liver with cream *(geschnetzeltes Kalbsfleisch)* and *Leberspiessli* (calf's liver cooked on a spit, with bacon). There is an extraordinary variety of *Wurst* (sausages). *Gnagi* (knuckle of pork, much enjoyed in Berne for a four o'clock snack), *Klöpfer* (saveloy) at Basel, *Schüblig* (long pork sausage) at Sankt Gallen, *Kalbsbratwurst* (veal sausage) at Zurich, *salsiz* (small salamis) in the Engadine. The national dish of German Switzerland is **Rösti,** potatoes boiled, diced, fried and finally baked with fried onion rings and bacon bits).

The French Swiss prefer smoked sausages with a stronger taste (*boutefas* in Payerne, *longeole* in Geneva). The monumental **Berner Platte** (Bernese Dish) combines bacon, sausages, ham, sometimes boiled beef, pickled cabbage *(Sauerkraut)* and potatoes.

Swiss rivers and lakes produce a wide variety of fish such as trout, pike, dace, tench, carp and perch (a speciality from Lake Geneva). All are seasoned according to local tradition.

Sweets and Desserts - Fresh cream enters into the composition of many sweets and desserts such as meringues and *Schaffhauserzungen* (baked biscuits with fresh cream). The kirsch-cake of Zug and the *Leckerli* of Basel – spiced bread made with honey and almonds – also have their faithful followers. Swiss chocolate, of time-honoured reputation, is used to make delicious cakes and sweets.

SWISS WINES

Switzerland's vineyards produce only 36% of the wine consumed nationally. Vaud's best-known white-wine vintages are Lavaux, Dézaley, Aigle and Yvorne. Fendant is the best known of the Valais wines. Dôle, the most popular red wine of Valais, is a fragrant, fruity blend of Pinot and Gamay grapes.

The Geneva canton produces white wines to accompany fish dishes: Perlan; Aligoté; Pinot Gris. Gewürztraminer and Sylvaner are well suited to desserts. Oeil de Perdrix, the rosé version of Pinot Noir, is best served chilled.

Although Cortaillod is a heavy red wine, most wines from Neuchâtel, such as Auvernier, Boudry and Colombier, are lighter whites drawn from a noble vine, the Chasselas, grown on chalky soil.

Ticino vines yield highly alcoholic wines, such as Mezzana and Nostrano, which are pleasant with dessert.

The red, white and rosé wines *(Süssdruck)* from the eastern region and the Alpine Valley of the Rhine are most appreciated for their light and subtle quality.

Terms Used in the Hospitality Industry

Bündnerstube – Traditional sitting room from the Grisons, furnished and decorated in accordance with the local custom.

Café – Tea room (in German-speaking Switzerland).

Carnotzet – In hotels of the Vaud and the Valais, a room where local cheese and wines are served.

Gasthaus – Inn (with restaurant if indicated).

Kurhaus – Spa. Usually a large isolated establishment with simple furnishings. There are also thermal and mountain *Kurhäuser*, used more as places to stay than as overnight stops.

Restaurant – Establishment serving lunch and dinner. In some German-Swiss towns, "restaurants" may provide only drinks, as in cafés, unless there is a notice saying *Speise-Restaurant*.

Wirtschaft – Very modest inn or pub, used mainly by local people.

Baden Houses and Covered Bridge
Bill Wassman / APA Publications

AARAU

Ⓒ AARGAU – POPULATION 15 229
ALT 383M/1 273FT

This is the capital of the Aargau canton, one of the richest in Switzerland, thanks to the textile and machine industries of the Aare and Rhine areas. It is pleasantly placed at the foot of the Jura. Formerly the capital of the short-lived Helvetic Republic, it became a separate canton in 1803. The best view of the old town is from the bridge spanning the River Aare. The town rises in terraces from the river and is dominated by the towers of the belfry, the church and the old castle.

Old Town

The narrow streets of this delightful quarter are lined with fine old houses, some adorned with oriel windows and wrought-iron emblems whose style recalls the long-standing Bernese domination; other façades are covered with frescoes, and roofs have stepped gables and eaves. The **Stadtkirche** (parish church) is surmounted by an elegant late-17C belfry. The fine Fountain of Justice (1643) stands in a small adjacent square and, nearby, there is a pleasant view of the countryside.

Excursion

Schönenwerd★
4.5km/3mi SW on ⑤, the Olten road. A modern quarter, owing its existence to the Bally boot and shoe factories, has grown up outside the old town of Schönenwerd, dominated by a 12C church.

Bally Schuhmuseum★★
Felsgarten House, Oltnerstrasse 6. 🔊 *Guided tours Jan to mid-Jul and mid-Aug to mid-Dec: last Fri of the month, 2pm and 4pm.* 💰 *No charge.* ☎ *062 858 61 00.*
The Bally Shoe Museum is in the Felsgarten House, where the founder of the firm lived and opened his offices and first workshops. It contains valuable collections tracing the history of footwear throughout the centuries and across cultures. The exhibition, the only one of its kind in Switzerland, includes corporate emblems, books on shoe craft, and royal and imperial orders for the manufacture of boots and shoes.

ADELBODEN★★

BERN – POPULATION 3 650
ALT 1 356M/4 446FT

Adelboden lies in the wide, sunny **basin**★ at the upper end of the Engstligen Valley. It is one of the highest of the fashionable resorts in the Bernese Oberland both in summer and in winter, and is known for its healthy and agreeable climate. The village clusters halfway up the slope, facing a majestic skyline of limestone mountains. The most striking feature is the snow-covered, flat top of the Wildstrubel (alt 3 243m/10 640ft), completing the great mountain circle of the Engstligenalp, from which the powerful Engstligenfälle bursts forth, leaping from a rocky shelf and forming a most impressive spectacle.

Sights

The Skiing Area

Adelboden skiing area, linked to that of Lenk, comprises 160km/99.5mi of pistes and some 50 lifts. Its highest point is Luegli (alt 2 138m/7 014ft); it is particularly suitable for intermediate skiers, who will enjoy the long treks through mountain forests.

Engstligenfälle★★★

Remember to bring warm, waterproof clothes and sturdy shoes. 4km/2.5mi along the Adelboden road, then access by cable car (ascent 5min).

From the top, the **view**★ of Adelboden is dominated by Gsür (2 708m/8 884ft), the Gross Lohner Massif, and the upper part of the Engstligen Falls. To the south extend the Engstligenalp pastures, lush with gentian, lying at the foot of Wildstrubel. Hikers can choose several **itineraries**, including those leading to Ammerten Pass (2hr climb 2 443m/8 015ft) and the **Ammertenspitz** summit (2hr 30min climb 2 613m/8 573ft), for a splendid **panorama** of Steghorn, Tierhorn, Les Diablerets and the Walliser Alpen. The most spectacular excursion leads down past the falls, featuring a vertical drop of 476m/1 562m *(1hr 30min on foot)*. From Engstligenalp, follow directions for "Unter dem Berg" and continue towards "Wasserfall."

After 30min, you will discover a breathtaking **view**★★★ as you approach the bridge spanning the falls, whose height and powerful flow is truly impressive. Follow directions for "Engstligenfall", within sight of the cable-car terminal. A steep, narrow path leads to luxuriant vegetation including Alpine columbine, a rare mountain species (slender stem 50cm/9in long with dark maroon petals). Finally, you reach the **belvedere**★★ overlooking the lower falls, which are equally spectacular. Return to the car park by following directions for "Unter dem Berg" *(10min)*.

AIGLE

VAUD – POPULATION 7 532
ALT 417M/1 369FT

A wine and industrial centre as well as a military depot, Aigle is a small, pleasant town at the junction of the Rhône Valley and the Ormonts Valley, surrounded by famous vineyards, which extend from the heights into the town itself. Stroll along the shaded Gustave-Doré Avenue (beside the torrent of the Grande Eau) and into the town centre by the unusual Jerusalem Alley (Ruelle de Jérusalem), with its covered wooden galleries decked with flowers. *Rue Colomb 5 – 1860 – ☎ (024) 466 30 00*

Castle

Like the town, this 13C feudal fortress is surrounded by vineyards. It originally belonged to the House of Savoy but was captured and rebuilt by the Bernese in the 15C. The recently restored stronghold retains its curtain walls, pepper-pot roofed towers, and turrets. It now houses period furniture and a local museum. The covered sentry-walk is decorated with frescoes depicting fruit and flowers.

Musée de la Vigne et du Vin

Open Jul and Aug, daily, 10am-6pm; Apr-Jun, Sep and Oct, daily except Mon, 10am-12.30pm, 2-6pm. Closed Nov-Mar. ≈9CHF. ☎ 024 466 21 30; www.chateauaigle.ch.

The Wine Museum is located in several rooms of the main building and three floors of the main tower. On display are glassware, coopers' casks, tubs, tools and labels from the 17C up to the present day. Note the two enormous early winepresses: a lever press dating from around 1600 and a screw press from 1706. There is also a luminous **tapestry** (1943) devoted to grapes and winemaking by Jean Lurçat.

LES ALPES VAUDOISES★★

MICHELIN MAP 729 F6-G6

The Vaud Alps are divided between the Rhône and Aare basins (Upper Sarine Valley). They owe their strong individuality to their landscape of wide green valleys and limestone escarpments, forming majestic snowy summits. Their mountain people speak French, are Protestant, and build houses like those of the Bernese Oberland. A striking feature of the local landscape is the extraordinary scattering of these chalets over the slopes above the Grande Eau and the Sarine.

The Ormonts and Enhaut district valleys around Lake Geneva and the Bernese Oberland are .dotted with holiday resorts such as Château-d'Oex or Les Diablerets. Higher up, on terraced sites 1 000m/3 280ft above the Rhône Valley and facing the Dents du Midi, Leysin and Villars-Chesières draw the world of sport and fashion.

1 Vallée des Ormonts★★

From Aigle to Saanen *45km/28mi – about 1hr 30min*
The Col du Pillon is usually blocked by snow from November to April.

Leysin✳
From the touring route, 4km/2.5mi by a road on the left before reaching Le Sépey.
The splendid terraced **site**★★ of Leysin, overlooking the Rhône Valley and facing the Dents du Midi, enjoys a mild climate and strong sun, an ideal location for either summer holidays or winter skiing. The next delightful sight is the village of Les Diablerets, at the foot of the escarpment bearing the same name.

Les Diablerets✳
Chief town of the Ormonts Valley. The resort is spread over a widening basin of meadows dotted with ash trees and maples. The **site**★★ is both delightful and impressive, with very fine chalets, built and decorated in the traditional style of the Bernese Oberland. Here the wall of the Les Diablerets Mountain curves deeply to form a cirque (Creux de Champ) between the Scex Rouge spur and the Culan.
Between Les Diablerets and the Pillon Pass, a bend in the ravine crossed by the Bourquin Bridge affords glimpses, between the trees, of white monoliths, formed by the dissolution of gypsum. On the opposite slope the Dard Torrent escapes in thin cascades from two overlapping rock **cirques**★.

The Ski Area
The Diablerets resort is renowned for its snowfields, spread out over three massifs: Le Meilleret (1 949m/6394ft), which can be reached by skiing from **Villars-sur-Ollon**★ (*see VILLARS-SUR-OLLON*), Isenau (2 120m/6 955ft at Le Floriettaz) and the Scex Rouge Glacier. In spite of its small size (50km/31mi of slopes) and somewhat impractical equipment, the resort offers several splendid slopes. Intermediate skiers will appreciate the Isenau area, the long forested pistes around Le Meilleret and especially

Address Book

For coin ranges, see the Legend on the cover flap.

TOURIST OFFICES

Les Diablerets – ☎ 024 492 33 58; www.diablerets.ch.

Leysin – ☎ 024 494 22 44 – Fax 024 494 16 16; www.leysin.ch.

Gstaad – Tourismusbüro Promenade – ☎ 033 748 81 81; www.gstaad.ch.

WHERE TO STAY

LES DIABLERETS

Hostellerie Les Sources – chemin du Vernex – ☎ 024 492 01 00; www.hotel-les-sources.ch – 48 rooms – open 1 Dec-7 Apr and 2 Jun-19 Oct. A hotel with highly affordable prices. Pleasantly situated near the village centre, overlooking the Diablerets Massif.

Hôtel des Diablerets – ☎ 024 492 09 09; www.hoteldesdiablerets.com – 59 rooms – open 20 Dec-15 Apr and 1 Jun-30 Sep. Treat yourself to one of the higher-priced rooms with sumptuous views of the glacier. Covered pool.

EATING OUT

LES DIABLERETS

Café de la Couronne – ☎ 024 492 31 75 – closed Wed in low season. Delicious homemade charcuterie.

Les Lilas – ☎ 024 492 31 34; www.hotelleslilas.ch – closed 22 May-8 Jun, Sun evenings and Mon in low season. This charming chalet converted into a guesthouse serves regional cuisine.

---

the red trail between Cabane and Oldenegg. Seasoned skiers can swoop along the **Combe d'Audon**★★, starting from Scex Rouge, which features high-quality snow and breathtaking vistas. Snowboarders will find snowparks laid out along the Isenau in winter and Scex Rouge in summer. The **Forfait Intégral des Alpes Vaudoises** ski pass grants visitors unlimited access to 220km/137mi of slopes and 77 cable cars covering Villars, Leysin and Les Mosses. Cross-country skiers have at their disposal 31km/20mi of pistes at high altitude as well as lower down in the valleys.

Scex Rouge★★★

Access: 35min by cable car from the Pillon Pass or by cable car leaving from Reusch. During the ascent, marmots and chamois goats take a backseat to the dramatic view of the Les Diablerets Basin and the splendid escarpment immediately before you reach the upper station. From here, a staircase *(open only in summer)* leads to the Scex Rouge Peak (alt 2 971m/9 747ft) where there is a magnificent **panorama**★★★: southwards, the Swiss Alps (Matterhorn) and French Alps (Mont Blanc) to the nearby peaks of Les Diablerets and the superb **Les Diablerets Glacier**★★ (an extension to the north of the Tsafleuron Glacier). Northwards the view extends to the Tornette and Palette peaks, which rise behind the Ormonts Valley.

Lac Retaud★

1.5km/1mi by a narrow mountain road from the Pillon Pass. This pretty sheet of green water fills a hollow opposite the double cirque of the Dard, dominated on the left by the Oldenhorn and on the right by the Scex Rouge. A third cirque lies between the spurs of the Oldenhorn (in the Oldenbach Valley) from Col du Pillon to Gsteig, ending in sight of the solidly buttressed Spitzhorn pyramid.

Gsteig

The rocky hanging valley farther upstream between the escarpments of the Spitzhorn and the Mittaghorn, and from which a powerful cascade flows, leads to the Sanetsch Pass, which used to be a well-travelled link between the Oberland and the Valais.

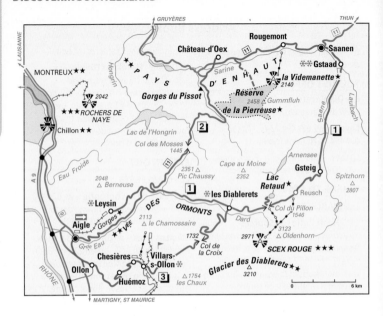

Gstaad✷✷ – ♿ *See GSTAAD.*

Saanen – ♿ *See SAANEN.*

2 Pays d'Enhaut★★

From Saanen to Aigle *45km/28mi – allow 1hr (not including visits)*

Lying between Saanen and Château-d'Oex, the short **Défilé des Allamans** marks the boundary between the cantons of Bern and Vaud as well as the switch from French to German, as the name of the hamlet suggests. The slim, rocky point aptly named Rubli (Carrot) continually catches the eye.

Rougemont
This charming village was the site of a Cluniac priory between the 11C and the Reformation. The church is typical of early Swiss Romanesque structures. Note the crane In the stained-glass windows – the mascot symbolising the Gruyères region.

La Videmanette★
Alt 2 140m/7 021ft. ⛰Access by cable car in 18min leaving from Rougemont.
The upper station is on top of the Videmanette Mountain, situated between the Rubli and Rocher Plat summits. From the restaurant's roof terrace, the **vista**★ encompasses *(right to left)*: the three summits of La Tornette, Les Diablerets, Lake Arnensee and Lake Retaud, behind the Gummfluh, the Oldenhorn Range, the Jungfrau Mountain range in the distance and, to the far left, the Eiger.

Réserve de la Pierreuse★
On foot: allow half a day.
At Les Granges bear left (⚠ *be careful: hairpin bend*) onto the downhill road from Gérignoz, which goes through a tunnel and crosses a bridge over the Sarine. Before a large sawmill bear right and take the road up the opposite side of the valley.

▶ *Leave the car before the Les Leyssalets Bridge and proceed on foot.*

This nature reserve, at the foot of the rocky north face of the Gummfluh, lies at an altitude of between 1 300m/4 264ft and 2 460m/8 068ft, a hilly **site**★ covering approximately 880ha/2 174 acres. The flora and fauna (spruce trees, ibexes, marmots) are protected. The twin Gummfluh peaks can be glimpsed through a gap formed by the tributary valley of Gérignoz.

Château-d'Oex – ⟨♿⟩ *See CHÂTEAU-D'OEX.*

Gorges du Pissot

A **viewpoint**★ on a curve allows you to appreciate the steepness and wooded nature of this rocky cleft, through which the Torneresse flows. After passing through the Pissot Gorges, the road curves to the beautiful, pastoral Etivaz Valley, at the end of which you will get a fleeting glimpse of a small peak, the Cape au Moine. You will then come to the extensive lowland of Mosses with its woods and fields.

At La Lécherette you reach the upper valley of the Hongrin where there is a reservoir. On the Ormonts slope the view extends downstream along the Comballaz to the icy domes of Les Diablerets; on the left, observe the Scex Rouge and the Oldenhorn. Looking down the Grande Eau Valley, you can pick out the spa and large hotels of Leysin and, on the horizon, the Dents du Midi.

Between Le Sépey and Aigle the road runs along a ledge above the wooded **Grande Eau Gorges**★, and after a few hairpin bends, goes down to the floor of the Rhône Valley. The town of Aigle, dominated by its castle, nestles in a vineyard setting.

Aigle – ⟨♿⟩ *See AIGLE.*

③ Croix Pass Road★★

From Aigle to Les Diablerets via Villars *29km/18mi – 1hr*

Aigle – ⟨♿⟩ *See AIGLE.*

From Aigle, the road runs through vineyards, orchards and meadows dotted with bee-hives, within sight of the snowy peaks of the Grand Muveran and Les Diablerets.

Ollon

This charming wine-growers' village is clustered about its church. The road climbs, tortuous but excellent, along a *corniche*. 3km/2mi after Ollon a superb **view**★★ opens onto the Grand Muveran and Les Diablerets, the Pas de Cheville Valley between.

Chesières; Villars-sur-Ollon – ⟨♿⟩ *See VILLARS-SUR-OLLON.*

After Villars, the climb is extremely steep (13%) and the Les Diablerets mountains fill the horizon with their snowy summits. At the **Col de la Croix** (alt 1 727m/5 666ft), the road offers superb views of the imposing mountain range before descending to the wide basin; the resort of Les Diablerets spreads out below.

Les Diablerets✳ **–** ⟨♿⟩ *See above: Vallée des Ormonts.*

ALPI TICINESI ★

LOCAL MAP SEE SANKT-GOTTHARD-MASSIV

The Ticino, the southernmost canton of the Confederation, is Italian-speaking and Roman Catholic, yet since the Middle Ages, it has remained politically attached to Switzerland. Essentially a mountainous region with the Lepontine Alps in the north, the canton is divided by three river systems, the River Ticino being the main one. It cuts into the southern face of the Sankt Gotthard from the Lombard Plain to the highest peaks of the Sankt Gotthard Massif. **The barrier formed by the massif shelters the shores of Lake Maggiore and Lake Lugano, which grace these resorts with a pleasant Mediterranean climate. This southernmost part of the Alps can be fully appreciated when taking the Sankt Gotthard and Lukmanier Pass roads as well as the Nufenenstrasse.**

The Sankt Gotthard Pass Road ★

See SANKT-GOTTHARD-MASSIV for the history of this road.
Most of the present siting dates from 1830 but extensive resurfacing and widening has improved it considerably. On the Ticino side the road is much faster than along the Reuss. Be forewarned that the Sankt Gotthard road carries heavy traffic. *The Sankt Gotthard Pass is usually blocked by snow from November to June.* The Sankt Gotthard road tunnel (16km/10mi) between Göschenen and Airolo, which opened in 1980, was surpassed in length in 2000 by the Laerdal tunnel (24.5km/15mi) in Norway.

From Andermatt to Biasca 65km/40mi – about 2hr

Itinerary ② (*see SANKT-GOTTHARD-MASSIV map*)

Andermatt ✴
Alt 1 436m/4 711ft. Andermatt lies at the junction of the Sankt Gotthard, Furka and Oberalp roads in a beautiful curve of the Urseren Valley, which is the heart of the Sankt Gotthard Massif. The life of the town flows along its narrow main street, sec-

tions of which still show the typical Italian **binario** (road with granite paving stones). In winter, when snow covers the neighbouring slopes, punctuated with anti-avalanche barriers, Andermatt is crowded with skiers attracted by its easy access and old-fashioned charm. The main ski resorts are in the Nätschen district (towards the Oberalp Pass), regularly served by local trains and chairlifts, as are the Gemsstock slopes, equipped with a cable car.

The last climb to the Sankt Gotthard begins at the foot of the ancient Hospental watchtower. The road climbs above the Urseren Valley, to the right of the Furka Pass, by the snowy Galenstock peaks, then into the Gams Valley.

Gemsstock★★

Allow at least 1hr there and back, including a 40min journey in cable car split up into two trips. Many opportunities for hiking.

Proceed to the upper terrace with its viewing tables. The dramatic **panorama**★★ sweeps over 600 summits in the distance. The Finsteraarhorn dominates the Bernese Oberland to the east. In the foreground, the Göschen Valley is overshadowed by Dammastock. To the south lie the Mont Rose and the spectacular range of Italian Alps.

Passo del San Gottardo

Alt 2 108m/6 919ft. Set in a rugged but breathtaking landscape of rounded rocks and scattered lakes, the pass owes its name to a chapel erected about 1300 in honour of St Gotthard, Bishop of Hildesheim (near Hanover). Situated at the top of the pass, the **Museo Nazionale del San Gottardo**★ (National Sankt Gotthard Museum, ○*Open Jun-Oct, daily, 9am-6pm. Film (25min).* ∞8CHF. ☎ *091 869 15 25*) traces the history of this strategic location, used by the Romans and which links together north and south, connecting Switzerland to the rest of Europe. Scale models, photographs,and other artifacts illustrate the road, the tunnel, flora and fauna, postal connections, the Sankt Gotthard Inn (where weary travellers were fed and given a bed) and the relevance of the pass, particularly to the Battle of Tremola on 24 September 1799, during which the French fought against the Russians and the Austrians.

Val Tremola

Access in summer only. 13km/8mi from the Sankt Gotthard Pass.

The road coils loop over loop within this steep corridor, which carries the alarming name of Trembling Valley. Seen from below *(stand on the disused bridge at the bottom of the ravine)* the road, with its interlaced sustaining walls, gives a good idea of the road-builders' audacity.

Museum and Hospice at San Gottardo

Heinz Schwab / Switzerland Tourism

The modern road, an exceptionally bold piece of work, avoids the difficult crossing of the Tremola Valley by a change of route. It follows the mountainside with only three hairpin bends – one of which is built partly on a curved viaduct, another is a **viewpoint**★ – and the third is a tunnel 700m/0.5mi long. The descent is very steep. The Upper Leventina lies wide open between slopes dotted with villages nestling at the foot of a campanile. Note the Ticino stone houses and Alpine chalets with wooden upper storeys.

> 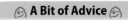 **A Bit of Advice**
>
> ### Mountain Roads
>
> The highway code states that on difficult mountain roads the ascending vehicle has priority.
>
> On "postal" roads drivers must comply with directions given by the drivers of the yellow post busses.

The Ambri-Piotta Basin, between woods of firs and larches, opens out between Airolo and the Piottino Defile. Below the Piottino Defile the valley is gradually shut in by steep spurs with wild ravines, whose torrents end in waterfalls.

Val Piora★
Alt 1 796m/5 900ft. 12min by funicular from the Ritom power station.
This is a pleasant walk along clearly laid-out paths, bordered by with charming Alpine lakes: the walk affords an opportunity to discover the local vegetation and the many wild animal species which inhabit the region.

Faido
Rich woodlands and gushing waters (La Piumogna Cascades), makes this township a splendid summer resort. The semicircular main square with shady lime trees, a statue dedicated to local glories, houses covered by curious conical stone roofs and dotted with outdoor cafés, compose a lovely Italian scene.

Biasca – *See below.*

The Lukmanier Pass Road★

From Biasca to Disentis/Mustér *66km/40mi – about 45min*

Itinerary 1 (*see SANKT-GOTTHARD-MASSIV map*)

The Lukmanier Pass is usually blocked by snow from November to May.

Biasca
Contrada Cavalier Pellanda 4 – 6710 – ☎ (091) 862 33 27
This small town, at the intersection of the Ticino Valley and the Brenno Valley, is dominated by the 12C **Chiesa dei Santi Pietro e Paolo** (*Contact the tourist office for entry*), hollowed out of the rock and accessible by a long stairway. The Romanesque church, made of local granite, has a tall bell tower with arches, its façade, decorated with a fresco partly worn away; the chapel is in the Baroque style with remains of interesting polychrome **frescoes** (14C-15C)

Malvaglia
The Romanesque **campanile**★ of the church is in the Lombard fashion, with the number of arches increasing as they approach the summit. It is by far the most graceful belfry in the Blenio Valley. The barrenness of the lower **Val Blenio**, accentuated by the destructive work of the tributaries of the Brenno, decreases beyond Dongio. A verdant basin opens out with the bold pyramid of the Sosto looming ahead.

Lottigna★

This village stretches along the valley in terraces. Fhe former Bailiffs' House (15C), decorated with the coat of arms of the first Swiss cantons, is now the **Musée du Blenio** (⏰*Open mid-Apr to 31 Oct, daily except Mon, 2-5.30pm.* ☞*5CHF.* ☎ *(091) 871 19 77; www.vallediblenio.ch)*. The museum houses historic tools, utensils and traditional regional costumes, religious art and a large arms collection (14C to the present day).

▶ *At Acquarossa bear left onto the small road that runs along the western side of Blenio Valley. Left of the church in Prugiasco, take the street that climbs, then narrows, and follow it for 2km/1mi. The sanctuary of Negrentino stands atop a grassy knoll.*

Chiesa Negrentino San Carlo★

30min on foot there and back. To visit, contact the Blenio Tourist office in Acquarossa. ☎ *(091) 871 19 77.*

This interior of this small 11C Romanesque church is painted with an admirable series of polychrome **frescoes**★★ (11C-16C). After leaving Castro and Ponto-Valentino, you reach Aquila and the direct road to Lukmanier. From Olivone to Acquacalda the road avoids the Olivone dead end in two series of hairpin bends separated by the Camperio shelf. Soon the **view**★ opens eastward to the snowy peaks of the Adula Massif.

Passo del Lucomagno

Alt 1 916m/6 286ft. The Lukmanier Pass marks the switch from one language to another – Romansh to Italian – and a cleavage between two types of local architecture. To the south, villages consist of groups of stone buildings around slender campaniles; to the north they feature wooden chalets and domed churches. The Lukmanier is the lowest of the Swiss transalpine routes, but owing to its roundabout approaches on the north slope of the Alps, international traffic uses the Sankt Gotthard. On the Rhine side, part of the high Alpine hollow is flooded by the waters of the Santa Maria Dam.

Between the Santa Maria Dam and Disentis/Mustér, beyond a valley dotted with clumps of dwarf alders and rhododendrons, the road crosses the clear Cristallina Rhine and, as conifers begin to reappear, enters the central basin of the Medel Valley. Sloping pastures cut by zigzag ravines, dark chalets and the domed belfry of Curaglia make this little mountain retreat an attractive **scene**★. Notice the silos in which grain ripens, after being harvested early because of the harsh climate.

Medelserschlucht

The Rhine Falls at Medel roar in this rocky cleft, where the road passes through many tunnels. The old road, which can now be followed only on foot after the lower entrance of the second tunnel (over 500m/0.4mi long), is more spectacular. Below, the Abbey of Disentis and the Tödi Massif appear in the gap of the Medel Gorges.

Disentis/Mustér✳ – ☙ *See DISENTIS/MUSTÉR.*

ALTDORF

Ⓒ URI – POPULATION 8 613
AND SANKT-GOTTHARD-MASSIV – ALT 462M/1 516FT

Altdorf, the key to the Sankt Gotthard Pass on the north side of the Alps, stands between Lake Lucerne and the defiles of the Upper Reuss Valley. It preserves all the dignity of a small, old-fashioned capital town. Travellers will notice the southern influences already apparent in restaurant menus, the presence of Ticino characteristics in the people and traces of the **binario** (Ⓖ *see ALPI TICINESI: Andermatt)*, all of which will prepare them for a greater change of scene.

Sight

Telldenkmal
The statue in honour of **William Tell**, the famous archer of Uri, stands in the main square of the town. The work dates from 1895 and is interesting chiefly for the fact that it created Tell's physical type, since made familiar all over the world by a postage stamp bearing his effigy. The statue of this national hero is appropriately erected in this canton, which was the first to throw off foreign control.

There is a small **Tell-Museum** (Ⓞ *Open Jul-Aug, daily, 9.30am-5.30pm; May, Jun and Sep to mid-Oct, daily, 10-11.30am and 1.30-5pm.* ⊜ *5CHF.* ☎ *(041) 870 41 55; www. tellmuseum.ch.)* at Bürglen on the Klausen Pass road (Ⓖ *see KLAUSENSTRASSE)*.

Excursion

Bauen★
10km/6mi NW. At the foot of the mountains, this lovely village nestles in a verdant, flowered landscape on the west bank of Lake Uri. The **site**★, with flower-decked hotels and chalets, and its foliage (pine, palm, banana and monkey puzzle trees), resembles a small Riviera resort thanks to its pleasant microclimate.

VAL D'ANNIVIERS★

This valley is known for the extraordinary nomadic habits of the people, continually on the move between the vineyards of the Rhône Valley, the main villages (Vissoie, for instance), mid-mountain pastures known as **mayens** and the Alps. The **Anniviers Valley attracts** enthusiastic mountaineers and skiiers to charming resorts like **Zinal.**

From Sierre to Zinal *49km/30mi – about 2hr 30min*

Itinerary ③ *(Ⓖ see Le VALAIS: map)*

Sierre – Ⓖ *See SIERRE.*

The route leaves the Brig road at the edge of Finges Forest and climbs quickly above the Sierre Basin, where the large aluminium works of Chippis are located. The twin towns of Montana and Crans stand high on the north slope of the Rhône Valley.

Niouc and its chapel mark the beginning of the way through the Anniviers Valley. Below, the Navisence flows in a deep ravine. Upstream the view is over the snowfields of Zinalrothorn and Ober Gabelhorn, on either side of the twin peaks of the Besso.

Vissoie
This lovely perched village is identified by its square feudal tower and small rustic church. Climbing the hairpin bends from Vissoie to St-Luc, travellers enjoy the **view**★★ the mountain skyline opens; the Matterhorn looms majestically in the distance.

St-Luc✳
This delightful hamlet has been converted into a winter sports resort. The viewing platform at the village entrance offers an impressive **view**★★ of the valley and the mountain range dominated by Mount Marais (2 412m/7 915ft) on the left and Mount Boivin (2 995m/9 825ft) on the right.
The road along the mountainside from St-Luc to Chandolin soon enters woods. During this run you will get splendid glimpses of the Anniviers Valley below, Sierre in the Rhône Valley and rising beyond the Wildhorn and Wildstrubel massifs.

Chandolin✳
Alt 1 936m/6 348ft. Chandolin is approached by the new village, a ski resort consisting of modern chalets built in accordance with local tradition. Continue on foot to the old village, dotted with quaint wooden bungalows, which is one of the highest permanently inhabited places in Europe. It clings to the slope that permits a splendid **panorama**★★ of the Valais Alps (from left to right: Zinalrothorn, Besso, Ober Gabelhorn, the Zinal Peak and the Dent Blanche).
Beyond Chandolin, the road climbs the west face of Roc d'Orzival, which at times becomes a breathtaking *corniche* overlooking the ravine. At the bottom, between magnificent rocky sides, flows the Navisence. Snowy crests block the horizon.

▶ *Return to Vissoie and drive south on the road to Grimentz.*

Grimentz✳
This lovely resort facing the Corne de Sorebois, which separates the Zinal and Moiry valleys, has preserved several *mazots* or *raccards* (🌓 *see illustration, Le Valais*), some of which date back to the 15C, and a beautiful **mansion** (1550). In summer, traditional festivals add to the atmosphere of the charming village. In mid-August, Grimentz is the end of the longest **mountain bike race** in the world, the famous Grand Raid Cristalp, which starts in Verbier. Mountain biking is one of the most popular activities in the resort, which has four waymarked trails, ranging in distance from 12km/7.5mi to 24km/15mi. The start of the **Bendolla** trail can be reached by cable car, at 400m/1 312ft above the resort.

Val de Moiry★
13km/8mi from Grimentz. This valley is an extension of the Val d'Anniviers. After 2km/1mi there is a lovely waterfall on the left, Grimentz on the right and the Dent Blanche ahead (appropriately named since *dent blanche* means white tooth). At 4km/2.5mi there is a **view**★ of Grimentz and the Anniviers Valley. Half a mile (1km) farther the **Moiry Dam** is visible in front of the Dent Blanche; from the middle of the dam (alt 2 249m/7 379ft) there is a **view**★ of the reservoir, the Pennine Alps and their glaciers. Continue along the road (🌀 *poor road surface – drive cautiously*), with its many small waterfalls. Overlooking the reservoir, at the end of the dam, there is a striking **view**★ onto the Moiry and **Zinal** glaciers. The road ends at a small lake facing the **Moiry Glacier**.

Walk to Cabane de Moiry★★★
Alt 2 825m/9 269ft. Allow 2hr 45min on foot there and back from the end of the road (🅿 car park at 2 409m/7 904ft).

The route first follows the left side of the Moiry Glacier at a reasonable gradient. It runs along a moraine, leading to a refuge after a steep climb. The Cabane de Moiry offers a magnificent **view**★★★ over the Pigne de la Lé (3 396m/11 143ft), Les Bouquetins (3 662m/12 015ft), Grand Cornier (3 962m/13 000ft), Dent des Rosses (3 613m/11 854ft) and the Pointe de Moiry (3 303m/10 837ft). The upper part of the Moiry Glacier sparkles under a thick layer of snow. Experienced hikers can continue (*an added 2hr 15min - follow the cairns and yellow signposts*) to the edge of the gla-cier, for pretty views of the Col de Pigne. In dry, favourable weather (enquire at the refuge beforehand), seasoned climbers may continue to the top. The final section involves walking on *névés* (☞ *remember to bring an ice pick or a stick*). The pass (alt 3 140m/10 303ft), dominated by the Pigne de la Lé, affords a superb sweeping **panorama**★★★ of the Zinal Valley (Weisshorn, Besso, Zinalrothorn).

▶ *Return to Grimentz and take the road to Zinal.*

Vallée de Zinal★★

The road offers a superb **view**: in the foreground lies the Zinal Valley with the town of Ayer high up on the east side, extended northwards by the Val d'Anniviers and in the far distance the snow-covered mass of the Wildstrubel. The valley, lined with spruce, then narrows and seems to shrink beside the overwhelming Weisshorn Mountain. After crossing the Navisence and passing the Pralong hydroelectric power station, the road passes through **Zinal**, a well-known mountaineering centre, and ends 2km/1mi farther on at Tsoudounaz, in a small corrie at the foot of the Zinal Glacier.

Zinal✳

Alt 1 670m/5 445ft. Located in an outstanding site high up in the mountains, Zinal is a small but pleasant resort frequented during both the summer and winter seasons. This tourist complex includes six villages: Ayer, Mission, Mottec, Curianey, La Combaz and Les Morands. Zinal is circled by the Imperial Crown, formed by the legendary summits of Weisshorn, Zinalrothorn, Besso, Obergabelhorn, Cervin and Dent Blanche. Since the 19C it has enjoyed a good reputation as a mountaineering centre. It also offers wonderful opportunities for walking and hiking, with a total of 200km/125mi of signposted paths. The **Lée copper mines** (Kupfermine), one hour's walk from Zinal, are open to the public (*visits must be booked at the tourist office*).

The **skiing area**, virtually unknown outside Switzerland, is powder paradise domi-nated by the Weisshorn. While there are slopes catering to all levels, Zinal has become a haven for freeriding. It is situated between 1 670m/5 479ft and 2 895m/6 835ft. A skiing pass also accesses the other facilities in the valley (Chandolin, St-Luc, Grimentz, Vercorin), including 46 ski lifts and around 200km/125mi of pistes. Cross-country skiers can enjoy a 12km/7.5mi circuit.

Soreboiss★★

Alt 2 441m/8 008ft. 🚠 *Access by cable car from Zinal: 5min.*
Lovely views of the Mont Durand, the Obergabelhorn, the rocky pyramid of Besso, the imposing Zinalrothorn and, farther to the left, the Weisshorn.

Walk to Le Petit Mountet★★★

This 4hr 30min walk from Sorebois should be made only in dry weather (☞ *be careful in early summer for the ground may be slippery*). The drop in altitude on the way down is 800m/2 625ft. After leaving the cable car, turn left. The path hugs the mountainside, affording wonderful views all along the way. After walking for about 2hr toward the refuge, you will enjoy a sweeping **panorama**★★★ of the Dent Blanche, Pointe de Zinal and Cervin. A steep descent leads to the Petit Mountet refuge (alt 2 142m/7 028ft); beyond, the route is pleasantly dotted with small waterfalls and thick vegetation.

APPENZELL

Appenzell lies at the foot of the lush Alpstein hills, a pastoral landscape at the heart of the "original eastern Switzerland" that its canton represents. It is a small, old-fashioned town which succeeds in reconciling rural and city life, a trait common to many Germanic countries. (It is a *flecken*, a word denoting communities that are neither towns nor villages.) 🛈 *Hauptgasse 4 – 9050 – ☎ (071) 788 96 41.*

The very name of Appenzell (*Abbatis cella*, the Abbot's cell) dates from the early settlement of the country by the monks of Sankt Gallen. The **Hauptgasse**★, the main street crossing the village, offers various temptations (embroidery shops, Appenzell cakes decorated with portraits of cowmen in yellow breeches and scarlet waistcoats). It lies between the church, with its astonishing Baroque embellishments, and the Löwendrogerie, whose curved gable bears a series of paintings of medicinal plants with this mournful comment: "Many plants against illness, none against death".

Address Book

🪙 *For coin ranges, see the Legend on the cover flap.*

TOURIST OFFICE

Appenzellerland Tourismus, *Hauptgasse 4 – ☎ 071 788 96 41 ; www. appenzell.ch.*

WHERE TO STAY

🛏🍽 **Schwägalp** – *Säntis – ☎ 071 365 66 00 ; www.saentisbahn.ch – 30 rooms* – Quaint wooden chalet nestling in a peaceful setting which has pretty views overlooking the terrace. Within walking distance of the Säntis ski resort.

🛏🍽 **Kaubad** – *☎ 071 787 48 44; www. hotel-kaubad.ch – 17 rooms* – This chalet is a haven of peace in a secluded spot surrounded by nature. Typical Swiss specialities at reasonable prices.

🛏🍽🍽 **Appenzell** – *Hauptgasse 37 – ☎ 071 788 15 15 ; www.hotel-appen-zell.ch – 17 rooms* – A cozy, welcoming establishment at the heart of Appenzell. The perfect base to rest after a challenging excursion.

🛏🍽🍽 **Säntis** – *Landsgemeindeplatz – ☎ 071 788 11 11; www.saentis-appensell. ch – 37 rooms* -Comfortable hotel with a romantic atmosphere and a wooden façade typical of the Appenzell region.

EATING OUT

🍽 **Rössli** – *Postplatz – ☎ 071 787 12 56 – 🕐 closed Mon, Tue and mid-Jan to mid-Feb.* Enjoy a card game with the locals at this typical old-fashioned café.

🍽 **Bären** – *Schlatt, 5km/3mi from Appenzell – ☎ 071 787 14 13 – 🕐 closed Tue, Wed, 11 Feb-1 Mar and 15-31 Jul.* Lovely views of the Alps and the valley from the terrace.

🍽 **Bären** – *Hauptstrasse, in Gonten, 6km/3.7mi from Appenzell – ☎ 071 795 40 10 – 🕐 closed Sun evenings and for three weeks from end of Mar.* Delicious regional specialities from the Appenzell area, served in a peaceful, rustic setting.

🍽🍽🍽 **Schäfli** – *in Störgel Nord, 3km/2mi from Teufen – ☎ 071 367 11 90; www.schaefli-stein.ch – 🕐 open Fri-Sat from 5.30pm, Sun from 11am, and during the week for groups of 12 or more.* This beautiful house, built in the Appenzell tradition, offers regional cuisine and the opportunity to discover the highest footbridge for pedestrians in Europe.

Sights

Appenzell Museum

🕐 *Open Apr-Nov, daily, 10am-noon and 2-5pm; Dec-Mar, daily except Mon, 2-5pm.*
🕐 *Closed 25 Dec, 1 Jan. ⊜5CHF. ☎ (071) 788 96 31; www.museum.ai.ch.*
Set up in the town hall and the adjoining house (1560), this museum focuses on with regional lore, including a collection of coins which the Inner-Rhoden people were able to mint for only five years (1737-42), a prison cell dating back to 1570, typical Appenzell costumes (featuring the sophisticated black tulle headdress), banners, a 16C triptych attributed to Jacob Girtanner and coffin-shaped hatchments (a bygone practice, they were once used to drive away evil spirits). The museum also boasts an Egyptian sarcophagus (c 1000 BC), found in a temple at Thebes.

Blaues Haus

🕐 *Open daily, 9am-6pm; Sun and hols, 10am-5pm. ⊜ No charge. ☎ (071) 787 12 84.*
The charm of this tiny museum, devoted to local crafts and folklore, is echoed by the formidable personality of its owner, an energetic woman who has painstakingly preserved all manner of exhibits relating to her native district, including the workshop of her late husband, a professional cabinetmaker, a collection of cave drawings, and embroidery from the Appenzell region.

Museum Liner

🕐 *Open Apr-Nov daily, 10am-noon and 2-5pm; Nov-Mar Mon-Sat 2-5pm, Sun 11am-5pm. ⊜9CHF ☎ (071) 788 18 00.*
This museum, housed in a postmodern building (1998) by the architects Annette Gigon and Mike Guyer, presents temporary exhibitions dedicated to work by local artists, such as the landscape painter Carl-August Liner (1871-1946) and Carl-Walter Liner (1914-97), an early exponent of Abstract art. A collection of modern art by painters such as Arp, Kirchner and Tapiès can also be admired in the museum.

Excursions

Hoher Kasten★★

Alt 1 795m/5 890ft. 7km/4mi southeast on the road to Weissbad and Brülisau. ⛰ Cable car leaves from Brülisau (alt 924m/3 030ft) every 30min. There and back ⊜26CHF. For information on operating periods, call ☎ (071) 799 13 22.
The ride up in the cable car (8min) offers a view below of spruce trees, mountain pastures and shepherds' huts and ahead to the massive limestone spur of the Hoher Kasten. The belvedere, with its attractive Alpine garden, is higher than the restaurant but easily accessible. It offers a magnificent **panorama**★★: west and northwest, the town of Appenzell and surrounding hills; to the east, the view plunges down to the Rheinthal and its river, winding from Lake Constance (north) to the Liechtenstein mountains (south), with the Austrian Alps in the background. The Alpstein Massif and its highest peak, Säntis, are clearly visible to the southeast. A waymarked path to Staubern and on to the lakes of Fälensee and Sämtisersee, as far as Brülisau has 14 information panels explaining the region's geology .

Ebenalp★★

Alt 1 640m/5 380ft. 7km/4mi – about 1hr 30min following the Weissbad-Wasserauen road to its terminus, plus 8min by cable car. ⛰Cable-car – Departures Jul-Aug, 7.40am-7pm; Jun and Sep, 7.40am-6pm, May and Oct, 8am-5.30pm, Nov-Apr, 8.30am-5pm. Fare there and back: ⊜24CHF. ☎ (071) 799 12 12.
This Alpine promontory is edged with cliffs jutting out over the Appenzell country. From Ebenalp you can return on foot *(about 1hr 30min)* to Wasserauen via the **tunnel-grotto of Wildkirchli** (80m/262ft long), where excavations have exposed traces of the oldest prehistoric settlement in Switzerland. The path passes the **Seealpsee**★, whose dark waters lie at the foot of the Rossmad.

APPENZELLERLAND★

(APPENZELL REGION)

The Appenzell region and the great Alpine combe of the Toggenburg (Upper Thur Valley) are separated by an administrative border. Appenzell has been a separate canton since 1513; Toggenburg remains under the control of Sankt Gallen, as it was when the famous abbey was at the height of its power. Nonetheless they form a single tourist area, for they are attached geographically to the pre-Alpine chain of the Alpstein, whose jagged crests, culminating in Säntis (alt 2 502m/8 207ft), rise above the Rhine Valley, facing the Vorarlberg Mountains.

Motorists crossing the Austrian frontier at St Margrethen-Höchst should take advantage of a visit to Sankt Gallen and leave road no 7 for one of the little winding roads to Trogen and Heiden, within sight of Lake Constance.

Life in the Appenzell

The soft, undulating landscape of green hills is dotted with farms and rich townships with their pretty, curvilinear gabled houses which still hold meetings of the traditional Landsgemeinden (&see Introduction: Government). These assemblies of peasants, who wear swords as a mark of their dignity as active citizens, take place in the Appenzell for the Inner-Rhoden half-canton (Catholic) at Trogen and at Hundwil for the Ausser-Rhoden half-canton (Protestant) (& see Calendar of Events). Traditions are still very much alive in the Appenzell: special dishes such as Appenzell fat cheese (one of the strongest Swiss cheeses) and small, dry sausages called *Alpenklübler,* plus the women's pretty ceremonial dress, characterised by a *coiffe* with immense tulle wings. Another long-standing custom to have survived is that of fine old-fashioned embroidery, which continues to flourish as a cottage industry in Inner-Rhoden.

① Sitter Valley and Stoss Road★

From Sankt Gallen to Altstätten *34 km/21mi – about 2hr*

Sankt Gallen★★ – *2hr.* & See SANKT GALLEN.

The recommended route from Sankt Gallen affords pleasant views all along the Sitter Valley. This is at first a deep ravine, but turns into a softly undulating depression dotted with traditional farms. Look especially for a group of buildings 1km/0.5mi southeast of the Hundwil junction.

Painted wooden panel (16C)

A. Magro/Appenzeller Volkskunde Museum

Stein

As you cross this village, located on a plateau (alt 823m/2 700ft) above its neighbours, there are sweeping views of the surrounding countryside. The **Appenzeller Volkskunde Museum** (🕐*Open daily except Mon morning, 10am-noon and 1.30-5pm, Sun 10am-5pm.* 🕐*Closed 25 Dec.* ✆*7CHF.* ☎ *(071) 368 50 56)* presents a reconstruction of a typical Alpine cheesemaking dairy *(production starts at 1.30pm)*, surrounded by traditional objects such as bells, saddles and casks. In the basement, two craftsmen demonstrate the functioning of a weaving loom and an embroidery hoop (superb jacquard fabrics). On the first floor, note the three 16C wooden panels, illustrated with naïve drawings, which were found in the nearby district of Gais.

A typical Appenzell gable

Jerry Dennis / APA Publications

Appenzell – 👣 See APPENZELL.

Gais

In the early 20C this market town was still drawing many seekers of whey cures. Admire the Baroque architecture of the curved-gabled houses on the main square.

Stoss★

In 1405 this plateau was the scene of a battle which secured the liberation of Appenzell from Austrian rule. To enjoy the distant **panorama**★★ of the Rheinthal and the Vorarlberg Alps, proceed towards the commemorative chapel and, 100m/110yd to its right, the obelisk marked out from afar by a clump of trees.

Altstätten

Altstätten lies at the heart of the Rheinthal on a warm inner plain with orchards, vineyards and crops of maize. It has a markedly medieval character: picturesque Marktgasse (Market Street), lined with pointed-gabled houses and pillared arcades for the convenience of pedestrians, who can walk under cover. The Engelplatz, with its flower-decked fountain and crooked houses, makes another pretty picture.

2 The Toggenburg★

From Appenzell to Buchs *62 km/39mi – about 2hr 30min*

Appenzell – 👣 See APPENZELL.

Urnäsch

The village is known for its **Museum für Appenzeller Brauchtum** (🕐 *Open Apr-Oct, daily, 1.30-5pm.* ✆*5CHF.* ☎ *(071) 364 23 22)*, a small folklore museum located in a 19C chalet with small, low-ceilinged rooms and crooked floors. There is a sumptuous collection of carnival costumes and extraordinary hats plus daily local costumes, jewels, pipes, paintings and painted figurines, bells and cowbells, as well as a carpenter's workshop. The second floor displays an Appenzell interior with painted furniture, complete with its box bed and the bedroom occupied by the cowherd; a music room; a dairy; and a collection of old wooden toys.

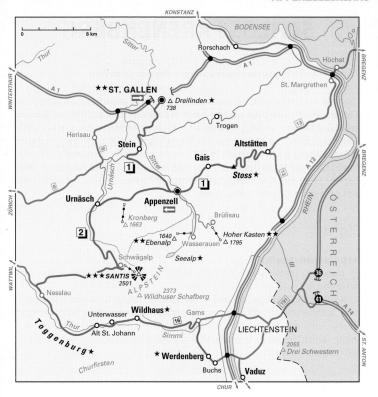

A short distance past Appenzell, between Urnäsch and Schwägalp, the road emerges from the bottom of a dell dotted with fir and ash trees, at the foot of the impressive cliffs of the north face of Säntis.

Säntis★★★ – 👣 See SÄNTIS.

The section from Schwälgalp to Nesslau leads along the southwest barrier of the Alpstein (Silberplatten, Lütispitz), where Alpine formations succeed the parklands. The spa of Rietbad is framed in a valley dotted with green knolls. Between Nesslau and Wildhaus, uphill from two wooded clefts, the High Toggenburg Valley spreads harmoniously, with dwellings whose walls are protected by weatherboarding. During the climb from Unterwasser *(facilities)* to Wildhaus, admire the deeply folded escarpments of the Wildhuser-Schafberg and the serrated crests of the Churfirsten. In conjunction with Alt St Johann, these two resorts exploit a vast snowfield.

Wildhaus★

The pleasant resort lies on the plateau separating the Toggenburg from the Rheinthal, within sight of the Wildhuser-Schafberg, the Churfirsten and the Drei Schwestern. Wildhaus is the birthplace of the great reformer **Ulrich Zwingli**, whose home may still be seen (⚬ *not open to the public*). From Wildhaus to Gams, the road dips towards the Rheinthal. From the hairpin bends immediately before Gams you will appreciate the size of this trough, dominated on its eastern side by the mountains of the Vorarlberg and of Liechtenstein. These are separated by the Feldkirch Gap, negotiated by the road and railway to the Arlberg region of Austria.

Werdenberg★ – 👣 See WERDENBERG.

SCHLOSS ARENENBERG

(ARENENBERG CASTLE) – THURGAU
1.5KM/1MI W OF ERMATINGEN AND N OF SALENSTEIN

The little Arenenberg Castle, surrounded by gardens and a fine park, stands on a terrace overlooking the western basin of Lake Constance, Untersee. Built in the 16C, it became, in 1817, the property of Queen Hortense, daughter of Louis Bonaparte. Hortense and her son, the future Napoleon III, spent every summer at Arenenberg until her death in 1837, and Empress Eugénie and the Prince Impérial stayed there frequently after the fall of the Second Empire. In 1906 Eugénie presented Arenenberg to the canton of Thurgau and it was transformed into a museum devoted to Napoleon.

Sight

Napoleonmuseum★
🕐 Open daily 10am-5pm. 🕐 Closed Good Friday, mid-Dec to mid-Jan and Mon mid-Oct to mid-Apr. ⊚10CHF. ☎ 071 663 32 60.
Works of art and furniture collected by the Bonapartes have remained in the castle. Note Queen Hortense's drawing room, furnished in the style of the period, and the library, bedrooms and boudoirs, which contain many mementoes of the imperial family. Queen Hortense's bedroom affords a sweeping **view** over Lake Constance and Reichenau Island.

GORGES DE L'AREUSE★

These gorges are part of the Val de Travers itinerary (🚶 see Val de TRAVERS).

🚶Hiking

▶ About 1hr on foot from Noiraigue railway station, where there is a car park.

Beyond the Plan-de-l'Eau hydroelectric power station the path descends to the heavily forested valley floor to follow the Areuse. Steep limestone sides of this V-shaped gorge rise to jagged crests. A viewpoint halfway offers a plunging view of the narrowest part of the gorge where the torrent gushes over cascades. An old humpbacked bridge adds a romantic touch to this attractive **beauty spot**★.

Champ-du-Moulin
A surfaced path leads through the woods to this hamlet.
The house, left of the path, is the place where the famous French philosopher **Jean-Jacques Rousseau** lived in exile in 1764. The Renaissance windows (1722) originally came from a house in Valangin. Beyond, the scattered hamlet of Champ-du-Moulin stands in a woodland setting at the southern end of the gorge. Climb back up to Champ-du-Moulin railway station *(30min on foot)* for another good view of the southern end of the gorge. Take one of the many trains back to Noiraigue, or walk back.

AROSA ✳ ✳

GRAUBÜNDEN – POPULATION 2 342
ALT 1 742M/5 715FT

The elegant resort of Arosa spreads its hotels in the Upper Schanffig Basin of the Plessur Valley. It charms the visitor at once with its setting of gently sloping woodlands, reflected in small lakes. 🛈 *Poststrasse – 7050 – ☎ (081) 378 70 20*

🅿 **Parking:** Everything in town is within walking distance, so park in the public area and leave your vehicle for the duration of your stay.

Access

From Chur to Arosa 31km/19mi – about 1hr.

The **Arosa road**★ (or **Schanfigg Valley road**), a high, winding, picturesque corniche along the Schanfigg, passes through flower-decked villages with quaint churches. During the last part, the road cuts through unusual sharp limestone ridges, which are convex and wooded on the north side and concave and barren on the south side. Note, on the outskirts of Langwies, the railway viaduct spanning the chasm; in summer this train is free, as are the resort's cablecars.

The Resort

The Chur road passes through **Aeusser-Arosa**, the chief centre of activity and location of the railway station and the lakes. The road emerges from the forest and ends at **Inner-Arosa**, where the upper depression of the Plessur (Aroser Alp) begins. The nearby centre of **Maran** is more isolated; visitors to Arosa walk to it along delightful, gently sloping paths through the woods (*Eichhörnliweg*: squirrel path). The settlement spreads over the open Alpine pastures. The Weisshorn cable car is the ski area's backbone in winter, Arosa's real season. Long, wide runs, some of which drop over 1 000m/3 280ft, make this resort ideal for the beginner or intermediate; the descent from the top of the Weisshorn is only for accomplished skiers and snowboarders. In January 2007, Arosa hosted the FIS Snowboard World Championships.

Additional Sight

Weisshorn★★

Alt 2 653m/8 704ft. 🚡 *Access in 20min by cable car.* 🕐 *Departure every 10min, 9am-5pm.* 🕐 *Closed mid-Apr to late Apr.* 🎫 *Fare there and back: 34CHF.* ☎ *(081) 378 84 84.*

The climb up to the mid-station, Law Mittel (alt 2 013m/6 640ft), offers wide vistas of Arosa, its lakes, verdant basin and mountains. From the top *(viewing table)* there is a magnificent **panorama**★★ of the Grison Alps' neighbouring heights and snowy ridges, blocked to the south by the Piz Kesch, Piz Ela and Erzhorn; Arosa is visible and Chur can be glimpsed to the northwest at the foot of Calanda Mountain.

ASCONA★★

TICINO – POPULATION 4 984
ALT 210M/689FT
TOWN PLAN IN THE MICHELIN GUIDE SWITZERLAND

Ascona's site on Lake Maggiore's shore resembles that of Locarno and its position at the mouth of the River Maggia. Like its larger neighbour, Ascona benefits from the river delta's flat lands, which provide a host of sporting facilities. This

Address Book

For coin ranges, see the Legend on the cover flap.

TOURIST OFFICE

Ente Turistico Lago Maggiore Ascona, Casa Serodine – ☎ *091 791 00 91; www.ascona.ch*

WHERE TO STAY

Al Faro – *Piazza G. Motta 27* – ☎ *091 791 85 15; www.hotel-al-faro.ch - 9 rooms –* open mid-Feb to late-Oct. The prettier rooms overlook the lake, well worth the extra expense to make your stay all the more enjoyable.

Al Porto – *Piazza G. Motta* – ☎ *091 785 85 85; www.alporto-hotel. ch – 37 rooms –* Simple rooms and rustic furniture. Drinks and meals are served on the terrace overlooking the lake.

Tamaro – *Piazza G. Motta 35* – ☎ *091 785 48 48; www.hotel-tamaro. ch - 50 rooms –* open 2 Mar-12 Nov. The main building is conveniently situated on the lakeside promenade (an annex with additional rooms is farther on). Pleasant inner courtyard and garden where meals are served.

Castello – *Piazza G. Mottta –* ☎ *091 791 01 61; www.castello-seeschloss.ch – 45 rooms –* open 1 Mar-9 Nov. If you want to treat yourself to something special, be extravagant and stay in this former medieval castle whose charm and romantic atmosphere have remained intact. Cosy rooms with period furniture. Outdoor pool.

IN LOSONE, 2KM/1MI NW

Albergo-garni Elena – *Via Gaggioli 25 –* ☎ *091 791 63 26 – Fax 091 792 29 22 – 20 rooms –* open 16 Mar-31 Oct. A hotel for low-budget

holidays, offering good service. Its two advantages are the swimming pool and peaceful atmosphere.

Casa Berno – ☎ *091 791 32 32 ; www.casaberno.ch – 62 rooms –* open Apr-Oct. Enchanting location near the panoramic Ronco Tour. Beautiful views of the mountains and lake. Peace and quiet guaranteed.

EATING OUT

Della Carrà – *Carrà dei Nasi* – ☎ *091 791 44 52 –* closed Sun (except Sun evening from Easter to Oct) and 1-20 Dec. Regional cuisine.

IN LOSONE, 2KM/1MI NW

Osteria Dell'Enoteca – *Contrada Maggiore 24 –* ☎ *091 791 78 17; www.osteriaenotecha.ch –* closed Mon, Tue and 1 Jan-7 Mar. A friendly osteria where meals are served in an enchanting garden.

IN PONTE BROLLA, 5KM/3MI N

Da Enzo – ☎ *091 796 14 75* – closed Wed all day, Thu at lunchtime and 15 Jan-1 Mar. Italian specialities in a lovely Ticino house nestling amid the greenery.

À BRISSAGO, 7KM/4.3MI W

Mirafiori – *Via Crodolo –* ☎ *091 793 12 34 –* open mid-Mar-Oct. Enjoy a good meal on the shaded terrace right on the edge of the lake.

Osteria Grotto Borei - *At Piodina 3km/2mi SW of Brissago* - ☎ *091 793 01 95; www.brissago.ch –* closed Thu, Dec-Feb; mid-Oct-mid-Nov open Fri, Sat and Sun only. Family business serving typical Ticino dishes. Splendid location in the mountains with pretty views of the lake.

colourful fishing village, long a favourite with artists, has become an important venue for cultural events (New Orleans Jazz Festival in July, Classical Music Festival in September).

The lake front, closed to cars, is a popular promenade area, dotted with lively restaurants and café terraces. During the high season, at night, strains of live music from nearby alleys and courtyards add to the festive atmosphere of the town. Regular boat trips leave for Locarno, Porte Ronco, the Brissago islands and destinations in Italy.

Sights

Santa Maria della Misericordia
Via delle Cappelle.
The church adjoins the cloisters of the Collegio Papio. Founded in 1399 and reconstructed in the 15C it is known for its 15C-16C display of polychrome **frescoes** in the nave and on the walls and vaulting of the chancel. The beautiful **altarpiece**, depicting the life of the Virgin is attributed to Giovanni Antonio della Gaïa – 1519.

Santi Pietro e Paolo
Piazza San Pietro.
At the heart of the town's narrow alleys, this parish church dedicated to St Peter and St Paul exhibits a fine altarpiece and splendid paintings by **Giovanni Serodine**, a pupil of Caravaggio. The beautiful mansion on the square, whose windows are decorated with sculpture, houses the Tourist Information Centre.

Excursions

Ronco Tour★★
17km/11mi – about 1hr 30min.   *See LOCARNO: Excursions.*

Isole di Brissago★
Boat service is available from May to Oct, daily, 9am-6pm. For information contact the Tourist office in Ascona or Losone or ask at the offices of Navigazione Lago Maggiore d'Ascona, at Ascona harbour. Exotic park, art exhibition. 7CHF. (091) 791 43 61.
The tiny Brissago islands (San Pancrazio and Sant'Appollinare) enjoy an exceptional climate and the larger of the two, San Pancrazio, is the most popular holiday destination for tourists staying in Ascona. The boat ride is one of the most pleasing features of the visit. The islands belonged to Baroness Antonietta de Saint-Léger, whose passion for botany turned San Pancrazio into a tropical garden; it has since become the Botanical Park of the Ticino canton. The mild climate permits cultivation of plant and flower species from all five continents year-round; they are carefully grouped according to their country of origin. Explanatory noticeboards in Italian, German and English enlighten visitors on varieties unknown in Europe. The tour also affords pretty views of the lake. The small shady beach has a distinctly tropical feel.

AUGST/AUGUSTA RAURICA★★

It is to the Roman general Munatius Plancus, a friend of Julius Caesar, that Switzerland owes the existence of the "Colonia Raurica" ruins, the oldest Roman settlement situated alongside the Rhine, founded in 44-43 BC. It is believed that the actual colonisation of the Augst site dates back to the year 10 BC.

- **P** **Parking:** There is ample visitor parking by the ampitheater.
- 🕐 **Organizing Your Time:** Allow most of a day as an excursion from Basel via train, bus no. 70, or motorway to exit Augst.
- **Kids** **Especially for Kids:** The animal park with pigs, sheep and small cattle.

A Bit of History

An important ancient city – By the year AD 200, Augst had grown to a city of 20 000 people and had become a prosperous centre for both trade and craft. Owing to its privileged location on the northern border of the Roman Empire, artistic activity thrived, as shown by the many imposing public buildings. Towards the end of the 3C, characterised by severe political unrest, most of the city was destroyed when the Alamans assaulted the defensive system, or *limes*. In order to keep control over this strategic passage of the Rhine, the army built the powerful Kaiseraugst stronghold slightly north of Augst soon after the year AD 300. Most of these fortifications remained standing after the fall of the Roman Empire and served to protect the local population during the early Middle Ages.

Excavation work – During the 16C, influenced by the doctrines of the great Basel humanists, the famous jurist **Amerbach** (🕐 *see BASEL)* was the first to carry out scientific research, making use of the excavation work formerly conducted by the tradesman Andreas Ryff, also a native of Basel. In 1839, the Historical and Archaeological Society of Basel (Historische und Antiquarische Gesellschaft zu Basel) commissioned research on the Roman city. From 1878 onwards, this ancient has been the object of in-depth investigations which have continued up to the present day.

Visit

Ancient ruins

👣 *Tour: 30min to 1hr, depending on the route. The ruins are signposted in French and German. A series of plans explains how buildings were laid out originally.* 🕐*Open Mar-Oct, daily, 10am-5pm; Nov-Feb, 10am-4.30pm.* ✂*No charge.* ☎ *(061) 816 22 22, www.baselland.ch.* Restored monuments include the **theatre**, the largest Roman ruin in Switzerland, with a seating capacity of 8 000. Today it is used as a venue for outdoor concerts and live performances. The administrative, political and religious core of the city was the **forum**, consisting of the basilica, the Temple of Jupiter

Roman mosaic

Römermuseum, Augst

and the **curia** (display of mosaics in the cellar). Markets and various local festivities were held at the forum. The **sewers** were designed to evacuate the waters from the central baths to s the Violental Valley; visitors may enter this huge cylindrical pipe *(diameter: 70cm/28in)*, with limestone walls and a sandstone paved floor. The amphitheatre was the scene of many games, races and fights between gladiators and wild beasts which invariably ended in bloodshed; it was built slightly away from the town centre so that the 5 600 or so spectators could leave the premises quickly and easily.

Römermuseum★★

&♿⏱ *Open Mar-Oct, daily, 10am-5pm, Mon 1-5pm; Nov-Feb, 10am-noon and 1.30-5pm.* ⏱ *Closed 1 Jan, 24, 25 and 31 Dec.* 🎫*7CHF.* ☎ *(061) 816 22 22.*

Adjoining the Roman House, the Roman Museum presents some of the 700 000 objects unearthed during the excavations. The **silver hoard**★★ discovered at the foot of the Kaiseraugst fortifications in 1962 features many precious objects, including 68 items of sumptuous tableware: dishes decorated with mythological scenes, tumblers, spoons, candelabra and platters. This treasure also contained three silver ingots which experts traced back to the year AD 350. It is thought that the treasure

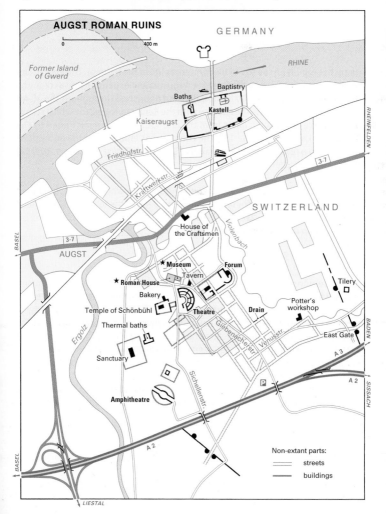

AUGST ROMAN RUINS

might have been buried during the Germanic invasion in AD 352-353. There is also a small **animal park** (haustierpark) 🧒 of old breeds, some threatened by extinction, including wooly-hair pigs, Alpine sheep and small cattle.

Römisches Wohnhaus★

🕐 *Same admission times and charges as the Römermuseum.*

This Roman House was a private residence and is considered to be a faithful reconstruction of the type common in Augst under the Roman Empire. The kitchen, dining room, bedroom, bathroom, workshop and shop contain authentic artefacts and utensils found on the site. The floor of the steamroom carries a diagram of an ingenious heating system devised by the Romans in which hot air circulated under the floor and between double walls. The right wall e bears a fragment of the famous **Gladiators' mosaic**, thought to be the largest and finest in the Roman city. It used to adorn the dining-room floor of a patrician villa nearby.

AVENCHES

VAUD – POPULATION 2 510
4KM/2MI S OF LAKE MURTEN – ALT 473M/1 574FT

Avenches is built on the site of the former capital of the Helvetii. The Roman city of Aventicum, founded by the Emperor Augustus and expanded into a colony by Vespasian, had some 20 000 inhabitants and flourished throughout the 2C AD and destroyed in AD 259. The château with the Renaissance façade which stands in the centre of the town dates from the late 13C. It was commissioned by the bishops of Lausanne. In the 16C, the château was enlarged by the authorities in Bern into a residence for their bailiffs. 🅱 *3 place de l'Église – 1580 – ☎ (026) 676 99 22, www.avenches.ch.*

The modern town is much smaller than the Ancient city, whose size can be judged from the excavated ruins. These became the property of the town in 1804. General Guisan, commander-in-chief of the Swiss army from 1939-45, was born here; his bust stands in the plaza in front of the post office.

A Bit of History

Roman legions – The town was defended by a ring of fortifications about 6km/4mi round, with walls over 7m/23ft high, crowned with battlements; semicircular towers abutting against the wall's inner surface were used as observation posts; one of them, the Tornallaz, is still standing but it has been badly restored. Visitors are allowed to visit the remains of the amphitheatre, the Roman arena (on the Fribourg road) and a large sanctuary known as the "storkery", of which only one pilaster has survived. Recent excavations have revealed the ruins of a portico and temple podium.

Amphitheatre – The amphitheatre is thought to date from the end of the 1C AD. Duels between gladiators and fights against wild animals were staged in this elliptical arena, which, in its heyday, was able to seat up to 16 000.

Sight

Musée Romain de Vallon★

🕐 *Open Apr-Sep, daily except Mon, 10am-noon and 1-5pm; Oct-Mar, 2-5pm.* 🕐 *Closed 1 and 2 Jan, 25, 26 and 31 Dec.* ⊜*4CHF.* ☎ *(026) 675 17 27.*

The museum is housed in a square tower, built in the Middle Ages over the main entrance to the amphitheatre. It contains objects discovered during the excavations. On the ground floor are displayed a very fine statue of a wolf suckling Romulus and Remus, several inscriptions, mural paintings and mosaics; an audio-visual presentation explains the history of Avenches. On the first floor, admire the copy of a golden bust of the Emperor Marcus Aurelius (the original is in the Musée des Beaux-Arts in Lausanne), along with some bronze pieces (Bacchus, Silenus, votive hand, Gaul divinity), marble sculptures (Minerva, Mercury, funerary art) and a collection of coins minted at Aventicum. The second floor displays old tools and pottery pieces recreating Roman daily life in Switzerland in a lively and evocative manner.

BADEN

AARGAU – POPULATION 15 984
ALT 385M/1 273FT

Baden lies at the foot of the last spurs of the Jura at a picturesque site★ on the banks of the Limmat. The spa and the industrial quarters extend below the old town, built on a promontory overlooking the river, dominated by the ruins of Stein Castle (Ruine Stein). This imposing fortress served as an arsenal and a refuge for the Austrians during their unsuccessful campaigns against the Swiss, which ended in the victories for Swiss independence at Morgarten (1315) and Sempach (1386). In 1415 the Confederates seized the city and burnt it. It was rebuilt in the 17C and destroyed again in 1712 by the people of Bern and Zurich.
🄸 *Bahnhofplatz 1 – 5400 –* ☎ *(056) 210 91 91.*

Known in Roman times as Aquae Helveticae and famous for its hot springs (47°C/116°F), Baden became one of Switzerland's most important spas towards the end of the Middle Ages. Famous personalities who have taken the waters here include the writers Goethe, Thomas Mann and Hermann Hesse, and the conductor Karl Böhm. Today, Baden is also a centre of electro-mechanical engineering.

Sights

Old town★

From the modern road bridge *(Hochbrücke)* there is a fine view★ of the old town. Its houses, with their stepped gables and fine brown roofs, pierced by many dormer windows, come down to the Limmat, which is crossed by an old covered wooden bridge *(Holzbrücke)*. The parish church *(Stadtkirche)* and the city tower *(Stadtturm)*, with a belfry and corner turrets with glazed tiles, dominate the whole scene.

Landvogteischloss

🕐 *Open daily except Mon, 1-5pm; Sat-Sun, 10am-5pm.* 🕐 *Closed public hols (except Easter Mon, Whit Mon and 1 May).* ⊜*7CHF.* ☎ *(056) 222 75 74, www.museum.baden.ch.*

The Bailiffs' Castle stands near the Holzbrücke, on the east bank of the Limmat. A **museum** (Historisches Museum) is housed in the keep, which served as a residence for bailiffs from 1415 to 1798. There are collections of weapons, period furniture, paintings and sculpture, pottery, bronze and coins of Roman origin, found in the district, and costumes of the Aargau canton.

Stiftung Langmatt Sidney und Jenny Brown★

Römerstrasse 30. Temporary exhibitions on the first floor. ⏱*Open Apr-Oct, daily except Mon, 2-5pm; Sat-Sun 11am-5pm.* 🎟*10CHF.* ☎ *(056) 222 58 42, www.langmatt.ch.*

The house formerly belonging to the industrialist **Sidney Brown**, whose name is perpetuated by the company ABB (Asea Brown Boveri), contains mostly Impressionist paintings, including two series by Renoir and Cézanne. There also are superb canvases by other famous artists: *Study of a Nude* by Degas, *Return of the Fishing Boats in Trouville* by E Boudin, *Chestnut Trees in Louveciennes* by Pissarro, *The Torments of the Seine* by Monet, sketches attributed to Henri Matisse, and noteworty pictures by Corot, Courbet, Fantin-Latour, Gauguin, Sisley and Vincent van Gogh. A small salon presents 18C French works (Fragonard, Greuze and Watteau) and landscapes by a native of Zurich, S Gessner.

The spa

Its 19 hot sulphur springs, yielding about 1 million litres/200 000 gallons of salty water a day, have the highest concentration of minerals of any spa in Switzerland. The spa specialises in the treatment of rheumatism, respiratory disorders and stress. The resort's public paths (Thermalbad) are situated on the Kurplatz. The Limmat-Promenade along the river affords a pleasant walk.

Excursion

Ehem. Zisterzienserkloster Wettingen★

🚹 *Alberich Zwyssigstrasse 81 – 5430 –* ☎ *(056) 426 22 11.*
3km/2mi S of Baden, between the railway and the Limmat. ⏱ *The cloisters can be visited Apr-Oct, Mon-Sat, 10-5pm, Sun, noon-5pm. Church:* 🎧 *Guided tours daily Apr-Oct, 2-5pm.* 🎟*5CHF.* ☎ *(056) 437 24 10.*

This former Cistercian abbey, founded by Count Heinrich von Rapperswil in the 13C, presently houses a school. The Gothic **cloisters** have been glazed and now display a collection of stained glass. The **interior**★ is richly decorated in Baroque style with frescoes, paintings, stucco and marble. Note the splendidly carved **choir stalls**★★ dating from the early 17C.

BASEL★★★

BASEL Ⓒ BASEL – POPULATION 166 074

Situated on the northwest border of Switzerland, facing Alsace and the Baden region, Basel is washed by the River Rhine at the point when it becomes navigable. The old town is part of Grossbasel (Greater Basel) is separated from Kleinbasel (Lesser Basel) by the wide river which opens up opportunities for maritime trade. The third largest city in the country, Basel is a vibrant cultural centre with over 30 museums: at present, new museums are opening at a rate of one every year. The city's prosperity is derived from banking, insurance, sea traffic and the primary sector, with a number of important chemical and pharmaceutical companies based here. Some 30 000 workers commute to Basel each day for work: approximately a third come from Germany and two-thirds from France, mostly from the Alsace region. 🚹 *Schifflände 5 – 4001 –* ☎ *(061) 268 68 68 – www. baseltourismus.ch.*

P **Parking:** Parking may be difficult to find in Old Town. See the map for outlying parking areas. A day-pass for public transport within the city is available for purchase from the tourist office.

◎ **Don't Miss:** The Kunstmuseum, the country's largest art museum.

◎ **Organizing Your Time:** Allow at least 4 hours for a walking tour of Old Town and the Kunstemuseum. To visit the majority of attractions mentioned, reserve 4 days plus an additional day for the Excursions.

Kids **Especially for Kids:** Basel's large zoo, situated southwest of Old Town.

◐ **Also See:** The Roman ruins of the nearby town of Augst.

A Bit of History

Origins – The city's origins date back to pre-Roman times, as testified by ruins of a fortified Celtic settlement dating from around 100 BC, excavated in the St Johann district. The Roman city of Augusta Raurica was later founded here in 44 BC. In 1032 Basel became part of the Germanic Empire but later came under the rule of a prince-bishop, vassal of the Emperor; these events are recalled in the town's coat of arms, which bears an episcopal cross.

From the Council of Basel to the Reformation – From 1431-48, the Council of Basel tried to reform the clergy and bring heretics back to the Church. However, its existence was threatened by serious disagreements dividing the Pope and his bishops. The Council offered the papal tiara to Amadeus VIII, Duke of Savoy, who took the title of Pope Felix V. It was only in 1501 that the city joined the Helvetic Confederation. An open city during the Reformation, Basel soon adopted the new confession advocated by Johannes Husschin, known as Œcolampadius. This former monk and priest preached moderate reform.

The industrial age – Because of its openness and geographical location, Basel welcomed many French Huguenots who had fled following the Revocation of the Edict of Nantes. They introduced silk weaving into Basel, paving the way for industrial expansion. The town started to manufacture ribbons, used for decorating hats and

Philipp Giegel / Switzerland Tourism

Musicians at the Carnival in Basel

The Carnival

The Basel Carnival dates back to the Middle Ages, the only Catholic celebration to have survived the Reformation in Protestant country. Created to mark the beginning of Lent, the carnival interrupts the daily life of the population with three days of processions and masquerades, meticulously governed by coded rituals.

On the first Monday (Shrove Monday), at 4 o'clock in the morning, all the lights are switched off and the "Morgestraich , a custom dating back to the 18C, heralds the start of the festivities. Participants, sporting masks and costumes and divided into "gangs" of 20 to 200 people, line up behind a coloured Chinese lantern which can reach 3m/10ft high. The procession then marches through the streets to the strains of fifes and drums, ending up in the local restaurants at 6 o'clock, where they are served onion pie and soup made with flour. These colourful displays of masks and musical performances – both highly organised and individually celebrated – continue to enliven the town until Wednesday. Tuesday afternoon is reserved for children; do not miss their procession.

crinolines, an activity in which it came to specialise. The industry of dyeing was introduced and began to expand; the creation of the Geigy factory in 1785 signalled the beginning of the chemicals industry in Basel. The golden age of the 18C has left its mark in the handsome Classical hotels built in the austere Huguenot style. During the 19C, the town expanded into the surrounding countryside. After a violent conflict, two half-cantons were created in 1883: Basel-Stadt (Basel Town, represented by a black crosier) and Basel-Land (Basel District, represented by a red crosier).

Basler dialect – Compared to other German-speaking areas, this dialect has slightly muffled vowels and is softer on the ear. Situated on the border of three countries, Basel borrows words from French, such as *Baareblyy* (*parapluie* – umbrella), *Boorpmenee* (*porte-monnaie* – wallet) and *Exgyysi* (*Excusez-moi* – Excuse me). Unusually, locals say *Aadie* derived from the French *adieu*, meaning goodbye, to say "hello".

Old Town★★★ *3hr*

Walking tours early May to mid-Oct, daily except Sun, 2.30-4.30pm; Jan-Apr and mid-Oct to late Dec, Sat, 2.30-4.30pm. Leave from the Tourist office. 15CHF. ☎ (061) 268 68 68; www.baseltourismus.ch

▶ *Take Münsterberg to Münsterplatz and admire the fine façade of the cathedral.*

Münster★★ (CY)
🕐 *Open mid-Apr to mid-Oct, Mon-Fri, 10am-5pm, Sat 10am-4pm, Sun 1-5pm; mid-Oct to mid-Apr, Mon-Sat, 11am-4pm, Sun and public hols, 2-4pm. ☎ (061) 272 91 57. Tower: Open mid-Apr to mid-Oct, 10am (1pm Sun) to 5pm (4pm Sat); mid-Oct to mid-Apr, 11am (2pm Sun) to 4pm. 3CHF. ☎ (061) 272 91 57.*
The great 12C cathedral was partly rebuilt in the 14C and 15C and restored in the 19C. It is built with red sandstone and surmounted by two Gothic towers (nice view of the city). Between the towers is a porch dating from the mid 13C. The recessed arches of the main doorway are decorated with small statues depicting prophets, angels and garlands of foliage and flowers.
Skirting the building to the left you reach the **portal** of Sankt Gallen (12C) showing Christ the Judge on the tympanum, the Wise and Foolish Virgins on the lintel and the Resurrection of the Dead over the main vault. There is a pretty **view**★of the Rhine, the town, the Black Forest and the Vosges from the Pfalz terrace. A narrow,

dark passage leads into 15C Gothic **cloisters**, extended by other cloisters dating from the same period.

The cathedral houses the **tomb of Erasmus**, the writer who made Basel a centre of Humanist learning, and who died here in 1536. Steps lead to the crypt, which houses tombs of the bishops of Basel from the 10C-13C. Vaulting is supported by thick, sturdy pillars, whose capitals are decorated with hunting scenes and legends.

▶ *Turn right into Augustinergasse.*

Augustinergasse is lined with 16C houses and decorated with a pretty fountain. Continue straight ahead by the **Rheinsprung**, an alleyway lined with half-timbered 15C and 16C houses, which

Münster- portal of Sankt Gallen

affords a good view of the Rhine, the town, the Mittlere Rheinbrücke and its chapel covered with glazed tiles. Near the terrace, note the two houses built in 1770: the **Blaues Haus** ("blue house", n° 16) and the **Weisses Haus** ("white house", n° 18). Flights of steps to the left as you descend the hill lead to the 14C **Martinskirche**; because of the excellent acoustics provided by its low ceiling, the church is a popular venue for concerts. The Rheinsprung slopes down to Eisengasse, a busy street lined with shops, which leads to the market square.

Marktplatz (BY)

Lined with corbelled houses, this square is the scene of a market held in front of the town hall near the 16C Wine-growers' Guildhall.

Rathaus (BY H)

Guided tours Thu, 6pm. No charge. Visitors must first call the Tourist office on ☎ (061) 268 68 68.

The town hall was erected between 1508 and 1514 in the Late Gothic style and enlarged and restored between 1898 and 1902. The façade is decorated with frescoes and flanked by a modern belfry adorned with pinnacles. In the inner courtyard, note the fresco on the theme, of justice by Hans Bock (1610) and a statue of the town's presumed founder, Munatius Plancus. The State Council Chamber is also open.

▶ *At the end of Marktplatz, turn left then right into Marktgasse (Market Street), which leads to Fischmarktplatz.*

Fischmarktplatz (Fish Market Square) (BY)

This lively sector of Basel's shopping district is ornamented with the Fish

The Rathaus

Market fountain (**Fischmarktbrunnen**), one of the most beautiful Gothic fountains in Switzerland. The fountain (11m/36ft high) is decorated with angels, saints and prophets. The original (1390), sculpted by Jacob Sarbach, is in the Historical Musem.

Old streets★ (BY)

Take Stadthausgasse on the left and continue along Schneidergasse (note the quaint Andreasplatz with its fountain decorated with a monkey eating grapes). This leads to **Spalenberg**, a steep picturesque street lined with art galleries and antique shops. Turn left into **Gemsberg** to a charming square lined with 13C and 14C houses and a flower-decked Chamois fountain. Turn into Untere Heuberg, a side street with attractive houses, then right into **Heuberg** where you see 13C and 14C residences; nos 24, 20 and 6 have retained the pulley systems once used to lift objects to the attic.

> ### Cakes and biscuits
>
> The *Lekerli*, a speciality of Basel since the Middle Ages, is a small but rich biscuit made from honey, flour, almonds, walnuts, orange and lemon concentrate, spices and eau-de-vie. It is sold in pastry shops all over town, including the **Läckerlihaus** (Gergerstrasse 57), which specialises in this particular biscuit. Local specialities served at Carnival time include the Fastnachtskiechli, a fried pastry sprinkled with sugar, and the Fastenwähe, a butter brioche flavoured with cumin.

Holbeinbrunnen (BY)

Left of Spalenvorstadt.

This 16C fountain portrays a bagpiper inspired by one of Dürer's engravings, and peasants dancing, based on a famous painting by Holbein the Younger.

Spalentor (ABY)

This fine monumental gate was built in 1398 and restored at the end of the 19C. Two battlemented towers frame the central part, which is crowned by a pointed roof with glazed tiles. The summit of the west façade is adorned with Basel's coat of arms.

▶ *Return to Spalenvorstadt and turn left at the road junction.*

Peterskirche (BY)

🕒*Open daily except Mon, 9am-5pm.* 📷 *Guided tours available; for further details, contact the tourist office on ☎ (061) 268 68 68 or the presbytery on ☎ (061) 261 87 24.* A Late Gothic church, St Peter's was built in pink sandstone. In the south aisle and in the chapel to the left of the chancel 14C-15C frescoes can be seen. On the left of the east end of the church, take **Petersgasse**, graced with medieval charm.

▶ *Blumenrain leads to the Mittlere Rheinbrücke giving access to the east bank of the Rhine. At the end of the bridge, go down some steps on the right.*

Oberer Rheinweg (CY)

This esplanade set along the Rhine affords a **view**★ of the area, especially from the **Wettsteinbrücke**: the panorama encompasses the old quarters of Basel, the towers and the east end of the cathedral, the Martinskirche, the city's palaces, and the small artisans' cottages by the water's edge. Narrow alleyways link the esplanade to Rheingasse, which leads to the **Theodorskirche,** where you find some fine late-14C stained glass windows and a bell tower dating from 1277.

▶ *With the old church on your right, cross the Wettsteinbrücke.*

St Alban District (St Alban Tal)

(**DY**) This district was named after the oldest convent in town, founded by the Bishop of Basel in 1083. Of the former building belonging to the order of Cluny, there remains only a wing of the Romanesque cloisters, added onto a private house and visible from the old graveyard of St Alban's Church (Gothic chancel and tower, 19C nave). It was in this residence that the painter **Arnold Böcklin** spent his childhood days. The traditional paper industry, dating back to the creation of a canal by monks in the 12C, is evidenced by a number of mills; there is a view over the canal and several mills at the beginning of the street, St-Alban-Tal.

Ferries across the Rhine

Since 1854, flat-bottomed ferries have operated a service across the River Rhine. There are now four separate routes and the ferry boats are named after the four brotherhoods of Kleinbasel. The boats have no engine, are propelled by the current and are guided by a cable stretched across the river. Tell somebody from Basel an implausable story and they are likely to reply "Tell that to the *Fäärimaa*" (ferryman).

Mühlegraben (E)
The heavily restored vestiges of the Basel ramparts were built in the 14C. The wooden wall-walk is a reconstruction of the original. Most of the medieval fortifications were destroyed after 1860, when the city expanded prompted by 19C industrialization.

Sankt Alban-Berg
Cross the canal, from where you see the foundations of the town's former fortifications; continue along the path up St Alban hill. At the top, St Alban gateway and its portcullis (Sankt Alban-Tor) built in the 13C, are surrounded by a pretty garden.

Museums

In Grossbasel

Kunstmuseum★★★ (CY)
♿ ⏱ *Open daily except Mon, 10am-5pm . 18CHF, no charge first Sun in the month.*
☎ *(061) 206 56 62 62, www.kunstmuseumbasel.ch.*
In this sprawling museum, which has a large collection of masterpieces, particular emphasis is laid on 15C-17C paintings and drawings from the Upper Rhine and the Netherlands. The museum boasts the world's largest collection of works by the Holbein family. Most of the early works shown here belonged to a Renaissance art collector from Basel, Basilius Amerbach, whose father was a friend of both Erasmus and Holbein. Donated to the city in 1661, they served as a starting-point for the creation of the museum, which also has a fine collection of 19C and 20C art.

Entrance courtyard, gallery, ground floor - Here stand sculptures by Rodin *(The Burghers of Calais)*, Alexander Calder *(Die Grosse Spinne)* and Edouardo Chillida and an extensive collection of works by **Arnold Böcklin**, a Basel native who produced many symbolic and mythological paintings. The Prints Gallery shows sumptuous collections of drawings and engravings in rotation.

The **First floor** covers 15C-17C art in the Upper Rhine, including a series of altarpiece panels, *The Mirror of the Holy Salvation*, by the Basel master **Konrad Witz** (c 1440-45). Characterised by a charming landscape, the panels are a careful study in composition and colour harmony. The Alsatian painter Martin Schongauer (c 1430-91), drawing

DISCOVERING SWITZERLAND

Museum Kleines/			Pharmazie-historisches			Schweizerisches Sport-		
Klingental	BX	M⁴	Museum	BY	M²	museum	AY	M¹⁰
Musikmuseum	BY	M³	Rathaus	BY	H	Skulpturhalle	AY	M⁵

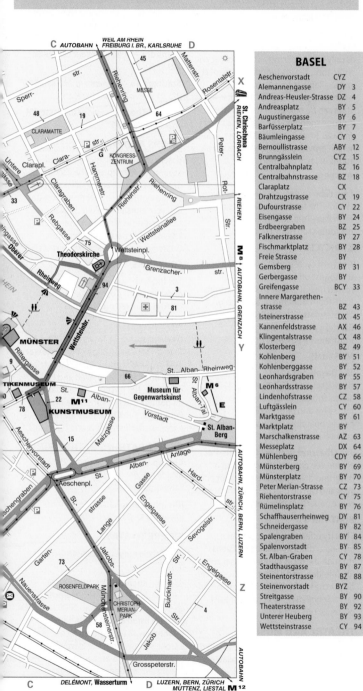

BASEL

Aeschenvorstadt	CYZ	
Alemannengasse	DY	3
Andreas-Heusler-Strasse	DZ	4
Andreasplatz	BY	5
Augustinergasse	BY	6
Barfüsserplatz	BY	7
Bäumleingasse	CY	9
Bernoullistrasse	ABY	12
Brunngässlein	CYZ	15
Centralbahnplatz	BZ	16
Centralbahnstrasse	BZ	18
Claraplatz	CX	
Drahtzugstrasse	CX	19
Dufourstrasse	CY	22
Eisengasse	BY	24
Erdbeergraben	BZ	25
Falknerstrasse	BY	27
Fischmarktplatz	BY	28
Freie Strasse	BY	
Gemsberg	BY	31
Gerbergasse	BY	
Greifengasse	BCY	33
Innere Margarethen-strasse	BZ	43
Isteinerstrasse	DX	45
Kannenfeldstrasse	AX	46
Klingentalstrasse	CX	48
Klosterberg	BZ	49
Kohlenberg	BY	51
Kohlenberggasse	BY	52
Leonhardsgraben	BY	55
Leonhardsstrasse	BY	57
Lindenhofstrasse	CZ	58
Luftgässlein	CY	60
Marktgasse	BY	61
Marktplatz	BY	
Marschalkenstrasse	AZ	63
Messeplatz	DX	64
Mühlenberg	CDY	66
Münsterberg	BY	69
Münsterplatz	BY	70
Peter Merian-Strasse	CZ	73
Riehentorstrasse	CY	75
Rümelinsplatz	BY	76
Schaffhauserrheinweg	DY	81
Schneidergasse	BY	82
Spalengraben	BY	84
Spalenvorstadt	BY	85
St. Alban-Graben	CY	78
Stadthausgasse	BY	87
Steinentorstrasse	BZ	88
Steinenvorstadt	BYZ	
Streitgasse	BY	90
Theaterstrasse	BY	92
Unterer Heuberg	BY	93
Wettsteinstrasse	CY	94

Address Book

PRACTICAL INFORMATION

PUBLIC TRANSPORT

One-way streets and car-free zones limit traffic in the centre of Basel, which is only accessible by foot, taxi or bicycle after 1pm. Tickets for public transport are available from automatic ticket vendors; a pass valid for one or several days can be bought at the tourist office. Anyone spending the night in a hotel in Basel Town is given a Mobility Ticket, which provides unlimited access to all forms of local transport.

BY FERRY

Four Fähri routes cross the River Rhine (5min). The ferries run daily in summer from 9am-7pm. In winter, the two middle routes run from 11am-5pm.

BY BICYCLE

A map of cycle routes is available from the tourist office. Bikes can be borrowed free of charge in summer from 8am-10pm from the railway station, Theaterplatz, Claraplatz and Schifflände; a deposit is charged. Visitors must show a passport or identity card.

MUSEUMS

The **BaselCard**, valid for one, two or three days (25CHF, 33CHF and 45CHF) allows tourists to visit a number of museums and offers reductions for hotels, boat rides, shows and other cultural events.

The **Oberrheinischer Museums-Pass** allows free entry to the museums in Basel and the surrounding area for one year and can be purchased at the tourist office or participating museums.

BOAT TRIPS

The city offers a number of boat trips, including dinner cruises, excursions through the locks between Basel and Rheinfelden, and night trips. Tickets can be purchased from Basel Personenschiffahrt, Schifflände, next to the tourist office; ☎ 061 639 95 00.

THEATRE AND MUSIC

A full list of cultural events is published in the magazine Basel Live, available from hotels and the tourist office.

Theater Basel – *Theaterstrasse 7 – ☎ 061 295 11 33; www.theater-basel. ch.* This theatre has an excellent reputation for opera, theatre and dance.

Komödie – *Steinenvorstadt 63 – ☎ 061 295 11 00.*

Stadtcasino – *Steinenberg 14 – ☎ 061 225 93 93; www.casinobasel.ch.*

Musical Theater – *Feldbergstrasse 151 – ☎ 061 699 88 99.*

SHOPS AND MARKETS

Basel's shopping district is centred around the Marktplatz. The Globus department store and smaller shops selling clothes, designer goods, crystal and souvenirsare on Freie Strasse and Gebergasse, as far as Barfüsserplatz. The Manor department store is on Greifengasse, in the St Alban district.

SOUVENIRS

The local emblem is the Basilisk, a type of dragon with a cockerel's head, which is often depicted on brooches.

MARKETS

General stalls: Barfüsserplatz, Thu, Jan to mid-Oct, 7am-6.30pm; **Food, flower and organic market:** Markplatz, daily, every afternoon; Mon, Wed and Fri, until 7pm. NB: prices are often based on pounds and not kilos. **Flea market:** Peterplatz, Sat. **Christmas market** – Dec, on Barfüsserplatz and Claraplatz.

PUBLIC BATHING IN THE RHINE

Rheinbad Breite – *St Alban-Rheinweg 195* ☎ *061 31125 75.* View of the cathedral.

Rheinbad St Johann – *St Johanns-Rheinweg* ☎ *061 322 04 42.*

WHERE TO STAY

🪙 *For coin ranges see Legend on cover flap.*

🍺🍺🍺 **Rochat** – *Petersgraben 23 – ☎ 061 261 81 40 ; www.hotelrochat. ch* – 50 rooms. Dating from 1899 and officially listed as a protected site, this hotel with a bright red façade is a stone's throw from the town centre. Light, quiet rooms at reasonable prices. The restaurant does not serve alcohol.

Wettstein – *Grenzacherstrasse 8* – ☎ *061 690 69 69 – Fax 061 691 05 45; hotel-wettstein@bluewin.ch – 42 rooms*. This hotel (no restaurant) is situated along the right bank of the Rhine, conveniently close to Wettsteinplatz. Easy access by public transport.

Baslertor – *Outside the town at Muttenz, 4.5km/2.8mi to the SE – St Jakobsstrasse 1* – ☎ *061 465 55 55; www.basel-hotels.ch – 47 rooms and 4 suites*. Modern, comfortable hotel with extremely good service for the price.

Drei Könige am Rheine – *Blumenrain 8* – ☎ *061 260 50 50; www.drei-koenige-basel.ch – 82 rooms and 6 suites* – This hotel, situated on the banks of the Rhine, is easily recognised by its imposing character and its distinctive ornamental façade featuring the "Three Kings". The old-fashioned yet civilised atmosphere evokes early 20C Europe. From the rooms overlooking the river, you can see boats gliding peacefully along the Rhine. Not surprisingly, such a refined establishment has welcomed such crowned heads and other celebrities as Voltaire, Napoleon, Metternich, Picasso, musicians such as Duke Ellington, Igor Stravinski and … the Rolling Stones. The restaurant serves traditional fare in elegance.

St Gotthard – *Central-bahnstrasse 13* – ☎ *061 225 13 13 – Fax 061 225 1314; www.gotthard.ch– 104 rooms*. Well located just opposite the railway station and close to a tramway stop. Easy access to the town centre. Delicious buffet breakfast.

EATING OUT

Löwenzorn – *Gemsberg 2-4* – ☎ *061 261 42 13; www.lowezorn.ch* – 🕐 *closed Sun and public hols, Easter and 24 Dec-5 Jan*. Traditional local cuisine served in an imposing mansion which used to be a guildhall, with a pretty inner courtyard.

St Alban-Stübli – *St Alban-Vorstadt 74* – ☎ *061 272 54 15; www.st-alban-stuebli.ch* – 🕐 *closed 23 Dec-9 Jan, Sun, Sat lunchtime and public hols*. Distinguished by its sign, this building is tucked away in a quaint, picturesque street. Meals at affordable prices.

Schlüsselzunft – *Freie Strasse 25* – ☎ *061 261 20 46; www.schluesselzunft.ch – Fax 061 261 20 56* – 🕐 *closed Sun and public hols*. This restaurant is housed in the former Locksmiths' Guildhall, originally built in the 15C. Meals are served in the attractive dining room where the faience stove is definitely the centre of attention.

Zum Goldenen Sternen – *St Alban-Rheinweg 70* – ☎ *061 272 16 66 – Fax 061 272 16 67* – 🕐 *closed Sun evening, Mon and 23 Dec-3 Jan*. On the banks of the River Rhine, under the chestnut trees, this is the oldest restaurant in Basel, opened in 1412. A ferry pulls in a few metres from the terrace. Fish specialities and seasonal cuisine are served in the dining hall, which features a splendid coffered ceiling.

Harmonie – *Petersgraben 71* – ☎ *061 261 07 18; www.harmonie-basel.ch*. This small, friendly restaurant, situated on Spalenberg Hill, is popular with locals. The restaurant serves generous portions of simple cuisine, featuring dishes such as Zurich-style veal, liver with rösti potatoes and a giant-sized im Schlüsseli salad.

Café Spitz – *Rheingasse 2* – ☎ *061 685 11 00; www.hotel-merta.ch* – 🕐 *Closed 25 Dec*. In 1833, this building housed the guildhall of the three brotherhoods of Kleinbasel, symbolised by their emblems: the savage, the lion and the griffin. Now well known for its excellent fish dishes, the restaurant has a terrace with splendid views of the Rhine.

Chez Donati – *St Johanns-Vorstadt 48* – ☎ *061 322 09 19; www.lestroisrois.com* – 🕐 *closed Sun, Mon, and mid-Jul to-mid-Aug*. A fashionable restaurant, decorated with lovely Murano glass lamps, serving fine Italian food and wine.

Waldhaus – *Birsfelden, 2km/1.2mi E* – ☎ *061 313 00 11; www.waldhaus-basel.ch* – 🕐 *closed Sun evenings, Mon and 23 Dec-11 Jan*. This old forest house stands in a park near the banks of the Rhine. Enjoy your meal in a quiet, secluded spot away from the bustle of the big city.

NIGHTLIFE

The bar of the **Drei Könige** (Mittlere Rheinbrücke) is very pleasant, especially in summer with its covered terrace overlooking the Rhine. The front page of the menu bears signatures and comments of famous people who have relaxed here. The **Schiesser** tea-rooms on the nearby Marktplatz have been serving delicious confectionery since 1870. Beyond the right bank of the river lies **Kleinbasel,** a district where nightlife is particularly active. In Clarastrasse, a lively shopping street, there are several popular places: **Mr Pickwick Pub** (British pub atmosphere), le **Plaza Club** and its thematic evenings (karaoke, concerts, shows) and the **Grischuna Bar** in the Hôtel Alexander (concerts every evening).

Near the railway station, you can have a cocktail in a discreet, refined ambience at the bar of the **Hotel Euler** (Centralbahnplatz 14). Those who like soft music and piano bars should visit the **Old City Bar** in the Hotel Hilton (Aeschengraben 31).

Le Caveau (Grünpfahlgasse 4, near the post office) offers a wide range of Swiss, French, Italian, Californian and other wines. In the heart of the old city, the **Atlantis** (Klosterberg 9) is reputed for its excellent jazz concerts, which can be appreciated from a mezzanine area or from seats around the stage.

EVENTS

The annual **International Art Fair** (Art Internationale Kunstmesse), the largest festival of its kind in the world, attracts collectors, brokers and art-gallery owners to Basel in June. The **Autumn Fair** has been held in the city since 1471: fairground rides and a big wheel are set up on several squares in the city, including the Barfüsserplatz, Kaserne and Mustermesse.

on the experience of Witz and his followers, depicts moving family scenes, notably in *Mary and Child in Their Room*. Next is Grünewald (1460-1528) and his *Christ on the Cross*, severely bruised and tortured with chilling realism, and his famous contemporary from Strasbourg, **Hans Baldung Grien** with his *Death and the Maiden* (1517). Niklaus Manuel Deutsch (c 1484-1530), a Bernese, is shown in his *Judgement of Paris* and *Pyramus and Thisbe*.

Hans Holbein the Younger (1497-1543), one of the greatest painters of all time, marked the peak of the Renaissance. His pessimistic and analytical art expresses reality in simple forms. Among the some 20 paintings is the admirable *Portrait of the Artist's Wife with her Children*, which conveys indescribable sadness, and *Portrait of Erasmus as an Old Man* with his shrewd gaze. Lucas Cranach the Elder (1472-1553) is present with *Virgin with Child Holding a Piece of Bread* and *Judgement of Paris*. Otherr contain 17C Dutch paintings, including an outstanding work by the young Rembrandt (1606-69), *David before Saul*.

Another section contains artists such as Rubens, Goltzius, Ruysdael, Brouwer and Stoskopff and by masters of Romanticism (Delacroix, Géricault, Daumier) and Realism (Courbet, Manet). These rooms also display a fine collection of Impressionist and Post-Impressionist art, with works by Monet *(Snow Scenes),* Pissarro *(The Harvesters)* and Sisley *(The Banks of the Loing at Moret)*; *The Racetrack* by Degas; *Young Girl Lying in the Grass* by Renoir; *Montagne Sainte-Victoire* by Cézanne; landscapes and portraits by Van Gogh; and several works by Gauguin, including *Nafea Faa ipoipo ("When Will You Marry?"),* an important painting dating from his Tahitian period, and major works by Caspar Wolf and Johann Heinrich Füssli. The Nazarenes are represented with pictures by Josef Anton Koch and Johann Friedrich Overbeck.

Second floor - A painting by Georg Baselitz *(Animals)* in the foyer marks the beginning of the remarkable 20C collection. Cubism, a movement created around 1908, is particularly well represented with canvases by Braque *(Landscape, Pitcher and Violin),* Picasso *(Bread Loaves and Fruit Bowl on Table),* Juan Gris *(The Violin)* and Fernand Léger *(The Woman in Blue)*. Fauvism and its distinctive technique of spreading vivid, bold colours can be admired in compositions by Matisse. German Expressionism is present with Franz Marc *(Tierschicksale)*, Emil Nolde *(Vorabend: Marschlandschaft)*, Kokoschka *(Die Windsbraut)* and Lovis Corinth *(Ecce Homo)*, Surrealism with Giorgio de Chirico, Salvador Dali, Miró, Max Ernst and Yves Tanguy. Some rooms contain Abstract art by Arp, Mondrian *(Composition in Blue, Yellow and White)*, Van Doesburg *(Composition in Black and White)*, Vantongerloo *(Enigmatic $L^2 = S$)*, Kandinsky and Schwitters, and works of Henri Rousseau, Marc Chagall and Paul Klee.

The museum also pays tribute to American art after the year 1945. Abstract Expressionism, also known as the New York School, is represented with works by Franz Kline *(Andes)* and Clyfford Still *(Painting)*; Color Field by Barnett Newman *(Day Before One, White Fire II)* and Mark Rothko *(Nᵒ 1)*; Minimal Art heralded by Frank Stella. Body Art saw a flourishing era with Sam Francis *(Deep Orange and Black)*, Cy Twombly *(Nini's Painting)* and Bruce Nauman. Pop Art is represented finds with pieces by Jasper Johns, Andy Warhol and Claes Oldenburg.

Museum der Kulturen★★ (BY M¹)

🕐*Open daily except Mon, 10am-5pm.* 🕐*Closed 1 Jan, 1 Aug, 24, 25 and 31 Dec.* 🎫*7CHF, no charge first Sun in the month.* ☎ *(061) 266 56 00; www.mkb.ch.*

The **Museum of Ethnography** houses the largest collection of its kind in Switzerland, with around 140 000 masks, arms, carvings, along with Oceanian and Pre-Columbian works of art. Of particular note is the Melanesian section (ground floor): a Papuan temple hut, masks, totems etc. There is also an interesting Indonesian collection exhibiting precious textiles. Other galleries display objects from Ancient Egypt, such as mummies and sarcophagi. Another section is devoted to European and Swiss customs and traditions, including popular religious art, rural life, and the carnival. There is also extensive **collections devoted to natural sciences** as well as a prehistory section. Exhibits include information on animals from the region, exotic species and dinosaurs, as well as live animals housed in terrariums.

Museum für Gegenwartskunst

♿🕐 *Open daily except Mon, 11am-5pm.* 🎫*10CHF.* ☎ *(061) 206 62 62.*

A modern, bright building next to a 19C factory provides a pleasant setting for the **Contemporary Art Museum**, part of the Fine Art Museum. It ouses temporary exhibitions on prominent contemporary art movements since 1960: Minimal Art, Conceptual Art, Arte Povera and Free Figurative Art and permanent works works by such artists as Frank Stella, Bruce Nauman, Cindy Sherman and Joseph Beuys. The vast white exhibition halls serve to enhance the monumental paintings on display.

Antikenmuseum Basel und Sammlung Ludwig★★ (CY)

♿🕐 *Open daily except Mon, 10am-5pm.* 🕐*Closed 1 Jan, 1, 9 May, and 24, 25 Dec.* 🎫*7CHF, no charge first Sun in the month.* ☎ *(061) 201 12 12.*

This is the only museum in Switzerland dedicated exclusively to the Ancient art of the Mediterranean. Its exhibits, largely donated by private collectors, cover five millennia, from 4000 BC to the 7C AD, and include artifacts from Greece, Rome, Egypt and other civilisations in the Middle and Near East. The exhibits are illuminated by subtle lighting, with panels providing information in German and English.

The Middle East, Cyprus and beginnings of Ancient Greece★★ (*Basement*)

Some 350 works illustrate the close ties between the island of Cyprus and the civilisations of the Near and Middle East – Iran, Mesopotamia, Syria, Urartu and Anatolia – with the Aegean. Even before the appearance of writing, the Iranian plateau was producing ceramics and objects made from fine bronze,often adorned with animal motifs, as shown in the superb cervid-shaped **vase**★ exhibited here (1300-700 BC). Also noteworthy are Syrian cups decorated with lions (8C BC), bronze caldrons from Urartu adorned with a bull's head, and votive statuettes from Cyprus, whose style is influenced by many countries, including Anatolia and Egypt (7C BC). The civilisations of the Near and Middle East also influenced Greek art, as shown by the containers with animal motifs displayed here (c 600 BC).

Ancient Egypt★★ (Basement)

This is the most important collection of Egyptian artefacts in Switzerland. This section is arranged in chronological order, with more than 600 exhibits on display. The Predynastic Period is represented by a simple but skilfully sculpted brown ceramic hippopotamus (c 3500 BC). A remarkable head in red jasper and a rare faïence statue of Ramses II with a falcon's head date from the Ramesside Era (c 1250 BC). Items dating from the New Kingdom include a make-up spoon representing a servant, and a box for *shabtis* – statuettes which represented the deceased (1303-1224 BC). An almost complete version of a Book of the Dead dating from the Ptolemaic Period (305-30 BC) is on one of the walls. The basement features works from **Roman and Hellenic times**: clay statuettes, small bronzes, funerary stelae from Phrygia, a scene representing Achilles and Penthesilea, and Roman tombs, including a fine marble sarcophagus decorated with the legend of Medea.

Archaic and Classical eras (Ground, first and second floors)

Exhibits include marble sculptures and bronze statuettes (600-300 BC). Note the funerary stela (480 BC), locally known as the "relief of the Basel doctor". A superb collection of vases (520-350 BC) includes works by an artist known as the "Berlin painter", as well as a huge amphora complete with lid, bearing the twin figures of Athena and Hercules, plus exhibits of jewellery and coins (Sicily and southern Italy). Another collection belongs to the Geometric (1100-700 BC) and Archaic (620-500 BC) eras, characterized by black figures set against a light clay background. They are shown together with weapons from ancient Greece and Italy, as well as Etruscan artefacts (votive statuettes and bronze miniatures).

Historisches Museum★ (BY)

🕐 Open daily except Tue, 10am-5pm. 🚫 Closed 1 Jan, Good Fri, 1 May, Ascension, 24 and 31 Dec. 7CHF, no charge one Sun a month. ☎ (061) 205 86 00, www.hmb.ch.
The Cordeliers belonging to the Franciscan Order occupied this old triple-aisle church (1231) until the Reformation in 1529. It is an imposing building, particularly suitable for presenting its prestigious art collections.

Near the steps leading downstairs stands a popular 17C *Lällenkönig* (King Lälli), with a small happy face, rolling eyes and protruding tongue. Downstairs, exhibits retrace the town's history since the days of the Celts, with strong emphasis on the 13C and the following centuries, when Basel became a truly independent city and was coveted by bishops and emperors, before it joined the Confederation. Besides this historical exhibition, reconstructed rooms (dining room, bedroom) present some fine period furniture. Also in the basement: precious non-religious objects (Erasmus's beaker, 1531; provost's crown, 1671) and the cathedral treasury (bust-reliquary of St Ursula in partly gilded repoussé silver and copper, 14C; monstrance of the Innocents or the Apostles in gilded silver, 1335-1340).

In the chancel, where stained glass and religious sculptures are exhibited, note the large altarpiece with panels from St Mary's Church in Calanca (Graubünden). This polychrome retable made in Ivo Strigel's workshop was carved out of limewood. The rood screen corridor is decorated with fragments of Konrad Witz's *Dance of Death* (15C), a famous fresco painted in the days of the Council of Basel. The north side aisle is devoted to the Basel Corporations. During the 18C, they numbered 15 and played a major role in the city's political, administrative, religious, social and economic life. The south aisle presents objects from the Upper Rhine region: splendid tapestries woven in Basel workshops (tapestry of the Garden of Love, 15C), sculpted or painted wooden chests with romantic motifs, bowls (note the hanap in pearwood with chiselled and gilded silver mounts given to Martin Luther by the Elector of Saxony Johann der Beständige in 1530), faience work for the ornamentation of stoves. In the nave, note the magistrates' stalls from Basel Cathedral (solid oak, 16C) and the 16C Holbein Fountain in painted sandstone, known as the Bagpiper's Fountain.

Musikmuseum (BY M³)

🕐 *Open daily except Mon and Tue, 2-6pm; Sun, 11am-5pm.* 🕐 *Closed most public holidays.* ⊜*7CHF, no charge one Sun a month.* ☎ *(061) 205 86 00.*

This museum, the largest of its kind in Switzerland, is part of the Historisches Museum. Its collection of 650 musical instruments is displayed in the Lohnhof, an old monastery, part of which dates back to the 11C. The building, for a long time used as a prison, was restored in 2000. The "Music in Basel" section presents musical instruments in their social context, with rooms dedicated to themes such as public concerts. Another section, "Concerto, Chorale and Dance", displays instruments played in different musical genres, including chamber music and religious music. "Parade, Celebration and Signals" exhibits instruments played during particular events, such as hunts or at royal courts. Visitors can listen to 200 extracts of music selected via an interactive display, which also provides information in a number of languages.

Karikatur & Cartoon-Museum (CY M¹¹)

Kids 🕐 *Open Wed-Sat, 2-5pm; Sun and public hols, 10am-5pm.* 🕐 *Closed during Carnival.* ⊜*7CHF.* ☎ *(061) 226 33 60.*

Set up in a superbly renovated old house, the Museum of Caricature and Comic Strip stands out because of its highly original and refreshing approach. Adults and children will enjoy leafing through original albums, drawn by some of the leading names in this field: Tomi Ungerer, EK Waechter, Claire Bretécher etc. Children can even try their hand at drawing in a special room set aside for this purpose.

Basler Papiermühle★★ (DY) (M⁶)

🕐 *Open daily except Mon, 2-5pm.* 🕐 *Closed 1 Jan, Carnival, Good Fri, Easter Sun and Whit Sun, Ascension, 1 May, 1 Aug, 24 and 25 Dec.* ⊜*12CHF.* ☎ *(061) 272 96 52; www.papiermuseum.ch.*

In 1980, this former flour mill attached to Klingental Convent, later converted into a paper mill (1453), was turned into a museum devoted to the many aspects of the paper industry. It provides a lively presentation of the history of paper and paper-related activities, laid out on four levels. As in former times, the mill is still operated by its paddle wheel. Each floor is devoted to a particular theme. Visitors can take part in the demonstrations and keep the objects they have made to remind them of their visit. They can choose between papermaking, fonts, typography and binding.

Pharmazie-Historisches Museum (BY M²)

🕐 *Open daily except Sun-Mon, 10am-6pm (5pm Sat). Guided tour first Sat in the month.* 🕐 *Closed public hols.* ⊜*5CHF.* ☎ *(061) 264 91 11, www.pharmaziemuseum.ch.*

The Apothecary Museum presents instruments and medicines used in bygone days as well as a carefully reconstructed alchemy laboratory and pharmacy, complete with 18C-19C wood panelling. The more unusual exhibits feature an 18C portable medicine chest from Japan (curious wooden valise fitted with small drawers) and a display cabinet devoted to Africa and its traditional remedies. Note the fine collection of jars dating from the 15C to the 19C.

Jüdisches Museum der Schweiz (BY M⁹)

🕐 *Open Mon and Wed, 2-5pm, Sun 11am-5pm.* ⊜*No charge.* ☎ *(061) 261 95 14, museum-judaistik@unibas.ch.*

This small museum is the only Jewish Museum in the whole of Switzerland. At the encouragement of Theodor Herzl, Jews from throughout Europe and America gathered in Basel to attend the first Zionist Congress, held in the Casino concert hall in August 1897. This momentous event marked a turning point in the long history of the Jewish community of Basel (the earliest Jewish settlements date back to the

12C and Hebrew books were printed here as early as the 16C) and is prominently mentioned in the museum. Exhibits are arranged in three groups: Jewish law, the Jewish year, and Jewish life, including kosher food and birth, wedding and death customs. Artifacts from Jewish communities around the world include tombstones from the Middle Ages, Persian amulets studded with precious stones and sumptuous 19C silver menorahs from Vienna, plus embroidered prayer shawls, inscribed and painted Torah scrolls (*Book of Law*), and passports from the Second World War with the telltale "J" stamped on them.

Haus zum Kirschgarten★ (BZ)

🕐 *Open daily except Mon, 10am-5pm, Sat 1-5pm.* 🕐 *Closed most public hols.* 7CHF, *no charge first Sun in the month.* ☎ *(061) 205 86 00.*

The museum is housed in a former 18C town house owned by the silk ribbon manufacturer JR Burckhardt. There is a fine collection of clocks, balance-cocks and watches from the 16C to the 19C, porcelain stoves and a large collection of porcelain figurines on the ground floor. Upstairs are drawing rooms adorned with Aubusson tapestries, pictures and French furniture; boudoirs; 18C and 19C costumes; a dining room; a music room; and a kitchen with a magnificent battery of copper pans and utensils. The third floor offers a collection of antique toys: dolls' houses, miniature carriages, rocking horses, boats and vintage cars. The basement contains porcelain and ceramics from Switzerland, Germany, France and China; and carved casks, one of which dates from 1723 and holds 10 000l/2 200gal.

Skulpturhalle (AY M⁵)

🕐 *Open daily except Mon, 11am-5pm.* 🕐 *Closed 1 Jan, 18 and 20 Feb, 29 Mar, 1, 9 and 20 May, 10 and 17 Jun, 24, 25 and 31 Dec.* No charge. ☎ *(061) 261 52 45.*

This museum is devoted to the art of moulding and displays many casts of Greek and Roman statues, including an impressive collection of plasters used for the Parthenon sculptures.

Schweizerisches Sportmuseum (AY M¹⁰)

🕐 *Open Tue-Thu, 10am-noon and 2-5pm, Sat 1-5pm and Sun 11am-5pm.* 5CHF. ☎ *061 261 12 21; www.swiss-sports-museum.ch.*

The Museum of Swiss Sport traces the sporting world since Antiquity. Winter sports practised on both snow and ice, national games (wrestling, hornus – 👤 *see Introduction*) and ball games (tennis, table tennis, golf) come to life via photograph, objects and equipment visitors can try out themselves, becoming hockey players, footballers or ice skaters. The cycling section features the legendary bicycle on which Albert Aichele broke the world record in Munich in 1888, reaching a speed of 38.07kph/23.7mph.

In Kleinbasel and on the right bank of the Rhine

Museum Kleines Klingental (BX M⁴)

🕐 *Open Wed and Sat 2-5pm, Sun 10am-5pm.* 🕐 *Closed 1 Jan, during Carnival, Holy Thu, Good Fri, Easter Mon, Whit Mon, 1 May, 1 Aug, 25 and 31 Dec.* No charge. ☎ *(079) 303 00 82.*

This museum is in an old Dominican monastery founded in the 13C and partly destroyed in 1860. A vaulted room in the shape of an inverted ship's hull exhibits a great many medieval sculptures taken from Basel Cathedral. These are either original works or replicas, made in red sandstone or wood: gargoyles, recumbent figures, freizes, low reliefs, statues (equestrian statues) etc. Other rooms present capitals and stalls as well as plasters casts of the St Gallen Portal and the main entrance to the cathedral, together with drawings and miniature models re-creating the old city.

In Riehen

Although this locality is a separate administrative division, its closeness to Basel makes it a suburb of the city.

▸ *Access by car via Wettsteinbrücke and Riehenstrasse. To avoid traffic and parking problems, visitors are advised to take tram n° 6 from Marktplatz.*

Fondation Beyeler★★

Tram n° 6, Fondation Beyeler stop. ◷ *Open daily, 10am-6pm.* ◷ *Closed 24-25 Dec.* ◖ *21CHF; reduced admission fees every Mon (except holidays).* ◖ *Guided tours available on request, contact* ☎ *(061) 645 97 00, www.beyeler.ch.*

For half a century, Basel art enthusiasts **Hildy and Ernst Beyeler** collected paintings and sculptures from celebrated 20C artists; they commissioned Italian architect **Renzo Piano**, who conceived the Georges Pompidou Centre in Paris, together with Richard Rogers, to design a museum to display this astounding private collection. This simple building (2 700m²/29 052sq ft) was constructed in 1997; three large bays open onto the lovely Berower Park, where a sculpture by Calder (*The Tree*, 1966) can be admired. A water garden evokes *Pond with Waterlilies* by Monet, a 9m/29ft triptych on display in the museum. A long glass roof supported by red porphyry walls provides excellent lighting.

Around 200 paintings and sculptures trace the development of modern art from Impressionism to Cubism. Famous works include *Seven Bathers* by Cézanne, *Wheatfield with Cornflower* by Vincent van Gogh, *Rouen Cathedral* by Monet, *Woman Reading* by Braque, *Hungry Lion Attacking Antelope* by Douanier Rousseau, *Woman in Green* by Picasso and *Interior with Black Fern* by Matisse. Abstract Art, which appeared in Russia before the First World War, with a strong emphasis on both shape and colour, is represented here by *Fugue* by Kandinsky and *Painting* n° 1 by Mondrian.

Tribute is paid to Switzerland in the works of Klee *(Diana, Ein Tor)* and Alberto Giacometti *(Seated Woman, Caroline, The Street)*. Post-war Abstract Art is represented by works of Mark Rothko, Robert Rauschenberg *(Windward)* and Roy Lichtenstein *(Girl with Tear III)*. One room is devoted to British artist Francis Bacon (1909-92), whose compositions are characterised by distorted perspective and hallucinatory themes *(Portrait of George Dyer Riding a Bicycle)*. Paintings by Jean Dubuffet, Georg Baselitz and Anselm Kiefer are also on display. Tribal art from Alaska, Oceania and Africa are displayed around the museum, interspersed with the paintings and sculptures.

Spielzeugmuseum★

Access by tram n° 6, Riehen Dorf stop. ◷ *Open Mon, Wed-Sun 11am-5pm, Sun 10am-5pm.* ◷ *Closed 1 Jan, Good Fri, 1 May, 1 Aug, 24-26 and 31 Dec.* ◖ *7CHF.* ☎ *(061) 641 28 29.*

The Toy Museum occupies a large section of Wettsteinhaus, a magnificently restored former mansion which belonged to Johan Rudolf Wettstein, mayor of Basel (1645-1666). The collections evoke carefree, childhood days: wooden and metal toys, lead and pewter figurines, board games, miniature theatres, string puppets, magic lanterns, dolls' houses and construction games. Exhibits illustrate the evolution of toy making and reflect the changes in trends and fashions throughout history. The mansion also houses the **Dorfmuseum**, devoted to daily life in Riehen and the **Rebbaumuseum**, which explains winemaking techniques and the art of oenology.

Right bank and environs

Museum Jean Tinguely (DY M⁸)

At the SBB train station, take tram n° 2 to Wettsteinplatz, then bus n° 31 in the direction of Habermatten/Hörnli and get off at the Museum Tinguely stop. ◷ *Open daily except Mon, 11am-7pm.* ◷ *Closed 1 Jan, Good Fri and 25 Dec.* ◖ *10CHF.* ☎ *(061) 681 93 20, www.tinguely.ch.*

The renowned Ticino architect Mario Botta designed this museum, located along the banks of the Rhine in Solitude Park, which features a long glassed-in ramp adjoining a construction in pink sandstone. This area, known as the *barca*, allows visitors access to the exhibition rooms (mezzanine) from the inside, while at the same time letting them gaze out at the nearby river.

The museum pays tribute to the great metal sculptor **Jean Tinguely**, a dominant post-war artist who conceived the famous "strange machines" (🕯️ *see FRIBOURG*). Each gallery is devoted to a specific period in the sculptor's life. The 1950s are represented by reliefs driven by engines (*Méta-Mécanique, 1955*). In the 1960s, Tinguely created objects from scrap metal, followed by machine-sculptures painted black. The 1980s are marked by large compositions such as *Lola T 180 - Memorial to Joachim B.* The machines can be operated by visitors in the way they choose. The upper floor displays letters and drawings as well as other sculptures like *Lotus and the Widows of Eva Aeppli, Hannibal II*, an impressive work reflecting Tinguely's obsession with death, and an unusual collection of philosophers' busts: *Friedrich Engels, Jean-Jacques Rousseau, Martin Heidegger* and *Henri Bergson*. The tour finishes where the most striking item in the huge room is unquestionably *Grosse Méta Maxi-Maxi Utopia* (1987), of which the artist himself said: "I would like to make something gay, something for children, who can climb and jump; I would like it to turn into something good, impressive, merry, wild, something suggesting a funfair...".

Kutschenmuseum (DZ M^{12})

♿🕐 *Open Wed and Sat-Sun, 2-5pm.* ✎*No charge.* ☎ *(061) 205 86 00.*

This museum, housed on an old estate in Brüglingen, exhibits 19C and 20C carriages and sleighs that once belonged to wealthy families from Basel. Shooting breaks, phaetons and landaus all demonstrate the skill of local carriage-makers. Other items include mail coaches, old fire engines and children's carriages and sleighs.

Additional Sights

Zoologischer Garten★★★ (AZ)

Kids ♿🕐 *Open May-Aug, 8am-6.30pm; Mar-Apr and Sep-Oct, 8am-6pm; Nov-Feb, 8am-5.30pm.* ✎*16CHF, 6CHF (ages 6-16).* ☎ *(061) 295 35 35, www.zoobasel.ch.*

This zoo of international renown was founded in 1874 and, with Bern, is one of the largest in Switzerland (13ha/32 acres). It includes more than 5 300 animals from each of the five continents. The zoo specialises in the reproduction and rearing of endangered species such as rhinoceroses, gorillas and spectacled bears. Its park, with ponds where swans, ducks, flamingoes and other exotic birds splash about, is equipped with restaurants, picnic spots and children's play areas. The children's zoo has young or newborn animals which children can pet, and ponies or elephants on which they can ride. Several buildings are entirely devoted to one species, such as the Monkey Pavilion, the Aviary, the Elephant House and the Wild Animal House. The **vivarium** houses 250 varieties of fish (sea and freshwater), 250 reptile species and 40 amphibian species, some of which are exceedingly rare. Before leaving, don't miss the zoo's star attractions, the several dozen or so penguins and king penguins.

Fasnachtsbrunnen (BY F)

The Carnival Fountain designed by **Jean Tinguely** (1925-91) is the centre of attraction on the esplanade in front of the municipal theatre. The artist studied at the local Academy of Fine Arts before leaving for Paris and establishing himself as a sculptor. Nine cleverly articulated metallic structures in perpetual motion provide a telling example of Tinguely's wit and ingenuity.

The Port (HAFEN) *via Klybeckstrasse*

(**BX**) Since the Middle Ages, the town has played a part in trade between the North Sea and the Mediterranean, Swabia and Burgundy. River navigation ceased following the building of the great Alpine roads and railway lines and it was not until 1906 that traffic resumed as far as Antwerp and Rotterdam. The city's main docks extend downstream as far as Kleinhünigen, where an obelisk and a viewing table mark the junction of the French, German and Swiss frontiers.

Proximity to the French and German borders precludes extending the port, which could only proceed if run by several countries, as is the case with the Blotzheim airport, which is run jointly with Mulhouse. The ports of Basel Town and Basel District (Basel-Stadt and Basel-Land) are equipped to handle the larger motor vessels and barges. Coal, hydrocarbons, grain, metallurgical products and industrial raw materials make up most of this traffic, which is mainly concerned with imported goods.

Boat trips

Tours of the harbour passing through the locks, May-Oct. Contact Basler Personenschiffahrts-Gesellschaft AG, Hochberstrasse 160, Postfach 4019. ☎ (061) 639 95 00/08.
In summer, there are tours of the port along the Rhine and the Kembs Canal. ♿ *For details of embarkation points see the town plan (BY).*

Siloterrasse Dreiländereck

In Kleinhüningen port, not far from the exhibition mentioned above, along the railway tracks. Access by a metal staircase, then a lift. 🕐 *Access to the terrace Mar-Nov, daily except Mon, and Dec-Feb, Tue, Sat-Sun, 10am-5pm. ☜4CHF. ☎ (061) 639 33 47.*
The silo terrace of the Swiss Navigation Company commands a wide **panorama**★ of the town and especially the port installations. Beyond them lies the plain of Alsace with the Vosges, the Black Forest and the Jura forming a backcloth. In fine weather, you can see the Ballon d'Alsace in the far distance (alt 1 250m/4 100ft).

Excursions

Augst★★: Roman Ruins – ♿ *See AUGST/AUGUSTA RAURICA.*

Liestal★

16km/10mi SE. 🚩 *Altmarktstrasse 96 – 4410 – ☎ (061) 927 65 20*
This charming locality, on a promontory between the Ergolz Valley and the Orisbach, is the chief town of the Basel District. Its main street (**Rathausstrasse**) lined with painted 19C houses, leads from the city's medieval gate to its red sandstone town hall, built in 1586 and extended in 1938. The town hall is decorated with Renaissance frescoes which were restored in 1900.

The **Kantonsmuseum Baselland** (🕐 *Open daily except Mon, 10am-noon and 2-5pm; Sat-Sun, 10am-5pm.* 🕐 *Closed 1 May and 1 Aug. 5. ☜18CHF. ☎ (061) 925 59 86)* on Zeughausplatz focuses on the natural environment and especially the ribbon-making industry, an important regional activity for over four centuries since it was introduced in 1550 by Huguenot refugees fleeing France. Silk ribbons, which were exported to England, France and even Australia, and reached a peak of popularity towards the late 19C. The successive stages of fabrication, ranging from design to the marketing, are illustrated with display cabinets and equipment.

On the heights of Schleifenberg, the Aussichtsturm belvedere affords a lovely **view** of the Rhine and, in fine weather, the landscape stretching to the Alps. The surrounding forests offer many pleasant walks. On summer Sundays, a little **steam train** (Waldenburger Dampfzug) links Liestal to Waldenburger, located 14km/9mi to the south.

Rheinfelden★ – 🍴 *See RHEINFELDEN.*

St Chrischona-Kapelle★
8km/5mi – allow 15min. Leave Basel by the road to Riehen. At the post office at Riehen turn right towards Bettingen.
The road runs through residential suburbs of Basel and Bettingen before climbing to St Chrischona Chapel. From a terrace nearby there is a **panorama**★ from Säntis in the east to the Jura mountain ranges in the west. Basel can be seen nestling in the Rhine plain.

Wasserturm Bruderholz★
3.5km/2mi. Leave Basel to the south;bear right in Jacobsbergstrasse to Bruderholz.
A water tower stands on the great Esplanade of the Battery, in memory of the redoubts built by the Confederates in 1815 during the last campaign of the Allies against Napoleon I. A stairway *(164 steps)* leads to the top of the tower, which commands a lovely **panorama**★ of Basel, the Birse Valley, the Jura and the Black Forest.

Muttenz
5km/3mi SE. In the town centre stands **Pfarrkirche**, a strange fortified church surrounded by crenellated circular walls; originally Romanesque, it was remodelled in the 15C and 16C. The small single nave, with its carved wooden ceiling, presents some superb fragments (restored) of early Renaissance religious frescoes.

Vitra Design Museum
In Weil am Rhein, Germany. Take tram n° 8 to Kleinünningen, then catch a bus. By car, follow the Riehenstrasse and the Riehenring towards Freiburg.
This startling white **building**★ is the work of the Californian architect Frank Gehry, the first example of his "deconstructivist" style in Europe. The museum houses furniture dating from the 1850s to the present day, a collection of lamps and other decorative objects from the early Functionalist period. Examples of Post-Modern design from the 1980s are also exhibited. Artists highlighted here include Charles and Ray Eames, Tietvield, Alvar Aalto and Mies van der Rohe. Exhibits are displayed in rotation and arranged by theme. The museum also hosts temporary exhibitions.

BEATENBERG★

BERN – POPULATION 1 266
ALT 1 150M/3 773FT

The winding but excellent road *(connecting to Scheidgasse in Unterseen)*, **climbing amid fir trees, offers good glimpses of Interlaken, the Jungfrau and Thun Lake. Beatenberg, a terraced resort, extending along more than 7km/4.5mi, consists mainly of hotels and holiday chalets nestling in the trees. It overlooks Thun Lake and, farther to the right, the Niesen; on the left one can admire the sweeping ranges of the Jungfrau and the Mönch. For an all-encompassing view, go up to the Niederhorn.** *10km/6.5mi from Interlaken;* ⛟ *access also by funicular from the Thun road.*

Niederhorn★★

Alt 1 950m/6 397ft. Access by chairlift. ⛟ *Chair-lift operates (generally) 8am-5pm in summer and 8am-6pm in winter.* 🚠 *Fare there and back: 34CHF.* ☎ *(033) 841 0841.*

From the summit *(viewing tables)* of this mountain covered with Alpine pastures is a spectacular **panorama**★★: south beyond Thun Lake onto the glaciers of the Jungfrau Massif; southwest onto the Niesen and far in the distance Mont Blanc, barely visible; west onto the summit of the Stockhorn; northwest as far as the Neuchâtel and Murten lakes; north onto the mountains preceding the Emmental; and east beyond Lake Brienz, onto the cliffs of the Brienzer Rothorn.

BELLINZONA★

Ⓒ TICINO – POPULATION 18 000
ALT 223M/732FT

Bellinzona is an essential point of passage for traffic using the Sankt Gotthard, Lukmanier or San Bernardino routes. It lies on the Italian side of the Alps and for 1 000 years has been a stronghold guarding the Ticino Valley. In 1803 it became the administrative centre of the canton, which took the name of the river. *Palazzo della Posta, via Camminata 2 – 6500 – ☏ (091) 825 21 31; www.bellinzonaturismo.ch.*

🕐 **Organizing Your Time:** Allow at least a 1/2 day to visit the three castles.

The Historical Centre

Collegiata dei Santi Pietro e Stefano
On Piazza della Collegiata, this church dedicated to St Peter and St Stephen stands out because of its imposing Renaissance façade carved out of Castione stone and adorned with a rose window. The Baroque interior houses a fine pulpit in glazed stuccowork imitating marble Fine frescoes decorate the side chapels, the most famous being the Angel Musicians, the work of Giuseppe Antonio Felice Orelli (c 1770). To

Castelgrande

Suisse Tourisme/Paris

Address Book

For coin ranges see Legend on cover flap.

TOURIST OFFICE

Bellinzona Turismo, Palazzo Civico, Via Camminata 2 – ☎ 091 825 21 31; www. bellinzona.ch.

WHERE TO STAY

☺☺ **Albergo Internazionale** *– Piazza Stazione 35 – ☎ 091 825 43 33 – 20 rooms.* In an old building of historical interest facing the station, the hotel offers modern, comfortable rooms, most with balconies.

☺☺☺ **Unione** *– Via Generale Guisan 1 – ☎ 091 825 55 77; www.hotel-unione. ch – 33 rooms – ⏰ closed 22 Dec-20 Jan.*

Conveniently situated near the town centre, this hotel offers good service for highly affordable prices. Meals can be served in the garden.

EATING OUT

☺☺ **Osseria Sasso Corbaro** *– In Castello Sasso Corbaro – ☎ 091 825 55 32 – ⏰ open 16 Mar-30 Nov.* A charming restaurant perched high up in a castle. Regional cuisine. Nice views of the town from the terrace.

☺☺☺ **Castelgrande** *– Salita al Castello (access by lift) – ☎ 091 826 23 53; www.castelgrande.ch – ⏰ closed Mon.* The restaurant lies within the ramparts of the former medieval fortress of Castelgrande. Wines bottled on the estate.

the right of the collegiate church, **Via Nosetto** features two unusual houses: one has a façade with alcoves containing busts of celebrities (Galileo, Dante, Petrarch, Aristotle, Volta) and at n° 1, the Red House or **Casa Rossa** is a replica of a Lombard cottage with its characteristic terracotta ornamentation.

Piazza Nosetto

This typical arcaded square and the surrounding streets are the scene of a well-known, lively market held on Saturday mornings, which attracts not only city crowds but also many people from the neighbouring villages.

Palazzo Civico

The town hall is heavily influenced by the Italian Renaissance and presents an elegant inner courtyard: the two rows of basket arches are decorated with drawings by Baldo Carugo depicting the city in bygone days. The third level is shaped as a gallery in which the columns are crowned with capitals. The stone staircase leads up to a superb coffered ceiling.

Teatro Sociale

Reopened in 1997 following extensive renovation, the Theatre of Bellinzona is the only existing neo-Classical theatre in Switzerland. Surmounted by a simple pediment, its elegant façade displays a row of four pilasters capped with Ionic capitals on the upper level.

The Castles

The city fortifications rested on three castles, two of which (Castelgrande and Castello di Montebello) were connected by walls, a great part of which can still be seen, even from a distance. These castles still bear the names of Uri, Schwyz and Unterwalden in spite of the bitter memories left in the country by the administration of bailiffs, appointed by the Forest cantons, who ruled the country.

Castelgrande

Recommended access by a lift situated on Piazzella Mario della Valle at the foot of the rock. ○*Open daily Apr-Oct, 10am-6pm and Nov-Mar,10am-5pm. Film (15 min).* ⊚*4CHF.*☎ *(091) 825 81 45.*

The oldest of the three castles is built on a rocky spur, its two quadrangular towers (Torre Bianca and Torre Nera) clearly visible from afar and from various vantage points in the town. The obvious defensive core of the city, hemmed in by steep cliffs, Castelgrande endowed itself with additional fortifications between 1250 and 1500 following the wars that ravaged the area. The Torre Nera marked the centre of the castle; from there the crenellated ramparts formed three inner baileys. Substantial restoration work was carried out between 1982 and 1992 under the supervision of the Ticino architect Aurelio Galfetti. Buildings in the south courtyard now house a restaurant and a reception area. In the south wing the **Museo Storico Archeologico** (Museum of History and Archaeology) contains rooms explaining the history of castles and a gallery devoted to the gold and silver coins minted in Bellinzona during the 16C. In 1503 the Uri, Schwyz and Nidwalden cantons decided to found a minting factory in Basel, which became famous throughout the Confederation.

Castello di Montebello★

Access by a ramp which starts from the railway station road (Viale Stazione). 🅿 *Car park.* ○ *Open Mar-Nov, daily, 10am-6pm.* ⊚*4CHF.* ☎ *(091) 825 13 42.*

This formidable citadel is typical of the Lombard military style in architecture. Built in the 13C by the influential Rusca family, the castle became the property of the Visconti in the late 14C. Under the reign of the Confederates in the 16C, it was renamed Castello di Svitto (Castle of Schwyz) and subsequently San Martino in the 18C. A drawbridge spanning the moat takes you to the defensive core of the stronghold, around which ramparts were erected in the 14C and 15C. The **Museo Civico** (Municipal Museum) presents ancient weapons and artefacts unearthed during digs carried out in the localities of Ticino, Gudo, Gorduno, Ascona, Giubiasco, Madrano etc.

Castello di Sasso Corbaro

Access by car from the castle described above. Take the steep Via Artore, then Via Bebedetto Ferrini on the right and Via Sasso Corbaro. 🅿 *Car park.* ○ *Open Mar-Oct, daily, 10am-6pm.* ⊚*4CHF.* ☎ *(091) 825 59 06.*

This castle is the highest of the three, an isolated fortress standing among chestnut groves. Built to a square plan, it was commissioned in the 15C by the Duke of Milan to consolidate the defensive network of the city, deemed too vulnerable at that spot. The terrace in the forecourt affords a beautiful **view**★ of the town and the Lower Ticino Valley as far as Lake Maggiore. Visit the **Museo dell'Arte e delle Tradizioni Popolari** (Museum of Popular Art and Tradition) installed in the keep. Room 3 (Sala Emma-Poglia) features a bedroom with fine wainscoting and a sculpted coffered ceiling taken from the residence belonging to the Poglia d'Olivone family. The following rooms display everyday objects which bring to life the Ticino region and its traditions.

Ravecchia

From Piazza Indipendenza, Via Lugano leads to the peaceful suburb of Ravecchia.

Santa Maria delle Grazie

Formerly attached to a 15C convent run by a minor order of monks, Santa Maria delle Grazie contains some interesting frescoes, including a poignant *Crucifixion Scene*, surrounded by 15 paintings illustrating the Life of Christ.

...gio

...all medieval church with its quadrangular belfry is worth visiting for its ...es...s. The façade presents a large portrait of St Christopher and a 14C *Virgin with Child* dominated by pink hues. As soon as you enter the church, you will notice the chancel decorated with fine mural paintings, enhanced by tasteful and discreet lighting. The pillars, too, bear paintings of St Agatha and St Bartholomew.

Villa dei Cedri

🕐 *Open Tue-Fri 2-6pm; Sat, Sun and public hols 11am-6pm.* 🕐 *Closed noon-2pm in autumn and winter and 2-3 weeks before each exhibition.* 🔖*8CHF.* ☎ *(091) 821 85 18; www.villacedri.ch.*

The Villa dei Cedri houses the municipal art gallery. This smart residential mansion nestling in a beautiful park displays collections mainly devoted to 19C and 20C figurative art from Switzerland and Italy bequeathed by private collectors. Paintings include such artists as Chiesa, Franzoni, Rossi, Foglia and Guido Tallone.

BERN★★★

BERNE Ⓒ BERN – POPULATION 130 000
PLAN IN THE MICHELIN GUIDE SWITZERLAND

The seat of the Swiss federal authorities, 70 embassies and the headquarters of several international organisations, Bern is situated on a spur overlooking a verdant loop of the Aare, facing the Alps. The old medieval town, a UNESCO World Heritage Site, is characterised by its 6km/4mi of arcades, home to a wide range of shops, making this one of the longest "shopping centres" in Europe. The town, with its attractive towers and flower-decked fountains, is best explored on foot: access by car to the city centre is restricted, giving the old town a rather provincial air, despite its lively atmosphere. Symbols on the trams and trolley buses remind visitors that Bern is the capital of Switzerland. 🏛 *Bahnhof – 3000 – ☎ (031) 328 12 12; www.berninfo.com.*

▶ **Orient Yourself:** Bern is best explored on foot. From the train station, walk along medieval arcaded streets.
😊 **Don't Miss:** The Zentrum Paul Klee, with some 4,000 works by this native son artist.
🕐 **Organizing Your Time:** Allow at least one day for museums and attractions in Old Town.
🧒 **Especially for Kids:** The Bear Pit in the center of town, where the heraldic animals will beg for carrots.

A Bit of History

Foundation of Bern – A 15C chronicle describes the foundation of the town by **Duke Berchtold V of Zähringen** in 1191 as follows: wishing to create a city, the duke asked for the advice of his huntsmen and his chief master of hounds. One of them answered, "Master, there is a good site in the river bend where your Castle of Nydegg stands". The duke visited the spot, which was then thickly wooded, and ordered that a moat be dug on the present site of the Kreuzgasse (a street running up to the cathedral). However, it was thought better to draw the line of the moat farther west, where the clock tower stands today. As game was very abundant the duke agreed with his advisers to give the new town the name of the first animal

Bill Wassman / APA Publications

The federal city of Bern

caught at the hunt. It so happened that this was a bear *(bär)*. The duke, therefore, named the town Bärn (Bern) and gave it a bear as its coat of arms. At the end of the 15C, the bear appeared in engravings of the town.

Expansion – From the 14C to the 16C, Bern followed a clever policy of expansion and played a dominant part in the Confederation. Many annexations, such as those of Burgdorf and Thun after the struggle with the Kyburgs, secured its hegemony on both banks of the River Aare. In the 15C the conquest of Aargau enabled it to extend to the Lower Reuss, and its resolute attitude in the Burgundian wars placed it in the front rank of Swiss cantons. In the 16C, by annexing the Gruyères and Vaud districts, Bern ruled over all the country between the Lower Reuss and Lake Geneva.

Bern in the Confederation – When the Constitution of 1848 was drafted after the defeat of the Sonderbund, Bern was chosen by common consent as the seat for the federal authority. The choice was amply justified on account of the leading political part the city had played for several centuries and its privileged position at the heart of the Confederation and at the dividing line between the Latin and Germanic cultures.

Though the city became the seat of the Federal Chambers, the civil service and the federal postal and railway services, this did not make it the administrative centre of its country in the manner of London and Washington. The federal system prevented any one town from enjoying political supremacy.

Ferdinand Hodler – One of the most important Swiss painters of the 20C, Hodler was born in Bern in 1853 (d 1918 in Geneva). Orphaned at the age of 12, he was apprenticed to Ferdinand Sommer, a painter of Swiss landscapes for tourists in Thun. At 19 he went to Geneva to copy the romantic landscapes by Calame. With the help of his profes-

> ☻ **A Bit of Advice** ☻
>
> **Swiss Pass:** This pass entitles tourists to travel freely throughout Switzerland, covering a total 20 000km/12 500mi network of rail, boat and coach transport, as well as tramway and bus routes in 35 towns. This pass (1st or 2nd class) can be bought for 4, 8, 15, 22 days or for one month. Available from train stations in most cities.
>
> **Visitor's Card:** This card, available from the town's tourist office (Bern Tourismus), grants you free and unlimited access to all forms of local transport.

sor Barthélemy Menn (1815-93), a student of Ingres and friend of Corot, Hodler broke with conventional painting. Among his many canvases painted at that time are portraits, some of which point to his later large, monumental masterpieces. A trip to Spain (1878-79) enabled Hodler to admire the technique of Velázquez. As a result his style evolved, his technique was perfected and his palette brightened. During this period Hodler painted many landscapes: the Alps and Thun Lake were his preferred subjects.

Although the major artistic currents (Realism, Symbolism, Art Nouveau) of the time are echoed in his works, from 1885 Hodler branched off to adopt Parallelism. This style can be found in his allegorical works (*Night*, 1889-90; *Day*, 1899-1900), as well as his historical canvases *(The Defeat at Marignano)*, which earned Hodler first prize in a 1897 competition organised by the Swiss National Museum in Zurich. Hodler no longer copied nature: his landscapes were simplified, shedding excessive ornamentation. Reflections mirrored in his lakes accentuated symmetry, and his inclination to paint in monochrome – blue was his preferred colour – confirmed the unity of his compositions. At the end of his life, Hodler was painting what he called "planetary landscapes", curious compositions consisting only of lines and space, with no trace of life or death.

Old Berne★★ *2hr 30min*

Tour of the town by bus (2hr) at 2pm daily from Apr-Oct; Sat only from Nov-Mar. ⊜24CHF. Tour of the old town on foot (1hr 30min) at 11am from Jun-Sep daily. ⊜16CHF. Contact the Tourist office for further information. ☎ (031) 328 12 12.

The old town, rebuilt in yellow-green sandstone after the terrible fire of 1405, is full of winding streets and terraced gardens overlooking the river. From Easter to the end of October the main monuments are floodlit until midnight. In the summer, the sound of horse-drawn carriages echo through the medieval streets.

Heiliggeist-Kirche (DZ)
This Baroque church was built between 1726 and 1729.
Spitalgasse is a bustling street lined with arcades which boasts many shops. A Piper's Fountain (16C and 19) stands in the centre.

Bärenplatz (DZ)
In former days, this square was occupied by a large bear pit. Today it is a vast esplanade, a lively meeting place surrounded by pavement cafés.

Käfigturm (DZ A)
This gate, built at the entrance to Marktgasse, marked the western boundary of the town from 1250 to 1350. It was restored in the 18C.

Marktgasse★ (DZ)
The smart and lively Marktgasse, with luxury shops and many florists' windows, is the main street of the old town. Fine 17C and 18C houses present a series of arcades, lending remarkable unity to the whole. The 16C-17C fountain (Seilerbrunnen) is dedicated to Anna Seiler, who in 1354 provided the town with its first hospital. Farther on, the Marksman's Fountain (Schützenbrunnen, 1543) depicts a standard-bearer with, between his knees, a small bear wearing armour and firing a gun. On Kornhausplatz, to the left, the Ogre Fountain (Kindlifresserbrunnen) represents an ogre devouring a small boy and holding other children in reserve under his left arm.

Zeitglockenturm★ (EZ C)

Guided tour May-Oct, daily, at 2.30pm; Jul-Sep, daily, at 11.30am and 4.30pm.
10CHF. ☎ (031) 328 12 12.

Known as the *Zytgloggeturm* in local dialect, this famous Bern landmark acts as the reference point from which all distances from the city are measured. Built between 1191 and 1250, the clock tower once marked the western limits of the city. Note the 15C Jack (on the Kramgasse side of the gate) and the two ducal crowns above the gilded clockface. Chimes strike at four minutes to the hour, and the many painted **figurines** (15C-17C) then start to move: the cockerel crows, flapping his wings, a procession of bear cubs march to the sound of pealing bells, followed by a second cock crow. The god Chronos turns his apron upside down and the large bell sounds the hour, struck by Hans von Thann, a knight made of lime wood and dressed in gilded armour. At the same time, Chronos counts the strikes and waves his sceptre, while the lion turns his head. The show ends with a third cock crow. A tour inside the **clock** enables visitors to admire its elaborate, sophisticated mechanism.

Bill Wassman / APA Publications

Kramgasse and Zeitglockenturm

Kramgasse★ (EZ)

Kramgasse is a more crowded extension of Marktgasse. Along Kramgasse notice the Zähringen Fountain (16C) with its bear wearing armour and holding the Zähringen coat of arms in his paw, and the Samson Fountain (16C), surmounted by a statue of the giant prising apart the jaws of a lion.

At n° 49 stands **Einsteinhaus** (*Open Apr-Nov, daily, 10am-5pm; Oct-Dec, Tue-Fri 10am-4pm. Closed public hols, Jan and Dec. 6CHF. Fax (031) 312 00 41*). It was here, on the second floor, that the great scientist Albert Einstein wrote his theory of relativity in 1905. Sixteen years later he was awarded the Nobel Prize for Physics for his outstanding research work on protons. The decor evokes the years Einstein spent in Bern (1902-09). Visitors are able to view his study and bedroom, which contained a writing desk where the physicist would work standing up, as well as a collection of portraits and photos. In 1909 Einstein was appointed Professor of Physics at Zurich University.

▶ *At the end of Kramgasse, turn left into Kreuzgasse leading to Rathausplatz.*

Rathausplatz is decorated with a fountain bearing a banneret (Vennerbrunnen) by Hans Gieng (1542).

Rathaus (EY H)

This is the seat of the Bern Municipal Council (legislative assembly of the city of Bern) and the Grand Council (legislative assembly of the canton). It was erected between 1406 and 1417 and has been heavily restored, although its double staircase and covered porch make it one of the most typical buildings in the city.

Return to Kreuzgasse which leads to Gerechtigkeitsgasse, where the **Justice Fountain** stands. Its shaft is crowned by a Corinthian capital (1543).

Nydeggasse, which is a continuation of Gerechtigkeitsgasse, contains the Church of the Nydegg (*Nydeggkirche*) built in the 14C on the foundations of a 13C fortress.

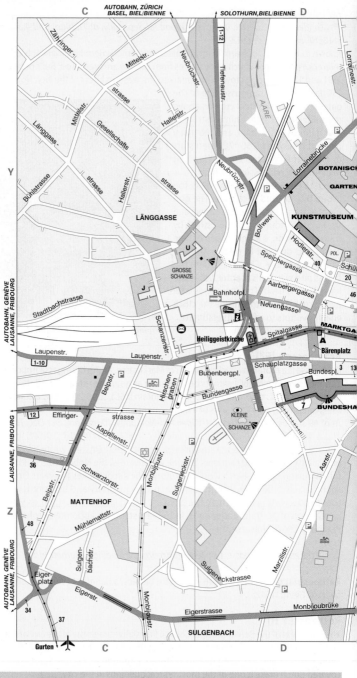

BERN			Christoffelgasse	DZ	9	Marktgasse	DEZ	
			Helvetiaplatz	EZ	10	Münstergasse	EZ	16
Amthausgasse	DEZ	3	Jubiläumsstrasse	EZ	12	Münsterplatz	EZ	18
Bärenplatz	DZ		Kochergasse	DEZ	13	Nägeligasse	DY	20
Brunngasse	EY	6	Kramgasse	EZ		Nydeggasse	FY	22
Bundesterrasse	DZ	7	Kreuzgasse	EZ	15	Rathausgasse	EY	28

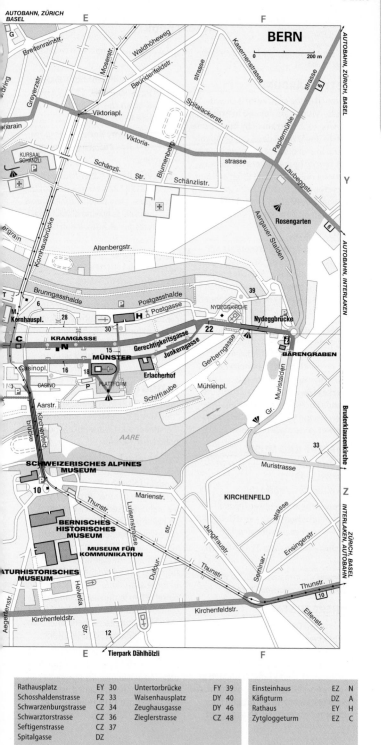

Address Book

🪙 *For coin ranges see Legend on cover flap.*

GETTING AROUND

As much of the city centre is closed to cars, visitors are advised to explore Bern on foot, by **tram** or by **bus**. Special passes (for 1, 2 or 3 days) can be bought at the tourist office or at hotels. A night bus service operates from the railway station until 3.15am on Fri, Sat and Sun. **Bicycles** can be rented from the railway station; b 0512 20 23 74. Cycle lanes are marked by yellow lines.

SHOPPING

The main **shopping streets** are Spitalgasse, Marktgasse, Kramgasse and Gerechtigkeitsgasse. Smaller specialist boutiques, selling antiques, wooden toys, and arts and crafts, can be found near the River Aare.

There are **markets** selling fruit, flowers, vegetables and various other articles every Tuesday and Saturday morning on Bundesplatz, Bärenplatz and Waisenhausplatz. The traditional **onion market (Zwiebelmarkt)** is the fourth Monday in November at various locations around the city. The **Christmas market** takes place on Münsterplatz.

THEATRE AND MUSIC

Stadttheater – *Kornhausplatz 20 – ☎ 031 329 51 11. www.stadttheaterbern.ch.*

Puppentheater *(Puppet Theatre) – Gerechtigkeitsgasse 31 – ☎ 031 311 95 85. www.berner-puppentheater.ch.*

Casino – *Herrengasse 25 – ☎ 031 311 42 42.*

Kursaal –*Kornhausstrasse 3 – ☎ 031 339 55 00. www.kursaal-bern.ch.*

WHERE TO STAY

🍴🍴 **Zum Goldenen Schlüssel** – *Rathausgasse 72 – ☎ 031 311 02 16 – Fax 031 311 02 16 – www.goldenerschluessel.ch – 48 rooms.* This reasonably priced and friendly hotel is situated in a picturesque street in the old town. A good restaurant on the ground floor, under the arcades, serves a range of meat (especially game) and vegetarian dishes.

🍴🍴🍴 **City am Bahnhof** – *Bubenbergplatz 7 – ☎ 031 311 53 77 – www.fassbind-hotels.ch – 113 rooms.* Modern hotel close to train station.

🍴🍴🍴 **Savoy Bern** – *Neuengasse 26 – ☎ 031 311 44 05. www.zghotels.ch – 94 rooms.*

🍴🍴🍴 **Berne** – *Zeughausgasse 9 – ☎ 031 329 22 22 – www.hotelbern.ch – 100 rooms.* Cosy hotel a stone's throw from the lively shopping district and its picturesque arcades. Piano bar in a sophisticated setting.

🍴🍴🍴 **Belle Époque** – *Gerechtigkeit 18 – ☎ 031 311 43 36 – www.belle-epoque.ch – 17 rooms.* As soon as you cross the threshold, you are transported back to the turn of the last century! "Toulouse Lautrec" bar and Art Nouveau furniture, decoration, vases and paintings. This elegant establishment could almost qualify as an art museum.

EATING OUT

On menus in Bern, Gschnätzeltes are "thin slices" or "émincé", Suurchabis is Sauerkraut and Gschwellti are potatoes boiled in their skins.

🍴🍴 **Kornhauskeller** – *Kornhausplatz 18 – ☎ 031 327 72 72; www.kornhauskeller.ch – 🕐 closed Mon lunchtime in summer.* In the early 18C, a warehouse used for storing wheat and wine was dug out beneath the old covered market. Converted into a village hall in 1896, it currently houses a restaurant. The paintings dating from that period are the work of the Bernese artist Rudolf Mänger. The huge barrel set up in the main dining hall can contain up to 41 055 litres! An unusual yet welcoming place where diners can sample traditional Bernese cuisine.

🍴🍴 **Harmonie** – *Hotelgasse 3 – ☎ 031 313 11 41 – 🕐 closed Sat evenings, Sun and Mon lunchtime.* Old-fashioned café, whose decor has remained exactly the same since 1915. Famous for its fondues.

🍴🍴🍴**Zum Äusseren Stand** – *Zeughausgasse 17 – ☎ 031 311 32 05 – 🕐 closed Sun.*This restaurant is housed in the former town hall where the Constitution of the Berne canton was first drawn up in 1831. In this building, representatives of 22 countries gathered in 1874 to found the Universal Postal Union. The huge dining hall upstairs, decorated in the Empire style, is reserved for formal banquets.

🍴🍴**Bar du Théâtre** – *Theaterplatz 7 – ☎ 031 312 30 31 – 🕐 closed Sun.* Informal establishment consisting of a bar and a large café installed in the former Music Academy of Bern.

🍴🍴**Brasserie Bärengraben** – *Muristalden 1 – ☎ 031 331 42 18.* Situated at the end of Nydeggbrücke, towards Bärengraben. Small, congenial restaurant with mouthwatering homemade desserts.

🍴🍴**Klötzlikeller** – *Gerechtigkeitsgasse 62 – ☎ 031 311 74 56 – 🕐 closed Sun in summer, Sun and Mon in winter.* A typical Bernese wine bar which has traditionally been run by women for over one hundred years: in 1635, there were more than 230 of these establishments in the city! The Klötzlikeller also serves light meals.

🍴🍴🍴**Gourmanderie Moléson** – *Aabergasse 24 – ☎ 031 311 44 63; www.moleson-bern.ch – 🕐 closed Sun and public hols.* Cosy, comfortable restaurant. Traditional cooking with an old-fashioned touch.

🍴🍴🍴**Zimmermania** – *Brunngasse 19 – ☎ 031 311 15 42 – 🕐 closed 8 Jul-5 Aug, as well as Sun, Mon and public hols.* The owner is said to be an authority on Beaujolais ... Put him to the test!

NIGHTLIFE

Klötzlikeller (Gerechtigkeitsgasse 62), the oldest tavern in town, serves wine by the glass in a cellar with rough stone walls. The standard Swiss aperitif is a glass of white wine served with thin slivers of cheese (rebibes).

The **Kursaal** (Schanzlistrasse 71-77) is a complex featuring games rooms, a bar, a piano bar, a nightclub and a cabaret (international variety shows).

Enjoy some good jazz at **Marian's Jazzroom** in the basement of the Hotel Innere Enge (Engerstrasse 54). Very popular among connoisseurs.

Nydeggbrücke (FY)

The bridge spans the Aare and affords an attractive **view**★ of the quarters huddled in the meanderings of the river and the wooded slopes which overlook it.

Bärengraben★ (FZ)

Kids 🕐 *Open 9am-5.30pm (4pm in winter).* 🆓*No charge.* ☎ *(031) 357 15 15.*
This bear pit confirms the fact that, since the end of the 15C, the bears of Bern have been local celebrities. They receive many visits, not only from tourists but also from the Bernese, who are particularly fond of them. Near the bear pit, the **Bern Show** uses video and an animated model to recount the history of the town.

▶ *Turn round. At the entrance to Gerechtigkeitsgasse turn left into Junkerngasse.*

Junkerngasse★

This street is lined with old houses. Note the **Erlacher Hof** at n° 47, a fine Baroque dwelling influenced by French architectural style, now home to the city hall. Approaching the cathedral from the east, there is a general view of the tall tower, the nave and flying buttresses, and the pinnacles surmounting the buttresses. Skirt the building to the left until you come to a fine terrace planted with trees and flowers. From the terrace there is a bird's-eye **view**★ of the Aare locks and, to the right, the Kirchenfeldbrücke Bridge, which spans the river over a distance of 40m/135ft.

Münster Sankt Vinzenz★ (EZ)

🕐 *Open summer, 10am (11.30am Sun)-5pm; winter, 10am-noon and 2-6pm (5pm Sat), Sun 11.30am-2pm.* 🕐 *Closed Mon.* 🚭 *No charge.* ☎ *(031) 312 04 62.*

One of the last great Gothic churches in Switzerland, generally called a cathedral, dates from 1421. Construction continued until 1573, and the bell tower, over 100m/328ft high, the highest in Switzerland, was only completed in 1893.

The splendid **tympanum**★★ of the main portal, by the Master Erhard Küng, was spared the destruction of the Reformation. It illustrates the Last Judgement (1495) with 234 figures, some of which are still painted. The Damned and the Elect are very realistically treated. There are statues of Prophets on the recessed arches, Wise and Foolish Virgins in the embrasures *(left and right respectively)* and *grisaille* frescoes dating from the early 16C on either side of the portal.

The nave is a vast structure with reticulated vaulting and 87 painted keystones adorned with coats of arms. The chancel has great 15C stained-glass windows by Hans Acker, depicting the Passion and the Crucifixion; other windows depict the Victory of the 10 000 Knights, and the Magi. Stalls, which date from the Renaissance (1523), are richly sculpted with scenes from everyday life.

Visitors who do not mind a climb can take the spiral staircase of 254 steps to the tower platform (🕐 *Open summer, daily except Mon, 10am (11.30am Sun)-4.30pm; winter, Tue-Sat, 10-11.30am and 2-3.30pm (4.30pm Sat), Sun 11.30am-1.30pm. Closes 30min before the cathedral.* 🚭*3CHF.* ☎ *(031) 312 04 63)* for a **panorama**★★ encompassing, in the foreground, the various quarters of the town, with their fine reddish-brown tiled roofs, many turrets and belfries, the bridges over the Aare and, in the background, the majestically spreading chain of the Bernese Alps.

▶ *On leaving the cathedral, cross Münsterplatz and turn left into Münstergasse (several narrow covered passages leading to Kramgasse) to Casinoplatz. Just before reaching the bridge (Kirchenfeldbrücke) take Bundesterrasse on the right.*

Bundeshaus (DZ)

🚶 *Guided tours (45min) daily except Sat-Sun, at 9am, 10am, 11am, 2pm, 3pm and 4pm, preferably at 11am and 2pm for individual visitors.* 🕐 *Closed public hols and during parliamentary sessions (access to the public galleries only during this period).* 🚭 *No charge.* ☎ *(031) 322 85 22.*

The Swiss Government (Federal Council) and Swiss Parliament (National Council and Council of the States) are housed in this heavy, domed building (1902), the design of which was inspired by the Florentine Renaissance. A guided tour describes the workings of Swiss democracy (🔍 *see Introduction*). The view from the terrace encompasses the Aare, the town and, in the background, the Bernese Alps.

▶ *Cross Kirchenfeldbrücke to Helvetiaplatz.*

Helvetiaplatz (EZ)

Several important museums stand in this square. The imposing monument symbolises the International Telegraphic Union founded in Paris in 1865. This bronze group with fountains was designed in 1915 by the sculptor Romagnoli from Ticino.

Museums

Kunstmuseum★★ (DY)

♿🕐 *Open daily except Mon, 10am-5pm (9pm Tue).* 🕐 *Closed most public hols.* 🚭*7CHF (price varies for temporary exhibitions).* ☎ *(031) 328 09 44.*

This Fine Arts Museum contains a splendid collection of 13C-20C paintings. Its renowned collection of works by **Paul Klee** has been moved to the new Zentrum

Paul Klee

Paul Klee was born in 1879 at Münchenbuchsee and spent his youth in Bern, where he painted scenes of the city and surrounding landscape: the meanders of the Aare, the Niesen mountains and the quarries at Ostermundigen. He was an ironic observer of social conventions and also drew caricatures. In 1906, he travelled to Munich, where he made contact with members of the Blauer Reiter movement, including Franz Marc, Wassily Kandinsky and Alexej von Jawlensky. A violinist and a poet, he taught in the Bauhaus (1921-33). Considered to be a "degenerate artist" by the Nazis, Klee saw his teaching contract at the Dusseldorf Academy terminated in 1933. He spent the latter part of his life in Bern, where he died in 1940. The Zentrum Paul Klee, a museum of 400 of his works, opened in Bern in 2005.

Paul Klee (👆 *see Zentrum Paul Klee, below*); that gallery space now is used for temporary exhibits.

Basement – Devoted to Italian Primitive artists of the 13C to 15C, including Fra Angelico *(Madonna and Child)* and Duccio, whose *Maestà* (c 1290) reflects the Byzantine style characteristic of the Sienese School and works by the Swiss Primitives (15C-16C), especially *Master with Carnation from Berne*. The 16C school also is represented by Bernese painter Niklaus Manuel Deutsch (c 1484-1530), whose style and composition were akin to the art of the Renaissance: *Triptych of St John the Baptist, St Luke Painting the Virgin, The Martyrdom of the 10 000 Knights of Mount Ararat*. Also note the two excellent portraits of Luther and his wife from the workshop of German painter Lucas Cranach. Adjoining rooms exhibit works by 17C artists from Bern.

Ground floor – The oldest wing presents works by 19C Swiss painters such as Caspar Wolf, Karl Stauffer, Arnold Böcklin and Franz Niklaus König. One room is devoted to **Albert Anker** (1831-1910), whose painting revolves around scenes of everyday life *(Old Man, Children from the Berne Crèche on an Outing)*.

First floor – A special exhibition is devoted to native-born artist **Ferdinand Hodler**. Along with great allegorical frescoes that reflect his concern for death *(Day, Night, Disillusioned Souls)*, visitors may admire his deeply nostalgic landscapes *(Thun Lake and the Stockhorn)*, as well as his portraits *(Young Girl with a Poppy)* and self-portraits (he depicts himself with wild, menacing features in *The Madman*). A whole room has been set aside for the work of Cuno Amiet, who favoured a palette of bright, vivid colours. The French School is represented by Delacroix, leading Impressionists such as Monet, Manet, Cézanne *(Self-portrait in a Felt Hat)*, Sisley, Pissarro, Renoir, Matisse *(The Blue Blouse)*, Bonnard *(In a Garden)*, and Utrillo, who painted scenes of Montmartre. Other galleries display Expressionist painters Chagall, Soutine and Modigliani, and a large collection of Cubist paintings by Braque, Picasso, Juan Gris and Fernand Léger *(Contrasts of Form)*, Kandinsky, Masson and Miró. Contemporary art is represented by Swiss artists Meret Oppenheim, Franz Gertsch and Markus Raetz, and the Americans Jackson Pollock and Mark Rothko.

Zentrum Paul Klee ★★

👆🕐 *Open Tues-Sun 10am-5pm (9pm Wed).* 🎫*14CHF.* ☎ *(031) 359 01 01, www.paulkleezentrum.ch.*

The Paul Klee Museum opened in 2005 to house more than 4,400 paintings *(Steinbruch, Monument in Fruchtland)* , gouaches, watercolours and drawings, plus archives and biographical material of one of the most significant and prolific artists of the 20C (1879-1940). The striving for colour effects gives rise to square paintings *(Pictorial Architecture in Red, Yellow and Blue)*, to Divisionist works (1930-32, *Ad Parnassum*) and paintings with figures and signs against a coloured background (*Flowers with Stone,*

1940). The collection is believed to be the largest single collection of a major artist in the world. The artwork is housed in a dramatic building designed by award-winning Italian architect Renzo Piano; three soaring hills of steel and glass offer natural light to showcase Klee's colorful creations, which seem to blend primitive art, surrealism and cubism with gentle humor and allusion to dreams. The main exhibits are in the center section; the other sections contain restaurants, shops, galleries and a performance theater. There is also a separate children's museum within the complex. Temporary exhibits focus on the connection between Klee and other artists, such as Kandisnky and Max Beckmann. The site includes a sculpture park. **Wege zu Klee** (Theme Path) from the city center to the museum is punctuated by additonal information about the artist and his works.

During the excavation, boulders buried by the retreating Aare Glacier more than 10,000 years ago were unearthed; these now form a natural landscape around ponds on the park-like site, which includes the 19C Villa Schöngrün, summer home of one of Bern's patrician families.

Bernisches Historisches Museum★★ (EZ)

◉ *Open Tue-Sun, 10am-5pm (8pm Wed). ⊜13CHF. ☎ (031) 350 77 11; www.bhm.ch.*
This neo-Gothic building built in 1881 contains a vast, historic, prehistoric, ethnographic and numismatic collection. On the lower mezzanine is the 18C Pourtalès Room, whose furniture once belonged to a palace in Neuchâtel. The upper mezzanine houses the Islamic-Oriental collection belonging to Henri Moser Charlottenfels. A miniature model of the city dating from 1800 is displayed on the first floor, together with the booty captured from the Burgundians at Grandson and Murten in 1476. It includes standards, embroideries and tapestries which belonged to Charles the Bold, Duke of Burgundy. Among the tapestries is one with the coat of arms of Philip the Good woven in a Flemish workshop in 1466. Other tapestries from Flemish looms attract attention by their fine design and rich colours. Examples are *The Judgement of Trajan and Herkenbald*, woven in the 15C and inspired by paintings by Roger van der Weyden; *The Magi* (1460), *The Thousand Flowers* from Brussels (1466), *The Life of St Vincent* (belonging to the cathedral), and others illustrating several episodes in the life of Julius Caesar. On the second floor is the giant scale (1752), which was made for the Bern arsenal and weighed cannons of 2 tonnes! The visit finishes with rooms illustrating the daily lives of the Bernese during the 19C and 20C, with reconstructions of a grocery shop, a dentist's surgery and a 1950s school room.

Schweizerisches Alpines Museum★★ (EZ)

◉*Open 10am (2pm Mon) to 5pm.* ◉ *Closed 1 Jan, 1 Aug, 24, 25 and 31 Dec. ⊜9CHF.*
☎ *(031) 350 0440.*
Thoroughly renovated between 1990 and 1993, the Swiss Alpine Museum is dedicated to the Alps, which cover 60% of the country's total area. Visitors view an audio-visual presentation called "A Mountainous Country." Several relief maps – the early ones date back to 1750 – connect the famous summits and their valleys: Bietschhorn, the Matterhorn, Dents-du-Midi, Jungfrau, Säntis, Bernina etc. A series of interactive booths focus on specific aspects of the exhibition (history, geology, transport and industry, tourism, climate, flora and fauna); all the commentaries are in German, French, English and Italian. On the first floor "Mountains seen through Maps" covers the 16C-18C and is followed by presentations on art, popular traditions and regional lore, as well as habitat. One room, decorated with a 1894 diorama by Ferdinand Hodler, *The Climb and the Fall*, evokes mountaineering sports, and the evolution of climbing gear and life-saving equipment in the Alps. In the centre there is a huge raised map of the Bernese Oberland. The top floor houses temporary exhibitions.

Naturhistorisches Museum★★ (EZ)

🄺🄸🄳🄲 ◉ *Open Mon 2-5pm, Tue-Fri 9am-5pm (6pm Wed), Sat-Sun 10am-5pm.* ◉ *Closed most public hols. ⊜8CHF. ☎ (031) 350 71 11/70 00; www.nmbe.ch.*

This is one of the largest natural history museums in Switzerland. On the ground floor, the fossil of an ichthyosaurus can be admired in the hall. The great Wattenwyl Hall is also remarkable: the African animals it contains are shown in their natural environment. On the ground floor dioramas display fauna from Asia. The first floor contains a fine collection of vertebrates taken from local fauna, and Arctic mammals. The biological nature of the whale is also outlined. The second floor is devoted to birds, reptiles, geology and insects. The third floor is reserved for collections relating to mineralogy and palaeontology.

Museum für Kommunikation★ (EZ)

&. ⊙ *Open daily except Mon, 10am-5pm.* ⊙*Closed 1 Jan, 24, 25 and 31 Dec.* ☜*13CHF.* ☎ *(031) 357 55 55; www.mfk.ch*

This modern, welcoming museum explains the history of communications from early smoke signals to the transmission of highly sophisticated digital systems. Special coverage is given to the history of postal institutions (founded in 1849) and philately (more than 500 000 stamps displayed). These permanent collections are regularly complemented by temporary exhibitions of great interest.

Additional Sights

Botanischer Garten★ (DY)

This vast botanical garden, with its fountains and pools, descends to the banks of the Aare in terraces. Some 6 000 plants, including a wide variety of Alpine species, grow in the garden, which covers an area of 2ha/5 acres. The seven greenhouses contain a collection of tropical plants, such as ferns, grasses and orchids.

Tierpark Dählhölzli★

Entrance in Jubiläumstrasse (EZ). Kids &. ⊙ *Vivarium open summer, 8am-6.30pm, winter 9am-5pm.* ☜*8CHF.* ☎ *(031) 357 15 15.*

This fine 13ha/32-acre zoo, overlooking the Aare, is home to a number of European and Nordic animal species, including otters, musk ox, lynx, wolves, bison, elk, reindeer and black grouse. The aviary contains hundreds of tropical birds, butterflies, rare specimens of local fauna, a termites' nest and an ant hill. There is also a children's playground and a picnic area.

Bruder Klausenkirche★

Leave by Muristrasse (FZ).

This church is dedicated to St Nicholas of Flüe, familiarly known in Switzerland as Bruder Klaus (Brother Nicholas). It is built on a broad esplanade and has a detached bell tower. With its simple lines it is one of the most representative specimens of modern architecture in Switzerland.

Rosengarten (FY)

The rose garden is planted with 200 different types of rose, 200 species of iris and 28 types of rhododendron. It offers a good overall **view**★ of the old town.

Excursions

Gurten★★

Alt 858m/2 815ft – 2.5km/1.5mi about 30min including 10min by funicular. Leave Bern by Seftigenstrasse (CZ), the Belp-Thun road, and at the entrance to Wabern turn right towards the lower funicular station. ⌁*Operates all year round.* ☜*4.50CHF one-way; 8CHF there and back.* ☎ *(031) 961 23 23.*

The Gurten, a magnificent belvedere with a **panorama**★★ of Bern and the Bernese Oberland, is a pleasant place in which to stroll; it also has facilities for children 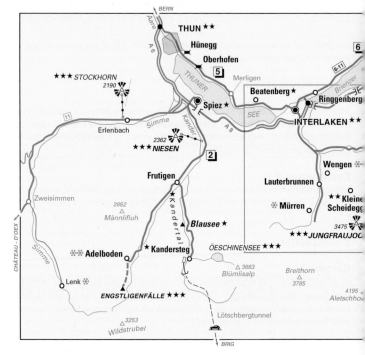.

Enge Peninsula

4km/2.5mi N, located in the first bend of the Aare. Leave Bern by the road to Biel. After the Tiefenau railway station, bear left and at a crossroads, bear right onto Reichenbach-strasse as far as a modern Protestant church (Matthäuskirche).

A board indicates the location of the archaeological remains of Enge: the ramparts of the ancient Helvetian town and Roman vestiges (1C). Behind the church are the ruins of a little oval amphitheatre, the smallest in Switzerland with a capacity of around 3 000; a couple of hundred yards farther on in the forest are the public baths.

BERNER OBERLAND★★★

BERNESE OBERLAND

The Bernese Oberland, a massif set in the heart of Switzerland, is bounded to the north by the crescent-shaped lakes of Thun and Brienz, to the east by the Graubünden, to the south by the Upper Valais and to the west by the Vaud and Fribourg Alps. It is rich with internationally famous sights, both natural – the Jungfrau and the Eiger, the Rhône Glacier, the Trümmelbach Falls and Thun Lake – and man-made – the resorts of Interlaken and Grindelwald and the Jungfraujoch, the highest rack railway in Europe.

For more than a century the dazzling view of the Jungfrau from the Höheweg promenade at Interlaken has been a lasting memory for visitors to this wonderfully scenic area. between the Aare and the Rhône. The region is also known as an international centre for mountaineering and has attracted many dedicated climbers.

A Bit of History

Conquest of the Eigerwand

One of the most dramatic climbs after the conquest of the Matterhorn was that of the north face of the Eiger (see INTERLAKEN). In 1858 the summit (3 970m/13 025ft) had been reached by the Englishman Barrington. The south and southwest spurs were conquered in 1874 and 1876. From 1935 onwards there were many deadly attempts to climb the north face: that year, two Germans were killed; the next year, three roped teams of Germans and Austrians fell to their deaths.

These tragedies raised such a storm of protest that cantonal authorities in Bern forbade any further attempt. The ban was lifted in 1937, marked by the failure of the Austrian Rebitsch and the German Wiggerl Vörg. However, the following year, Vörg and his companion, Anderl Heckmair, made secret preparations for an attempt. Though two Austrians, Kasparek and Harrer, started before them, they overtook them on the second day and decided to join forces with the rival team. Their slow and difficult progress, threatened at every step by the danger of storms and avalanches, was watched anxiously from the valley. Thanks to international press and radio, the whole world eagerly awaited details of their progress. When they surmounted the final crest, blinded by fatigue and storm, they were not even immediately aware of their victory! Their difficult descent by the west face, in the midst of a blizzard, sealed the success of their expedition.

Driving Tours

Recommended itineraries

Organised from longest to shortest. See names in the index.

Jungfrau Region★★★

Tour by car, cable cars and train from Interlaken – allow 2 days.

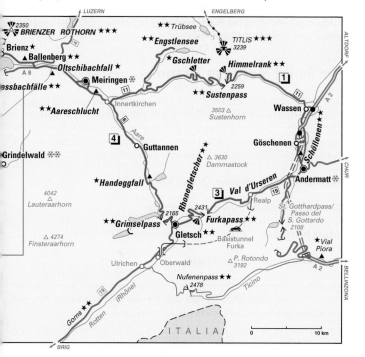

Round Tour of the Three Passes (Grimsel, Furka, Susten)★★★

Starting from Interlaken allow at least 1 day. This includes the itineraries **4**, **3** and **1** (👣 *see below*).

1 Sustenpasstrasse★★★
From Andermatt to Meiringen – about 2hr 30min.

2 Kandertal★
From Spiez to Kandersteg – about 2hr 30min.

3 Furkapasstrasse★★★
From Gletsch to Andermatt – about 2hr 15min.

4 Grimselstrasse★
From Meiringen to Gletsch – about 1hr 30min.

5 Thuner See★★
From Thun to Interlaken – about 1hr.

6 Brienzer See★
From Interlaken to Meiringen – about 45min.

Blue Thistle

MICHELIN

BERNINASTRASSE★★★

THE BERNINA ROAD

This magnificent mountain road climbs up the Bernina Valley as far as the pass and then descends along the Poschiavo Valley to Tirano; it links the Engadine in Switzerland to the Valtellina in Italy.

From Sankt Moritz to Tirano *56km/34mi – about 2hr*

Itinerary **7** *(👣 see GRAUBÜNDEN map)* 😊 *It is inadvisable to start across the Engadine slope late in the afternoon; it will be difficult to see the Morteratsch. The Bernina Pass is usually blocked by snow from October to May. The pass road is not cleared at night. The railway – the highest in Europe without racks – runs all year round. The Swiss customs control is at Campocologno and the Italian control at Piattamala.*

Sankt Moritz☀☀☀ – *1hr 30min.* 👣 *See SANKT MORITZ.*

▶ *Leave Sankt Moritz in the direction of Pontresina.*

Muottas Muragl★★ – *Access and description see MUOTTAS MURAGL.*

Pontresina☀☀ – 👣 *See PONTRESINA.*

Between Pontresina and the Chünetta road fork, the valley quickly becomes wilder. The three glittering peaks of the Piz Palü appear to the right of the Munt Pers, and farther to the right, the snowy summits of the Bellavista.

Heinz Schwab / Switzerland Tourism

Bernina Railroad near Morteratsch Glacier

Chünetta Belvedere★★★

Alt 2 083m/6 832ft. From the Bernina road 2km/1mi there and back – plus 1hr on foot there and back.

After branching off on the road to the Morteratsch Glacier, leave your car before the wooden bridge leading to Morteratsch station. Cross this bridge and the railway track and after passing a bed of stones brought down by the torrent, take a path going uphill to the right, under the larches. After 20min, at the second fork, when the view opens out, turn right to climb to the viewpoint.

From there you will see the grand picture formed by the **Morteratsch Corrie**, over-looked from left to right by the Piz Palü, the Piz Bellavista, the cloven summit of the Piz Bernina (highest point: 4 049m/13 284ft), the Piz Morteratsch with its heavy snowcap and the Piz Boval. The lower end of the glacier dies away in the foreground; it is framed by terminal moraines and divided longitudinally by a central moraine. The **view**★★ is splendid after two hairpin bends. To the right of Bellavista the glorious twin peaks of the Bernina Massif – Piz Bernina and Piz Morteratsch – appear. From the latter the Morteratsch Glacier descends– a truly breathtaking sight. After this the road emerges into the Upper Bernina Depression.

Diavolezza★★★

Alt 2 973m/9 754ft. About 1hr there and back from the Bernina road, including 9min by cable car. Operates in summer only 8.15am-5pm. Fare there and back: 28CHF. ☎ (081) 842 64 19.

For generations of mountaineers and skiers the Diavolezza refuge (now a restau-rant) has been the starting-point of one of the most famous glacier runs in Europe. Thanks to a cable car, tourists can now reach this high mountain pass and admire its spectacular glacier landscape. Take in the splendid **view**★★★ encompassing the Piz Palü, Piz Bellavista, Piz Zupó, Crast Agüzza (easily identifiable because of its white peak), Piz Bernina, Piz Morteratsch and the Boval refuge.

Walk to Munt Pers★★★

Alt 3 207m/10 522ft. 1hr 15min from Diavolezza.

Follow the rocky path to the right of the restaurant, clearly signposted in orange. The outstanding **panorama**★★★ seems even more impressive than the one from Diavolezza. You can see the localities of Pontresina and Celerina to the north, the

Piz Lagalb and the Lago Bianco to the east, the Italian Alps (snow-capped summit of Ortier) to the south and the dazzling Morteratsch Glacier to the west.

Piz Lagalb★★

Access by cable car in 8min; leave from Curtinatsch. ○ *Departures every 30min, Nov-Apr, 9am-noon and 1-4pm, hours may vary with the seasons.* ○ *Fare there and back: 21CHF.* ☎ *(081) 842 65 91.*

Through a rocky terrain *(15min there and back on foot)* one reaches the snowy peak of the Piz Lagalb (alt 2 959m/9 708ft) from which a **panorama**★★ reveals about 40 of the main peaks in the Grisons: to the southwest, the Diavolezza Range and its northern glaciers; to the south a lovely green lake, Lago Bianco, and other lakes (natural); to the right of the Diavolezza, the small Lej de la Diavolezza sparkles at the bottom of a crater-like pit. Farther on, where the road begins to skirt the first lakes of the Bernina, the Piz Cambrena, in its turn, stands out clearly.

Passo del Bernina★★

Alt 2 328m/7 638ft. After leaving the valley, followed throughout its length by the railway and in which the Lago Bianco lies, the road climbs to the Bernina Pass from which there are clear **views**★★★ of the Piz Cambrena and its glacier.

Alp Grüm★★★

Alt 2 091m/6 860ft. From the "Ospizio Bernina" station (accessible by car along a downhill road starting from the Bernina Pass), about 1hr there and back, including 10min by rail. ○ *4.40CHF for a one-way ticket.*

A well-known viewpoint overlookins the Palü Glacier and the Poschiavo Valley.

From the Bernina Pass to the Rösa Plateau the road dips into the Agone Valley, framed between the warmly coloured slopes of the Piz Campasc and Cima di Cardan. It then follows a winding course, taking advantage of every natural feature to maintain a practicable gradient. Looking back, the Cambrena group offers glimpses of its glaciers. Forest vegetation is once more reduced to a few stunted larch. You will make your entry into La Rösa facing the majestic, rocky Teo cirque.

From La Rösa to Poschiavo the wooded slopes, clothed with spruce, grow darker. 1km/0.6mi after two hairpin bends, in a section where the road winds above a green valley, a widely sweeping stretch of corniche reveals, lying below, the villages of San Carlo and Poschiavo, overshadowed by the icy shoulder of the Pizzo Scalino.

Poschiavo

Tall, uniform buildings with regularly spaced windows quite unlike those in the Engadine, is typically transalpine in style. The early 16C church of San Vittore on the main square shows the peculiar position of the Grisons as a transitional area for men and goods and for artistic influences. Although the low-pitched roof and slim campanile with five storeys of arches is Lombard style, the intricate star vaulting, most remarkable in the chancel, derives from a typically Germanic style belonging to the last Flamboyant Gothic period (*see Introduction*). **Lago di Poschiavo** (a hydroelectric reservoir) is the best feature of the Poschiavo-Miralago section. Very high on the steep and wooded eastern slope stands the steeple of San Romerio.

Miralago

From this hamlet, whose name ("look at the lake") refers to the **view**★, upstream is your last glimpse of a mountain skyline.

MINE DE SEL DE BEX★

VAUD

This 300-year-old **salt mine** is still fully operational and produces 150 tonnes of salt daily. The salt is obtained through traditional means: a stream of fresh water is injected into the salt rock, flooding every crevice, until the brine shows a salt content of 30%. This technique is known as leaching. Water is then evaporated through boiling, leaving a salt deposit at the bottom of the container.

Visit

🚶 *Guided tours (1hr 45min) Apr-Oct at 9.45am, 11.15am, 2.15pm and 3.45pm.* 🕐 *Closed Mon except in Jun, Jul and Aug. Visitors must book ahead of time.* ⌬*18CHF.* ☎ *(024) 463 03 30; www.mines.ch.* The mine consists of 40km/25mi of galleries, shafts, passageways and steps, originally hollowed out by chisels and sledgehammers. Part of the mine has been made into a **museum** which can be visited on foot and in a small train, including a permanent exhibition in a former brine reservoir first excavated in 1826. Exhibits include tools and machinery which have served the mining industry over the past centuries.

BIEL/BIENNE★

BERN – POPULATION 49 802
ALT 438M/1 437FT

Lying at the foot of the last spurs of the Jura and on the shore of the lake that bears its name, Biel is a good excursion centre and its beach, not far from Nidau, is much appreciated. The city marks the linguistic frontier between French and German (👉 *see Introduction: Language and religion)*: **one third of the inhabitants speak French. The modern lower town contrasts with the old quarters of the upper city.** 🛈 *Zentralstrasse 60 –* ☎ *(032) 032 329 84 84; www.biel-seeland.net.*

Life at Biel – The population of Biel has increased ten-fold within a century, thanks to the watch and clock industry, which still employs about 6 000 people. The first Omega watch factory was set up here in 1879. Other industries have been established to ward off possible economic crises (precision machine-tool works, wire-mills and graphic art workshops). Biel is also a shining example of successful bilingualism, even by Swiss standards: German and French are official languages on an equal footing, with street signs in both languages. It is not unusual to come across two locals conversing without difficulty, each in his own language. In summer, the place to see and be seen is **Strandboden**, the park on the lake.

Sights

Museum Schwab★
🕐 *Open daily except Mon, 2-5pm, Sun and public hols, 11am-5pm.* 🕐 *Closed 1 Jan, 24 and 31 Dec.* ⌬*5CHF.* ☎ *(032) 322 76 03.*
Here are housed collections made from discoveries by Colonel Schwab (1803-69), a pioneer in the research of the prehistoric epoch in Romansh Switzerland. The museum

Fontaine de la Justice

Suisse Tourisme/Paris

contains the best-known examples of the lake-dwellers' era. Artifacts uncovered in the lakes of Biel, Neuchâtel and Murten are displayed alongside those from the Gallo-Roman settlement at Petinesca and La Tène (excavated by Schwab in 1857).

▶ *From the museum go along Seevorstadt (Faubourg du Lac), then take Burggasse (Rue du Bourg) on the left into the old town.*

Old Town★

This section of town is very picturesque. Visitors will find many fountains and façades decorated with remarkable wrought-iron signs, often painted in bright colours. On the main street, **Burggasse**, stand the town hall, notable for its stepped gable and façade adorned by windows with red sandstone mullions, and a Fountain of Justice dating from 1744. **Obergasse** is lined with houses influenced by both Bernese and French architectural styles. To the right, the houses are arcaded and accessible directly from street level; to the left, short flights of steps lead to the house entrances.

Ring

This charming square was the centre of old Biel when the town was governed by the prince-bishops of Basel, from the 11C to the Revolution. Justice was rendered here; the accused appeared before members of the Council seated in a semicircle, and it was from this arrangement that the Ring drew its name. In the middle of the Ring is the curious **Banneret Fountain** (1546), symbolising the militia and war. The houses, with their arcades and turrets, form a fine architectural group. Note the massive tower of the Gothic Church of St Benedict and the frescoes to the left as you enter. The highly decorated corner house with a turret is particularly attractive. Now home to the local registry office, it was once the forest workers' house.

Obergasse leads to **Juraplatz**, another picturesque square surrounded by arcaded houses. Note the beautiful Angel's Fountain (1480), decorated with an angel holding a lamb in its arms, which it is protecting from the devil.

▶ *Then take Untergasse which leads to the lake district.*

Excursions

Sankt Petersinsel★★ – 👌 *See BIELER SEE.*

Taubenlochschlucht★
2.5km/1.5mi – about 1hr 30min. Leave Biel by Madretschstasse and the road to Solothurn and Zurich, and at Bözingen take a path just before the Suze Bridge, near a wire-mill. These gorges, often wild and mysterious, are served by an excellent tourist path.

Magglingen★
8km/5mi – about 30min. Leave Biel by the road to Delémont and 200m/220yd after going under a bridge between two bends, turn left into the byroad to Evilard.
At Magglingen, also known as Macolin, you will find an extensive **panorama**★ of the Swiss plateau, the lakes at the foot of the Jura and the Alps. Magglingen is known for its Federal School of Gymnastics. 🚡 *It is accessible by funicular from Biel (west on the town plan).*

Aarberg
11km/7mi south (road n° 22). A canal links this small yet prosperous town to Biel Lake. The upper town, joined to the lower town by a covered bridge (16C) spanning the River Aare, is well worth a visit. Its main square, **Stadtplatz**★, oblong in shape and paved, is embellished with two flower-decked fountains and lined with classical façades and a small 15C church (restored). A picturesque second-hand fair is held annually on the last weekend in April.

BIELER SEE★

LAKE BIEL

Lake Biel is of glacial origin. It stretches for 15km/9mi at the foot of the Jura and was once larger than now; when water level dropped about 2m/7ft in 1878, it uncovered a score of lake-dwellings on the south shore. At the same time some of the waters of the Aare were deflected from the lake. "The shores of Lake Biel are wilder and more romantic than those of Lake Geneva ... but they are not less smiling", wrote French philosopher Jean-Jacques Rousseau. The north shore, with villages such as La Neuveville nestling amid vineyards, is more picturesque.

Visit

Sankt Petersinsel★★
By boat from Biel or la Neuveville. Allow half a day for the whole excursion. 🕐 *Departure from Biel Apr to mid-Oct, 9.45am-4.45pm (times vary according to the season).* 🎫*Fare there and back: 30.40CHF.* ☎ *(032) 329 88 11. Departure from La Neuveville Apr to mid-Oct, 10.30am-5.15pm (times vary according to the season: weekends only in winter).* 🎫 *Fare there and back: 18.40CHF from La Neuveville.* ☎ *(032) 329 88 11.*

St Peter's Island, at the extreme southwest end of the lake, effectively became a peninsula when the lake's water level was lowered, but it has retained its former name of island. In the autumn of 1765 it was visited by **Jean-Jacques Rousseau**, who recalls his idyllic stay there in *The Confessions* and in *Musings of the Solitary Walker*. The visitor can easily walk round the north side of the island and enjoy pretty glimpses of the lake, especially towards the village of Ligerz (Gléresse). After seeing the small landing stage used by Rousseau, you will come to the house in which he lived. St Peter's Island and its neighbour, the small **Rabbits Island** (joined to the shore by a strip of marshy land since the waters of the lake were lowered), are nature reserves, providing a delightful haven of peace for migratory birds, hare and deer.

North shore★
In this French-speaking section of the lake are some charming old towns.

Cressier
Set back from the lake, this wine-growers' village has preserved some of its old buildings; on Rue des St-Martin there is a house (1576) with an oriel window and the Vallier Château (1610) with its pointed turrets lies nearby.

Le Landeron
Nearer to the lake, this small hamlet is hemmed in by vegetable gardens and orchards. The charm of this village lies in its unique long shaded square adorned with two fountains with bannerets. It is defended at each end by a fortified gate (1659 north side, 1596 south side) and lined with old houses. The town hall (15C) is built onto the Martyrs Chapel. At n° 36 note a house dating from 1550.

La Neuveville – (*See La NEUVEVILLE.*

BREMGARTEN

AARGAU – POPULATION 5 177
ALT 386M/1 266FT

Bremgarten is built at the base of a bend in the Reuss, which encircles its walls. In the days of the Habsburgs it served as both a fortress and a bridgehead. Although less imposing, its site may be compared to those of Bern and Fribourg.

Visit

From the Lucerne road, or from Casinoplatz, there is a fine **general view** of the old town, whose roofs rise in terraces above the river. The river can be crossed on a 16C covered bridge; in the middle stand two small chapels. Fortified towers – the Obertor (Upper Gate) and the Hexenturm (Witches' Tower) – and attractive houses featuring oriel windows and overhanging roofs form an interesting tableau.

BRIENZ★

BERN – POPULATION 2 229
ALT 570M/1 871FT

Brienz lies along the shore of its lake, facing the Giessbach Falls, whose muffled roar can be clearly heard in the town. It is one of the best preserved, old-fashioned summer resorts in the Bernese Oberland. The town is a great woodcarving centre and a technical school was founded here to keep up the tradition as well as a music academy for stringed instruments. Most of the carvings of bears in all sizes and positions sold as souvenirs come from local workshops. 🛈 *Hauptstrasse 143, Brienz – 3855 – ☎ (033) 952 80 80, www.alpenregion.ch.*

Sights

Brienzer Rothorn★★★

Alt 2 350m/7 710ft. Allow 3hr there and back (2hr 20min by rack railway). 🕐 *Operates Jun-Oct, 7.30am-5.30pm.* 🚠 *Fare there and back: 72CHF. For further information, call ☎ (033) 952 22 22, www.brienz-rothorn-bahn.ch.*
Panoramic view of the Bernese Alps, Lake Brienz *(Brienzersee)* and Hasli.

Giessbachfälle★★

Impressive group of cascades in a wooded setting.

Starting from Brienz

Allow 2hr there and back, including 45min by boat and funicular. 🕐 *Daily service during summer season.* 🚠 *From Brienz, fare there and back: 10.80CHF by boat in 2nd class, 4.50CHF by funicular.*
Main platform of Brienz-Bahnhof.

Swiss Museum of Rural Architecture

Starting from Interlaken

About 3hr there and back, including 2hr by boat and funicular. ☞From Interlaken, fare there and back: 21.20CHF by boat in 2nd class, 4.50CHF by funicular. Contact the tourist office ☎ (033) 952 80 80. Separate Interlaken-Brienzersee or Bönigen embarkation stages.

Ballenberg (Swiss Museum of Rural Architecture)★★

2.5km/1.5mi. Leave Brienz east on the Hofstetten road which branches left off the main street (follow directions for Freilichtmuseum). &. ☉ Open mid-Apr to Oct, daily, 10am–5pm. ☞18CHF. ☎ (033) 952 10 30; www.ballenberg.ch

In a vast and superb wooded setting designed for pedestrians, this open-air museum, opened in 1978, is spread out over 80ha/200 acres. There is a free shuttle service bus between the west (nearest Brienz) and east entrances. Genuine examples of regional architecture from practically all the country's cantons were transported here and re-assembled piece by piece, along with ancient furniture. Wiithin each building are daily demonstrations of crafts, from needlework to wood sculpture, and an Alpine cheese dairy, bakery and blacksmith. Divided into 13 groups by geographical origin, the traditional rural houses are connected by paths complete with picnic spots, play areas and small enclosures with 250 domestic animals.

The most noteworthy buildings are: the Chaux-de-Fonds multi-purpose dwelling, typical of the Haut-Jura district; the Oberentfelden (Aargau) chalet (1609) crowned by a huge thatched roof; the half-timbered Old Bear Inn moved from Rapperswil; the chalet from Ostermundigen, with its *trompe-l'œil* windows beneath the gable; the imposing farmhouse from Lancy, originally a small outbuilding containing a winepress; the Richterswil house with pretty half-timbering, built in the Zurich area around 1780; the 17C dwelling from Erstfeld, a masterpiece of Late Renaissance "Sankt Gotthard" style; and the Adelboden chalet (17C), notable for its lovely beams. Three inns serve traditional cuisine and shops sell local craftwork, usually made on the premises.

Brienzer See★

Shorter, narrower, perhaps less picturesque but nonetheless wilder than Thun Lake, Lake Brienz is linked to its "twin" by the River Aare.

North shore★

From Interlaken to Meiringen – 30km/19mi – about 45min – & Local map see BERNER OBERLAND. From Interlaken to Ringgenberg the road runs through woods, climbing to the last slopes of the Harder.

Ringgenberg

From the lake shore, there are attractive views of the lake and the mountains immediately overlooking Interlaken. The building was erected in the 17C on the ruins of a castle (Burg) whose keep was used again in the building of the belfry. Between Ringgenberg and Brienz, especially on the Oberried-Brienz section, the view opens out over **Brienzer See**, enclosed by the Brienzer Rothorn Chain and the foothills of the Faulhorn. The best place to stop is 600m/0.3mi northeast of Oberried, where you return to the lake shore. From this point you will begin to see, upstream, the Sustenhörner Range, which reaches its highest point of 3 503m/11 490ft in the dome-shaped Sustenhorn, and Brienz in the distance.

Brienz★ – & See above.

After Brienz, the road follows the flat valley of the Aare. Among the cascades which spray down the nearby cliffs, the **Oltschibach Falls**★ are the most noteworthy.

Meiringen★ – & See MEIRINGEN.

BRIG

VALAIS – POPULATION 11 597
ALT 681M/2 234FT –
TOWN PLAN IN THE MICHELIN GUIDE SWITZERLAND

Brig is located at the confluence of the River Rhône and River Saltine. This charming town is a lively stopping-place at the junction of the Simplon road and the road to the Rhône Glacier and the Furka. The railway station is important, as it stands on the frontier at the north end of the Simplon Tunnel, the longest rail tunnel in the world (19.8km/12mi). *Banhnofplatz 1 – 3900 – ☎ (027) 921 60 30*

A Bit of History

The King of the Simplon

Brig owes its great attraction to the ideas and ambitions of **Kaspar Jodok von Stockalper** (1609-91) who came from a Valais family, traditionally the guardians of the Simplon Defile. Through his enterprise Stockalper amassed great riches from the trade route over the Alps during the Salt Monopoly. He was courted by emperors and kings but his wealth and success made him enemies and he fled to Italy, leaving his proud fortress unfinished. He returned to Brig to die a respected but ruined man.

Sight

Stockalperschloss

Guided tours (45min) May-Oct, daily except Mon, every hour from 9.30-11.30am, and 2.30-4.30pm, no visit at 4.30pm in May and Oct. ☜5CHF. ☎ (027) 921 60 30.
Once the largest private residence in Switzerland, it can be recognised from afar by its three towers with bulbous domes, standing where the road to the Simplon begins. The first building you encounter as you come from the centre of Brig is the Stockalper family dwelling (early 16C), flanked by a fine watchtower. The imposing main building (built over the original warehouse by the "Great Stockalper") features eight storeys, including cellars, linked to the smaller house by a picturesque gallery with two tiers of arcades. The main **courtyard**★ is surrounded by open galleries in two or three storeys. The three towers arranged around it, with their plain stonework, stand in sharp contrast to this elegant building.

Excursion

Thermalschwimmbäder (Thermal baths)

5km/3mi W of Brig, between Viège and Gamsen. Situated at the foot of the Lötschberg, these are the largest thermal baths in Switzerland (2 000m² /21 520sq ft in the open air). The water here is changed daily and reaches temperatures of 27°C/80°F - 37°C/98°F. Visitors can relax in the Grotto pool or the Olympic pool, or tackle the longest water slide in the Alps (182m/596ft).

BRUGG

AARGAU – POPULATION 9 113

Founded by the Habsburgs in the early 12C, the "city of the bridges", which stands at the confluence of the River Aare and the River Reuss, has preserved many of its old buildings. An important industrial town, Brugg plays a central role in the country's road and railway network.

Old Town

Leave your car in one of the car parks (fee) located outside this area.
Among the monuments still standing in the old city are the Archive Tower, the Storks' Tower (Storchentum) and the imposing 12C and 16C Black Tower, **Schwarzer Turm**, which overlooks the bridge spanning the Aare. This vantage point affords a good view of its wooded banks and old houses. Note the 16C former town hall and the Late Gothic Protestant church with its 18C interior. On the pretty Hofstatt, a paved square embellished with a white fountain, you will find the former 17C arsenal and the old storeroom, dating from the 18C.

Vindonissa-Museum

Open daily except Mon, 10am-noon and 2-5pm. Closed 1 Jan, Good Fri, Easter Sun, 1 May, 24-25 and 31 Dec. 5CHF. (056) 441 21 84.
Housed in the museum are the finds from the Roman site of Vindonissa: jewellery, arms, coins, statues, pottery, glasswork, plus articles made from wood and leather. Note the 4C skeleton of a Roman woman in a sarcophagus and the model of the Vindonissa military camp. Outside is a lapidary museum (stelae, votive inscriptions).

Additional Sights

Kloster Königsfelden – *See Kloster KÖNIGSFELDEN.*

Vindonissa: Roman Amphitheatre
At Windisch 1km/0.5mi via the Zurich road, then to the right of Königsfelden Church take Hauserstrasse.
This is the most important find of the Vindonissa site, a military camp which, in the 1C AD, was the Roman headquarters for the whole of Switzerland, on the present-day site of Windisch. The huge oval amphitheatre with its double wall of ashlar stone (average height 2m/6.5ft) had an estimated seating capacity of 10 000.

> **EATING OUT**
> **Schloss Restaurant** – 056 41 76 73; www. schlosshabsburg.ch. Enjoy a meal in the former fief of the Habsburgs or sip a glass of wine in the weinkeller.

Excursion

Schloss Habsburg
3km/2mi SW. Take the road to Aargau then follow signs to Schinzach Bad.
A narrow country lane wends its way to the castle, which is set up on a spur and which has been converted into a restaurant. In former days, it was the cradle of the Habsburg dynasty: several members of this illustrious family were to influence the course of European history for many centuries. Note the family tree and map illustrating the possessions acquired by the Habsburgs on European territory.

The keep houses an exhibition on the castle's architecture and the restoration work that has been carried out on it throughout the centuries. Climb the wooden staircase: the **view** at the top encompasses the surrounding countryside, cut across by the pretty meanderings of the River Aare.

BRUNNEN

SCHWYZ – POPULATION 6 232
ALT 439M/1 440FT

Brunnen is one of the major resorts of Lake Lucerne; **Hans Christian Andersen**, the author of fairy tales, visited often on holiday. Until the opening of Axenstrasse, Brunnen was a key port for traffic between the Schwyz and Uri cantons and a major transit point on the Sankt Gotthard route. It is busy today because tourists on the great transalpine route (road n° 2, through Arth) and those on the coast route (through Vitznau) come together here.

Brunnen deserves a stop for its **site**★★ at the head of the wild Lake Uri (Urnersee), in the heart of picturesque and historical Switzerland. It was here after the victory at Morgarten in 1315, the three cantons of Uri, Schwyz and Unterwalden renewed their pact of mutual assistance (& *see Introduction: History*).

Quays★★

From the shaded quay, the extension of the Axenquai Promenade eastwards below Axenstrasse, there is a sweeping **panorama**★★ of Lake Uri, lying like a fjord between wild mountain spurs. The dominant feature is the Uri-Rotstock, whose bare twin peaks rise above a small glacier.

In the foreground, on the opposite shore, the tender green of the historic field of **Rütli** (Grutli for the French Swiss) shows up against the wooded slopes of the Seelisburg spur. At the extreme point of this promontory you can see the natural obelisk known as the **Schillerstein**, erected by the "early Cantons" in memory of Friedrich von Schiller, whose "Wilhelm Tell" provided the basis for Rossini's famous opera.

A short trip in a motor boat will give a closer view; & *see VIERWALDSTÄTTER SEE.*

Address Book

Tourist office – Verkehrsbüro, *Bahnhofstrasse 15* – ☎ *041 825 00 40; www.brunnentourismus.ch.*

WHERE TO STAY

⊜⊜⊜ **Weisses Rössli** – *Bahnhofstrasse 8* – ☎ *041 820 11 22 – 17 rooms* – ⊶ *closed for renovation. Reopening Jun 2007.* Frescoes evoke the memory of Louis II of Bavaria, who once stayed at the hotel. The first-floor salon is decorated in blue and white, the official colours of Bavaria, and, naturally, the most prestigious room is the one which was occupied by the sovereign.

⊜⊜⊜ **Schmid und Alfa** – *On the lakeshore* – ☎ *041 820 18 82; www.schmidalfa.ch – 28 rooms* – ⏱ *closed Tue and Wed from 1 Mar to Easter.* The best rooms overlook the lake, from where, on a fine day, you can make out the Rütli and the memorial to Schiller on the opposite shore. This is the heart of Switzerland and the excellent service at this modern, comfortable hotel will make your stay even more appealing.

BULLE

FRIBOURG – POPULATION 10 861
ALT 769M/2 523FT

Bulle is the capital of the "green Gruyères", one of the most attractive districts in Switzerland with its peaceful scenery and quaint folklore. The market town deals in timber and cheese plus the black-and-white Fribourg cattle. *Avenue de la Gare 4 – 1630 – ☎ (026) 912 80 22*

Sights

Musée Gruérien★★

Open daily except Mon, 10am-noon and 2-5pm; Sun and public hols, 2-5pm: Closed 1 Jan and 25 Dec. 6CHF. ☎ (026) 912 72 60, www.musee-gruerien.ch.
Founded by the writer **Victor Tissot**, the Museum of the Gruyères Region is in the basement of a modern building at the foot of the castle. Exhibits are superbly arranged and include some 10 000 pieces of rural furniture, craft objects and documents illustrating the cycle of the seasons. The first section contains several reconstructed peasant interiors, including a cheese room and a typical Fribourg house. Note the pyramid-shaped fireplace in one of the kitchens and painted scenes of the life of the prophet Elijah in one of the bedrooms. Myriad objects highlight the **folklore of the Gruyère region**. Large paintings (19C) known as "poyas" (from the verb *poyî*, " to move up the mountain") show the herds being led up to mountain pastures. One of these is by a master of the genre, Sylvestre Pidoux. The *armaillis* (cowherds) are depicted in their *bredzon* (short jacket with puffed sleeves), with their *loyi* (bag of salt) slung over their shoulder. Also admire the large variety of fine **old furniture**: tables, beds, chests, wardrobes, sideboards, decorated cribs, and chairs, such as the 16C bench from Fribourg. The 18C Gruyères **regional costumes** are also worth noting as well as the wax crèches from the same period. Also on display are 18C-19C medallions on cut-out paper, religious statues, church plate (gold monstrance dated 1752), cowbells and horns from the Alps and a diorama of the local fauna. The second section contains 16C-17C engravings and paintings from the Italian School. Also represented are the French School, with works by Corot and Courbet, including a lovely portrait of a young Bulle girl, and the Swiss School (Vallotton, Alexis Grimou), and the painted cupboard by Netton Bosson.

Castle

This imposing 13C building, flanked by four round towers, was built for Bishop Boniface of Lausanne in the style of Burgundy and Savoy, like the castles of Rolle and Yverdon-les-Bains. Two coupled shields bearing the two cauldrons of Fribourg are painted on the walls.

Cailler, Suchard, Kohler, Nestlé, Lindt, Tobler...

Attractive presentations and mouth-watering contents characterize the high-quality confectionery of Swiss chocolate makers, many of whom have been making chocolate since the 19C. As in the case of a good wine, one should savour the aroma and taste. Dark, white or milk chocolate comes in many forms – cakes, mini-slabs, figurines, sweets and in a variety of shapes – and is often combined with various other ingredients such as nuts, raisins or ginger.

BURGDORF

BERN – POPULATION 14 379
ALT 533M/1 749FT

Burgdorf, at the entrance to the Emmental (the Valley of the Emme, famous for its pastures and its cheese industry - ⚓ *see EMMENTAL*), is a busy little town in the canton of Berne. The modern district, with its large textile works, is overlooked by the old quarter, crowned by its castle. ▯ *Poststrasse 10 – 3400 –* ☎ *(034) 422 24 45.*

Castle

This massive brick building was erected by the dukes of Zähringen at the end of the 12C and passed to the Bernese in 1384.

Museum

🕐*Open Apr-Oct, daily, 2pm (11am Sun)-5pm; Nov-Mar, Sun only, 11am-5pm.* ⚓*5CHF.* ☎ *(034) 423 02 14.*

The museum occupies three floors in the tower. Visit the Knights' Hall, with fine old furniture, Emmental costumes, porcelain, a collection of musical instruments and mementoes of **Johann Heinrich Pestalozzi**, who worked here from 1799 to 1804. From the top floor there is an attractive **view** of Burgdorf and the Bernese Alps.

Excursions

Lueg Belvedere★

Alt 887m/2 910ft. 8.5km/5.5mi – about 30min. Leave Burgdorf by the road to Wynigen.
On leaving town you will cross two ferro-concrete bridges over the Emme. After 1.5km/1mi take a narrow, winding road to the right which passes through Gutisberg; after leaving a byroad to Wynigen on your left, park the car. You reach the top of the bluff along a very steep path among fir trees. A monument commemorating the Bernese cavalry (1914-18) has been erected on the open space; from here the semicircular **panorama**★ includes, in the foreground, a landscape of fields and fir trees, and the Jura and the Bernese Alps on the horizon.

Sumiswald

16km/10mi E. Leave Burgdorf by road n° 23 to the south and bear left at Ramsei.
This pretty Bernese village has fine wooden houses characteristic of the region: a large façade carries one or two tiers of windows close together; the overhanging roof is immense; the gable is often painted and decorated with designs in bright colours. The **Kramerhaus** and the **Zum Kreuz Inn** are quite remarkable.

CELERINA

GRAUBÜNDEN – POPULATION 1 209
6KM/3.5MI NE OF SANKT MORITZ

Celerina (Schlarigna in Romansh) lies at the foot of the larch-clad ridge separating the Samedan Basin from the upper levels of the High Engadine lakes. It is rather like an annex of Sankt Moritz in regard to sports opportunities: In the Cresta quarter, where the great hotels of the resort are found, the famous bobsleigh and "skeleton" runs end. Nearer the banks of the Inn, an attractive group of typical **Engadine houses** make up old Celerina. 🏠 7500 – ☎ (081) 830 00 11.

San Gian

🕐 *Open summer, Mon 2-4pm, Wed 4-5.30pm and Fri 10.30am-noon; winter, Mon and Wed 2-4pm and Fri 10.30am-noon.* ⚒ *Guided tours in summer only (mid-Jul to mid-Sep, Wed 4-4.30pm.* ☎ *(081) 830 00 11.*
Standing alone on a mound to the east of Celerina, the uncrowned tower of St John's Church is a familiar landmark of the Inn Valley, dating back to Romanesque times, with a 15C painted ceiling and frescoes.

Excursions

Excursions which start in Sankt Moritz can also be followed from Celerina.

LE CHASSERAL★★★

BERN
12KM/7MI SE OF ST-IMIER – LOCAL MAP SEE LE JURA SUISSE

Le Chasseral (alt 1 607m/5 272ft) is the highest point of the northern Jura and commands a justly famous panorama of the Swiss Alps. Hardy motorists can cross the Swiss Jura by the route shown below. *A chairlift from Nods enables visitors to reach the summit more quickly.*

From St-Imier to la Neuveville *33km/21mi – about 1hr 30min*

Itinerary 7 *(*⚐ *see Le JURA SUISSE map)*
😊 *The road (4CHF) is narrow and generally blocked by snow between December and mid-May (April on the south side).*

St-Imier

This bustling watch and clock-making centre is located on the south face of Mount Soleil. St-Imier's past is recalled by the Tower of St Martin (or Queen Bertha), the bell tower, all that remains of an 11C church destroyed in 1828, and its 12C former **Collegiate Church** (now a Reformed Church). The interior features a narthex with archaic capitals (heads on the right), an apse with oven vaulting and a chancel with ogive vaulting and mural paintings (Evangelists, Christ in Majesty in a mandorla).

▶ *Leave St-Imier by the Neuchâtel road. 1km/0.5mi beyond Les Pontins, turn left onto the Chasseral road.*

This road, after following the line of a typically Jurassic fold (⚐ *see Introduction)*, comes out on the upper ridge.

▶ *On reaching this upper ridge, turn left towards the Hôtel du Chasseral where you can leave the car.*

Panorama★★★

The Hôtel du Chasseral, situated just below the route's highest point, marks the end of the public thoroughfare. The nearby viewing table allows visitors to take their bearings on the main peaks of the Bernese and Valais Alps and the Mont Blanc Massif. This wonderful backcloth extends for some 250km/156mi.

The motorist with a little time to spare can walk to the Chasseral beacon *(1hr there and back by a wide, gently sloping path)* near a Swiss postal service's telecommunications relay station. From the beacon you get a **circular view**★★★ of the horizon, extending from the Swiss Alps to the northern Jura, the Vosges and the Black Forest.

▶ *Return to the car and make for the fork, where you turn left towards Nods, Lignières and La Neuveville.*

Before reaching La Neuveville there are good views of Lake Biel and Lake Neuchâtel from the road's hairpin bends.

La Neuveville – 🦽 *See La NEUVEVILLE.*

CHÂTEAU-D'ŒX

VAUD – POPULATION 3 078
LOCAL MAP SEE LES ALPES VAUDOISES – ALT 1 000M/3 281FT

Château-d'Œx (pronounced Château Day) is the capital of the Enhaut district, a section of the Sarine Valley between the Tine defile and the Bernese border. It is a little pre-Alpine mountain centre which has long lived apart, spreading its chalets and hotels at the foot of the last wooded slopes of the Gummfluh and the Vanils. This is a typical Vaud Alps family resort, highly popular because of the many watersports facilities it offers. 🄸 *La Place – 1837 –* ☎ *(026) 924 25 25; www.chateau-doex.ch.*

Château d'Œx organises an international hot-air balloon meeting each year in mid-January. The venue for this colourful event is at the junction of the Saanen road and the one to Col des Mosses.

Sight

Musée d'Art Populaire du Vieux Pays d'Enhaut★
🕐 *Open daily except Mon, 2-5pm.*
🕐 *Closed 1 Jan, Easter and 25 Dec.*
🄴*5CHF.* ☎ *(026) 924 65 20.*
Located in a three-storey building, the museum illustrates the region's rich historical past (12C-19C). Exhibits include parchment, engravings, drawings, photographs, popular or religious works of art, weapons, beautifully carved tools, old-fashioned utensils and other objects, painted or inlaid furniture, and reconstructed interiors: blacksmith's forge, peasant's kitchen, bourgeois kitchen, and bedrooms belonging to a herdsman and a weaver. Stained glass, a fine collection of 19C paper cuttings and black

J. Anseaume/MICHELIN

Round the World in a Hot-Air Balloon

On 28 January 1998, French navigator Olivier de Kersauzon lit the burners of *Breitling Orbiter 2* with the Olympic flame, which had been specially brought from Lausanne for the occasion. At precisely 9.56am, the Swiss hang-gliding specialist Bertrand Piccard (whose grandfather Auguste Piccard invented the bathyscaph), Belgian Wim Verstraeten and Andy Elson from Great Britain slowly rose into the air in a pear-shaped Rozier balloon made of aluminium and filled with helium. This non-stop flight around the world, which seemed to spring from the pages of a Jules Verne novel, would last three weeks and follow a specific flight path – Italy, Greece, Cyprus, Israel, Saudi Arabia, India, China, the Pacific Ocean, California, Florida, Bermuda Islands, Canary Islands and North Africa – achieving an unprecedented feat in the history of aviation. The mission suffered a serious setback when Chinese authorities denied them access for national security, despite strong diplomatic pressure from the International Olympic Committee, and the *Breitling Orbiter 2* team was forced to abandon the operation. Then, China changed its mind and gave permission for the balloon to fly over the country, but it was too late. The delays incurred by China's indecision slowed the flight so the balloon could no longer reach the jet stream, a narrow belt of high-altitude, fast-moving winds which would have propelled *Breitling Orbiter 2* over the Pacific Ocean at around 200kph/125mph. The team nonetheless continued their flight and eventually landed in Burma after 9 days, 17 hours and 51 minutes, having covered altogether 8 473km/5 270mi. Although they failed to complete their full orbit, they did succeed in establishing a new world record for living in a hot-air balloon. On 20 March 1999, Bertrand Piccard and British pilot Tony Brown finally achieved their world record round-the-word flight in *Breitling Orbiter 3*.

bobbin pillow lace are also worth noting. Reconstituted in two separate pavilions are a chalet which housed herders up in the mountain pastures: note the cheese room with its gigantic copper cauldron (800l/176gal), and the carpenter's workshop. Also part of the museum, but located at the end of the town, is the **Étambeau Chalet**, which houses artefacts of regional architecture. Visitors are also shown the cheese cellar and the barn, which houses an exhibition on Alpine transport.

LA CHAUX-DE-FONDS

NEUCHÂTEL – POPULATION 36 931
ALT 992M/3 254FT – TOWN PLAN IN THE MICHELIN GUIDE SWITZERLAND

La Chaux-de-Fonds is the biggest watch and clockmaking centre in Switzerland as well as being one of the most important towns for the Swiss farming industry. It is the main town of the Neuchâtel mountains, and lies in an upper valley of the Jura. The town was almost entirely destroyed by fire in 1794 and afterwards rebuilt to a geometrical plan. The cradle of the clockmaking industry since the early 18C, this city also plays an important part in the production of microtechnology, electronics and mechanics, as well as in the tertiary sector.
🛈 *Tour Espacité, Place Le Corbusier – 2300 – ☎ (032) 919 68 95.*

La Chaux-de-Fonds has another claim to fame: the local printing house **Courvoisier** issues postage stamps for the Confederation as well as for many foreign countries, including Finland, Morocco, Jordan, Nepal, Thailand and the United Arab Emirates. Like many localities in the Swiss Jura, La Chaux-de-Fonds welcomes workers coming from the nearby Franche-Comté; a railway line linking Besançon to La Chaux-de-Fonds came into service again in 2000.

Local celebrities

La Chaux-de-Fonds is the native town of the automaton maker **Pierre Jaquet-Droz** (1721-90), the painter Léopold Robert (1794-1835), automobile designer **Louis Chevrolet** (1870-1941) and writer Frédéric Sauser, better known as **Blaise Cendrars** (1887-1961), who, with Guillaume Apollinaire, heralded the age of Surrealism. Like his literary work, his personal life was governed by his overriding passion for travel, both across land and in his own mind.

The Cradle of Clockmaking

From Geneva to the Jura

In the 16C this craft, which had already existed for over a century, was given a new impetus. The reformer Calvin, influential in Geneva, compelled the goldsmiths to turn their attention to making watches, forbidding them to make "crosses, chalices and other instruments of popery and idolatry". The development of this budding industry was spurred on by the arrival in Geneva, about 1587, of French Huguenots driven from their country. Clockmaking soon spread from Geneva to the Neuchâtel Jura.

Daniel Jean Richard and the horse dealer

In 1679 a horse dealer returning to the Neuchâtel mountains from London brought back a watch which was admired by everyone until, one day, it stopped. The people of Sagne, a village near La Chaux-de-Fonds, advised him to have his watch examined by Daniel Jean Richard, who was said to be highly skilled. He managed to repair the watch, studied its mechanism and decided to make watches himself. This he did, using tools of his own design, and subsequently settled at Le Locle, where he trained many others. The watch industry was to gradually spread throughout the Jura.

Le Corbusier

Charles-Édouard Jeanneret was born on 6 October 1887. After studying painting and architecture at the local art school, he embarked upon a European tour. In 1918 he gained recognition as a painter and published the *Purist Manifesto* with Amédée Ozenfant. "After Cubism" advocated formal simplicity, economy of means and mathematical precision without denying emotion. The same principles were to guide his work as an architect. In 1920 he changed his name and became known as Le Corbusier. The same year, together with Ozenfant and the poet Paul Dermé, he founded the literary magazine *L'Art Nouveau*, which remained in circulation until 1925.

Le Corbusier was an inventive man who believed in structuring man's habitat along vertical lines. He invented the "living machine", which illustrated his views on the relationship between society and technology. His accomplishments in the field of community housing stand out on account of their revolutionary conception; he established an artful balance between the different elements, combining a variety of building materials and using light to enhance the cement blocks and exploit their full potential. His work was by no means limited to Europe and many examples of his creative genius can be seen in Russia, Brazil, Japan and India. Strongly criticised or highly praised, Le Corbusier remains one of the undisputed masters of 20C architecture and his impact on modern urbanism was considerable. He died in 1965.

A "Le Corbusier Route," illustrating his achievements in the area, can be obtained from the Tourist Information Centre.

Collection Musée International d'Horlogerie

Collection Musée International d'Horlogerie

A world-famous industry

Most of the watchmaking industry today is concentrated in French-speaking Switzerland, and especially in the Jura. Many firms are located in La Chaux-de-Fonds, Le Locle, Biel, Neuchâtel, Solothurn and Granges. They employ about 32 000 white-collar employees and manual workers. Workshops have sophisticated technical equipment which enables them to produce a quantity of high-quality watches. However, perfection has always been very important to Swiss watchmakers. At present the precision tolerance for the industry's working parts is of the order of 1/400th of a millimetre – 1/10 000th of an inch. In certain workshops, the daily production of 1 000 workers could be carried away in a jacket pocket. Precision has improved with the introduction of computer technology. Together with chemical products and machinery, clockmaking is one of the country's largest export industries. It plays a major role in the economy, and in spite of fierce competition from Japan and Southeast Asia, it remains a key factor in the stability of Switzerland's balance of trade.

Musée International d'Horlogerie★★ 1hr

&. ① *Open daily except Mon, 10am-5pm and Dec 24, 25, 31, Jan 1.* 15CHF. *(032) 967 68 61; www.chaux-de-fonds.ch.*

Founded in 1902, this fascinating International Museum of Horology has been housed since 1974 in basement rooms with the entrance on the north side of the park.

The museum illustrates the ways of measuring time chronologically from Antiquity to the present, with more than 3 000 items from all over the world. The theme is "Man and Time". The museum also has a centre for the restoration of antique clocks and watches; be sure to stop at the glassed-in workshops to watch craftsmen working. Via a footbridge crossing over striking clock mechanisms you reach the main gallery, with early instruments for measuring time and Renaissance, 17C (exquisite enamel watches) and 18C instruments. Marine chronometers, watches from the Neuchâtel region and other countries, as well as unusual astronomical instruments, musical clocks and amusing 19C automata are also displayed.

Continue on to the centre of scientific clocks and watches (astronomical, atomic and quartz-crystal clocks). The belfry offers a pleasant view of the museum's park; proceed into a raised gallery which introduces modern clockmaking techniques. Outside is the imposing **Carillon**, a 15t tubular steel structure made by the sculptor Onelio Vignando erected in 1980. Every quarter hour it chimes (the tune varies according to the season) and at night it offers a captivating light show.

Additional Sights

Musée des Beaux-Arts★

♿ ⏱ *Open daily except Mon, 10am-5pm.* ⏱*Closed 1 Jan and 25 Dec.* 📷*15CHF.* ☎ *(032) 967 60 76; www.chaux-de-fonds.ch.*

Built in the 1920s in the neo-Classical style, the Fine Arts Museum is devoted to regional art in Switzerland and abroad. Beyond the imposing entrance hall embellished with mosaic tiling and sweeping staircase enhanced by carved balusters, rooms display works by such La Chaux-de-Fonds artists as Charles L'Eplattenier *(Springtime, The Doubs River)*, François Barraud *(Self-Portrait)*, Charles Humbert *(Friends)* and Charles-Édouard Jeanneret, later known as Le Corbusier *(Woman in Bathrobe, The Musicians)*. Elsewhere, daily lives and working conditions of the local population are vividly illustrated by such artists as Édouard Kaiser *(Engraver's Workshop, Box Maker's Workshop)*, Albert Anker *(The Grandparents)* and Édouard Jeanmaire *(Leaving the Stables)*. Swiss painting is represented by the work of Félix Vallotton *(Nude with Green Scarf)* and Ferdinand Hodler *(Marignan Warriors)*.

The prestigious **René and Madeleine Junod Collection** features masterpieces of Modern Art, in particular from France: Delacroix *(St Sebastian Released by the Saintly Women)*, Renoir *(The Colettes)*, Derain *(L'Estaque)*, Matisse *(Young Girls in a Garden)*. It also includes pictures by Liotard *(Marie Favart)*, Constable *(Dedham from Langham)* and Van Gogh *(Young Girl with Tousled Hair)*. Abstract art is present with painters belonging to various movements that blossomed after 1950: Manessier *(The Passion of Our Lord Jesus Christ)*, Bissière *(The Angel in the Cathedral)* and Graeser, Christen and Glattfelder for Concrete Art in Switzerland.

Musée d'Histoire Naturelle

On the 2nd floor (lift) of the main post office. 🧒 ⏱ *Open daily except Mon, 2-5pm; Sun and public hols 10am-noon and 2-5pm.* ⏱ *Closed 1 Jan and 25 Dec.* 📷*6CHF.* ☎ *(032) 967 60 71.*

The Museum of Natural History houses a wonderful collection of stuffed animals. Various Swiss and exotic species (of African origin, particularly from Angola) of mammals, birds and reptiles are exhibited in of dioramas of their natural setting. A room devoted to marine fauna displays several hundred types of seashells.

Musée d'Histoire

⏱ *Open daily except Mon, 2-5pm ;Sat, Sun and public hols 10am-5pm.* ⏱ *Closed 1 Jan and 25 Dec.* 📷*6CHF (032) 967 60 88; www.chaux-de-fonds.ch.*

The Local History Museum is housed in a former mansion used for the meetings of the town council. A collection of 17C to 19C Neuchâtel interiors are on show on the first floor: bedrooms with sculpted ceilings, kitchens complete with cooking utensils etc. The Medal Room presents collections of local and foreign coins, along with medals bearing the effigy of famous personalities from Switzerland (Calvin, General Dufour, Le Corbusier) and abroad (Abraham Lincoln, Louis XVI, Queen Victoria).

Bois du Petit Château

Enter by Rue du Docteur Coullery. ⏱ *Zoo open 8am-7pm (5pm in winter).* 📷*No charge.* ☎ *(032) 968 52 62.* ⏱ *Vivarium open 9am-noon and 2-6pm (5pm in winter).* 📷*No charge.* ☎ *(032) 968 11 55.*

Take a stroll around this pleasantly shaded park and zoological garden, where the different species, including deer and wolves, are separated by enclosures. Reptile and insect lovers will be delighted to discover the **vivarium**.

Musée Paysan

SW of the town, at Rue des Crêtets 148. ⏱ *Open Apr-Oct, daily except Mon, 2-5pm; Nov-Mar, Wed, Sat-Sun, 2-5pm.* ⏱ *Closed 1 Jan, Mar and 25 Dec.* 📷*6CHF.* ☎ *(032) 926 71 89.*

The Peasant Museum is located in an old Jura farmhouse (1612). Although restored, the farmhouse has preserved some Gothic elements (mullioned windows on the ground floor) of the original 1507 building. It is an imposing shingled structure with its triangular gable and discreet, carved decoration. The interior has a pine framework with a large central fireplace. The life of a wealthy 17C farmer is re-created. There is a clockmaker's workshop, a cheese room, a still, as well as furniture, utensils, tools, and porcelain stoves. Local lacemakers can be seen at work on the first Sunday of every month. The life of peasants is illustrated by temporary exhibitions held every year.

Excursions

Le Locle – *8km/5mi SW.* 👣 *See Le LOCLE.*

La Sagne
10km/6mi S and after 4km/2.5mi by a road on the right which runs along the railway line.
Fine 16C-18C Jurassian farms are interspersed along the road. Daniel Jean Richard was born in this village in the 17C. The church (15C and 16C) was partially restored in 1891 and more thoroughly in 1952 and 1983. The nave features ogive vaulting. Modern windows are glazed in plain glass in pale shades of green, yellow, grey and violet.

Vue des Alpes Road★★

From La Chaux-de-Fonds to Neuchâtel

22km/14mi – about 45min. Itinerary 8 (👣 see Le JURA SUISSE: Tour). Motorists coming from France are advised to approach La Chaux-de-Fonds through Morteau and Le Locle. This route will enable you to admire the Doubs Falls as you cross the frontier.
On leaving La Chaux-de-Fonds, when going up to the Vue des Alpes, there will be attractive glimpses of the Les Ponts Valley (on the north side of the pass), whose flat pale green floor cuts into the wooded slopes around it.

Vue des Alpes★
Alt 1 283m/4 209ft. The viewing table will enable the visitor to fit names to the peaks in this tremendous **panorama**★: Finsteraarhorn, Jungfrau, Weisshorn, Dent Blanche and Mont Blanc. The best light is in the late afternoon.

Tête de Ran★★
Alt 1 422m/4 655ft. From the Vue des Alpes, 2.5km/2mi to the Tête de Ran Hotel, plus 30min on foot there and back to reach the summit, climbing straight up the steep ridge overlooking this hotel on the right.
Lovers of panoramic views may prefer this view *(steep stony path)* to that of the Vue des Alpes: Tête de Ran is better placed for a wide view of the Jura ridges in the foreground (Val de Ruz, Chasseral and Chaumont Chains), even though fir trees hide the view to the northwest; most of Lake Neuchâtel can be seen. On the way down through the fir trees of the southern slope are interesting views of the **Ruz Valley** depression. This immense "ship's hold" has struck geographers with the regularity of its features: *ruz* has, therefore, become a scientific term to describe the first stages of erosion on the side of a mountain (👣 *see Introduction*).

Valangin

This picturesque little town nestles at the foot of an attractive 12C and 15C castle protected by an imposing curtain wall with towers (levelled). The 16C Gothic collegiate church (inside, interesting tombs and funerary plaques), the town gate with a clock tower and 16C to 17C houses make a nice, old-fashioned picture.

Between Valangin and Neuchâtel the road follows the wooded Seyon Gorges.

Neuchâtel★★ – *2hr 30min.* 👤 *See NEUCHÂTEL.*

CHÂTEAU DE CHILLON★★

VAUD
LOCAL MAPS SEE LAC LÉMAN AND MONTREUX

Chillon Castle is built on a rocky islet; its towers are reflected in the waters of Lake Geneva. The picturesque **site★★** lies at the centre of the lake, within sight of Montreux, the French shore and the Alps: the Dents du Midi are clearly visible. The first fortress was built in the 9C to guard the road from Avenches to Italy, which crossed the Great St Bernard after skirting Lake Geneva. The castle became the property of the bishops of Sion, who enlarged it, and then of the counts of Savoy from 1150. It took on its present appearance in the middle of the 13C.

"The Prisoner of Chillon"

The castle and its dungeons have been used as a state prison more than once, but **François de Bonivard** remains its most famous prisoner. Bonivard attempted to introduce the Reformation when he was Prior of St Victor at Geneva. His theories displeased the Duke of Savoy, a staunch supporter of Catholicism. Bonivard was arrested and cast into the castle dungeons which have borne his name ever since. He lived chained to one of the pillars – the pillar is shown to visitors – and it is said that his footprints can still be traced in the rock. He remained there for four years until he was freed by the Bernese in 1536. When **Lord Byron** visited Chillon in 1816

Château de Chillon

Franziska Pfenniger / Switzerland Tourism

on a pilgrimage to Clarens, which was the setting of Rousseau's *La Nouvelle Héloise*, he commemorated the captivity of Bonivard in a poem, *The Prisoner of Chillon*, which contributed to making the castle the most popular monument in Switzerland.

Visit *allow 1hr*

🕑 *Open Apr-Sep, 9am-6pm; Mar and Oct 9.30am-5pm; Nov-Feb, 10am-4pm.* 🕑 *Closed 1 Jan and 25 Dec.* 🎟10CHF. ☎ *(021) 966 89 10, www.chillon.ch.*

The drawbridge which once spanned the moat has been replaced by an 18C bridge. The dungeons, used as magazines for the Bernese fleet in the 17C and 18C, have fine ogive vaulting and are hewn from the rock. While he was visiting the prison, Byron carved his name on the third pillar in Bonivard's cell.

The Great Hall of the Bailiffs, which bears the coat of arms of Savoy, is enhanced by a magnificent ceiling and an imposing 15C fireplace. Other interesting ornamental features are the oak columns, the fine set of furniture and the collection of pewter. The former Banqueting Hall (Aula Nova), decorated with timber roofing in the shape of an inverted ship's hull, houses the museum; the collections comprise pewter, armour, furniture and weapons (a musket inlaid with bone and mother-of-pearl). The Camera Paramenti served as a guestroom when the dukes of Savoy ruled the town. The walls of the vast Knights' Hall, also called the Coat of Arms Room are hung with heraldic insignia of the Berne bailiffs of Vevey; note the wooden throne and the dresser containing pewter pots. It leads to the Duke's Bedroom or Camera Domini. You also may visit the chapel (painted murals), the Justice Hall or Large Room of the Count, formerly used for parties and formal receptions (splendid black marble columns), the Clerks' Hall and the Lapidary Museum, displaying stones found in the moat and maquettes showing the successive stages of construction of the castle. The top of the keep (🔎 *difficult access by a narrow staircase*) commands lovely **views**★★ of Montreux, Lake Geneva and the Alps. The visit ends with a section of the wall-walk and two fortified towers, converted into a prison during the 17C.

CHUR★

© GRAUBÜNDEN – POPULATION 31 185
LOCAL MAP SEE GRAUBÜNDEN – ALT 585M/1 919FT

Chur lies in the Rhine Valley at the crossroads of Latin and German influences and since the 16C has been the historical, administrative and religious capital of the Graubünden. It is built a short distance from the Rhine on a mound of rocky debris formed by a tributary of the Plessur. 🔖 *Grabenstrasse 5 – 7000 – ☎ (081) 252 18 18; www.churtourismus.ch.*

To thehe east of Chur, the first hairpin bend on the road to Arosa (Arosastrasse) provides an ideal **viewpoint**★ of the whole town and its many belfries, set against a backdrop of steep rocky ridges, covered with the eternal snow of the Calanda.

Sights

Old Town

The old town (reached by climbing a stairway and passing under an old gateway known as Hoftor) is grouped around St Martin's church below the cathedral and the bishop's palace. Chur remains a cathedral city with narrow streets with fine houses, occasionally flanked by towers, pretty squares with fountains adorned with flowers and the arms of the Graubünden canton, and finally the 15C town hall (Rathaus), all of which make for a picturesque scene.

Kathedrale

The Cathedral of Our Lady was built in a mixed Romanesque and Gothic style in the 12C and 13C. The exterior was remodelled after a fire in 1811, and restored in 2007. The tower is crowned with a domed belfry, the porch adorned with painted recessed arches. The nave, which is roofed with ribbed vaulting, is very dark, lit only by clerestory windows on the south side. The interior, restored in the 1920s, features massive piers, surmounted by fine, if somewhat unusual capitals. The chancel contains a 15C **triptych★** in carved and gilded wood at the high altar; it is dedicated to Our Lady and is the largest Gothic triptych in Switzerland. Four 13C statues depicting the Apostles are arranged on either side of the altar.

Domschatz

Guided tours by appointment only daily except Sun, 10am-4pm. ◔ *Closed Good Fri and Corpus Christi.* ⬭1.48CHF. ☎ (081) 252 92 50/19 70.

The treasury includes reliquaries from the Carolingian period and the Middle Ages and valuable reliquary-busts. The Bishop's Palace **Hof** (Z) is an elegant 18C edifice.

Rätisches Museum

◔ *Open daily except Mon, 10am-5pm.* ◔ *Closed most public hols.* ⬭6CHF. ☎ (081) 257 28 89.

This museum is housed in the late 17C Buol Mansion. It contains interesting displays of folklore relating to the canton, a prehistory collection and historical specimens.

Bündner Kunstmuseum

◔ *Open daily except Mon, 10am-5pm (8pm Thu).* ◔ *Closed most public hols.* ⬭ 8CHF. ☎ (081) 257 28 93.

Most of the works displayed in the Fine Arts Museum are by 18C to 20C artists and sculptors from the Graubünden by birth or adoption: Barthelemy Menn, Angelica Kauffmann, Giovanni Segantini – and contemporaries, namely Giovanni, Augusto and Alberto Giacometti, and E-L Kirchner.

Lenzerheide Road★ – Schyn Gorges

Round Tour starting from Chur *73km/45mi – about 3hr*

Itinerary ⑤ *(☙ see GRAUBÜNDEN map)*
After leaving Chur from the south, the uphill road, which becomes very steep, soon gives a general view of the town and the little Calenda Chain in the background. Higher up, emerging from the first wooded section, the slope becomes gentler and you can look down on the opening of the **Schanfigg** *(☙ see AROSA)* and the spa at **Passugg**, which has given its name to one of the most popular Swiss table waters. Then, as you ascend the Rabiusa Valley, you will see the ruins of Strassberg Tower standing out below the village of Malix. The small resorts of **Churwalden** – preceded by a solitary church on the edge of the forest – and **Parpan**, mark the end of this route, which leads through open country to the Lenzerheide Plateau forming the watershed and language boundary between German and Romansh.

Lenzerheide-Valbella✳✳

The twin resorts of Lenzerheide and Valbella are located in Lenzerheide Valley, their modern buildings are set in a hollow (at an altitude of 1 500m/4 900ft; the hollow forms the top of the first ridge crossed by the road from Chur) enhanced by two lakes. It owes its popularity to the charming **parklike country★** which the motorist will appreciate between Valbella and Lenzerheide-Centre. In winter the smooth slopes encourage downhill skiing, especially on the Piz Scalottas and the Stätzerhorn. A long chain of chairlifts reaches up the 2 861m/9 382ft of the Parpaner Rothorn.

Parpaner Rothorn★★

Access by cable-car in 15min from Lenzerheide-Valbella. Departures every 20min, 8.10am-12.10pm and 1.10-5.10pm. Closed mid-Apr to late Jun. Fare there and back: 30CHF. ☎ *(081) 385 03 85.*

The climb above the fir trees as far as Scharmoin (alt 1 900m/6 234ft) gives way to barren slopes before reaching the rocky peak of the Parpaner Rothorn (alt 2 861m/9 382ft). The superb **view**★★, which to the west reveals the Valbella hollow, its resort and clear lake, is blocked to the east by the snowy summits of the Weisshorn, Tschirpen and Aroser Rothorn.

For a more open view, walk *(15min return)* to a nearby mountain top such as the Ostgipfel (alt 2 899m/9 511ft). From Lenzerheide to Lenz, approaching the chapel of San-Cassian, the view opens out towards the depression of the Oberhalbstein, its entrance narrowed between the wooded foothills of the Piz Mitgel and the more pasture-like slopes of the Piz Curvèr. The first Romansh houses, giving a foretaste of the Engadine style, (*see Introduction: Rural architecture*) can be seen at **Lenz**.

Brienz

The church is worth visiting for the sake of its **altarpiece**★ (1519) with Flamboyant decorations, representing the Virgin surrounded by saints. Notice St Luzius, the evangelist of Rhaetia, who is depicted with the insignia of royalty.

From Lenz to Tiefencastel the road descends into the Albula Valley, which until the very end seems uninhabited; higher up, however, the perched villages of Mon and Stierva are a welcoming site on the ledges dominated by the Piz Curvèr. The fine mountain group of the Piz Mitgel stands out clearly. After two hairpin bends, the white church of Tiefencastel, a favourite subject for amateur photographers, looms into sight. Farther on, the belfry of **Mistail** marks one of the oldest churches in the Grisons (Carolingian period).

Tiefencastel – *See SANKT MORITZ: Julier and Albula Pass Roads.*

From Tiefencastel to the Solis bridges, the Albula Valley narrows and the Piz Mitgel mountain group can be seen. The Albula then plunges into the Schyn Gorges.

Soliser Brücken★

These structures comprise an impressive group. From the road bridge you can appreciate the boldness of the railway viaduct, whose central span of 42m/137ft rises 89m/292ft above the bed of the River Albula.

Schinschlucht

The vegetation clinging to the rocky walls of this formidable gorge makes it difficult to appreciate how deep it is. The most impressive section is the crossing of the lateral Mutten Ravine *(Tobel)*.

Thusis – *See SAN BERNARDINO-STRASSE.*

The road from Thusis to Chur is described under SAN BERNARDINO-STRASSE.

COLOMBIER

NEUCHÂTEL – POPULATION 4 610
7KM/4MI W OF NEUCHÂTEL

This village near Lake Neuchâtel is renowned for its white wines. It is dominated by its imposing castle, built in the 15C in Late Gothic style and enlarged during the two following centuries. In 1762 the philosopher **Jean-Jacques Rousseau** stayed at the castle, which remained the property of the counts of Neuchâtel for many years. Today the building is a barracks and military museum.

Museum

🐾 *Guided tours (1hr 15min) Mar-Oct: Wed-Fri at 3pm and first Sun in the month at 2pm and 3.30pm.* 🎟️*No charge.* ☎ *(032) 843 97 00, www.military.ch.*
On the first two floors the vast common rooms, reserved for officers, have timber ceilings and monumental chimneypieces. Patriotic frescoes adorn the walls of the Knights' Hall on the first floor (mobilisation of the Swiss army in 1914) and, on the second floor, important historical events in medieval Switzerland are highlighted. Also displayed are hundreds of arms (14C-20C), either cutting and thrusting weapons or firearms, armour, flags and regimental memorabilia (portraits, uniforms etc). A large gallery on the third floor exhibits cannons. There is also a display of textiles made in the area in the 18C and 19C, painted with an Indian pattern.

COPPET

VAUD – POPULATION 2 389
LOCAL MAP SEE LAC LÉMAN – ALT 380M/1 246FT

This little town is crossed from end to end by a main street lined with arcaded houses built after the invasion by Bernese troops in the 16C.

Château

🐾 *Guided tours (35min) mid-Apr to Oct, 2-6pm (last admission 30min before closing time).* 🎟️*8CHF.* ☎ *(022) 776 10 28.*
Rebuilt in the 18C, the château overlooks Lake Geneva and is surrounded by a charming park. It once belonged to Jacques Necker, a banker from Geneva who was Minister of Finance to Louis XVI. His dismissal by the king in 1789 was one of the decisive moments which drove France to revolution. In 1786 his daughter Germaine married the Swedish ambassador in Paris. Mme de Staël spoke out against Napoleon's regime and was duly sent into exile; she fled to Coppet, where she remained until the Restoration. Endowed with a lively personality, she welcomed many intellectuals of the day, and wrote *Corinne, Ten Years in Exile, Literature Seen in Relation to Social Institutions* and her often sweeping cultural critique, *On Germany,* which has as much to say about French politics and society as about Germany's nascent national identity. Coppet soon became a sort of literary principality, dubbed "the States General of Europe" by Stendhal, frequented by celebrities such as Benjamin Constant, Lord Byron, Schlegel, Chateaubriand and Mme Récamier.

The château has remained in the same family ever since. The interior is lavishly decorated. The Louis XVI and Directoire furniture was taken from Mme de Staël's Paris residence. The rooms remain unchanged since the Revolution. Visitors are shown round the library, Mme de Staël's bedroom, Mme Récamier's suite and, on the first floor (fine wrought-iron staircase), the Great Salon embellished with Aubusson tapestries and a Portrait Gallery displaying works by Duplessis, Gérard, Carmontelle and Mazot. In the park, in a grove near a shaded path, lie the remains of Mme de Staël and other members of her family.

CRANS-MONTANA✳✳

VALAIS

ALT 1 500M/4 921FT – TOWN PLAN IN THE CURRENT MICHELIN RED GUIDE SWITZERLAND

This resort, formed by the neighbouring towns of Crans and Montana, extends for 2km/1.2mi along a wooded plateau dotted with small lakes, facing the impressive backdrop of the Valais Alps. Seen from Montana, the Valais Alps give the impression of rising from the near background whereas in fact the Rhône Valley lies between them and the observer. ◨ *Avenue de la Gare, Montana – 3962 – ☎ (027) 485 04 04,* ◨ *Crans-sur-Sierre – 3963 – ☎ (027) 485 08 00, www.crans-montana.ch.*

Its splendid location, facing due south at an altitude of 1 500-1 700m/4 900-5 600ft, was initially responsible for the development of luxury hotels and sanatoria between the two wars. It was here that **Katherine Mansfield** stayed in 1921 and wrote some of her charming stories *(The Garden Party, The Doll's House)*. Renowned for its skiing, Crans-Montana attracts visitors, who can spend their time away from the slopes playing golf or squash, or window-shopping in the many luxury boutiques. Despite its cosmopolitan attractions, the resort lacks the charm of a traditional Alpine village. However, in summer waymarked footpaths allow visitors to escape the modern buildings and busy roads in search of more typically Alpine scenes. *A map of footpaths (a total of 280km/175mi) is available from the tourist office.*

The skiing area at Crans-Montana

The skiing area of Crans-Montana, consisting of 160km/100mi of slopes served by 41 lifts, including four gondolas, is one of the most important in Switzerland. It is especially popular among beginners and intermediate skiers for its of wide, groomed trails. Experts will find many off-piste opportunities,tree skiing through the forest and some mogul sections around Bella Lui and La Toula. However, the most superb skiing slopes are on the Plaine Morte, which offers opportunities for skiing both in winter and summer, and where the vertical drop is considerable (1 500m/4 920ft to the resort). There are also opportunities for **cross-country skiing**, with 50km/31mi of loops extending over the lovely wooded plateau of Crans at Aminona and the Plaine Morte Glacier. A funicular (12min) connects Crans-Montana with Sierre.

Montana

13km/8mi from Sierre, either by funicular or car. The road to Crans-Montana from Sierre is a succession of hairpin bends, climbing through vineyards and then pastures. On reaching Montana, motorists wishing to return to the floor of the Rhône Valley by a different road can find their way down along the by-road from Crans to road n° 9 – an interesting route which offers fine views of the Pennine Alps.

Aminona

Alt 1 515m/4 969ft. This small modern resort, to the east of Montana, is the departure point for the **centenary walk**, designed in 1993 to commemorate the resort's centenary. This easy walk (4hr 30min there and back) winds its way through parks and forest and crosses Crans-Montana by La Comba (1 428m/4 684ft) and Les Mélèzes (1 450m/4 756ft). Three orientation boards give information on the surrounding peaks of Brigue and Martigny. *A bus service operates back to the resort.*

Petit Bonvin★★

Alt 2 400m/7 873ft. Access by cable car from Aminona. **View**★★ of the Crans-Montana surrounded by spruce, the Bella Lui, the Grand Combin and the Dent Blanche.

Vermala★★

Alt 1 670m/5 479ft. 1.5km/1mi. Leave your car below the Café-Restaurant du Cervin and go to the viewpoint on the right, at the edge of a small escarpment.
Enjoy a bird's-eye view of the Rhône Valley with a sweeping panorama of the high summits enclosing the Val d'Anniviers (especially the Weisshorn and the Zinalrothorn and, in the far distance, the Matterhorn).
Housed in an old Alpine chalet, the small **Colombire Museum** recalls life in the mountains in the 1930s, with information on cheese-making and other rural activities. *Snacks available, guided walks at dawn, plus a typical mountain breakfast.* This chalet is the departure point for the **Bisse du Tsittoret**, an easy walk suitable for children across fields and through woodland *(4hr 30min there and back)*. Take the path towards the Marolires, Courtavey, Colombire caves and the Tièche (alt 1 969m/6 458ft).

Plaine Morte★★★

9min by the Violettes Express cable car reaching an altitude of 2 267m/7 437ft. The **view**★★ of the Dom, Zinalrothorn, Gabelhorn, the Matterhorn and Dent Blanche is particularly beautiful.

▶ *Then take the Funitel to reach Plaine Morte. 5min on foot up a short but steep slope.*

The summit (alt 3 000m/9 843ft) affords an exceptional **panorama**★★★ of the Valais Alps. To the southwest loom the Grand Combin, Mont Blanc and, on the distant horizon, the Meije (on the frontier with the southern French Alps). To the north extends the gently sloping Plaine Morte Glacier, dominated by the Wildstrubel (3 243m/10 637ft).

Plans Mayens★★

Alt 1 622m/5 322ft. 1.5km/1mi. You may stop at the edge of the road, beside the terrace of the Restaurant du Mont-Blanc.
A wide panorama of the Valais Alps extends to the Mont-Blanc Massif in the distance. A picturesque walk (3hr 30min) can be followed from here along the old **Bisse du Ro** up to Er de Chermignon (1 733m/5 684ft). ⊘ *The path is steep in parts and not suitable for children or those who suffer from vertigo.* Follow the path near the Hôtel de la Dent-Blanche. Return to Crans-Montana via Pra du Taillour and the Pas de l'Ours.

Crans-sur-Sierre

The resort of Crans (alt 1 460m/4 788ft) was founded in 1929 in the immediate neighbourhood of Montana. It has rapidly expanded to include a number of renowned Alpine golf courses (18 and 9 holes) and a good selection of hotels and guesthouses. Delightful, easy walks in the area make it a much sought-after country resort.

Bella Lui★★

Alt 2 543m/8 340ft. Access by cablecar. 1hr 30min there and back. Cable-car leaving from Crans and Montana. Service to Cry d'Er 8.30am-4.30pm, Jul to mid-Sep. Departure every 20min. 22CHF there and back. (027) 485 89 10.

Stop at Croix (or Cry) d'Er (alt 2 263m/7 422ft with TCS viewing table) for a magnificent ascent by cable car over the Rhône Valley, with a great panorama of the Valais Alps. To reach Bella Lui by foot, take the path from Vermala to Cry d'Er (2hr 45min) around Mont Lachaux, then carry on to Bella Lui (45min).

DAVOS★★★

GRAUBÜNDEN – POPULATION 13 000
ALT 1 560M/5 120FT

Davos is the main resort of the Graubünden region, situated in the heart of the one of the most famous skiing areas in Switzerland. The pastel-shaded façades of the town extend for over 3km/1.8mi, in an area renowned for its dry, clear air. Davos established itself as a cure town in 1860, during the Belle Époque period when it became very popular with the British. It was here that Robert Louis Stevenson wrote *Treasure Island* in 1881; other literary visitors include Thomas Mann, who drew on his impressions of the town and countryside in *The Magic Mountain*. ⓘ Promenade 67 – 7270 – ☎ (081) 415 21 21, ⓘ Bahnhofstrasse – 7260 – ☎ (081) 415 21 21, www.davos.ch.

▶ **Orient Yourself:** The main funiculars, Parsenn and Strela are like bookends to the city.

ⓟ **Parking:** There is ample parking in garages throughout the city.

ⓓ **Don't Miss:** The cosmopolitan nightlife, with clubs and casinos.

Davos, with a population of 13 000, covers a large area (260km²/100sq mi) in a stunning location, surrounded by mountain peaks up to 3 000m/9 840ft in altitude. The highest town in Europe, it is a busy resort throughout the year, with hotel accommodation for 24 000 visitors, and a high proportion of luxury hotels.

Philipp Giegel / Switzerland Tourism

View of Davos

The capital of world economy

The **World Economic Forum** is held in February every year at Davos, bringing together around 2 000 heads of state, politicians, economists and business people from around the world. The original idea was launched by Klaus Schwab, a lecturer on corporate strategy, who decided to bring together leading company managers in an informal manner in 1970. The first meeting was held in Davos in January 1971, the year in which Klaus Schwab founded the European Management Forum, which was subsequently renamed the World Economic Forum in 1987. In 2000, the conference was attended by the American President Bill Clinton. In 2001, Davos was the scene of violent clashes between police and pressure groups opposed to globalisation; as a result, the Forum was held in New York the following year.

The site

The village of Davos developed in the 13C on the floor of the mountain valley in which the Landwasser flows before plunging into the Zügen defile. The torrents rush into this basin from the southeast; the Flüelabach, the Dischmabach and the Sertigbach, in particular, have made gaps which bring much sunshine to the resort between mountains which might screen it on that side. To the northeast, beyond Lake Davos, equipped for aquatic sports, the gentle, wooded slope towards Wolfgang offers easy access to the Prättigau (towards Klosters). The site is dominated by the Flüela Schwarzhorn (3 146m/10 318ft) and the Alpihorn (3 006m/9 859ft).

The resort

The resort extends between Davos-Dorf and **Davos-Platz**, the chief administrative centre. Around the central square stand the most important public buildings of the old village: the Church of St John (Sankt Johann) and the town hall. The main road through the town is the Promenade, busiest around the Europe Hotel. Davos has the largest **natural skating rink** in Europe and is renowned for its giant **sledge runs**: Rinerhorn and Wiesen (2 505m/8 216ft and 3 500m/11 480ft long respectively), and Schatzalp (2 500m/8 200ft in winter and 600m/1 968ft in summer). During the winter, when snow usually covers the ground from December to April, 80km/50mi of footpaths remain open to walkers. In summer, visitors can choose from 450km/281mi of marked **paths** and superb **mountain bike trails**, including the route (14km/9mi) from Weissfluhjoch to Klosters, with an altitude difference of 1 463m/2 340ft.

The skiing area – 44 ski lifts serve 320km/200mi of pistes, which run through pine and larch woods over a difference in altitude of 1 600m/5 248ft as far as Klosters (see KLOSTERS), a village-resort popular with the jet set. The area extends over 7 massifs, most of which are linked by train or bus, rather than by ski lifts. The main section is **Parsenn**✳✳✳ (120km/75mi of pistes), accessible by funicular from

The Magic Mountain by Thomas Mann

The great German writer Thomas Mann, winner of the Nobel Prize of Literature in 1929, spent time in Davos in 1911 visiting his wife in the Graubünden resort. His stay at the Am Stein villa, close to a sanatorium, inspired him to write *The Magic Mountain (1924)* in which Hans Castorp leaves his native Hamburg to visit his cousin Joachim at the international Berghof sanatorium. Hans is fascinated; succumbing to its charm and atmosphere, he ends up living there for seven years instead of the three weeks initially planned, before the First World War drags him onto the battlefields. Today the Waldsanatorium is the Waldhotel Bellevue, which still houses patients' rooms on the first floor. In the corridor, a photograph shows Thomas Mann in baggy trousers, standing next to his friend Herman Hesse, on skis. The reading room is named The Magic Mountain. The Schatzalp funicular climbs up to the Berghotel, on a promontory. With its cream façade and quaint balconies, the building was once the Berghof sanatorium, the setting for Mann's novel.

Davos-Dorf, which has earned the town its current reputation: skiers leaving from Weissfluhgipfel or Weissfluhjoch will discover splendid, beautifully maintained snowfields of surprising variety suitable for all levels of expertise. The advantages of this particular massif are the excellent facilities and the wide range in altitude: from the top (2 844m/9 331ft) you go down to 810m/2 658ft in Küblis (train journey back) or even 190m/624ft in Klosters. Most slopes offer hiking paths with lovely views in the lower sections; the longest run (12km/7mi) is from the top of Parsenn to Kublis.

Jacobshorn offers 45km/28mi of pistes characterised by a difference in height of 1 000m/3 280ft, some of which should only be tackled by experienced skiers. This massif is particularly popular with snowboarders. The remaining massifs are smaller and farther away from Davos: **Pischa** (1 800m/5 906ft to 2 483m/8 146ft) on the Flüelapass road, **Rinerhorn** (1 450m/4 757ft to 2 490m/8 169ft) at Glaris and **Madrisa** (1 120m/3 674ft to 2 600m/8 530ft) at Klosters-Dorf.

Davos is also famous for its 75km/47mi of pistes for **cross-country skiing** between Wolfgang and Glaris, which follow the lake shores before reaching the lateral valleys of Flüela (used for international competitions), Dischma and Sertig.

Sights

Kirchnermuseum
Ernst-Ludwig Kirchner (1880-1938), a leading German Expressionist painter, left Berlin in 1917 to settle in Davos. In 1936, his intense artistic style was declared "degenerate" by the Nazis. Kirchner was badly affected by this condemnation of his art and committed suicide in Davos two years later. This museum *(n° 67 on the Promenade)* houses the world's largest collection of works by Kirchner, including *Davos in Summer*. It also hosts regular temporary exhibitions.

Hohe Promenade★
1hr on foot there and back.
The promenade is a perfectly planned road, level and sometimes under trees, kept clear of snow in winter. This walk begins in Davos-Dorf by the road behind the Arabella Sheraton Hotel (near the Parsenn funicular station) or from Davos-Platz by a steep path which continues the lane to the church.

Alpinium
At Schatzalp, alt 1 900m/6 232ft. Take the funicular from Davos-Platz. A number of footpaths cross this large **botanical garden**, which enjoys lovely views of the Landwasser Valley. From the garden, waymarked paths lead to Podestatenalp, Lochalp, Grüenialp, Erbalp, Stafelalp and Davos Frauenkirch (approximately 4hr). It is also possible to walk back into Davos along the easy Eichörnli path (45min).

Hikes and Viewpoints

Weissfluhgipfel★★★
Alt. 2 844m/9 331ft. Allow 1hr 30min there and back (or a whole day if you opt for a long walk, see below). Departure every 15min, Jul-Oct and Dec-Apr, 8.15am-5pm. Fare there and back: 32CHF. (081) 415 21 21.
From Davos-Dorf, take two successive funiculars to **Weissfluhjoch Pass** (2 662m/8 758ft). The trip affords lovely **views**★★ over Davos and its lake as well as Dürrboden Valley. Then take the cable car. From the summit, there is a **sweeping panorama**★★★ of the surrounding landscape: to the west, beyond the arid slopes of the Parsenn (in summer), you will glimpse Chur, the Arosa resort nestling in its wooded setting with Jungfrau in the distance: to the north Klosters and Silvretta (Austria); to the east Flüelatal; and to the south the Bernina Massif.

Walk from Weissfluhjoch to Davos★★
Allow 3hr 30min without breaks (difference in height 1 000m/3 280ft).
Walk to the Parsennhütte refuge *(45min)* along a steep, stony path, passing pretty Lake Totalspee half-way down. Inexperienced hikers may take the cable car. On reaching the lower station (300m/300yd ahead), bear right and take **Panoramaweg★★**, a smooth path flanked by benches following the mountain slope and offering superb **views★★** of Lake Davos, Dürrboden Valley, Pischa and Silvretta. After walking for about 1hr 15min, turn left and proceed towards the intermediate platform of the funicular. Continue in the direction of Büschalp 1850, with its dreamlike setting, then go back down to Davos-Dorf or Davos-Platz *(allow 1hr 30min)*.

Jacobshorn★★
Alt. 2 590m/8 497ft. 🎿 *Allow at least 1hr there and back. Access is by 2 funiculars, then 5min on foot up a steep incline.* 🕐 *Year-round service leaving every 15min, 8.30am-5pm.* 🚡 *Fare there and back: 32CHF.* ☎ *(081) 415 21 21.* There is a **panorama★★** over the whole Davos and Klosters area as well as Sertig Valley.

Schatzalp★
Alt. 1 863m/6 110ft. *45min there and back including 5min of funicular (Schatzalp-bahn) leaving simultaneously from Davos-Platz and Schatzalp.* 🕐 *Open Apr-Oct, daily, 9am-5.30pm (2am Dec-Apr).* 🚡 *Fare there and back 13CHF.* ☎ *(081) 415 52 80; www. schatzalp.ch*
The vicinity of the Schatzalp Hotel commands fine views of Davos' main valley and its narrow side valleys. A charming Alpine garden *(alpinum)* lies nearby *(10min there and back)*.

Dürrboden Valley★★

Road to Dürrboden★★
12km/7.5mi from Davos. Allow 20min.
This narrow road running along the peaceful waters of the Dischmabach wends s through a heavenly setting: lovely pastures dotted with woods, cottages and hillocks, with the Scaletta Glacier in the far distance. To fully enjoy these natural beauties, make good use of the hiking and biking trails that have been marked out for visitors.

Walk to Grialetschhütte★★
Alt. 2 542m/8 340ft. Park the car at the end of the road to Dürrboden (2 007m/6 584ft).
Walk up the gentle slope *(allow 1hr 45min)* facing the Scaletta Glacier until you get to **Fuorcia da Grialetsch Pass★★**. From there it is easy to reach the refuge, charmingly surrounded by a cluster of lakes. This is a typical bare mountain **setting★★** that contrasts sharply with the luxuriant vegetation thriving down in the valley. The Scaletta and Grialetsch Glaciers are overlooked by Flüela Schwarzhorn and Piz Vadret. To get a **bird's-eye view★★** of the whole area, continue the ascent towards the glacier for 20min and take in the sweeping panorama of the valley and lakes. Go back down along the same route.

The Zügen and Flüela Pass Roads★★

Round Tour Starting from Davos *135km/84mi – allow one day*

Itinerary 1 *(🧭 see GRAUBÜNDEN map)*
Leave Davos by ③.

Frauenkirch

The small church has an avalanche screen. The nearby houses with larger wooden superstructures herald the German architecture of Prättigau for tourists coming from the opposite direction.

Zügenschlucht★

You will pass alongside the defile on the way to Bärentritt (see below).

The clear, leaping waters of the Landwasser seethe impressively through this defile. The Zügen, neighbouring avalanche corridors, are often disastrous in winter.

Bärentritt★★

2hr on foot there and back by the old road to the Zügen taking the exit east of the tunnel (on the Davos side). Park the car at Schmelzbaden.

From this point – a projecting parapet forms a belvedere that marks the beginning of the Zügen defile. There is an impressive downward view of the confluence 80m/262ft below, of the Landwasser and of the torrent forming the Sägetobel Cascade on the right. Coming out of the deep Tieftobel Ravine, you will see below you the **Wiesen Viaduct**★ (length 210m/689ft, central span 55m/180ft, height 88m/288ft), one of the largest structures of the Rhaetic railways.

After Schmitten the view plunges to the left onto the Albula and the Landwasser; on leaving Davos, you descend its tributary stream. As far as Tiefencastel the larch woods follow a landscape of deep ravines *(tobel)*; the last of these level with Surava, serves as a backdrop for the ruins of the feudal **Belfort Castle**, a fortress perched on an escarpment.

Brienz –   *See BRIENZ.*

Tiefencastel –   *See SANKT MORITZ: Albula Pass Road.*

▶ *From Tiefencastel to La Punt, the itinerary (Albula road) is described under SANKT MORITZ and from La Punt to Susch under ENGADIN.*

Susch

A village whose two towers (the church belfry and a tower with a bulbous steeple) stand out in front of the last wooded slopes of the Piz Arpiglias. Officially starting from Susch, the Flüela Pass Road soon overlooks this village. The first series of hairpin bends climbs quickly above the rugged Susasca Valley. Beyond, on a 4km/3mi long corniche section, the **view**★ opens out over the icy corrie enclosing the desolate combe of the Grialetsch Valley completely covered with the greenish debris of landslides. On either side of a well-marked snowy gap you will recognise the Piz Grialetsch (on the right) and the Piz Vadret (on the left). Two hairpin bends bring the road to the entrance of the deserted Chantsura combe, overlooked by the Schwarzhorn.

Beyond Chantsura, after two more hairpin bends, a distant gap downstream invites a stop to enjoy the white, high-perched form of **Schloss Tarasp** (Tarasp Castle) against the background of the Lower Engadine Dolomites. Nearer but less distinct, the grey Steinsberg Tower guards the town of Ardez.

Flüelapass

Alt 2 383m/7 818ft.   *May be closed temporarily when there is an avalanche risk.*

Two lakes, a hospice and traces of landslides from the Schwarzhorn and the Weisshorn characterise the barren landscape of the Flüela Pass. The descent to Davos follows a long, monotonous corridor. After the second bridge spanning the Flüela – notice here the first Arolla pines, outposts of the forest zone – the crests of the Weissfluh appear, well-known to the skiers of Davos. Beyond Tschuggen, the valley becomes more welcoming with flower-strewn fields, larch and fir woods all the way to Davos.

DELÉMONT

C JURA – POPULATION 11 396
ALT 436M/1 430FT

Until 1792 Delémont was the summer residence of the prince-bishops of Basel, whose crosier appears in the arms of the town. Today it owes its importance to its watch and precision-instrument factories. Since 1978 it has been the capital of the new canton of Jura. ▯ *12 place de la Gare – 2800 – ☎ (032) 422 97 78.*

Old Town

The old or high town, on either side of rue du 23 Juin, has kept its monumental gates, 16C Renaissance fountains and noble 18C classical buildings. The bishops' castle, the Church of St Marcellus and the town hall are the most representative buildings of the old town of Delémont, as is the **Hôtel de Ville** *(town hall)* with its outside staircase, Baroque doorway and noteworthy interior decoration.

Musée Jurassien d'Art et d'Histoire
🕐*Open daily except Mon, 2-5pm.* 🕐*Closed 1 week between Christmas and New Year.* 🎟*6CHF.* ☎ *(032) 422 80 77, www.mjah.ch.*
The regional Art and History Museum contains archaeological finds from the prehistoric to the Merovingian Era discovered in the area (bronze and terracotta Roman statuettes), ancient religious objects (parish treasure in the basement: 7C silver and enamelled crosier), mementoes of Napoleon, and examples of local crafts and furniture including 17C: furnishings in the prince-bishops' Portrait Gallery, 18C dining room; third floor: 18C bedroom and folklore and works by artists from the Jura).

Chapelle du Vorbourg
2km/1mi NE. To arrive at the pilgrimage centre of Our Lady of Vorbourg use the shaded road lined with Stations of the Cross, offering good views of Delémont. The chapel stands in a wild and wooded site overlooking a deep valley. It contains Baroque altars and walls covered with 18C and 19C ex-votos.

DENT DE VAULION★★★

VAUD
15KM/9MI SW OF VALLORBE
LOCAL MAP SEE LE JURA SUISSE – ALT 1 483M/4 865FT

Dent de Vaulion, one of the steepest summits in the Swiss Jura, offers a sweeping panorama of the Alps, from the Jungfrau to the Meije and the Joux Valley.

Climb to the Dent

From the road from Romainmôtier to L'Abbaye, 5km/3mi – allow 45min.
The access road, tarred as far as the chalet on Dent de Vaulion, branches off from the main road on the ridge between the Vaulion Valley and the Joux Valley. It soon becomes very narrow *(passing only possible at certain points)*. From the chalet you can see your way to a signpost marking the summit *(viewing table)*.

Panorama★★★

The great glory of this view is the Mont-Blanc Massif beyond the mists of Lake Geneva; the first ridges of the Jura towards the Joux Valley and its lakes are also a majestic sight. Beware of the alarming precipice, a sheer drop of over 200m/600ft.

DISENTIS/MUSTÉR✳

GRAUBÜNDEN – POPULATION 2 209
ALT 1 133M/3 717FT

Disentis, the centre of Romansh culture and a health resort, is the small capital of the Upper Grisons and Oberland Valleys, colonised in the Middle Ages by the monks of St Benedict. From its terrace it overlooks the junction of the Tavetsch Rhine, flowing down from the Oberalp Pass to the west and the Medel Rhine from Lukmanier Pass to the south. In summer those who like an excursion involving little effort will find here a whole series of short walks complete with belvederes and painted chapels. In winter skiers are offered a network of ski lifts which take them up to the runs at an altitude of 3 000m/9 240ft.

Sight

Abbey and Klosterkirche

This is one of the oldest Benedictine institutions in Switzerland, dating from the 8C. The buildings, originally used by the monks as a school, are 17C, 19C and 20C. The abbey, from which the town derives its Romansh name of Mustér, forms a massive quadrilateral ensemble of buildings lying on the flank of a long, rugged Alpine slope, whose summit is shaded by forests. The **Abbey Church**★ **(Klosterkirche),** an imposing Baroque church (1695-1712) flanked by two towers with bulbous domes, has a bright interior with well-placed tribunes. The two tiers of windows are invisible from the nave in accordance with the Baroque rules of indirect lighting. The stucco and paintings on the vaulting were restored in the first quarter of the 20C.

Oberalp Pass Road★

From Disentis/Mustér to Andermatt *31km/19mi – about 1 hour*

Itinerary 5 *(* see SANKT-GOTTHARD-MASSIV map)
The Oberalp Pass is usually blocked by snow from November to May; when the pass road is closed a train ensures the transportation of cars between Andermatt and Sedrun. In winter the train runs between Andermatt and Sedrun. For the timetable and reservations (obligatory) call ☎ (041) 888 75 11 or ☎ (081) 920 47 11.
The most notable features of the trip through the Oberalp Pass (alt 2 044m/6 704ft), which is largely covered by a lake, are the following:

◆ **the upper exit from the Sedrun Basin**: after Camischolas, the road bends to enter a wooded area with a charming view of the villages of **Val Tavetsch,** where the Vorderrhein rises. The villages stand on green terraces cut by sharp-edged ravines.

◆ **the descent from the Oberalp to Andermatt**: the **view**★★ soon encompasses the pastoral slopes of the Urseren Valley as far as the Furka Gap and looks down on Andermatt, clustering at the foot of the Urseren Forest, which has been ravaged by avalanches (notice the many protective walls on the slope).

Andermatt❄ – 🖑 *See ANDERMATT.*

Vorderrhein Valley★

From Disentis/Mustér to Reichenau

52km/32mi – allow half a day. Itinerary 🔳 *(🖑 see SANKT-GOTTHARD-MASSIV map)*
Just after leaving Disentis from the northeast, upstream from the modern road bridge and railway viaduct which span the Russeinbach Ravine, stands an old covered bridge now disused. Farther on, the elegant bulbous belfry of Somvix is noteworthy.

Trun
The imposing mass of the **Cuort Ligia Grischa** (black and white shutters) (🕐 *Open mid-Apr to Nov, Mon, Wed, Sat and the second and last Sun of the month 2-5pm.* *Guided tours available (1hr) at 2pm, 3pm and 4pm.* ☜*5CHF.* ☎ *(081) 943 23 09/33 88*), a former residence of the abbots of Disentis built in 1674, once housed the Parliament and Law Court of the League. Inside, the apartments open to visitors include the Abbot's Bedchamber, with 17C panelling, and the Law Court decorated in the Baroque style. The maple tree planted at the entrance to the village, in the enclosure adjoining the 18C Chapel of St Anne (modern commemorative paintings), grew from a seedling from the Maple of Trun. It was in the shade of this sacred tree – as strong a symbol to the people of Graubünden as the Oak of Guernica is to the Basques (🖑 *see The Green Guide Spain*) – that the Pact of the Grey League was solemnly confirmed in 1424.

Ilanz
Ilanz is the only place in the Grisons Oberland which bears the official title of "town". It was the former capital of the Grey League, founded here in 1395 (🖑 *see GRAUBÜNDEN*), Disentis being considered more of a religious capital. The most picturesque quarter, reached by crossing the bridge over the Rhine and following the exit route towards Vals or Vrin, has retained its 17C mansions with Baroque ornamentation, especially the Casa Gronda (black and yellow shutters) with its corner turret, window grilles and finely decorated door frames.

Vals
20km/12mi from Ilanz.
A detour along a charming, winding road in the Valsertal Valley leads to this spa resort (alt 1 248m/4 093ft), which nestles among a grandiose cirque of mountains. **Felsen-Therme**★ was the first spa to be built in natural stone. Opened in 1996, it was designed by the famous Swiss architect Peter Zumthor. The walls of this cube construction are made of quartzite, extracted from within the valley. The spa's sophisticated facilities include an indoor pool (32°C/89°F), an open-air pool (36°C/96°F), saunas, a cold plunge pool and a "musical" grotto which plays "mineral" music composed by Fritz Hauser.

▶ *Retrace your steps to Ilanz.*

Versam road★
From Ilanz to Bonaduz 21km/13mi.
The road offers vistas of the Rhine Gorges and the Bifertenstock (Tödi Massif) Crests, to the left of the Vorab. The clearing just before the village of Versam is a good place to stop for a **view**★ of the Vorab group, with its great plateau glacier, on the left, and

the Ringelspitz on the right. In the foreground stands the Flimserstein promontory, girdled with imposing cliffs.

The narrow road is soon suspended on a ledge along the flank of white precipices (a curious phenomenon caused by erosion) formed by the Rhine and its tributary, the Rabiusa, and runs through debris brought down by the Flims landslide.

▶ *Return to Lanz and the Reichenau road.*

From Laax to Trin, the landscape, which becomes rough and thickly wooded, reveals the original chaotic formation of the great flow of debris coming down from the Sardona Range into the Rhine Valley. Below the road the dark waters of the small Lake Cresta will be seen. The obstruction created by the Flims landslide compels the road to cross a very steep ridge of which the summit is marked by the resort of Flims at an altitude of 1 103m/3 618ft.

Flims✳✳ – 🚡 *See FLIMS.*

The widest views on this trip are seen during the descent from Trin (a pretty village high up in the mountains) to Reichenau. This is the time to look at the Reichenau Basin, where the Vorderrhein (Outer Rhine), just freed from its gorges, joins the Hinterrhein (Inner Rhine) emerging majestically from the Domleschg Basin, near Bonaduz.

Reichenau

With its three bridges forming a triangle enclosing the confluence of the Vorderrhein and the Hinterrhein, this little settlement – consisting of a castle and its outbuildings *(partly converted into an inn)* – owes its existence to a site exceptionally convenient for collecting tolls. It is still an important road junction at the fork of the main roads to the Domleschg (Thusis) and the Grisons Oberland (Disentis/Mustér). During the French Revolution, buildings here were occupied by an Institute of Education. Louis-Philippe d'Orléans, the future King of France, spent his first winter in exile here (1793-94), teaching languages, history, geography and mathematics under the pseudonym of Chabaud-Latour.

BASSINS DU DOUBS★★

The name Bassins du Doubs (Doubs Basins) designates the area which includes the widest part of the gorges of the River Doubs, Lake Brenets (called Lake Chaillexon on the French side) and Chatelot Dam. It establishes the boundary between France and Switzerland for 43km/27mi, is more accessible to the motorist and offers more belvederes on the French side (🚡 *see The Green Guide Burgundy Jura*), whereas the Swiss side offers pleasant boat trips on Lake Brenets.

From Les Brenets to the Doubs Fall

🚶 *On foot (by a forest path bordering the east bank) 2hr 15min there and back or 1hr plus return trip by boat. By boat: 1hr there and back plus 20min there and back on foot.* 🕐 *Summer service May–Sep, departures every 45min starting at 10am.* 🎫 *Fare there and back: 12.50CHF.* ☎ *(032) 932 14 14; www.nlb.ch.*

Les Brenets

A small border town pleasantly terraced on the slopes which plunge into the lake of the same name. **Lac des Brenets**★ called Lac de Chaillexon on the French side, this lake was a bend in the Doubs transformed into a reservoir following a series of landslides. It is 3.5km/2.5mi long and averages a width of 200m/656ft. At one point its sides become extremely narrow, forming two basins: the first (average depth 10m/33ft) spreads over an area between gently smiling slopes; the second (average depth 30m/99ft) flows between abrupt limestone cliffs – crowned with fir, Norway spruce and beech trees – the crests of which, here and there, are said to resemble famous people in profile (Louis-Philippe, Calvin and others). The federal cross painted onto the rock face in 1853 and the so-called Grotto of the King of Prussia can be seen on the Swiss side.

Saut du Doubs★★★

The waterfall can be reached by the landing stage which marks the end of the lake, via a forest path. This famous waterfall, the overfall of Brenets Lake, 27m/89ft high, is far more spectacular when it is seen from the French side (*description in The Green Guide Burgundy Jura*). The site is heavily wooded.

From Les Brenets to Les Roches de Mauron

11km/7mi – allow 1hr

Les Brenets – See above.

After leaving Les Brenets in the direction of Le Locle, bear left at the crossroads onto the road towards Les Planchettes. The road passes through woods, climbs to the plateau, and arrives near the hamlet of Les Recrettes.

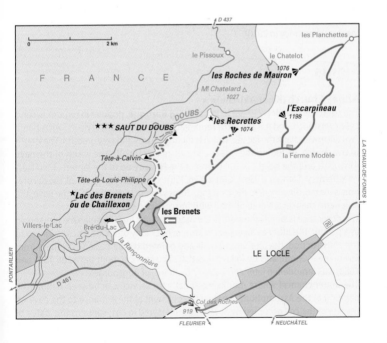

Les Recrettes viewpoint★
Alt 1 074m/3 524ft. 30min on foot there and back.
From the belvedere there is a good **view**★ onto the loop of the Doubs made by Châtelard Mountain on the French side and the hinterland covered with fir trees and pastures. Just before the farm *(Ferme Modèle)* bear left onto a path *(private: close the gates after you)* and continue along it for about 700m/0.5mi until you are right by the cliff.

Les Roches de Mauron
Alt 1 076m/3 530ft. Walk to the viewpoint near the restaurant, from where there is a plunging view onto the Doubs, hemmed in by the Châtelard Promontory and the Chatelot Dam.

EINSIEDELN★★

SCHWYZ – POPULATION 11 995
ALT 881M/2 890FT

The small town of Einsiedeln, a pleasant winter or summer resort, lies in a district of rugged hills and pinewoods intersected by torrents. It is the most famous and most frequented place of pilgrimage in the whole of Switzerland.  *Hauptstrasse 85 – 8840 – ☎ (055) 418 44 88.*

The church and monastery buildings were built on the site of a monastery founded in 934 by Otto I and Duchess Reglinde of Swabia, and subsequently burnt down several times. The town's main street runs into the west side of the huge square on which the abbey church stands. The façade of the Benedictine abbey overlooks a great semicircular parvis, edged with arcades, in the centre of which stands a fountain in honour of the Virgin. It is in this impressive setting that performances of *The Great Theatre of the World* by Calderón de la Barca take place every five years (next performance in 2010).

Sights

Abbey Church (Klosterkirche)★★
The church was built (1719-35) in **Vorarlberg Baroque**, popular in regions around Lake Constance, and it is the most remarkable example of this style in Switzerland. Two tall towers flank the façade, which is slightly convex and very graceful. The length of the church, including the upper chancel, is 113m/370ft, the width of the nave 41m/131ft and the height of the Dome of the Nativity up to the lantern 37m/118ft (Westminster Cathedral 93m/306ft x 47m/156ft x 85m/280ft). Above all, the decoration is extraordinarily rich: the vaulting, domes and octagonal roof of the nave, the aisles and chancel are embellished with frescoes and stuccoes.
This decoration is largely the work of the Asam brothers from Bavaria. One was known as a painter, the other as an expert in stucco, but many other artists contributed to the construction: the altars were built and painted by the Carlone brothers from Sciara (near Como) and by Milanese artists. The chancel, built between 1674 and 1680, was remodelled later and painted by Kraus, of Augsburg.
The upper chancel where monks meet daily for service can be seen behind the painting of the Assumption. The Holy Chapel, built at the entrance to the nave on the site of the cell occupied by St Meinrad, martyred in 861, contains the statue of Our Lady of Hermits, an object of special veneration for pilgrims.

Grosser Saal

🕐 *Open 1.30-6pm.* 🕐 *Closed when concerts are scheduled.* 🚌 *3CHF.* ☎ *(055) 418 62 40.*

The Abbey Great Hall ,on the second floor of the monastery buildings,is reached by skirting the church to the right. Enter the first door on the left, in the courtyard. It was built at the beginning of the 18C and is decorated with stuccowork and frescoes by Marsiglio Roncati of Lugano and Johannes Brandenberg of Zug. Exhibitions are held on a regular basis, displaying items from the monastery's different art collections.

EMMENTAL ★

The Emmental, whose name immediately brings to mind the well-known Swiss cheese, is a large valley to the east of the canton of Berne and bordered by the River Aare and the canton of Lucerne. It is cut across by the River Emme, a tributary of the Aare, into which it flows east of Solothurn. Originating in the Hohgant Massif north of Lake Brienz, the River Emme crosses first a mountainous area, whose slopes are covered with fir trees and pastures, and then runs through an area of forests and fields dotted with flower-decked chalets. The area's wealth comes from forestry, crop farming and cattle raising.

Sights

Burgdorf; Lueg Belvedere ★ – 🚶 *See BURGDORF.*

Hasle

On the west bank of the River Emme, this village is linked to the Rüegsauschachen (east bank) by a remarkable **covered bridge** (1838). Built entirely of wood, the bridge crosses the river in one span. The Protestant church, a former chapel rebuilt in the 17C, is worth noting. Inside are small 17C stained-glass windows, heraldic bearings and 15C frescoes showing the Last Judgement and the Crucifixion.

Emmental Cheese

Emmental cheese is to German Switzerland what Gruyère cheese is to the French cantons. It is the most widely exported of all Swiss cheeses: its enormous wheels, hard interior with large irregular holes (Gruyère is more compact and has fewer and smaller holes) and hazelnut taste are known throughout the world.

Jegenstorf

The houses in this cheerful, flowered town cluster around a Late Gothic church, with a saddleback roof and a shingled bell tower. The interior is decorated with woodwork; the stained-glass windows are 16C-18C. The town's **château** (🕐 *Open mid-May to mid-Oct, daily except Mon, 10am-noon and 2-5pm.* 🚌*7CHF.* ☎ *(031) 761 01 59*), an 18C town house added to a feudal tower, stands in a small wooded park and presents temporary exhibitions in lovely 18C period rooms.

Kirchberg

The Protestant church, built in 1506 and since restored, overlooks the village. Its apse contains 16C and 17C stained-glass windows: the north side windows depict St George slaying the Dragon and the Bernese coat of arms; the south side shows a Virgin in Majesty. The stained glass in the central windows is modern.

Langnau im Emmental★ – 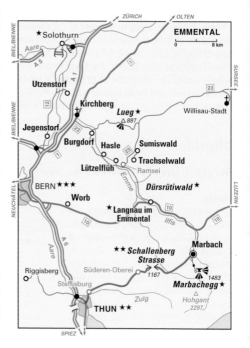 See LANGNAU IM EMMENTAL.

Lützelflüh

This lovely village on the Emme has a church which was built in 1494 (modernised). Inside the church are six old stained-glass windows and an organ loft (1785). Outside the door is the tomb of Albert Bitzius (pseudonym of Jeremias Gotthelf), pastor and writer during the 19C.

Marbach – See MARBACH.

Sumiswald – See BURGDORF: Excursions.

Trachselwald

The 17C Reformed church with its 18C bell tower, has in its nave a curious painted ceiling and in its apse an intriguing Baroque mausoleum (1695). Outside the village, on a wooded slope, stands a gracious 15C **castle**, which, although it has been restored, has kept its 12C tower *(access by a covered stairway)*. Schloss, ⊙ *Open Mon-Sat, 9am-6pm, Sun noon-6pm.* ∞ *No charge.* ☎ *(034) 431 21 61.*

Utzenstorf – See UTZENSTORF.

Worb

This bustling, industrial centre is dominated by its two castles (12C and 18C) and by its Late Gothic church (carved stalls, 16C and 17C stained-glass windows in the apse).

BARRAGE D'EMOSSON★★

24KM/15M SW OF MARTIGNY

A winding road (8km/5mi, closed in winter) leads from Le Châtelard, on the border between Switzerland and France, via Finhaut to the Émosson Dam. As the flower- and pine-tree lined road nears the dam, there are extensive views towards Mont-Blanc in the distance. The dam – the second largest in Switzerland after the Barrage de la Grande Dixence – was a joint Franco-Swiss project (1967-72). It harmonises perfectly with its rocky, mountainous setting.

Access by funicular★★

From **Le Châtelard-Giétroz** take the funicular (the steepest in the world, with a gradient of 78%) which goes from the C.F.F. (Swiss Railway) power station to the water tower, and which offers lovely **views** of the Rhone Valley to one side and Mont Blanc to the other (*Access by funicular from Châtelard-Château d'Eau, Emosson train and Emosson mini-funicular* – Operates June to mid-Oct, 9.30am-12.30pm and 1.30-5.30pm. *44CHF there and back.* ☎ *(027) 769 11 11; www.chatelard.net).* A little train runs from here to the base of the dam. A second funicular, known as "Le Minifunic",

then leads to the Gueulaz Pass (alt 1 970m/6 461ft). Inaugurated on the occasion of the 700th anniversary of the Swiss Confederation in 1991, this ingenious piece of engineering can rise to a height of 260m/854ft in 2min.

View★★

From the dam, there is a magnificent view of the Mont-Blanc Massif (right to left) from Aiguilles Rouges to the Mont Blanc, including Mont Maudit, Mont Blanc du Tacul, Aiguille du Midi, Aiguille du Dru, Aiguille Verte, the Aiguilles du Chardonnet and Argentière, Aiguille du Tour and Le Tour Glacier and Grands Glaciers.

Above the café-restaurant stands the modern Chapelle Notre Dame des Neiges (Chapel of Our Lady of Snow), whose interior features pretty stained-glass windows depicting Alpine flowers and animals.

The dam

Alt 1 850m/6 068ft. Open May-Oct (exterior). For further information, contact the Parc d'attractions on ☎ (027) 769 11 11.

The vaulted dam of Emosson rises to 180m/590ft just below the Gueulaz Pass (alt 1 970m/6 463ft). The reservoir has a capacity of 225 million m³/7 946 million cu ft and a surface area of 327ha/808 acres. It replaced the old Barberine dam which now lies 42m/138ft below the surface of the water when it is at its highest level. The water in the lake comes mostly from the Mont-Blanc Massif, on the other side of the valley. The sub-glacial water is collected at a higher altitude than the dam and is then transported here via underground tunnels and siphoned up to the lake.

The hydroelectric power station on the upper stage at Châtelard-Vallorcine is in French territory; the Swiss power station on the lower stage (la Bâtaz) lies on the floor of the Rhône Valley. Annual production of some 850 million kWh is shared between the two national electricity companies EDF (France) and ATEL (Switzerland).

Climbing the dam

In 1996, a climbing route was opened on the smooth side of the dam by climbers Marc Volorio, Paul Victor Amaudruz, Samuel Lugon Maulin and Thierry Amaudruz from the Valais region. This is the highest artificial climbing wall in the world, with two sloping sections, a vertical section and two final sections which curve back at 13m/42ft over a height of 60m/197ft. Around 600 synthetic resin footholds have been screwed into and stuck onto the concrete wall. This spectacular 150m/492ft route is very popular with experienced climbers.

Walks

Emosson Lakes★

3-4hr walk, there and back.

A wide paved path crosses the dam, leading to a route which follows the left bank of the **Lac d'Emosson**. The tranquil lake, surrounded by greenery and overlooked by the Cirque du Fer à Cheval in France, is almost Scandinavian in feel. The **Lac du Vieux Emosson** stands at the western end of the lake. The path climbs up to the Vieux Emosson Dam, where there is a snack bar. From here, there are fine views of the Cirque du Cheval Blanc (alt 2 831m/9 285ft) and the Pointe de Finive (2 625m/8 610ft).

In the footsteps of the dinosaurs★★

5-6hr walk, there and back. 🖐 *It is strictly forbidden to remove rocks or stones.*

Follow the left bank of the Lac d'Émosson (🕭 *see above*). At the end of the lake, a footpath signposted to Col de la Terrasse climbs up to this protected site (alt 2 400m/7 872ft) discovered on 23 August 1976 by the French geologist Georges Bronner. The site contains more than 800 fossilised dinosaur footprints, left over 250 million years ago, before the Alps even existed. The dinosaurs stood at a height of 3-4m/10-13ft and weighed several tons. They have left prints 10-20cm/4-8in long and 5cm/2in deep. The space between the prints shows that these animals had a stride of up to 2m/6ft.

Experienced walkers can continue towards the Crête de **la Veulade** (alt 2 491m/8 170ft). A path (🖐 *caution: there is sometimes snow here even in summer*) then heads down to the Gorges de la Veulade. Overlooked by the Grande Perche, the path leads to the Col du Passet and then heads back to the Barrage d'Émosson.

ENGADIN★★★

Engadine, traditionally approached by the High Road, presents a different landscape from that of the great, deep valleys of the Alps, where basins and gorges often alternate in a somewhat monotonous manner. Since the altitude averages 1 500m/4 900ft (1 800m/5 900ft in Upper Engadine) motorists travelling from the north through the Julier or Albula Pass will experience only a modest fall in ground level. As for motorists coming from Italy through the Maloja Pass, they drive into the cradle of the Upper Inn without any change of level.

In these conditions, the Engadine Mountains, despite their 4 000m/13 000ft height (Piz Bernina: 4 049m/13 284ft) look as though they have lost their lower slopes. They are admired mainly for the splendour of their glaciers. Besides the lovely landscapes, the main asset of this area is undoubtedly its continental mountain climate, almost entirely protected against disturbances from the sea. The weather is varied and characterised by clear skies, and dry, light breezes. The rarefied air causes radiant sunshine which, in winter, is intensified by the reflection of the snow, and the resort of Sankt Moritz has rightly adopted the sign of the sun as its logo.

From Sankt Moritz to Soglio *33km/21mi – about 1hr 30min*

Itinerary 4 (🕭 *see GRAUBÜNDEN map*)

Romansh in the Engadine

Both Italian and German are spoken in the Engadine Valley, in addition to **Romansh**, which was declared the fourth official language of the Swiss Confederation in 1938. Romansh, a Rheto-Romance language, is distantly related to French and Italian, and is spoken by 40 000 people in the Grisons. Here, the word for bread is *pan*, and child is *uffant*. Romansh developed as a result of the conquest of Rhaetia 2 500 years ago by the Roman legions of Tiberius and Drusus. Latin was mixed with the local languages, evolving into the Romansh dialects spoken today. There are two main dialects: *putèr* is spoken in the Upper Engadine Valley and *vallader* in the lower valley.

Sankt Moritz✳✳✳ – *1hr 30min.* 🔊 *See SANKT MORITZ.*

As you leave Sankt Moritz the snowy peaks of the Piz de la Margna puncuate the horizon.

Piz Corvatsch★★★

🚡Access by cable car in 16min; leave from Surlej (to the left of Lake Silvaplana which is reached by the causeway). 🕐 *Departure every 20min 8.10am (8.20am in winter) to 5pm Jul to mid-Oct and Dec-Apr.* 🚠*Fare there and back: 34CHF.* ☎ *(081) 838 73 73.*
The ride up to the mid-station of Murtel (alt 2 702m/8 865ft) offers views onto Lake Silvaplana and Lake Sils. The upper station is situated below the superb ski jump formed by the Piz Corvatsch (alt 3 451m/11 319ft). Go to the panoramic terrace, which commands a splendid **overall view**★★★ of the surrounding landscape. To the east you can see the glaciers of the Piz Tschierva, Morteratsch, Palü, Bernina, Scerscen and Roseg; you can just make out the Italian Ortier Massif in the far distance. To the northwest, one overlooks the Engadine Valley and its lakes, dominated by the Piz Lagrev, Julier, Bever and Ot. And in the background, one can make out the Säntis and, farther east, the Jungfraugruppe and the Sustenhorn.

The skiing area

Piz Corvatsch is the departure point for several splendid pistes boasting an excellent snow cover. Moderate slopes are perfect for intermediate skiers, who can feast their eyes on the breathtaking landscapes around them. The Hahnensee piste, the only really steep one, runs from Giand'Alva (2 643m/8 671ft) down to St-Moritz-Bad, ending in a forest. Two ski lifts leaving from Alp Margun above Surlej will take you to the Sils area, which offers some fine easy slopes, the highest point being Furtschellas (2 800m/9 185ft). There is a lovely route through the woods towards Sils. Unfortunately, the ski lifts are rather old and not too comfortable.

Walk to Piz Murtel★★★

Alt 3 433m/11 262ft. Enquire beforehand about conditions of access (ice and snow) and, if necessary, ask to be accompanied by a mountain guide. Go down all the steps until you reach the glacier. There is a steep walk in the snow for 45min to reach the top (🥾 *remember to bring stout mountain boots*).

Walk to Fuorcia Surlej★★

Alt 2 755m/9 038ft. This is an easy, gentle walk, leaving from the intermediate station of Murtel. From the pass, where a refuge has been set up, there is a lovely **view**★★ of the Bernina Massif. You can return to Surlej on foot *(2hr 30min)* via Hahnensee. This will take you along a rocky path affording a beautiful **panorama**★★★ of four lakes: Sils, Silvaplana, Champfer and Sankt Moritz.

Lucia Degonda / Switzerland Tourism

Lake Sils and Piz de la Margna

Walk to Chamanna Coaz refuge★★★

Alt 2 610m/8 562ft. Remember to bring stout shoes and a walking stick. Allow 5hr not including stops. The walk is exhausting, especially on the way down. Enquire beforehand about times of buses and carriages to get back to Surlej in the late afternoon. This is one of the most challenging and popular walks in the area, after you have climbed Piz Corvatsch and reached Fuorcia Surlej early in the morning.

Starting from the pass, the clearly signposted path follows the mountain slope, offering an increasingly stunning **view**★★★ of the glacial corrie coating the valley, dominated by Piz Roseg. After following the path, enhanced by burbling streams and waterfalls, for 2hr you will the refuge, nestled in a secluded **setting**★★ amid mountain tops. The Roseg and Sella Glaciers plunge down towards a vast white lake.

Retrace your steps and after about 15min bear right towards Pontresina (Puntraschigna). The 40min descent along a stony path towards Lake Vadret is very steep and trying. The impressive tongue of ice ending in the lake, dotted with ice floes, is a truly arresting sight. Continue following the stream and notice that the flora gradually becomes more lush: alpine meadows, mountain flowers, larch and pine trees. After 1hr 30min, you reach a hotel (alt. 2 000m/6 561ft) that marks the end of this wonderful outing. Do not miss the striking **panorama**★★★ of glaciers standing out against bursts of vegetation, basking in the glowing sunset. At the hotel, treat yourself to a carriage ride to Pontresina, then catch a bus back to Surlej.

The road runs along the foot of the slopes of the Upper Inn Valley and skirts **Lake Silvaplana**★★ and **Lake Sils**★★.

Sils★

This quiet, elegant resort in the Upper Engadine includes the two townships of Sils-Baselgia and **Sils-Maria**※, situated at the beginning of the Inn Valley in thickly wooded countryside. The two lakes and the soft lines of the landscape, both in the main valley and in the tributary **Fex Valley**, which is also very wide, contribute to the restful atmosphere of the resort. In spite of the large hotels of Sils-Maria, which stand out between the trees, across the way at the foot of the slope, visitors can take in a view to the south of the very wide glacier gap at the beginning of the Fex Valley from between the lakes. The German philosopher **Friedrich Nietzsche** (1844-

1900) spent seven summers here (1881-88) and found inspiration for many of his most famous works during his walks along the lakeshore. Photos, letters and other mementoes can be found in the house where he stayed, which has been converted into a museum and which stands near the Church of Sils-Maria.

Passo del Maloja

Alt 1 815m/5 955ft. The Maloja Pass, the lowest one between Switzerland and Italy, establishes the actual boundary of the Engadine and is the watershed between the Danube and the Italian sides of the Grisons. Downhill from the pass the **Val Bregaglia**★★ (Bergell) is the continuation of the Inn Valley. A series of hairpin bends leads you to Casaccia, which marks the junction with the old Septimer road from Bivio. Beyond rises the Piz Cacciabella, distinguished by its small rounded snowcap. Downhill from Löbbia, the **view**★ opens towards Stampa and Vicosoprano framed on the slope facing north by magnificent fir woods interspersed by pale green clumps of larches. The villages between Vicosoprano and Promontogno – including Stampa, Giacometti's native village – show the waning influence of the Engadine style (tall houses with deep, sunken windows, narrow, cobbled streets; and groups of little barns with rows of open gables). Even the Alpine flora gives way to chestnut groves, vineyards and orchards.

La Porta

This bottleneck in the valley, fortified since Roman times, marks the natural frontier between Alpine and southern Bergell. The Castelmur Keep stands on a spur above the Romanesque campanile of Nossa Donna. The former road, higher and still clearly visible, cut through the promontory more directly and passed through the former ramparts, substantial traces of which remain. Castelmur was the key to the Obere Strasse on the Italian side. Constant improvements to this road during the Middle Ages were heavily financed by the lords of the domain.

Soglio★★

Access by a narrow and very steep byroad.
The **site**★★ of this village is one of the most picturesque in the Bergell. It stands on a terrace surrounded by chestnut groves facing the rocky cirque that closes off the Bondasca Valley. The smooth slopes of the Pizzo Badile are among the most amazing in the Alps. Standing out against the houses which cluster around the church and its Italian-style campanile, the noble façades of several Salis palaces (one is now the Hotel Palazzo Salis) conjure memories of a Grisons family best known overseas, since many of its members made their career in the diplomatic service.

From Sankt Moritz to Martina 78km/49mi – about 3hr

Itinerary 4 (👣 *see GRAUBÜNDEN map*)

Sankt Moritz✳✳✳ – *1hr 30min.* 👣 *See SANKT MORITZ.*

After the wooded slope separating Sankt Moritz from Celerina, the road goes along the lower plateau of the Upper Engadine.

Celerina/Schlaringa – 👣 *See CELERINA.*

Zuoz★★ – 👣 *See ZUOZ.*

Between Punt Ota (the traditional boundary between Upper and Lower Engadine) and Zernez, the valley narrows and near Zernez the Piz Linard looms into sight.

Susch – ⬤ See DAVOS: Excursions.

Beyond Susch, after a widening of the valley, commanded from its terrace by the village of Guarda, the road runs through another narrow section where, in places, it overlooks the gushing waters of the torrent from a height of about 150m/500ft.

Guarda★

Excursion from Giarsun, 2.5km/1.5mi plus 30min sightseeing.
With its fountains, houses decorated with sgraffiti and family coats of arms over the doors, and its steep, narrow streets paved with cobblestones, Guarda is regarded as a typical village of the Lower Engadine. Notice the **Steinsberg Tower** standing upstream on a rocky hill, against which the white village of Ardez is built.

Ardez

This village at the foot of the Steinsberg is worth a stop for its painted houses with charming flower-decked oriel windows. The theme of Original Sin has enabled the decorator of the "Adam and Eve House" to paint a study of luxuriant foliage.
Between Ardez and Schuls the corniche road overlooks a third wooded defile, sinking finally towards its floor. From the start it offers a first glimpse of the proud **Schloss Tarasp** (Tarasp Castle). The many mountain crests of the Lower Engadine Dolomites (Piz Lischana and Piz St Chalambert Mountains) follow one another in the distance as far as the Swiss, Italian and Austrian frontier ridges.

Scuol/Schuls✳ – ⬤ See SCUOL/SCHULS.

Downhill from Schuls, the valley narrows between the crest line marking the Italian side on the right and the slopes streaked with torrents descending from the Silvretta Massif on the left. An itinerary towards the Dolomites to the south passes via the Reschenpass.

ENGELBERG✳✳

OBWALDEN – POPULATION 3 452
ALT 1 002M/3 287FT

Engelberg stands on a site which, although surrounded by heights, is nonetheless sunny. It is the great mountain resort of central Switzerland, engaged in both tourist and religious activities. A swimming pool, tea rooms, tennis courts, and a skating rink are found alongside one of the large, imposing Benedictine abbeys which lie concealed in the high valleys of Switzerland. 🛈 *Klosterstrasse 3 – 6390 – ☎ (041) 639 37 37*

The mountaineer has only to choose between the glacier formation of the Titlis and the jagged crests of the Spannörter and Uri Rotstock, whereas the walker, using the ski lifts which have made a reputation for local technology in the winter season, can easily reach attractive sites such as those of Trübsee and even the Titlis.

Sights

The skiing area

Engleberg-Titlis is the largest ski resort in Central Switzerland, with 82km/51mi of pistes for 26 ski lifts, including the famous rotating lift, Rotair, with skiing and snowboarding year-round (depending on conditions) on the glacier. The slopes are interesting because of the difference of height they offer, along with a wide choice of landscapes and pistes and vast snowfield on the Stotzig Egg. There is some 40km/25mi of loops for cross-country skiers in the direction of Trübsee.

Kloster

Guided tour of monastery (1hr) Tue-Sat, 10am and 4pm; monastery and exhibition hall (1hr 30min) Wed and Sat at 4pm. ☜6CHF (monastery), 8CHF (monastery and exhibition hall). ☎ (041) 639 61 19.

The monastery, founded in the 12C, ruled over the whole valley until the French invasion of 1798. Today most of the buildings are used as a religious college. One of the rooms displays an unusual collection of liturgical objects from the 11C to the 20C. The **church**, which also serves the parish, features the arrangement and decoration peculiar to the 18C Baroque School. The organ is one of the largest in Switzerland.

Excursions

Titlis★★★

Alt 3 239m/10 627ft. Allow 3hr there and back, preferably during the day, when you can combine the climb with a long walk. Remember to wear warm clothes, stout mountain shoes and a pair of sunglasses. ◷Operates Dec-Oct, 8.30am-4.50pm. ☜Fare there and back: 76CHF. ☎ (041) 639 50 50. ⚞A pivoting cable-car, the "Rotair" operates on the upper section between Strand and Titlis. The journey takes 5min. The rotation of the cabin gives passengers a spectacular panoramic view; there is a restaurant at the top.

The cable car service to Trübsee, split up into two journeys, commands overall **views**★ of Engelberg and its green pastures. Then take another cable car to Stand (2 450m/8 038ft): the splendid **views**★★ of Trübsee and the Titlis Glacier can be seen from above thanks to *Rotair*, an incredible cable car fitted with, revolving cabins (**views**★★ of Lake Engtsien). From the terrace (alt 3 020m/9 909ft) enjoy the breathtaking **panorama**★★★ of Sustenhorn dominating a rough mountain range, the steep rocks of Wendenstöcke and Reissand Nollend and, farther west, the Valais Alps (Dom) and the Bernese Oberland (Jungfrau). A number of curious sights will delight visitors: an ice grotto, a panoramic window hollowed out of the south slope, 45m/145ft beneath the ice.

You are advised to climb up to the viewpoint and its viewing table *(10min)*. A ski lift for children leads to a sledge piste. Experienced hikers who want a broader **bird's-eye view**★★★ should proceed to the summit *(40min)*, taking care to observe the safety rules. From Stand, there is a panoramic route that takes you back down to Trübsee *(1hr 15min)*, offering lovely **views**★★ of the valley, interspersed with explanatory panels about the geology of the area.

Trübsee★★

Alt 1 764m/5 786ft. ⚞Access in 5min after the second journey in cable car.

Lying at the foot of the Titlis Glacier framed by rocky summits, this is one of Europe's most beautiful mountain lakes. Go on a **tour of the lake**★★, proceeding towards the right (allow 1hr 10min) and appreciate the pretty path enhanced by clumps of spruce and rhododendron.

Joch Pass and Engstlensee★★

⚞About 40min by chair-lift there and back and a 1hr 30min walk.

Southwest of Trübsee, take the chair-lift to **Joch Pass**★★ (alt. 2 207m/7 241ft), where mountain bike trails have been laid out. Go down using another chair lift (access to a snowpark in winter) and you will discover the superb site of **Lake Engstlensee**★★, with Lake Tannen in the background. Go down towards the tip of the lake. If you undertake a long walk lasting a whole day, you may reach the twin lakes **Tannensee**★ and **Melchsee**★ (👣 *see MEIRINGEN*).

Fürenalp★★

Alt 1 850m/6 069ft. 🚠*Access by cable car. 3.5km/2.2mi E of Engelberg.*
The route leading to this rocky outcrop perched up high affords spectacular **views**★★ of the whole glacial cirque lining the valley, with its waterfalls, peaks and glaciers.

Walk to Stäfeli★★

1hr 45min on foot and 5min by cable car.
From Fürenalp, bear right onto a gently sloping path bordered by yellow gentian and herds of cows. Continue to walk straight on until you catch sight of Abnet village: proceed towards it bearing right. For a hair-raising experience, jump into the small cable car that will take you to Stäfeli, dropping by 300m/985ft amid sheer cliffs. You will eventually get back to your point of departure by a smooth path flanked by steep slopes, in an austere but verdant landscape cut across by a stream.

Brunnihütte★

Alt 1 860m/6 102ft. 🚠*Access by cable car, then by chair lift. Allow 1hr there and back.*
You will enjoy a **view**★ of the whole valley.

Walk to Rugghubelhütte★★

Alt 2 294m/7 526ft. Make your way down the right-hand path following the mountain slope, bordered with luxuriant alpine flora *(30min)*. Proceed straight until the refuge *(1hr 15min)*. The early part of the climb offers fantastic **views**★★ of the Titlis, Grosser Spannort and the massive Hahnen barrier. On reaching the top, enjoy views of Gemsispil, Reissend Nollen and the Bernese Alps in the distance. Continue for 100m/100yd beyond the refuge for a **sweeping panorama**★★ including the Griessenfirn Glacier and Wissigstock. Return the same way, then go towards Ristis *(2hr altogether)* by a good path in a charming bucolic **setting**★★. Finish the outing by cable car.

Schwand★

4km/2.5mi N – allow 1hr.
Schwand is approached by a steep, narrow road from where there are unencumbered views of the ring of mountains (you can turn below the chapel at Schwand). A fine Alpine beauty spot within sight of the Titlis.

ERLENBACH

BERN – POPULATION 1 668

Several **houses**★ of the most majestic Bernese type lend distinction to the entrance to this village on the Spiez side (👣 *see Introduction: Rural architecture*). From the central crossroads a curious covered wooden staircase leads to the terrace on which the church stands.

Stockhorn★★★

🚠 *Access by cable car (25min).* 🕐 *Operates May-Oct, 8.10am-5.40pm; Dec to mid-Mar, 11.10am (9.10am Sat-Sun)-5.10pm; mid-Mar to late Mar, Sat-Sun, 9.10am-5.10pm.* 🎫*43CHF there and back.* ☎ *(033) 681 21 81.*

From the top of Stockhorn (alt 2 190m/7 185ft) is one of the loveliest panoramas in the Oberland. You may even see the surefooted chamois near its peak. From Erlenbach to the mid-station of Chrindi (alt 1 637m/5 374ft), the cable car goes through a small, deep valley carved out by a torrent and lined with fir trees and chalets. Between Chrindi and the upper station (alt 2 139m/7 018ft) you fly over the lovely Stockensee, a pool of emerald green water *(angling)* occupying a glacial hollow. From the upper station, walk *(15min there and back)* to the summit of the Stockhorn *(viewing table below, south side)*, surrounded by grassy and wooded slopes, for the splendid **panorama**★★★: to the north, Thun and part of its lake; to their left, Lake Amsoldingen and Lake Allmendingen; to the south, Stockensee and on its right and higher up the smaller Oberstockensee; Erlenbach, between the Walpersbergfluh and Mieschfluh peaks; and all around, forming a majestic backdrop, the legendary white summits of the French and Swiss Alps from the Jungfrau to Mont Blanc.

ESTAVAYER-LE-LAC

FRIBOURG – POPULATION 4 156
ALT 454M/1 489FT

The little town of Estavayer is built on a hill overlooking the south shore of Lake Neuchâtel. It has preserved its medieval city look (ramparts, towers, old houses). Its pleasure-boat harbour makes it a popular resort among water-sports enthusiasts. 🛈 place du Midi – ☎ (026) 663 12 37, www.estavayer-le-lac.ch.

Église St-Laurent

A Late Gothic church crowned with a large square tower at the transept crossing. Inside, the **chancel** is embellished with fine 16C stalls and a painted and gilded high altar in the Baroque style, enclosed by an elaborate wrought-iron screen.

Museum

🕐 *Open Mar-Oct, 9-11am and 2-5pm; Nov-Feb, Sat-Sun only, 2-5pm.* 🕐 *Closed Mon Mar-Jun and Sep-Oct and public hols (except Easter Mon, Whit Mon and the Jeûne Fédéral day).*🎟 *4CHF.* ☎ *(026) 663 24 48.*
This stately mansion (1435) built in yellow sandstone and featuring tiered bay windows was once used to store the tithes contributed by the local population. At present it houses a Regional History Museum: remarkable collection of stuffed frogs parodying human scenes (a political gathering, a game of cards), impressive collections of weapons and early engravings, reconstruction of an old kitchen and its utensils, exhibition room devoted to railway transport (Swiss trains, lanterns).

WHERE TO STAY

🍽🛏**Hôtel du Lac** – *1 place du Port* – ☎ *026 663 52 20* – Fax *026 663 53 43* – *32 rooms.* Splendid location at the water's edge, offering lovely views of the lake and pleasure-boat harbour. On a fine day, settle in a deckchair and soak up the sun on the terrace.

EATING OUT

🍽**La Gerbe d'Or** – *5 rue Camus* – ☎ *026 663 11 81* – 🕐 *closed Sun and Mon (except Sun evening Jul-Aug), 26 Feb and 6 Mar.* Traditional cuisine with a large choice of dishes.

FLIMS⋇⋇

GRAUBÜNDEN – POPULATION 2 425
ALT 1 103M/3 618FT

The resort of Flims is divided into two sections: **Flims-Dorf**, the traditional residential section, whose mountain houses stand on open ground at the foot of the Flimserstein Cliffs (or Crap de Flem); and **Flims-Waldhaus**, where hotels are scattered over a forest of conifers on a low ridge connecting the Flem Valley to the basin in which the delightful Lake Cauma lies (beach with water warmed by underground hot springs).

Thickly wooded slopes which undulate between this point and the bottom of the Vorderrhein Gorges recalls the chaotic appearance of this area in prehistoric times, when an enormous landslide along the axis of the present Flem Valley blocked the Rhine Valley and forced the river to find a new course. The terraced site of Flims, its southern exposure and woods suitable for walking, make it much sought-after as a family resort, with many marked trails for hiking and biking enthusiasts, including some accessible by cable car. Swimming is another popular activity because of the proximity of Lake Cresta and Lake Cauma, whose shimmering waters remain beautifully warm all summer. However, the favourite season here is clearly winter, characterised by a lively, festive atmosphere and a majority of young visitors.

The skiing area

Commonly known as **Alpenarena**, it incorporates three resorts, Flims, Laax and Falera, and is said to be among the largest in Switzerland (220km/137mi of pistes and around 30 ski lifts). Spread out over 4 summits,including the Vorab Glacier, it features altitudes ranging from 1 100m/3 608ft to 3 000m/9 843ft. It is possible to move around by skiing along the many narrow tracks linking together the massifs. These pistes are particularly suitable for intermediate skiers (Crest da Tiarus and Crappa Spessa on Crap Masegn, Curtgani on Crap Sogn Gion and Naraus). Experienced skiers can tackle the few steep slopes such as Fatschas, Sattel, Alp Ruschein and Stretg (**views**★ from the forest). The area is s several snowparks and has become extremely popular with snowboarders; the towns of Flims and Laax host some of the most prestigious snowboard events in November and April.

Sights

Cassons Grat★★

Leave from Flims; ⛷ *the ascent takes 30min by chairlift and then by cable car.* 🕐 *Departures every 30min, 8.30am-5pm.* 🎫 *Fare there and back: 38CHF (summer), 59CHF (winter).* ☎ *(081) 927 70 01.*

The ride up in the chairlift, at least as far as the first station (Foppa: alt 1 424m/4 672ft), is enchanting; you look down on green pastures, luxurious Engadine chalets adorned with flowers, and spread out in the background are the two built-up areas of the resort. After Foppa the terrain becomes more desolate, however, a promising **view**★ develops – it is at its best at the second station (Naraus: alt 1 850m/6 070ft) – onto the shelf of Flims and the snowy ridges appearing in the distance. The cable car *(after change)* stops at Cassons (alt 2 637m/8 652ft) after having hugged the magnificent Flimserstein Cliffs. Go on foot *(15min there and back)* to Cassons Grat (alt 2 700m/8 858ft), where the Swiss flag flies; enjoy the superb **view**★★ south towards the Rhine Gap and the Grisons Alps, blocked to the north by ravine-like ridges.

Crap Masegn★

Leave from Murschetg (3.5km/2.3mi SW on the road to Oberalppass); ⛷ the ride takes 25min by cable car. 🕐 *Open daily, 8.30am-5pm. Departure every 15min.* 🚠*Fare there and back: 24CHF.* 🕐 *Does not operate mid-Apr to mid-Jun and mid-Oct to mid-Dec.* ☏ *(081) 927 70 01.*

During the ascent of the Vorab, a landscape of fir trees, chalets and grazing cows unfolds before you, but from the mid-station of Crap Sogn Gion (alt 2 213m/7 261ft) onwards the terrain becomes more barren. The **view**★ from the upper station of Crap Masegn (alt 2 472m/7 110ft) passes from the desolation of the surrounding peaks (Fil de Rueun, Vorab and Siala) to Flims below in the Vorderrhein Valley, the Rhine's main headstream. *A cable car continues up to the Vorab (alt 2 570m/8 432ft) and its glacier (summer skiing).*

Skiers may go right to the top (3 018m/9 902ft) in a ski lift and admire the sweeping **panorama**★★ of Alpenarena, Graubünden to the south and Glarus to the north.

ROUTE DE LA FORCLAZ★★

The convenience of a direct link between the resort of Chamonix and the great Valais road junction of Martigny makes the Forclaz Pass Road one of the great international routes of the Alps.

From Vallorcine to Martingny

▶ *26km/16mi – about 45min – tour of the Émosson Dam and trek to the Trient Glacier not included. The road is narrow between Vallorcine and the Swiss frontier. Customs controls at Le Châtelard. From Vallorcine (* 👣 *see The Green Guide French Alps) the road runs boldly through the Tête Noire defile.*

Défilé de la Tête Noire★

The most impressive section of this gorge is between the Roche Percée Tunnel and the hamlet of Tête-Noire. Note the picturesque village of Finhaut.

Barrage d'Émosson★★ – 👣 See Barrage d'ÉMOSSON.

To reach the pass the road then turns back into the high pastoral combe of Trient, fissured at the foot of the Trient and Grands Glaciers, which are separated by the Aiguille du Tour.

Col de la Forclaz

Alt 1 527m/5 010ft. To the south the view is cut off by the detached crests of the Aiguille du Tour (visible on the extreme left, above the Grands Glacier). To the north the snowy peaks of the Bernese Alps seldom emerge from the bluish mist which rises from the great Valais Depression on fine summer days. The rocky Pierre-Avoi Peak, between the valleys of the Rhône and the Drance, is easier to distinguish.

From the Forclaz Pass, many long signposted walks (*Information on trails is available from the Marécottes tourist office* ☏ *(027) 761 31 01*) are available in the midst of the Valais mountains to visitors keen on wild nature. One of these walks, leading to the **Trient Glacier**★ (*allow 3hr there and back, inaccessible in winter because of snow*) follows an outflow channel (natural duct draining glacier waters towards the valley) along the mountainside and through a forest of larch, spruce and arolla pines. The path offers an open view of the Grands Glaciers and Dzornevattaz Valley, and the Pétoudes d'En Haut and Herbagères pastures below the Balme Pass. The ascent towards the Trient Glacier is breathtaking. The tongue of snow – a massive powdery stretch which appears to have frozen in mid-air like a lava flow – sparkles with bluish tints as one gradually draws nearer.

Halfway up the mountain, enjoy a well-deserved break at the Trient refreshments stall: This former refuge, rebuilt after an avalanche in 1978, was used in the late 19C as accommodation for workers farming the ice for commercial use. From the pass to Martigny the view of the Martigny Basin and the gap formed by the Valais Rhône really opens out only 2.5km/1 1.5mi below the ridge. The rocky snag-like Pierre-Avoi is still prominent in the foreground; soon you will pick out the narrow furrow of the Drance forming a way through to the Great St Bernard. The site of Martigny and the La Bâtiaz Tower become visible where the road runs between vineyards.

Martigny – *1hr 30min.* 👣 *See MARTIGNY.*

LES FRANCHES MONTAGNES★

The high plateau of the Franches Montagnes (average altitude 1 000m/3 281ft) between the Doubs Valley and Mount Soleil Chain is one of the most original districts in the Swiss Jura. Its low houses, pastures dotted with fir trees and natural parks where bay horses and milch cows graze, are most attractive.

Tourism flourishes in winter because of the popularity of cross-country skiing. The chief town of the district is **Saignelégier**, well-known throughout the Jura for its August Horse Fair (👣 *see Calendar of Events*). Many fine trips can be made locally, especially to the **Corniche du Jura**★ (👣 *see below*) or in France, to the **Corniche de Goumois**★★ (👣 *see The Green Guide Burgundy Jura*). The latter is a particularly picturesque route, which for 3km/2mi offers superb views of the gorges below *(the best viewpoints have protective railings).*

Corniche du Jura★
Itinerary J (allow 30min – 👣 see Le JURA SUISSE: Tour).
At the foot of the Rangiers Sentinel (Sentinelle des Rangiers) branch off into the St-Brais road along the crest between the Doubs Valley and the Sorne or Delémont Valley; the latter is dotted with thriving industrial villages.
To see the floor of the Doubs Valley towards St-Ursanne, halt at the viewpoint 100m/328ft after passing under a electric cable.

Muriaux
2km/1mi SW of Saignelégier.
A striking building reminiscent of a 1930s factory houses the **Musée de l'Automobile**. (♿🕐 *Open Apr-Oct, 10am-noon and 1.30-5.30pm, Sun and public hols 10am-6pm; Nov-Mar, Sat, 1.30-5.30pm, Sun and public hols 10am-noon and 1.30-6pm.* 🕐 *Closed 1 Jan and 25 Dec.* 🎫*8.88CHF.* ☎ *(032) 951 10 40; www.musee-muriaux.ch).* Around 50 cars, in good working order, dating from the turn of the last century to the present, are displayed, with information on the technical characteristics of each. The most remarkable vehicles are a number of coupés and cabriolets: Zèbre 1913, Peugeot 402, AC Cobra 1966, an elegant Talbot Lago Record (1952) conceived by the Swiss bodywork specialist Graber, Rolls-Royce 20/25 from 1930 and a 12 cylinder 1931 Cadillac Fleetwood.

FRIBOURG★★

© FRIBOURG – POPULATION 34 217
ALT 640M/2 100FT
PLAN IN THE MICHELIN GUIDE SWITZERLAND

Fribourg is a remarkable **site**★★ on a rocky spur circled by a bend of the Sarine. The old quarters extend from the river to the upper town; bristling with church towers and monasteries, they still bear the appearance of a medieval city. Fribourg boasts many **sculpted fountains** gracing the squares and along the streets, built during the Middle Ages as outlets for the many springs which supplied the town with water. Later, in the 15C, they were adorned with elegantly chiselled basins and stone columns, the work of such renowned artists as Hans Geiler, Hans Gieng and Stephan Ammann. *1 avenue de la Gare – 1700 – ☎ (026) 350 11 11; www.fribourgtourism.ch.*

The deeply sunken course of the river still marks the boundary between the two great ethnic and linguistic communities of Switzerland: places on the west bank of the river carry French names, whereas the hamlets on the east bank are named in German. *Bolz*, a dialect which mixes the two languages, can be heard in the city. Every three years the city of Fribourg hosts an international exhibition of photography.

A Bit of History

From its foundations to the Reformation – In 1157 **Berchtold IV of Zähringen** founded Fribourg at a ford on the Sarine and made it a stronghold to command this important thoroughfare. After the Zähringen family died out, the town changed hands several times. It passed to the Kyburgs and then to the Habsburgs but finally preferred the rule of Savoy to that of Berne. Fribourg joined the Confederation in 1481 after having acquired extensive lands in the Vaud Country. Here the Reformation had no decisive influence and the Catholic Restoration inspired by Father Canisius reaffirmed the already deeply Catholic feelings of the town, which became the seat of the Bishopric of Lausanne, Geneva and Fribourg.

A bastion of Catholicism – In the 17C many religious orders were added to those already settled in Fribourg during the 13C: Franciscans, Jesuits and other communities made it the Catholic capital of Switzerland. Among the most famous and brilliant establishments were the College of St Michael, founded by the Jesuits, the Capuchin Church and Monastery, the Franciscan Monastery and the Monastery of Maigrauge, built by the Cistercians in the 13C.

The university – In 1889 the foundation of a Catholic state university gave a new impulse to the crucial role played by religious instruction in modern times. Fribourg University, one of the most prestigious seats of learning, still enjoys an excellent reputation in Switzerland and abroad. Its five faculties (theology, law, social and economic sciences, languages and natural science) and 15 independent institutes (computer technology, journalism etc.) welcome students from all over the world.

Overview★★ *30min by car*

Starting from place de l'Hôtel de Ville, cross the Zaehringen Bridge. From this great stone structure you can get a **view** down the deeply sunken course of the Sarine towards the small covered bridge, Pont de Berne, and the new Gottéron Bridge.

Address Book

SHOPPING

The main shopping streets are **boulevard de Pérolles,** from the train station to the jardin des Pérolles, **rue de Romont, rue St-Pierre** and **rue de Lausanne.** There is a **vegetable and flower market** on place Georges-Python every Wednesday morning and on place de l'Hôtel-de-Ville on Saturdays. Regional produce can be bought from **La Clef du Pays**, 4 route des Alpes.

THEATRE AND MUSIC

Aula Magna, avenue Louis Weck-Reynold.

Église St-Michel: classical music.

Centre Frison, route de la Fonderie: modern music.

Le Nouveau Monde, Arsenaux 12A: jazz, rock, salsa, reggae etc.

WHERE TO STAY

🍽️🍽️🍽️ **Hôtel Alpha** – 13 rue du Simplon (2nd floor) – ☎ 026 322 72 7 , www.alpha-hotel.ch– 27 rooms – 🕐 closed 24 Dec-2 Jan. Conveniently located 275m/300yd from the train station.

🍽️🍽️🍽️ **Hôtel de la Rose** – 1 rue de Morat – ☎ 026 351 01 01, www.hotelrose.ch – 40 rooms – Located a stone's throw from the Cathédrale Notre-Dame and the Église des Cordeliers.

🍽️🍽️🍽️🍽️ **Hôtel du Sauvage** – 12 Planche-Supérieure – ☎ 026 347 30 60 , www.hotel-sauvage.ch – 17 rooms – This hotel in the heart of the old city is easy to spot because of its sign. It offers a choice of different rooms, each with its own personality and charm.

EATING OUT

🍽️ **Buffet de la Gare CCF** – Place de la Gare – ☎ 026 322 28 16. Reasonably priced buffet cuisine.

🍽️🍽️ **Auberge du Chasseur** – 10 rue de Lausanne – ☎ 026 322 56 98 – 🕐 closed Mon. Try the delicious home-made fondues and raclettes.

🍽️🍽️🍽️🍽️ **La Cigogne** – 24 rue d'Or – ☎ 026 322 68 34 – 🕐 closed Sun and Mon and last two weeks Feb and first two weeks Sep, Bistro near Pont de Berne in the old district providing good, affordable cuisine.

🍽️🍽️ **L'Épée** – 39 Planche-Supérieure – ☎ 026 322 34 07 – 🕐 closed mid-Jul- to mid Aug, Mon evenings and Tue. Carefully prepared dishes at reasonable prices.

🍽️🍽️ **Grand Pont "La Tour Rouge"** – 2 route de Bourguillon – ☎ 026 481 32 48 – 🕐 closed Apr 8-23, Oct 14-29, Wed and Sun evenings. Traditional restaurant and brasserie (La Galerie). Terrace commanding nice views of the Sarine River and the old city.

🍽️🍽️🍽️ **Auberge de Zaehringen** – 13 rue de Zaehringen – ☎ 026 322 42 36 , www.auberge-de-zaehringen.ch– 🕐 closed Sun and Mon. Lovingly prepared cuisine in a delightful 13C setting, the oldest house in the city, overlooking the Sarine. Tourists may choose between the restaurant (La Galerie) and the more informal Brasserie. Splendid tapestries from the Gobelins workshops.

NIGHTLIFE

The **Rock Café** features rock 'n' roll music and decor: gold and platinum records and instruments which belonged to famous performers (Johnny Hallyday, Elton John etc).

Near pont de Zaehringen, in the street bearing the same name, the **Golden Gate** (enter through the Auberge de Zaehringen) offers a pleasant 13C setting (rough walls with pebble masonry, sturdy wooden beams and pillars).

In the vicinity of place de Notre-Dame: the **Gothard** (typical fondue from the Fribourg area) with its young, trendy crowd; **Les Arcades**, a more restful restaurant and bar; **La Cave** (basement dance hall situated below the Hôtel de la Rose) has a fine vaulted cellar with thick stone walls and opens its doors at 10pm, although the place livens up later in the night. **Paddy Reilly's**, an Irish pub, offers a remarkable choice of beers and live folk music on weekends, is the place to go, especially on St Patrick's Day, when the atmosphere is at its wildest. The **Baccara** nightclub in the **Hôtel au Parc** has a disc jockey.

Turn to the right onto route de Bourguillon, passing between the Red Tower (Tour Rouge) and the Cats' Tower (Tour des Chats), relics of the former ramparts.

From the Gottéron Bridge *(leave the car in the small parking area to the left just after the bridge)*, you can admire the beautiful **panorama**★★ of the roofs of Fribourg. About 600m/660yd after the bridge turn sharply to the right onto Beau Chemin and pass under the Bourguillon Gate (Porte de Bourguillon – 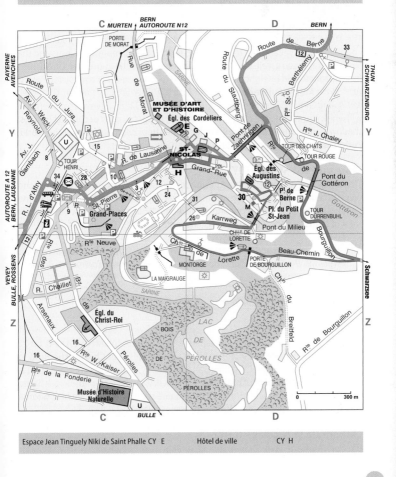 *traffic forbidden on Sundays*). The wooded land surrounding Loreto Chapel – a classical building inspired by the famous Italian sanctuary in the Marches region – offers several interesting **views**★ of the city and its natural site. A steep slope will take you down to the old town.

Old Town★ *allow 30min on foot*

▶ *Park your car before Berne Bridge (Pont de Berne) along chemin de la Patinoire.*

FRIBOURG					
Alpes, Rte des	CY 3	Hôpital, R. de l'	CY 15	Romont, R. de	CY 28
Europe, Av. de l'	CY 8	Industrie, R. de l'	CZ 16	Samaritaine, R. de la	DY 30
Gare, Av. de la	CY 9	Lausanne, R. de	CY	St-Jean, Pont de	DY 31
Georges-Python, Pl.	CY 10	Neuveville, R. de la	CY 24	Tavel, Rte de	DY 33
Grand-Fontaine, R. de la	CY 12	Pérolles, Bd de	CZ	Tivoli, Av. de	CY 34
		Planche Supérieure	DY 26		

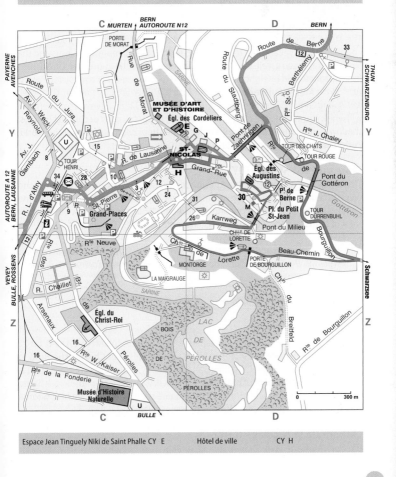

Espace Jean Tinguely Niki de Saint Phalle	CY E	Hôtel de ville	CY H

Pont de Berne (DY)
A charming wooden bridge with oak supports spans the River Sarine .

▶ *Start walking up rue d'Or.*

On the corner you will find the Auberge de la Cigogne (Storks' Inn), which was once a hostelry attached to the Augustinian convent. The façade features a Rococo mural representing a group of storks.

▶ *Turn right into rue des Augustins.*

Église des Augustins (DY)
The interior of the church, commissioned by the mendicant orders, presents a large nave divided into four bays, separated by Gothic arches resting on spherical pillars. The furnishings are characteristic of the Baroque period. The wooden retable surmounting the high altar – gilded and painted to resemble marble – is the work of Peter and Jacob Spring: three levels, two of which feature niches flanked by columns, portray religious scenes, mostly taken from the Life of the Virgin. The two retables placed at the entrance to the chancel were executed by the Ryeff workshops. The one on the right features an elegant polychrome composition, *Virgin and Child*. On the square is an annex to the church: a gallery with six arcades, supporting a first floor reinforced by half-timbering.

Rue de la Samaritaine
This steep, paved street will return you to place du Petit St-Jean. The Samaritans' Fountain (1551), yet another token of Hans Gieng's talent, represents Jesus and the Samaritan at Jacob's well. Level with the fountain, note the impressive Late Gothic façade, punctuated by eight picture windows embellished with Flamboyant tracery. At n° 34 the **Musée Suisse de la Marionnette** (Open daily, 10am-5pm. Closed Jan, during Carnival, Easter and 25 Dec. 5CHF. (026) 322 85 13; www.marionette.ch) will whisk you away to the magic world of dolls, puppets, paper or chiffon figurines, shadow pantomimes, masks and similar games from countries all over the world. Performances can be arranged on a regular basis.

Place du Petit-St-Jean (DY)
This square, located south of the Auge district, extends up to the Pont de Berne and owes its name to St-Jean-de-Jérusalem, a former Knights' Chapel built in the 13C and demolished in the 19C. The Fontaine de Ste-Anne (1560), a tribute to the city's patron saint of tanners, is the work of Hans Gieng; note the lovely façade at n° 29.

▶ *Go back to the car and drive to the new part of town via the Pont de Berne, rue des Forgerons, the Tour des Chats, the road to Stadtberg and the Zaehringen Bridge.*

New Town★ *2hr 30min*

Hôtel de Ville★ (CY H)
The town hall stands near a square famed for its lime tree, planted, it is said, on 22 June 1476 to celebrate the victory of the Confederates over **Charles the Bold** in Murten. This fine, early-16C building, and its canopy and double staircase (17C) is dominated by a large roof of brown tiles. The belfry and its Jack-o'-the-clock figure are crowned with pinnacle turrets. On the square stands the Fountain of St George (1525), featuring a group of sculptures by Hans Geiler.

Cathédrale St-Nicolas★ (CDY)
 Open Mon-Sat, 9am-5.45pm; Sun, 12.30-8pm.

The cathedral rears its fine Gothic tower above the roofs of the old town. The first stone was laid in 1283; the cathedreal was intended to take the place of the church built a century earlier by the founder of the town, Berchtold IV of Zähringen. began. The far end of the church was altered in the 17C by the rebuilding of an apse with three walls and five bays to replace the flat east end. The tower, 76m/250ft high, was built in the 14C, on the octagon completed c 1490 with a crown of pinnacles in the style of the period.

The **tympanum**★★ of the main porch, surmounted by a rose window, is devoted to the Last Judgement: Heaven and Hell are shown on either side of the Weighing of Souls; the archivolts portray the Angels, Prophets and Patriarchs; the doorway, the Apostles. The sculptures in the south porch date back to the 14C. Inside, a square vestibule is formed by the lower part of the tower, with side walls adorned with fine arcades, precedes the ogive-vaulted nave. Pictures from the 17C adorn the corner-pieces of the great arcades, which is surmounted by clerestory windows (the work of Alfred Manessier in 1983). The aisles, which also feature ogive vaulting, are lit by windows designed by the Polish painter Mehoffer.

The side chapels (16C and 17C) received Baroque altars in the mid-18C. The chancel, with a Gothic wrought-iron screen, is adorned with 15C **stalls**★ representing the Prophets and Apostles. A beam supports a large Calvary carved in the first half of the 15C. To the right, the Chapel of the Holy Sepulchre contains a fine **Entombment** (433) and more stained glass by Alfred Manessier. The late-15C font on the south side of the chancel is made of finely carved stone. Its wooden cover is 17C. The organ, which was one of the glories of Fribourg in the 19C, was built in 1834.

Musée d'Art et d'Histoire★ (CY)

&♿🕐 *Open daily except Mon, 11am-6pm (8pm Thu).* 🕐 *Closed 24-26, 31 Dec, 1 Jan.* 📞 *8CHF.* ☎ *(026) 305 51 40.*

The collections displayed in the Hôtel Ratzé, an elegant Renaissance building (16C), and in a former slaughterhouse converted in 1981, illustrate the art and history of Fribourg from its origins down to the present day. Many exhibits date back to the Middle Ages, a period rich in artistic events. Note the Late Gothic collections of remarkable works of art executed by local artists such as Martin Gramp, Hans Fries, Hans Gieng and Hans Geiler. Fries – the city's official poet from 1501 to 1510 – exerted a strong influence over his contemporaries and several of his works are on display. The 17C is present with works by Pierre Wuilleret and Jean-François Reyff, the 18C with paintings attributed to Gottfried Locher. In the room devoted to regional guilds and associations, a series of engravings and watercolours present the city of Fribourg and its canton. The artefacts displayed in the archeological section can be traced back to prehistoric times, ancient Rome and the early Middle Ages.

The stone museum set up in the former slaughterhouse features a fascinating collection of fourteen **15C stone statues**★ taken from the Cathedral of St Nicholas, depicting the Annunciation and the Apostles. Visitors may also admire a splendid 11C Crucifixion scene from Villars-les-Moines and a group of 16C sculptures attributed to Hans Gieng, contrasting sharply with the monumental compositions of Jean Tinguely. The rest of the exhibition consists of a rare collection of objects in silver and gold (14C-18C), some stunning pieces of Burgundian jewellery (7C-8C) and works by Marcello (the pseudonym of the native artist the Duchess Castiglione Colonna, née Adèle d'Affry), extremely popular during the last century. A number of 19C and 20C works, including several by Eugène Delacroix, Félix Vallotton and Ferdinand Hodler, are in the attic room above the former slaughterhouse.

Église des Cordelier (CDY)

A Franciscan community settled in Fribourg in 1256. The monastery buildings were completed about the end of the 13C and remodelled in the 18C. The monastery, which then had a superb bookbinding workshop and the richest library in town, received popes, cardinals, emperors and princes passing through Fribourg.

The first chapel on the right contains a gilded and carved wood **triptych**★ made in about 1513 for Jean de Furno, which shows Alsatian influence. The central panel depicts the Crucifixion, with Mary Magdalene at the foot of the Cross; the panel on the left shows the Adoration of the Shepherds, and that on the right, the Adoration of the Magi. The folding shutters on the left illustrate the Annunciation; those on the right present a pretty Coronation of the Virgin.

The **chancel** is a good example of 13C Franciscan architecture, with four keystones in the vaulting bearing the symbols of the Evangelists. It contains oak **stalls**★ dating from c 1280. On the left of the chancel is the altarpiece of St Anthony, known as *The Death of the Usurer*, painted in 1506 by the Fribourg artist Hans Fries. The picture illustrates the words of the Gospel: "Where a man's treasure is, there will his heart be too". Over the high altar stands the magnificent **altarpiece**★★ by the Masters of the Carnation, painted at Solothurn and Basel in 1480 by two artists who signed their works with red and white carnations. The picture is very large (8 x 2.7m/26 x 8.5ft) and was installed il during the restoration of 1936 replacing a 1692 Baroque altarpiece. The central scene represents a Crucifixion; it is flanked by four Franciscan saints: St Bernardine of Siena, St Anthony of Padua, St Francis of Assisi and St Louis, Bishop of Toulouse. The Adoration of the Shepherds is on the left shutter, that of the Magi on the right; the background suggests the Fribourg Alps. Folding shutters feature an Annunciation in their centre, St Elizabeth of Hungary, patroness of the Franciscan Third Order, on the right, and St Clara of Assisi on the left.

Espace Jean Tinguely - Niki de Saint-Phalle (CY E)

&♿⏰ *Open Wed-Sun, 11am-6pm (8pm Thu). ⬤6CHF. ☎ (026) 305 51 40, www.fr.ch.*
The former tram depot designed in 1900 by the Fribourg architect Léon Hertling has been converted into a vast gallery displaying the works of the famous artists Jean Tinguely and Niki de Saint-Phalle; and temporary exhibitions. Fronted by an

Jean Tinguely – Sculptor and Experimental Artist

Born in Fribourg in 1925, Jean Tinguely began studying painting at the Academy of Fine Arts in Basel. He soon found the courses too conventional and he moved to Paris in 1953. Throughout his life, his conception of art and his passion for games and movement – reflected in his "strange machines" – marked him as an eccentric endowed with a fervent imagination. Even his earliest creations, mobiles of geometrical figures, stood out from the work of his contemporaries. In 1959 his *Metamatics* could be seen as a reaction against abstract art. After producing compositions made of wire, sheet metal and cardboard boxes, he turned towards discarded objects like cogs and engine parts which he combined with wood and fabric to make frightening machines; he staged live "happenings" at which these contraptions would self-destruct. In 1960, when he presented his work *Tribute to New York* at the Museum of Modern Art of New York, the destruction of this extraordinary piece required the intervention of the local fire department.

Later, influenced by the principles of Nouveau Réalisme and by Dadaism and its principal exponents, Marcel Duchamp and Picabia, Tinguely broke with tradition by creating large, extravagant machines which showed a strong sense of humour. In 1983, in collaboration with Niki de Saint-Phalle, he produced the Stravinsky Fountain, a highly original and amusing structure commissioned by the City of Paris, which now stands in a small pond next to the Georges Pompidou Centre.

In later years, Tinguely's work took on sombre overtones, resulting in scenes verging on the macabre (his exhibitions in Venice in 1987 and at the Georges Pompidou Centre in Paris in 1988). "Death has visited me, Death has caressed me. I turned her threats into a celebration, a burlesque dialogue", the artist declared shortly before the end of his life. Jean Tinguely died in Bern on 30 August 1991. He was a major figure in contemporary sculpture who strongly influenced the artistic conceptions of his time.

imposing façade and decorated with neo-Baroque gables, the gallery permanently houses the Niki de Saint-Phalle donation. The artist (Jean Tinguely's wife, who died in 2002) conceived her *Monumental Relief* especially for this new cultural venue: a series of 22 brightly coloured tableaux evoking Jean Tinguely's stay in Fribourg (left-hand wall as you enter). In the middle of the room, the central sculpture, *Retable to Western Opulence and Totalitarian Mercantilism,* is one of the many large altarpieces that Tinguely started making in 1981. This huge machine, which grinds into motion at regular intervals, is decorated with toys and various objects symbolising the wealth of Western society. Visitors may also admire *Mythology Wounded*, a work jointly signed by both sculptors, as well as *The Avalanche* and *The Waterfall*.

Grand-Places (CY)

The ornamentation of the fountain was conceived and executed by the sculptor **Jean Tinguely**. The monument on the left commands a view of the rooftops of the old town, dominated by the Gothic tower of the Cathédrale St-Nicolas.

Musée d'Histoire Naturelle (CZ)

In the Faculty of Science on the route de Marly (not on the plan) via the boulevard de Pérolles. ♿🕐*Open daily 2-6pm.* 🕐 *Closed 1 Jan, Good Fri and 25 Dec. The museum closes at 4pm on 24 and 31 Dec.* ☜ *No charge.* ☎ *(026) 300 90 40.*

The Natural Science Museum occupies seven rooms on the first floor. The first rooms display fossils (geological and palaeontological sections), a relief model of the Aletsch Glacier and its region, and a splendid collection of minerals, along with a reconstruction of a crystal cave. The other rooms, impressive by their size, are devoted to zoology. Stuffed specimens of local fauna are presented in their natural setting and a diorama shows visitors a variety of bird species, complete with their recorded songs. Other displays include animals from the five continents, namely fish, reptiles, invertebrates and shellfish. The fascinating world of insects is given special attention: morphology, reproduction, evolution of the species, recorded stridulations of the grasshopper and cricket, and studies conducted under a microscope.

Excursions

Schwarzsee★

27km/17mi – about 1hr. Leave Fribourg by the road to Bourguillon (DZ) and then road N 74.

When you reach Tafers, turn right on to a picturesque road offering charming views towards the Berra on the right and towards the Guggershorn on the left.

After Plaffeien, a pretty village of varnished wooden chalets, the road climbs through the Sence Valley to end at the **Black Lake** (Schwarzee – *angling*) in a pretty mountain **setting**★. A pleasant resort has grown up beside the lake.

Barrage de Rossens★

Round tour of 55km/34mi. Leave Fribourg by road n° 12. After 13km/8mi take the Rossens road on the left.

A large dam was built across the Sarine in 1948, upstream from the village of Rossens. It is of the arched type, 320m/1 049ft long and 83m/272ft high. The 14km/8.5mi-long reservoir, forming a magnificent pool in a pretty, steep-sided setting, is known as **Lake Gruyères**. To enjoy a good view, follow the road on the right towards Pont-la-Ville. At La Roche take road n° 77 on the right and cross the lake at Corbières. At Riaz you rejoin road n° 12 to Fribourg.

Abbaye de Hauterive

7km/4mi SW of Fribourg by the road to Bulle (CZ). After 4.5km/3mi take the Marly-le-Grand exit and turn right. *Guided tour (1hr), Mon-Sat, 2-5pm, Sun and public hols, 10.45-11.30am.* *(026) 409 71 02.*

After Chesalles, a road on the left leads to the abbey, which stands in a loop of the Sarine. The Cistercian abbey, founded in 1138 by 12 French monks, was secularised in 1848 but resumed the life of prayer and work in 1939. It is the oldest remaining Cistercian abbey in Switzerland. Situated on the route to St-Jacques-de-Compostela, it extends hospitality to pilgrims or other travellers wishing to go into retreat.

The church, built in 1160, has undergone many alterations, especially in the 14C and 18C. It was furnished with stained-glass windows (14C and 15C) in the chancel with fine stalls with panels carved with human figures and crowned with open-work canopies, a 16C mural painting and in the north side aisle the recumbent figure of a knight whose feet rest on a lion. The monastery buildings were rebuilt in the 18C, with a Baroque façade. Inside, the main staircase is adorned with elegant wrought-iron balustrades. The Gothic **cloisters**, entirely remodelled in the 14C, are roofed with painted groined vaulting featuring finely carved keystones.

FURKASTRASSE★★★

THE FURKA ROAD

The view of the Rhône Glacier and the summits of the Bernese Oberland make this high-altitude itinerary unforgettable.

From Gletsch to Andermatt *32km/20mi – about 2hr 15min*

Itinerary (see BERNER OBERLAND map)

Gletsch★★ – *See GOMS.*

Leaving Gletsch, you will be charmed by the sight of the Rhône Glacier, which can be seen from the ledge to where it ends as a frozen cataract between rounded rocks.

Rhonegletscher★★ (Hôtel Belvédère) – *See GOMS.*

The road across the slopes reveals distant views of the Bernese and Valais Alps. To see the **panorama★★★** at its widest, stop near the fork of a small military road (*closed to traffic*) 1.5km/1mi before reaching the pass and walk a little way through the fields. You will see the snow-clad peaks of the Weisshorn and the Mischabel shining in line with the gap formed by the Conches Valley (*see GOMS*). Nearer, towards the Grimsel Pass, the barren sides of the great peaks loom above the 4 000m/13 123ft line of the Bernese Oberland.

Furkapass★★

Alt 2 431m/7 975ft. During the season of heavy snow, generally Nov-May, cars are transported by rail, from the stations at Oberwald or Realp. Departures every hour from 6am at Oberwald (6.30am at Realp) to 9pm at Oberwald (9.30pm at Realp). *30CHF includes car and passengers. Jun-Sep: 25CHF.*

Stop at the Hôtel Furkablick to admire the majestic Galenstock at close range. The **Furka Pass** is the highest shelf of the great longitudinal furrow that divides the Swiss Alps from Martigny to Chur. It is an essential route for tourist communications

Rhône Glacier

Bill Wassman / APA Publications

between Romansh Switzerland, the road junction of Andermatt and the Graubünden (Grisons). Since 1982 a railway tunnel through the pass has been opened linking Oberwald to Realp. The **steam train** linking Realp to Gletsch has resumed its services thanks to the relentless dedication of many volunteers. At present the 13.3km/8.12mi journey lasts for 1hr 35min but a final link-up with Oberwald will soon be completed. The steam engine, originally designed for the Furka Pass in 1913, was bought back from the Vietnamese authorities and has now been lovingly restored to give it a new lease on life.

From the pass to the Hôtel Galenstock, the road, after a long gentle slope above the deserted valley of Garschen, skirts the foothills of the Galenstock, the most familiar peak on the run. The **panorama**★★ opens out on the forbidding **Val d'Urseren**, with the three villages of Realp, Hospental (marked by an old watch tower and a church) and Andermatt. In line with them, in the background, you will see the zigzags of the Oberalp road. Andermatt is within easy reach.

Andermatt★ – *See ANDERMATT.*

GENÈVE★★★

GENEVA – Ⓒ GENÈVE – POPULATION 173 519
ALT 375M/1 227FT
PLAN IN THE MICHELIN GUIDE SWITZERLAND

An exceptional location makes Geneva one of Switzerland's most privileged cities; it is blessed with a mild climate and its natural environment is carefully protected to guarantee the best possible living conditions. The result is that, despite its cosmopolitan and international atmosphere and sprawling residential suburbs, Geneva retains the feel of a small and pleasant town. Geneva is the second seat of the United Nations (after New York) and houses the headquarters of several specialised UN agencies devoted to economic issues and social and humanitarian causes (disarmament etc), and international bodies such as the European Centre for Nuclear Research, the International Committee of the Red Cross and the International Labour Organisation. Clustering around its cathedral, remains the town of Calvin and the stronghold of the Reformation. The metropolis of French-speaking Switzerland, it is an intellectual city which has welcomed many naturalists and teachers. It is also known for its busy streets and shopping centres. A very Helvetian atmosphere of order and discipline binds these three Genevas into one. Visitors will be charmed by the opulent mansions, the harbour and its fountain, and the shimmering shores of the lake, set against a backdrop of lush vegetation and wooded mountains. 🅘 *Rue du Mont-Blanc 18 – 1211 –* ☎ *(022) 909 70 70, www.geneva-tourism.ch.*

▶ **Orient Yourself:** The city nestles around the southwest corner of Lac Leman, much of which is bordered by broad pedestrian walkways.

🅿 **Parking:** There is a fine network of public transportation in the centre city and neighboring towns (Montreux, Vevey).

🆚 **Don't Miss:** The *Jet d'Eau* (Water Fountain), a man-made geyser that sends up a 400-foot fountain over the lake, the city's symbol.

Geneva and the Jet d'Eau

Lucia Degonda / Switzerland Tourism

Address Book

TRANSPORT

PUBLIC TRANSPORT

The public transport company Transports Publics Genevois (TPG) operates the city's tram, bus and trolleybus network. The city is divided into zones (zone 10 is the city centre; zones 21, 31 and 41 cover the suburbs; while zones 51, 61 and 71 are in France). The lines serving zone 10 are numbered (1, 2, 3 etc), those serving zones 21, 31, 41, 61 and 71 are identified by letters (A, B, C etc), and line 51 is operated by Transports Annemassiens Collectifs (TAC).

Information and tickets are available from TPG agents at Cornavin Railway Station, Rond-Point de Rive and Bachet de Pesay. The main ticket office can be contacted at ☎ 022 308 34 34 (Mon-Fri). Tickets and day passes can also be purchased from automatic ticket machines at bus stops in zone 10, as well as from licensed vendors around the city.

A day pass is 6CHF for one zone (eg zone 10) and 12CHF for more than one zone.

BOATS

The two banks of the lake are connected by boat, with departures every 10min from 9am-7pm. Line M1 operates between Pâquis and Molard, and M2 from Pâquis to Eaux-Vives.

SHOPPING

The main shopping areas, with a huge range of stores to suit all tastes and budgets, are in the following streets:

NORTH BANK - Quai des Bergues, quai du Mont-Blanc and rue du Mont-Blanc.

Department store: Manor (6 rue Cornavin).

SOUTH BANK - Rue du Rhône, rue de la Confédération, rue du Marché, galerie Jean-Malbuisson, rue Neuve du Molard, rue de la Croix-d'Or (which includes the Confédération Centre shopping mall), rue de Rive, cours de Rive and rue de la Corraterie.

Department store: **Globus** (48 rue du Rhône and rue de la Confédération).

MARKETS

Geneva has several colourful local markets, offering visitors the chance to soak up te atmosphere of the city.

NORTH BANK

Place de la Navigation – Tue and Fri, 8am-1pm: fruit and vegetables.

Place de Grenus – Sat, 8am-1.30pm: fruit and vegetables.

SOUTH BANK

Plaine de Plainpalais – Geneva's largest markets are held in this square. Tue and Fri, 8am-1pm; Sun, 8am-6pm: fruit and vegetables. Wed and Sat, 8am-5pm: flea market; wide selection of antique and second-hand goods.

Boulevard Helvétique – Wed, 8am-1pm; Sat, 8am-1.30pm: fruit and vegetables.

Place de la Fusterie – Wed and Sat, 8am-6.45pm: fruit and vegetables. Thu, 8am-7pm: handicrafts. Fri, 8am-6.45pm: second-hand books.

Place du Molard – A flower market is held in this square almost every day.

THEATRE AND MUSIC

Grand Théâtre – *5 place Neuve – ☎ 022 418 30 00. Reservations ☎ 022 418 31 30, www.genevaopera.ch.* Modeled after the Paris Opera, this well-known theatre hosts performances of opera, ballet and music.

Bâtiment des Forces Motrices – *2 place des Volontaires – ☎ 022 322 12 20. www.bfm.ch.* An annex to the Grand Théâtre, this is a venue for plays, opera and conferences. Excellent acoustics.

Comédie de Genève – *6 boulevard des Philosophes – ☎ 022 320 50 01, www.comedie.ch.* Contemporary and classical drama.

Les Salons – *6 rue Bartholoni – ☎ 022 807 06 30. Reservations ☎ 022 807 06 33, www.les-salons.ch.* Musical performances and plays by modern authors.

Théâtre le Poche – *7 rue du Cheval-Blanc – ☎ 022 310 37 59, www.lepoche.ch.* This small theatre in the old town has developed a reputation for its contemporary works, with a focus on experimental drama.

Casino-Théâtre – *42 rue de Carouge – ☎ 022 839-21 02, www.theatre-confiture.ch.* Satirical reviews, operetta and variety shows.

Forum Meyrin – *1 place des Cinq-Continents, Meyrin – ☎ 022 989 34 34.* The theatre's varied programme includes drama, dance and classical and modern music.

Théâtre de Carouge – *39 rue Ancienne, Carouge – ☎ 022 343 43 43 – www.theatredecarouge-geneve.ch.* This renowned theatre offers a varied international programme of drama, with works by classical and modern playwrights, including Racine, Molière, André Roussin, Chekhov, Goldoni and Pirandello.

Victoria Hall – *14 rue du Général-Dufour – ☎ 022 328 35 73;* ⏱ *closed for refurbishment until Jan 2007.* For over a century this impressive auditorium with its superb acoustics has hosted classical concerts by the Orchestre de la Suisse Romande and visiting orchestras, performing many traditional favourites.

Conservatoire de Musique – *Place Neuve – ☎ 022 319 60 60 – www.cmusge.ch .* Classical music concerts performed by renowned soloists.

FOR CHILDREN

Les Marionnettes de Genève – *3 rue Rodo – ☎ 022 418 47 77 – www.marionnettes.ch.* This puppet-theatre group presents works by the Grimm Brothers, Russian fairy tales and contemporary stories written by the group. Not to be missed by children of any age.

Am Stram Gram – *56 route de Frontenex – ☎ 022 735 79 24 – www.amstramgram.ch.* Traditional favourites for children and parents alike. The repertoire includes Beauty and the Beast, Peter Pan and Robinson Crusoe.

⛏ *For coin ranges, see Legend on the cover flap.*

WHERE TO STAY

⛾ **City Hostel Geneva** – *2 rue Ferrier – ☎ 022 901 15 00 – www.cityhostel.ch– 57 rooms (dormitory style and private).* This hostel is in a good location, just five minutes' walk from Cornavin railway station. Each room has a washbasin; toilets and showers are on the landing. Kitchen available for guest use. A good address for those on a tight budget.

⛾ **Luserna** – *12 avenue Luserna – ☎ 022 345 46 76 – www.hotel-luserna.ch – 33 rooms –* Situated in a quiet residential district, this small, simple hotel was built at the beginning of the 20C. The hotel has a large garden, overlooked by the guest rooms. The least expensive rooms have a washbasin, but no toilet or shower.

⛾⛾ **Les Tourelles** – *2 boulevard James-Fazy – ☎ 022 732 44 23 – www.lestourelles.ch – 23 rooms –*Excellent value given its location on the banks of the Rhône. Simple rooms which are refurbished regularly.

⛾⛾ **Bel'Espérance** – *1 rue de la Vallée – ☎ 022 818 37 37 – www.hotel-bel-esperance.ch – 39 rooms –* Traditional establishment with an interesting location half way between the old city and the shores of Lake Geneva.

⛾⛾⛾ **Le Montbrillant** – *2 rue de Montbrillant – ☎ 022 733 77 84 – www.montbrillant.ch – 82 rooms –* A comfortable hotel in a 19C building directly behind Cornavin station. The rooms are soundproofed; those on the top floor decorated with wood panelling. No parking facilities.

⛾⛾⛾ **Mon Repos** – *131 rue de Lausanne – ☎ 022 909 39 09 – www.hmrge.ch – 85 rooms –* Cosy, traditional hotel near Lake Geneva, standing opposite the Mon Repos park. Convenient location near UN headquarters and other international organisations.

⛾⛾⛾ **Strasbourg** – *10 rue Pradier – ☎ 022 906 58 00 – www.hotel-strasbourg-geneva.ch – 51 rooms –* Comfortable hotel at the top of rue du Mont-Blanc near the railway station but away from the bustling Place Cornavin and rue des Alpes, a one-way street which channels traffic from the lake shores towards the station.

⛾⛾⛾⛾ **Du Midi** – *4 place Chevelu – ☎ 022 544 15 00 – www.hoteldu-midi.ch – 89 rooms –* Just off quai des Bergues, surrounded by lively narrow streets, this is an ideal starting-point for visiting the old quarter and the right bank of the city.

⊜⊜🖥 **Suisse** – 10 place Cornavin – ☎ 022 732 66 30 – www.hotel-suisse. ch – 57 rooms – Facing the station, on the corner of rue du Mont-Blanc and its pedestrian zone. At the end of this main street lie the harbour, the landing-stages and, on the left bank, the old city. Restaurant with flower-decked terrace.

⊜⊜🖥 **Cornavin** – 23 boulevard James-Fazy – ☎ 022 716 12 12 – 162 rooms – Completely renovated and modernised in 1999; upper floors have beautiful views of the lake. Rooms are spacious and soundproofed, with cherry-wood furniture and light, airy bathrooms. Note the unusual 30m/98fthigh clock, whose clockface is on the 8th floor. The panoramic breakfast room is on the same floor.

⊜⊜🖥 **La Cigogne** – 17 place Longemalle – ☎ 022 818 40 40; www. relais-chateau.com – Fax 022 818 40 50 – 47 rooms – Luxury hotel at the heart of the old city offering excellent service with a personal touch. Cosy rooms with quality furniture and original decoration. Quiet, peaceful atmosphere.

⊜⊜🖥 **Les Armures** – 1 rue du Puits-Saint-Pierre – ☎ 022 310 91 72 – www.hotel-les-armures.ch - 28 rooms – Sophisticated 17C hotel with great charm close to the Cathédrale Saint-Pierre. An unforgettable experience.

EATING OUT

At lunchtime, many restaurants offer reasonably priced menus or "plats du jour" (dishes of the day), which include a main dish and a salad, for around 20CHF. À la carte dinner with good wine can easily cost around 70-80CHF.

⊜ **Globus** – 48 rue du Rhône. ⏲ Department store restaurant open Mon-Sat lunchtime. Good food at reasonable prices. Fresh ingredients, served buffet-style, and hot dishes cooked to order.

⊜⊜ **Aux Halles de l'Île** – 1 place de l'Île – ☎ 022 311 52 21. Situated on an island in the middle of the River Rhône. Very popular at lunchtime, with its magnificent panoramic dining room

overlooking the river. The restaurant serves simple, traditional cuisine and offers a number of different menus. Jazz some nights of the week.

⊜⊜ **Le Vallon** – 182 route de Florissant – ☎ 022 347 11 04 – ⏲ closed 23 Dec-3 Jan, last two weeks Apr, mid- Jun to mid-Jul, and Sat and Sun. A small restaurant with informal decor situated at Conches 5km/3mi southeast of Geneva.

⊜⊜🖥 **Café Papon** – Old town. 1 rue Henry-Fazy – ☎ 022 311 54 28 – ⏲ closed Sat lunchtime in winter, and Sun. In part of the historical building housing the town hall and gives onto a pretty, shaded square. Rustic dining hall with bare stone walls and undeniable charm. The clientele includes local politicians.

⊜⊜🖥 **Le Lacustre** – Quai du Général-Guisan – ☎ 022 312 21 13. ⛔ Closed for renovation. Opposite the Île Jean-Jacques Rousseau on the south bank of the Rhône, this restaurant has an attractive outdoor terrace for the summer months. Brasserie-style decor in the dining room. Try the fillets of perch, served with different sauces.

⊜⊜🖥🖥 **La Favola** – Old town. 15 rue Jean-Calvin. ⏲ closed 1-15 Aug, Sat lunchtime and Sun. Booking recommended. ☎ 022 311 74 37. This attractive restaurant is in a 17C building with a wooden façade. One dining room is on on the ground floor and one on the first floor, linked by a narrow spiral staircase. The restaurant serves well-presented, inventive cuisine from Ticino.

IN CAROUGE

⊜⊜ **La Bourse** – 7 place du Marché. ☎ 022 342 04 66. This restaurant serves traditional cuisine on the ground floor and pizzas and meat pierrades in the vaulted basement.

⊜⊜ **Café Les Négociants** – 29 rue de la Filature – ☎ 022 300 31 30 – ⏲ closed Tue. Good food at reasonable prices. Customers can select wine directly from the wine cellar, or order by the glass.

⊜⊜🖥 **L'Ange du Dix Vins** – 31 rue Jacques-Dalphin – ☎ 022 342 03 18 – ⏲ closed 21-30 Apr, 29 Jul to 20 Aug, Christmas and New Year. Two dining rooms, one of which is bistro-style.

Good service and fine cuisine, including some delicious desserts.

NIGHTLIFE

At night, the neighbourhood between Cornavin station and Les Pâquis is always bustling with people on account of the many cinemas, bars, pubs and restaurants, mainly serving exotic food.

The **Les Brasseurs** (place Cornavin) micro-brewery produces its own beer on the premises, and has a brewing room and fermentation vats. If there are several of you and you manage to get a seat, it's worth ordering a *colonne* of beer, which comes in either 3-litre or 5-litre measures. Three types of beer are on offer: *blonde, blanche* and *ambrée.*

The **Casino de Paris** on Quai du Mont-Blanc is known to attract a lively crowd. If you prefer the tango, cha-cha or the waltz, visit to the **Palais Mascotte** (rue de Bern) after 10pm.

In the old district, centered around Place du Bourg-de-Four, the **Mortimer** is an unusual place with its collection of advertising posters, its early gadgets and its splendid zinc counter. In summer, enjoy a drink on the terrace of the **Clémence** (fountain and huge chessboard).

For Irish beer and ambience, try the busy **Flanagan's Irish Pub** (4 rue du Cheval Blanc), which often hosts live music. The fashionable **Demi-Lune** café (3 rue Étienne-Dumont) attracts an international clientèle, especially late in the evening. Decor is traditional, in keeping with its location in the old town, and the atmosphere jazz-inspired. A range of snacks, including tapas, salads and hamburgers, are served until 11.30pm.

There are also several smart cinemas and establishments around place du Molard, popular at aperitif time or later in the evening. These include the **Brasserie Lipp** (8 rue de la Confédération), the antechamber of world finance and trade.

Many of the stylish cafés in the Eaux-Vives quarter are patronised by foreign dignitaries or executives. **La Coupole** (116 rue du Rhône) features two types of atmosphere, depending on your mood. For an aperitif or after-dinner drink, the comfortable **Café or American Bar** has a large choice of alcoholic and non-alcoholic cocktails, and a wide selection of fine whiskies. If you feel like dancing, climb the stairs to the café's nightclub, **Le Dancing**. L'**Opéra Bouffe,** in avenue de Frontenex, is a favourite haunt among artists, journalists and intellectuals, with opera music playing in the background.

OUTSIDE GENEVA

Head out on the Thonon road to Vésenaz, where you can't miss **Le Trois-Huit** café on the side of the road. With their leather armchairs and sofas, the **Night Café** and **Bibliothèque** (open 7pm-5am) have a cosy, almost British ambience. From 10pm, the Night Café alternates as a piano-bar and disco-bar with a live DJ; on Sunday afternoons it holds tea dances. The **Bibliothèque** (lined with bookshelves, as the name suggests), is quieter and more suited to a drink and a chat. The café has a good choice of drinks, with over 70 different types of blended and pure malt whiskies.

In France, in **St-Julien-en-Genevois** (going southbound along motorway A 40 then N 201 in the direction of Annecy), the **Macumba** is a the largest nightclub complex in Europe, with 17 themed club rooms and 7 restaurants (*tel. 33 4 5049 2350, www.macumba. net*). The nightclub is very popular on Saturdays, with people coming here from miles around. Eat at the **Grill, La mère Marie** and the **Spaghetti Bar,** before hitting the dance floor. Choose between the **Club Tropical** (salsa, Caribbean and reggae), the **Macumba** (techno), the **Empire** (rock and disco), the **Bal** (accordion music), the **Irish Pub** (karaoke), the **Club 30/40** (American music), and **Roger's Club,** (variety music with a band).

🕐 **Organizing Your Time:** At least 3 days for the city and its museums, excursions to nearby vineyards and summits, and a lake cruise.

Kids **Especially for Kids:** the Natural History Museum, with dinosaurs, reptiles and minerals.

A Bit of History

2000 Years of History – The first settlement here dates from around 3000BC. It became a Roman city when Julius Caesar drove off an attack by the Helveti and its strategic location on the banks of the Rhône caused the city to be conquered by reconquered repeatedly, by Burgundians, Francs, Merovingians, Carolingians, and in 1032, Germanic emperors; all this time the city was ruled by its bishops. Geneva developed into an important commercial center in the Middle Ages, but its independence was threatened by Savoy, whose princes tried unsuccessfully from the 13C-15C to control it. The city's autonomy was saved in the early 16C by the intervention of the Swiss cantons of Fribourg and Bern, and Geneva became a republic in 1535. Geneva's coat of arms reflects its status until then as an Imperial town (half-eagle) and a bishopric (symbolised by a golden key).

The Town of Calvin – From 1532 onwards reform was preached successfully in Geneva by French humanists. Shortly after Calvin settled in the town (1536), he dictated laws, decreed laws, built new ramparts, welcomed Marot, Theodore Beza and others and sentenced the Spanish doctor Miguel Serveto to be burnt at the stake for his religious opinions. Meanwhile, the dukes of Savoy could not resign themselves to the loss of their state's leading city, and in 1602, Charles-Emmanuel delivered an unexpected night attack on Geneva. This was the famous unsuccesful attempt at scaling the rampart walls *(L'Escalade)*, which the Genevese still commemorate annually (🕐 *see Calendar of Events)*. The first flood of Protestant refugees to Geneva in the mid-16C followed by second wave at the end of the 17C fleeing Louis XIV's persecution of Protestants in France turned the city into a beacon of faith and learning.

Geneva, Capital of the Mind – Intellectual life flourished in the 18C: Jean-Jacques Rousseau, Mme d'Epinay, the banker Necker and his daughter Germaine (the future Mme de Staël), Dr Tronchin, the mountaineer and man of science, De Saussure, the painter Liotard and Voltaire were citizens of Geneva by birth or by adoption. Diderot and D'Alembert had several volumes of their controversial 18C French encyclopaedia, *L'Encyclopédie*, printed here from 1777 to 1779. The city was annexed by France in 1798 and for 16 years the town was the capital of the French *département* of Léman. It joined the Swiss Confederation, after the collapse of the Napoleonic Empire, in 1815, when the unification treaty was signed. In 1846, a revolution led by James Fazy overthrew the government of the Reforation and established the constition that is still in force today. Geneva's tradition of intellectual and religious freedom set the stage for its becoming an international city: Henri Dunant (1828-1910) had governments sign the Geneva Convention in 1863, limiting the effects of war, which led to the creation of the International Red Cross and cemented the city's reputation of a center of peace and humanism and commerce, including watch-making.

Harbour and Lake Shores★★ *3hr*

🚶 *Walking tours at 10am every Sat. Cultural tours mid-June to Sep, daily except Sun at 10am; tour varies depending on the guide. For information, call ☎ (022) 909 70 30.*
One of the most famous landmarks of Geneva is the harbour and its magnificent **Jet d'Eau**, whose great white plume marks the city from afar. It is now the emblem of

GENÈVE

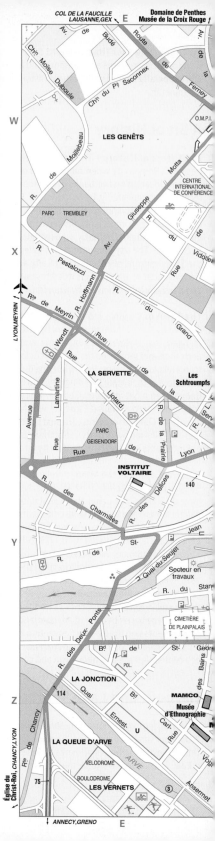

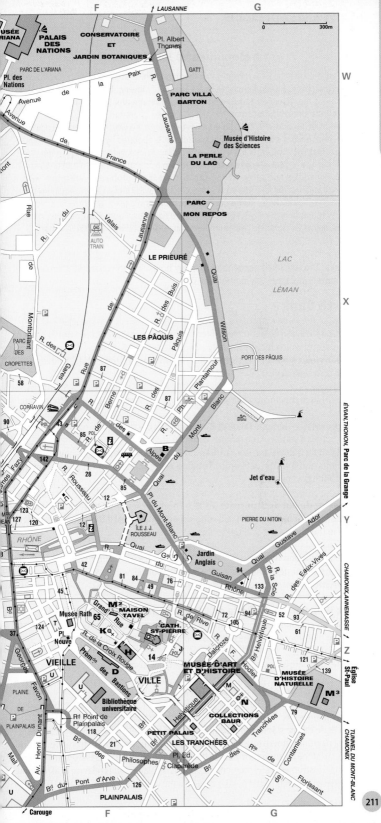

A Monumental Jet of Water

Most big cities boast a recognisable landmark which identify it: the Eiffel Tower in Paris, London's Big Ben, New York's Statue of Liberty, Rome' Colosseum, Athens has the Acropolis and Geneva has…its monumental jet of water. It gushes not from the earth but from the lake at a speed of around 200kph/125mph to a height of 140m/460ft. This gigantic white column, on which the Genevese pride themselves and which tourists flock to admire, is operated by a powerful pumping system driven by electrical engines which draw in lake water and shoot it into the air at a rate of 500l a second. The water falls in a fine spray which, if a strong wind is blowing, can take tourists by surprise! To avoid any problems, particularly with boats crossing the lake, the jet is subject to strict wind and weather regulations. A meteorological centre inside the machine room and a team of technicians are on duty to monitor the city's symbol. The *Jet d'Eau* is traditionally turned on on the first day of the Salon de l'automobile in March, and operates until 31 October.

Geneva. The lake itself, teaming with many boats, including paddle steamers and the famous *mouettes*, is a memorable sight.

North Bank

Take a walk along Quai du Mont-Blanc, which runs parallel to the north bank of the lake and which features stately mansions decked with flags. The route offers distant **views**★★★ of the surrounding mountains (Voirons, Môle, Salève, Mont Blanc on a clear day).

▶ *Start from the junction formed by the bridge, the street and Quai du Mont-Blanc.*

The prow of the **Île Jean-Jacques Rousseau** juts out downstream from the bridge. On it stands a statue of the famous writer.
The Quai du Mont-Blanc is a bustling centre of activity, frequented by both local residents and tourists, who enjoy strolling along the lake shores and visiting the cafés and souvenir shops.

Mausolée du Duc de Brunswick (FY B) – The mausoleum of Charles II of Brunswick (b 1804, d in Geneva in 1873), a distinguished benefactor of the town, was built in 1879 in the style of the Scaliger tombs in Verona.

▶ *Proceed along Quai Wilson, the continuation of Quai du Mont-Blanc, or go to the Débarcadère des Pâquis and use the "Mouettes Genevoises", a regular shuttle service linking several points of the harbour.*

Parc Villa Barton, La Perle du Lac and Parc Mon Repos★★ (GWX)
These three connected parks form the finest landscaped area in Geneva. There are elegant mansions within the gardens and around its permiter.

Farther on there is a good view of the **Little Lake** towards Lausanne.

Musée d'Histoire et des Sciences (GWX)
🕐 *Open daily except Tue, 10am-5pm.* 🕐 *Closed 1 Jan and 25 Dec.* ✍No charge.
☎ (022) 418 50 60.
In La Perle du Lac stands the stately Bartholoni Villa (1825), lavishly decorated with mural paintings, now a museum devoted to scientific equipment from the 18C and 19C. One of the rooms pays tribute to the Genevese physicist De Saussure (inventions, personal instruments and mementoes); others display exhibits relating to astronomy

(sundials, planetaries), navigation (sextants, compasses) and surveying (theodolites). Other historical medical artefacts include stethoscopes, portable first-aid kits), electricity and electromagnetism, meteorology (thermometers, barometers) and physics (models of steam engines, various measuring devices, including an acoustic spoon used for calculating the speed of sound crossing water).

Conservatoire et Jardin Botanique★ (FW)

🕐 *Open Apr-Oct, daily, 8am-7.30pm; Oct-Mar, daily, 9.30am-5pm. Greenhouses open daily except Fri, 9.30-11am and 2-4.30pm.* 🍽️ *Guided tour Tue at 12.30pm, May-Oct, by appointment.* 🎫*No charge.* ☎ *(022) 418 51 00, www.ville-ge.ch.*

This 17ha/42-acre garden is both a pleasant recreational spot and a living museum of the plant kingdom. It features a **rock garden★★**, where the different plants are divided into geographical groups, a deer pen and aviary, and a series of hothouses with a superb winter garden, containing many luxuriant species from both equatorial and tropical countries. Noticeboards direct visitors to the most interesting flower varieties. There are more than 16,000 plant species from around the world and the herbarium of 5.5 million samples makes it one of the five largest in the world.

South Bank

▶ *Start from Pont du Mont-Blanc*

The quays running along the south of the lake are flanked by lawns planted with trees and decorated with pretty flower beds.

Jardin Anglais (GY)

A floral clock dominates the part of the English garden which looks out onto Quai Général-Guisan. The clock consists of 6 500 different flowers and symbolises the expertise of Geneva's clockmaking industry. The terrace affords an interesting panorama of the harbour and, farther back, the Jura mountain range. For a good, close-up view of the fountain, situated at the end of the Jetée des Eaux-Vives, take a walk along Quai Gustave-Ador. There, an impressive collection of sailing boats are moored to an artificial marina, confirming Geneva's reputation as an important yachting harbour.

Parc de la Grange★ (GY)

It features the finest rose garden in Switzerland (flowering season mid-June) and, in the centre of the grounds, an elegant 18C residence.

Next to it lies the charming **Parc des Eaux-Vives★**.

The Last Days of Sissi

Elisabeth, Empress of Austria and Queen of Hungary, wife to Emperor Franz-Joseph, died in Geneva in 1898. Just as she was stepping onto a boat, Sissi, as she was affectionately known by the population, was stabbed in the heart by the Italian anarchist Luigi Lucheni. She staggered on board and then collapsed. She was rushed to the private suite which she occupied at the Hôtel Beau-Rivage, on Quai du Mont-Blanc, but died of her wounds soon afterwards. The 100th anniversary of her death was commemorated in Austria and Hungary and also in Geneva. The Hôtel Beau-Rivage organised an exhibition devoted to the sovereign including her poems, which she had bequeathed to Switzerland. A bust in her memory stands along the lake opposite the hotel.

Boat trips

Many choices are available to visitors, from a quick trip round the harbour to a grand tour of the lake. ⟲ *See Lac LÉMAN.*

Old Town ★ *1hr 30min*

(**H**) With its narrow cobbled streets, the old town is a labyrinth of architectural gems spanning the 12C-18C, and is dotted with fine restaurants and vibrant bistros and cafes.

Place Neuve
This large square, dominated by the bronze equestrian statue of General Dufour, a Swiss hero of the 19C, is surrounded by several stately buildings: the Academy of Music, founded in the 19C by Jean-François Bartholoni, the Grand Theatre (19C) and the Rath Museum.

Musée Rath
♿🕐 *Open daily except Mon, 10am-5pm, Wed noon-9pm.* 🕐 *Closed 1 Jan, 25 Dec and between temporary exhibitions.* 🎟*Between 5CHF and 10CHF (depending on exhibition).* ☎ *(022) 418 33 40, www.mah.ville-ge.ch.*
This museum, fronted by a portico, was built in the 19C in Greek classic style. It features temporary exhibits organised by the Art and History Museum. Special emphasis is placed on archeology and ancient art and on contemporary and modern art.

Promenade des Bastions
This public garden, laid out in the 18C, follows the former lines of fortification of the town. On the right, beyond the huge plane tree, stand the university buildings and library.

Monument de la Réformation★
This monumental wall (over 100m/329ft long) was built against a 16C rampart and kept deliberately plain. The great statues of the four Genevese reformers Farel, Calvin, Beza and Knox stand in the centre underneath the motto *Post Tenebras Lux.* The memorial (erected 1917) and its other statues and low reliefs with explanatory texts recall the origins of the Reformed Church and its repercussions in Europe. In front of it the arms of Geneva – bishop's key and imperial eagle – appear on the pavement between the Bear of Bern and the Lion of Scotland.

Bibliothèque Universitaire
🕐 *Open daily except Sun, 9am-noon and 2-6pm, Sat 9am-noon only.* 🕐 *Closed Easter, 1 May, Ascension, Whitsun, 2nd Thu in Sep and school hols.* ☎ *(022) 418 28 00.*
The Ami-Lullin library room is reserved for a permanent display of manuscripts, books and archives relating to the history of the Reformation and literary life in Geneva. The room named after **Jean-Jacques Rousseau** contains personal mementoes belonging to the writer (manuscripts, prints and a bust by Houdon).

▶ *Leave the Promenade des Bastions by the gate leading into rue St-Léger, opposite the Place Neuve. Then turn left and take the road which passes under the bridge.*

Place du Bourg-de-Four
This picturesque square, located in the heart of the old town, was used for markets and trade fairs during the Middle Ages. Some of the old buildings, many of which were inns, have kept their original signs. The fountain in the middle of the square is

decorated with flowers and surrounded by cafés, art galleries and antique shops. It is a favorite meeting point for the city's inhabitants.

▶ *Follow rue de l'Hôtel-de-Ville on the left, cross Place de la Taconnerie on the right.*

Cathédrale St-Pierre★

🕐 *Open Jun-Sep, daily, 9am-7pm, Sun and public hols, 11.30am-7pm; Oct-May, daily, 10am-noon and 2-5pm, Sun and public hols, 11.10am-12.30pm and 1.30-5pm.* ☎ *(022) 311 75 75.*

This vast cathedral, erected 12C-13C, partly rebuilt during the 15C, has been a Protestant church since 1536. It was given a surprising neo-Grecian façade in the 18C. The interior is plain but impressive. It was here that John Calvin preached his fierce, protesting sermons; you may see Calvin's seat, , 15C stalls and the tomb of the Duke de Rohan, who was the head of the Reformed Church in France during the reigns of Henri IV of Navarre and Louis XIII. The Chapelle St-Pierre or Chapelle des Macchabées opens out of the first bay in the south aisle. It is an elegant structure in the Flamboyant Gothic style, built by Cardinal de Brogny at the beginning of the 15C and heavily restored in the 19C in the neo-Gothic tradition after designs by the famous architect Viollet-le-Duc.

North Tower

🕐 *Same opening times as the cathedral (last admission 30min before closing time).* 🎫 *2CHF.*

The top of the tower commands a superb **panorama**★★ of Geneva, the lake, the Jura and the Alps.

▶ *Once out of the cathedral you come to the Cour St-Pierre.*

Archaeological site★

🕐 *Open Tue-Sun, 10am to 6pm. Last admission 30min before closing time.* 🕐 *Closed Mon except Easter and Whitsun.* 🎫*3.5CHF.* ☎ *(022) 311 75 75.*

In front of the west face of the Chapelle des Macchabées a staircase leads down to the archaeological site found under the present cathedral. A chronological itinerary leads the visitor through the excavations, some of which date back over 2 000 years. Eleven excavation zones have been marked out in the subsoil, with information panels in different colours representing different periods of history. A first church and baptistery were built in the late 4C and this site has been a major centre of Christian worship worship undergoing constant changes ever since: three episcopal churches and the baptistery were replaced by an imposing cathedral (c 1000) flanked by cloisters. Its walls were used as foundations for the present cathedral, whose construction began in 1160.

Cross Cour St-Pierre and turn right into rue du Soleil-Levant. On the corner of the street stands a bronze statue of the Prophet Jeremiah, executed by Rodo.

▶ *Rue du Soleil-Levant leads into rue du Puits-St-Pierre.*

Maison Tavel★

♿ ⏱ *Open daily except Mon, 10am-5pm.* 🚫*Closed 1 Jan and 25 Dec.* 🎫*Temporary exhibition: 3CHF.* 🔊 *For guided tours, contact* ☎ *(022) 418 37 00.*

This house is the oldest in Geneva. After the great fire of 1334 – which ravaged more than half the town – it was rebuilt and gradually acquired its present appearance. Its elegant stone façade, broken by three rows of picture windows and flanked by a turret at one corner, features amusing stone effigies representing heads of animals and human beings. A niche above one of the windows on the first floor carries the sculpted coat of arms of the Tavel family, a branch of the Genevese aristocracy who gave their name to the house. Displays focus on the history of Geneva between the 14C and 19C. The town's ramparts, architecture, religious and political activities, and day-to-day life are vividly evoked through l collections of coins, early photographs, locks, door panels and roof ornaments. Everyday objects, printed calico and paper wall hangings are displayed in a prettily furnished apartment. Admire the fine services made of silver and pewter, of which Geneva was once an important manufacturing centre. On the top floor is a striking relief map attributed to the Genevese architect Auguste Magnin (1842-1903), presenting the town as it was in 1850 (copper roofs, zinc buildings and fortifications).

A few steps from the Maison Tavel, on the opposite side of the street, the arcades of the **former arsenal** house the last remaining cannon of the Republic of Geneva (♿ *see Introduction: History*). The walls carry modern mosaics executed by Cingria, illustrating three phases in the town's history.

Hôtel de Ville (H)

The town hall dates from the 16C-17C and the oldest section, the Tour Baudet, was built in 1455. Go into the courtyard to see the curious cobbled ramp which allowed people to be carried on litters to the upper floors. On the ground floor you can visit the **Alabama Room** (🔊 *Guided tours (15min) by appointment only.* ⏱ *Closed Sat-Sun and public hols. Contact the Geneva Tourist office on* ☎ *(022) 909 70 70 or the State Chancellery reception staff at the town hall on* ☎ *(022) 319 21 11 or (022) 327 41 11*) where the first Convention of the Red Cross, known as the **Geneva Convention**, was signed in 1864.

Grand'Rue

This picturesque street, one of the best preserved in the old city, offers visitors a remarkable choice of bookstores, art galleries and antique shops. Several buildings are associated with famous people: n° 40 is where **Jean-Jacques Rousseau** was born; the great actor **Michel Simon** (1895-1975) was born at n° 27. When you reach the place du Grand-Mézel, ornamented with a flower-decked fountain, turn left to **Rue des Granges** (FZ 65), lined with large, comfortable residences in the style of French 18C architecture. The Hôtel de Sellon at n° 2 houses the **Musée-Fondation Zoubov** (🔊 *Guided tours (50min) mid-Jun to late Sep, Mon-Fri 3.45pm; Oct to mid-Jun, Thu at 6pm, Sat at 2.30pm and 3.30pm.* 🎫*5CHF.* ⏱ *Closed two weeks at Easter and three weeks at Christmas.* ☎ *(022) 311 92 55.*) made up of Countess Zoubov's personal mementoes and brought back from her many trips abroad, including *cloisonné* enamels from Peking and painted enamels from Russia (imperial palaces of St Petersburg). Furniture pieces signed by the greatest 18C French cabinetmakers, portraits executed by court painters such as Vigée-Lebrun, the Baron Gérard, Lampi the Elder and Lampi the Younger, as well as sumptuous carpets and tapestries decorate the various rooms of the Hôtel: the private entrance, the dining hall, the vast lounge, the bedrooms and the boudoir of Catherine II. At n° 7 stands the house where **Albert Gallatin** (1761-1849) was born, who emigrated to America and became an American statesman, including as peace commissioner to Ghent in 1814.

Église St-Germain (FZ K)

🕐 *Open by appointment. Contact M. le curé J-C Mokry, Passage du 1er août, 1212 Grand-Lancy.* ☎ *(022) 794 06 54.*

This 4C-5C basilica was extended in the 14C and 15C. The belfry, façade and east end were renovated when the building was restored in 1959. The interior is lit by modern stained-glass windows. There are remains of a late-4C altar. A canopied fountain surmounted by a sundial stands against the east end of the church.

▶ *Turn right into rue Henry-Fazy.*

Pass under the Porte de la Treille. The Tour Baudet (1455), which houses the Executive Council Chamber, stands on the left.

▶ *Follow on the right the Promenade de la Treille which slopes down steeply to the Place Neuve.*

The International District

Place des Nations (FW)

This huge square borders on Ariana Park and the modern buildings of international organisations and banks. Note the tall, concave structure, made of blue-tinted glass, which houses the WOIP (World Organisation of Intellectual Property) headquarters. In front is a tiered waterfall flanked by bronze copies of the naiads originally conceived for the Neptune Fountain in Florence.

Musée Ariana★★ (FW)

♿🕐 *Open daily except Tue, 10am-5pm.* 🕐 *Closed 1 Jan and 25 Dec.* 💰5CHF. ☎ *(022) 418 54 50.*

The museum, founded by Gustave Revilliod (1817-90), after whose mother Ariane Revilliod-de-la-Rive it was named, was built by Émile Grobety between 1879 and 1884 in the style of an Italian palace. The collections provide a riveting illustration of 10 centuries of ceramics in Europe, Asia and the Middle East, from the first earthenware pieces (a 9C bowl from Mesopotamia) to Italian Renaissance maljolica and Delft earthenware up to early Meissen pottery at the beginning of the 18C. Other displays also show how the Chinese and Japanese porcelain production that was exported to Europe developed from the 16C to the 18C. An educational area explains firing and glazing techniques; another section concentrates on the production of European glassware between the 16C and the 19C. Several rooms are devoted to Swiss manufacturers (Winterthur earthenware, terracotta from Bern and porcelain from Geneva, Nyon and Zurich) as well as European ceramics from 1900 to 1940, plus numerous sketches and cartoons. The superb gallery with torsade columns exhibits Swiss and European glasswork and also features a tea shop. The building also houses the headquarters of the International Academy of Ceramics.

Palais des Nations★★ (FW)

Entrance at 14 avenue de la Paix, Portail de Pregny. ♿👣 *Guided tours (1hr) daily in Jul and Aug, 10am-5pm; Sep-Jun, 10am-noon and 2-4pm.* 🕐 *Closed Sat-Sun from Nov to Mar and for two weeks before Christmas.* 💰10CHF. ☎ *(022) 917 48 96, www.unog.ch.*

The palace, which stands in Ariana Park, was built between 1929 and 1936 as the headquarters of the League of Nations. Since 1946 it has been the second centre of

Armillary sphere in front of UN Headquarters

Bill Wassman / APA Publications

the United Nations, the seat of which is located in New York City. A new wing added in 1973 is said to be one of the most active conference centres in the world. The **Salle des Pas-Perdus**, adorned with various kinds of marble donated by UN member countries, leads into the great **Salle des Assemblées** (capacity 2 000 people) where plenary meetings are held. Pass along a gallery onto which several meeting rooms open, to reach the **Salle du Conseil** where the most important conferences take place. It is also known as the Spanish Room in honour of Francisco de Vitoria, who is considered by many to be the founder of international law. The Spanish artist José Maria Sert decorated this room with huge frescoes depicting the technical, social and scientific achievements of mankind. The visit ends with a film explaining the role of the United Nations Organisation and its famous peacekeeping forces.

Park
These relaxing grounds, covering 25ha/60 acres, are planted with cedars, cypresses and many other fine species. The park features several works of art: a bronze armillary sphere bequeathed by the United States in honour of President Woodrow Wilson, an arrow-shaped monument donated by the Soviet Union to celebrate the conquest of space and a bronze sculpture christened *Family*, the work of Edwina Sandys, offered to Geneva during the International Year of Childhood (1979). Seen from the park, the huge mass of the Palais des Nations, built in limestone, travertine and a variety of marble materials, offers a powerful, imposing image. The upper part of the terrace affords a nice view of Lake Geneva and the Mont-Blanc mountain range.

Musée International de la Croix-Rouge et du Croissant-Rouge★
Access to the museum is through the Avenue de la Paix (EW).   *Open daily except Tue, 10am-5pm. Closed 1 Jan, 24, 25 and 31 Dec. 10CHF. (022) 748 95 25, www. micr.org.*

The Geneva Escalade

This traditional festival commemorates the successful defence of the town against the Savoyards who attemped to scale (escalader) the walls. Celebrations include a torchlight procession with the Genevese in period costume through the narrow streets of the town and along the banks of the Rhône. The procession stops along the way when a herald on horseback reads out the official proclamation claiming victory over Savoy. Local confectioners make chocolate cauldrons, symbolising the heroic deed of one semi-mythical Genevese housewife who put the enemy to flight by pouring the boiling contents of a cauldron over their heads. Fireworks and a religious service in the Cathédrale St-Pierre complete the day's festivities.

In the entrance hall, a bronze sulpture by the US sculptor George Segal entitled *The Petrified* symbolises the violation of human rights.

The Genevese businessman **Henri Dunant**, who witnessed the Battle of Solférino, when the French and the Piedmontese engaged in hostilities against the Austrians in 1859, decided to launch a movement to aid the wounded (40 000 men were killed or wounded in one day during the battle). Four years later, he founded the Red Cross. These historical facts are shown in a panoramic diorama; at the end of the presentation the screen opens onto the figure, *Henri Dunant Writing*, executed by George Segal. Also on display in the room is the uniform worn by Napoleon III during the battle. Eleven exhibition areas, harmoniously combining light, glass and concrete, describe the activities of the **Red Cross** and the **Red Crescent** throughout the world (during the Russo-Turkish war between 1870 and 1875, the Muslim Turks were given permission to replace the cross by a red crescent on a white background). The Wall of Time is a chronology of the major events associated with the Red Cross: relief to victims of wars and natural disasters, support to hostages and political prisoners, efforts to contribute to their release. An impressive archive system, featuring over 7 million cards, lists the names of men and women detained in prison camps during the First World War. Visitors can also enter a $4m^2/4.5$sq yd area, the replica of a real cell in which 17 prisoners spent up to 90 days. After five years of pressure by the Red Cross, the country concerned abolished this type of detention. A series of films and computer terminals supply more detailed information about the action of the Red Cross. The museum provides a moving insight into the history of mankind, inviting both respect and contemplation.

Museums of the South Bank

Musée d'Art et d'Histoire★★ (GZ)

🕐 *Open daily except Mon, 10am-5pm.* 🕐 *Closed 1 Jan and 25 Dec.* 🈺 *No charge for the permanent collection.* ☎ *(022) 418 26 00.*

The Art and History Museum collections present an encyclopedic outline of the history of civilisation, from prehistoric times up to the 21C. The largest sections are devoted to archaeology and painting. Collections of applied art include exhibits dating from the 12C-19C: sculpted furniture (15C-18C), stained glass from the Middle Ages, weapons (guns, pistols with carved ivory butts) and armour made between the 12C and the 18C. Several rooms of a castle have been reconstructed, complete with raised panelling and 17C furniture. One room presents Byzantine and Coptic archaeology. There is also an exhibition on art in Western Europe during the Late Middle Ages.

Archaeology – Several rooms in succession are devoted to prehistory (objects of local origin), Egypt, Mesopotamia, the Near East, Greece, Rome and the Etruscans. The Numismatic Room contains a wide range of ancient monetary weights and coins.

Painting – The celebrated altarpiece by **Konrad Witz** (1444), one of whose panels shows the New Testament story of the miraculous draught of fishes, is generally held to be the first exact representation of landscape in European painting: Geneva and Le Môle can be glimpsed in the background. Other rooms pay tribute to the Italian and Dutch Schools. These are succeeded by pictures of the 17C and especially the 18C. Largillière and his rather contrived, brightly coloured paintings *(Allegorical Portrait of Françoise Turettini as Diane the Huntress)* precedes two great 18C artists in pastel. There are a number of masterpieces by Quentin de la Tour, including *Abbot Hubert Reading*, picturesque and true to life, as well as the delicate and impish portrait of Belle de Zuylen. The second pastellist is the Genevese artist Liotard, whose extravagance was well-known to all European society. His portrait of Mme d'Epinay is astonishingly fresh. Another of his works *(Still-Life with Game of Lotto)* is a wonderful complement to the two other still-life paintings by the same artist. The 19C section shows some luminous landscapes by Corot, works by the Genevese artist Toepffer, as well as several pictures by Hodler, whose fierce, powerful technique is illustrated by two portraits *(View of Lake Geneva and Mont Blanc, The Port of Geneva at Dawn)*. Tribute is paid to the Impressionist movement, with works by Pissarro *(The Harbour in Rouen)*, Monet *(Peonies)*, Cézanne *(The House in Bellevue)*, Renoir *(Summertime)* and Sisley *(The Lock at Moret-sur-Loing)*.

Collections Baur★ (GZ)

○*Open daily except Mon, 2-6pm (8pm Wed).* ⌚*Guided tour first Wed of the month.* ○*Closed 1 Jan and 25 Dec.* ⊜*5CHF.* ☎ *(022) 346 17 29, www.collections-baur.ch.*
This museum, housed in a 19C mansion, is devoted to art from the Far East amassed over a half-century by Swiss collector Alfred Baur (1865-1951) plus temporary exhibitions. The permanent collection features porcelain, stoneware, celadon and jade combining purity of form, richness of colour and delicacy of decoration from the 10C to the 19C.. These show the evolution of ceramic art in China, from the T'ang (618-908) to the Ch'ing dynasty (1644-1911). Japanese exhibits include sabres, 18C porcelain, lacquer ware, netsuke carved woodenand buttons from the Tokugawa (1615-1868) or Meiji periods (1868-1912).

Muséum d'Histoire Naturelle★★ (GZ)

♿○ *Open daily except Mon, 9.30am-5pm.* ○ *Closed 1 Jan and 25 Dec.* ⊜ *No charge.* ☎ *(022) 418 63 00.*
The Natural History Museum was originally founded in 1820, when a decree led to the creation of an academic museum, which subsequently became the one we know today. The collections are outstanding and the care with which they are arranged

General Dufour, a National Hero

Guillaume-Henri Dufour was born in 1787 in Germany to Swiss parents in exile. He attended military studies in Paris and became an officer in Napoleon's Grand Army, resigning his commission in 1817 to return to Switzerland, where he was appointed captain in the federal forces and *chef du génie genevois*. He helped to found the Military Academy at Thun in 1819 and was a military instructor until 1830; soldiers he trained included Prince Louis Napoleon Bonaparte, the future Emperor Napoleon III. Dufour reorganised the armed forces and was appointed Chief of Staff, commanding the Swiss Army against the rebels of separatist Catholic cantons in the Sonderbund War (1847). Between 1832-64 he surveyed Switzerland, publishing a series of topographical maps on a scale of 1:100 000, known as the Dufour Map. Perhaps his most enduring legacy was the national flag, officially recognised by the Diet on 21 July 1840. When he died on his estate at Contamines in 1875, he was honoured with a hero's funeral. The highest point of Mount Rosa, Pointe Dufour (alt 4 634m/15 202ft), was named in his honour.

makes for a highly interesting visit. It is the largest such museum in the country. The ground floor is devoted to regional fauna (birds and mammals in their natural environment recreated by man: a forest clearing, the water's edge etc). The first floor, set aside for tropical birds and mammals, takes visitors, from the African savannah to the South and North Pole, not forgetting Asia and Latin America. You can see several species of tiger, some of which have become extinct, as well as the dodo, a bird which used to inhabit the Mauritius and Réunion Islands, whose weight prevented it from flying. It became extinct in the 17C-18C. The second floor shows reptiles and amphibians from around the world.

> ### 😊 Swiss Motorways 😊
>
> In Switzerland motorway signs feature a green background and not a blue one as in other European countries. The maximum speed limit is 120kph/74mph. There are no tolls on Swiss motorways but an annual road tax (vignette) is levied on all vehicles using Swiss motorways. This stamp costs 40F or 27 Euro and must be affixed onto the windscreen. It can be purchased from the Swiss National Tourist Office before leaving or at border crossings, petrol stations and post offices.

The third floor focuses on palaeontology, geology and mineralogy, giving a chronological account of the history of the earth, making reference to the other planets of the universe, meteorites and the continental drift. Note the dinosaur display with its huge triptych in the background, explaining three prehistoric ages: the Secondary Era with dinosaurs, the Tertiary Era with strange, giant mammals and the end of the last Ice Age with landscapes of the Geneva region. Another fascinating exhibit is the fossil of a *xiphactinus audax*, a predatory fish from the Cretaceous period (96 to 75 million years ago), which lived in warm seas and which grew up to several metres lin length. The section devoted to the *Hominidae* is illustrated by Lucy, who was discovered in Ethiopia in 1974 and whose origins are thought to go back some 3.5 million years.

The fourth floor focuses on the geology of Switzerland. Most interesting is a relief map, at a scale of 1:100 000, which clearly shows the three main geographical regions: the Swiss Jura, the Middle Country and the Alpine range.

Patek Philippe Museum★★ (EZ M⁴)

♿🕐 *Open Tue-Fri, 2-5pm; Sat, 10am-5pm.* 🕐 *Closed public hols.* 🎫*10CHF* ☎ *(022) 807 09 10, www.patekmuseum.com.*

The history of Patek Philippe began in 1839, when Antoine Norbert de Patek founded a watch and clock manufacturers with his compatriot, François Czapek. Czapek retired in 1845 and the French watchmaker Adrien Philippe, inventor of the keyless watch, joined the company, which soon built an international reputation for unparalleled technical expertise and aesthetic style. A beautifully restored factory now houses the Patek Philippe Museum, which exhibits a collection of magnificent timepieces collected over a period of 30 years. Each floor focuses on a particular aspect of watch-making and history.

More than 400 tools dating from the first half of the 18C to the beginning of the 20C can be seen on the ground floor, in a reconstruction of an old workshop once used for making clocks, jewellery, engravings and enamel pieces.

Take the lift to the third floor, which houses the library, containing more than 4 000 works on horology. The history of the company is presented here, with a section dedicated to Antoine Norbert de Patek and a section dedicated to Patek Philippe's many prestigious customers, who included Queen Victoria and the emperor of Ethiopia, Haile Selassie. Note also "La Bratine", a set of 12 carved vodka glasses in vermeil and enamel, a gift of the Russian Tsar Nicolas II on 15 April 1904. The second floor has a splendid 16C-19C collection of masterpieces of Genevese and European horology, including luxury items and unusual watches made for the Chinese and Turkish markets. Two of the oldest pieces are a German drum-watch and a watch in the shape of the cross of the Holy Spirit Order made by Abraham Cusin. Also noteworthy are the ingenious automated models. The pistol with a singing bird, made c 1810 by the Genevese watchmaker Rochat, is in engraved gold, adorned with pearls and enamel, with a watch built in on the rounded section of the butt. Moses, another masterpiece, is the work of a Locle workshop (1815-20); the water can even be seen gushing from the rock. Another section displays miniature portraits painted on enamel; the subjects include George Villiers, the Duke of Buckingham, Louis XIV, the Marquise de Sévigné and Charles-Edward Stuart. The first floor is dedicated to items produced by Patek Philippe from 1839 to the present day, including pocket watches, wrist watches and commemorative pieces. The *Calibre 89* with 33 functions, 2 clock faces, 24 hands, 8 discs and 1 728 different parts is the most complicated watch ever made.

Musée de l'Horlogerie et de l'Émaillerie★ (GZ)

 Closed for renovation until 2009. ☎ *(022) 418 64 70.*

Housed in an elegant 19C mansion, this museum is dedicated to the science of horology from its origins up to the present day. It also illustrates the Genevese art of enamels, applied to the ornamentation of watches, jewellery, portraits and snuffboxes between the 17C and 20C. The 15C-18C period is represented by sundials, hourglasses, clocks (18C wooden clocks and astronomical clocks with automatons), and especially clocks made in Geneva (ornamental pieces shaped as shells and insects, executed 1830-70). On the same floor, visitors are enlightened about the different techniques of this delicate art, which flourished in Geneva soon after 1650. The collections on display demonstrate the fine draughtsmanship, bold colours, extreme precision and high degree of mastery which characterise the art of enameling (snuffboxes, painted enamels, watches etc). One display cabinet regularly showcases the work of contemporary Geneva enamellers; a second one presents the recent achievements of newly trained jewellers from the Academy of Decorative Arts in Geneva. The first floor displays 19C and 20C enamelled clocks from Geneva, often equipped with musical mechanisms, as well as a fine collection of clocks from Geneva and European countries. The top floor houses a reconstruction the workshop that belonged to the famous watch and clock repairer **Louis Cottier**.

Additional Sights

Les Schtroumpfs (EX)

North bank, rue Louis-Favre and rue I.-Eberhardt.

These modern housing blocks (1982-89) in the Grottes district near Cornavin Station bring to mind the work of the Spanish architect Gaudí. The multicoloured buildings, designed by Robert Frei, Christian Hunziker and Georges Berthoud, seem to have come straight from the pages of a fairy tale. The mass of mosaics and wrought-iron work, coupled with the extravagantly shaped arabesque forms, combine to produce an architectural ensemble that stands out in the urban landscape of the city.

Musée Barbier-Mueller (FZ M²)

 Open daily, 11am-5pm. *5CHF.* *Guided tour by appointment only.* ☎ *(022) 312 02 70; www.barbier-mueller.ch.*

It presents in rotation sumptuous collections relating to the earliest known cultures of the five continents. The impressive display of sculptures, ceramics, jewels, ornaments and material is enhanced by the judicious layout and lighting.

Cathédrale Orthodoxe Russe de l'Exaltation de la Sainte-Croix (GZ N)

 Open daily except Mon, 9.30am-noon and 2.30-5pm in summer; 2.30-5pm only in winter. ☎ *(022) 346 47 09.*

This beautiful Russian Orthodox church dates from the late 19C. The golden domes of its cupolas are an attractive feature of this residential district. The building, in the style of old Moscow churches, reproduces the plan of a Greek cross. Inside, walls, vaulting and pillars are ornamented with paintings inspired by Byzantine art. The nave is separated from the chancel by the iconostasis, forming five arches in Carrara marble, finely carved and adorned with icons. In the centre stands the sacred doorway, carved in cypress pine, gilded with intricate relief work.

Musée d'Ethnographie (EZ)

🕐 *Open daily except Mon, 10am-5pm.* 🎟*5CHF for temporary exhibitions, no charge for permanent collections.* ☎ *022 418 45 50.*
The Museum of Ethnography presents miscellaneous collections from all over the world, featuring both works of art and simple objects for everyday use. It also hosts temporary exhibitions, each focusing on a specific theme or ethnic group.

Grande Synagogue (EZ)

🕐 *Open daily for services at 7.15am, tours by appointment.* ☎ *(022) 736 96 32.*
This magnificent old synagogue (formally the **Beth Yaakov Synagogue**) was built in 1858-59 when the Geneva government finally allowed minorities to build religious buildings within the city walls. It was the first synagogue built in Switzerland, designed by Swiss architect Jean-Henri Bachoven (1821-89) and underwent a major restoration in 1997. The predominantly Moorish design is crowned by a prominent dome over an octagonal base. The exterior is dominated by Moorish-style arched windows and doors and fortress-like crenelated ramparts. The façade is fine brickwork in stripes of pale orange and white, with several six-pointed Star of David windows; curved windows outlined with decorative brickwork further accentuate the exterior. Inside, the Holy Ark (containing the Torah and other religious texts) is situated within the soaring dome, which is ornamented by a set of concentric white arches. The Grand Synagogue influenced the design of other synagogues built in Switzerland during the late 19C (Basel in 1868, Porrentruy in 1874, Sankt Gallen in 1881 and Zeurich in 1884), and those as far away as New York City. It serves Geneva's Ashkenazi community, whose ancestors were driven out of Muslim Spain in the Middle Ages, hence the Moorish architecture.

MAMCO (EZ)

🕐 *Open Tue-Fri, noon-6pm; Sat-Sun, 11am-6pm.* 🕐 *Closed 1 and 2 Jan, Good Fri, 1 May, 1 Aug, first Thu of Sep (Jeûne Genevois) and 25 and 26 Dec.* 🎟*8CHF.* ☎ *(022) 320 61 22, www.mamco.ch.*
This **Museum of Modern and Contemporary Art**, housed in an old factory, displays recent avant garde works (post-1960), taken from over 40 private and public collections, both in Switzerland and abroad. Relying for the most part on unusual or relatively unknown artists, the museum's aim is to surprise and provoke visitors, whether they be seasoned critics or simply amateur art lovers. Start by visiting the fourth floor, set aside for temporary exhibitions, and do not hesitate to read the information cards in each room or, better still, canvass the views of the staff, who are sure to have an opinion!

Institut et Musée Voltaire★ (EY)

🕐 *Open daily except Sun, 2-5pm; Ascension, Whit Mon and Jeûne Genevois, 2-6pm.* 🕐 *Closed 2 Jan, Good Fri, Easter Mon, 24-26 and 31 Dec.* 🎟*No charge.* ☎ *(022) 344 71 33.*
"Les Délices" – Voltaire's residence in Geneva (1755-65) has become a centre for research into his life and the period in which he lived. The Institute, which published the very first edition of the author's vast correspondence and which houses an impressive library, presents a series of exhibits retracing the career of **François-Marie Arouet**, the famous author better known as Voltaire. Displays contain an

original edition of *Candide*, and handwritten documents, mainly letters signed by or addressed to Voltaire (including one of the last letters sent to him by King Frederick II of Prussia). Another curiosity is the collection of 199 wax seals bearing his heraldic insignia he used in his correspondence. Among the portraits of the author, note the painting by Largillière, representing him at the age of 24 *(ground floor)* and a terra-cotta replica of Houdon's famous statue *Voltaire Seated (first floor)*. An audio-visual presentation *(45min)* enlightens visitors on Voltaire's stay in Geneva.

Église St-Paul

Leave by rue de la Terrassière (GZ).

This church will appeal to visitors interested in contemporary religious art by virtue of Maurice Denis' contribution to its interior decoration after 1915: the nave is enriched with 14 stained-glass windows and the canvas adorning the apse illustrates the life of St Paul in the form of a superb triptych.

Église du Christ-Roi

At Petit-Lancy by the road to Chancy (EZ).

The bell tower of this modern, suburban church is linked to the rest of the building by a peristyle. The interior consists of a spacious **nave**★ with coffered vaulting and exposed beams. The south wall is decorated with a fresco by Beretta, while the north wall is pierced with a stained-glass window designed by Albert Chavaz. In the chancel, ending in a flat chevet, a huge triptych is embellished with a fine tapestry by Alice Basset.

Domaine de Penthes

In Pregny-Chambésy, 18 chemin de l'Impératrice. Enter by avenue de la Paix (EW), *north of the local map, then take the route de Pregny.* This hilly park, covering an area of 12ha/30 acres, is planted with fine beech trees.

Musée des Suisses à l'Étranger★

🕐 *Open Apr-Dec, Tue-Sun, 10am-noon and 2-6pm, Jan-Mar, Wed-Sun, 10am-noon and 2-5pm.* 🕐 *Closed over Christmas and New Year hols.* 🚃*5CHF.* ☎ *(022) 734 90 21.*

Penthes Château, initially built in the 14C and extensively remodelled up to the 19C, welcomed the Duchess of Orléans and her sons, the Comte de Paris and the Duc de Chartres in 1852 and now houses a museum devoted to Switzerland's relations with the rest of the world from the Middle Ages to today, focusing on economic, military, diplomatic, scientific, cultural and literary aspects of Swiss society. Emphasis is on the Franco-Swiss alliances from 1444 to 1830, and on the armed forces or famous Swiss personalities who served the European powers. In the Le Fort Room, enhanced by delicate wainscoting, are a several portraits worth noting and an oval embossed silver platter depicting the oath of alliance taken by Louis XIV and the Swiss cantons after a tapestry by Le Brun. The first floor captures the French Revolution and its tragic result for Louis XVI's Swiss Guards, the French Occupation and the role of the Swiss regiments during the Empire, as well as traditions followed by the Papal Guard, founded during the 16C (👆 *see Le VALAIS).* Mementoes of Beatus von Fischer, Switzerland's first postmaster, and of the national postal system, are presented in the Salon des Dieux, decorated with lovely **woodwork**★, seven gilded and painted panels representing the Gods of Olympus, taken from Reichenbach Château near Bern. The exhibition rooms on the second floor are devoted to Swiss celebrities who acquired a worldwide reputation: archaeologists (Burckhardt), leading figures in industry and aeronautics (Breguet), forerunners of the modern banking system (Necker), diplomats (Gallatin) and statesmen (Haldimand), writers (Blaise Cendrars), scientists and physicians (De Haller), artists (JH Füssli) and famous women (Sybille Merian).

Musée Militaire Genevois

🕐 *Open Apr-Dec, Tues-Sat, 2-5pm; Sun 10am-noon and 2-5pm.* 🕐 *Closed during Christmas hols.* 🎫 *No charge.* ☎ *(022) 734 48 75.*

The former stables of Penthes Château presently house a small museum which explains the history of the Genevese troops from 1814 to 1815, when Geneva joined the Confederation, up to the present day. The landmarks in Geneva's military history are illustrated through collections of arms, equipment, documents and around 30 figures in uniform.

Musée International de l'Automobile★

Palexpo, halle n° 7, along the bypass on the road to Ferney (EW). Leave your car in car park P26. ♿🕐 *Open Tues-Fri 1:30pm-6:30pm, Sat-Sun 10am-6pm.* 🎫*12CHF.* ☎ *(022) 788 84 84, www.cilma.ch.*

Laid out over two 7 000m²/8 300sq yd exhibition areas, the Automobile Museum presents around 400 vehicles in chronological order, grouped together by make and country of manufacture. All the cars are in perfect condition. General Patton's Jeep, Mussolini's Fiat, General Guisan's Buick, Stalin's Zis, as well as a Cadillac and a Ferrari which belonged respectively to Elvis Presley and Sophia Loren, are y the star attractions. Of particular note are the Swiss models (Ajax, Felber, Monteverdi etc) and the superb Italian machines such as Ferrari, Lamborghini and Maserati, to name but a few. Finally, a number of exceptional automobiles will not fail to seduce even the most hardened professionals: three Bugatti T35 models (1926, 1927 and 1929), Voisin C14 (1930), Auburn Speedster (1932), Hispano-Suiza (1934), Alfa-Romeo 2500 (1939), Allard 81M (1945), Facel-Vega HK500 (1959) Austin Healy MKIII (1967), and a gull-wing Mercedes-Benz SLR McClaren (2005).

Excursion

Carouge★ (FZ)

S of Geneva. Founded in the late 18C by Victor-Amadeus III, Duke of Savoy and King of Sardinia, the town has often been in conflict with its neighbour Geneva. Many left puritan Geneva to enjoy themselves in the cabarets and inns of Carouge. The town was annexed to the Geneva canton in 1816 by the Treaty of Turin. The old district still has streets which were laid out in the 17C. The cafés, restaurants, antique shops and artists' studios of Carouge attract Geneva residents, who enjoy strolling down its pretty streets.

GLARUS

Ⓒ GLARUS – POPULATION 5 753
ALT 472M/1 549FT

Glarus lies in a deeply ravined **site**★ at the foot of the Vorder Glärnisch Cliffs. Since its old quarters were destroyed by fire in 1861 it has had the appearance of a busy city, built on a regular grid plan. The great Zaunplatz holds the canton's open-air assemblies known as Landsgemeinde (♿ *see Introduction*) every year on the first Sunday in May.

A Hive of Industry

The row of factories, which gives a peculiar character to the Linth Valley as the main artery of the Glarus canton, recalls the valleys of the Vosges. In the 18C Pastor Andreas Heidegger introduced cotton spinning into the area. The town enjoyed its golden age about 1860 when printing on cloth was introduced. Indian fabrics made in the area then flooded the Eastern market, as the weavers of Glarus excelled at this technique. Today Glarus is still the only industrial mountain canton in Switzerland. This municipality is also a tourist area, however; a resort such as **Braunwald** keeps up the traditions of the canton, which was a pioneer of mountaineering (the very first shelter of

> ### Schabzieger
>
> One of the local specialities of the Glarus canton is *Schabzieger*, a green, cone-shaped cheese with no crust or eyes, made with skimmed milk and crushed herbs. It owes its spicy flavour to one of its ingredients, *ziegerklee*, a leaf belonging to the clover family.

the Swiss Alpine Club was built in the Tödi Massif in 1863) and skiing (the very first Swiss Ski Championship was held at Glarus in 1905). Music Festivals at Braunwald are extremely popular events and attract many music lovers each year.

Excursion

Klöntal★

13km/8mi – about 45min. Leave Glarus by the road to Zurich, then make for Riedern. In this village follow the road straight on to the Klöntal, running up the Löntsch Valley.
At the top of a steep climb under beech trees Lake Klöntal (alt 848m/2 781ft) which was enlarged when the dam was built. The Glärnisch's jagged steep slopes, rent by inaccessible ravines, plunge from a height of 2 000m/6 500ft into the lake waters. The road climbs to follow the lake shore and after the second hairpin bend halt at a bench; facing you is a superb **view**★★ of the Klöntal.

GOMS★★

The road, as it climbs up the Upper Rhône Valley, enters mountainous terrain; it serves the numerous resorts and ski lifts hanging on the side of the Aletschhorn Massif. Conches Valley (**Val de Conches** in French or **Goms** in German) begins at Fiesch.

From Brig to Gletsch *54km/32mi – about 2hr*

Itinerary ④ (♿ see Le VALAIS map). The road that follows the Furka-Oberalp railway at a distance may be blocked by snow between Brig and Oberwald for short periods.
The Upper Rhône Valley comprises four levels which cause the river to drop by 1 000m/3 000ft.

Brig – *45min. ♿ See BRIG.*

From Brig to the Grengiols fork, the road runs close to the foaming Rhône at the bottom of a narrow, winding cleft. It passes by the large, isolated Baroque **Hohen Flühen Chapel** and serves the lower stations of the Riederalp-Greicheralp cable car (starting from Mörel) and that of **Bettmeralp**. These lines serve a high Alpine plateau (alt 2 000m/6 500ft), wonderfully situated within view of the Valais Alps and close to the Aletsch Glacier, the most extensive in the Alps (169km²/65sq mi with its tributaries).

Daybreak on the Eggishorn above the Aletsch Glacier

Philipp Giegel / Switzerland Tourism

Riederalp✷, Moosfluh★★

⛰Access to Riederalp by cable car from Mörel; access to Moosfluh by chair-lift from Riederalp. 🕐 *Operates in summer, 8am-5pm; winter, 9am-4.30pm.* 🚡*13CHF there and back. For information on periods of closure, call* ☎ *(027) 928 68 11.*

Located in a **site**★ overlooking the Rhône Valley on the valley's north side, the **Riederalp**✷ chalets and hotels are terraced, beginning at 1 930m/6 332ft, and face the mountain range separating Switzerland from Italy. Above its westernmost point stands Villa Cassel, a Victorian-style mansion (1902), now the centre of the Aletschwald Nature Reserve with exhibitions on the nature reserve and its larch and arolla pine forests, which are among the highest in Europe. Visitors can also learn about the history of the Aletsch Glacier, which can be visited on excursions organised by the centre. The centre's Alpine garden is open to the public.

▶ *From the cable car's arrival station, walk (a few minutes) to the chairlift's departure station to go to Moosfluh.*

The chairlift passes by the mid-station of Blausee, located between two small lakes, before arriving at the upper station of **Moosfluh**★★ (alt 2 335m/7 661ft), set amid a jumble of green rocks and dominates the spectacular curving form of the **Grosser Aletschgletscher**★★★, immediately to the north at the foot of the slopes and tributary glaciers of the Aletschhorn Massif, as well as the Rhône Valley to the south. The valley's second level stretches from Lax to Fiesch and is marked by the appearance – confirming a gain in height – of arolla pines and small barns on piles *(raccards)*. This section marks the start of the Upper Rhône Valley, known as the Conches Valley. Below, in a gorge section, the Rhône is joined by the tributary River Binna. Farther up the valley, when Fiesch comes into view, it is possible to look up the Fieschertal Valley, on the left, and see in the far distance the snowy peak of the Finsteraar-Rothorn.

Eggishorn★★★

Alt 2 927m/9 603ft. ⛰*Access by cable car from Fiesch.* 🕐 *Departures every 30min, 8am (7.30am Jun-Oct) to 6pm.* 🕐 *Does not operate in May and Nov.* 🚡*Fare there and back: 42.80CHF.* ☎ *(027) 971 27 00.*

The first stage takes you up over a spruce forest and a scree of greenish-coloured, jagged rocks. From the upper station (alt 2 869m/9 423ft) there is a superb **panorama**★★★; below in the immediate foreground the Aletsch Glacier, the Fiesch Glacier, a nearby cascade farther round to the right, and of all the other neighbouring mountain peaks. For an even wider view, climb to the top of one of the three mounds of scree which are quite close to the station. The Eggishorn summit is marked by a cross (🔺 *difficult clamber*). After the next change in level beyond Fiesch, the view extends back downstream to the snow-covered slopes of the Weisshorn (alt 4 505m/14 780ft).

After a few hairpin bends notice the village of **Mühlebach**, the birthplace of Cardinal Schiner, on the opposite slope.

Bellwald★

🔺*Access by a winding road 8km/5mi or by cable car from Fürgangen.*

A small summer and winter resort, Bellwald (alt 1 600m/5 249ft), with its old larch wood chalets and hotels set on a curved terrace, presents a wide aerial **view★** of the Conches Valley – from Fiesch to Brig – over the Eggishorn (identified by its cross), above and to the right of the Wannenhorn Massif and its glaciers and left onto the Alps of the Italian frontier. The **Richinen and Steibenkreuz chairlift** (🕐 *Operates in winter from 9.15am-4.15pm, in summer from 9am-noon and 1.15-5.30pm. Ask for information on closed periods.* 🎫*16CHF.* ☎ *(027) 971 19 26)* offers a pleasant excursion above the grassland with a close-up view of the Wannenhorn Glaciers and the majestic Matterhorn in the distance. The valley opens out again beautifully. The third level is the longest in the Conches Valley. The Alpine combe now offers a bare, open landscape; the total lack of enclosures, the lone trees and scattered chalets makes for striking views. The villages with their blackish wooden houses adorned with geraniums are grouped around slim white church towers. Upstream, to the right of the Galenstock summit, you will glimpse the Furka Gap, although the pass itself is out of sight.

Reckingen

The Baroque church of Reckingen is the most agreeably proportioned in the Conches Valley. It was built in the 18C to the plans of the parish priest, **Jean-Georges Ritz**, one of a family of artisans who made sculptured altars for many churches in the district. The name of this family has become world-famous since one of its members, **César Ritz** (b 1850 in Niederwald, d 1918), achieved eminence as a hotel-keeper. The **Seilers**, who made Zermatt prosperous and built the two hotels near the Rhône Glacier (at Gletsch and at the Belvédère) were also from the Conches Valley.

Münster

This large village stands at the foot of the cone of debris, which is covered with fan-shaped patches of tillage. The church with its conical-shaped spire is worth visiting for its Flamboyant **altarpiece★** dedicated to the Virgin, the work of an artist of Lucerne (1509). Beyond Ulrichen the valley becomes wilder; the stone houses of **Obergesteln**, have a stark appearance at first sight, and the Muttenhörner still seems to block the valley completely. Above **Oberwald**, the last village in the Conches Valley, looking down on the village's little church with its stone avalanche screen, the road, now quite mountainous, slips into a defile which gets more barren as the Rhône leaps from fall to fall, and emerges on the fourth level into the Gletsch Basin, in sight of the Rhône Glacier, source of the great river.

Gletsch★★

Alt 1 759m/5 771ft. At the junction of roads from the Furka Pass, the Grimsel Pass and the Conches Valley (Upper Valais) lies Gletsch, on the floor of a desolate basin once covered by the tongue of the Rhône Glacier. Higher up, on the road to the Furka Pass (🔺 *see FURKASTRASSE*), the setting in which the Hôtel Belvédère stands draws many sightseers. This well-known stop offers a sweeping **panorama★★** of the Bernese and Valais Alps plus the **Rhonegletscher★★** in which an **Ice Grotto★** (Eisgrotte 🕐 *Open Jun-Oct, 8am-7pm (7.30pm Sat-Sun).* 🎫*5CHF.* ☎ *(027) 973 11 29)* has been carved out, its walls reflecting a lovely bluish light.

BARRAGE DE
LA GRANDE DIXENCE★★★

The new Grande Dixence Dam, the greatest feat of civil engineering the Swiss have ever undertaken, is of the dead-weight type and 284m/932ft tall. The first Dixence Dam, 87m/285ft, completed in 1935, had a storage capacity of 50 million m³/1 765 million cu ft feeding the Chandoline power station on the floor of the Rhône Valley opposite Sion with an average fall over 1 750m/5 700ft. This was already the most powerful hydroelectric installation in Switzerland and the biggest head of water in the world.

The Grande Dixence Dam
400m/0.3mi downstream from the original work, at an altitude of 2 365m/7 759ft (crest of the dam). The dam has been built up in stages to a height of 284m/932ft, more than two and a half times the height of St Paul's Cathedral in London. About 6 million m³/208 million cu ft of concrete were required – enough to build two Great Pyramids. A further part of the project involved drilling about 100km/60mi of underground tunnels to bring water from the foot of the Matterhorn Glacier. The water was then distributed not only to the new power station at Fionnay in the nearby Bagnes Valley, but also to the Riddes-Nendaz and Chandoline power stations in the Rhône Valley. The hydroelectric output of Switzerland has been increased by an annual 1 600 million kWh.

GRANDSON★

VAUD – POPULATION 2 473
ALT 440M/1 442FT

Situated near the southern end of peaceful Lake Neuchâtel, not far from the foothills of the Jura, the little town of Grandson was the backdrop to a major historical event: the humiliating defeat suffered by Charles the Bold, Duke of Burgundy, in 1476.

Sights

Castle★★
🕐 *Open daily Apr-Oct, 8.30am-6pm; Nov-Mar, Mon-Sat, 7.30-noon and 1:30-5pm, Sun and public hols, 8.30am-5pm.* 🕐 *Closed 1 Jan and 25 Dec.* 🎫*12CHF, no charge first Sun in Dec.* ☎ *(024) 445 29 26.*
The first stronghold was built at the beginning of the 11C by the lords of Grandson, but the castle as we know it today dates from the 13C. After 1476 Grandson became the property of the town of Bern and Fribourg; the castle became the bailiffs' residence and was rearranged inside. Its high walls, large round towers and a covered watch-path, occupy a remarkable **site**★★ on the shore of the lake. There are rooms of historic interest and collections of ancient arms. The wall-walk particularly should be seen, also the Knights' Hall (fine Renaissance stalls), a museum devoted to the Burgundian wars (dioramas) and to Charles the Bold, the great armoury, the fortresses' museum, the dungeons and the chapel as well as a museum devoted to the Grandson District. An **Automobile Museum** occupies the basement. The collection

---

The Battle of Grandson

Charles the Bold, Duke of Burgundy and rival of the King of France Louis XI, longed to recreate former Lotharingia, which extended from the Alps to the North Sea including the Swiss Confederation. In 1476, the duke's troops besieged the city of Grandson and its castle and the garrison was forced to surrender. Charles the Bold ordered his enemies hanged. The Confederates raised an army of around 18 000 men and marched on Grandson. It was a cruel, bloody battle. The Confederates defeated the Burgundians, who only survived by fleeing. Charles abandoned s the whole of his camp: horses, artillery, and his precious treasure, which accompanied him on all his campaigns. This bitter Battle of Grandson is a famous landmark in Swiss history and has inspired many authors, novelists and playwrights.

---

includes an 1898 Delahaye as well as the 1927 white Rolls-Royce Phantom which once belonged to Greta Garbo.

Église St-Jean-Baptiste

The church is half-Romanesque, half-Gothic, with a striking contrast between the very simple nave and the chancel, which is lit by many stained-glass windows. A fine fresco depicting the Entombment is in the chapel on the south side of the chancel. The acoustic drums are also noteworthy. Leave the church, go around to the east end and the fountain (1637); then, to the right of the church, note the former Bailiff's House, which has a sun with a human face supported by savages, wearing loincloths and brandishing clubs, carved on its pediment.

Excursion

Champagne

6km/3.7mi N. The most outstanding feature of this small village is its cellar, where you will be able to taste white champagne wine. Obviously, this beverage bears no relation to the famous bubbly from France that all celebrations call for! But each town is entitled to its own name…

COL DU GRAND-ST-BERNARD★

VALAIS AND ITALY

ALT 2 469M/8 100FT

The Great St Bernard hospice stands in a rocky gully, almost continually swept by an icy wind, on the edge of a lake which is frozen, on average, 265 days in the year and where the winter season lasts for more than eight months. The refuge exemplifies the survival of an admirable Christian tradition of assistance and hospitality. For nine centuries, the monks established here by St Bernard from Aosta – regular canons belonging to the Augustinian Order – have taken in, comforted and rescued travellers in winter. A statue in honour of this "Hero of the Alps" has been erected at the summit of the pass, on Italian soil.

Hospice

The hospice is open throughout the year to all travellers seeking a quiet haven. In the hallway stands the marble statue commissioned by Napoleon in honour of General Desaix, who died at the Battle of Marengo in 1800. The hospice was founded in 1050 as a refuge for those who had suffered at the hands of bandits or been victims of the mountain. Before the road, all supplies had to be carried by mules. The hospice continues to offer accommodations and meals to skiers, hikers and climbers, as well as a warm, cosy welcome to all visitors.

St Bernard Dog

Church

This 17C Baroque church, fully incorporated into the hospice, was built on top of an early 13C sanctuary, presently serving as the crypt. The high altar is graced with statues of St Bernard and St Augustine. The carved walnut stalls and the painted vaulting in the chancel, wildly ornate with strong, bold colours, are characteristic of the Baroque period. The Holy Trinity is pictured surrounded by scenes taken from the New Testament: the Adoration of the Three Wise Men, the Annunciation and a Nativity scene. To the left, the altar of St Bernard, bearing the gilt walnut casket containing the remains of the illustrious saint.

Treasury

It features a fine collection of sacred objects: a 13C polychrome bust-reliquary of St Bernard, sculpted in wood and ornamented with embossed gold and precious stones, a silver pilgrim's cross gilded and studded with gems (13-14C), a Virgin and Child dating from the 15C and an illuminated 15C breviary.

ROUTE DU GRAND-ST-BERNARD★

The Great St Bernard Pass, connecting the valleys of the Drance and Dora Baltea, carries the most historic transalpine route. The great tradition of hospitality has continued here since the 11C and such popular memories as that of Napoleon's crossing of the Alps in 1800 have drawn crowds. The opening of the tunnel beneath the pass has helped to separate the mass of hurried tourists crossing the frontier from the genuine pilgrims.

From Martigny to the Great St Bernard Pass

55km/34mi – about 3hr 30min. Itinerary 1 *(& see Le VALAIS map)*
Once beyond the fork in Bourg-St-Bernard the road demands careful driving because of its numerous bends. When the road is blocked by snow, tourists should travel via the tunnel. Swiss and Italian customs control are at the top of the pass in summer. Those using the tunnel will find the customs control all the year round at Gare Nord in Switzerland and Gare Sud in Italy.

Martigny – *1hr 30min. & See MARTIGNY.*
A short distance after Martigny, the road follows the deeply sunken Drance Valley as far as Les Valettes. The smallest valleys are still planted with vines and fruit trees (& *see Le VALAIS: "A first taste of Provence"*).

Address Book

For coin ranges, refer to the Legend on the front flap.

WHERE TO STAY

Glacier – *Endweg* – ☎ *033 853 10 04 – Fax 033 853 50 04 – www. glacierhotel.ch - 19 rooms* – This restored chalet, situated below the ski resort, is the starting-point for many excursions. The quiet, peaceful terrace commands magnificent views of the Eiger.

Fiescherblick – *Haupt- strasse* – ☎ *033 853 44 53 – www. fiescherblick.ch - 25 rooms* – This old, partly restored chalet serves generous helpings of tasty regional cuisine. Quiet, restful atmosphere, superb views and warm welcome guaranteed.

Alpenhof – ☎ *036 853 52 70 – Fax 036 853 19 15 – 13 rooms* – Simple, comfortable chalet with pretty rooms nestling at the foot of the ski runs. The restaurant serves local produce grown on the premises. Peaceful atmosphere and nice views of the Alps.

Gletschergarten – ☎ *033 853 17 21 – www.hotel- gletschergarten.ch – 26 rooms* – A romantic and private setting, this is a charming flower-decked wooden chalet with a cosy atmosphere. If you dream of warming your toes before a blazing fire after a long trek in the snow, this is definitely the place for you.

Road to Mauvoisin

75km/46.6mi from Les Valettes – about 3hr 30min.
Road n° 21 as far as Sembrancher wends its way between the River Drance and the railway line.

Round tour of the passes★

Starting from Sembrancher.
When the weather is fair this excursion is very pleasant. The road continues through Vollèges (elegant bell tower), **Le Levron** (terraced mountain village), the passes of Le Lein (a rocky larch-filled hollow), Le Tronc and Les Planches (restaurant) and the tiny village of Vens *(join the road to Mauvoisin)*. It is a forest road at the beginning *(unsurfaced for 5km/3mi between Le Levron and Les Planches Pass)*, becomes a corniche and then passes through woods of fir trees and larches. It affords splendid **views**★ of the neighbouring valleys, the Pierre Avoi Mountain (northeast), the snowy sum- mits of the French Alps (Mont Blanc) to the southwest and the Pennine Alps (Grand Combin) to the southeast.

Verbier✳✳✳ – *Starting from Bagnes.* *See VERBIER.*

▶ *From Bagnes return to the Drance Valley.*

Barrage de Mauvoisin★★★

Alt 1 961m/6 433ft. The Mauvoisin Dam, which blocks a wild ravine in the Upper Bagnes Valley, is one of the highest arched-type dams in the world (237m/778ft). This huge wall has created a reservoir of 180 million m^3/40 000 million gal of water to feed the turbines of the Fionnay and Riddes power stations.

▶ *At Mauvoisin, make for the visitors' car park halfway between the hotel and the dam. After parking the car, take the path to the crown of the dam.*

Walk to the Chanrion refuge★★

This strenuous walk *(6hr)* affords nice views of the lake but requires hikers to be in excellent physical condition. It is possible to spend the night at the refuge to spread the outing over two days. Bear right and proceed down the long covered passageway

(30min) then continue around the lake by a smooth path, walking for more than an hour. At the tip of the lake, you discover the Bec de Chardoney and the Bec de l'Épicourne. Go up to the refuge (1hr 30min) by following the words "piétons" on rocks, then the "red and white" signposting. On reaching the top (alt 2 462m/8 077ft), enjoy the **view**★★ of the Épicourne Glacier and, to the west, Mont Avril, Tour de Boussine, Combin de Tsessette (4 141m/13 600ft) and Tournelon Blanc, forming an imposing rocky barrier. The setting is enhanced by Lake Chanrion, where many plant and flower species thrive in this ideal location. Follow a charming path until the Col de Tsofeiret; the first part is relatively easy and offers **views**★ of the Brenay Glacier. The pass (alt 2 635m/8 645ft) affords a lovely **view**★ of Lake Tsofeiret. The expedition finishes by going down the gentle slope (2 hours or more), glimpsing plunging **views**★★ of Lake Mauvoisin along the way.

Road to Champex★★
The small road from Les Valettes to Champex is difficult. There are 22 hairpin bends, mostly sharp and awkward above the Durnant which flows through 1km/0.5mi of the impressive gorges *(sightseeing facilities; inexperienced mountain drivers are advised to take the route via Orsières, see below).*

Champex★★
Alt 1 465m/4 806ft. Champex stands high above the Orsières Basin at the mouth of a deep wooded valley containing a delightful lake. It is an elegant resort which in summer combines the pleasures of the beach and good views. Its watery mirror reflects the majestic series of snowy summits of the Combin (Combin de Corbassière on the left, Grand Combin on the right). Those in search of views can see the range at their leisure while strolling along the Signal road connecting the hotel-belvederes of the resort. An alpine garden is open to visitors in summer.

La Breya★★
Alt 2 374m/7 787ft. 1hr 30min there and back, including 15min by chairlift. Operates from mid-Jun to late Sep, 8.30am-12.30pm and 1.30-4.30pm, winter 9.15am-4.30pm. *Fare there and back: 12CHF; 151CHF for a 6-day pass.* (027) 783 13 44.
A pleasant ascent by chairlift above Lake Champex; panorama of the Valais Alps. From Champex to Orsières, the winding, surfaced road, well laid out, within sight of the Combin Massif and the Valais foothills of the Mont Blanc sloping down to the Ferret Valley, lies between broad fields of strawberries. The scenery is wonderful.

Orsières
The small town lies at the bottom of a hollow where the Ferret Valley, after following the whole Valais face of the Mont-Blanc Massif, joins the Entremont Valley. The church has preserved its rustic belfry in the Lombard Romanesque style, although much damaged by the weather. Among the Valais foothills of the Mont Blanc which overlook the Ferret Valley, you will see the snowy peak of the Portalet in the distance; the great pyramid of the Catogne stands out clearly; Mount Vélan rises behind the triangular Petit Vélan.
The road passes **Bourg-St-Pierre** on its right, with its rust-coloured roofs nestling at the mouth of the Valsorey Valley and its waterfall. After crossing the Valsorey and its gorges, the road overlooks the Les Toules Dam of which there is a magnificent view *(a small section of the old pass road from Bourg-St-Pierre before you reach the dam is not surfaced).* Afterwards glaciated and striated rocks and rifts filled with landslides make the landscape more harsh.

Bourg-St-Bernard
The ski lifts (cable car towards the Menouve Pass) in this frontier resort at the entrance to the tunnel is the small winter sports resort, Super-St-Bernard. The last section is

through the sinister Combe des Morts, swept by avalanches. To the left of the Vélan rises the fine smooth ice cap of the Grand Combin.

Tunnel du Grand-St-Bernard

Entrance at Bourg-St-Bernard. 🚘 *Cars: 27CHF one-way, 38CHF there and back; motorbikes: 15CHF one-way, 20CHF there and back.*

In view of the ever-increasing road traffic between the Rhône Valley and the Aosta Valley and to overcome the problem of snow blocking the road through the pass for over six months of the year, the Swiss and Italian governments combined to build a road tunnel, from 1959 to 1964, which would be open all year round and shorten the distance from Basel to Turin to 450km/281mi. Some sections of the road on the Italian side are not protected. Throughout the length of the road you can admire the daring construction of this highway, with its viaducts high above the Artanavaz Gorges. Access roads on either side of the tunnel are generally covered and have a maximum gradient of 6% (1 in 16); they lead from below Bourg-St-Pierre on the Swiss side and above St Oyen on the Italian side.

After the Combe des Morts, it is a fast run to the Great St Bernard Pass (Col du Grand-St-Bernard).

Col du Grand-St-Bernard★ – 💧 *See Col du GRAND-ST-BERNARD.*

GRAUBÜNDEN★★★

GRISONS

Three languages, two churches more or less equally represented and a political evolution towards democracy similar to that of the original cantons make the Grisons, the largest Swiss canton, a true model of the Confederation. This is undoubtedly the part of Switzerland where the traveller can enjoy the most complete change: the Engadin, with the charm of its clear blue skies and open countryside, is the tourist lodestar of this little mountain state astride the Alps.

Geographical Notes

The Grisons, locally referred to as Graubünden, contain the sources of the Rhine and Inn. These two upper basins are separated southwest of the Silvretta by the large mountain range dotted by the Piz Linard, Piz Kesch, Piz Err and Piz Platta summits. Between these summits the valleys of the Flüela, the Albula and the Julier open up. This large Alpine area forms a vast semicircle marked out from west to east by the great Oberalp, Sankt Gotthard, San Bernardino, Maloja, Bernina and Umbrail passes. The Vorderrhein takes its source in the Oberalp cirque and runs from Disentis/Mustér along the Grisons Oberland; the Hinterrhein comes down from the Adula Glaciers. They meet at the foot of Reichenau Castle. The Upper Inn Valley (the river joins the Danube at Passau on the borders of Germany and Austria), because of the Engadin, is also part of ancient Rhaetia.

A Bit of History

The territory of the Grisons canton corresponds with the most mountainous parts of ancient **Rhaetia**, whose "Welsch" tribes originally peopled the area between Lake Constance and Venetia. The Upper Valleys of the Rhine and the Inn, protected from

Philipp Giegel / Switzerland Tourism

National Park Museum in Zernez

Germanisation, remained Romansh-speaking districts whose language, derived from Latin, was officially recognised as the fourth Swiss national language in 1938.

A Transit Area – Under Roman rule and throughout the Middle Ages, Rhaetia, being crossed by the High Road – the **Obere Strasse** (the Julier and especially the Septimer Pass) – and the Low Road – the **Untere Strasse** (Splügen Pass) – monopolised nearly all transalpine traffic through the present territory of the Confederation. The great advantage of the High Road is that there are few passes, so frequent along transalpine roads. The only comparable route was farther west along the Great St Bernard road. The present network of transalpine roads through the Grisons results from the implementation of a programme jointly financed by Switzerland, Austria and Piedmont between 1818 and 1823.

Driving Tours

Recommended Itineraries

Organised according to time (longest to shortest).

1 The Zügen and Flüela Pass Roads★★

Round tour starting from Davos – allow one day. 🚷 *See DAVOS.*

2 Route du Grand-St-Bernard★★

Road from Bellinzona to Chur – allow one day. 🚷 *See Route du GRAND-ST-BERNARD.*

3 Julier and Albula Pass Roads★

Round tour starting from Sankt Moritz – about 5 hours. 🚷 *See SANKT MORITZ.*

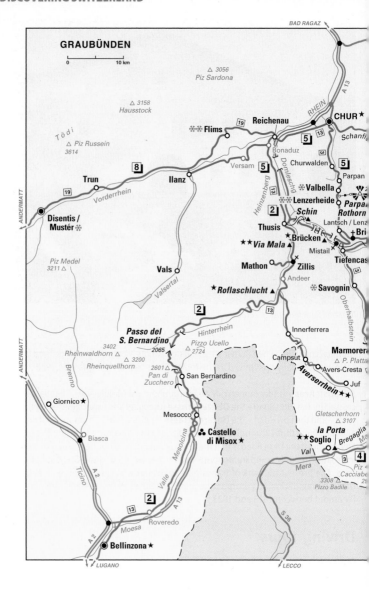

4 Engadin★★★

Upper Engadine (Bregaglia Valley): road from Sankt Moritz to Soglio – about 1hr 30min. Lower Engadine (Inn Valley): road from Sankt Moritz to Martina – about 3hr. 🕭 See ENGADIN.

5 Lenzerheide Road, Schyn Gorges★

Round tour starting from Chur – about 3hr. 🕭 See CHUR.

6 Ofen Pass Road (Swiss National Park and Müstair Valley)★

Road from Zernez to the Umbrail Pass – about 2hr 30min. 🕭 See ZERNEZ.

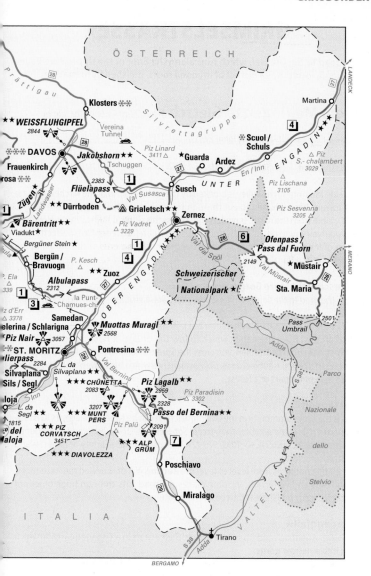

7 Berninastrasse (Bernina Valley and Poschiavo Valley)★★★
Road from Sankt Moritz to Tirano – about 2hr. 👤 *See BERNINASTRASSE.*

8 Vorderrhein Valley★
Road from Disentis/Mustér to Reichenau – about 1hr 45min. 👤 *See DISENTIS/MUSTER.*

9 Schanfigg Road★
Road from Chur to Arosa – about 1hr. 👤 *See AROSA.*

GRIMSELSTRASSE ★

The road to the Grimsel, which runs along the floor of the Upper Aare Valley (Haslital), introduces a district of rounded rocks, polished by former glaciers.

From Meiringen to Gletsch *37km/23mi – about 1hr 30min*

Itinerary 4 *(& see BERNER OBERLAND map)*

Meiringen★ – *& See MEIRINGEN.*

Outside Meiringen, the valley is blocked by the rocky mound of the Kirchet. Though the torrent has managed to cut through this bolt in the well-known Aare Gorges (not visible from the road), travellers must cross this ridge at high altitude. However, this enables you to get attractive glimpses between the trees of the perfectly level basin of Innertkirchen, dominated by the great escarpments of the Burg and the pyramid of the Bänzlauistock.

Aareschlucht (Aare Gorges)★★
From the road to the Grimsel, 1km/0.5mi plus 30min visit. & See MEIRINGEN: Excursions.
The valley loses its pastoral character but patches of vegetation still flourish among slabs of rock. After the bends which follow the bridge at Boden and 1.5km/1mi downstream from Guttannen, you cross the Spreitlauibach by a reinforced concrete gallery. This ravine is subject to terrible avalanches which have swept the whole area clean except for part of a forest.

Guttannen
This is the only community in the Oberhasli which can be called a village. Its **Kristall-museum** (🕐 *Open Jun-Sep, daily except Sat-Sun, 8am-5pm; Oct-May, Sat-Sun, open by appointment. ⊙3CHF. ☎ (033) 973 12 47*) displays a wide variety of minerals and crystals.
The climb continues from level to level in a **setting**★★ of rounded greenish rocks, snowfields and waterfalls. In some places the road cuts through huge blocks of extraordinarily polished, light-coloured granite.

Handeggfall★
The River Arlenbach and River Aare mingle their waters in a Y-shaped cascade which falls into a narrow gorge.
After the turquoise sheet of the reservoir-lake of **Räterichsboden** comes the great artificial lake of Grimsel, whose muddy waters are held back by two dams anchored to the Nollen Rock – the site of a hotel which took the place of the Grimsel hostel, now submerged. In line with the drowned valley, the **view**★ reaches the crests of the Finsteraarhorn (alt 4 274m/14 022ft, highest point of the Bernese Alps) in the distance.

Grimselpass★★
Alt 2 165m/7 103ft. A "Lake of the Dead" recalls the fighting between the Austrians and the French in 1799. From the mound behind Hotel Grimselblick, the **view**★★ includes the desert region where the Rhône rises, the Belvedere Hotel – the only visible human habitation – near the Rhône Glacier and, from left to right, the snowy Galenstock summit, the foot of the Rhône Glacier, the Furka Gap and its long, bare, monotonous crests stretching between the Upper Valais and the Piedmontese Toce

Valley. Facing northwest you will see in the far distance the walls of the Lauteraa (alt 4 042m/13 261ft).

The road then drops towards the **Gletschboden**, a desolate valley floor. The country loses its Arctic character and becomes more typically Alpine. The road develops hairpin bends on the Meienwand slopes and the terminal cataract of the Rhône Glacier, comes into sight, overlooked by the snowy dome of the Galenstock. You will also see Gletsch in the distance.

Gletsch★★ – 👌 *See GOMS.*

GRINDELWALD★★

BERN – POPULATION 3 930
ALT 1 034M/3 392FT

On an unforgettable site, Grindelwald, the Eiger village, is the only great mountain resort in the Jungfrau area which can be reached by car. It therefore attracts not only holidaymakers – mountaineers or skiers depending on the season – but also crowds of day trippers from the Interlaken area. The bustling crowds which, on fine winter or summer days, surge exuberantly along the little town's main street, plunge the newcomer straight into the atmosphere of an Alpine capital. Events throughout the year include the famous **World Snow Festival**, held each January on the natural skating rink at the heart of the village: several teams from different countries make ice and snow sculptures.

The majestic Grindelwald Glacier

🐾 **Don't Miss:** The Jungfraujoch – Top of Europe, from where you can see the longest glacier in the Alps. On the way to the top you pass Kleine Scheidegg with a spectacular view of the famous Eiger-Monch-Jungfrau triptych.

The Skiing Area

The Grindelwald skiing area, linked to those of **Wengen** and **Mürren**, consists of about 200km/125mi of slopes suitable for downhill skiing, served by 49 ski lifts, and dominated by the hulking grandeur of the Eiger. Surprisingly, many of the pistes in this staggeringly steep terrain are mild enough for intermediate level skiers and snowboarders. The Bodmi area is for novices, where lifts rise to First and Oberjoch (alt 2468m/8098ft) before opening onto vast, sunny snowfields. The descent between Oberjoch and Grindewald via piste 22 offers superb **views**★★ of the surrounding landscape and quaint villages. A carving piste and a snowpark have been laid out at the top. Kleine Scheidegg offers opportunities for splendid walks towards Grindelwald, especially at sunset. Seasoned skiers should choose the "Lauberhorn Rennstrecke" slope above Wengen, often used in official competitions for Alpine skiing. Steep and challenging slopes can be found on the Schilthorn Massif (including the Eiger Glacier), which is somewhat difficult to reach (train ride followed by a bus and 4 separate funiculars) but boasts the best pistes. For cross-country skiers, 35km/22mi of loops are available between Grindewald and Burglauenen. Despite the low altitude, the snow coverage is usually satisfactory at the bottom of the valleys because there is little sunlight during the winter season.

The area also offers many opportunities for hikers, with 80km/50mi of marked out trails and 20km/12.5mi of pistes for sledges. One recommended route is to walk up to Faulhorn from First (*2hr 30min -* 👣 *see below*) and then to go back down to Grindelwald by sledge via Bussalp; this 12.5km/8mi itinerary is the longest sledge piste in Europe.

The area boasts an important Sports Centre (Centre Sportif) with facilities for a number of sports, a skating rink, indoor swimming pool, curling rink, gymnasium, etc.

Site★★★

The site of Grindelwald combines a foreground full of country charm – fields planted with fruit trees or maples and containing pretty dwellings – with a grand rocky barrier stretching from the shoulder of the Wetterhorn to the pyramid of the Eiger. On one hand are the high mountains, a playground for mountaineers or skilled skiers; on the other, between the Grosse and Kleine Scheidegg Ridges, with the Faulhorn in between, is an immense amphitheatre-like shape of Alpine pastures and woods perfectly suited to cross-country skiing. Access is provided by the Wengernalp railway—much appreciated by skiers in early spring—which serves the high altitude annexe of the Kleine Scheidegg, and by the chain of chair-lifts at First.

Cable-Car Viewpoints

Jungfraujoch★★★

👣 *See JUNGFRAUJOCH. Allow at least one day for this exceptional excursion. We recommend that you choose the round tour of the Jungfrau by railway (👣 see Interlaken: Kleine Scheidegg).* 🚠 *Circular ticket Interlaken-Jungfraujoch-Interlaken: 172CHF; when taking one of the two first morning trains (Nov-Apr) and the trains with direct interconnection: 126CHF. Ticket for departure from Lauterbrunnen: 148CHF; when taking the two first trains: 154CHF. Ticket for departure from Grindelwald Grund: 149CHF; when taking the first train and return until noon (May-Oct): 103CHF. Circular ticket Interlaken-Kleine Scheidegg-Interlaken (not going up to Jungfraujoch): 68CHF.*

Männlichen★★★

⚠Access by the longest cable car ride in Europe (6.2km/4mi), 15min on foot from the centre of the resort. Allow 2hr there and back including 1hr by cable car. The main attractions of this summit are the walks and hikes that it offers (👣 see below).

The final platform (alt 2 227m/7 306ft) commands a splendid view of Grindelwald, at the foot of the Wetterhorn and the Schreckhorn. Go to the nearby viewpoint dominating the Lauterbrunnen Valley. **Panorama**★★★ of the legendary Eiger-Mönch-Jungfrau triptych, the sparkling Silberhorn, Breithorn and, down below, the village of Wengen, with Lake Thun lying to the north. To enjoy a complete circular view of your surroundings, climb up to the top of the Männlichen (alt 2 343m/7 687ft). The view is quite clear to the north.

First★★

⚠Access by cable car. Allow 1hr 30min including 1hr by cable car. The excursion can be combined with a walk (👣 see below). 🕐 Operates from 8am or 8.30am, times vary according to the season. 🕐 Closed in Nov and Apr. 🎫 Fare there and back: 50CHF. ☎ (033) 828 77 11.

When you reach the third section (alt 2 168m/7 113ft), go to the restaurant's panoramic terrace *(viewing table)*. Magnificent **view**★★ of the Grindelwald Basin in its wooded setting and the summits of the Wetterhorn, Grosser Fiescherhorn, Eiger, Jungfrau, Morgenhorn and Schreckhorn, hemmed in by the Upper and Lower Grindelwald Glaciers. The Titlis and the Sustenhörner can be glimpsed in the far distance. Lush pastures extend to the northwest, at the foot of the Faulhorn (note the hotel right on top).

🚶 Hiking Trails

Grindelwald is a great rambling and climbing centre, offering all types of excursions of varying degrees of difficulty (300km/187mi of paths at an altitude of 1 000-3 600m/3 280-11 810ft). Some of the more interesting circuits are listed below. There are also 100km/62mi of marked trails for mountain bikes.

Faulhorn★★★

⚠Access to First by cable car. 2hr 20min climb (500m/1 640ft difference in altitude). Inexperienced hikers can stop at Bachalpsee (50min easy walking).

Bachalpsee★★ is one of Switzerland's most beautiful lakes. It affords a spectacular **view**★★, enhanced by the twinkling reflections of the mountain cirque. From the verdant shores of the lake, you can admire the jagged crest of the Finsteraarhorn, framed between the Schreckhorn and the Fiescherhorn. The climb to Faulhorn is along a steep but even path. At the top (alt 2 681m/8 795ft), you reach one of the highest mountain hotels in Europe, and certainly the oldest (opened in 1832). Sweeping **panorama**★★★ of the Bernese Oberland. To the south, you can see First, the Mönch and the Breithorn. To the north, you overlook Lake Brienz and Lake Thun, lying at the foot of the Brienzerrothorn and the Niederhorn respectively. In the far distance, farther east, note the Pilatus and Rigi peaks.

From Faulhorn to Schynige Platte★★★

3hr 15min walk with a 600m/1 969ft difference in altitude. 🚶 This excursion is for experienced hikers only (sturdy mountain boots necessary) and can be undertaken after the walk to Grindelwald. 🌧 Do not attempt to go in wet weather. The return to Grindelwald is by train (enquire beforehand about times).

The fascinating **path along the crest** offers a wonderful panorama at all times. After one hour's walking, heading towards the Mädlenen Restaurant, the rocky track becomes more tiring and more difficult to negotiate. It commands nearby **views**★ of Lake Sägistal and the formidable slopes of the Faulhorn. It then wends its way through mountain pastures before revealing a fantastic **panorama**★★★ of the Jungfrau Massif, extending from the Schreckhorn to the Morgenhorn. On reaching the Schynige Platte, those climbers who still have some energy left will discover an Alpine garden.

▶ *The climb down to Wilderswil is by rack railway. Then take the train back to Grindelwald.*

Mönchsjochhütte★★★
Alt 3 629m/11 905ft. 1hr climb. Access from Jungfraujoch (see *JUNGFRAUJOCH*).

Stieregg and Bänisegg★★
Access to Pfingstegg (alt 1 391m/10 078ft) in 4min by cable car. Allow 1hr climb to reach the Baregg Restaurant (260m/854ft difference in altitude) and an extra 1hr to get to Bänisegg (160m/525ft difference in altitude).

From Pfingstegg, look for an overall **view**★ of Grindelwald and the First area and an even path following the mountain slope. After 30min, you will admire a fantastic **view**★★ of the Lower Grindelwald Glacier and especially Fieschergletscher. Note the waterfalls gushing down the slopes of the Eiger. The path now becomes steeper and leads past local flora (orchids, rhododendrons, and forget-me-nots) and the occasional sheep. Allow 1.20 hrs to reach the Baregg Restaurant (alt 1 650m/5 413ft) commands an even more impressive **view**★★ of the majestic glacial cirque dominated by the Grossfiescherhorn (alt 4 048m/13 280ft).

Experienced hikers who do not suffer from vertigo and who are equipped with proper mountain boots can continue towards Schreckhornhütte. Although it is still wild, the setting now features more and more species of regional flora and fauna. After a series of short ups and downs, the path follows a very steep course to reach Bänisegg (alt 1 807m/5 927ft). From a bend to the left, you can discover the long ice

Lucia Degonda / Switzerland Tourism

Kleine Scheidegg with Eiger lookout tower

tongue of the Ischmeer. It is a truly breathtaking **site**★★, with the Fins looming at a height of 4 274m/14 021ft.

▶ *Go back down along the same path (1hr 30min).*

From Pfingstegg, you can reach the **Milchbach Chalet** by a gently sloping track *(allow 1hr).* This route will take you past the mineral paradise of Breitlouwina (Gesteinparadies Breitlouwina), characterised by a remarkably wide range of sediments dating from several million years ago. View of the Upper Grindelwald Glacier, in which an **ice cave** has been set up. Visitors will be impressed by the blue ice walls of the cave, which is almost 30m/99ft deep. Allow an extra 20min to climb down to the Hôtel Wetterhorn, where a bus will take you back to Grindelwald.

From Männlichen to Kleine Scheidegg★★
Take the Männlichen cable car. 1hr 15min walk along an easy, pleasant path (170m/558ft difference in altitude).
All along the way, there are superb **views**★★ of the Eiger, Mönch, Jungfrau and Grindewald Basin.

▶ *From Kleine Scheidegg, continue with the walk to Eigerwand or return to Grindelwald by train.*

Eigerwand★★
Access to the Eigergletscher resort (alt 2 320m/7 611ft) by train. Allow 2hr for the climb down to Alpiglen (700m/2 297ft difference in altitude). Good mountain boots essential. Do not stray from the beaten track, which cuts across a protected area for local fauna.
Follow the railway tracks for 100m/328ft going downwards, then cross them and take the "Eiger-Trail" itinerary on the right. Walk a short distance up to the foot of the Eiger. The path goes through steep Alpine pastures and mounds of fallen rocks, following the imposing mountain face, offering pretty views of Grindelwald and the Wetterhorn. Reaching a steep slope, it leads to the Alpiglen pastures (alt 1 615m/5 297ft). The climb down can be undertaken on foot or by train.

Gletscherschlucht★
2.5 km/1.5mi – on a very narrow road beginning at the far end of the village, on the right, after a church, plus 30min sightseeing. ⏱ *Access from beginning May to mid-Oct, 10am-5pm; mid-Jul to late Aug, 9am-6pm (9pm Tue and Thu); Sep-Oct, 10am-5pm.* ⏱ *Closed in winter.* ⊛6CHF. ☎ *(033) 853 60 50.*
A rocky fissure, at the bottom of which the tail of the Lower Grindelwald Glacier (Unterer Grindelwaldgletscher) appears as a narrow strip of ice. This impressive geological formation was once described by Byron as a "frozen hurricane".

GRUYÈRES★★

FRIBOURG – POPULATION 1 412
ALT 830M/2 657FT

This little fortified town is perched on a hill in a harmonious landscape. It charms visitors to Romansh Switzerland by its friendly atmosphere, derived from the time when the whole Sarine Valley lay under the benevolent rule of the counts of Gruyères (12C-16C). 🛈 *1663 –* ☎ *(026) 921 10 30.*

Arrival

P *Cars should be parked outside the town (car park).* Visitors will immediately be charmed by the locality of Gruyères, which they approach by its main street. It is lined with old houses with twin windows and wide eaves, and slopes down to the town fountain before rising again towards the castle.

Go up to the castle on foot, noticing on the right the old grain measures hollowed out of a stone block, and then, on the left, the house with delicately carved 16C window frames of the jester Chalamala, who became famous at the court of the counts of Gruyères.

Sights

Castle★★

Guided tour (1hr) Apr-Oct, 9am-6pm; Nov-Mar, 10am-4:30pm. Last admission 30min before closing time. ◷ *Closed 1 Jan and at Christmas.* ⊛ *6CHF.* ☎ *(026) 921 21 02; www.gruyeres.ch/chateau/.*

The former castle of the counts of Gruyères now belongs to the Fribourg canton. Most of it dates from the late 15C (façades on the courtyard of the main dwelling). The internal arrangement recalls both the feudal period (kitchen and guardroom) and 18C refinements. Their decoration, more or less tasteful, is largely the work of the Bovy family, a dynasty of artists who saved the castle from destruction in the 20C and welcomed many foreign artists (namely Corot). The heraldic crane of the counts of Gruyères can be seen in many places, over doors, in stained-glass windows and on firebacks. The most valuable pieces assembled here are the three mourning **copes**★ of the Order of the Golden Fleece, used by almoners of Charles the Bold to celebrate masses for the repose of knights who died in the campaign of 1476. These sumptuous vestments became, for the people of Fribourg, their most glorious trophy of the Battle of Murten. Four 16C Flanders tapestries depicting scenes from the Old Testament are displayed in the count's bedroom, whose ceiling is typical of the Savoyard period. In the Baroque Salle des Baillis, note the impressive sculpted wood furniture. The Salle des Chevaliers, notable for its size and decoration, has a coffered ceiling with hanging keystones and walls painted with scenes illustrating the history of the counts' lands.

Chapelle St-Jean

The 15C chapel stands on a pleasantly terrace within view of the Lower Gruyères (Bulle-Broc district), partly drowned by the reservoir of the Rossens Dam, and of the two graceful Dent de Broc peaks. Near the chapel, on the ramparts, is a splendid view of the surrounding area, including the Moléson and the Jura chain (viewing table).

Musée HR Giger

◷ *Open summer, 10am-6pm; winter, daily except Mon, 11am-6pm.* ⊛ *10CHF.* ☎ *(026) 921 22 00, www.hrgiger.info.*

This museum is a must-see destination for fans of science-fiction films. Housed in Château St-Germain, the museum is dedicated to Swiss sculptor HR Giger, who created the *Alien* life forms. The *Birth Machine* sculpture at the entrance sets the tone for a visit, which includes a room dedicated to the movie, with various sketches used for the film, paintings, sculptures and unique pieces of furniture made from glass, plexiglass, polyester, metal and rubber and artifacts from the artist's other major works, *Species*, *The Spell I-IV* and *Harkonnen*.

▶ *Follow the main street again. In this direction it offers a view of the Moléson (see below), the most typical Gruyères peak. Turn to the right in front of the fountain.*

Address Book

For coin ranges, see the Legend on the front flap.

WHERE TO STAY

Those wishing to sample local specialities should taste these dishes: the traditional fondue and raclette, jambon (ham) and meringue à la crème de la Gruyère (sweet topped with cream).

Auberge de la Halle – ☎ *026 921 21 78*. Restaurant with a rustic setting offering regional dishes and a charming atmosphere.

Fleur de Lys – ☎ *026 921 82 82* - www.hotelfleurdelys.ch – *11 rooms* – *closed Feb and Nov-Easter*. Rooms decorated with pretty wainscoting Large, rustic dining hall where traditional meals are served.

Hôtel de Ville – ☎ *026 921 24 24* – www.hoteldeville.ch – *8 rooms* – *closed 1-20 Dec and 3-17 Jan*. Located in the main street, this old-fashioned, rustic hotel has a restaurant which serves regional cuisine.

Le Chalet – ☎ *026 921 21 54* – *closed 25 Dec*. A country chalet serving local cuisine in the heart of the town centre.

Hostellerie de St-Georges – ☎ *026 921 83 00* – www.st-georges-gruyeres.ch – *14 rooms*. Old inn dating back to the 16C. Peace and quiet guaranteed. Lovely views of the ramparts and surrounding mountains.

Maison du Gruyère

1km/0.5mi away, at the entrance to Pringy. Open 9am-7pm (6pm Oct-Mar). 5CHF ☎ (026) 921 84 00, www.lamaisondugruyere.ch.

This former industrial cheesemaking factory houses a demonstration cheese dairy. The ground floor contains the cellars where the cheeses are stored. The first floor features the ripening area, an exhibition on local customs, a videotape explaining cheesemaking techniques and galleries overlooking the demonstration area where Gruyère is made in wheels of 35kg/77lb. Exhibits reverberate with the sounds of cheesemaking, inlcuding cowbells and the sound of the rushing mountain streams where cows spend their summer pasture; another exhibit focuses on the aromas of the high pastures.

Excursion

Moléson-sur-Gruyères

6 km/4mi to the SW. 1662 – ☎ (026) 921 85 00

This pretty village features a **Fromagerie d'Alpage** (*Open mid-May to Oct, 9.30am-6pm. 2.50CHF. By prior appointment to Madame Sylvia Magnin on ☎ (026) 921 10 44; www.fromagerie-alpage.ch*), an Alpine cheese dairy set up in a 17C chalet, with a roof made up of 90 000 shingles. After an audio-visual presentation of regional specialities, visitors are shown the humble sleeping quarters of a local cowherd *(armailli)*. Then they can watch a cowherd prepare Gruyère cheese according to traditional methods, baking it in an old-fashioned stove fuelled by firewood. Fresh products are kept in the milk room and the more mature cheeses are stored in the salting house, a small square building with a shingle roof located near the farm.

A cable car will take you up to the **Observatoire de Moléson** (*Cable-car leaving from Moléson-Village: does not operate from Easter to mid-May and mid-Oct to mid-Dec. The observatory is open from mid-Dec to mid-Apr, 9am-4.30pm; mid-May to mid-Oct, 9am-6pm (11pm Fri and Sat in Jul and Aug). Evening introductory sessions to astronomy, by appointment 5pm-9am. 65CHF. ☎ (026) 921 29 96*) (alt 2 002m/6 500ft), which commands a panoramic view of the Gruyères area and the Swiss plateau. The observatory organises evening classes on the subject of astronomy (telescopes). During the winter season 35km/20mi of carefully marked-out ski runs are available to tourists.

The La Locanda restaurant in Moléson village is the setting for the **Historial Suisse**, (🕐 *Open daily except Tue, 8am-9pm.* 🕐 *Closed Nov.* 🚫 *No charge.* ☎ *(026) 921 32 63.*) a wax museum whose figures evoke prominent personalities in Swiss history from St Maurice to Henri Dunant.

GSTAAD✳✳

BERN – POPULATION 2 000
ALT 1 080M/3 543FT

Gstaad lies on the boundary between the Bernese and Vaud Alps at the junction of four gently sloping valleys including: the Upper Sarine Valley, the Lauenen Valley, the Turbach Valley and the Saanenmöser Depression. The resort, with its carefully restored old chalets and many luxury boutiques, is pleasing for its restful setting and the variety of its sporting and social facilities. Popular with celebrities in winter, Gstaad offers a number of pleasant walks in summer: explore the **Eggli** (alt 1 557m/5 106ft) and the nearby plateau, accessible by cable car. Helicopter rides of the area are available from Gstaad-Grund heliport.

The Skiing Area

Thanks to the blue trains of the local railways, the resort shares with Saanenmöser (alt 1 272m/4 173ft – facilities) and even with Zweisimmen (equipped with a large cable car for ascents to the Rinderberg) a magnificent ski area served by about 60 ski lifts. There are more than 85km/53mi of groomed local runs and more than 250km/155mi in the region, which encompasses six ski resorts with inteconnected lifts. The Eggli (alt 1671m/5483ft) has good, long intermediate runs and connects with nearby Rougemont. Wassergrat (alt 1942m/ 6372ft) is for intermediates and experts, offering both open snowfields and piste routes through the trees. Cross-country skiers can enjoy 100km/62m of classic tracks and 40km25mi of skating tracks.

A Selection of Ski Resorts

Resort	Altitude	Resort	Altitude
✳ Arosa:	1 742m/5 715ft	✳ Sankt Moritz:	1 856m/6 089ft
✳ Crans-Montana:	1 500m/4 921ft	✳ Wengen:	1 275m/4 183ft
✳ Davos:	1 563m/5 128ft	✳ Zermatt:	1 620m/5 315ft
✳ Gstaad:	1 080m/3 543ft		

VAL D'HÉRENS★★

The Hérens Valley is one of the most accessible of the lateral valleys in French-speaking Valais. The Évolène district, located in a very fine setting of high mountains, overlooked by the Dent Blanche (alt 4 357m/14 290ft), has retained many traditional local customs. Sights like that of haymaking between Évolène and Les Haudères are among the most attractive in picturesque Switzerland. When you see the women working in the fields or driving herds of cows, you are often tempted to forget the rigours of their mountain life. The men seldom feature in these pastoral scenes. Most of them find work in local timber yards or factories.

The Skiing Area
In winter, skiers can tackle 100km/65mi of downhill runs, two cross-country skiing tracks (33km/20mi) and two open-air ice rinks.

From Sion to Les Haudères *29km/18mi – about 2hr*

Itinerary 5 *(* 👆 *see Le VALAIS map)*

Sion★★ – *3hr.* 👆 *See SION.*

From Sion, crossing the Rhône and leaving on the right the Chandoline power station, fed by the Grande Dixence Dam, the road climbs in hairpin bends, affording good views of the site of Sion, marked by the fortified heights of Valère and Tourbillon. On arriving at Vex, the first village in the Hérens Valley, the superb rock pyramid of the Dent Blanche begins to emerge from the Ferpècle Corrie.

Barrage de la Grande Dixence★★★ – 👆 *See Barrage de la GRANDE DIXENCE 16km/10mi from Vex by a narrow road – allow 2hr.*

The road, which runs almost horizontally along a ledge, approaches the ravines overlooking the confluence of the Borgne and the Dixence. The eye will be caught by the astonishing ridge of broken country from which the Pyramids of Euseigne spring.

Pyramides d'Euseigne★
The road passes through a tunnel under the crowned columns cut out by erosion from masses of soft morainic debris and saved from destruction by their unstable, rocky crowns. The valley shrinks and the gradient grows steeper. Arrival in the Evolène Basin is marked by the reappearance of the Dent Blanche. To the right of the Dent Blanche, in the foreground, stand the twin sharp-edged pyramids of the Dents de Veisivi.

Évolène★
Alt 1 400m/4 592ft. The tall, flower-decked **wooden houses★★** of this charming resort, some of which date back to the 16C, are among the finest in the Valais. Évolène is a popular mountaineering centre (Mount Collon and the Dent Blanche Massifs) with a climbing school in the village.

Les Haudères
The chalets stand in picturesque disorder.
From here roads lead to **Ferpècle** (alt 1 770m/5 807ft; 9km/5.5mi from Les Haudères), at the foot of the Dent Blanche, and Arolla (12km/8mi) at the foot of Mont Collon. The road passes through the hamlets of La Sage, Villa and La Forclaz, with their beautiful slate-roofed chalets, and offers clear views of the Upper Hérens Valley.

Walking in the Val d'Hérens

Walk to Alpe Bricola★★
Alt 2 415m/7 923ft. Park the car at Salay/Ferplècle. 2hr 15min up, 1hr 30min down. A comparatively easy ascent.
This outing offers lovely **views★★** over the glaciers of Ferplècle, Mont-Mine and La Dent Blanche. For a sweeping panorama of the landscape, continue to climb a little higher towards the Dent Blanche Hütte refuge.

Walk to the Cabane des Aiguilles Rouges★★

Alt 2 810m/9 219ft. 3hr up, 2hr down. Check timetables in advance to get back to Arolla from La Gouille hamlet in the evening. Park the car at the foot of the Guitza ski lift. This lovely route requires considerable stamina over a variety of landscapes.

Leaving behind the ski lift, proceed up a steep forest path commanding magnificent **views**★★ of Pointe de Tsa, Mont Collon and Pigne d'Arolla to a lovely path crossing an Alpine lawn *(avoid the winding lane)*. After about one hour, you reach the pretty perched village of **Remointse de Pra Gra** (2 479m/8 133ft), built entirely in stone and the traditional rough-hewn tiles called *lauzes*, nestling in its lovely site. Start climbing towards the refuge, lying in its rocky setting at the foot of the Aiguilles Rouges of Arolla (follow red signs when crossing the chasms). The refuge affords a **sweeping panorama**★★ of the whole valley: the Aiguille de la Tsa, Pointe des Genevois, Dent de Perroc and La Grande Dent de Veisivi form a huge, formidable-looking stone barrier.

The descent is steep and very picturesque, leading down to the shores of the charming **Lac Bleu**★★ (2 090m/6 856ft), with its crystal-clear waters, enhanced by a leafy setting of larch trees. Treat yourself to a **tour of the lake**★★ to take in all its shimmering reflections. Walk down to La Gouille hamlet and catch a bus back. You are advised not to take the path going from Lac Bleu to Arolla, as it is both tiring and dangerous.

Walk to the Pas de Chèvres★★

Alt 2 855m/9 366ft. 2hr up, 1hr 30min down, difference in height 850m/2 789ft. Park the car on leaving Arolla, just before you get to the highest chalet.

Follow the lane for 50m/55yd, then take the steep path on the right, facing the slope, until you reach the broken-down hillocks *(40min)*. Take the path opposite that winds its way through an open **landscape**, skirting the impressive Tsijiore Nouve Glacier and Pigne d'Arolla (3 796m/12 454ft). Around 30 min later, after crossing a track, the path becomes steeper. At the next fork, turn left. The pass offers beautiful **views**★★ of Mont Collon and the Aiguille de la Tsa, the two most striking features of the Arolla Valley, and the sight of Mont Blanc de Cheilon and its glacier, the lake and the Cabane de Dix, huddled atop a rocky outcrop. Go back down along the path on the right in the middle section, near the ski lift.

HÖLLOCHGROTTE★

SCHWYZ

The Hölloch Cave is known for the size of its galleries, the number of its naturally formed chambers and the beauty of its concretions. It is also the largest cave in Europe and, as a geological phenomenon, it enjoys a worldwide reputation.

Access

On the way out of Schwyz, take the Muotatal road which is narrow until Hinterthal, then cross the river and turn left into a steep uphill road going to Stalden *(signpost: Stalden-Hölloch)*. Leave the car near the Gasthaus zur Höllgrotte where the guide lives, and walk to the entrance to the cave.

Visit

Torches, hard hats and waterproof boots are strongly recommended. Guided tour *(1hr 30min) Jun-Sep, Wed-Fri at 10.30am, 1.30pm and 4pm, Sat-Sun at 10am, 1pm, 3pm and 4pm; Oct-May, by appointment only.* 14CHF. (041) 390 40 40.

Since 1949, the Hölloch Cave has been the scene of continuous exploration. Only 1km/0.5mi of the galleries are open, though more than 147km/91mi have been mapped. This natural underground architecture is fascinating; there are few stalactites or stalagmites, but by contrast there are delicate, fairylike concretions in the form of roses, chandeliers and seashells, which seem to soften the grim walls of the great gulfs in the cave and the ever-increasing number of erosion holes. The "Altar" (Autel) and the "Great Pagoda" (Grande Pagode) deserve special attention.

INTERLAKEN★★★

BERN – POPULATION 5 056
TOWN PLAN IN THE MICHELIN GUIDE SWITZERLAND

Interlaken is the tourist centre of the Berner Oberland. It is renowned for its superb view of the Jungfrau Massif, which is home to the highest railway station in Europe (☼ see JUNGFRAUJOCH). Framed between the small wooded ranges of the Rügen and the Harder, the town extends over the low plain of the Bödeli, formed by deposits from the Lombach in the north and the Lütschine in the south. These finally divided the single lake (into which the Aare used to flow between Meiringen and Thun) into two distinct sheets of water, Lake Thun and Lake Brienz (Thunersee and Brienzersee). *Höheweg 37 – 3800 – ☎ (033) 826 53 00, www.interlakentourism.ch.*

▶ **Orient Yourself:** Interlaken has two train stations, West and Ost. West station goes to the city centre; take Ost station for excursions to nearby villages and peaks such as Grindelwald and Junfraujoch.

🅿 **Parking:** There is parking at the Ost train station.

☺ **Don't Miss:** An excursion to one of the majestic summits: Schilthorn, Junffrau, Eiger.

The Latin sound of the name Interlaken recalls the clerical origin of the town; it grew up between the lakes from the 12C onwards, around an Augustinian monastery of which traces, like the cloister gallery, can still be found in the block of buildings

---

Address Book

☼ *For coin ranges, see the Legend on the cover flap.*

WHERE TO STAY

⊝⊜⊜ **Seehotel** – *Seestrasse 22 – ☎ 033 822 07 70 – Fax 033 822 07 40 – www.seehotelterrasse.ch - 40 rooms* – Hotel with terrace situated on the shore of the lake. Peace and quiet guaranteed.

⊝⊜⊜ **Beau Site** – *Seestrasse 16 – ☎ 033 826 75 75 – www.beausite.ch – 50 rooms* – Superb views of the Jungfrau. Enjoy the pleasant garden after a hard day's trekking in the snow.

⊝⊜⊜ **Goldey** – *Obere Goldey 85 – ☎ 033 826 44 45 – www.goldey.ch – 41 rooms* – Lovely hotel at the water's edge. The starting-point for many excursions, it will provide a warm, cosy welcome when you return at the end of the day.

⊝⊜⊜ **Hirschen** – *In Matten, Hauptstrasse 11 – ☎ 033 822 15 45 – www.hirschen-interlaken.ch – 25 rooms* – Attractive wooden chalet typical of the region, dating from the 16C. Breathtaking panorama of the Jungfrau range from the terrace. Traditional cuisine. Restful atmosphere and great charm.

formed by the castle and the Protestant church. The resort is extremely popular in the summer months, when its many souvenir shops are busy with tourists.

Sights

Höheweg★★

This famous avenue is bordered on one side by the lawns and flower beds of the Höhematte, on the other by a row of grand hotels and behind them, the casino (Kursaal). The promenade links the urban centre of Interlaken West with the much more scattered township of Interlaken East. It offers dazzling **views**★★★ of the Jungfrau, through the opening of the lower Lütschine Valley. It is pleasant to stroll beneath the trees, glancing at the pavilion of meteorological instruments or the well-known floral clock in the casino gardens. A second attraction on the opposite bank of the River Aare is the open-air swimming pool and miniature golf course. These are both popular weekend activities during the summer season.

Kirche von Unterseen

With its rustic tower crowned by a steeply pitched roof, this building with the Mönch (on the left) and the Jungfrau (on the right) in the background makes an attractive **scene**★★.

Touristikmuseum

At Unterseen Obere Gasse 26. ○ *Open May to mid-Oct, daily except Mon, 2-5pm.* ◌*5CHF.* ☎ *(033) 826 64 64, www.unterseen.ch/museum.*
A charming renovated 17C residence with old timber beams up to 20m/60ft long houses a small museum which retraces the development of tourism in the Jungfrau region from the beginning of the last century to the present day. Exhibits illustrate a century of road transport in the Oberland: the Habkern postal carriage, models of other postal vehicles and the first bicycle to have been used in Interlaken. The milestone *(studenstein)* indicated the distance and length of time required for those on foot to reach Bern. Other displays illustrate the expansion of the hotel industry (accommodation in private homes, inns and hotels) and development of the railway network (model of a locomotive from the Brünig Pass's rack railway). They also feature nautical instruments and furnishings (compass, first-aid kit, siren, wheel) grouped together in the boat section. The most interesting exhibit is undoubtedly a miniature model of the *Bellevue*, the very first boat to sail on Lake Thun. There are additional displays on winter sports, with a section on development of skis and sledges, the growth of mountain railways such as those on the Giessbach, Wetterhorn and Jungfrau, and the sport of mountaineering. The top floor is reserved for temporary exhibitions.

Excursions

By Funicular or on Foot

Schynige Platte★★

Alt 2 101m/6 891ft. About 4hr there and back, including 2hr by rack railway starting from Wilderswil station. ○ *Operates Jun-Oct. Departure every 50min, 8am-6.30pm.* ◌ *Fare there and back: 55CHF.* ☎ *(033) 828 72 33.*
This climb is especially suited to tourists who have no time to venture farther into the Jungfrau Massif. Schynige Platte is one of the most popular destinations for holidaymakers staying in Grindelwald (& see GRINDELWALD).
Near the upper station, an Alpine garden and a botanical section have been laid out over an area of 8 000m²/9 570sq yd, presenting some 500 varieties of flowers

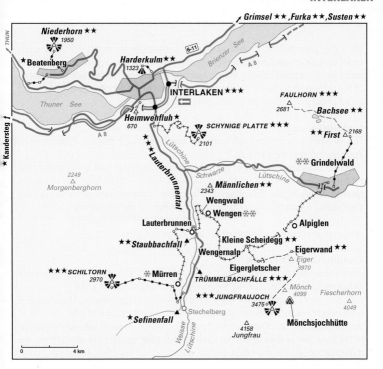

(edelweiss, gentian), plants and ferns. The panoramic terrace of the hotel affords easy access to the nearest summit (alt 2 076m/6 812ft – viewpoint overlooking the Jungfrau, Interlaken and its lakes). Note the Alpine dairy on the Iseltenalp, where fresh dairy produce is made daily day (milk, butter, cheese and serac).

Harderkulm★★

Alt 1 323m/4 341ft. ⚓About 1hr there and back, including 10min by funicular from Interlaken East. ⏰Operates daily, Apr-Oct, 8.10am-5.45pm. Departures every 20 or 30min. ✆Fare there and back: 25CHF. ☎ (033) 828 73 39.
A small park near the lower funicular station is home to a variety of animals typically found in the Alps. From the panoramic restaurant at the summit, there is a clear view of the two Interlaken lakes and the Jungfrau Massif.

Heimwehfluh★

Alt 670m/2 218ft. 1hr to 2hr there and back, including 5min by funicular. ⏰ Operates mid-April to late Nov, 8.30am-5.30pm. Departures every 15min. ✆Fare there and back: 11CHF. ☎ (033) 822 34 53.
A cool, shady hill overlooking Lake Thun and Lake Brienz.
There are many shaded walks, especially on the slopes of the Rügen or the Harder.

By Car or by Cable Car

Beatenberg★; Niederhorn★★ – ⚓ *Access and description see BEATENBERG.*

Lauterbrunnental★★★

18km/11mi – about 3hr including 2hr 45min cable car and sightseeing. Leave Interlaken to the south on the Grindelwald road. The road runs into the wooded Lütschine defile, losing sight of the Jungfrau for the time being.

▶ *At the road fork at Zweilütschinen, go straight ahead to Lauterbrunnen.*

The valley soon widens, framed, as you go upstream, by the huge rock walls which make the Lauterbrunnen Gorge a classic example of the glacial feature: a U-shaped valley (*illustration see Introduction: Alpine relief*). Ahead, on either side of the slopes of the Schwarzmönch, appear the snowy summits of the Jungfrau (on the left) and those of the Mittaghorn-Grosshorn group (straight ahead).

Lauterbrunnen

This village has heavy through traffic. Motorists who wish to go to Wengen must leave their cars in the car park.

Here the **Staubbachfall**★, which Byron compared to the "tail of the pale horse ridden by Death in the Apocalypse", plunges 300m/1 000ft from the terrace at Mürren, dissolving almost entirely into fine spray. In line with the valley you will see the Breithorn summit, clearly detached to the right of the Grosshorn.

▶ *Leave your car in the Trümmelbachfälle car park.*

Trümmelbachfälle★★★

3hr to 4hr on foot there and back. *Open Jul and Aug, 8am-6pm; Apr, May, Sep and Oct, 9am-5pm.* 11CHF. Take waterproof garments. *(033) 855 32 32.*

A lift passing through the rock leads to the beginning of the galleries. These are well sited over the winding fissure where the Trümmelbach leaps and boils, forcing its way through a series of great eroded potholes. On returning to the lower entrance of the funicular, be sure to walk up the path to the left (to the right when facing the mountain) to see the incredible gush of water coming from the second last falls of the Trümmelbachfälle.

Lucia Degonda / Switzerland Tourism

Lauterbrunnen – View of the Staubbachfall

Return to your car and drive up the valley to Stechelberg, the Mürren-Schilthorn cable-car station and the place from where you can see, to the south *(1km/0.5mi)* the lovely, almost vertical **Sefinenfall**★.

Mürren❋ – *Access: 10min by cable car.* See MÜRREN.

Schilthorn★★★
Round trip about 2hr including 1hr cable car via Stechelberg. Operates from 6.25am-11.25pm. Fare there and back: 89CHF. For information on periods of closure, call (033) 856 21 41. See MÜRREN: Excursions.

Grindelwald❋❋
20km/12mi to the SE – about 3hr to 4hr. See GRINDELWALD.
At Zweilütschinen turn left into the Schwarze Lütschine Valley. This is less steep-sided than the Lütschine Valley through which you have just come. After climbing the ridge, created by a former moraine, following a series of hairpin bends, you will begin to see the impressive mountain setting of Grindelwald. From left to right the following will appear in succession: the Wetterhorn group, with the great snowfield of the Grindelwald Firn, the beginning of the Upper Grindelwald Glacier (Oberer Grindelwaldgletscher), the Mettenberg, the Lower Grindelwald Glacier (Unterer Grindelwaldgletscher) and finally, at the end of the long rock face, the pyramidal shape of the Eiger.

Tour of Three Passes (Grimsel, Furka, Susten)★★★
191km/119mi – allow a whole day (start in the early morning). Leave Interlaken to the southwest on the Meiringen road (see MEIRINGEN), then follow the roads to the Three Passes, preferably beginning with the Grimsel Pass Road (see GRIMSELSTRASSE).

Kanderstal★
43km/27mi – about 3hr. Leave Interlaken by the road to Spiez. See KANDERSTEG.
The road follows the south shores of Thun Lake which lies opposite the wooded Nase promontory and the Beatenberg terrace. After Därlingen a corniche section reveals the whole of the lake and town of Thun in the distance.
At Leissigen take the road to the left towards **Aeschi**, crossing the ridge between the lake and the Kander Valley. The Aeschi **panorama**★ is a pleasantly wide view; the village marks the top of the climb.
After discovering the pretty mountain setting of Thun Lake you will catch sight of the gigantic Niesen Peak and – through the Kiental Gap – the three snow-covered Blümlisalp Peaks. *The rest of the excursion, from Reichenbach to Kandersteg, is described under KANDERSTEG.*
After going up to Lake Oeschinen return to Interlaken via Spiez. *For other excursions from Interlaken into the Bernese Oberland, see the list of recommended itineraries under BERNER OBERLAND.*

Round Tour of the Jungfrau by Railway★★★

This panoramic tour is magnificent, but quite expensive. Reductions are available on the first train of the morning: ask for a Good Morning Ticket. Allow a whole day for the tour and choose a day when the atmospheric conditions are the best possible in order to enjoy spectacular scenery; a veil of cloud on the summits is enough to spoil the excursion. Wear warm clothes, and if you want to go out into the open, take sun-glasses and wear sturdy shoes.
The first part of the journey is to Kleine Scheidegg, where passengers change trains. The train then makes its way through tunnels cut into the Eiger, stopping occasionally to allow passengers to admire the glaciers, and eventually reaches the **Top of Europe** station (alt 3 454m/11 329ft). Some of the slopes along this unforgett-

The Highest Railway Station in Europe

In 1893 Adolf Guyer-Zeller, an industrialist and member of the Mountaineering Club, had the idea of extending the Wengernalp railway by building a tunnel through the Eiger. The line would then continue across the Mönch to the heart of the Jungfrau, where a lift would take visitors to the summit. With wind, snow, avalanches and fog making working conditions difficult, the construction of the railway was to take 16 years. Hundreds of workers with mules and carts besieged the region between the Kleine Scheidegg and the Eiger Glacier every summer, when provisions were brought in and stored for the winter. Adolf Guyer-Zeller's thorough design even included large panoramic windows cut into the rock to allow visitors to admire the glaciers. The line was opened on a national holiday, 1 August 1912 … and in dense fog.

able route have gradients of 25%, (💧 *for a description of the Jungfrau summit, see JUNGFRAUJOCH*).

Lauterbrunnen – 💧 *See INTERLAKEN: Excursions.*

The excursion to the **Trümmelbachfälle**★★★ should not be missed. It takes about 1hr to 2hr from Lauterbrunnen. *Use the postal van connecting with the trains from Interlaken.*

Wengwald
Alt 1 182m/3 878ft. Between this stopping-place and Wengen the route offers a splendid **view**★★★ of the Lauterbrunnen rift; the **Jungfrau** emerges in the distance. This is flanked on the right by the Silberhorn, a dazzling white, conical snow peak.

Wengen✱✱ **–** 💧 *See WENGEN.*

Wengernalp
Alt 1 873m/6 145ft. A wild site at the foot of the rock and glacier slopes of the Jungfrau. The deep Trümmelbach Gorge in the foreground makes the height of this wall of rock even more impressive, and it is rare to pass here during the warm part of the day without seeing an avalanche.
To the left of the Jungfrau you will recognise the snowy cleft of the Jungfraujoch – the terminus of the excursion (the Sphinx observatory is visible) – and then the Mönch, the Eigergletscher Glacier and the Eiger.

Kleine Scheidegg★★
Alt 2 061m/6 762ft. This mountain resort, isolated on the ledge linking the Lauterbrunnen Valley to the Grindelwald Valley, is a favourite with skiers, who find abundant snow here even late in the season. In summer it is frequented by tourists seeking tranquillity. Tourists who do not go up the Jungfraujoch may admire the Grindelwald Basin and pick out the Eiger-Mönch-Jungfrau group in excellent conditions by going up to the **belvedere**★★ on the north side of the pass *(1hr to 2hr on foot there and back).*

Eigergletscher
Alt 2 320m/7 612ft. This stop near the snout of the Eiger Glacier, much broken and stained with morainic deposits, marks the beginning of the underground section, 7km/4mi long, which leads to the Jungfraujoch. In spring, great numbers of skiers come here.

Eigerwand★★

Alt 2 865m/9 400ft. The station is cut out of the rock. Ventilating bays giving on to the north face of the Eiger afford a bird's-eye view of the Grindelwald Basin and the Interlaken district. The situation is all the more impressive when you remember the dramatic efforts of mountaineers to conquer this rock wall, which was only climbed for the first time in 1938.

Eismeer★★★

Alt 3 160m/10 367ft. The second stopping-place during your ascent to the Jungfrau. Superb **view** of seracs and the Schreckhorn.

Jungfraujoch★★★ – 🕓 *See JUNGFRAUJOCH.*

Alpiglen

Alt 1 616m/5 302ft. After this resort the railway line, which hitherto has skirted the foot of the Eiger, dips towards the broad and verdant Grindelwald Basin, where the outlying fields, dotted with houses, reach out to the rock base of the Wetterhorn. Ahead is the pastoral plateau of the Grosse Scheidegg (Great Scheidegg).

Grindelwald✲✲

Alt 1 057m/3 392ft at the station. 🕓 *The resort and the best excursions (to First, the Bachsee and the Glacier Gorge) are described under GRINDELWALD.*

Boat Trips

Many steamer and motor-boat services are run during the season on Lake Thun (Thuner See – landing stage in the Interlaken Westbahnhof) and on Lake Brienz (Brienzer See – landing stage behind the Interlaken Ostbahnhof or at Bönigen), enabling everyone to go on trips which include stopping-places like the **Giessbachfälle**★★ which is the most interesting sight on the shores of Lake Brienz, or to enjoy evening cruises. Lovers of aquatic sports will find sailing and water-skiing schools and boats for hire at the base at Neuhaus, on Lake Thun.

KARTAUSE ITTINGEN★

ITTINGEN CHARTERHOUSE – THURGAU

5KM/3MI NW OF FRAUENFELD

The Ittingen Charterhouse stands on a hill overlooking the Thur Valley, surrounded by vineyards. It was founded in 1152 as an Augustinian priory dedicated to St Lawrence and became affiliated to the Carthusian Order in 1461. The monastery was almost entirely rebuilt between the 16C and 18C. A foundation (Stiftung Kartause Ittingen) was established in 1977 to administer the old monastery, which has been carefully restored and now houses two museums run by the canton of Thurgau. The building is also occupied by a hotel, restaurant and pottery and furniture workshops. Surrounded by its own agricultural land, including 8ha/20 acres of vines, the monastery enjoys a peaceful location, with magnificent views extending as far as the Alps. The foundation, which also administers a nature reserve (14ha/34 acres), has details on walks in the area: ask for a map at reception.

Access

From Frauenfeld, take the road to Stein am Rhein and follow signs to Kartause Ittingen. The old charterhouse is situated in the small village of Warth. Direct buses run from Frauenfeld to Warth (10am-2pm; journey time 15min). 🛈 *At Frauenfeld Railway Station,* ☎ *052 721 31 28, www.frauenfeld.ch.*

Walking Tour *approximately half a day*

▶ *Walk through the porch to the ticket office, situated in the building to the left. The tour starts at the end of the courtyard, to the right.*

Ittinger Museum
☎ *(052) 748 41 41, www.karthause.ch.*

A small cloistered gallery surrounds the garden where the monks were buried. The history of the charterhouse, from the pillages of the 15C to 18C prosperity, is explained in the old cellar. In the 19C, monasteries were abolished in Thurgau and their property confiscated by the State. The charterhouse became the property of the Fehr family, whose 19C living room can still be seen: a portrait of Emperor William II is a reminder of a visit he paid here. The museum collections – paintings, models and furniture – provide an insight into the austere life led by the monks, who renounced all worldy pleasures. In the refectory where the monks met for meals on Sundays, without breaking their vow of silence, the decoration is decidedly religious in tone, right down to the biblical scenes on the faience stove. One of the cells is dedicated to St Bruno, who founded the Carthusian Order in the 11C. Note also the carved **stalls** dating from around 1700 in the chapter house, as well as the religious works of art from Ittingen in the sacristy. A small chapel on the first floor contains a Baroque display cabinet of relics. The guestrooms within the charterhouse have beautiful painted ceilings, 18C four-poster beds and **faience stoves** decorated with emblems and landscape scenes.

Church★

This Baroque church is striking for its exuberant décor: the interior is covered with frescoes recounting the life of St Brun, red-veined green and white stuccowork, statues and cherubs. Farm workers sat slightly apart from the rest of the church; the gallery was reserved for guests. The superb **choir stalls**★ were sculpted in the 18C. The main altar is adorned with Rococo-style ornamentation. There is no organ in the church as the Carthusian monks sang unaccompanied chants.

Address Book

Concerts – *These are held ten times a year, always on a Sunday. Chamber music festival at Easter.*

WHERE TO STAY

🛏🛏 **Gästehaus** – ☎ *052 748 44 11 – Fax 052 748 44 55 – www.kartause.ch.* The hotel run by the foundation, which has 33 double and 15 single rooms, is situated in a warm, modern building, with attractive wood decoration.

EATING OUT

🍽🍽 **Zur Mühle** – *In the courtyard, on the right.* This restaurant, housed in one of the buildings belonging to the foundation (1870), offers a reasonably priced menu, with an emphasis on local ingredients. Visitors are also allowed to picnic in the garden of the cloisters.

GOURMET SHOP

Delicium – 🕐 *Open Mon, 1-6pm; Tue-Fri, 9.30am-12.15pm and 1.30-6pm; Sat-Sun, 10am-12.15pm and 1.30-6pm.* This attractive shop sells cheese, cold meats, bread, vegetables, honey and wine produced either in the Charterhouse or in other monasteries.

Kunstmuseum des Kantons Thurgau

This art gallery houses a collection of 20C paintings, most of which are Swiss in origin. Artists exhibited include Adolf Dietrich, with work inspired by the landscapes of Thurgau, Carl Roesch, Ernst Kreidolf and Hans Brühlmann. Of particular interest is the *Self-portrait* by Helen Dahm. Temporary exhibitions of contemporary art are held in the basement.

Klostergarden

The cloisters garden overlooks the surrounding countryside and is planted with herbs and rose bushes. The plant "labyrinth", a symbol of human destiny, was laid out according to a 9C design.

JAUNPASSSTRASSE

JAUN PASS ROAD

The **Jaun Pass Road** is the most mountainous in the Fribourg Alps. For the sightseer it combines lakes, rocky crests and stretches of pasture.

From Spiez to Bulle *63km/39mi – about 2hr 30min*

Spieza – 👓 *See SPIEZ.*

Just beyond Spiez, between Wimmis and Reidenbach, the Simme Valley – to which the Port, a rocky defile cut through the Burgfluh barrier, marks the lower entrance – appears as a corridor through lush countryside showing highly developed agriculture. Many covered bridges (👓 *see Introduction: Picturesque Switzerland*) span the torrent. To the east the great cone-shape of the Niesen is prominent for a long time in the background.

Erlenbach; Stockhorn★★★ – 👓 *See ERLENBACH.*

From Reidenbach to the Jaun Pass, the road, making many hairpin bends in open country, offers steadily lengthening views of the valley, dotted with red roofs, in which the embanked Simme flows. The snows of the Wildhorn sparkle on the horizon due south.

From the Jaun Pass (alt 1 509m/4 951ft; winter sports) to Jaun, the road is less winding but steeper than on the Bernese side. It includes several fine high corniche sections opposite the deeply riven escarpments of the **Gastlosen**, where the people of Fribourg practise rock-climbing.

Jaun

This little town, quite close to the dividing line between Romansh and German Switzerland, still features several fine old chalets and a church with a traditional shingle roof. The site is deeply shut in and is cheered by its generous cascade.

Charmey

The **Musée du Pays et Val de Charmey** in the tourist office houses a collection of objects relating to life in the region, including wooden utensils used in the dairy industry, articles made from woven straw and hunting weapons.

Pont du Javroz★

Leave the Jaun Pass for a moment to take the road to Cerniat; park the car in the car park on the right and go a few steps to the belvedere. The reinforced concrete arch with a span of 85m/275ft crosses the deep Javroz Valley at a height of 60m/200ft where the river begins to flow into the artificial Montsalvens Lake. As far as the Montsalvens Tower, whose ruined walls recall the feudal past of the Counts of Gruyères, the **Jogne Valley** (Jauntal – now Romansh-speaking) remains wide and open, its lower slopes disappearing under the waters of the many-armed lake formed by the Montsalvens Dam. As in other parts of the Alps, farmers here used to use curious vehicles (half-sleighs, half-carts) well suited to local surfaces to gather in the crops. At Charmey on the second Sunday in October there is a race of these vehicles.

The road becomes very hilly between Montsalvens and Bulle as it descends to the floor of the ravines through which the Jogne and the Sarine flow, and then crosses these torrents. It then affords pleasant views of the Gruyères district.

Broc

From the garden in front of the town hall, you will enjoy a lovely **view**★ of the Gruyères area with the three familiar summits of the Vanil Blanc, Vudalla and Moléson as a backdrop. The **Nestlé chocolate factory** is open to the public (short film and tasting).

Electrobroc, (🕐 *Daily except Sun, March-Dec except public hol), 9am-noon and 1.30-5pm. Audio-guides.* 🕮 *No charge.* ☎ *(026) 352 52 52)*, next to the factory, is run by the Fribourg electricity company and introduces visitors to the world of electricity, with information on consumption, distribution and production, as well as explaining how a hydroelectric plant works. The tour finishes with an impressive audio-visual display of the effects of lightning.

Bulle – 🕭 *See BULLE.*

Gruyères★★

Extra distance 7km/4mi – allow 1hr for sightseeing in Gruyères.

VALLÉE DE JOUX★★

The jewel of the Vaud Jura, the Joux Valley and its lake, presents an agreeable stop on an otherwise hilly road linking the French border to Lake Geneva.

From Vallorbe to Nyon *57km/36mi – about 3hr*

Itinerary ② *(🕭 see Le JURA SUISSE map). The Marchairuz road (Le Brassus to St-George) is usually blocked by snow from November to April.*

Vallorbe – 🕭 *See VALLORBE.*

From Vallorbe, the road, climbing quickly up the side of the steep, wooded slope overlooking the source of the Orbe, skirts the foot of the Dent de Vaulion escarpments.

Dent de Vaulion★★★

▶ *From Le Pont, 12km/7mi – about 30min – by the Vaulion road and then the road to the Dent, on the left, plus 30min on foot there and back.* ♿ *For access and description see DENT DE VAULION.*

Vallée de Joux★★

The road then leads into the Joux Valley gently hollowed out between the minor ranges around Mont Risoux and Mont Tendre. After the small Lake Brenets and the villas and hotels of Le Pont (facilities) scattered around it, Lake Joux, the largest of the Jura lakes, appears. Its calm waters are frozen during the long harsh winter. Until a few years after the First World War this ice, cut into regular blocks, was stored at Le Pont in underground ice-houses before being sent to Paris by rail.

Follow the south shore, bordered by wooded hills, wide pastures and hospitable villages, which are both pleasant country resorts and small industrial centres employed in watch and clock-making. The **Espace Horloger de la Vallée de Joux** (🕐 *Open daily except Mon, 2-6pm.* 👓 *8CHF.* ☎ *(021) 845 75 45)* at **Le Sentier** introduces visitors to the famous names of clock-making in the region (Audemars Piguet, Blancpain, Braguet etc) through a display of splendid clocks and watches dating from the 16C-19C. The museum also contains a reconstruction of a typical watchmaker's workshop. The climb from Le Brassus (facilities) to the Marchairuz Pass affords pleasant views of Lake Joux and its valley, closed by the bold spur of the Dent de Vaulion.

Combe des Amburnex

Tour from the pass road, 8.5km/5mi. The road to the Amburnex Combe begins a little below the Marchairuz Pass, on the slope of the Joux Valley. Close the gates behind you. Take care not to drive on the grass. Military area. Tourists looking for a quiet, secluded stop will find it here. On the Nyon side, this run affords wonderful views of Mont Blanc in two different sections:

● **Between the pass and St-George** – the descent through the woods is interspersed with wide, flat clearings from which glimpses of Lake Geneva and the great lakeside towns (Lausanne, Thonon, Geneva) can already be had. Geneva is easy to recognise in summer, thanks to the jet of its great fountain;

● **Between St-George and Nyon** – Mont Blanc is nearly always visible.

Zoo de la Garenne

🕐 *Open daily, 9am-6pm (5.30pm Dec-Feb).* 👓 *10CHF.* ☎ *(022) 366 11 14.*
This small zoo presents mostly European species (wolf, lynx, eagle etc). The hairpin section between Burtigny and Begnins offers particularly open **views**★★ of the Savoy shore of Lake Geneva – with its towns and mountains (from left to right: Den d'Oche, Voirons, Salève), and the crests of the Jura, forming a rampart above the Gex district. Nyon is close by.

Nyon★ – *1hr.* ♿ *See NYON.*

JUNGFRAUJOCH★★★

BERN
ALT 3 475M/11 401FT

This mountain resort, now marketing itself as **Top of Europe**, is the highest in Europe to be served by a **rack railway**. It presents a memorable and grandiose setting hemmed in by high mountains, with spectacular views of the surrounding mountain glaciers. The site includes the famous summits of Mönch, the Eiger and the Jungfrau, as well as the Aletsch Glacier, and has been a UNESCO World Heritage Site since 2001. This is the first natural region in Switzerland – 539km²/208sq mi in the Bern and Valais cantons – to be declared a World Heritage Site.

Tour of the Jungfrau by railway★★★
Departure from Interlaken or Grindelwald (🕭 *see INTERLAKEN: Excursions).* Because of the crowds, it is advisable to start out early in the morning *(allow at least 3hr).*

Sphinx-Panoramaterrasse★★★
Alt 3 571m/8 435ft. Access by the fastest lift in Switzerland (108m/355ft gained in 25 seconds with a maximum speed of 6.3m/20ft a second halfway up), then by 19 steps. Breathtaking **panorama** of the Aletsch Glacier as it flows majestically like a wide river, sparkling among the rocky peaks. It is framed by the Mönch (4 099m/13 447ft), the Fiescherhorn (4 049m/13 282ft), the Aletschhorn (4 193m/13 755ft) and the Jungfrau (4 158m/13 641ft). To the north, the steep Guggigletscher Glacier can be seen inching its way towards the Kleine Scheidegg. The view includes the Schilthorn, the Niesen, Interlaken and the Faulhorn. The crests of the Jura, the Vosges and the Black Forest can be glimpsed in the far distance.

A restaurant serving drinks and light meals is located at the summit of the Jungfraujoch. The Sphinx houses a research laboratory and an astronomical cupola. The pure quality of the air and easy access by railway are undeniable assets to carry out scientific experiments.

Bill Wassman / APA Publications

View of Jungfrau

Aletschgletscher★★★

Go back down by lift and follow directions for Aletschgletscher. You will reach the glacier itself, used as a piste for summer skiing (gentle slope with a ski lift covering a distance of around 100m/330ft). It is also possible to fly over the Jungfrau Massif in a small plane (☞ *60CHF to 200CHF depending on the circuit*).

Eispalast★

10min access on foot and 15min visit. The Ice Palace is a grotto carved out of the ice containing a great many sculptures, mainly depicting animals.

Walk to the Mönchsjochhütte★★★

Alt 3 629m/11 905ft. This walk up the glacier is clearly marked out and can be undertaken by any hiker wearing good mountain boots (☺ *do not stray from the beaten track – crampons are not necessary*). One hour's energetic walking up a steep slope will take you to a stunning **setting**★★★ and then to the small refuge at the foot of the Mönch. The pass (Obere Mönchsjoch) commands a pretty **view**★★ of the Schreckhorn.

▶ *Walk back along the same path.*

LE JURA SUISSE★★

The Swiss Jura, however fine its great panoramas may be, is more than a mere viewing point for the Alps and deserves more than a quick run. From the parallel valley to the cross valley and from parkland to forest the motorist will find here – especially in the Bernese Jura – a whole series of sites making a harmonious transition from the Burgundian lands of the Saône Plain to the German culture of the Swiss Mittelland.

The Swiss Shield

In the past the Jura has been more often a protective *glacis* for the Confederation than a stronghold of democracy. It has remained as politically divided among surrounding towns as it was when the princes of Neuchâtel or the bishops of Basel held the keys to the main routes through it. Thus, we may speak of the Vaud Neuchâtel, Bernese, Solothurn and Basel Juras in spite of the creation of the Jura canton in 1978. This political division has not greatly hampered the economic progress of the Swiss Jura, secured since the beginning of the 18C by the watch and clockmaking industry, which originated at Le Locle and La Chaux-de-Fonds.

Crossing the Jura

Motorists coming from France would be well advised to follow, towards the end of their run, the roads giving very open views of the Swiss Plateau (Mittelland) with its lakes and the Alps. The itineraries along the Pichoux Gorges, the Vue des Alpes or the Joux Valley are especially suitable. The Chasseral road, between St-Imier and Lake Biel is certainly worthy of inclusion in any list of roads crossing the Jura, if only for the wide panorama to be seen from its upper level. Other crossings of the Jura also offer sustained scenic interest over short sections, for instance the road from La Cure to Nyon via St-Cergue (n° 90), an alternative to the Faucille road which is recommended, especially in winter, for its surface; the road from Vallorbe to Lausanne via Cossonay (n° 9), which forms a balcony over the Vaud district is within sight of the Mont Blanc; and the roads from Pontarlier to Yverdon-les-Bains via Ste-Croix, from Pontarlier to Neuchâtel via the Travers Valley (n° 10) or via Le Locle and the La Tourne Pass (D 437).

Driving Tours

1 Weissensteinstrasse★★
Road from Porrentruy to Solothurn – about 4hr 30min. ♿ *See WEISSENSTEINSTRASSE.*

2 Vallée de Joux★★
Road from Vallorbe to Nyon – about 3hr. ♿ *See Vallée de JOUX.*

3 Val de Travers
Road from Fleurier to Noiraigue – about 3hr. ♿ *See Val de TRAVERS.*

4 Bassins du Doubs★★
Tour by boat, car or on foot – about 2hr 30min. ♿ *See Bassins du DOUBS.*

5 Gorges du Pichoux★
Road from Biel to Porrentruy – about 2hr 30min.
♿ *See Gorges du PICHOUX.*

6 Passwangstrasse★
Road from Œnsingen to Basel – about 2hr 15min.
♿ *See PASSWANGSTRASSE.*

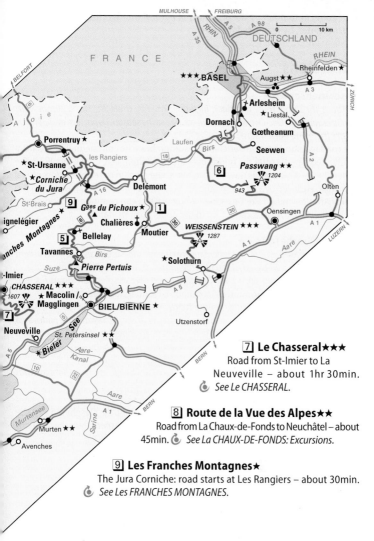

7 Le Chasseral★★★
Road from St-Imier to La Neuveville – about 1hr 30min. ⓒ *See Le CHASSERAL.*

8 Route de la Vue des Alpes★★
Road from La Chaux-de-Fonds to Neuchâtel – about 45min. ⓒ *See La CHAUX-DE-FONDS: Excursions.*

9 Les Franches Montagnes★
The Jura Corniche: road starts at Les Rangiers – about 30min. ⓒ *See Les FRANCHES MONTAGNES.*

KANDERSTEG★

BERN – POPULATION 1 129
ALT 1 176M/3 858FT

Lying at the foot of rugged escarpments, which frame the snow-peaks of the Blümlisalp to the east and dip into a green Alpine basin, Kandersteg is best known today for its position at the north end of the **Lötschberg Tunnel**. This railway tunnel, 14.6km/9mi long (Kandersteg-Goppenstein), has created, since 1913, a direct link between Bern and the Rhône Valley and can also convey cars. As a mark of the close co-operation between Eurotunnel and the Swiss railway system, one locomotive of the Bern-Lötschberg-Simplon train has been given the name *Eurotunnel*. Likewise, one of the engines which carries passengers across the Channel is called *Lötschberg*. ⓘ *Apply for information from the Swiss National Tourist Information Centres or at railway stations.* The life of the locality is kept going in summer by the proximity of natural wonders like Lake Oeschinen and, in winter, by facilities for skiers.

Excursions

Oeschinensee★★★

About 1hr 30min there and back, including 7min by chair-lift, plus a 20min walk. Operates from Dec-Oct; times vary according to the season. Departure every 30min. Fare there and back: 18CHF. ☎ (033) 675 11 18.

The road leading to the lower chair-lift station branches off the main road from Kandersteg directly after the bridge over the Oeschinenbach, on the left. From the upper station a road leads down to the lake shore *(bear to the right at a fork after a 5min walk)* encircled by a vast amphitheatre of cliffs, crowned by the snowy Blümlisalp Peaks. After reaching Lake Oeschinen, good walkers can continue to Kandersterg by the direct road, others can return to the upper chairlift station.

Walk to Oberbergli★★★

Not to be attempted in wet weather. Sturdy mountain shoes are necessary. Allow at least 3hr 15min or even a whole day if you plan to climb up towards the Blüemlisalp refuge.

A path *(good condition)* skirts Lake Oeschinen and reveals splended **views**★★★ of the steep surrounding summits: Doldenhorn, Fründenhorn, Oeschinenhorn and Blüemlisalphorn. This imposing mountain cirque is cut across by four glaciers. At the far end of the lake, a steep path leads to Oberbergli. To enjoy a sweeping panorama of the glacier, continue climbing for 1hr (*very steep slope)* towards the Blüemlisalp refuge until you reach a small lake.

▶ *Come back down the same way until you reach Oberbergli, then turn right towards Heuberg.*

The mountain path affords magnificent **views**★★★ of Lake Oeschinen and the vertiginous cliffs. *Tourists should be extremely cautious, especially in the company of children, since the narrow track follows the edge of the precipice.*

Klus★★

2.5km/2mi – plus 1hr on foot there and back.

Follow the main road towards the floor of the valley and leave your car at the lower cable-car station at Stock. Then continue to climb, on foot, a little road which will soon cling to the rocky wall before entering a tunnel over the Klus, a wild gorge where the Kander, flowing down from the Gasterntal, rushes downwards. Go on to the bridge over the Kander after a second tunnel. Sure-footed tourists will prefer to descend by the steep path, sometimes wet with spray, which leaves the road between the two tunnels.

KANDERTAL★

From Lake Thun to Lake Oeschinen this valley is divided into two sections orientated differently: firstly the Frutigtal which goes southwest as far as Frutigen; then the Kandertal which goes south to Kandersteg.

From Spiez to Kandersteg *39km/25mi – about 2hr 30min*

Itinerary [2] (see BERNER OBERLAND map). This excursion ends in a cul-de-sac at Kandersteg, but the railway is fitted out to take cars through the Lötschberg Tunnel emerging in the Valais.

Spiez★ – *See SPIEZ.*

Crossing the spur which separates Spiez from the Kander, the road, situated halfway up the slope, drops towards the valley floor and begins to encircle the huge Niesen Pyramid, which has almost geometrically precise lines.

Climb to the Niesen★★★

Alt 2 362m/7 749ft. From Mülenen station, about 2hr there and back, including 1hr by funicular. Operates Jun-Nov. Departure every 30min (or 15min if busy), 8am-5pm (enquire in advance). Fare there and back: 43CHF. (033) 676 11 12.
The funicular rides above the Frutigtal and stops at Schwandegg (alt 1 669m/5 474ft), before continuing to Niesen Kulm, from where there is a magnificent **panorama**★★★ of the Berner Oberland, Lake Thun, the Mittelland and the Jura. A footpath leads to the summit *(allow half a day)*, where visitors will find a hotel-restaurant. Ahead, through the Kiental Gap, the three identical snowy Blümlisalp peaks gradually appear. They are best seen from around Reichenbach.

The Longest Flight of Steps in the World

A total of 11 674 stairs have been built in order to link Mülenen to Mount Niesen. Naturally, for reasons of security, access is forbidden to tourists. However, a race was organised in 1990 and it took the winner 52 minutes to get to the top. Quite a record!

Beyond Reichenbach, the valley, known as the Frutigtal, opens out. Among the houses scattered on the slopes are many new buildings, which must conform strictly to the traditional architecture of the Bernese Oberland. Just before Frutigen you will see shining ahead and to the left, at the end of a new panorama along the Kander Valley, the Balmhorn and Altels ice fields.

Frutigen

15min on foot there and back to go up to the church (following the Adelboden road for a moment and then turning up the first ramp to the right).
This large village at the confluence of the Kander and the Engstligen, a torrent flowing down from Adelboden, is the best-equipped medium altitude resort in the Lötschberg district. The church is built high up within view of the Balmhorn and the Altels. It enjoys a delightful **setting**★ among the lawns and trees of its close.

Adelboden** – *See ADELBODEN.*

Crossing the Kander at the foot of the Tellenburg ruins – the picture formed by this tower and the railway viaduct has been widely distributed by local tourist publicity – you approach the Bühlstutz ridge. This separates the Kandergrund shelf from the Kandersteg Basin and compels the Lötschberg railway to make a hairpin loop around the Felsenburg ruins, which stand out clearly on their rocky spur.

Blausee★

About 45min walk and trip by boat. Nature reserve open from Apr-Oct, 9am-5pm (Nov-Mar 10am-5pm). Admission 4.50CHF, including boat trip. 033 672 33 33.
This site comprises not only a little lake with incredibly clear, blue water, lying deep in the forest within view of the snowy Doldenhorn summit, but also a mass of rocks

among the woods, a trout farm and a restaurant. The road now takes on the Bühlstutz ridge in a more austere landscape of fields and woods dotted with rocks. At last you emerge into the Kandersteg Basin with steep slopes laced with waterfalls.

KIPPEL

VALAIS – POPULATION 370

The remote Alpine valley **Lötschental**★ remained cut off from the outside world until the Lötschberg railway tunnel was built between Kandersteg in the north and Goppenstein, in 1913. The River Lonza flows southwards through the valley to join the Rhône. In the past, when it was extremely difficult to maintain an open road in the lower sections of the valley, because of the frequent avalanches, the main access was by passes at an altitude of 2 500m/8 200ft. The people of this remote valley remain very attached to their traditional way of life and it is well worth leaving the Valais to visit Kippel.

Access
From the road fork at Gampel to Kippel 12km/7.5mi – about 45min.
The road climbs the steep and wild gorge of the Lower Lonza, with below, the many bridges of the Lötschberg railway. Beyond Goppenstein the road enters the great and gently spreading combe of the Upper Lötschental.

Kippel★
This is the most typical village in the valley, and visitors not pressed for time may want to spend the whole day here. In the area around the church are numerous blackened **wooden houses**★★ with delicate friezes of dog-tooth and rosette patterns. The crowds which gather for High Mass make Sundays and feast days most spectacular events for lovers of folklore, but the Corpus Christi Procession *(see Calendar of events)*, with its procession of God's Grenadiers, is the most colourful spectacle. For this occasion flags are flown and the local men bring out their old-fashioned trappings including plumes, bearskin caps and belts.

Blatten
4km/2mi from Kippel.
This short excursion enables the tourist to discover the beauty of this valley, which becomes ever more rugged.

KLAUSENSTRASSE★★

KLAUSEN PASS ROAD

The Klausen Pass Road connects the Reuss Valley (Uri Canton) to that of the Linth (Glarus Canton). It combines nearly all the physical and economic features of mountainous Switzerland. Within less than 50km/31mi the traveller passes from a high, wild primitive Alpine combe (Urner Boden) to one of the most industrial valleys in the range (Linth Valley).

From Altdorf to Lindthal *48km/30mi – about 2hr*

The Klausen road is closed to vehicles with a trailer. The Klausen Pass is usually blocked by snow from November to May.

Altdorf – *See ALTDORF.*

It is only a short distance from Altdorf to the next stopping-place.

Bürglen

Bürglen is said to be the birthplace of **William Tell** and the village now has a **Tell Museum**. The exhibits include a host of documents, chronicles, sculptures, paintings and other items relating to Switzerland's legendary hero over the past 600 years.
Between Bürglen and Unterschächen, the road, lined by a series of chapels, runs at first along the verdant cleft through which the Schächen rushes. This widens upstream and is then covered with birch, maple and fruit trees, but the south slope, quickly becoming barren, gives a foretaste of harsher sections.
From Unterschächen to the pass, two big hairpin bends facing the mouth of the Brunnital, a tributary valley ending in a cirque at the foot of the Ruchen and the Windgällen precipices, lead to Urigen, the starting-point of a magnificent **corniche section**★★. From then on there is a bird's-eye view of the wild cul-de-sac of the Upper Schächental, enclosed by the gigantic Chammliberg Cliffs. The bend marked by a single rock on the side of the escarpment (600m/0.4mi above the first tunnel) forms a **viewpoint**★ overlooking the Stäubi Waterfall (Stäubifall) and the hamlet of Aesch, 400m/1 312ft below. The great snow-laden corniches of the Clariden can be seen behind the Chammliberg Cliffs.

Klausenpass★

Alt 1 948m/6 391ft. Motorists usually stop below the summit on the Schächental slope, at the Klausenpasshöhe Hotel.
From a spot near the hotel you can see, from left to right, the snowy crests of the Clariden, the Chammliberg Cliffs, the double Schärhorn peak, the rocky points of the Windgälen and finally, in line with the Schächen Gap, the Uri-Rotstock Massif on the horizon. After passing the huts of Vorfrütt, where herdsmen shelter during the summer, you will be able to admire the north face of the Clariden and the Chlus, a corrie streaked by two cascades.

Post bus at Klausenpass

Heinz Schwab / Switzerland Tourism

Urner Boden★

The run along the bottom of this very regular cleft offers the motorist a long level stretch, unexpected at this altitude (1 300-1 400m/4 250-4 600ft). The belfry of the main hamlet, standing in the middle of the hollow, behind a clump of fir trees, is an attractive feature of the run down from the Klausen Pass. There are more hairpin bends as far as Linthal. The Linth Valley, both agricultural, and industrial, now opens out below, abutting the walls of the Selbsanft (Tödi Massif) upstream.

KLOSTERS✳✳

GRAUBÜNDEN – POPULATION 3 894

Klosters (alt 1 194m/3 917ft) nestles in a valley below Davos (see DAVOS), but unlike its neighbor, has remained a traditional Alpine village. In the setting, still quite rural, of the Prättigau, the resort is ideal for both summer and winter holidays. In summer the Silvretta summits, jutting up on the horizon, are enjoyable expeditions for mountaineers.

In winter, skiers using the cable cars from Gotschnagrat and Madrisa or the railway shuttle service between Klosters and Davos can reach the famous Parsenn snowfields; skiers in search of more challenging terrain should proceed to the Weisspfluhgipfel (alt. 2844m/9328ft). In March and April, spring skiing weeks are organised as excursions led by guides in the Silvretta and Vereina Massifs. Klosters has been fashionable with the rich and famous since the 1950s. Celebrities who have spent time here include Gene Kelly, Vivien Leigh and Audrey Hepburn. The Prince of Wales is also a regular visitor to the resort.

KLOSTER KÖNIGSFELDEN

ABBEY OF KÖNIGSFELDEN – AARGAU
WEST OF BADEN BETWEEN BRUGG AND WINDISCH

The Franciscan abbey of Königsfelden was founded in 1308 by Queen Elizabeth and the Habsburg family on the spot where King Albrecht I was assassinated by Duke Johann of Swabia. The monastic buildings presently house a psychiatric hospital.

Klosterkirche

 Open Apr-Oct, Tue-Sun, 10am-5pm, Nov-Mar, 1p-4pm. Closed 1 and 2 Jan, Good Fri to Easter Sun, 24, 25 and 26 Dec. 5CHF. (056) 441 88 33.
A pretty park is the setting for this large Gothic church. The nave, lit by clerestory windows, has a flat wooden ceiling, aisles are decorated with painted wooden panels representing portraits of knights

Stained glass window

and coats of arms. A memorial in the nave recalls that Königsfelden became the burial place of the Habsburgs. The long **chancel**★ is lit by 11 windows of which the **stained glass**★, made between 1325 and 1330, forms an interesting series. You will recognise the Childhood of Christ, the Passion, scenes from Lives of the Saints and Death of the Virgin. The colours, in which a silvery-yellow predominates, are iridescent.

KREUZLINGEN

THURGAU – POPULATION 17 735
ALT 407M/1 335FT

The Swiss town of Kreuzlingen is built on a former moraine of the Rhine Glacier. It forms a single town with the German city of Constance, divided only by the frontier. The town owes its name to a relic of the Holy Cross (Kreuz), which was brought back from the Holy Land in the 10C and deposited in the basilica.

Ehem. Klosterkirche St Ulrich
This basilica was built in the 17C and the Baroque interior decoration completed in the following century. The building was damaged by fire in 1963 and restored in 1967. The Olive Grove Chapel (Ölbergkapelle) contains an extraordinary group of 250 carved wooden figurines set in curious rock work, representing scenes taken from the Passion. These figurines are about 30cm/12in high and were carved in the early 18C by a Tyrolean sculptor. The work took no less than 18 years. The chancel has a fine wrought-iron parclose screen.

Excursion

Gottlieben
4km/2mi W by road n° 13. Gottlieben lies at the western end of the arm of the Rhine joining the Untersee, or lower lake, to the main basin of Lake Constance. It has a 13C castle, remodelled in the 19C. In the 15C the building was used as a prison for the deposed Pope John III and for the Czech reformer **Jan Hus**. Prince Louis-Napoleon Bonaparte, the future Napoleon III, lived here from 1837 to 1838.
Near the castle stands an attractive group of half-timbered houses.

LANGNAU IM EMMENTAL★

BERN – POPULATION 8 790

The picturesque town of Langnau lies on the banks of the Ilfis (spanned by a covered bridge), a tributary of the River Emme. Its commerce is based on forestry and Emmental cheese (main exporting centre for the latter). 🄸 *Schlossstrasse 3 – 3550 – ☎ (034) 402 42 52.*

Heimatmuseum
🕐 *Open Apr-Oct, daily except Mon, 1.30-6pm.* ☜*4CHF.* ☎ *(034) 402 18 19.*
Housed in a 16C chalet, the Chüechlihus displays local crafts (porcelain, glasswork) and objects representing regional industries including workrooms,

a room furnished in 18C painted wood, household utensils, clocks, musical instruments and old military uniforms.

Across from the museum, the 17C Reformed Church has its original elaborate stone pulpit and a dozen small stained-glass windows emblazoned with heraldic emblems.

Dürsrutiwald★
3km/2mi N (to the right of the road to Burgdorf).
This forest of giant pine trees on a hill offers pleasant views of the Langnau Valley.

LAUSANNE★★

Ⓒ VAUD – POPULATION 114 518
ALT 455M/1 493FT
PLAN IN THE MICHELIN GUIDE SWITZERLAND

Lausanne is a welcoming, cosmopolitan city, much loved by its university students and its high society, who enjoy the scenic views of the lake and the surrounding Alps. The city is built on uneven ground. After being confined to the promontory of the present city for several centuries, Lausanne spread southwards to the delightful shores of Ouchy, a former fisherman's hamlet. Its new quarters contrast sharply with the old, steep, narrow streets which lead to the cathedral.
🄸 *4 place de la Navigation – 1000 – ☏ (021) 613 73 73; www.lausanne-tourisme.ch.*

- 🅿 **Parking:** Leave the car; use the rapid subway between lakefront and city centre.
- 🐾 **Don't Miss:** The Olympic Museum in a beautiful park on the lake.
- 🕐 **Organizing Your Time:** Allow at least two days for the museums and a lake excursion.
- 🕭 **Also See:** Palud Square with its 17C City Hall and Fountain of Justice (1726).

The life of the city is concentrated within Place de la Riponne, rue du Bourg, Place Saint-François, rue du Grand-Chêne and Place Bel-Air. These are joined by the Grand Pont, spanning the valley where the Flon torrent once flowed.
An important centre for both art and entertainment, Lausanne has acquired a worldwide reputation for the famous ballet troupe directed by Maurice Béjart and the classical concerts performed by the French Swiss Orchestra and the Chamber Orchestra of Lausanne. The Palais de Beaulieu and the Théâtre Municipal are frequently used to host dance performances and musical shows.
The municipality of **Vidy**, part of Lausanne, enjoys Olympic status since it houses the International Olympic Committee (IOC), which was founded in 1894 by Baron Pierre de Coubertin, whose belief in sportsmanship became famous as "it's not the winning but the taking part". The Olympic Museum, opened in Ouchy in 1993, has made Lausanne the world capital of the **Olympic movement**.

A Bit of History

Early days – Recent excavations show Lausanne was originally built on the site of the present city, perched on the promontory where Neolithic skeletons have been uncovered. Southwest (at **Vidy**), part of the former Roman Lousonna has been excavated. Of particular interest is a section of Roman road, located exactly where the Geneva-Lausanne motorway is today.

Cathedral City – At the end of the 6C Bishop St Marius, came to live in Lausanne; the first cathedral was built two centuries later. In the Middle Ages, religious leadership combined with economic and political expansion: the quarters of Place de la Palud, the Bourg, St-Pierre, St-Laurent and St-François were added to the town. In the 13C many religious orders settled here and the Prince-Bishop Guillaume de Champvent consecrated the new cathedral; later Pope Gregory X dedicated it in the presence of Emperor Rudolf I of Habsburg. The city or upper town was the religious and intellectual centre; commercial activities flourished in adjoining districts.

From the Reformation to Bernese domination – The Reformation scored a sweeping success at Lausanne; it was preached there by Guillaume Farel, one of Calvin's friends. In 1536 the town and all of the Vaud Country were occupied by the Bernese, who had already been converted. All of Lausanne's churches except for the cathedral and the Church of St Francis disappeared, one by one. In 1723 the Bernese harshly suppressed an attempt by the Vaud people to regain their independence; Davel, the instigator of the revolt, was beheaded at Vidy. It was not until 1803 that the Vaud region attained political autonomy, with Lausanne as its capital. In 1874 it became the seat of the Federal Court of Justice.

The Age of Enlightenment – The 18C was an era of prosperity. Lausanne came under French influence; Voltaire stayed in the city, where his play *Zadig* was performed. Byron and Shelley visited Lausanne in 1816, as did Wordsworth in 1790 and 1820; Dickens resided here twice: in 1846, where he was visited by, among others, Thackeray and Tennyson; and again in 1853. It was during his stay in Lausanne (1921-22) that TS Eliot wrote *The Waste Land*, which secured his international reputation.
Literary salons flourished. Benjamin Constant, author of *Adolphe*, was born in Lausanne in 1767. The university, partly installed in the 16C Academy, brilliantly perpetuated these traditions. Enthusiastic publishers helped its fame: Sainte-Beuve delivered his speech on Port-Royal at Lausanne, Gide adapted his *Caves du Vatican* as a play for a students' society. The best known local figures, however, were Dr Tissot, who lived in the 18C and was known as the "Healer of the Sick of Europe", Dr Jules Gonin, an eye surgeon who specialised in operating on detached retinas, and Maurice Lugeon (d 1953), an outstanding geologist and an authority on the Alps.

Ouchy★★

Ouchy is linked to Lausanne by its *métro*, an electrically-driven funicular once known as the "rope" (cable-driven) and later as the "tyre" (mounted on wheels). Ouchy – a famous hotel resort and popular spot for Sunday strollers – is also one of the liveliest navigation centres on the lake. The large sailing port adjoining Place de la Navigation has been refurbished and is now reserved for pedestrians, who can enjoy its charming fountains and four giant chess games. Many leisure boats are also available for cruises. The shaded quays, adorned with tropical plants and flowers, stretch for over 1km/0.5mi and are prolonged eastward by the lakeside path. This charming route offers lovely **views**★★ of the harbour, Lake Geneva and the Chablais mountains.

Musée Olympique★★

 🕒 *Open 9am-6pm (8pm Thu).* 🕒 *Closed Mon from Oct-Apr (except Easter Mon), 1 Jan and 25 Dec.* ⊛*14CHF.* ☎ *(021) 621 65 11.*
This museum enjoys a privileged location on the shores of Lake Geneva, a charming landscape laid out as a public garden enhanced by statues, fountains and multi-coloured pavilions. The **park**, planted with evergreens, Italian cypress, juniper and magnolia, extends across terraced slopes, offering nice views of Lake Geneva and the Savoy Alps in the distance. All along the path to the museum entrance (420m/1 378ft, the length of an Olympic stadium), a series of statues symbolises the marriage of

Address Book

SHOPPING

Most main shopping streets are located in the old district and include: place St-François, rue des Terreaux, rue de l'Ale, rue Mauborget, rue Chaucrau, rue St-Laurent, rue de Bourg, rue St-Jean and rue St-François. **Department store:** Innovation (rue Centrale).

THEATRE AND MUSIC

The high season is September to June.

Théâtre Arsenic – *57 rue de Genève* – ☎ *021 625 11 22, www.theater-arsenic. ch.* Centre of Contemporary Drama.

Théâtre Vidy-Lausanne – *5 avenue E.-Jacques-Dalcroze* – ☎ *021 619 45 44, www.vidy.ch.* Stage performances.

L'Octogone – *41 avenue de Lavaux-Pully* – ☎ *021 721 36 20.* Theatre, concerts, dance.

Le Petit Théâtre –*3 place de la Cathédrale* – ☎ *021 323 62 13, www.lepetittheatre.ch.* Theatre, plays for children.

WHERE TO STAY

🕯 *For coin ranges, see the Legend on the cover flap.*

🍽 **Les Pierrettes** – In *Saint-Sulpice, route Cantonale 19* – ☎ *021 691 25 25.* Conveniently situated at the western entrance to Lausanne. Each room has a private terrace with a table and garden chairs. Relax on the lawn or by the outdoor pool in summer.

🍽 **Les Voyageurs** –*19 rue Grand-St-Jean* – ☎ *021 319 91 11, www.voyageurs. ch – 33 rooms* – This hotel, nestling in the old part of Lausanne, is an ideal starting-point to discover the city on foot.

🍽 **Agora** – *9 avenue du Rond-Point* – ☎ *021 555 59 55, www.fhotels.ch. – 81 rooms* – Modern hotel decorated in bold colours: blue, pink and silver. Large rooms. The lobby features a sculpture of white marble.

🍽 **Alpha-Palmiers** – *34 rue du Petit-Chêne* – ☎ *021 555 59 99 – 205 rooms* –Convenient location in a lively shopping street, a stone's throw from a multiplex cinema (6 screens). Traditional cuisine. Fondue, raclette and other Swiss specialities at the Carnotzet.

🍽 **Aulac** – In *Ouchy, 4 place de la Navigation* – ☎ *021 612 15 00, www. aulac.ch – 84 rooms* – Hotel situated just opposite the lake, near the landing stage for excursions to Évian (trip there and back overnight).

🍽 **City** – *5 rue Caroline* – ☎ *021 320 21 41, www.fhotels.ch – 51 rooms* – Located near the Pont Bessière (no restaurant).

🍽 **Angleterre et Résidence** – In *Ouchy, 11 place du Port* – ☎ *021 613 34 34, www.laresidence.ch – 75 rooms* – Three imposing pavilions exuding great charm, including an 18C hôtel particulier, located just off the lakeshore. Outdoor pool and ornamental garden. Complete the experience with delicious meal at the gourmet restaurant.

EATING OUT

🍽 **Brasserie Bavaria** – *10 rue du Petit-Chêne* – ☎ *021 323 39 13* – 🕐 *closed Sun, closed Sat in summer.* On the boundaries of the old city, an old-fashioned restaurant with a nostalgic decor serves sauerkraut and cold meats made from pork. Remarkable choice of beers.

🍽 **Port de Pully** – *rue du Port 7, In the port of Pully, skirting the lake to the east* – ☎ *021 728 78 78* – 🕐 *closed Mon.* Charming establishment facing the marina. Dining choices are brasserie, traditional restaurant or rotisserie.

🍽 **Le Lacustre** – In *Ouchy, on the landing stage, quai Dapples* – ☎ *021 617 42 00* – 🕐 *closed mid-Dec to mid-Feb.* The Brasserie offers nice views of the lake while the Café Français gives onto the park. Both establishments serve traditional fare.

🍽 **Café Romand** – *2 place St-François* – ☎ *021 312 63 75, www. caferomand.ch* – 🕐 *closed Sun and public hols.* Typical old Lausanne brasserie gathers a local crowd. Traditional food and Swiss specialities. A lively meeting-place in the evening.

🍽 **La Petite Grappe** –*15 Cheneau du Bourg-* ☎ *021 311 84 14;* 🕐 *closed Sun.* Bistro-style restaurant with plain, reasonably priced lunch meals; evening menus vary.

🍴🍷 **Mövenpick** – *In Ouchy, 4 avenue de Rhodanie* – ☎ *021 612 76 12. La Pêcherie restaurant* ⏰ *closed in Jul and Sat lunch.* Pleasant location facing the lake and its marina. La Pêcherie is one of several restaurants where meals are served in a pleasant setting. Large choice of dishes. In the restaurant Le Général, where prices are more affordable, the life of General Guisan is illustrated with paintings and panels displayed on the walls.

🍴🍷🍽 **À la Pomme de Pin** – *11 rue Cité-Derrière* – ☎ *021 323 46 56* – ⏰ *closed Sat at lunchtime, Sun, public hols and 24 Jul-20 Aug.* A friendly establishment in a narrow street lying behind the cathedral. Clients can choose between two dining rooms: simple fare in the café or a more elaborate and more expensive meal in the restaurant.

NIGHTLIFE

Nestling in its superb setting on the shores of the lake, the **Ouchy** district is extremely lively, both during the day and at night. On a fine day, you can enjoy the many pavement cafés and their sunny terraces. Those yearning for an English atmosphere can go to **Sherlock's Pub** in Avenue de Rhodanie, where a disc jockey will liven up the evening. For beer drinkers, the **Bavaria** (rue du Petit-Chêne), one of the oldest cafés in town (1872), offers a selection of 22 different beers. Finally, for those who appreciate jazz, the **Pianissimo** (rue des Deux-Marchés) with its outstanding pianist is definitely the place to go; live concerts of jazz-soul and occasionally rock are held at the **V.O.** (Place du Tunnel). The old vaults of a 14C cellar are the hallmark of the unusual **Disco Zille** (Rue Cite-Devant 10).

sport and culture. Part of the museum has been built underground to preserve the natural environment.

The modern ensemble, inspired by a Greek temple, is the work of architects Pedro Ramirez Vázquez (who designed the National Anthropology Museum in Mexico City) and Lausanne native Jean-Pierre Cahen. In front of the white marble façade (the stone is from the Greek island of Thassos), two rows of four columns carry the names of the towns which have hosted the Olympic Games and the names of the Olympic Committee presidents. In a granite bowl, decorated with allegorical motifs illustrating the myth of Prometheus, the Olympic flame burns forever.

Ground Floor – Largely devoted to the history of the Games, with particular emphasis on ancient Greece. Superb works of art evoke the origins of the Games: terracotta figures, marble and bronze sculptures, vases decorated with figures of athletes, gold laurel wreaths and *strigils* – scraping instruments used by athletes for removing the combination of oil, sand and perspiration from their bodies. Also on display: all the torches that have carried the Olympic flame, from the Berlin Games of 1936 to the present. Other exhibitions focus on the life and achievements of **Baron Pierre de Coubertin** (furniture and personal mementoes), the various International Olympic Committees and the IOC presidents (a video film presents the world events that marked their epoch). Note two fine bronze statues – *The American Athlete* by Rodin and *The Archer* by Bourdelle. Additionally, there are displays on the cities of forthcoming Games: Beijing (Summer Games - 2008), Vancouver (Winter Games - 2010).

Suisse Tourisme

Olympic flag

Level 1 – One side is devoted to the Summer Games, the other to the Winter Games. Videos enable visitors to relive

The Olympic Museum in Lausanne

great moments of Olympic history and share the physical effort and strong emotions experienced by top-level athletes. Opening and closing ceremonies are re-enacted on huge screens and interactive terminals provide answers to thousands of questions about the Games, the different events, the athletes, the records, etc. The Philatelic and Numismatic Department boasts a remarkable collection of stamps, coins and medals bearing the effigy of the Games.

Cafeteria and Terrace – **View** of the park, the lake and the mountains. Sculptures by Botero *(Young Girl with Ball)*, Niki de Saint Phalle *(The Football Players)* and Eduardo Chillida *(Lotura)*.

Musée de l'Élysée
Open daily 11am-6pm. ⌨8CHF, no charge first Sat in the month. ☎ (021) 316 99 11.
This large, late-18C villa with its sculpted façade is surrounded by a small park which slopes down to the lakeside and is shaded by chestnut, pine and cedar trees full of squirrels. The building houses a Photography Museum which presents large-scale temporary exhibitions of 19C and 20C prints.

Old Town *2hr*

Tours (2-3hr) from May to Oct every Tue and Fri at 3pm, ⌨34CHF. For further information, contact Lausanne Tourist Office on ☎ (021) 613 73 66; www.lausanne-tourisme.ch.

Place de la Palud (BX 70)
Lined by old houses and by the Renaissance façade of the town hall, which proudly bears the arms of the city of Lausanne, this square is adorned with the charming Fountain of Justice (16C-18C). Nearby, at n° 23, an animated clock strikes the hours of the day, exhibiting a gallery of historical figures. The curious covered **staircase** beyond the fountain leads through to the cathedral. In the past these steps led to the entrance of what was known as the Cité du Marché.

Musée Historique de Lausanne (BX M¹)
Open Tue, Wed, Thu 11am-6pm; Fri, Sat-Sun 11am-5pm. Closed Mon (except in Jul and Aug), Good Fri, Easter Sun-Mon, Ascension Thu and Whit Mon. ⌨8CHF. ☎ (021) 315 41 01, www.lausanne.ch/mhl.

J.J. Strahm/CIO-Musée Olympique

Rooms of the former bishop's palace have been restored to house these collections, which recall the town's history from prehistoric times to today. The first section, devoted to geology, prehistory and the Middle Ages, features a vast miniature model of the city as it was in 1638. The Bern period (17C-18C) is liberally illustrated with documents and objects relating to politics, agriculture and everyday life. The advent of the railway and its consequences on the political scene, expansion of tourism and business (banks, insurance companies) are among the many chapters that make up the fascinating history of the town. Several 19C displays include a general store, grocery shop, printing house and photographer's studio. Note the safe which once belonged to the Kohler House (1828), with its original and elaborate ironwork.

Cathedral★★ (CX)

🕐 *Open 7am-5.30pm (7pm in summer).* ☎ *(021) 316 71 61.*

This is the finest Gothic building in Switzerland. Its construction began during the episcopate of St Amadeus (1145-59) and was completed in the mid-13C; it was consecrated in 1275 and entirely restored in the late 19C. The east end, the oldest part of the building, abuts two picturesque square towers and is dominated by the lantern-tower at the transept crossing. Both it and the bell tower are reminiscent of Anglo-Norman architecture, clearly marking the transition from Romanesque to Gothic.

The **south door**, known as the Painted Doorway, is adorned with a fine group of 13C sculptures similar to those of the Île-de-France. The pillars supporting the roof bear figures of the Prophets (Isaiah, David and Jeremiah); near the door, the Forerunners (Moses, John the Baptist, Simeon); on the right, three of the Evangelists (St Matthew, St Luke and St Mark); in the background, three Apostles (St Peter, St Paul and St John). The lintel is carved with low reliefs, Death and the Assumption of the Virgin. The Montfalcon Doorway, in the center of the main façade, is named for the bishops Aymon and Sébastien de Montfalcon (1517, restored in the early 20C). Three 13C statues, two of which are sadly decapitated, represent the Virgin, Solomon and the Queen of Sheba. In a chapel on the right, murals (1505) portray the life of the Virgin Mary.

The interior shows Burgundian features such a narthex with no side chapels. Other features are influenced by the English Gothic style: the gallery runs below the clerestory windows. Note the original arrangement of sturdy columns, alternating with pairs of slender pillars. The rare and unusual 13C **stalls**, feature exceptionally fine figures on the cheek pieces. Other stalls, in the Flamboyant style (16C), are in the St-Maurice chapel. In the south arm of the transept a 13C rose window, *Imago Mundi* (elements, seasons, months and signs of the Zodiac), is remarkably harmonious and decorative. It was already well known in the 13C, for Villard de Honnecourt drew it in his *Album*, the first collection dealing with Gothic architecture and decoration. In the chancel rests the tomb of Othon I of Grandson, who embarked on a brilliant career at the English court and became a close friend of Edward I. He died in 1328. In the ambulatory note the tomb of the 13C bishop-builder Roger de Vico-Pisano.

Lausanne is one of the last towns to maintain a nightwatch. From the top of the cathedral tower the nightwatchman cries the hour between 10pm and 2am.

Tower

Access to the stairway (232 steps) at the end of the south aisle. ◔ *Ascent 8.30-11.30am and 1.30-5.30pm (4.30pm in winter), Sun 2-5.30pm (4.30pm in winter).* ◔ *Closed 1 and 2 Jan and 25 Dec.* ▣ *2CHF.* ☎ *(021) 316 71 61.*

From the top of the tower there is a fine **view**★ of the town, Lake Geneva and the Alps. The parvis of the cathedral affords bird's-eye views of the town and the lake. Go round the cathedral and take on the left of the east end, rue Cité-Derrière, a small medieval street decorated with wrought-iron signs.

Château St-Maire (CX)

This 15C brick and stone castle was originally the residence of the bishops of Lausanne and then the Bernese bailiffs. The cantonal government sits there today. The terrace affords a sweeping **view** of the Lausanne rooftops and Lake Geneva.

▶ *Continue along rue Cité-Derrière. Then turn left into avenue de l'Université, which leads to Place de la Riponne, situated at the foot of the promontory.*

Palais de Rumine (BX)

Built in the early 20C in the Italian Renaissance style, thanks to a generous legacy bequeathed by Gabriel de Rumine. It houses the library and these five museums:

Musée des Beaux-Arts

♿ ◔ *Open Tue and Wed, 11am-6pm; Thu, 11am-8pm; Fri, Sat-Sun and public hols, 11am-5pm.* ◔ *Closed 1 Jan and 25 Dec.* ▣ *6CHF, no charge first Sun in the month.* ☎ *(021) 316 34 45. Each year temporary exhibitions are held around a specific theme or artist.*

Most of the paintings in this Museum of Fine Arts in the first three rooms are the work of Swiss nationals, many of whom were born in the region. Paintings from the 18C (note the watercolours by Ducros, which were the first acquisition of the museum) are followed by the works of Charles Gleyre (*Le Coucher de Sapho*), who received many leading Impressionists in his Paris studio. Among those who depicted their own country are Romansh landscape artists such as De la Rive, Diday, St-Ours, Calame, and natives from the Vaud area: Bosshard, Biéler and Bocion (70 pictures of the countryside around Lake Geneva, showing great sensitivity). The more recent works are by the German Swiss painter Hodler (*Bleu Léman*) and the Lausanne artist Félix Vallotton, of whom the museum possesses the largest **state collection**★. This section ends with some of the most prestigious French painters, namely Largillière, Géricault, Courbet, Cézanne, Bonnard, Renoir, Degas, Matisse, Marquet, Vlaminck, Vuillard and Utrillo. Also, sculptures of Rodin and Giacometti, now seen as classics, are exhibited alongside more recent works by Nauman and Boltanski.

Musée de Géologie

First floor, on the left. ◔ *Open daily except Mon, 11am-6pm (5pm Fri and Sat-Sun).* ◔ *Closed 1 Jan and 25 Dec.* ▣ *4CHF, no charge first Sun in the month.* ☎ *(021) 316 33 90.*

The Geological Museum contains rock specimens from the Jura, the Alps, Lausanne and surrounding region, plus relief models of the Jura, the Simplon and the Matterhorn. One section is devoted to the Quaternary Era in the Vaud canton, including the skeleton of a mammoth discovered near Le Brassus, in the Jouy Valley, in 1969.

Musée de Paléontologie
On the right, opposite the Geological Museum.
A collection of plant and animal fossils, mostly European, are on display, alongside molluscs and skeletons of birds and mammals.

Musée de Zoologie
Second floor. Same hours as the Musée de Géologie.
The main gallery of the Zoology Museum houses specimens of flora from countries all over the world. On the left is an interesting room of comparative anatomy between Man and the animal race. On the right is a display of all the vertebrates found in the Vaud region: birds, insects, fish, and species commonly found in forests and at high altitudes. Of particular interest is the colony of Mexican ants busy at work in their natural setting, a carefully reconstruction of their natural tropical environment. The central gallery of the museum is devoted to mineralogy.

Salle d'Archéologie et d'Histoire
Sixth floor. Same hours as the Musée de Géologie.
The History and Archaeology Museum displays artifacts discovered during excavations of local sites. Many of the objects found near the lakes of Geneva, Lausanne and Murten feature tools and ceramic pieces from the Bronze Age, Celtic tombs, a gold bust of Marcus Aurelius and jewellery and weapons dating back to the 5C-7C.

Additional Sights

Collection de l'Art Brut★ (AX)
🕐 *Open daily except Mon, 11am-6pm.* 🎫*8CHF.* ☎ *(021) 315 25 70; www.artbrut.ch.*
The four floors of this unique museum – housed in the former stables of Beaulieu Château (18C) – present 1 000 objects (out of some 5 000) collected by the painter Jean Dubuffet since 1945 and donated to the city. The paintings, drawings, sculptures, modelling and embroidery are all made with unexpected materials and are the work of schizophrenics, inmates confined to prison cells or psychiatric hospitals, spiritualist mediums and others. Their spontaneous art, while reflecting their own individuality, is reminiscent of the modern works attributed to "genuine" artists such as Surrealist, Abstract and Naïve painters. Some of these strange objects are quite exciting and possess strong artistic appeal: carved wood by Clément, painted fabric by Madge Gill, drawings by Guillaume Pujolle *(The Eagles)*, Woïfli, Aloïse and Scottie Wilson, sculptures by Filippo Bentivenga, huge sketches by Jaki, illustrated books by Metz, paintings by Walla.

Fondation de l'Hermitage (CX)
2 route du Signal. 🕐 *Open for exhibitions only, daily except Mon, 10am-6pm (9pm Thu).* 👣 *Guided tours (1hr) Thu at 6.30pm and Sun at 3pm.* 🎫*15CHF.* ☎ *(021) 320 50 01; www.fondation-hermitage.ch.*
Surrounded by a fine park with rare species of trees, the former home of the Bugnions (a family from Vaud) was built in about 1841. Since 1984 it has been the setting for large temporary exhibitions on art and history.

Vue du Signal★★ (CX)
Alt 643m/2 109ft. This belvedere *(viewing table, telescope)*, near a small chapel, affords a pleasant **view** of Lake Geneva, the Savoy, Fribourg and the Vaud Alps and, in the foreground, the historic centre of Lausanne. Half a mile away lies the **Lac de Sauvabelin** and its reserve for deer and ibexes, a popular place for weekend strollers.

LAUSANNE

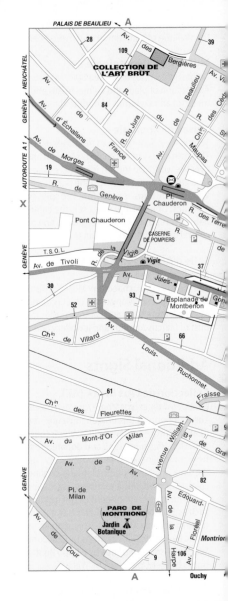

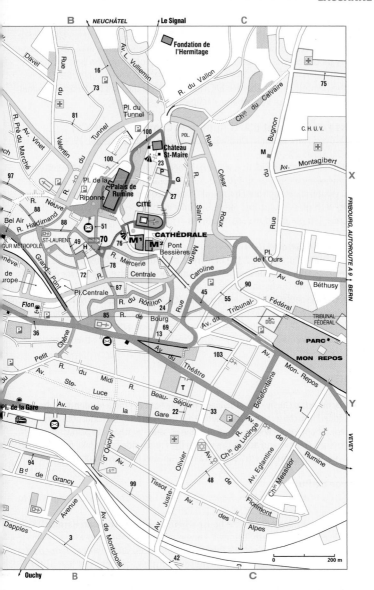

LAUSANNE

Parc Mon Repos (CY)

In this pleasant landscape garden stands the Empire-style villa where Voltaire once lived and which housed an Olympic Museum dedicated to the memory of **Baron Pierre de Coubertin**, founder of the modern Olympic Games, who lived in Lausanne for many years and is buried there. This French aristocrat largely contributed to reviving the Olympic spirit in the late 19C. To the north of the park the Federal Tribunal, the supreme court of Switzerland, occupies a large building.

Musée de Design et d'Arts Appliqués Contemporains (CY)

  🕐 *Open 11am-6pm.* 🕐 *Closed Mon (except Jul and Aug), 1 Jan and 25 Dec.* 🖮 *8CHF.* ☎ *(021) 315 25 30.*

The former Gaudard residence, which has been admirably restored, is the setting for this museum devoted to design and contemporary art. The presentations include early exhibits coming from Egypt and China (Jacques-Édouard Berger Collection), along with glass sculptures made by contemporary artists in Europe, Asia and America. Temporary shows are organised in rotation.

Parc de Montriond (AY)

On this spot where, in 1037, the first Truce of God was proclaimed in the district; there is a great esplanade reached by a ramp and a staircase. The **view**★★ extends southwards over Ouchy, the shores of Lake Geneva (Lac Léman) and to the Alps. One section of the park is by a **botanical garde**n (🕐 *Open May-Sept, daily, 10am-6.30pm; Mar-Apr and Oct, daily, 10am-5.30pm.* 🖮 *No charge. Museum open by appointment.* ☎ *(021) 316 99 88)*, consisting of an arboretum, an alpine garden with mountain flora, flowers, succulents and a variety of medicinal, carnivorous and aquatic species.

Pully

(**BY**) *by avenue d'Ouchy.* The old village of Pully has become a residential suburb of Lausanne. From the terrace of the Church of St Germain (Gothic in origin but very much altered) a charming **view**★ opens out onto the pleasure-boat harbour below, the eastern part of Lake Geneva and across the way to the French side of the lake from Évian to Meillerie. In the church precincts stand a museum and the remains of a Roman villa.

Musée de Pully

  🕐 *Open daily except Mon, 2-6pm.* 🕐 *Closed Easter, Christmas and according to temporary exhibitions.* 🖮 *5CHF.* ☎ *(021) 729 55 81.*

The museum is located near the house where **Charles-Ferdinand Ramuz** (1878-1947) lived until his death. This well-known novelist collaborated with Stravinsky, for whom he wrote *The Soldier's Tale*; he also produced such works as *Terror on the Mountain* and *Beauty on Earth*. The museum displays souvenirs of Ramuz (photographs, manuscripts, original works), together with paintings by R Domenjoz, M Borgeaud, V Milliquet, and by many other contemporary artists from Pully (including: J Lecouttre, P Besson, F Simonin, M Pellegrini). Visitors may also admire clay sculptures by Derain and precious objects (writing desk, model of royal barge) which belonged to the King of Siam, a resident of Pully between 1925 and 1945.

Villa Romaine

  🕐 *Open Apr-Oct, daily except Mon, 2-5pm; Nov-Mar, Sat-Sun2-5pm.* 🕐 *Closed Easter and Christmas.* 🖮 *2.50CHF.* ☎ *(021) 728 33 04 or 729 55 81.*

Located under the terrace of Le Prieuré Hotel (the pink paving reproduces the outline of the Roman walls). What has been revealed of this vast and rich 2C domain is the summer residence, which is a small building with an apse made of a double semi-circular wall about 3m/10ft high and decorated on its inner wall with a polychrome **fresco** more than 20m²/215sq ft depicting chariot races.

Excursions

Lutry

4km/2.5mi by avenue de l'Élysée (DZ – plan of Ouchy), then take road n° 9.
Pleasantly located on the shores of Lake Geneva (small sailing harbour, view of the Alps), this village and its maze of narrow streets deserve a short visit. The main square, embellished with a fountain, features a church with a white façade and fine Romanesque porch. Inside admire the carved wooden stalls and flower motifs painted on the vaulting. As you leave the village, notice an imposing fortified castle (now a centre for social services and healthcare) dominating the vine-covered slopes.

Échallens

15km/9mi by avenue d'Échallens (AX) then take road n° 5.
Located in a fertile cereal-growing agricultural area, this small town boasts a fascinating **Maison du Blé et du Pain** (🕐 *Open 8.30am-6pm.* 🕐 *Closed Mon and two weeks at the end of the year.* 👁 *8CHF.* ☎ *(021) 881 50 71)*, set up in a restored 18C farmhouse. The daily lives of peasants, millers and bakers throughout the ages are illustrated by a diorama, a collection of farming tools (seeders, ploughs, harrows), granaries and a display of different types of baking ovens and mills (manual, mechanical, grinding, and cylinder mills). At the end of the visit, rolls, loaves and croissants are prepared and baked before your eyes.

Zoo de Servion

Kids *18km/11mi by the road to Bern (CX).* ♿ 🕐 *Open 9am-7pm (6pm in winter). Last admission 1hr before closing.* 👁 *10CHF.* ☎ *(021) 903 16 71.*
This estate is home to a wide range of animal species from countries all over the world. After the Monkey Pavilion (comical black and white-ringed marmosets, so-called because of the tufts of fur around their ears), visitors enter the tropical hothouse where exotic birds live in natural conditions (Chinese crested mynahs, African spur-winged plovers etc). Alongside the Ostrich Pavilion you will find Chilean flamingos, as well as crowned cranes and pink-backed pelicans from Africa. Next come the red deer, American buffaloes, brown bears and wolves. The last two species to be visited are the mighty Siberian tiger and the energetic wallaby. The park also features several recreational areas for picnics and outdoor games.

LAC LÉMAN★★★

LAKE GENEVA

The Swiss shore of Lake Geneva, known to the French as Lac Léman, spreads its great arc fringed with vineyards successively along the last slopes of the Jura, the ridges of the Swiss Plateau and the foothills of the Vaud Alps. This shore, especially in the Vevey-Montreux section, became, after Jean-Jacques Rousseau had stayed there, the refuge of the Romantics. The pilgrimages which became more and more frequent among nature lovers started a great tourist industry.

Hydrographical Notes

From the Geneva Fountain to Chillon Castle – In all the Alpine range there is no lake that can rival that of Geneva, with its depth of 310m/1 018ft and area of 58 000ha/143 323 acres. The lake is crescent-shaped, 72km/45mi long and 13km/7.5mi across at its widest point, between Morges and Amphion. The Little Lake between

Geneva and Yvoire is usually considered separately from the Great Lake. The latter is the widest section, within which another Upper Lake can be seen off Vevey-Montreux. For centuries Lake Geneva has been an exceptional study centre for f naturalists established at Geneva since the Reformation. Since the line of Swiss altimetry was fixed at the Niton Rock (alt 374m/1 227ft above the level of the Mediterranean at Marseille), a rock emerging from the water in the port of Geneva, the level of the lake may be regarded as the general standard of altitude in Switzerland.

The folding of the Alps in the Tertiary Era reversed the incline of the valleys, causing the waters to ebb and lakes to form along the edge (Lake Lucerne and Lake Geneva). The lake absorbs the waters of the Valais Rhône: their **meeting** can be observed from terraces or summits overlooking Vevey and Montreux. The powerful muddy flow seems to be completely engulfed; in reality, it does not mix with the lake water immediately and a layer of muddy river water remains at a depth of about 20m/65ft until autumn, when the lake cools and mixes the river flow, purifying and regulating the Rhône water. The lake deptch is gradually decreasing due to silt deposits from the Rhône and the deepening of the river bed.

Exchange of heat between the lake waters and the atmosphere produces a very mild **climate**, especially in early spring and late autumn. The latter season on the Riviera of the Vaud canton is well-known abroad. We also recommend a tour at the time of the grape harvest along the routes described below.

Tour by Boat

In addition to the following itineraries, the corniche section of the motorway connecting Vevey and Rennaz affords wonderful views of the Upper Lake.

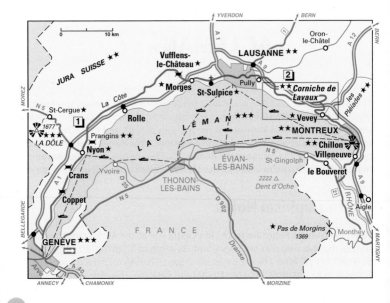

The lake by boat

The steamers of the Compagnie Générale de Navigation on Lake Geneva call regularly on the Swiss and French shores, offering many trips. Among the available excursions are the afternoon trips called the Tour of the **Little Lake** (Petit Lac – starting from Geneva) and the more interesting Tour of the **Upper Lake** (Haut Lac – starting from Ouchy-Lausanne). A round trip of the lake takes 11hr-12hr.

Tour of the Vineyards

From Geneva to Lausanne *70km/43mi – about 3hr*

Genève★★★ – *2hr.* ♿ *See GENÈVE.*

▶ *Leave Geneva by the shore road to Lausanne (which does not leave Geneva's built-up area until after Versoix).*

Coppet – *30min.* ♿ *See COPPET.*

Crans – ♿ *See NYON: Excursions.*

Nyon★ – *1hr.* ♿ *See NYON.*

▶ *Leave Nyon by ⑤, heading towards Aubonne.*

On leaving the charming port of Nyon and after Luins and the enchanting little church standing alone among the vines in a clump of cypresses, it is a fast trip to Bursins and then on to Mont-sur-Rolle. Besides the Savoy shore of the lake – with Thonon – and the summits of the Haut-Chablais, you see the Vaud shore from Rolle Bay to the Naye Rocks with Lausanne in between. The south-facing hills which slope down to the lake are one of the great wine-growing areas of Switzerland.

Rolle

This town lies on the north shore of Lake Geneva halfway between Geneva and Lausanne. The 13C **castle** built by a Prince of Savoy is triangular, with a large tower at each corner. On a small artificial island is an obelisk erected to the memory of **General Frédéric de Laharpe** (1754-1838), a tutor of Tsar Alexander, who promoted the independence of the Vaud and is a founding father of the Helvetian Republic. The road from Mont-sur-Rolle to Aubonne reveals typical villages surrounded by vineyards such as Féchy. The **views★★** open out towards the Little Lake as far as Geneva (fountain) and the Salève. Immediately after leaving Aubonne, towards Lavigny, the crossing of the Aubonne Ravine offers an attractive general view of the town.

Vufflens-le-Château★

Vufflens Castle is one of the proudest buildings in all of Switzerland. It stands on a plateau overlooking the ravine of the Morges, with a fine view of the Jura, Lake Geneva and the Alps. The castle belonged to a Savoy family and was entirely rebuilt with brick in the 15C in the Italian tradition and extensively restored in the 19C. The castle consists of two quite distinct parts. The massive square keep, with four towers, rises well above the rest to a lantern turret at a height of 60m/200ft. Decorative brickwork and machicolations add an attractive note to this imposing fortress. The entrance courtyard separates the keep from the living quarters with its four unusual slender towers each sporting a machicolated ruffle terminating in pointed roofs.

Morges★ – ♿ *See MORGES.*

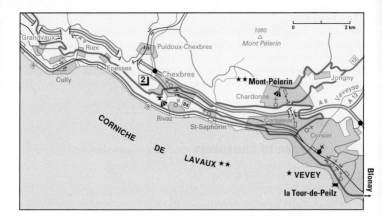

▶ *Between Morges and Lausanne leave road n° 1 to make a detour through St-Sulpice.*

St-Sulpice★

The little **St-Sulpice Church**★ – Protestant since the 16C – is a pure specimen of Romanesque in a rustic and peaceful **setting** within sight of Lake Geneva and the Savoy Alps. The only traces of the former Romanesque church – originally a Benedictine priory – are the chancel, the transept and the crossing with a tower above. The interior is austere and simple but tempered by multicoloured decoration.

▶ *Return to road n° 1 for the drive to Lausanne.*

② The Lavaux Corniche★★

From Lausanne to Villeneuve *39km/24mi – about 1hr 30min*

The road described below, which crosses the motorway after the La Croix crossroads, is the same road that is sandwiched between the motorway and the coastal road (n° 9) as far as the outskirts of Vevey. If traffic is too heavy, take the small road from Chexbres to the Puidoux railway station (5km/3mi), which then links up with the road described. It, too, borders and overlooks the motorway. The motorway offers splendid views, but the views are often interrupted by the many tunnels.

▶ *Leaving from Ouchy, you can always join up with the tour at Grandvaux by taking the coastal road n° 9. After leaving Lutry, turn left into the "Route de la Petite Corniche", then follow directions to Riex.*

Lausanne★★ – *1hr.* 🕭 *See LAUSANNE.*

▶ *Leave Lausanne by avenue de Béthusy going towards La Rosiaz.*

After this the road runs through a residential suburb and wooded ravines and emerges on a gently undulating slope planted with fruit trees within view of the Upper Lake and its Savoy shore. This is marked from left to right by the Meillerie Cliffs, the green undulations of the Gavot Plateau (behind Évian) and the Drance Delta.
After the crossroads at La Croix, the whole of the Great Lake (Grand Lac) can be seen: the curves of the Vaud shore make a bend at the foot of the Jura, beyond the houses of Lausanne. The Yvoire Point juts out from the far shore. Sadly, the once familiar sight of stately lateen boats with great white sails is now a thing of the past.

▶ *After a steep descent you will cross the motorway and railway.*

The road then enters the Lavaux vineyard, praised by Ramuz, the writer from the Vaud. Its slopes plunge down into the Upper Lake opposite the precipitous shores of Savoy. Then come the wine-growing villages of Riex and Epesses enclosed by terraces of vines. The slope steepens and you enter the Le Dézaley district. Where the road skirts a sharp little spur, a **viewpoint**★★ offers the Valais Rhône Valley through a gap in which the snowy Grand Combin summit appears in the distance. Beyond are the towns of Vevey and Montreux. They cover every bend in the shore at the foot of the characteristic Dent de Jaman and the cliffs of the Naye Rocks. During the last corniche section, between Chexbres, Chardonne and Vevey *(belvederes with benches; the first one has a viewing table)* look out for the Dents du Midi.

Vevey★; Mont-Pèlerin★★
1hr 30min (for both Vevey and Mount-Pèlerin Resort). 👤 *See VEVEY.*

Montreux★★ – 👤 *See MONTREUX.*

Château de Chillon★★ – *1hr.* 👤 *See Château de CHILLON.*

Villeneuve
Located at the east end of the lake, this small town with vestiges recalling its ancient past has a pleasant lake front. The Grand'Rue, bedecked with multicoloured banners in summer, has kept its old narrow houses fronted by wooden gates. Several shops have façades decorated with quaint wrought-iron signs. Near the Place du Temple and its pretty fountain stands St Paul's Church (12C), noted for its stained-glass windows. Not far from the station, an unusual town hall has been set up in the former chapel of the hospital. Many world celebrities fell in love with the town and decided to make it their home. Among those whose name will forever remain associated with Villeneuve were writers like **Byron** (one hotel is named after him), Victor Hugo, Romain Rolland (he lived here (1922-38); a villa in the grounds of the Byron Hotel carries his name), and painters like Oskar Kokoscha (he died here in 1980).

▶ *When you leave Villeneuve, turn right and take the road to Noville, then cross the Rhône and turn right again towards Le Bouveret (road n° 21).*

Le Bouveret
🚉 *Bâtiment CFF – 1897 –* ☎ *(024) 481 51 21.*
This village a few miles away from the French border is the seat of the **Swiss Vapeur Parc** (🕐 *Open mid-Mar to mid-Oct, daily, 10am-6pm; early Apr to mid-May, 1.30 (10am Sat-Sun) to 6pm; mid-Sep to 31 Oct, 1.30-6pm.* 🕐 *Closed Nov-Mar.* 💰13CHF. ☎ *(024) 481 44 70; www.swissvapeur.ch).* Along a circuit set up on the shores of the lake, near the sailing harbour, miniature trains circulate in a reconstructed railway in the midst of lush vegetation. Travellers may be seated on board small carriages driven by steam locomotives (Pacific 01, Waldenbourg 030 etc) – a great favourite among children.

🄺🄸🄳🅂 If you or your children enjoy both water sports and big thrills, be sure to visit **Aquaparc** (🕐 *Open daily 10.30am-8.30pm (9.30pm Fri, Sat and school holidays.* 💰 *Admission for 5hr: 40CHF.* ☎ *(024) 482 00 00; www.aquaparc.ch).* The braver will venture into Jungle Land, the shy ones will stop in Paradise Land and tiny tots will go straight to Captain's Kids Land.

EATING OUT-LA BOUVERET
Rive-Bleue – *La Lagune, route de la Plage –* ☎ *024 481 17 23.* A welcoming dining hall extended by a terrace facing Lake Geneva. Traditional cuisine characterised by a wide choice of dishes.

LENK

BERN – POPULATION 2 439
ALT 1 068M/3 504FT

Lenk is located in a vast basin surrounded by lush green cow pastures and is crossed by the Simme (canalised) which rises only a couple of kilometres south in the snowy Wildstrubel Range. It is a charming resort, with an attractive town centre planted with trees and and dotted with impressive, flower-decked villas.
www.lenk-semmental.ch.

As a spa, the town's sulphurous springs cure patients of ailments of the joints and the respiratory system. Lenk also has excellent leisure facilities, including an indoor swimming pool, tennis courts, a riding school, ice rink and climbing wall, as well as opportunities for mountain biking, paragliding and rafting. A total of 200km/125mi of footpaths lead around the lake and into the mountains.

The Skiing Area
In winter, the town's network of 56 lifts takes the walker or skier to the nearby slopes of Metschberg, Betelbert (family skiing), Mülkerblatten and the challenging pistes at the Metsch.There are more than 74km/110mi of prepared winter hiking and snowshoeing trails, both near the village and at higher elevations. Lenk is linked to the Abelboden ski resort.

Sights

Simmenfälle
4km/2.5mi plus 10min on foot there and back. Leave the car in the car park to the left of the restaurant and follow the signposts indicating Barbarabrücke.
Powerful and noisy, the Simme Falls tumble down the rocky face of the Wildstrubel. Because of the fir trees you can only see the base of the falls; return to near the restaurant to see the top.

Iffigenfall★
2.5km/1.5mi plus 45min on foot there and back.
Leave Lenk to the south on the road to Iffigen. Park the car at the end of the surfaced road (falls visible) and walk up the road for 2km/1mi *(rocky and steep – 15% – traffic permitted only for large trucks and at fixed hours).* From a bend to the left admire the falls tumbling down (80m/262ft).

LEUK

VALAIS – POPULATION 3 253
ALT 750M/2 461FT

Leuk lies in terraces halfway up the slope above the Rhône Valley at the mouth of the Dala Gorges. The little town has a severe setting characteristic of the southern Valais due to the barrenness of the slopes and heavily modelled summits. From the castles' esplanade at the entrance to the town there is an astonishing **view★** of the valley floor. The great fluvial cone of rubble from the Illgraben, covered with mingled heath and forest vegetation (Forest of Finges or Pfynwald) stands below; the rubble is familiar to all Swiss school children as an example of fluvial deposition. This obstruction still forms the natural boundary between the French-speaking Central Valais and the Upper Valais with its German-Swiss culture.

The Castles

Their names recall the titles of functionaries of the Bishop of Sion, who used to live there. The first stronghold encountered on entering the town is the **Château des Vidommes**: vidames were secular deputies appointed to command armies or to represent the interests of French abbots or bishops under the Ancien Régime. This building has become the town hall. The tall 16C structure and its stepped gables flanked by watchtowers recall, in a much more graceful and original style, the building at Sierre of the same name. Farther on, the 15C **Château des Majors** still features its square crenellated tower.

Excursions

Leukerbad✵
15km/10mi N by the direct route – allow 30min (🔗 see LEUKERBAD).

Albinen
Leukerbad can also be reached through the quaint village of Albinen, whose wooden houses, perched on the nearby slopes, appear to defy the laws of gravity. The narrow, winding road to Leukenbad offers plunging **views** of the valley below.

LEUKERBAD ★

VALAIS – POPULATION 1 600
ALT 1 411M/4 628FT

This high-altitude spa was discovered by the Romans. It nestles in a grandiose **site**★, overlooked by the Gemmipass and approached from Leuk via a narrow, often vertiginous road. It was this austere landscape that inspired French author Guy de Maupassant to write his fantastic tale, *L'Auberge*. Bare rocky peaks overlook the valley, which is dotted with attractive chalets and pastureland. 🄑 ☎ *027 472 71 71; www.leukerbad.ch.*

The **Skiing Area** (*50km/31mi of downhill runs and 25km/15mi of cross-country tracks*) extends across the Gemmi and Torrent ranges, at an altitude between 1 400m/4 592ft and 2 800m/9 184ft. Leukerbad is particularly renowned for its **spa**, the largest in Europe, whose sulphurous, calcareous and gypsum-rich waters are recommended for the treatment of rheumatism, circulatory diseases and skin problems. The resort is popular year-round with tourists, who come here to bathe in thermal waters (51°C/124°F at source and between 28°C/82°F and 44°C/111°F in the pools).

Spas

Burgerbad
This spa complex houses an indoor thermal bath and a pool for children, a gym and a bar-restaurant. Outdoor facilities include a swimming pool, two thermal baths, a 70m/230ft water slide, jacuzzis, a footbath and a sauna in a grotto.

Hikers in the Gemmi region above Leukerbad

Lindner Alpentherme

Opened in 1993, this fitness centre has indoor and outdoor thermal baths, a swimming pool, plus a complex where the visitor can choose between showers, hot-air baths, massage, steam baths, jacuzzis and cold-water baths.

Excursion

Gemmipass

Alt 2 314m/7 590ft. Linked to Leukerbad by cable car, this pass begins in Kandersteg in the Bernese Oberland and ends on the slopes of the Valais in a vertiginous road cut out of the rock, offering superb **views**★ of the Valais and Bernese Alps.

LIECHTENSTEIN

The Principality of Liechtenstein is a fragment of the former Germanic Confederation, whose territory extended from the east bank of the Rhine to the Vorarlberg Mountains. The little state was made a sovereign principality by Emperor Charles VI in 1719 to benefit Prince Jean Adam of Liechtenstein; it owes the preservation of its statute largely to the wise policy followed by Prince Johann II (the Good), whose reign (1858-1929) was the longest of any Western European sovereign except Louis XIV (1638-1715). Franz-Joseph II, who ruled the country from 1939 to 1989, has been succeeded by his son, Hans Adam II.

After 1919 Liechtenstein loosened its last bonds with Austria and concluded monetary, postal, customs and diplomatic conventions with the Swiss Confederation; today it is to all intents a part of the Swiss economic sphere. The dividing line between the Germanic and Rhaetic civilisations is, however, clearly marked by the southern boundary; large villages scattered among the orchards at the foot of a castle or around churches with pointed spires make a contrast with the Grisons cities closely gathered among their vines.

General Information

Size: 160km²/61.5sq mi

Population: 32 800 in 2000

Altitude: From 430m/1 410ft to 2 559m/8 393ft at the Grauspitz

Official abbreviation: FL (number plates)

Official language: German

Religion: Catholicism (majority)

Government:
- Constitutional monarchy
- The Parliament or Diet is composed of 25 members elected for four years.
- The Government, elected for four years, is composed of five members: the Head of State, his deputy and three Federal advisors (Federal councillors).

There are no formalities on passing from Switzerland into Liechtenstein.

Vaduz *1hr 30min*

Städtle 37, Postfach 139 – 9490 – ☎ (00423) 239 63 00, www.welcome.li.
Lying at the foot of the imposing **castle**, the residence of its princely family *(☛ not open to the public)*, the capital city and seat of the present government has become a busy international tourist attraction.

Post Office
Philatelists collect stamps issued by this small state. The post office is as great a feature of interest as the Postage Stamp Museum *(☝ see below)*.

Musée des Beaux-Arts du Liechtenstein
♿ 🕐 *Open daily except Mon, 10am-5pm (8pm Thu). 🕐 Closed 1 Jan, 24, 25 and 31 Dec. ✆ 8CHF. ☎ (00423) 235 03 00, www.kunstmuseum.li.*
This Fine Arts Museum is devoted primarily to paintings and 20C graphic artwork. It houses some of the works taken from collections belonging to the Prince of Liechtenstein. There is also a fine outdoor sculpture park dotted with modern works.

Liechtensteinisches Landesmuseum
Städle 43, Vaduz. 🕐 Open Tues-Sun 10am-5pm (Wed to 8pm). 🕐 Closed 24, 25, 31 Dec and 1 Jan. ✆ 8CHF. ☎ (00423) 239 68 20, www.landesmuseum.li.
In the restored buildings of an old inn, this museum covers the important periods of the principality's history. There is a relief model of the country, a mineralogy collection and a display of art from the prehistoric age, the Bronze Age, the Roman era (coins, objects), and the Alemannic period (jewellery, arms). Also exhibited are arms (medieval cutting and thrusting weapons, 16C-18C firearms), utensils, local folk art, works of art (16C paintings, German religious sculpture) and cult objects.

Briefmarkenmuseum
🕐 *Open daily, 10am-5.30pm (5pm Nov-Mar). 🕐 Closed 1 Jan and 25 Dec. ✆ No charge. ☎ (00423) 236 61 05.*
Located in a small gallery of the Fine Arts Museum *(☝ see above)*, this museum highlights the principality's philatelic art and the history of the country's postal system (stamp collections). Temporary exhibitions are regularly organised.

South of Vaduz

From Vaduz to Maienfeld
16km/10mi – allow 45min

▶ *Leave Vaduz to the south on the Triesen road.*

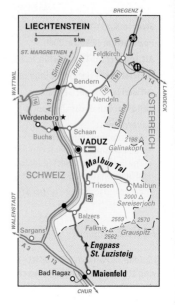

Malbuntal
15km/9mi from Triesen.
In the heart of the country, this road climbs to the corrie at the foot of the Sareiser Joch (alt 2 000m/6 562ft), part of the Vorarlberg foothills and which can be reached on foot or by cable car from Malbun.

Engpass Sankt Luzisteig
This fortified defile momentarily leaves the warm, wide Rhine Valley, only to return to it immediately. Hemmed in between the Fläscherberg height and the steep and often snowy escarpments of the Falknis, this defile was of strategic importance so long as the road that follows it was the only road suitable for motor vehicles between Austria and the Grisons. The route is still barred today by a line of fortifications, some of which were built in 1703 (most of the others were built 831-37).

On the Grisons side of the Luzisteig Pass, the road is steep and runs through woods. For a stop you may choose the shady clearing among oak trees,  1km/0.5mi from Maienfeld where a **Heidi Fountain** (Heidibrunnen) serves as a memorial to Johanna Spyri (1827-1901), a popular Swiss writer of the *Heidi* children's books.

LOCARNO ★★

TICINO – POPULATION 14 371
TOWN PLAN IN THE MICHELIN GUIDE SWITZERLAND

Locarno lies in the hollow of a sunny bay which curves more sharply as the delta formed by the River Maggia juts into the waters of one of Italy's most famous lakes, **Lago Maggiore ★★★**. Sheltered by the Alps, Locarno enjoys an exceptional climate in which hydrangeas, magnolias and camellias blossom as early as March. This is a beautiful town with pleasant walks among the gardens, along the lakeshore, on the vine-covered slopes of Orselina and in the Cardada Hills. 🛈 *Largo Zorzi 1 – 6600 – ☎ (091) 791 00 91, www.maggiore.ch.*

Sights

Piazza Grande
This paved oblong square in the old district is an important place in the life of the city. The Piazza Grande is frequented by locals, who enjoy coming here for a stroll, as well as by tourists, attracted by the shopping arcades, cafés and restaurants, especially in summer when the sunny pavement terraces overflow with people. The old houses with balconies painted in pastel hues add charm to the whole scene. Each August,

The Pact of Locarno, or How to Maintain Peace in Europe

In October 1925, Locarno was at the center of international politics. World attention was focused on the Palais de Justice, where delegations from France, Great Britain, Germany, Italy, Belgium, Poland and Czechoslovakia attended a conference led by their respective foreign ministers Aristide Briand, Austen Chamberlain, Gustav Stresemann, Vittorio Scialoja, Émile Vandervelde, Alexander Skrzynski and Edvard Benes. Seen as a sequel to the 1924 London Conference, which stipulated that the Ruhr area be evacuated within a year and that Germany join the League of Nations, the Locarno Conference led to the signing of a treaty on 16 October 1925. Germany recognised its borders with France and Belgium and the demilitarised zone included in the 1919 peace treaty concluded in Versailles. Germany also agreed not to alter her western borders through military action. For his key role in the negotiations and final peace agreement, the head of the British delegation, Austen Chamberlain, was awarded the Nobel Prize for Peace in 1925.

The Pact of Locarno was hailed as a resounding success by the international press. It introduced a new era of peaceful cohabitation and Lord d'Abernon, the British ambassador in Berlin, wrote: that it "marks a significant turning-point in the history of post-war Europe. It symbolises the abolition of the dividing line between the conquerors and the conquered." The treaty was ratified in London on 1 December 1925. Briand, Chamberlain and Stresemann met regularly to supervise its implementation and to pave the way for economic cooperation between countries. Germany was accepted into the League of Nations in 1926, signifying reconciliationit seemed that the future would be free from international tension. But in 1936 Hitler violated the treaty by occupying and remilitarising the Rhineland, plunging Europe, and, indeed, the world, into a bloody war three years later.

film buffs meet in Locarno to attend the **International Film Festival**, when Piazza Grande becomes a huge open-air cinema screen. To the east the square is extended by Largo Zorzi: on one side it is flanked by pretty lawns and fine trees and ends at the landing stage from which boat trips on the lake can be organised.

Castello Visconteo

🕐 *Open Apr-Oct, daily except Mon, 10am-noon and 2-5pm.* 🕶 *7CHF.* ☎ *(091) 756 31 70/80.*

The castle is named after the Visconti, a famous Italian family who ruled over Milan from the 13C to 15C. These were troubled times because of the feud between the Guelfs, who supported the emperor, and the Ghibellines (the Visconti), who favored papal supremacy. Ticino became involved in the conflict, and in the 14C the castle was heavily fortified by the Viscontis. In 1439 the castle fell to Count Franchino Rusca, who continued its fortification. His son Jovanne converted it into a residential palace; there remain some fine sculpted coffered ceilings which can be admired during a tour of the Museo Civico e Archeologico. The Municipal and Archaeological Museum, is devoted to the region's Iron and Bronze Age, Roman period (fine collection of glassware) and Middle Ages. There is also a fine collection of ceramics and 18C clothing and porcelain figures. One room is devoted to the Pact of Locarno through photographs and press articles.

Chiesa San Francesco

Consecrated in 1230 by Uberto di Monserrato, the Bishop of Como, the church attached to the former Franciscan convent was extensively restored in the 16C. The austere interior features a nave and two side aisles separated by five twin columns made of granite from the Ascona area. Note the wooden vaulting in the nave and side aisles crowned by Romanesque barrel vaulting. The upper section of the chancel is decorated with a large fresco depicting the Annunciation of the Virgin.

Address Book

SHOPPING

The main shopping streets are Via della Stazione, Via della Ramogna, Via Sempione, Via Cattori, Via D. Recinto, Via F. Balli and Piazza Grande.

THEATRE

Teatro di Locarno (Largo Zorzi).

👁 *For coin ranges, see the Legend on the front flap.*

WHERE TO STAY

⊜⊜⊟ **Palmiera** – *Via del Sole 1* – ☎ *091 743 14 41 – Fax 091 751 43 63 – 33 rooms –* ⏱ *open mid-Mar to mid- Nov.* A charming and quaint hotel, surrounded by a garden planted with palm trees. Most rooms have a balcony overlooking Lake Maggiore.

⊜⊜⊟ **Piccolo Hotel** – *Via Buetti 11* – ☎ *091 743 02 12, www.piccolo-hotel. ch. – 21 rooms –* ⏱ *open mid-Mar to mid-Nov.* Good prices and service at this hotel away from the town centre. No restaurant.

⊜⊜⊟ **Dell'Angelo** – *Piazza Grande* – ☎ *091 751 81 75, www.hotel-dell-ange-lo.ch. – 55 rooms –* Centrally located at the heart of the new town, this hotel is a good starting-point for discovering the old quarter or to simply go window-shopping beneath the arcades of Piazza Grande. The top floor has a terrace offering nice views of the town and lake. Good service for the price.

⊜⊜⊟ **Hotel du Lac** – *Via Ramogna 3* – ☎ *091 751 29 21, www.du-lac-locarno. ch. – 31 rooms.* Located in the pedestrian area near Piazza Grande, barely 5min from the Madonna del Sasso funicular and near the landing for delightful boat trips on the lake. Several rooms overlook the lake. No restaurant.

⊜⊜⊟ **Alba** – *At Minusio, 2km/1mi E* – *Via Simen 58 – ☎ 091 735 88 88, www. albahotel.ch. – 36 rooms –* ⏱ *closed 1-15 Mar.* A modern hotel with a swim-ming pool and a garden for restful summer afternoons. All rooms have balconies offering lakeside views. No restaurant.

⊜⊜⊟ **Dellavalle** – *In Brione, 4.5km/2.8mi E, via Contra 45 – ☎ 091 735 30 00, www.dellavalle.ch – 50 rooms–* ⏱ *closed Jan-Mar.* Peace and quiet are guaranteed in this comfortable establishment providing lovely views of the lake and surrounding mountains. Fitness devotees will enjoy the gymnasium and its facilities.

EATING OUT

⊜⊜⊟ **Muralto** – *Piazza Statione 8* – ☎ *091 743 01 81 –* ⏱ *Closed Jan to early- Mar and at lunchtime.* Settle on the terrace and watch dusk slowly descend on the peaceful waters of the lake.

⊜⊜⊟**Campagna** – *In Minu-sio, 2km/1mi E – Via Rivapiana 46* – ☎ *091 743 20 54 –* ⏱ *closed Tue, and Wed evening.* This typical Ticino grotto has been converted into a restaurant with rustic decor. Eating at granite tables outdoors, in the shade of the trees, can be a charming experience.

NIGHTLIFE

Enjoy an apéritif in a typical setting at **Alle Grotto** (in the Grand Albergo Locarno complex, access by Via della Stazione). On weekends, there is live music at **Cantina Canetti** (Piazza Grande 20), a well-known wine bar which has retained its old-fashioned charm. The **Kursaal** casino (Largo Zorzi) attracts the late-night crowd with its discotheque and slot machines.

In the Muralto district, along the lake shores, the **Al Pozz** (Viale Verbano 21) is a bar offering musical entertainment, with strong emphasis on the accordion, the mandolin and the guitar. A little farther on, the **Bussola** is for dedicated jazz enthusiasts.

Casa Rusca

Piazza Sant'Antonio. ⏱ *Open Apr-Jun and Aug-Nov, daily except Mon, 10am-5pm.* 👛 *7CHF.* ☎ *(091) 756 31 85/70.*
The house is a fine example of a 17C patrician residence. The beautiful inner courtyard is surrounded by baskethandle arcades laid out on three levels. The exhibitions, renewed on a regular basis, are devoted to modern and contemporary art and always

Film Festival on the Piazza Grande in Locarno

Heinz Schwab / Switzerland Tourism

focus on the work of a specific artist. In the past, the Casa Rusca has been associated with painters such as the Italian Enrico Baj, Ferdinand Hodler, Cuno Amiet and Claude Baccalà (from the Ticino area). Traditionally, these artists are expected to donate one of several of their works to the museum. For instance, two ceramic sculptures by Enrico Baj stand on either side of the entrance: *Adam and Eve, Love and Psyche*.

Boat Trips on Lake Maggiore

Visitors to Locarno can spend a pleasant afternoon relaxing on a boat, gliding along the water's surface. There are several boat trips available, ranging from a simple crossing ending at the pontoon on the opposite shore (Magadino), at Ascona or Brissago, to a proper excursion, including a visit to Stresa and the Isole Borromee.

Excursions

Madonna del Sasso★
At Orselina. Recommended access by funicular. Lower station at Via della Stazione.
This church, frequented by many tourists and pilgrims, stands on the summit (355m/1 165ft) of a wooded spur which can also be reached by car along the hairpin bends of the Via ai Monti della Trinità. At the upper level, stairs lead down to the basilica (excellent bird's-eye views). In 1480, the Virgin appeared before the brother of Bartolomeo of Ivrea, a monk from the San Francesco convent in Locarno, who had gone into retreat on the Sasso della Rocca. A chapel was erected to commemorate the vision. In the courtyard (bronze statue by Giovanni Manzù, *Il Frate*), follow directions for the "Chiesa". Before reaching the church, you can see several chapels containing groups of wooden sculptures (Chapel of the Pietà, Chapel of the Last Supper, Chapel of the Holy Spirit). The **Church of the Annunciation** features an imposing doorway consisting of an arcaded gallery embellished with murals. The Baroque interior is

particularly interesting forits frescoes and works of art, such as the *Flight into Egypt*, a retable painted by Bramantino (1522) and a *Descent from the Cross* (left side aisle) by Antonio Ciseri, a 19C Ticino painter born in Ronco. The nearby loggia along the church commands a pretty **view**★ of Locarno and Lake Maggiore.

Return to the courtyard to visit the **museum** set up in Casa del Padre, the oldest section of the convent buildings. It presents 18C sculptures, liturgical objects (busts-reliquaries, chandeliers, silver crucifix), ex-votos, a breviary taken from the former San Franciscan convent and an illuminated gradual from the 15C. Leaving the church, you can return either by funicular or on foot, following directions for Locarno via Crucis. This will take you along the path traditionally used by pilgrims. The steep climb down, dotted with Stations of the Cross, offers interesting views of the lake.

Cimetta★★

🚡 *Chair-lift leaving from Cardada –* 🕐 *Operates Mar-Oct, 9.15am-12.30pm and 1-5pm.* 🕐 *Closed Nov.* 🎫 *35CHF there and back.* ☎ *(091) 735 30 30; www.cardada.ch.*

The funicular going to the Madonna del Sasso is continued by a cable car which in 10 minutes climbs the **Alpe di Cardada** (alt 1 350m/4 428ft) from where there is a very extensive **view**★★. From Cardada a chairlift goes to the top of the Cimetta (alt 1 672m/5 482ft) and a fine **panorama**★★ of the Alps and Lake Maggiore.

Ronco Tour★★

▶ *17km/11mi – about 1hr 30min – by a corniche road between Ronco and Porto Ronco on which it is difficult to pass. The trip is very pleasant in the late afternoon. Leave Locarno to the southwest by the Ascona road.*

Soon after the great bridge over the Maggia, turn right towards Losone. In this village, after the church, turn left (road to Ascona and Veritá Mountain) and right (road to Ronco) at the next crossroads. After running through a small valley containing a sawmill and a flour mill, leave the Arcegno road on your right and follow directions for Monte Verita. At the next fork bear right.

The *corniche* byroad, emerging from chestnut woods, opens out above Lake Maggiore and immediately affords a series of beautiful **bird's-eye views**★★. Below, in succession, you will see Ascona, the two wooded **Isole di Brissago** (👓 *see ASCONA*) and finally the lakeside town of Brissago. You come into sight of Ronco.

Along Lake Maggiore

Jerry Dennis / APA Publications

Ronco

The village clings to the flank of a slope in a typically Mediterranean **setting**★★. The church terrace makes a good belvedere, offering a pretty view of Lake Maggiore, the small Brissago Islands and Monte Gambarogno. Taking a winding road downwards you can rejoin the road running along the lake at Porto Ronco; turn to the left. This road has several sections cut out of the rock. The scenery is charming as you approach the attractive village of Ascona.

Ascona★★ – 👣 See Ascona.

Valle Maggia★★

28km/17.5mi NW until you reach Bignasco. First take the road to Ascona, then follow directions.

This valley, the most important one in the Locarno region, is also one of the deepest on the southern slope of the Alps. The landscape gradually changes as the road climbs north. The valley is wide at low altitude, with the steep cliff face jutting almost vertically, but narrows farther on, taking on Alpine features with pine and larch forests carpeting the mountain side. Most of the villages have retained their rustic appearance: old houses with stone walls, roofs covered in gneiss. As in the Valais canton, you often come across chalets mounted on piles, known as *raccards* or *torbas*, which were used as lofts (👣 *see Le VALAIS*).

▶ *Turn right into a narrow road which branches off the main road.*

Maggia

The starting-point for many excursions, the village of Maggia has a lovely church, **Santa Maria delle Grazie**, which stands on the edge. Its most notable features are the 16C **frescoes**★ adorning the apse and the walls of the nave and a fine collection of ex-votos painted by Giovanni Antonio Vanoni (1810-86). This artist born in the small neighbouring hamlet of Aurigeno decorated a great many churches in the Ticino region. The valley becomes narrower and the river bed is littered with huge boulders. Beyond Someo, the **Soladino Waterfall** is on the left.

Cevio

The administrative centre of the Valley Maggia is known for its **Bailiffs' House** (16C), set back behind the main square. The façade is decorated with the coats of arms of the different bailiffs who occupied the premises. On leaving the village, you can visit the **Museo di Vallemaggia** (👣🕐 *Open Apr-Oct, daily except Mon, 10am-noon and 2-6pm, Sun 2-6pm.* ✏*5CHF.* ☎ *(091) 754 13 40/23 68; www.museovalmaggia.ch*). The museum is divided into two sections. A Folklore Museum in Palazzo Franzoni illustrates the costumes and local crafts of this secluded area. Another display concerns the extraction and use of granite and serpentine, a rare type of rock that is easy to work and that encouraged the development of local craft. The quarrying of serpentine (deposits at Valle di Peccia, Valle Rovana, Valle Verzasca and Centovalli) ended in the 19C. The second part of the museum lies nearby: the Casa Respini-Moretti is devoted to the Mogheno necropolis discovered in 1994 while a house was being built.

In the hamlet of Rovana (road to Busco/Gurin), near the bridge spanning the river, the church **Beata Vergine del Ponte** is a fine example of Baroque architecture. The interior is lavishly ornamented with stuccowork and frescoes.

Bignasco

The confluence where the River Maggia (or Lavizzara) meets the River Bavona. Choose between two itineraries: Val Lavizzara or Val Bavona.

Val Lavizzara
17km/10.5mi until Fusio.

Peccia
This village is renowned for its marble. The quarry is located near the small hamlet of Piano di Peccia. The marble is taken to Peccia, where it is worked. The shades go from white, as in the case of Carrara marble, to grey, with blue, brown or even pink streaks. The road continues to climb, forming hairpin bends.

Mogno
Soon after the bridge, take a small road on the right to the chapel, designed by Ticino architect Mario Botta. The white and grey stone building, shaped as a truncated pyramid, replaces the former church, swept away by an avalanche in 1986.

Fusio
Perched at an altitude of 1 280m/4 199ft, at the foot of a rocky spur, Fusio is the highest village in Val Lavizzara, with many fine old houses. During the high season, you may continue beyond the dam lake (Lago Sambuco). The road becomes steeper and narrower, with more bends (*caution is required here as there is no parapet and only room for one car to pass at a time*). The vegetation is scarce and the landscape appears barren. There are breathtaking views all the way up to the small mountain lakes. The silence is impressive.

▶ *Return to Bignasco.*

Val Bavona
12km/7.5mi until you reach San Carlo, where the road ends. This wild area is characterised by high cliff faces and huge boulders which accumulated after a series of rockfalls, especially around **Cavergno**. All along the route, you will drive through charming villages with typical 16C architecture.

Foroglio
The most attractive feature of Foroglio, the starting-point for many mountain walks, is its waterfall. Leave the car near the bridge, cross the river and follow the green signpost "Punto Panoramico" near the restaurant. The path leads to the foot of the waterfall, whose gushing waters form an imposing sight.

Sonlerto
Built in the midst of fallen rocks which cut across the valley, this little village is worth visiting. The church and its campanile, the fountain, the houses and the torba make a charming picture. The road wends its way upwards along a sinuous course. As it crosses the river, it gets closer to the huge mass of rock looming on the horizon.

San Carlo
From the last village in Val Bavona, a cable-car will take you to Mont Robiei (1 894m/6 213ft). Experienced climbers may reach the summit on foot and proceed until they reach the three small mountain lakes: Zött, Robiei and Bianco.

Bosco/Gurin★
43km/26.7mi. Take the road to Valle Maggia and in Cevio turn left. For the description of the itinerary up to Cevio, see above.
Follow the road and its hairpin bends through Alpine landscape to Linescio, then Cerentino. The countryside becomes more ragged and opens onto Bosco/Gurin, a cirque of Alpine pastures. This wild "world's end" is often part of the difficult official circuit of the Swiss Cycling Tour for experienced cyclists.

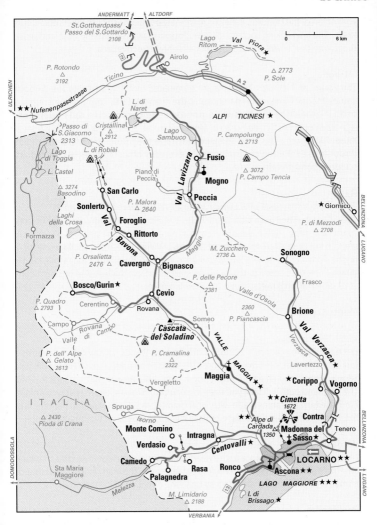

The highest village in the Ticino area (1 503m/4 930ft) is unique: it is the last remaining Walser village where the local population still speaks Gurinerdeutsch or Walser Deutsch, a German dialect which incorporates Italian words. The Walser probably settled here around the 13C, coming from the Upper Valais to cultivate and defend land belonging to Italian lords. These rugged mountain people, who lived in a state of serfdom, enjoyed certain privileges in return, such as the free hereditary loan of land. The church terrace commands a plunging view of the Lower Valley with wooden houses built on stone bases. A fine old mansion, the **Walserhaus** (🕐 *Open mid-April to Oct, daily except Mon, 10-11.30am and 1.30-5pm, Sun 1.30-5pm.* ✆ *3CHF.* ☎ *(091) 754 24 23; www.walserhaus.ch*), contains an Ethnographical Museum explaining the history and traditions of the Walser (household objects, early trades, costumes, religious rites etc).

Centovalli★

19km/11.8mi W. Leave Locarno by the road to Ponte Tresa. At Ponte Brolla, turn left.

The region of the Hundred Valleys is extremely popular with both hikers and nature lovers. The train linking Locarno to Domodossola (Italy) makes many stops and allows those who don't have a car to discover a highly attractive area.

Intragna

The village and its narrow streets are dominated by the campanile. The Baroque church features fine mural paintings in the chancel. To the right of the church, a small alley leads to the **Museo Regionale delle Centovalli e del Pedemonte** (🕙 *Open Easter to Oct, daily except Mon, 2-6pm.* 🎟 *5CHF.* ☎ *(091) 796 25 77; www. museo100valli.ch*). This little museum illustrates the history and life of the region through an exhibition of farming tools, everyday objects, costumes, sacred art, sculptures and paintings.

Rasa

Access by cable car (Funivia Verdasio-Rasa). Allow 10min there and back.
The village perched at an altitude of 900m/2 953ft presents many old stone houses. To the left of the church, a path leads to a fountain and some benches. From there you can enjoy an interesting view of the Lower Valley, lake and the villages nestling on the slopes. From right to left, you will see Verdasio, Borgnone, Lionza and, farther down, Comedo. Several paths for hikers start from Rasa, such as that of Pizzo Leone *(3hr)*, which affords pretty views of Lake Maggiore.

Monte Comino

Access by cable car (Funivia Verdasio-Monte Comino) to the right of the road. Allow 15min there and back.
From the upper station (1 200m/3 936ft), a path wends its way down, towards a fork branching off into two directions. The right-hand path leads to Madonna della Segna, a small church fronted by a porch with three arcades dating back to 1700. The left-hand path will take you to an inn or *grotto* where hikers may stay the night. From the terrace (tables made with local granite), there is a sweeping panorama of the whole valley. The tiny village of Rasa can be glimpsed on the opposite slope.

Verdasio

Leave the car at the entrance to the village and continue on foot through a charming ensemble of narrow streets and vaulted passageways. The road climbs down towards a small reservoir, then snakes its way up in the direction of Palagnedra.

Palagnedra

The village architecture—one or two-storey houses scattered over pastureland— provides a striking contrast with the other localities in the area. Nearby, a curious building stands out because of its unusual decoration, consisting of coats of arms, painted columns and balustrades. The road passes the rocky bank of Borgnone.

Camedo

This is the last Swiss village, separated from Italy by a bridge, the Ponte Ribellasca.

Val Verzasca★

25km/15.5mi NE.
After **Tenero**, a small village surrounded by vineyards, the road climbs towards the gigantic concrete mass of the Contra Dam.

Contra Dam

Leave the car by the roadside and walk up to the dam, which dominates the valley from a height of over 200m/656ft, built over a lake 5km/3.5mi long. In the centre of the dyke, a contraption has been set up with the inscription "007 Bungy Jumping," used in bungee jumping competitions and films (the famous scene in the James

Bond movie *Goldeneye* was shot here). The best record to date is a 220m/722ft jump in 7.5 seconds!

The road skirts the dam, climbs upwards and goes through several tunnels.

Vogorno

The houses are built on the mountain side. The church, entirely white with a stone campanile, presents a fine fresco in the Byzantine style. About 2km/1mi farther on, take a narrow road on the left which climbs up the opposite side of the valley.

Corippo★

This picturesque village is one of the most popular stopping-places for tourists. The setting is truly magnificent. Note the splendid panorama of the Lower Valley and the lake. Near the church stands the tiny *Sala Communale*. Amateur painters will appreciate the charm of this quaint locality, with its narrow alleys and old stone houses, some of which have wooden balconies.

▶ *Return to the main road, which crosses the river over a bridge with twin arches. The landscape becomes more barren and the river snakes through huge boulders.*

Brione

Situated on a plateau where the Osola stream and the River Verzasca converge, this village is famous for its granite quarries. It is also a starting-point for many hiking excursions. The parish church boasts some beautiful 14C **frescoes**★ attributed to one of Giotto's pupils from the Rimini School, centering on religious themes (*The Last Supper, Presentation of the Virgin, etc*). The small castle with corner turrets (formerly the Trattoria del Castello) was once the private residence of the Marcacci barons of Locarno. Before reaching Frasco, you will see a waterfall on the right.

Jerry Dennis / APA Publications

Corippo

Sonogno

🅿 *Car park (fee) at the entrance to the village.*

The last village in Val Verzasca spreads its stone houses at the foot of a rocky barrier. The **Museo di Val Verzasca** (🕐 *Open daily May-Oct, 1-5pm.* 🎫 *4CHF.* ☎ *(091) 746 17 77*) is a small Museum of Ethnography devoted to regional crafts, farming, costumes and sacred art. Walk up the main street near the church you can see an early bread oven which is still used. The chancel in the church contains frescoes painted by Cherubino Pata, a pupil of Courbet who was born in Sonogno. A Madonna di Loreto, a Black Virgin with Child cloaked in a long silver cape, is in an alcove behind the altar.

LE LOCLE

NEUCHÂTEL – POPULATION 10 413

This small town nestling in the Jura Valley and linked to Franche-Comté by the Rock Pass (Col-des-Roches) owes its prosperity to **Daniel Jean-Richard**, a young goldsmith who introduced the art of clockmaking into the area during the 18C.

🛈 *31 rue Daniel-Jean Richard – 2400 –* ☎ *(032) 931 43 30.*

Sights

Musée d'Horlogerie★

🕐 *Open May-Oct, 10am-5pm; Nov-Apr, 2-5pm only.* 🕐 *Closed Mon (except on public hols), 1 Jan and 25 Dec.* 🎫 *7CHF.* ☎ *(032) 931 16 80, www.mhl-monts.ch.*

The **Château des Monts** is an elegant 18C mansion on the heights of Le Locle, surrounded by a lovely park. The site houses a museum containing many superb artifacts from many countries and is seen as the indispensable complement to the Horology Museum of La-Chaux-de-Fonds. The ground floor is a showcase for 18C interior decoration: a large drawing room, an antechamber, a panelled dining hall, a library – all tastefully furnished and decorated – provide the charming setting for a splendid collection of clocks delicately worked in silver and gold. The AL Perrelet Room illustrates the history of clockmaking from the very first timepiece with automatic rewinding to the tiniest digital watch. The Maurice-Yves Sandoz Room presents clocks with miniature automatons, like the Carabosse fairy, a gilt copper figure portraying an old woman walking with great difficulty. The second floor explains the science of horology (old instruments, clocks, watches, chronometers, precision tools etc). Look around the workshop of a local clockmaker, faithfully reconstructed.

Musée des Beaux-Arts

🕐 *Open daily except Mon, 2-5pm.* 🕐 *Closed 24 Dec-2 Jan.* 🎫*6CHF.* ☎ *(032) 931 13 33, www.mbae.ch.*

In addition to rooms devoted to Swiss painting and sculpture in the 19C and 20C (Girardet, Koller, Kaiser, Mathey), the Fine Arts Museum features an interesting display of work by foreign artists including *Richard Wagner* by Félix Vallotton, *The Studio* by Alberto Giacometti, *First Snowfall* by Lermite, *The Dancing Stars* by Dufy, *Portrait of Claude* by Renoir.

Moulins Souterrains du Col-des-Roches

🎧 *Guided tours (1hr) May-Oct, daily at 10:15 and 11:30 am and 1:30, 2:45 and 4pm; Nov-Apr, Sat and Sun at 2:15, 3:30 and 4:15.* 🎫 *9CHF.* ☎ *(032) 931 89 89; www.lesmoulins. ch.* ❄*The temperature is 7°C, so be sure to wear warm clothes.*

Built in the 16C to use the waters of the Le Locle Valley as a new energy source, these underground mills expanded rapidly from the mid-17C to the late 19C: the gushing waters of the river activated huge wheels, which in turn operated beaters, baking ovens and sawmills. In the early 20C the mills were turned into slaughterhouses, subsequently abandoned, and then restored to their former glory. Exhibitions explain different types of mills, their roles and mechanisms. The downstairs grotto is certainly worth a visit, featuring numerous wells and galleries that the men had to dig with their bare hands. The grotto also contains several remarkable pieces of machinery (gear mechanisms, flour mills, saws, superimposed wheels).

LUGANO

TICINO – POPULATION 25 949
ALT 273M/896FT

The Queen of the Ceresio lies at the end of a beautiful bay framed between the wooded Mount Brè and Mount San Salvatore. It faces south and is an ideal tourist and health resort for its temperate climate, particularly appreciated in spring and autumn. There are beaches, tennis courts, 18-hole golf course, riding, boating and casino. Lugano is a convenient excursion centre for visiting the Ticino's three lakes: Maggiore, Lugano and Como. *Palazzo Civico, Riva Albertolli – 6900 – ☎ (091) 913 32 32, www.lugano-tourism.ch.*

- ▶ **Orient Yourself:** The most popular tourist attractions are between the train station and the Museo Civici de Belle Arti, close to the lakefront.
- P **Parking:** The town center is car-free
- ◉ **Don't Miss:** Villa Favorita, one of the largest private art museums in Europe.
- ◷ **Organizing Your Time:** Allow at least two days for museums, lake excursions.
- Kids **Especially for Kids:** The adventure playground in the Parco Civico
- ◔ **Also See:** Swissminiatur, small replicas of important sights, in a lakeside park.

Lago di Lugano★★

The greater part of Lake Lugano lies within Switzerland. The Italians, who call it Ceresio, have only the northeast branch (Porlezza), part of the southwest shore (Porto Ceresio) and a small enclave on the east shore (Campione d'Italia). Lake Lugano looks wilder than Lake Maggiore and Lake Como. It is set among the steep but beautiful slopes of the Alps, on which the silvery leaves of olive trees make pale patches. It is irregular in shape, with a total length of 33km/21mi and a maximum depth of 288m/947ft or 150 fathoms. Unfortunately, a causeway carrying the Sankt Gotthard road and railway cuts it into two basins. From the municipal park up to Paradiso, the splendid shaded promenade following the lake shore is an ideal place for a leisurely stroll as it offers a variety of interesting viewpoints. Sit on one of the benches and enjoy the restful sight of pleasure boats gliding along the rippling waters.

Parco Civico★★ (ABX)

Not far from the Palais des Congrès, this delightful public garden laid out around the lake is definitely worth a visit. During the summer season and providing the weather is fair, one can attend open-air concerts in the park. Several statues (*Socrates* by the Russian sculptor Antokolsky) and fountains lend charm to the delightful setting. Kids Children will appreciate the adventure playground, the aviary and the deer enclosure.

Address Book

SHOPPING

The town centre, cut by narrow streets, many of which are closed to traffic, is a great shopping area featuring attractive boutiques with eye-catching window displays **(Via Nassa, Via Pelissa, Piazza Cioccaro)**. In the **Quartiere Maghetti** is a modern shopping complex laid out over several levels.

THEATRE AND MUSIC

The high season runs from May to October, when a great many performances are held at the Palais des Congrès or on squares throughout the town (Piazza della Riforma, Piazza Maghetti or Piazza della Chiesa Santa Marta).

WHERE TO STAY

Owing to its ideal location, Lugano offers many opportunities for leisure activities and for boat trips on the lake or into the mountains, where spectacular panoramas can be had. As in many resorts with a prestigious reputation, prices are comparatively high and some visitors may prefer to stay outside the town.

⊖⊖ **Motel Vezia** – *In Vezia, Via San Gottardo 32* – ☎ *091 966 36 31, www. motel.ch.* – *50 rooms* – 🕐 *closed mid-Dec-Jan.* Convenient, comfortable hotel with large car park and soundproof rooms. Garden with heated pool.

⊖⊖⊖⊖ **Delfino** – *Via Casserinetta 6* – ☎ *091 985 99 99, www.delfinolugano. ch.* - *51 rooms* – 🕐 *open Mar-Nov.* In the Paradiso quarter, away from the lake. Excellent service for a decent price. Terrace with solarium and pool, a definite asset for the summer season.

⊖⊖⊖⊖ **Colibri** – *In Aldesago, 6km/3.7mi E* – *Via Bassone 7* – ☎ *091 971 42 42, www.hotelcolibri.ch.* – *30 rooms* – 🕐 *closed Jan and Feb.* A delightful setting atop the Monte Brè, commanding splendid views of the lake, the town and the Alpine range, especially from the terrace near the swimming pool.

⊖⊖⊖⊖ **Ticino** – *Piazza Cioccaro 1* – ☎ *091 922 77 72, www.romantikhotels. com* – *18 rooms* – 🕐 *closed in Jan.* This historic 14C residence nestles at the heart of the old quarter, among pedes-trian streets dotted with fashionable boutiques. A touch of romanticism in a modern city.

EATING OUT

⊖⊖ **Osteria Ticinese Da Raffaele** – *Via Pazzalino 19* – ☎ *091 971 66 14* – 🕐 *closed Sat lunchtime, Sun and end-Jul to end- Aug.* A typical osteria characterised by its friendly, congenial ambience.

⊖⊖ **Trani** – *Via Cattedrale 12* – ☎ *091 922 05 05* – 🕐 *closed Sun.* In a steep, narrow street in the old city, this typical osteria serves regional cuisine complemented by lively country wines.

⊖⊖ **Grotta della Salute** – *In Massagno, 2km/1mi NW, Via del Sindicatori 4* – ☎ *091 966 04 76* – 🕐 *closed Sat, Sun, mid-Dec to mid-Jan and mid-to-end-Aug.* Reasonably priced menus offering regional specialities which vary by season.

⊖⊖ **Locanda del Boschetto** – *Via Boschetto 8 (Cassarina)* – ☎ *091 994 24 93* – 🕐 *closed Mon and 1-15 Nov.* A rustic setting and lovely flower-decked terrace. A good address for fish and seafood dishes.

⊖⊖⊖ **Osteria Calprino** – *Via Carona 18 in the Paradiso district* – ☎ *091 994 14 80, www.osteriacalprino.ch* – 🕐 *closed Wed.* Three small, cosy rooms, one of which has an open fireplace where polenta is cooked in the winter season. Reservations are recommeded.

NIGHTLIFE

The Paradiso area offers several fashionable and pleasant choices: the **Golfe** (Riva Paradiso 2), **Charlie's Pub** (Via Guisan 10) and the **Karisma Pub** (Via Geretta 6). In the town centre, sample delightful Ticino wines at the **Bottegone del Vino** (Via Magatti) or the **Trani** (Salira Mario e Antonio Chiattone).

Corso Pestalozzi becomes especially lively after 11pm, when crowds pour out of the **Corso Cinema** and settle down for a drink at the **Etnie** in the Maghetti district or for one of the tempting ice creams at the pavement café Vanini, on Piazza della Riforma. The **New Orleans** (Piazza Indipendenza) has a combination of live music and DJs.

Santa Maria degli Angioli (Z)

This former convent church, begun in 1499, contains three fine **frescoes**★★ by Bernardo Luini (c 1480-1532). The most impressive represents a *Passion*, striking on account of its huge size and great expressiveness. Below it are pictured St Sebastian and St Roch. In the first chapel on the right, note the fresco *Virgin with Child and St John*, which was taken from the cloisters; its beauty is said to be "worthy of the great Leonardo". The nave bears a representation of the Last Supper.

Museo d'Arte Moderna (AX)

🕐 *Open mid-Mar to late Jun and in autumn, daily except Mon, 9am-7pm.* 🔖 *11CHF.* ☎ *(058) 866 69 08; www.mdam.ch.*

Set up in the Villa Malpensata, the Museum of Modern Art hosts temporary exhibitions of an exceptionally high standard. Painters such as Francis Bacon, Nolde, Soutine, Rouault and Botero were revealed to the public during retrospective shows held here, which brought together works that had been lent by other museums or borrowed from private collections.

Paradiso (AX)

This district, a perfect holiday destination, is populated by luxury hotels, restaurants, cafés, nightclubs, fashionable boutiques and a dock for boat trips on the lake.

Monte San Salvatore★★★

Alt 912m/2 996ft. 🚡 *45min there and back, including 20min by funicular, starting from the Paradiso quarter (**AX**).* 🕐 *Operates mid-Mar to mid-Nov. Departure every 30min.* 🔖 *Fare there and back: 20CHF.* ☎ *(091) 985 28 28; www.montesansalvatore.ch.*

An admirable view of Lugano, its lake and the Bernese and Valais Alps (belvedere with viewing balconies). You can return to Lugano from the summit by marked paths.

The Town Centre

The Old City★

🔖 *Guided tours of the town Apr-Oct, Mon, 9.30-11.45am. Contact the Tourist office:* ☎ *(091) 913 32 32.*

Its pedestrian streets, steep alleys and flights of steps make for an interesting walk or shopping expedition. **Via Nassa** and its arcades flanked by elegant boutiques form the main axis. On **Piazzetta San Carlo** note the Surrealist sculpture by Salvador Dalí called *The Dignity of Time*. Via Nassa leads to **Piazza della Riforma**, a huge, lively square with outdoor cafés and the Municipio (town hall). In early July, during **Estival Jazz**, the square is swarming with jazz lovers enjoying live performances. **Via Pessina** is a narrow passageway with many grocery stores offering tasty, fresh produce displayed on colourful, sweet-smelling stalls. Also of note are **Piazza Cioccaro** (funicular serving the train station), with the **Palazzo Riva**, a fine patrician villa with wrought-iron balconies, and **Via Cattedrale**, a steep alleyway leading up to the cathedral. The **Quartiere Maghetti**, defined by the Corso Pestalozzi to the north, is a modern district of boutiques, cafés, restaurants and a cinema.

San Lorenzo (Y)

The cathedral was built in the Romanesque style and it presents an elegant façade in addition to three doorways embellished with fine Renaissance motifs. The south aisle contains the Chapel of Santa Maria delle Grazie, a splendid example of Baroque decoration. At the far end of the cathedral stands a marble tabernacle by the Rodari brothers from Maroggia (16C). The esplanade commands a lovely view of Lugano and its lake.

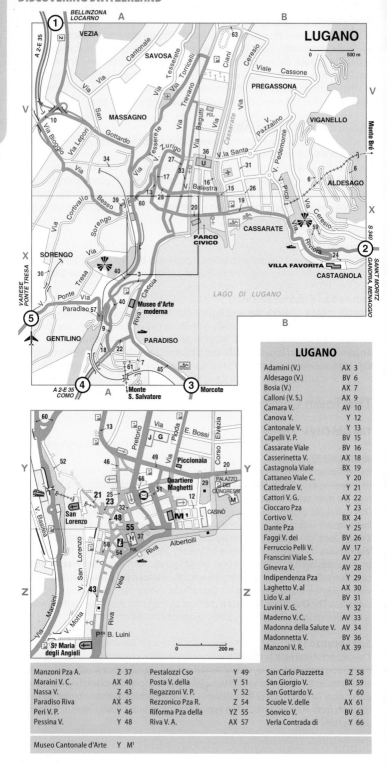

LUGANO

Piccionaia (Y)

At the junction between Corso Pestalozzi and Via Pioda, in the northeast corner.
This lovely house, known by its Italian name, meaning "dovecote", is said to be the oldest in the city. It has a façade embellished with painted friezes.

Museo Cantonale d'Arte (Y M[1])

🕐 *Open daily except Mon, 10am-5pm, Tue 2-5pm.* 🕐 *Closed Christmas and New Year's Day.* 🚌 *10CHF (permanent and temporary collections).* ☎ *(091) 910 47 80, www. museo-cantonale-arte.ch.*
Installed in a former palace, the Museum of Municipal Art mainly presents temporary exhibitions of excellent quality, displaying the work of artists from Switzerland and, more specifically, the Ticino area.

Excursions

Villa Favorita★★ (BX)

At Castagnola. Take bus n° 1 leaving from Piazza Manzoni and get off at Villa Favorita.
🚗*It is advisable to take the bus since the car park can only accommodate a few cars.*
🕐 *Open Apr 15-Oct 31, Thurs-Sun 10am-5pm,* 🚌*12CHF.* ☎ *(091) 971 61 52.*
A narrow garden park overlooking the lake over a distance of 1km/0.5mi, planted with boxwood, cypress, palm and monkey puzzle trees and graced with statues, leads to this late-17C mansion featuring three staggered storeys and crowned by a birdcage. Although the greater part of the remarkable collection of paintings gathered since 1920 by Thyssen-Bornemisza, the famous German steel industrialists, has been transferred to the Thyssen-Bornemisza Museum in Madrid, the Villa Favorita regularly holds exhibitions of works taken from this collection, concentrating on a given theme or artistic style (e.g. 19C and 20C American artists Andrew Wyeth, Winslow Homer and Edward Hopper).

Villa Heleneum – Museo delle Culture Extraeuropee (BX)

Take bus n° 1 leaving from Piazza Manzoni. Get off at San Domenico, then continue on foot for 5min along Via Cortivo. 🕐 *Open Tue-Sun, 2-7pm.* 🚌*8CHF.* ☎ *(058) 866 69 60.*
On the edge of the lake, a neo-Classical mansion houses the **Museum of Non-European Cultures**. The collections are laid out on three levels. The ground floor is devoted to Oceania and Southeast Asia. The first floor focuses on New Guinea and the different regional cultures which make up its identity. The second floor is divided into themes, adopting a comparative approach on issues such as death, fertility

Jerry Dennis / APA Publications

Villa Favorita – garden overlooking the lake

and power. Each display is amply illustrated with explanatory panels and objects, including finely carved wooden sculptures with unusual shapes.

Monte Brè★★

Alt 925m/3 051ft. About 1hr there and back, including 30min by funicular, starting from Cassarate (BX). ⤢Access by funicular from Cassarate via Suvigliana, 9.10am-6.15pm. Departures every 30min. ☞19CHF there and back. ☎ (091) 971 31 71.

You can also go by car, by taking the road to Castagnola and then following the directions. The summit is very sunny and affords fine views of the lake and the Alps (many hiking tours in the area) from the terraces.

By Car or Rack Railway

Monte Generoso★★★

Alt 1 701m/5 581ft. The excursion takes a full half-day. 15km/9mi by ③ and the road to Como as far as Capolago, where you turn right to reach Riva San Vitale.

Riva San Vitale

This village is worth a visit for its 5C baptistery *(battistero)*, in an octagonal room near the parish church. Remains of 11C frescoes adorn part of the walls. At the opposite end of the village, the Chiesa Santa Croce (16C) can be recognised by its octagonal dome; note the sculpted wooden door with grotesque faces. The interior, designed after a square plan, features fine mural paintings.

▶ *Return to Capolago where you will leave the car and take the rack railway. Allow 2hr there and back.*

Monte Generoso★★★

Rack-railway from Capolago – Departure every hour from early May to late Oct. ◷ Open in winter except Mon-Tue and Nov. ☞ Fare there and back: 46CHF. ☎ (091) 648 11 05. From the summit the splendid **panorama**★★★ extends over the Alps, Lugano, the lakes and the Lombardy Plain to the distant Apennines on a clear day.

Swissminiatur★

Kids 7km/4.5mi S. ♿ ◷ Open mid-Mar to 31 Oct, 9am-6pm. ☞ 15CHF. ☎ (091) 640 10 60; www.swissminiatur.ch.

This replica of the main sights of each Swiss canton is a joy to children and grown-ups alike. Spread over 1ha/2.5 acres of verdant and flowery land on the edge of the lake, the exhibit displays the country's main tourist attractions reproduced in miniature (monuments carved out of stone, mountains, bridges, sites etc) and evokes the country's main economic activities. The trains (3km/2mi network), boats and cable cars all function.

Morcote★★

Round trip of 26km/16mi – about 3hr – starts along a fairly hilly road. Alternative access by boat from Lugano – ◷ Operates Apr-Oct. Tour lasts for approximately 1hr. Other boat excursions available: Gandria, Porlezza (Italy) etc. Information on trips (with or without lunch on board) and cruises is available from Società Navigazione del Lago di Lugano. ☎ (091) 971 52 23; www.lakelugano.ch.

▶ *Leave Lugano through Paradiso, then take the high road to Morcote by ③.*

This route via Pazzallo and Carona offers magnificent **bird's-eye views**★★ of the lake and distant glimpses as far as the Monte Rosa Massif.

Carona

At the entrance to the village, lined at intervals with picturesque houses, the **Chiesa San Giorgio** (16C) is crowned by an octagonal dome and contains interesting 16C **frescoes**★. They include a *Last Supper,* a *Descent from the Cross,* a *Beheading of St John the Baptist,* a *Last Judgement,* an *Assumption* and a *Baptism of Christ.* Adjoining the church is a portico with Tuscan columns, decorated with heraldic arms and *trompe-l'œil* paintings.

On leaving the locality, follow directions for **Madonna d'Ongero**. You can leave the car at a car park and continue on foot along a forest path. A wide path with Stations of the Cross leads to the church, which has a portico and an octagonal dome. The interior is heavily ornate, with abundant frescoes and stuccowork.

Return to the road to Morcote; after a few miles you can stop at a roadside belvedere (two benches) to enjoy a splendid view of the lake.

Morcote★★

The Lombardic arcaded houses of this village, dubbed the Pearl of the Ceresio, are reflected in the calm waters of Lake Lugano at the foot of the last slopes of Mount Arbostora carpeted with Mediterranean flora. By a staircase and alleys offering many vistas you will reach the **Church of Santa Maria del Sasso** containing splendid 16C frescoes and a fine organ case made of wood (note the carved heads). Go through the church to see the baptistery (Battisteri da Sant Antoni) ornamented in the Baroque style (painted ceiling, altar decorated with angels and cherubs). The lake, the church, the baptistery, the cypresses and a cemetery form a remarkable **picture**★★.

Morcote and its church Santa Maria del Sasso

Franziska Pfennifer / Switzerland Tourism

▶ *Return to Lugano taking in the road along the lake shore, which is most attractive.*

Monte Lema★

17km/10.5mi NW via Bioggio. Leave Lugano by ⑤.
From Bioggio the road winds through woods before entering Cademario.

Cademario

From this terraced village there is a nice view (especially near the parish church) of the plain below, part of the west side of Lake Lugano and the surrounding mountains. As you leave the village following directions to Lugano, the old **Chiesa di San Ambrogio** (*For information, call ☎ (091) 605 68 30*) stands alone with its campanile in the Lombardy style and its façade with partly-erased 15C frescoes. Inside are interesting 13C polychrome frescoes.

Miglieglia

At the foot of the wooded Monte Lema lies the village and its church, St Stefano (15C). The interior houses 16C-17C frescoes: note in the chapel across from the side entrance God the Father above Mary in prayer then visited by the Holy Ghost; in the chancel are Evangelists and their symbols, the Nativity and Crucifixion, under a Christ Blessing (in the vaulting).

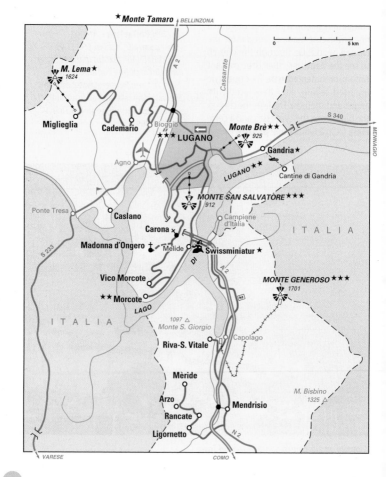

Mario Botta

Born in 1943, Mario Botta is unquestionably one of the most talented and renowned architects of his time. After studying technical design in Lugano, he attended the Institute of Architecture at Venice University. Influenced by Le Corbusier and Louis Kahn, with whom he had worked, he became one of the foremost representatives of the Ticino School. His work aims for a harmonious balance between landscape and architecture, with a curved perspective and compact shapes. His major accomplishments are the school at Morbio Inferiore (1972-77), the Arts Centre in Chambéry (1982-87), the Médiathèque in Villeurbanne (1984-88), the Museum of Modern Art of San Francisco (1990-94), Évry Cathedral (1995), the Tinguely Museum in Basel (1996), the Chiesa Santa Maria degli Angeli at Monte Tamaro (1996) and the Dürrenmatt Centre in Neuchâtel (2000).

Monte Lema★

Alt 1 624m/5 328ft. ⛷ *Access by chair lift from Miglieglia. Departure every 30min 9am-5pm.* ⊙ *Does not operate from mid-Nov to Mar.* 🎫 *Fare there and back: 22CHF.* ☎ *(091) 609 11 68.*

The climb, above a landscape of fern and rocks, presents a bird's-eye view of Miglieglia and the Church of St Stefano. From the restaurant of the upper station climb to the top *(20min there and back along a steep path)* between a television relay station and a large metal cross for a **panorama**★ which extends westwards to Lake Maggiore and the Monte Rosa and eastwards to Lake Lugano and the Monte Generoso.

Monte Tamaro★

15km/9mi NW. Leave Lugano by ④ and take the motorway towards Bellinzona. Turn off at Rivera. Reach Alpe Foppa by cable car (20min).

Although it looks like a fort, it is the **Chiesa Santa Maria degli Angeli**, designed by the famous Ticino architect Mario Botta, who was commissioned by the cable car owner to pay tribute to his late wife. A long upper passageway ends in a belvedere decorated with a metal cross supporting a bell. You can also reach the church via the lower passageway, whose ceilings are embellished with paintings by Enzo Cucchi (the same artist decorated the interior). Notice the two hands symbolically united on a blue background, lit by a luminous source from above. The curved walls present two rows of 11 windows (each one illustrates a scene taken from the Life of the Virgin), which make for a light, radiant atmosphere.

Alpe Foppa (alt 1 530m/4 018ft) is the departure point for many excursions. You can also hire cross-country bicycles or go paragliding from there. The Monte Tamaro summit (alt 1 960m/6 397ft) commands a sweeping **view**★ of Lake Lugano, Lake Maggiore, the Monte Rosa and the Matterhorn. A 4hr walk will take you to the top of the Monte Lema.

Caslano

5km/3mi SE. Leave Lugano by V on the plan, heading towards Ponte Tresa.

Switzerland is invariably associated with chocolate and for those who have a sweet tooth, the visit to a chocolate-making factory is a must. Near the Italian border, the firm **Alprose** welcomes visitors to its **Museo del Cioccolato** (⊙ *Open daily, 9am-6pm (Sat-Sun 5pm).* ⊙ *Closed 2 Jan, 1 Nov and 24 Dec. Film (20min). Shop.* 🎫*4CHF.* ☎ *(091) 611 88 56; www.alprose.ch).* The museum unveils the world of chocolate before your eyes, starting with the cocoa plantations in Amazonia and ending with present-day manufacturing and marketing techniques. An upper passageway enables you to observe the methods of fabrication from above. All aspects of the industry are covered: milk, white or bitter chocolate, small squares to have with coffee, and drinking chocolate, a warm nectar with an enticing aroma. The tour ends with a tasting session.

Le Mendrisiotto
25km/15.5mi S. Leave Lugano by ④ on the plan, then follow directions for N 2.

Mendrisio
This is the town where the famous Ticino architect **Mario Botta** was born. The old city is dominated by the imposing neo-Classical Chiesa Santi Cosma e Damiano (19C) and its characteristic dome. It is reached by a monumental flight of steps; at the foot of these, a square tower is a remainder of the city's medieval ramparts. Note the fine Baroque palace nearby. Take the charming Via San Damiano, continued by Via Stella, which leads to the oratory of Madonna delle Grazie (13C) and its interior featuring naïve ornamentation. Behind the oratory, on Piazza dei Serviti, the former convent house contains the Museo d'Arte, which stages temporary art exhibitions.

Ligornetto
Ligornetto is the birthplace of the Ticino sculptor **Vincenzo Vela** (1820-91), a legendary figure in the region. His villa has been converted into a museum tracing his life and work.

Rancate
This village is certainly worth a detour, if only to visit the **Pinacoteca Cantonale Giovanni Züst** (🕐 *Open Mar-Jun and Sep-Nov, daily except Mon, 9am-noon and 2-5pm; Jul-Aug, daily except Mon, 2-6pm.* 🎟 *7CHF.* ☎ *(091) 646 45 65)*, which presents a fine selection of works executed by Ticino artists from the 17C to the 20C. The paintings of Antonio Rinaldi, characterised by their grace and strong romantic atmosphere, are given pride of place in Room 3 on the ground floor *(The Kitten, Portrait of Angiolino)* and in Room 6 on the first floor (portraits: *Sketch for a Portrait, The Shepherd* and a religious study, *The Holy Virgin*). Giuseppe Antonio Petrini (1677-1758) is represented with the intensely moving *L'Addolorata*, displayed in Room 7 on the first floor. The work of Giovanni Serodine (1600-30) shows the undeniable influence of Caravaggio in its subtle use of light and shade, especially in *St Peter Imprisoned*.

Arzo
At the entrance to this small hamlet lies a marble quarry carved out of the hillside. It is fascinating to observe how the marble is extracted and how it is cut into slabs by means of powerful electric saws. The bell tower of the Baroque church is decorated with marble tiles coming from that particular quarry.

By Boat

The steamer services on Lake Lugano, which you can make an hour's trip at short notice or a complete half-day tour, are among the resort's top attractions.
In addition to the localities below, steamships on Lake Lugano stop regularly at Porlezza Ponte Tresa, Campione etc. A grand tour of the lake, called Grande Giro del Lago, starts from Lugano. It is advisable to check departure times if you wish to combine the tour of Gandria with that of the Museum of Swiss Customs, in which case allow 3hr.

Gandria★
1hr there and back, if you do not go ashore.
Amid a maze of stepped streets this village, with terraces planted with geraniums, trellises, leafy bowers, arcaded houses and a small Baroque church form a charming picture appreciated by artists and tourists.

WHERE TO STAY IN GANDRIA
🛏🛏 **Moosmann** – ☎ *091 971 72 61 – Fax 091 972 71 32 – 29 rooms* – A friendly, welcoming hotel with quiet terrace and garden on the shores of the lake. The best rooms have balconies overlooking the lake.

Museo Doganale Svizzero

At Cantine di Gandria on the south shore of the lake (access by boat 1hr 45min there and back, including visit to the museum). Accessible by boat only. 🚤 *Tours Apr-Oct, 1.30-5.30pm.* 🎫 *No charge.* ☎ *(091) 910 48 11.*

Located on the lake shore in a former Swiss customs post (kitchen, bedroom and office), the museum explains the role, past and present, of the customs officer (maps, photographs, boards, models dressed in uniform). Beneath the verandah is an amazing car, illustrating the incredible number of tiny hiding places that can be found in an automobile. Othere exhibits focus on the perilous role they played during the Second World War, the most common devices (traps, weapons, trick objects) used by smugglers, drug dealers and forgers (false passports, fake Lacoste and Levi's garments). It also presents the highly sophisticated means used by customs officers to foil smugglers. Perhaps the museum's most unusual exhibit is the Zodiac submarine seized in 1946: its metal tubes were stuffed with salami! Under the eaves are temporary exhibitions on Swiss customs: recruitment and training techniques at the Liestal School near Basel and the role of women in this profession.

Morcote★★ – 👟 *See above.*

LUZERN★★★

LUCERNE Ⓒ LUZERN – POPULATION 60 000
ALT 436M/1 430FT
PLAN IN MICHELIN GUIDE SWITZERLAND

Lucerne is a picturesque town of squares and churches, with two attractive covered wooden bridges and an octagonal tower overlooking the River Reuss. The tenth most visited city in the world, it nestles in a remarkable site at the northwest end of Lake **Lucerne**, dominated by Mount Pilatus and Mount Rigi. Its location on the important north-south transport axis, between the Swiss Plateau and the Alps, helped spur its development. Its reputation has been further enhanced by a music festival held since 2000 in the cultural centre built by Jean Nouvel.
🛈 *Zentralstrasse 5 (in the railway station) – ☎ (041) 227 17 17, www.luzern.org.*

▸ **Orient Yourself:** The two medieval covered wooden bridges that connect the old and new parts of the city are the main focal points of Lucerne. Take a 2hr guided city walk leaving from the tourist office (👟 *see above*) at 9:45 daily May-Oct and Sat Nov-Apr, 🎫18CHF.

🅿 **Parking:** Old Town is pedestrian-only, and attractions beyond walking distance are easily accessible by public transportation.

👁 **Don't Miss:** Strolling across the covered bridges that are the city's icons.

🕐 **Organizing Your Time:** Allow at least two days to stroll the streets and visit the museums.

Kids **Especially for Kids:** The sprawling transportation museum, Verkehrshaus, includes the opportunity to experience the weightlessness of space travel.

👟 **Also See:** Mount Pilatus, Rigi.

A Bit of History

Early History to Middle Ages – There was probably a small settlement near the lake during Roman times or earlier. The St. Leodegar monastery has existed since the early 8C. An important marketplace developed around the Reuss Bridge, which connected the monastery, attached to the Alsatian abbey of Murback, with the feudal court to the south. Historians regard 1178 as the year of the city's birth, when the parish was transferred from the monastery to the city. With the opening of the Sankt Gotthard route around 1220, the town became an important staging-point between Flanders and Italy, and the first city fortifications were built

Lucerne was sold to Rudolf von Habsburg in 1291. The city population protested limits on its autonomy and in 1332 pledged a treaty with the Waldstätten (the "forest cantons" around Lake Lucerne), an important political and commercial alliance that helped ensure the survival of the young Confederation (formed in 1291). The Confederation victory at Sempach (1386) permanently freed Lucerne from ties to Austria, and the town's influence and affluence grew, funded by lucrative contracts to supply Swiss mercenaries for foreign armies. When the Reformation began, Lucerne led the Catholic resistance. In 1574, the Jesuits opened their first college in German-speaking Switzerland and built a church, the first Baroque construction erected in the country. Because the city voted against the Federal Constitution in 1848, it was bypassed as the nation's capital for Bern. In the mid 19C, Lucerne gratefully seized upon opportunities offered by tourism to recapture some of its lost glory.

Development of Tourism – Lucerne remained a small town, with just 4,300 inhabitants, at the end of the 18C; that changed with the arrival of tourists beginning in 1830. The Nationalquai and the esplanade by the Jesuit church were laid out during this period, fine hotels were built and the first steamboats began operating on the lake. In 1868, Queen Victoria booked a holiday in Lucerne, using a pseudonym. Lucerne was popular with American soldiers following the Second World War. Today, Lucerne welcomes over five million tourists every year, a quarter of whom are Swiss.

Lucia Degonda / Switzerland Tourism

Luzern with Wasserturm and Kapellbrücke

Address Book

SHOPPING

The main shopping area is the pictur-esque, pedestrian streets in the old town, with its traditional atmosphere.

Department stores: Jelmoli (Pila-tusstrasse 4), Manor Warenhäuser (Weggisstrasse 5), Au Bon Marché (Kapellgasse 4). A well-stocked fruit and vegetable market is on the right bank of the Reuss River every Tues and Sat.

THEATRE, MUSIC, CINEMA

Stadttheater – *Theaterstrasse 2 – ☎ 041 228 14 14; www.luzerner-theatre.ch.*

Cinema - ABC, Moderne and **New Rex** in Pilatusstrasse.

For coin ranges, see the legend on the front flap.

WHERE TO STAY

Goldener Stern – *Burger-strasse 35 – ☎ 041 227 50 60 , www.goldener-stern.ch – 13 rooms.* Ten min-utes from the railway station, next to the the Franciscan church, this simple, family-run hotel has well-maintained rooms at reasonable prices for Lucerne.

Himmelrich – *Schatten-bergstrasse 107 in Himmelrich, 7km/4.3mi SW – ☎ 041 310 62 62 – 25 rooms.* - Peaceful atmosphere and splendid views of Lucerne, its lake and the moun-tains of Central Switzerland. The terrace is very pleasant in the summer.

Krone – *Weinmarkt 12 – ☎ 041 419 44 00 – www.krone-luzern.ch. – 25 rooms* – Situated in the heart of the old town, this modern, tastefully furnished hotel has spacious rooms. The breakfast room overlooks the Wein-markt, a pedestrian square with real medieval charm.

Cascada – *Bundesplatz 18 – ☎ 041 226 80 88 , www.cascada.ch – 62 rooms* – Comfortable rooms plus a private car park, 400m/440yd from the station. The Boléro restaurant serves Spanish specialities.

Seeburg – *Seeburgstrasse 61 at Ost going towards Meggen (north shore of the lake) – ☎ 041 375 55 55 – www.hotelseeburg.ch – 58 rooms.* A handsome, beautifully preserved resi-dence with old-fashioned charm. The best rooms look onto Lake Lucerne and Mount Pilatus. Lakeside garden with a charming creek for mooring boats, two restaurants and a lively lounge.

MOUNTAIN HOTELS

Book a few days ahead and enjoy the privilege of waking up at sunrise at an altitude of 1 797m/5 895ft or even 2 120m/6 955ft! *See RIGI and PILATUS.*

EATING OUT

Schlössli Utenberg – *Uten-bergstrasse 643 (4km/2.5mi NE heading towards Dietschiberg) – ☎ 041 420 00 22, www.schloessli-untenberg.ch – closed Mon, Tue.* An 18C mansion built in the Baroque style houses this ideal lunch-spot. Admire the 18C faience stove (1758) on the first floor. Pretty terrace views of the city and its lake.

Schwendelberg – *Horw – ☎ 041 340 35 40 – www.schwendel-berg.ch – closed Easter-Sep; rest of year: Tue and Wed.* Traditional gasthaus offering peace and quiet. Sweeping panorama of Lake Lucerne and the Swiss Alps.

Rathaus-Brauerei – *Unter der Egg 2 – ☎ 041 410 52 57, www.rathausbrau-erei.ch. Open to 12:30 am Apr-Oct.* This brewpub is beneath the former town hall, along the banks of the River Reuss. Access is through the arcades.

Stadtkeller – *Sternenplatz 3 – ☎ 041 410 47 33 , www.stadtkeller.ch– closed Sun and Mon in winter, and in Nov and Feb.* A local tavern with a colourful atmosphere. Musical enter-tainment inspired by Swiss folklore.

Galliker – *Schützenstrasse 1, near Kasernenplatz – ☎ 041 240 10 02 – closed Sun and Mon.* Small, cosy and friendly establishment where you immediately feel at ease.

Wilhelm Tell – *Schweizerhofquai – ☎ 041 410 23 30.* Huge steamboat, many of which used to be seen gliding on Lake Lucerne. From the bar, you can glimpse the machinery which once operated the paddle wheels. The Art Nouveau dining hall adds a touch of refinement.

Au Premier – *In the main train station* – ☎ *041 228 91 91.* Modern restaurant with a warm welcome.

NIGHTLIFE

Situated on the seventh floor of the Hôtel Astoria (Pilatusstrasse 29), the **Penthouse**, with its soft background music, is a favourite haunt among the young. In the same street, the Hôtel Schiller (Pilatusstrasse 15) offers two different bars: the **Grand Café** in an old-fashioned setting and the **Cucaracha**, a bar with a Mexican touch.

On the shores of the lake, both the **Hôtel National** and the **Hôtel Palace** feature a piano bar (Haldenstrasse 4 and 10 respectively), as does the **Casino**, which also has a large room where weekend shows are held.

In the old town, enjoy a good fondue to the strains of folk music at the **Stadtkeller** (Sternenplatz 3). The **Movie Bar** (Weinmarkt), whose decor will delight film buffs, attracts a casual crowd and offers a great variety of wines and beers. In the basement, you can order dishes bearing the name of a famous film: try Al Capone, Jaws or Love Story.

For dancers and nightclub goers, the **Wall Street** offers live music in Kriens, a few miles away from Lucerne. **Pravda Dance Club** (Pilatus-strasse 29) is one of the hippest in the city.

LUCERNE FESTIVAL

On 25 August 1938, Arturo Toscanini conducted *Siegfried* by Wagner in Tribschen Park. This performance marked the beginning of the **Lucerne Festival**, dedicated to classical and contemporary music, which now attracts over 110 000 people every year. The festival holds events at Easter, during the summer (around 30 concerts in August and September) and in November (piano recitals). For further information, contact Hirschmattstrasse 13, 6002 Luzern; ☎ (041) 226 44 80; www.lucernefestival.ch; ticketbox@lucernefestival.ch

CARNIVAL

The Fasnacht carnival lasts for one week from the Thursday before Shrove Tuesday until Ash Wednesday. During this colourful event, the Guggenmusigen, a type of brass band, stages a huge concert before marching through the streets of the old town.

Altstadt (Old Town)★★ *3hr*

The old town is built on the side of the mountain and is partially surrounded by vestiges of the old fortifications, of which seven large square towers remain. Access to the town by water was protected by covered wooden bridges built across the river.

North Bank

▶ *Start from Schwanenplatz (Swan Square).*
Head towards Kapellplatz, fronted by the impressive 18C Sankt Peterskapelle. The chapel was built on the site of an earlier church, originally built in the 12C.

Kapellplatz

The centre of the square is adorned with the Fritschi Fountain (Fritschibrunnen) which represents carnival, spring and joy. **Fritschi** is a legendary character in whose honour a carnival has been held since the 15C. The Kapellgasse, a lively street lined with shops, leads to **Kornmarkt** (Grain Market), a square built in the 16C. A market is held here on Tuesdays and Saturday mornings.

Altes Rathaus★

This handsome Renaissance town hall was built by Anton Isenmann from 1602 to 1606 and is flanked by a tall, square tower, although its roof is in the style of a Bernese farmhouse. The building overlooks the Kornmarkt and was once used as a grain storehouse. The Gasthaus zu Pfistern, to the right, has a fine painted façade. To the left, the Am Rhyn town house is home to the **Picasso Museum** (& see Museums).

▶ Take Kornmarktgasse, and through an alleyway on the right, to Hirschenplatz.

Hirschenplatz (Stag Square)

This square is lined with attractive, restored houses with painted façades, which are adorned with wrought-iron signs. Goethe stayed at the Goldener Adler in 1779.

Weinmarkt (Wine Market)★

The old houses in this pretty square, which are covered with paintings and decorated with many signs and flags, were once the seats of the various guilds. Note the Scales' Mansion, and the Wine Market Pharmacy (Weinmarktapotheke) built in 1530. The Gothic fountain represents warriors and St Maurice, patron saint of soldiers. The original is currently displayed in the Regierungsgebäude.

Follow Kramgasse to **Mühlenplatz** (Mills Square) which dates from the 16C. There is a fine view of the Spreuerbrücke, the old houses on the opposite bank of the Reuss and, in the distance, of Gütsch Hill.

Spreuerbrücke

This covered bridge, part of the fortifications of the old town, spans an arm of the River Reuss. It was built in 1408 and restored in the 19C. In German, *Spreu* means "chaff": the bridge was the only point where chaff and dead leaves could be thrown into the river. A small chapel (1568) stands in the middle of the bridge. The decoration of 67 painted panels representing a Dance of Death was executed in the 17C

ALTSTADT		Rössligasse	V	Kornmarktgasse	V
		Pilatusstrasse	V	Kapellgasse	V
Weggisgasse	V	Kramgasse	V	Gerbergasse	V

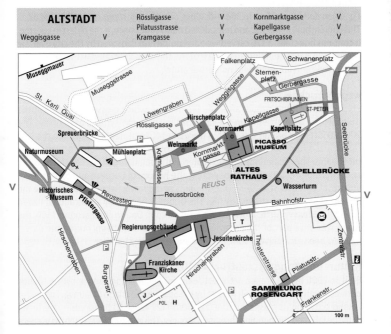

by Caspar Meglinger. From the bridge, there is a good view of the quays of the old town and of the façade of the Jesuits' Church.

▶ *Beyond the bridge, follow Pfistergasse.*

South Bank

Pfistergasse
N° 24, formerly the Arsenal, from 1567 to 1983, now houses the **Historisches Museum** (🕭 *see Museums*).
On the quay, (Reuss-Steg), charming houses with oriels, painted façades and flower-decked fountains; on the left are the towers from the old town fortifications.

Jesuitenkirche
Built in 1666 by Pater Christoph Vogler, this was the first church in Switzerland built in the Jesuit style. The plain façade is framed between two tall towers surmounted by domed belfries, and the **interior**★ is nobly proportioned. The high altar is adorned with a huge pink marble stucco altarpiece. Stucco in the nave is inspired by Rococo art. Paintings on the ceiling, also from 1750, depict the Apotheosis of St Francis Xavier, the patron saint of the church: camels and elephants remind parishioners he was a missionary in India and Asia. The second chapel on the right houses the remains of **Nicholas of Flüe**, the only Swiss saint (🕭 *see VIERWALDSTÄTTER SEE and SACHSELN*).

▶ *On the right of the church, take Bahnhofstrasse to the Government Palace.*

Regierungsgebäude
This building with ornate stonework in Florentine Renaissance style (1557-64) for the bailiff, Ritter. Since 1804 it has housed the cantonal government. In the inner court stands the original Weinmarkt Fountain (🕭*see above*) which dates back to 1481.

Franziskanerkirche★
🕓 *Open daily except Sat, 10.30am-6.30pm, Sun 12.30-6.30pm.* ☎ *(041) 210 14 67.*
This church, built in the 13C and remodelled many times since, is the oldest in Lucerne. It contains fine stalls, a 17C carved wooden pulpit and flags won by the city over the centuries. A Baroque chapel to the rear of the church is decorated with stucco in the Italian style and adorned with numerous angels.

Kapellbrücke★
This covered bridge, rebuilt after the fire of 1993, which crosses the Reuss at the point where it emerges from the lake, has become the symbol of Lucerne. The 200m/656ft long bridge was built in the early 14C to protect the town on the lake side. It was adorned with about 100 paintings on the wood triangles formed by the roof beams. These paintings were executed at the beginning of the 17C and restored at the turn of the last century, depicting the history of Lucerne and Switzerland, and of St Leger and St Maurice, patron saints of the town. Replicas now replace the panels which were destroyed by fire. The bridge is flanked by an octagonal tower, called the **Wasserturm**, crowned with a tiled roof. Dating from around 1300, the tower was once part of the defensive fortifications of the town; during the past it has also been an archives room, a prison and a torture chamber.

Kultur- und Kongresszentrum★★ (DZ)
Built in 2000 by the French architect Jean Nouvel, this conference centre blends perfectly with the station built in 1991 by the Spaniard Santiago Calatrava. The centre is solid but light, its glass structure (12 000m²/129 120sq ft) harmonising perfectly with the lake and surrounding mountain scenery. The interior offers splendid **views**★

of Lucerne and the lake, framed by stainless steel girders like a series of postcards. The centre houses the Kunstmuseum (👁 *see Museums*), and a concert hall (capacity 1 840), where the Lucerne Festival is held. An attractive, brightly coloured café on the ground floor also enjoys fine views of the lake shore.

Around Löwenplatz

▶ *Leave Schwanenplatz (DY) and follow St-Leodegarstrasse as far as the Hofkirche.*

Hofkirche★ (DY)
🕐 *Open 10am-5.30pm.* 🐾 *Guided tours available by request.* 🕐 *Closed Nov-Feb, noon-2pm.* ☎ *(041) 410 52 41.*
This collegiate church is dedicated to St Leger (Leodegar), the patron saint of the town, which is said to derive its name from him, founded in 735. In 1633 all except the Gothic towers were destroyed by fire and it was rebuilt in the Renaissance style. It is a huge building, reached by a monumental stairway, and is surrounded by Italianate cloisters, containing tombs of the old families of Lucerne. The **interior**★ is spacious and well proportioned, in the late Renaissance style. The chancel is enclosed by a wrought-iron grille and furnished with ornate stalls. Gilded and figured altarpieces adorn 10 of the altars (Pietà in the south aisle; *Death of the Virgin* in the north aisle). The organ (1650) is one of the best in Switzerland.

▶ *Take Löwenstrasse up to Löwenplatz, where the Bourbaki-Panorama (see Museums) is housed in a domed building. Take Denkmalstrasse up to the Lion's Monument.*

Löwendenkmal (DY)
Known as the Lion's Monument, this statue was carved out of the sandstone cliff face in 1821. It portrays a dying lion with a spear embedded in its left flank and its right paw protecting a fleur de lys. The sculpture (9m/29ft long) commemorates the Swiss Guards, whose task it was to protect the royal palace in Paris during the French Revolution: about 850 mercenaries were either killed during the Storming of the Tuileries in August 1792 or guillotined soon after. The monument was the brainchild of Karl Pfyffer von Altishofen, a Swiss officer who survived the massacre. American writer Mark Twain described it as "the saddest piece of stone in the whole world".

Gletschergarten★ (DY)
🧒 🕐 *Open Apr-Oct, 9am-6pm; Nov-Mar, 10am-5pm. Film (12min).* ⊜*12CHF.* ☎ *(041) 410 43 40.*
In 1872, JW Amrein-Troller, a bank clerk, bought a meadow outside Lucerne with the intention of building a cellar. During construction work, 32 different cavities were discovered, hollowed out from the sandstone by the Reuss Glacier 20 000 years ago, when ice covered the entire plain as far as the Jura. Amrein-Troller built a park around this geological site, which is particularly popular with children.
Deep crevasses in the sandstone show how the glacier started to melt at the end of the Würm period 20 000 to 15 000 years ago. The powerful flow of water, stones and sand – 10 times greater than that of the River Reuss today – created the famous glacial potholes, one of which is 9.5m/29.5ft deep and 8m/28ft wide. The heaviest blocks, smoothed by the water, remained at the bottom of the potholes.
In the **museum**, **glacier science** is explained in an easy and accessible way, showing how glaciers are formed and displays of Swiss glaciers. Visitors can touch "cold" ice from Polar glaciers and the more "temperate" ice from Alpine glaciers. Displays document the life of glaciers, animal species, such as the glacial flea (2mm/0.08in long), The region's geological history, which was still subtropical 20 million years ago, iss demonstrated by fossils marked with prints of palms and birds. Othere exhibits include an old relief model of Central Switzerland, made in 1786 by Ludwig Pfyffer von Wyher; models of traditional houses and a reconstruction of a peasant's bedroom.

The second floor is dedicated to old Lucerne, via lithographs, models and reconstructions, including the Biedermeier bedroom of Marie Amrein-Troller.

After the museum, enjoy a **panoramic walk** with views of Lucerne and Mont Pilatus in the beautiful gardens, planted with Alpine flowers. The gardens also house an unusual **Moorish-style hall of mirrors** built in 1896 for the Geneva National Exhibition. The Alpineum is situated opposite the glacier garden.

▸ *Return through Löwenplatz to Alpenstrasse, turn right into Hertensteinstrasse.*

Musegg Ramparts (CY)
🕐 *Open Easter to All Saints, 7.30am-7pm.* 🚫 *No charge.*

The remains of the fortified city walls (800m/880yd in length) include nine watch and defensive towers, dating from around 1400. Since their construction, only one tower has undergone restoration work. Three of the towers are open to the public: **Schirmerturm**, rebuilt after the fire in the spring of 1994; **Zitturm**, which has the oldest clock tower in Lucerne (1535); and **Männliturm**. The towers offer superb **views**★ of the town and the lake in its memorable mountainous setting.

Sankt Karlikirche
This modern church was built by the architect Metzger in 1934. The porch is surmounted by great statues of the four Evangelists. Inside is decorated with frescoes and lit by yellow and purple stained-glass windows.

The Lakeshore★★

The **Schweizerhofquai** replaced the third covered bridge in Lucerne during the 19C. Planted with trees and flanked by mansions, both the Schweizerhofquai and the **Nationalquai** afford admirable **views**★★ (DY) of the town site and Lake Lucerne, and beyond of the Alpine range stretching from the Rigi to the Pilatus *(viewing tables)*. At the end of Carl-Spittelerquai are pleasant green lawns and the Lido beach.

Museums

Old Town

Sammlung Rosengart★★ (DZ M⁴)
🕐 *Open Apr-Oct, 10am-6pm; Nov-Mar, 11am-5pm.* 🚫 *15CHF.* ☎ *(041) 220 16 60, www.rosengart.ch.*

This art gallery was opened in 2002 by Angela Rosengart, daughter of the art dealer Siegfried Rosengart; this great collector had already donated a number of works by his friend Picasso to the town (🕐 *see Picasso Museum*). Like her father, Angela Rosengart has demonstrated her attachment to Lucerne through this generous donation of more than 200 modern works of art dating from the 19C and 20C, including paintings by Picasso, Klee and Chagall. More than 100 **works**★★ by **Paul Klee** are displayed in the basement. The collection includes ink drawings such as *Belebte Strasse* (1910) and watercolours such as *St Germain bei Tunis* (1914); occasionally the artist combines the two techniques (*Modebild*, 1922). Among the many graphic works, *Bild mit Hahn* (1919) and *Bergdorf* (1934) are particularly worthy of note.

On the ground floor, the stunning **Picasso collection**★★★ (over 80 works of art painted after 1938) includes many Cubist paintings, such as *Violin at the Café* (1913). Portraits of Nusch Éluard, Dora Maar and Marie-Thérèse Walter, painted in the 1930s and 1940s, are exhibited along with *Woman and Dog Playing*, a painting inspired by Françoise Gilot (1953). *The Studio* (1954) is that of the Villa Californie in Cannes. Other interesting works include *Jacqueline's Profile* (1957) and *Women in Hats* (1961,

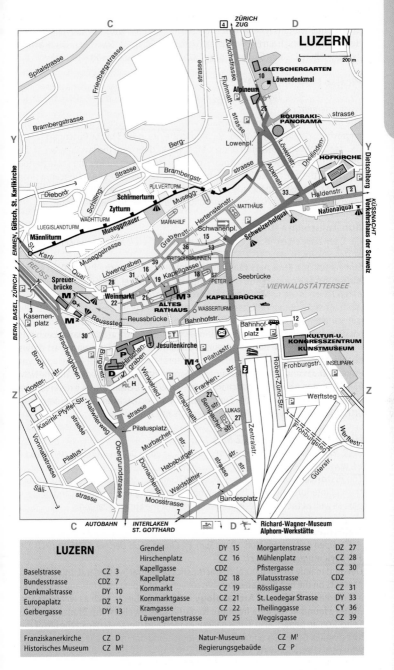

1963). In *Déjeuner sur l'herbe* (1961), inspired by Manet's famous painting, Picasso himself is depicted on the right. Other paintings are also enriched by references to the great masters: note the *Portrait of a Painter after El Greco* (1950) and *Rembrandtesque Character and Love* (1969).

The first floor is devoted to Impressionist works by artists such as Monet, Pissarro, Renoir, Bonnard and Cézanne (*L'Estaque, the village and the sea*, 1882). Léger (*The*

Staircase, 1914) and Matisse (Lemons and Saxifrage, 1943) are also well represented, as is Braque with his lyrical Pot and Ivy (1950). Thirteen works by Chagall are also displayed, ranging from Evening at the Window (1950) to Red Sun (1983). Other artists exhibited here include Seurat, Vuillard, Utrillo, Dufy, Rouault and Kandinsky.

Picasso Museum (CZ M³)

🕐 Open Apr-Oct, 10am-6pm; Nov-Mar, 11am-5pm . 8CHF. ☎ (041) 410 35 33; www.rosengart.ch.

The attractive house (Am Rhyn-Haus) contains a small collection of lithographs, engravings, ceramics by Picasso, donated to the city in 1978 by the Rosengart family (👉 see Sammlung Rosengart above). Most works date from the last 20 years of the artist's life. The museum also houses photographs taken during the same period (1956 until the artist's death in 1973) by the American David Douglas Duncan, a close friend of the artist, and include portraits of Picasso, whose creative genius seemed inexhaustible at over 70 years of age, and his last muse, Jacqueline Roque.

Kunstmuseum★ (DZ)

🕐 Open daily except Mon, 10am-5pm (8pm Wed). 🕐 Closed 7, 11 and 12 Feb, 24 and 31 Dec. 10CHF. ☎ (041) 226 78 00.

Since 2000, the **Fine Arts Museum** has been housed on the fourth floor of the **Kultur- und Kongresszentrum** designed by Jean Nouvel. The museum's 19 rooms extend over an area of 2 100m²/22 596sq ft and are decorated in a neutral, almost Abstract style, with a polished concrete floor, white walls and artificial light. The permanent collection of mainly Swiss paintings from the 18C-20C is exhibited in rotation alongside temporary exhibitions of contemporary art. Permanent exhibits include works by the Romantic painter Johann Heinrich Füssli, whose art draws heavily on theatrical effects; landscape painters from the School of Geneva, such as François Diday and Alexandre Calame; the Symbolist Ferdinand Hodler; and the Nabi Félix Vallotton (👉 see Introduction: Art in Switzerland). Other artists exhibited here include Vlaminck, Soutine, the Expressionist Max Pechstein and the contemporary artists Joseph Beys, Paul Thek, Franz Gertsch and Jeff Wall.

Historisches Museum (CZ M2)

♿🕐 Open daily except Mon, 10am-5pm. 🕐 Closed 25 Dec. 10CHF. ☎ (041) 228 54 24, www.hmluzern.ch.

The **Historical Museum** displays 16C and 17C armour, traditional dress, reconstructions of interiors, such as a 19C hotel room, pertaining to the political and military past as well as the former economic activities of the Lucerne canton.

Naturmuseum (V)

♿🕐 Open daily except Mon, 10am-5pm. 🕐 Closed 24, 25 Dec. 6CHF. ☎ (041) 228 54 11, www.naturmuseum.ch.

Devoted mainly to the natural characteristics of central Switzerland, this museum presents on the first floor an extensive collection of Alpine minerals and fossils and a remarkable **Gallery of Archaeology** exhibiting objects such as weapons and pottery found in the area from the Neolithic lake dwellers, the Bronze Age and Celto-Roman period. Also in this gallery, models and dioramas depict the life of the lake dweller. On the second floor are zoological and botanical collections as well as aquariums, terrariums etc.

Around Löwenplatz

Bourbaki-Panorama★ (DY)

🕐 Open 9am-6pm. 8CHF. Contact the tourist Office ☎ (041) 227 17 17, www.bourbakipanorama.ch.

A glass building houses this huge **circular canvas** (1 100m²/1 300sq yd) painted by Édouard Castres. The canvas hangs on the second floor, attached by hundreds of magnets, and depicts one of the last episodes of the Franco-Prussian war. During the winter of 1870-71, the French army, commanded by General Bourbaki, were entirely surrounded in the French Jura, resulting in 87 000 demoralised soldiers fleeing into Switzerland. They were disarmed and sent to different areas of Switzerland until March, when France paid more than 12 million francs for their internment.

Édouard Castres, who was employed as an auxiliary by the Red Cross, had first-hand experience of the war. He began work on the Bourbaki canvas in 1881 in collaboration with 10 other painters, including Ferdinand Hodler. Characters made of resin seem to step out of the painting, which is movingly realistic, made more so by the whinnying of horses and rumble of canons on a soundtrack accompanying the painting.

The **Bourbaki Museum** on the ground floor provides a thorough portrayal of the Franco-Prussian war of 1870-71, with information given in three languages, and includes an audio-visual presentation; "picture boxes" of the main protagonists in the conflict; and propaganda papers and military uniforms, including those of the Zouaves and the Turks, conscripts from the French colonies.

Alpineum (DY)

In this museum, situated opposite the Glacier Garden, the most famous peaks of the Swiss Alps have been painted in three-dimensional form by Ernst Holder and his son. The summits depicted include Mount Pilatus, Mount Rigi, the Jungfrau, Monte Rosa, Gornergrat, Breithorn and the Matterhorn.

Outside the Town Centre

Verkehrshaus★★★

Lidostrasse 5 (near the lake) by Haldenstrasse (DY). *Bus nos 6 and 8; Verkehrhaus bus stop.* &. 🅺 🕐 *Open daily Apr-Nov, 10am-6pm; Dec-Mar, 10am-5pm.* ⊗24CHF. ☎ *(08) 48 85 20 20.*

This museum illustrates the **history of transportation** in Switzerland. The different sections are housed in a dozen separate buildings dotted around a park, which is interspersed with play areas and snack bars.

Rail transport – A 8 000m²/9 568sq yd exhibition area featuring 1 000m/3 280ft of railway tracks is presents the largest collection in the country. Exhibits include the locomotive belonging to the Vitznau-Rigi, the very first rack-railway in Europe, dating back to 1873. Nearby, you can admire the C/6, Switzerland's largest steam engine and the legendary Be 6/8, better known as the Crocodile. The remarkable display of electric engines illustrates the leading role played by the Confederation in the history of train transport around the turn of the 20C. Famous locomotives and self-propelled vehicles manufactured subsequently such as CFF's Red Arrow (*Flèche Rouge*), BLS's Blue Arrow (*Flèche Bleue*) and Landi-Lok's AE 8/14 are given pride of place. Exhibits also include tramcars from several Swiss cities and an impressive collection of miniature trains of varying sizes. There is also a lively presentation of the building of the St-Gotthard Tunnel: visitors are invited to settle in a carriage and be guided through the various stages of this exciting project, accompanied by typical sounds and smells.

Road transport – This dramatic changes during the course of the 19C and the 20C are illustrated by the sledge used by the Simplon Post Office and the Grimsel horse-drawn carriage evoke the era prior to motorisation. The impressive Halle du Transport Routier contains more than 30 automobiles that illustrate the role played by the Confederation in this thriving industry. The most remarkable exhibit is probably the 1905 racing car designed by Genevese manufacturers Charles and

Frédéric Dufaux, presented alongside several Weber, Turicum, Pic-Pic and Martini models. Note the replica of a Benz tricycle dating from early days of motorisation. From the dandy horse to the scooter, two-wheeled vehicles are represented by 50 or so bicycles, including a number of Swiss models.

Halles Com 1+2 – This section devoted to the history of communication is equipped with radio, television and videoconference facilities as well as interactive systems that enable visitors to experiment with the latest techniques in this field.

Aviation and Space Travel Hall – The history of aviation emphases Switzerland's role: the first biplane in which Arnaud Dufaux flew over Lake Geneva in 1910, Swissair's DC 3, the supersonic carrier CV 990 Coronado, plus hot-air balloons, hang-gliders, microlites and other types of aircraft. Exhibits include several genuine models, namely a Fokker F-VII, a collection of 200 miniature models and 30 engines or turbines. Visitors can venture into a flight simulator and experience G-forces and take over controls or they can pose for a photograph on board the Blue Box. In the control tower, a radar console designed for controlling air traffic gives you an idea of the complexities of modern safety conditions at airports. On the second upper level, the **Cosmorama**, whose presentation *Crystal Moon Express* boasts numerous special effects that plunge you into the fascinating world of asteroids and outer space, including experiicnging weightlessness.

Planetarium ZEISS Longines – Beneath a huge cupola lies a perfect replica of the firmament, where the life of the planets and their movements will be explained to you.

Navigation, cable cars, tourism – The ground floor exhibits the machinery of the paddle steamer *Pilatus* (1895), one of the legendary boats to glide on Lake Lucerne. The Navigation Section *(first floor)* presents a remarkable collection of reduced models and nautical instruments evoking the progress of navigation through the centuries. Note the shipowner's office, containing a wide range of miniature ships, marine books and seascapes donated to the museum by shipowner Philipp Keller in 1980. The multimedia show **Nautirama** retraces the history of navigation on Lake Lucerne, covering all aspects, ranging from cargo vessels to sailing boats. The cable car section displays a cabin of the first public aerial cable car (1908), which transported passengers to the Wetterhorn, and the ultra-modern cabin of the cable car, built in 1984, linking Spielboden to Langfluh near Saas Fee. The tourism section displays the country's most typical products and activities and **Swissorama**, a multivision show, illustrates its most famous sites.

IMAX Cinema – Films shown here are projected onto a huge circular screen (25m/82ft x 19m/62.5ft), accompanied by a powerful soundtrack of 22 000 watts. The cinema can be visited separately from the museum.

Hans Erni Museum – The museum houses over 300 canvases by contemporary painter Hans Erni, a native of Lucerne. The most striking exhibit is *Panta Rhei*, a huge mural painting on show in the auditorium which depicts the great thinkers and scientists of the Western world, from Antiquity to the present day.

Richard Wagner-Museum

Access by boat from the landing-stage near Seebrücke. By car leave the town by Hir-schmattstrasse (DZ); at the Bundersplatz take Tribschenstrasse and follow directions to Tribschen. Bus n°s 6, 7 or 8; bus stop Wartegg. 🕐 *Open mid-Mar to 30 Nov, daily except Mon, 10am-noon and 2-5pm. Open Easter Mon.* 🎟 *6CHF.* ☎ *(041) 360 23 70.*

The composer's house, where he lived from 1866 to 1872, stands on a promontory in the centre of a large park that slopes down to the lake. The composer produced some of his major works here, *(The Master Singers, The Twilight of the Gods, Siegfried)* and it was here that he married Cosima, Franz Liszt's daughter and where he received Nietzsche. The ground floor houses original scores and artifacts including Wagner's death mask, a plaster of his right hand, family photos and letters, and the **Érard piano** that accompanied the composer on his trips to Venice and Vienna. Information is given in three languages and music by Wagner is played in the museum. There is also collection of musical instruments dating from the 17C-19C, including elegant stringed instruments, and African drums.

Richard Wagner Museum, Tribschen

Boat Trips

With the world's largest fleet of steamers on an inland lake and comfortable saloon boats, the Lake Lucerne Navigation Company links Lucerne and the famous lakeside holiday resorts, offering cruises with commentary on sites charged with history, dinner cruises with music in summer, links or combined trips with all the cable-cars and funiculars in the region and also the "William Tell" express for a trip in a first class carriage equipped with panoramic windows on the Sankt Gotthard line. In high season, the boats from Lucerne to Flüelen and Lucerne to Alpnachstad leave approximately every hour. ☎ (041) 367 67 67; www.lakelucerne.ch

Constantly changing views of Lake Lucerne make a trip on its waters a continual delight, even in stormy weather. Starting from Lucerne the complete tour of the lake in a comfortable boat with a restaurant takes around 6hr. These outings introduce visitors to some of the most treasured historical sights, including the William Tell Chapel and the Schillerstein Obelisk. It is also possible to combine a mini-cruise with a train journey through the mountains: such is the case with the William Tell Express, which links Lucerne with the Ticino canton.

Excursions

Dietschiberg★★
Alt 629m/2 064ft. At the station, take bus n° 14 and get off at the Konservatorium stop. From there it is a 20min walk, following signposts to Utenberg and Golfplatz. By funicular from Felsental, on the north bank: to get there, follow the lakes hore (off the map by DY) as far as Carl-Spitteler-Quai, then take Gesegnetmattstrasse.

Splendid **panorama**★★ of Lake Lucerne, with Lucerne and the Pilatus on the right, the Rigi on the left and the Bernese and Glarus Alps on the distant horizon *(viewing tables).*

Gütsch★
Alt 523m/1 716ft. Allow 30min there and back, including 3min by funicular (station on Baselstrasse). Leave by Hirschengraben (CY). ⊶Temporary closure at time of going to press. ☎ (041) 249 41 00.

From the terrace of the Gütsch Castle Hotel which crowns this wooded hill on the left bank of the Reuss, the **view**★ extends over the fortified town, the lake and Alps.

Pilatus★★★

15km/9mi about 3hr, including 1hr by rack railway. Michelin map 729 I5. Leave Lucerne and take the motorway in the direction of Interlaken. 11km/7mi farther, after a long tunnel, turn right towards Alpnachstad. At Alpnachstad take the Pilatus rack railway.
🚶 *The excursion is described under PILATUS.*

Bürgenstock★★

16km/10mi S by Obergrundstrasse (CZ). Michelin map 729 J4. You can go up the Bürgenstock either by car from Stansstad (6km/3mi along a steep, narrow road) or by funicular from the landing stage at Kehrsiten-Bürgenstock in 7min. Services connect with the steamers.

The name Bürgenstock is given to a massive, wooded, rock ridge and also applies to a group of hotels perched 500m/1 500ft above the central junction (Chrüztrichter) of the lake. A favourite walk here is along the **Felsenweg**★★ (about 30min), a corniche making a panoramic circuit around the Hammetschwand spur. The summit (1 128m/3 700ft) can be reached by a lift up the mountainside.

Rigi★★★

24km/15mi – about 3hr, including 1hr by mountain railway. Leave Lucerne by Haldenstrasse (DY), road n° 2. Leave the car at the Arth-Goldau station and take the Rigi railway to its terminus at Rigi-Kulm.

🚶 *The rest of the excursion is described under RIGI.*

Alphorn-Werkstätte at Kriens

3km/1.8mi S of Lucerne. By car, follow signs to the Schweighof industrial area (off the map by DZ). Catch bus n° 1 from the railway station, then bus n° 16 to Oberkuonimatt station, getting off at Schweighof. 🕐 *Open Tue-Fri, 8am-noon; Sat, 9am-noon.* 🆓 *No charge.* ☎ *(041) 340 88 86.*

This workshop produces the famous Alpine horns (3.20m/10ft-3.60m/12ft) used traditionally by Swiss shepherds and now exported as far as Japan. A short video (in German) explains how the horns are made: first, sections of spruce or fir are dried, then stuck together and hollowed with a milling-cutter; the two halves of the tube are then soldered together with rings and a length of hand-rolled bamboo placed around the horn. A collection of horns is displayed in the workshop.

MARBACH

LUZERN – POPULATION 1 366

Adjacent to the Entlebuch Valley, Marbach is a good departure point for excursions. Note the large Catholic church with its richly adorned Baroque interior.

Excursions

Marbachegg

🚡 *Gondola operates daily mid-Mar to late Oct.* 🕐 *(Opening hours vary) until 5.30pm.* 🕐 *Closed Oct 30 to 1 Dec.* 🎫 *35CHF and up.* ☎ *(034) 493 33 88, www.marbach-lu.ch.*
The cable car leaves Marbach, rides over a countryside made up of spruce forests and meadows, and arrives *(12min)* at the Marbachegg Mountain where the village of Lochsitenberg (alt 1 483m/4 865ft) is perched. The restaurant's terrace commands a lovely **view**★ of the area. From east to south the following can be seen: the Schrattenflue Cliffs, flanked on the right by the Schibengütsch; on the horizon gleam the shiny white Fiescherhorn and Eiger peaks and in the foreground the snowy torrents

of the Hohgant summit. Just below is a fine wooded valley. From Marbachegg, a path leads to Obere Habchegg (1 407m/4 614ft) at the foot of the Schrattenfluh. Another path skirts the side of the Schibengütsch down to Kemmeribodenbad *(3hr 30min)*. In winter, the **ski area** offers both downhill and cross-country trails.

Schallenberg Pass Road★

33km/20.5mi from Marbach to Thun.

This picturesque road winds along the foot of the Hohgant and between peaks bordering the Emmental to the south, with good glimpses of the Schrattenfluh, the Hohgant and, after the narrow Schallenberg Pass (alt 1 167m/3 829ft) and a lovely spruce forest, the peaks of the Jungfrau Massif. Starting at Süderen Oberei, villages alternate with meadows and fir trees; the road then skirts the deep, wooded Zulg Valley (left) with a view of the Rüti peak.

▶ *After Kreuzweg continue to Steffisburg, the industrial centre of Thun; on the left note Thun Castle. Continue to Thun.*

Thun★★ – 🕭 *See Thun*

MARTIGNY

VALAIS – POPULATION 13 956

ALT 476M/1 562FT – TOWN PLAN IN THE MICHELIN GUIDE SWITZERLAND

The town of Martigny, dominated by the Tour de la Bâtiaz and surrounded by vineyards, is an international road junction and a choice stopping-place for tourists. In this elbow of the Valais Rhône, where the Drance joins it, the flow of traffic from the Simplon and the Great St Bernard routes, and that from the Forclaz Pass all converge. 🛈 *9 place Centrale – 1920 – ☎ (027) 721 22 20, www. martignytourism.ch.*

Martigny boasts several stone ruins dating to Roman times. Forum Claudii Augusti was a small town situated in the Forclaz Pass, linking Italy directly to France. Originally founded between 41 and 47 AD, under the Emperor Claudius, it was renamed Forum Claudii Vallensium (🕭 *the tourist office organises archaeological tours).*

Sights

Tour de la Bâtiaz

20min on foot there and back by chemin du Château.

Set in a strategic site, high on a rocky promontory, the circular keep and its defensive wall are all that remain of a 13C fortress. From the tower there is a lovely **view**★ of the Martigny Basin and surrounding vineyards.

▶ *Just before the bridge, turn right along the west bank of the river.*

Chapelle Notre-Dame-de-Compassion

This 17C sanctuary contains an elegant Baroque gilt altarpiece and an unusual collection of ex-votos in the form of small paintings.

▶ *Cross the 19C wooden covered bridge (pont couvert) to avenue Marc-Morand.*

The 16C **Grand'Maison**, recognisable by its elegant spire-like shingle roof, was a hostel where a number of 18C and 19C European notables stayed. On the right, at the beginning of avenue du Grand-St-Bernard, is a powerful bronze bust of a woman symbolising Liberty by Courbet.

Return to Place Centrale and enter the 19C town hall (H) to see the brilliant **stained-glass window**★ (55m²/592sq ft) which illustrates the Rhône contemplating the Drance. There are also other fine stained-glass windows which depict the Four Seasons, the Zodiac etc, all the work of **Edmond Bille**, the painter from the Valais.

▸ *Continue to the Église Notre-Dame-des-Champs on Place du Midi.*

Église Notre-Dame-des-Champs

Rebuilt in the 17C in the Tuscan style and flanked in the 18C by a neo-Gothic bell tower (50m/164ft high), outstanding features are a monumental doorway with finely carved panels, 17C baptismal font, pulpit carved by local artisans, 18C statues of the Apostle, and a large Crucifix dating to 1495.

Go as far as rue des Alpes to see the restored **Maison Supersaxo**, an interesting example of 15C architecture. Take rue de la Délèze, rue Octodure, and rue du Forum, which passes in front of the Forum Claudii Vallensium, a Gallo-Roman site .

▸ *Continue along rue du Forum to the modern building which houses the museum.*

Fondation Pierre Gianadda★★

& ◷ Open Jun-Oct, 9am-7pm; Nov-May, 10am-6pm. ⊜18CHF. ☎ (027) 722 39 78, www.gianadda.ch.

Léonard Gianadda opened this cultural centre named for his brother, who died in a tragic accident. It is built around the site of an ancient Celtic temple, the oldest of its kind in Switzerland. In addition to permanent collections, there are temporary exhibitions of works by such renowned artists as Goya, Renoir, Picasso, Klee, Braque, Degas, Manet, Dufy, Kandinsky, Van Gogh, Miró and Modigliani.

The **Gallo-Roman Museum**, in galleries overlooking the Roman ruins, displays statuettes, coins, jewellery, domestic utensils and fragments of sculpted stones dating back to the 1C-4C. Especially worth noting are the bronzes of Octodurum, including the tricorn head of a bull.

The **Automobile Museum** presents unique early vehicles, still in perfect working order, dating from 1897 to 1939. The oldest is a 1897 Benz with a maximum speed of 25kph/15.5mph. All the great names of the car industry are represented: Rolls-Royce (1923 model in polished aluminium which travelled to Mandelieu, on the French Riviera, in 1988), Bugatti, De Dion-Bouton, Delaunay-Belleville (1914-17

H. Preisig/Foundation Pierre Gianadda

Martini 1903

torpedo commissioned by the Tsar Nicholas II for his hunting parties; delivery was cancelled on account of the Russian Revolution). The museum also displays cars made in Switzerland: Pic-Pic (1906 double-phaeton), Sigma (1910-11), Martini (1912 torpedo), Fischer (1913 six-seater torpedo) and Stella (1911).

The **Louis and Evelyn Franck Collection**, features Impressionists, including prominent works by Cézanne, Van Gogh, Ensor, Van Dongen and Picasso. The **Garden**, is as open-air sculpture museum, dotted with archaeological ruins and more modern works by Henry Moore *(Reclining Figure)*, Joán Miró *(Head)*, Brancusi *(The Big Rooster)*, Dubuffet *(Contortionist Element of Architecture V)*, Segal *(Woman with Sunglasses on Park Bench)* and Rodin *(Meditation Scene with Arm)*.

Every year, from April to October, an exhibition dedicated to Leonardo da Vinci is held in the old arsenal of the foundation, with facsimiles and models.

▶ *Turn left into chemin de Surfrête, then left again into route du Levant.*

Amphithéâtre Romain

The **Roman Ampitheater** dates back to the 2C and bears witness to the prosperity of the Roman community that was here. Excavation work exposed ruins of residences, temples and public baths. The ampitheater has been restored and is the site of open air shows, concerts, and re-enactments of Roman gladiator fights and races. Originally the podium was surmounted by a parapet to protect spectators from the wild beasts. Six ramps led to the *cavea*, where members of the public sat on wooden steps. A number of *carceres* opened into the arena; these small cells were used for storing equipment and locking up the animals. The *pulvinar*, or official tribune, is located above one of these cells. It is approached by a long vaulted corridor.

▶ *Turn around; route du Levant leads back to Place du Bourg.*

Place and rue du Bourg

Pleasant small square with its turreted house (1609 heavily restored) and picturesque street. On the left note the old town hall (Maison de Commune du Quartier du Bourg – 1645) with arcades supported by seven marble columns.

St. Bernard Dog Museum

Kids ♿ *Route du Levant 34 in the old Arsenal building adjacent to the Roman Ampitheater; take the CFF bus to Pierre Gianadda Foundation.* ◷ *Open daily, 10am-6pm.* ≋*10CHF.* ☎*(027) 720 49 20, www.musee-saint-bernard.ch.*

This modern museum, which opened in 2006, is dedicated to the history of the Great St. Bernard hospice and pass and the history and role of the legendary St. Bernard dogs; it replaces an antiquated facility adjoining the hospice on the pass (*see Col du GrandSt-Bernard*). Art objects and other items include 19C paintings and statues from the Brienz School, plus artifacts from the thousands of merchants, pilgrims, soldiers,migrants and smugglers who have been welcomed at the hospice, which was founded in 1050 as a refuge for victims of crime and victims of the harsh mountain itself. Visitors can watch the dogs inside the museum and outside from a footbridge. There are special programs and exhibits for children, and a picnic area nearby.

Excursion

Vallée du Trient★
 See Vallée du TRIENT. Head NW from Martigny along the St-Maurice road.

MEIRINGEN★

BERN – POPULATION 4 637
ALT 595M/1 952FT

Meiringen is the chief town in the Hasli Valley (the Upper Aare Valley – above Lake Brienz). It is an important tourist centre as the starting-point for excursions to the Aare Gorges and the Reichenbach Falls and also a convenient stop on the Grimsel and Susten roads. *Bahnhofstrasse 22 – 3860 – ☎ (033) 972 50 50*

Visit

On the square named after the Scottish novelist **Arthur Conan Doyle** (1859-1930), the creator of Sherlock Holmes, stands a bronze statue of the celebrated fictitious detective by the English sculptor John Doubleday. Conan Doyle, who loved Switzerland, was made an honorary citizen of Meiringen.

The **Sherlock-Holmes-Museum** (*Open May-Oct, daily except Mon, 1.30-6.30pm; Oct-Apr, Wed and Sun, 4.30-6.30pm. 3.80CHF.* ☎ *(033) 971 41 41*) is an imaginative reconstruction of the famous, fictitious London drawing room at n° 221B Baker Street. It contains memorabilia belonging to the sleuth and his faithful assistant, Doctor Watson. In 1891 Holmes fell to his death in the Reichenbach Falls in a struggle with Professor Moriarty. But fortunately for his readers, who

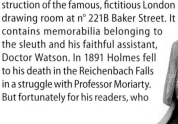

Musée Sherlock-Holmes, Meiringen

refused to accept the demise of their hero, Conan Doyle resurrected his character a few years later.

Kirche

The church (1684) is in part of the village where wooden houses recall old Meiringen, ravaged by fire in 1879 and 1891. This is the fifth church built on this spot, succeeding others swept away by the flooding of the Alpbach, a torrent which forms a waterfall behind the building. For this reason, its imposing detached Romanesque tower has foundations over 7m/23ft deep. During restoration the remains of the original 11C structure, now the crypt, and a series of Romanesque frescoes in the upper church, representing scenes from the Old Testament, were discovered.

Excursions

Planplatten★★

Alt 2 245m/7 365ft. *1hr by ski lift, then cable car (3 sections).*
Stunning **route**★★ overlooking pretty pastures and forests. When you reach the top, bear right towards the viewing table. Superb **panorama**★★ presenting many different landscapes: to the east the summits and glaciers of Rhonestock, Sustenhorn and Wendenstöcke, to the south the sparkling, snow-capped peaks of the Bernese Alps (Wetterhorn, Schreckhorn, Finsteraarhorn), to the west Lake Brienz and to the north the Glogghüs dominating the Alpine gorges around Meiringen.
Planplatten is a popular departure point for microlite flying and hang-gliding and as a starting-point for hikes and walks. Less experienced hikers can stop after reaching the two lakes Tannensee and Melchsee *(allow 5hr);* those in excellent physical condition can continue on the route described below.

Walk to the lakes and Hochstollen★★★

▶ *Leave Planplatten early in the morning to allow enough time to catch the last cable car back at the end of the day. Allow 5hr to 6hr depending on your choice of route, not including stops. It is essential to wear shoes with non-slip soles.*

Walk to **Balmeregg** (alt 2 255m/7 397ft) in 1hr by a track following the mountain slope. **View**★★ of the three lakes (Engstien, Tannen and Melch), the Titlis and Wendenstöcke. Pretty **mountain path**★★ heading towards **Tannensee**★, then a flat track until **Melchsee**★ *(allow 1hr 30min; to save 1hr, go directly from Balmeregg to Melchsee).* Bear left and walk round Melchsee: the lovely postcard view from the tip of the lake is enhanced by shimmering **reflections**★★ on the Titlis. Climb up to small **Blausee**★. The route becomes very steep and after 1hr you will reach **Abgschütz Pass** (2 263m/7 421ft), which commands a heavenly **view**★★. However, you will be able to get an even broader **panorama**★★★ of the surrounding landscape if you go up to **Hochstollen** (2 481m/8 140ft, marked out by a cross) along a strong, impressive incline. There are splendid views of the lakes and the Bernese Oberland, from the Eiger to Finsteraarhorn. Panoramic descent towards Käserstatt until you get to the track running down the slope before joining up with a path leading to **Mägisalp** (1 689m/5 543ft, allow 45min). Take the two cable cars to go back to the car park.

Aareschlucht★★

2km/1mi, plus 30min sightseeing. The road to the gorges' car park branches off from the Grimsel road (n° 6) on leaving Meiringen for Innertkirchen, 200m/220yd upstream from the bridge over the Aare.
The gorges cut by the Aare through the Kirchet bolt between Meiringen and Innertkirchen, are among the most popular curiosities in the Bernese Oberland. The viewing galleries lead into the narrowest part of the gorges, the walls of which, sometimes

sheer, sometimes polished and hollowed by erosion (traces of potholes and glaci-ated rocks), are very impressive. Stranger still is the dim light in the depths of the cleft where the jade-green stream of the Aare flows.

▶ *After about 1.5km/1mi within view of a tributary waterfall you arrive at the far end of the gorge (the last hairpin bend before Innertkirchen).*

Rosenlauital★★
12km/8mi – about 1hr – by a very narrow mountain road (passing is impossible between stops). The road is stony, sometimes walled-in and very steep on leaving Willigen. Cars for six or more people are not allowed through.

▶ *Leave Meiringen by the Grimsel road.*

At Willigen, turn right toward Rosenlaui which, after a series of sharp hairpin bends, enters the lonely Reichenbach Valley, dominated by the extraordinary rock forma-tions of the Engelhörner. Soon you will see ahead, from left to right, the Rosenlaui Glacier, the Wellhorn and the Wetterhorn. A bridge over the bed of the Reichenbach leads to the fields of Gschwandtenmad and a striking **view**★★★: the rocky shoulder of the Welhorn behind fir woods to the right of the Rosenlaui Glacier. This flanks the icy cone of the Wetterhorn, which stands above the Grosse Scheidegg Depression, a broad shelf over which you can walk from Rosenlaui to Grindelwald.

Rosenlaui
This mountaineering resort has given its name to a climbing school which has trained several guides for the conquest of the Himalayas. Here tourists may visit the **Glet-scherschlucht**★ (🕐 *Open daily from May-Oct 9am-5pm (6pm in Jun, Jul and Aug).* 🎫 *6CHF.* ☎ *(033) 971 24 88)*, the glacier gorges hollowed out by the waters from the melting ice of the Rosenlaui Glacier (🚶 *45min of rather difficult walking).* The scenery now becomes quite rocky. On arriving at Schwarzwaldalp, at the end of the road suitable for cars, you will find a slope wholly planted with maples.

Reichenbachfälle★
1km/0.5mi, plus 30min there and back, including 10min by funicular. Leave Meiringen by the road to Grimsel. After the bridge over the Aare, turn to the right and leave your car at the Reichenbach funicular station. 🕐 *Operates mid-May to mid-Oct, every 15min from 8.15-11.45am and 1.15-5.45pm.* 🎫 *One-way: 5CHF, there and back: 7CHF.* ☎ *(033) 972 50 50.* Crossing the lower falls on a viaduct, the funicular ends at a terrace from where you can admire the great Reichenbach Waterfall, the site of the fictional disappearance of Sherlock Holmes and Moriarty.

CASTELLO DI MISOX★

GRAUBÜNDEN
LOCAL MAP SEE GRAUBÜNDEN

The feudal ruins of Misox Castle, the most impressive in the Grisons, commands the Mesolcina Valley and the San Bernardino Defile from a high rocky peak. This massive fortified group, where the heavy shape is broken by the vertical lines of a graceful campanile, once belonged to the counts of Sax-Mesocco. The castle was sold in 1483 to the Trivulce of Milan and dismantled by the Grisons Leagues in 1526 (🕼 *see Introduction).* It was saved from complete destruction by the intervention of Swiss students in 1924.

Walking Tour *allow 30min*

Santa Maria del Castello

The key is available at the "cancelleria comunale" in Mesocco. ☎ *(091) 822 91 40.*
This chapel with a heavily pierced Romanesque campanile at the foot of the castle contains an interesting series of 15C **frescoes**★. St George slaying the Dragon is depicted with the features of a very young knight. St Bernardino of Siena, patron saint of the valley – the San Bernardino Pass was named after him – is the thin-faced monk, surrounded by rays of light. The symbolism for months of the year, on the lower panel, mingles scenes of courtly love with those of rural life in the Alps.

Castle

Access by the footpath from behind the chapel to the entrance drawbridge.
The most remarkable feature of this fortress is the Romanesque campanile of its chapel, with five storeys of arches. To enjoy a superb **bird's-eye view**★ of the Mesolcina Valley and the village of Soazza, turn left as soon as you find a gap between the ruined buildings and make for an uncrowned wall on the edge of the escarpment, the top of which can be reached by a staircase without a balustrade.

MONTREUX★★

VAUD – POPULATION 21 476
ALT 398M/1 305FT
PLAN IN THE MICHELIN GUIDE SWITZERLAND

Thanks to its beautiful **site**★★ and pleasant surroundings—which have won literary fame since **Jean-Jacques Rousseau** chose the village of Clarens, now a suburb, as the setting for *La Nouvelle Héloïse*—Montreux is the most frequented resort on Lake Geneva and has acquired an international reputation. It stretches along the shores of a large bay facing south and rises in tiers to heights covered with woods and vineyards which shelter it from winds. Its sumptuous palaces and Edwardian hotels are reminiscent of the French Riviera. It is an important cultural city, hosting many festivals and major world events such as the International Choral Festival (the week following Easter), the Golden Rose Television Festival (spring), a jazz festival (July) and the September Musical Concert (*see Calendar of Events*). 🚩 *5 rue du Théâtre – 1820 –* ☎ *(021) 962 84 84, www.montreux-vevey.ch.*

▶ **Orient Yourself:** The broad lakeside promenade may be the city's real center.
👁 **Don't Miss:** Chillon Castle, immortalised by the Lord Byron poem.
🕐 **Organizing Your Time:** Allow two-three days for the city and nearby excursions, more if you are attending the world-famous Montreux Jazz Festival.
Especially for Kids: The Museum of Food at former Nestlé headquarters in nearby Vevey, easily reached by public transportation.

Many local trains leave Montreux station for the nearby summits, offering panoramic views of Geneva, the Mont Blanc, the Matterhorn: the two most famous are the Montreux-Oberland Bernois (MOB) and the Montreux Crystal Panoramic Express (*it is necessary to reserve*). Steamboat cruises are available for tours of the Upper Lake. Or, you can walk up through old Montreux to the terrace of the church for a lovely **view**★★ of the district of Clarens-Montreux-Territet and the lake with the Château de Chillon on its rocky islet, the mountains of the Savoy Chablais and the sparkling Dents du Midi.

The Vaud Riviera

The mildness of its climate (average annual temperature 10°C/50°F) makes Montreux a year-round resort and earns it the name of Vaud Riviera for its lake shore. This exceptional climate, said to be by far the mildest on the north side of the Alps, produces varied and luxuriant vegetation: vines grow at an altitude of nearly 600m/2 000ft, walnut trees up to 700m/2 300ft and fruit trees up to 1 000m/3 250ft. Fig, bay, almond and mulberry trees and even cypresses, magnolias and palm trees flourish on the lakeshores at truly Mediterranean temperatures. In spring, the fields overlooking the town are covered with narcissi, which lend a special charm to the hillsides.

Musée du Vieux-Montreux

40 rue de la Gare. 🕐 *Open Apr-Oct, daily, 10am-noon and 2-5pm.* 🎫 *6CHF.* ☎ *(021) 963 13 53.*

In the heart of the old quarter, the museum installed in two fine wine-growers' houses (17C) presents a lively account of the region's eventful history. Prehistoric times, Roman era, Middle Ages, reconstruction of domestic interiors and workshops from different centuries, the expansion of tourism prompted by the residence of illustrious personalities, technology and communications, coins, architecture and town planning are some of the themes presented on three levels, explaining the development of the city of Montreux throughout the ages.

Audiorama

At Montreux-Territet, route de Chillon, Villeneuve. ♿🕐 *Open daily except Mon, 1-6pm.* 🎫 *10CHF.* ☎ *(021) 963 22 33.*

The **Swiss National Audio-visual Museum** is housed in a large room with magnificent Art Deco glasswork on the second floor of the old Grand Hôtel, once a favourite with Empress Elisabeth of Austria. Major events in the history of radio and television are presented here, with displays of radios, gramophones, phonographs, record players and video recorders. The development of studio recording, the first program broadcast through Eurovision, and the first colour pictures are explained through equipment used at the time. The Champ-de-Mars to Lausanne transmitter (1922), created to ensure aircraft security on the Paris-Lausanne route, can be seen on the ground floor.

Lucia Delgonda / Switzerland Tourism

Montreux

Address Book

SHOPPING

Many shops and boutiques are on avenue des Alpes, Grande-Rue, avenue du Casino and rue de la Paix.

Department store: Innovation (avenue du Casino).

THEATRE AND MUSIC

Théâtre du Vieux-Quartier –36 *Rue du Pont –* ☏ *021 961 11 32, www.theatre-de-montreux.ch.*

Auditorium Stravinski – *95 Grand-Rue –* ☏ *021 962 21 19.*

ё *For coin ranges, see the Legend on the front flap.*

WHERE TO STAY

◯◍ **Hôtel du Pont** – *12 rue du Pont –* ☏ *021 963 22 49 – 10 rooms* – Congenial establishment in the old district, at the foot of the funicular. Restaurant offers traditional cuisine and Italian specialities.

◯◍ **Hôtel de Sonloup** – *At the Col de Sonloup, 8km/5mi N –* ☏ *021 964 34 31 –www.sonloup.ch – 22 rooms –* ⏱ *closed Dec to late- Mar.* This secluded, blissfully quiet hotel on the heights has tastefully furnished rooms in the rural tradition. Tourists without a car can reach the hotel by taking the panoramic train MOB.

◯◍◍ **Auberge des Planches** – *2 rue du Temple –* ☏ *021 963 49 73 - www.montreux.ch/auberge-des-planches – 36 rooms –* ⏱ *closed Jan.* Located on a steep street on the outskirts of town. Rooms tend to be large and decorated in rustic style. The Don Chico Restaurant has a Mexican decor and serves typical dishes from Mexico.

◯◍◍◍ **Golf-Hôtel René Capt** – *35 rue de Bon-Port –* ☏ *021 966 25 25 - www.golf-hotel-montreux.ch– – 75 rooms –* ⏱ *closed 22 Dec to mid-Jan.* Away from the bustling town centre, this hotel has a pretty garden overlooking the lake shores.

◯◍◍◍ **Masson** – *In Veytaux, 5 rue Bonivard –* ☏ *021 966 00 44 - www.hotelmasson.ch – 31 rooms –* ⏱ *open Apr- Oct.* The oldest hotel in Montreux (1829) has undeniable charm, evoking the splendor of bygone times. The small garden is perfect for long, relaxing afternoons in the shade.

◯◍◍◍ **Eurotel Riviera** – *81 Grand-Rue –* ☏ *021 966 22 22 – 152 rooms.* Centrally located hotel with a pontoon for mooring boats and the choice between two restaurants: the Bel-Horizon and the Matara.

◯◍◍◍ **Eden Palace am Lac** – *11 rue du Théâtre –* ☏ *021 966 08 00 – www.edenmontreux.ch – 101 rooms –* ⏱ *closed 21 Dec to 10 Jan.* Who hasn't dreamed of spending the night in a sumptuous, turn-of-the-century palace? The rates may seem outrageously high but they are definitely worth it. The Victorian architecture, period furniture, lofty rooms, gastronomic cuisine and romantic atmosphere will transport you back in time, while offering all the advantages of modern sophistication!

EATING OUT

◯◍◍◍ **Le Museum** – *40 rue de la Gare –* ☏ *021 963 16 62 – www.museum-montreaux.ch – closed Sun and Mon.* This former convent house dating back to the 13C features three fine dining halls with vaulted ceilings. Fondue, raclette and grilled meat are served in a rustic decor with an open fireplace.

◯◍◍ **Caveau des Vignerons** – *30 bis rue Industrielle –* ☏ *021 963 25 70 –* ⏱ *closed Sun, one week at Easter and first two weeks Aug.* Decor focuses on grapes and the art of oenology (display of tools used during grape harvesting). The restaurant serves fondue, raclette and meat on hot slates, and local wines.

◯◍◍ **Restaurant du Montagnard** - *In Villard-sur-Chamby, 7km/4.3mi N –* ☏ *021 964 36 84 -* ⏱ *closed Mon, Tue and in Jan and Feb.* A genuine 17C mountain farmhouse serving traditional fare. Lively evenings with folk music.

◯◍◍ **Auberge de la Cergniaulaz** – *In Les Avants, 8km/5mi N by the Col de Sonloup and the road to Orgevaux –* ☏ *021 964 42 76 –* ⏱ *closed Mon, Tue and Jan-Mar.*

Set in a typical chalet in the heart of the mountains, this auberge has a wide choice of tasty country dishes chalked up on a board. A popular restaurant where it is advisable to reserve a table.

NIGHTLIFE

The Grand-Rue is a lively area with live music: the **Sunset Bar and Piano Bar,** located in the Hôtel Royal Plaza (no 97) and **Harry's New Yor**k Bar (in the Raffles Le Montreaux Palace Hotel, no 100) offers and hundreds of cocktail varieties.

At night, a lively, bustling crowd can be found in rue du Théâtre, where the **Casino de Montreux** complex (9 rue du Théâtre) caters for all tastes: for instance, the **Montreusien** piano bar for a quiet, cosy drink. **Le Piano Bar** (in the hotel Mirador Kempinski, Mont-Pelerin) is a stylish bar with fireplace, breaktaking view of Lake Geneva, and more than 70 varieties of champagne.

Excursions

Rochers de Naye★★★
2 042m/6 699ft. About 3hr there and back, including 2hr by rack railway. In summer, an old-fashioned steam train departs every hour, except at noon, from 9.05am-5.05pm. In winter, last departure at 305pm. 🚂 *Fare there and back: 45CHF. Other tourist train – Montreux, Bernese Oberland – MOB: 12 panoramic-express trains per day in summer, Sat-Sun all year round.*

During this trip you will enjoy the hill sites of **Glion** (alt 689m/2 260ft), a pleasant country holiday resort at medium altitude, and of **Caux** (alt 1 050m/3 448ft), another balcony-resort with a tourist reputation of long standing. From the summit of Rochers de Naye you will enjoy a bird's-eye view east of Lake Geneva and a splendid panorama of the Bernese, Valais and Savoy Alps and the Jura.

Château de Chillon★★
3km/2mi S. It can also be reached on foot by following the shores of the lake. ♿ *See Château de CHILLON.*

Avants-Sonloup Tour★★
25km/14mi – about 1hr. Follow the route marked with arrows on the plan above. Leave Montreux by the route marked Les Avants-Fribourg.

On the left, the road overlooks the town and the lake; the Château du Châtelard, with its large rectangular 15C crenellated tower, stands out on the crest of a vine-clad slope. Climbing steeply, the road affords fine views of the lake and the Alps.

▶ *4km/2mi from Montreux turn right towards Chernex-Les-Avants, then left 200m/220yd farther on before Chamby (two bends) and cross the railway line, and another right turn for Les Avants.*

Les Avants★
Alt 968m/3 175ft. This small resort overlooked on the southeast by the Dent de Jaman and the Naye Rocks is beautifully sited.

Col de Sonloup
Alt 1 149m/3 770ft. A fine **view**★ of the Rochers de Naye, the Dents du Midi and the Savoy Alps.

▶ *The return to Montreux is via the villages of Saumont, Chamby and Chernex. Narrow at first, this road reveals new glimpses of the lake and of the Vevey-Blonay region.*

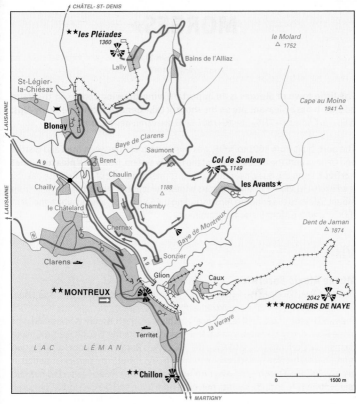

Les Pléiades Tour★★

▶ *36km/22mi – plus 30min on foot there and back. To get to Saumont follow the directions explained above. Turn right at Saumont towards Bains de l'Alliaz and then take the road which climbs steadily among fields and fir woods to the hamlet of Lally, where you will leave the car. You can also reach Lally by rack railway from Blonay.*

Les Pléiades★★

From Lally 30min on foot there and back.

From the Les Pléiades summit (alt 1 360m/4 462ft) you will see a fine **panorama**★★ of Lake Geneva, the Molard, the Dent de Jaman, the Rochers de Naye, the Savoy Alps and the Mont Blanc Range.

Return by the Blonay road which gives frequent glimpses of the lake and reveals, to the right, **Château de Blonay**, dating back to the 11C.

▶ *Shortly after Brent, turn right to return to Montreux.*

MORGES ★

VAUD – POPULATION 13 747
ALT 378M/1 240FT

The little town of Morges is an important wine-growing centre on the Vaud hillside. It has a pleasant site on the shore of Lake Geneva, facing the Savoy Alps.
🛈 *Rue du Château – 1110 – ☎ (021) 801 32 33, www.morges-tourisme.ch.*

The port, built from 1691 to 1696, was busy with trade between the Vaud district and Geneva until the development of the railway system. Now, it is a **pleasure-boat harbour**. From the quay, near the castle (a former residence of the Bernese bailiffs) is an excellent **view**★ of the lake at its widest point and beyond it of the Alps, from Mount Salève to the Fribourg Alps, including the Savoy Alps, among which the Dent d'Oche and the Mont Blanc are prominent.

Visit

Musée Alexis-Forel★★
54 Grand'Rue. ◷ *Open Wed-Sun 2-6pm.* ◷ *Closed Easter Mon, Whit Mon and 1 Aug.*
👓 *6CHF.* ☎ *(021) 801 26 47, www.museeforel.ch.*
Founded by the engraver **Alexis Forel** and his wife, the museum is housed in part of the Blanchenay Mansion, a handsome residence from the 15C, 17C and 18C. Note the panelled ceilings (15C and 16C), the 17C carved Burgundian doors and the two monumental fireplaces. Each exhibition room pays tribute to a particular period in history: 15C-19C French and Swiss furniture, most of which Forel collected himself; mementoes (17C and 18C salons), porcelain from Nyon and the East India Company; 16C-19C glasswork, 18C and 19C silverware. An exhibition of dolls occupies two floors, displaying numerous 18C-20C pieces together with their accessories.

Castle
◷ *Open Jul and Aug, daily except Mon, 10am-5pm; Sep-Jun, daily except Mon, 10am-noon and 1.30-5pm, Sat-Sun and public hols 1.30-5pm.* ◷ *Closed Easter Mon, Whit Mon and from mid-Dec to 31 Jan.* 👓 *7CHF.* ☎ *(021) 316 09 90, www.chateau-morges.ch.*
Built on a strategic location west of the town, this massive 13C fortress, flanked by four circular corner towers defining four bulwarks arranged around a central courtyard, houses the collections belonging to three museums.

The **Swiss Figurine Museum** *(ground floor)* presents a series of dioramas with lead or tin soldiers which illustrate major historical events from Antiquity to the 19C, including Babylon, the Aztec rebellion against Spanish settlers, the Field of the Cloth of Gold and the Berezina Crossing on Napoleons's retreat from Russia. Each figurine has been painstakingly reconstructed with minute attention to detail.

The **Vaud Military Museum** *(ground floor and first floor)* presents an exhaustive collection of the weapons, uniforms and types of headdress associated with the Swiss army from Napoleonic times through the present day, including the Pope's famous Swiss guard. A succession of rooms recreate particular periods of history: , the Tower of Justice or the Tower of Torture, the Davel Room, devoted to Major Jean-Daniel Abraham Davel, a Vaud patriot executed in 1723 for having fought against the Bernese authorities, or the room paying tribute to General Guisan, Commander-in-Chief of the Swiss army between 1939 and 1945 (military record, personal belongings).

Address Book

For coin ranges, see Legend on front flap.

WHERE TO STAY

△**Campsite** – ☎ 021 801 12 70. Outstanding location on the very shores of Lake Geneva.

◯◯◯◯ **Hôtel du Mont-Blanc** – Quai du Mont-Blanc – ☎ 021 804 87 87 – www.hotel-mont-blanc.ch – 46 rooms – All the rooms overlook Lake Geneva.

Small, cosy bar on the first floor. For meals, you can choose between the first-floor gastronomic restaurant Les Guérites and Le Pavois, which caters for a simpler, less sophisticated clientele.

◯◯◯◯ **La Fleur du Lac** – 70 route de Lausanne – ☎ 021 811 58 11 – www.fleur-du-lac.ch – 30 rooms – This hotel with large, comfortable rooms is a haven of peace and well-being. Flower-decked terrace and pretty garden on the lake shore.

The **Artillery Museum**, set up in a series of fine cellars enhanced by barrel vaulting, displays around 40 real exhibits along with miniature models which explain the development of this weapon: early artillery pieces from the 16C, mountain artillery carried by beasts of burden, 75mm field canon and carriage; an unusual boule-shaped 12mm mortar able to revolve around its axis, adjustable on slopes, with a range of 3km/2mi.

VAL DE MORGINS★

The Morgins Pass is the only international route in the pre-Alpine Chablais Massif joining the pastoral valleys of Dranse d'Abondance and Morgins, with their many large chalets. On the Valais side it is a modern road offering views of the Dents du Midi.

From Monthey to Châtel 34km/21mi – about 2hr

Itinerary 8 (see Le VALAIS map). Swiss customs control near the pass, French customs at Vonne.

On leaving Monthey the road climbs quickly in hairpin bends above the Rhône Valley, overlooked (going upstream) by the summits of the Les Diablerets, Grand Muveran and Dent de Morcles. Ahead, in line with the Illiez Valley, are the snowy Dents Blanches and Dents du Midi. Fields planted with walnut trees succeed vineyards.

Champéry★★

Champéry lies on the mountainside at the beginning of the **Val d'Illiez★★**, in the shadow of the Dents du Midi Range. The resort clusters around its single narrow street and exudes a family atmosphere despite its international clientele. It is a favourite place for rock-climbers. A local feature is the church **belfry** roofed with a curious pierced stone crown. In winter the Panachaux Basin, served by several ski lifts, offers fine, sunny slopes to skiers.

The skiing area

Champéry is an impressive resort within the group known as **Portes du Soleil**★★. This Franco-Swiss resort is among the largest in the world, with an estimated 650km/404mi of slopes ranging from 900m/2 953ft to 2 300m/7 546ft, a comparitively low altitde that creates a shortened season. It is particularly suitable for intermediate skiers. The smaller Champéry section offers splendid skiing opportunities: the famous bumpy descent at Pas de Chavanette is one of the most challenging in Europe, and the long red piste leading to Grand Paradis, serviced by the Ripaille ski lift. Other sections such as Les Crosets or Avoriaz are far easier to reach.

Croix de Culet★★

From Champéry, about 45min, including 15min by cable car and 1hr on foot. Jul-Aug, departure approximately every 30min, 9am-5.30pm; Jun, Sep and Oct, departures approximately every hr, 9am-5pm; Dec to mid-Apr, 9am-5pm. 🕐 *Closed late Oct to the beginning of the skiing season.* 🚡 *15CHF there and back.* ☎ *(024) 479 02 03.*

From the upper station of the Planachaux cable car, climb on foot, along the crest, to the cross (alt 1 963m/6 539ft). There is an open view of the various peaks of the Dents du Midi, Mount Ruan, Dents Blanches and the Vaud Alps.

The road continues to make hairpin bends, offering a widening **view**★ of the Rhône Valley, to the south of the Illiez Valley, the Dents du Midi Cliffs and, to the right of these, Mount Ruan. The road then becomes a corniche above the wooded ravine of the Vièze; it then reaches the floor of the softly shaped Alpine combe of the Morgins Valley. Here, chalets nestle under wide-eaved roofs covered with shingles; their two-storey balconies have a double overhang, forming a gallery.

Morgins❋

This peaceful mountain resort is restful both in summer and in winter.

Pas de Morgins★

Alt 1 369m/4 491ft. The road, falling slightly, slips into this forest dell containing a small lake in which fir trees are reflected. Southeastwards, in the middle distance, the Dents du Midi summits can be seen. The steeper descent into the Dranse d'Abondance Valley reveals the majestic **site**★ of Châtel. Ahead, the horizon is now barred by the slopes of Mount Chauffé (left) and the Cornettes de Bise (right).

MOUDON

VAUD – POPULATION 4 425
ALT 522M/1 713FT

Situated in the centre of the rich agricultural area of the Broye Valley, Moudon was an important stop on the road between Rome and Vindonissa (Windisch, near Brugg) in Gallo-Roman times and enjoyed great prosperity under the counts of Savoy (14C): most of the buildings which give the town its medieval air date from that time. From the bridge over which the N 1 secondary road crosses the Broye, there is, in the foreground, a pleasing view of the old quarter with its 15C-17C houses. These with great overhanging roofs, stand huddled at the foot of the hill crowned by the old Rochefort and Carrouge castles and the ancient Broye Tower. 🛈 *Place de la Douane – 1510 – ☎ (021) 905 88 66.*

Sights

Église St-Étienne

This church, built in the 13C and early 14C, testifies to Moudon's importance during the Savoyard period. It is flanked by an imposing fortified belfry, once part of the town walls. The Gothic nave, roofed with vaulting, bearing coats of arms, has lovely stained-glass windows and an organ (1764). The chancel contains fine stalls (early 16C and early 17C). Original 16C frescoes, which have undergone extensive restoration, are noteworthy.

Rue du Château

▶ *Start from Place de la Grenette.*

This is the main street of the old quarter. At the beginning of the street is an amusing fountain depicting Justice (polychrome statue sheltering four little magistrates under its robe). Farther along, the 12C Broye Tower (in ruins) stands on the right of the street, which is lined on either side by houses dating from the 15C, 16C and 17C; note the Bernese-style house at n° 34, with a terrace under the eaves. Midway to the left the view overlooks the river, spanned by a covered bridge; at the end of the street are the museums (on the right) and a second fountain (1557) called Moses.

Musée du Vieux-Moudon

🕓 *Open Apr to late Nov, Wed, Sat and Sun , 2-6pm.* ⊛*5CHF, 8CHF (combined ticket with Musée Eugène-Burnand).* ☎ *(021) 905 27 05.*
Housed in the 13C Maison de Rochefort in the upper town, this museum is dedicated to local and regional history, including a notary's study full of documents; weapons (flint shotguns, blunderbusses, halberds etc); and a kitchen amply supplied with accessories (coffee roasters, mincers, salt mills). Additional sections are dedicated to the town (old wrought-iron signs that once hung outside cafés in Moudon, finials and paintings) and rural areas (tools, ploughing instruments and cow bells). A spiral staircase leads to the first floor, where a model of the town as it was in 1415 is displayed. The large drawing room, once used for music, reading and board games, is decorated with painted tapestries (18C). The faience stove bears the coat of arms of Sigismond de Cerjat, who lived in the house 1729-31. Another room focuses on antique trades (iron-working and carpentry), flax and hemp, and military life. Attractive 18C Moudon tiles are particularly noteworthy.

Musée Eugène-Burnand

🕓 *Open Apr-Nov, Wed, Sat-Sun, 2-6.30pm.* ⊛*5CHF, 8CHF (combined ticket with Musée du Vieux-Moudon), no charge (under 16). Visit by appointment 10 days in advance to the tourist office on* ☎ *(021) 905 88 66.*
The Bâtiment du Grand'Air houses works by Eugène Burnand, who was born in Moudon in 1850 and died in Paris in 1921. His trips to Provence inspired paintings such as *Paysages de Camargue* and *Troupeaux de chevaux en Camargue* and his friendship with the Provençal writer Frédéric Mistral led to his illustration of the poet's famous work *Mireille*. Among his large works, the most famous depicting rural themes are *Le Labour dans le Jorat* (1916), *Les Glaneuses* (1880), *Le Paysan* (1894) and *La Ferme Suisse* (1882). Among his religious works, *La Voie Douloureuse* (1903), which depicts Jesus being led to Calvary (the woman kneeling is the artist's wife), is worthy of note. Historical paintings include his major work *La Fuite de Charles-le-Téméraire* (1895), with its the skilful portrayal of faces, especially that of Charles the Bold.

Excursion

Lucens
5km/3mi NE on the Payerne road.
This small town is associated with Sherlock Holmes, as the son of Sir Arthur Conan Doyle, author of the adventures of the famous English detective, once owned the château here. He donated many of his father's things to the town and founded a museum. The **Musée Sherlock Holmes** (🕓*Open Wed and Sat-Sun, 2-5pm.* ⊛*4CHF.* ☎ *(021) 906 73 33)* is dedicated to the work of Conan Doyle and his well-known hero.

Exhibits include an armchair, desk, personal items, copies of letters, clothes and a large table around which famous guests including Winston Churchill and Rudyard Kipling once sat; photos of the writer are also on display. Holmes's drawing room at 221B Baker Street has been reconstructed according to the detailed descriptions given in Conan Doyle's novels, and has been filled with objects recalling the famous detective and his friend, Dr Watson.

MUOTTAS MURAGL★★

GRAUBÜNDEN

The grassy ridges of Muottas Muragl, easily reached by funicular from the Samedan Basin, form the classic belvedere of the Upper Engadine.

Climb to Muottas Muragl★★

From the lower station at Punt Muragl, about 1hr there and back, including 30min by funicular. 🚠 *Operates from June to mid-Oct and Dec-Apr. Departure every 30min, 8am–11pm.* 🚠 *Fare there and back: 22CHF in winter, 26CHF in summer.* ☎ *(081) 842 83 08.* From the upper station (hotel), at an altitude of 2 453m/8 048ft there is a **view**★★ of the Upper Engadine Gap, framed by the small Piz Rosatsch and Piz Julier ranges. The string of lakes between Sankt Moritz and the Maloja are also clearly visible. Farther left are the Roseg corrie and the shining peaks of the Bernina Massif: Piz Morteratsch, Piz Bernina and Piz Palü. Many tourists will enjoy walking on this high ground, famous for its flora and fauna, along broad, gently sloping paths superbly sited on the mountainside, such as the Hochweg.

Muottas Muragl

Franziska Pfenniger / Switzerland Tourism

Walk to Pontresina★★

Allow one day to ascend by funicular to Muottas Muragl, walk to, and then tour Pontresina village. From Muottas Muragl, allow at least 2hr 30min on foot.

The classic route is through peaceful pastureland to Alp Languard *(3hr on foot)*, offering superb **views**★★ of the Roseg and Morteratsch glaciers and the Pontresina Valley. The climb down from to Pontresina can be done on foot or by chairlift. You may, however, decide to stop at the Unterer Schafberg Restaurant perched at a height of 2 231m/7 318ft *(1hr on foot before reaching Alp Languard)* before heading directly for Pontresina through the forest *(45min)*. From Pontresina, a path following the bed of the valley will take you to the foot of the funicular *(45min)*, wending its way through many houses whose architecture is typical of the area.

MÜRREN

BERN
ALT 1 638M/5 374FT

Perched on a shelf of Alpine pasture forming a balcony overlooking the steep cleft of the Lauterbrunnen Valley, Mürren faces a series of giant peaks carved out of rock or ice: from left to right, the view encompasses the Eiger, the Mönch, the Jungfrau, the Breithorn, and the Gspaltenhorn range (far right).

The **site**★★ of this village, completely free of car traffic, and its surrounding ski slopes, which bristle with every conceivable obstacle, account for the resort's popularity. The development of tourism in the area was largely due to the British, who came here at the turn of the last century to indulge in their favourite winter sports and succeeded in recreating a cosy, congenial atmosphere. It was here that the Kandahar Ski Club was founded in 1924; it was to lead to the famous **Arlberg-Kandahar competition**, now regarded as the unofficial world championship of the Alpine countries.

Approach

Motorists are advised to drive to Stechelberg, at the end of the Lauterbrunnen Valley road. There, take the Schilthorn cable car to Mürren. You can also drive to Lauterbrunnen and park the car before taking the funicular to Grütschalp. From there a train will take you to Mürren.

Excursion

Schilthorn★★★

Alt 2 970m/9 744ft. About 1hr 15min including 17min by cable-car leaving from Mürren. There is also a cable car leaving from Stechelberg down in the valley.

From the top, in a desolate landscape of torrents and scree, is a **panoramic view**★★★ of the Jungfrau Massif with only the Lauterbrunnen cleft between that and the observer. Part of Lake Thun is visible. The panoramic restaurant features a popular revolving plateau; it makes a complete turn in 55min. This aluminium establishment with a futuristic look and exceptional location is famous and familiar for its role in the James Bond film *On Her Majesty's Secret Service*; several scenes were shot on the premises (1967-68). Every year in January the locality hosts **Inferno**, an Alpine skiing competition in which contestants race from the Schilthorn summit down to Lauterbrunnen, a 16km/10mi circuit and a vertical drop of 2 134m/7 000ft in barely 20min! Seasoned skiers can follow the route on other days without racing.

MURTEN★★

FRIBOURG – POPULATION 5 478
ALT 458M/1 503FT

Overlooking the east shore of the lake that bears its name, Murten has a yachting marina which attracts visitors. It is famous in history for the defeat of Charles the Bold by the Swiss. This former fortified city, which has kept most of its ramparts and towers, exudes picturesque charm. *Französische Kirchgasse 6 – 3280 – ☎ (026) 670 51 12.*

Murtensee

This peaceful, oblong stretch of water runs parallel to the northern part of Lake Neuchâtel and is linked to it by the Broye Canal. Lake Murten, swarming with fish, has a migratory bird sanctuary on its north shore and a beach (facilities) on its south shore. It is bordered on its eastern side by the town of Murten.

Old Town

Hauptgasse

The main street runs through the heart of the old town and displays a fine degree of unity with arcaded houses, overhanging roofs covered with brown tiles, fountains and the Bern Gateway, surmounted by a graceful pinnacle.

▶ *Take Deutschekirchgasse which starts just before the Berntor, go around the German Protestant church, behind which a wooden stairway leads to the walls.*

Stadtmauer★

Take the wall-walk, covered with an attractive timber roof, to the right. It affords pretty views over the clustering roofs of the old town, the castle and the lake. Mount Vully and the Jura foothills rise on the horizon. At the end of the wall-walk, climb the tower for views of the castle and the lake in the distance.

▶ *Retrace your steps and leave the wall-walk by the square tower.*

Schloss

Built in the 13C by Duke Peter of Savoy, this is a grim, imposing castle. From the inner court there is a fine view of Lake Murten and the Jura.

Historisches Museum

⊙Open Apr-Oct, daily except Mon, 2-5pm; Mar, Apr, Oct and Dec, daily except Mon, 2-5pm; Jan and Feb, Sat-Sun, 2-5pm. ⊜6CHF. ☎ (026) 670 31 00, www.museummurten.ch.

The historical museum is located in the town's former watermill, restored to its 18C glory. On five levels are exhibited: prehistoric and Gallo-Roman relics (pottery, arms, jewellery); objects evoking local history from the Middle Ages to the 18C (coins, pewter, glassware, stained-

The Battle of Murten

Anxious to revenge his defeat at the hands of the Swiss Confederates at Grandson in 1476, the Duke of Burgundy, **Charles the Bold**, hastily raised a new army. From Lausanne, he marched on the Broye Valley and laid seige, suffering a second defeat by the Confederate Army two weeks later. Hemmed in by the lake, nearly 8,000 of the duke's troops perished.. Many drowned in the lake; Charles himself was able to flee. A rich booty of fabrics, furs and arms fell into the hands of the victors. A model of the battle is displayed at the Swiss National Museum in Zurich.

glass windows, utensils), Burgundian treasures (swords, armour, cannon) and exhibits on the crucial Battle of Murten.

Rathausgasse

This street passes the town hall, an attractive arcaded building dating from the 16C, and leads to the small **French church**, with its single nave and ogival-vaulted choir. A balcony to the side of the church affords splendid views of the lakes and the foothills of the Jura mountains in the distance.

▷ *Französischegasse leads to the Berntor and back to the main street.*

MÜSTAIR

GRAUBÜNDEN – POPULATION 840

Chief town of the **Val Müstair**, Müstair is the only part of Swiss territory in the Adige Basin. The church, according to tradition, was founded by Charlemagne; it stands at the end of the village on the Italian side still enclosed in the boundaries of the Abbey of St John the Baptist (a Benedictine monastery). It is one of the most ancient buildings in Switzerland.

Church★

🐾 *Guided tours available. Contact Kurerein Müstair on ☎ (081) 858 50 00.*

The nave, originally built in the style of a basilica, was transformed in the 15C into a vaulted Gothic structure with two aisles. The **frescoes**★★ on the walls are listed as a UNESCO World Heritage Site and are the most imposing cycle of wall paintings in the Confederation: some have been transferred to the Swiss National Museum in Zurich. This painted decoration goes back to Carolingian times (early 9C), and is partially covered by Romanesque frescoes (1150-70) which are in good condition. Among the other works of art are a 12C statue of Charlemagne.

NEUCHÂTEL★★

see over

Ⓒ NEUCHÂTEL – POPULATION 31 553
ALT 440M/1 444FT

Neuchâtel enjoys a charming site between its lake, with 4km/3mi of quays, and Chaumont Hill. The pleasant, attractive town stands in the middle of vineyards; its pale ochre houses prompted Alexandre Dumas to say it was carved out of a pat of butter. The silhouettes of the collegiate church and the castle dominate the scene. ⓘ *Hôtel des Postes – 2000 – ☎ (032) 889 68 90, www.neuchateltourisme.ch.*

Lake Neuchâtel

This is the largest wholly Swiss lake, being nearly 38km/24mi long and 8km/5mi wide. It is teeming with fish. Canals used by pleasure boats join it with Lake Biel and Lake Murten. Its iridescent waters and hilly, vine-clad shores are favourite subjects for painters and writers; André Gide is one of many to have been inspired in the past.

A Bit of History

Middle Ages - The name Neuchâtel is derived from a structure built as a stronghold during Burgundian rule (1011). Later, the town became the property of the French Orléans-Longueville family. It is said that in order to celebrate his entry into the town during a 1657 visit, Henri II of Orléans had 6 000l/1 300 gallons of the local red wine poured into the Griffin Fountain, which still stands in rue du Château. Neuchâtel became the personal property of the King of Prussia after 1707.

Struggle for independence – After being placed under the rule of Marshal Berthier (Chief of Staff of Napoleon I) as a principality (1806-14), Neuchâtel joined the Swiss Confederation in 1815 and was then in a peculiar political position as a Swiss canton bound to the King of Prussia. An independence effort in 1831 failed, but succeeded in 1848, and the Republic was proclaimed. The King of Prussia finally recognised the canton's independence in 1857 but kept the courtesy title of Prince of Neuchâtel. The French spoken at Neuchâtel is considered by many to be the purest in Switzerland. Neuchâtel today is an important watch and clock research centre, whose observatory gives the official time to all of Switzerland. It is also a wine market—a great wine harvest procession takes place here in September.

Old Town

Old town★ (BZ)

🔊 *Guided tours – (1hr) mid-May to Oct, at 5.30am.* 💶 *5.05CHF. Contact the tourist office.*

A picturesque quarter (rue du Château, rue du Trésor, rue du Seyon, rue du Pommier, rue des Moulins) with old houses, 16C and 17C fountains (Fontaine de la Justice, Grand-Rue; Fontaine du Banneret, on the corner of rue du Château and rue du Trésor; Fontaine du Lion, on the corner of rue du Temple-Neuf and rue du Bassin) and defensive towers, extends between the town hall (1788), a classical building by the architect and painter Paris (1747-1819), from Besançon, and the group formed by the collegiate church and the castle. On the oblong Place des Halles (Market Square) are 17C houses, and, at the far end, the Renaissance house Maison des Halles is flanked by turrets and bearing the shield with the fleur-de-lis of the Orléans-Longueville family. In the summer, the square is a popular meeting-place and outdoor cafés are busy until late in the evening.

Collegiate Church and Castle★

🔊 *Guided tour (45min) Apr-Oct, Mon-Sat at 10am, 11am, noon, 2pm, 3pm, 4pm; Sun and public hols at 2pm, 3pm, 4pm.* 💶 *No charge.* ☎ *(032) 889 60 00.*

These two curious buildings form a single monumental ensemble. The **collegiate church** is a fine 12C and 13C construction with multicoloured glazed tiles, and was heavily restored during the 19C. A statue of the reformer **Guillaume Farel** (1489-1565) faces the main church entrance; his sermons led the population of Neuchâtel to adopt the Protestant religion. The nave, with its ribbed vaulting, is typical of the Gothic style. At the transept crossing is a lantern-tower. Under an arcade in the chancel, the cenotaph of the counts of Neuchâtel (14C) is a striking example of medieval sculpture: this superb stone composition comprises 14 stiff, impressive polychrome statues depicting knights and noblewomen at prayer. The south portal, Romanesque, decorated with archivolts and carved capitals, is flanked by the statues of St Peter and St Paul.

The **Castle** (15C and 16C, restored), once the residence of the Neuchâtel lords, today is the seat of the cantonal government; it retains vestiges of the 12C: the Romanesque gallery pierced by seven blind bays in the southwest façade. The main entrance gate, evidently defensive, is flanked by two crowned towers and embellished with broken arches. Under the passageway, the arms of Philippe de Hochberg, Lord of

Neuchâtel, can be seen. In the northern wing, the first to be built, you may visit the former kitchen area, the antechamber (clock by Jacquet-Droz, *The Blessing of the Plough in Franche-Comté*, painted by Robert Ferrier), the semicircular Great Council Hall, seat of the cantonal government (115 members elected for four years – note the stained-glass windows by Georges Froidevaux, representing municipal coats of arms), a small room with barrel vaulting which once housed regional archives, and the Knights' Hall, the largest room in the castle, used for receptions (fine ceiling, arms on either side of the fireplace, portraits of all the State Councillors). In the south wing visitors are shown the room named after Mary of Savoy, niece to Louis XI and wife to Count Philippe de Hochberg (the count's arms hang above the stone fireplace), the Philippe de Hochberg Gallery, where State Councillors meet, and the States' Room or Tribunal Room, whose walls recount the history of the Neuchâtel district (emblazoned coins). The wall-walk offers lovely views of the town.

Tour des Prisons

🕐 *Open Apr to Sept, 8am-6pm.* ⊙ *1CHF.* ☎ *(032) 717 76 02.*

At the foot of the hill on which the castle stands, in rue Jehanne-de-Hochberg, there is a high crenellated tower known as the Prison Tower. Its base is the oldest piece of architecture in the town. The interior contains two wooden dungeons used until 1848 and two maquettes of Neuchâtel from the late 15C and late 18C. The viewpoint affords a fine **panorama** of the collegiate church, the town and the lake.

Musée d'Art et d'Histoire★★ (CZ)

Start from the Fine Arts section. ♿🕐 *Open daily, except Mon, 11am-6pm.* 🕐 *Closed 1 Jan, 24, 25 and 31 Dec.* ⊙*7CHF, no charge Wed.* ☎ *(032) 717 79 20, www.mahn.ch.*

Fine Arts (*Upper floor*) – A sweeping staircase decorated with allegorical frescoes by Paul Robert and stained glass by Clement Heaton leads to this part of the museum, which was used to house temporary exhibitions during Expo 02. A retrospective of Swiss painting now occupies five exhibition halls, presenting works by Léopold Robert (*Weeping Woman at the Water's Edge*), Ferdinand Hodler (*Autumn Evening*) and Albert Anker (*Bernese Peasant Reading his Newspaper*). Another room contains the Amez-Droz bequest, largely devoted to French Impressionism (*The Boat-Workshop* by Monet).

History and Decorative Arts (*Ground floor and mezzanine*) – A series of large and small galleries display objects evoking regional crafts and retrace the history and lifestyle of the canton via collections of gold and silver plate (cups of the various guilds), coins and porcelain. Gallery 4 includes timepieces from Neuchâtel and three delightful **automata★★**, marvels of ingenuity made in the 18C by Jaquet-Droz and Sons as well as by Jean-Frédéric Leschot: they are the Musician, the Writer and the Draughtsman. Also, you can admire old glassware, arms and 16C-17C stained glass ornamented with municipal coats of arms. Do not miss the admirable **Strübin Collection★**, presenting weapons, armour, helmets and uniforms from the French Revolution, the First Napoleonic Empire, the Restoration and the Second Empire.

A. Rentsch / Switzerland Tourism

Automaton: The Writer

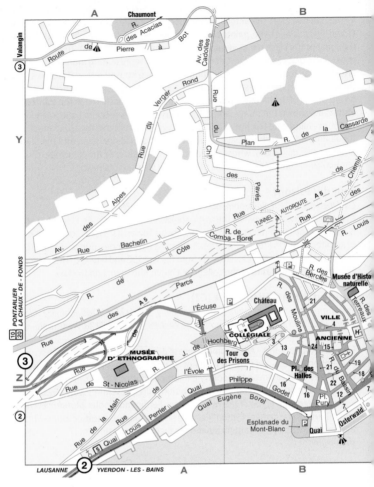

Musée d'Ethnographie★ (AZ)

⏰ *Open daily except Mon, 10am-5pm.* ⏰ *Closed 1 Jan, 24, 25 and 31 Dec.* ⊕*8CHF, no charge Wed.* ☎ *(032) 718 19 60; www.men.ch.*

The Museum of Ethnography is housed in a late-19C villa surrounded by a park. The modern annexe is used exclusively for temporary exhibits focusing on a specific theme: the northern façade is embellished with a huge mural painting, *The Conquests of Man,* executed by the Swiss painter **Hans Erni**.

Ground floor rooms are dedicated to Ancient Egypt, with collections of *shabti* statuettes and funerary boats, wooden sculptures dating from the 6th and 10th Dynasties, and exhibits explaining the ritual of mummification (also carried out on animals). Another room displays artifacts from the Himalayas, including Tibetan statues and a collection from Bhutan. On the first floor is the private study of the great traveller and collector Charles-Daniel de Meuron (1738-1806), containing exotic objects encountered on his many voyages: Hawaii fan, Chinese porcelain, quiver with arrows etc. This floor also houses traditional ethnographical collections, with exhibits that include a Tuareg tent, spears, Angolan musical instruments, masks from New Caledonia, Nigeria and Angola, a reliquary head from Gabon and an androgynous "Uli" statue from New Ireland, near Papua New Guinea.

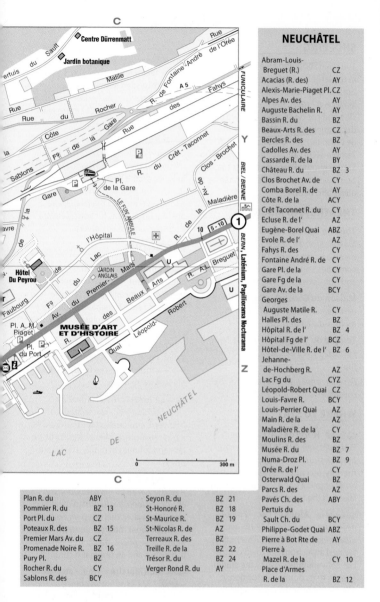

Quai Osterwald (BZ)

Viewing table. Superb **view**★★ of the lake and the Alpine range.

Musée d'Histoire Naturelle (BZ)

&. © *Open daily except Mon, 10am–6pm.* © *Closed 25 Dec.* ☞ *8CHF, no charge Wed and mid-May to late Oct.* ☏ *(032) 717 79 60, www.museum-neuchatelle.ch.*
The **Natural History Museum** is housed in the former School of Commerce, an imposing 19C residence built with yellow brick. In addition to exhibitions of mammals, it presents several species of aquatic and sylvan birds, displayed in dioramas which reproduce their natural setting; note the recordings of the different songs – twitters, squawks and screeches.

Address Book

SHOPPING

The main shopping area is concentrated in the largely pedestrianised old town, bordered by rue du Coq-d'Inde, rue de la Place-d'Armes, rue de l'Hôtel-de-ville and rue de l'Écluse. The two main department stores, **Migros** (12 rue de l'Hôpital) and **Globus** (14 rue du Temple-Neuf) are also located here. On Saturdays, the **Place de Halles** market brims with regional produce, cheese, olives and people.

THEATRE AND MUSIC

Théâtre du Passage – *Passage Max-Meuron,* ☎ *(032)717 79 07, www. theatredupassage.ch.* This theatre hosts comedies and dramas by both Swiss and non-Swiss playwrights.

Maison du Concert – *Rue de l'Hôtel-de-Ville* – ☎ *(032) 724 21 22 - www. maison-du-concert.ch.*

Temple du Bas, *Rue du Temple-Neuf* – ☎ *032 717 79 07.* Classical and choral music.

For coin ranges, see the Legend on the cover flap.

WHERE TO STAY

◌◌◌ **Hôtel des Arts** – *3 rue Pourtalès* – ☎ *032 727 61 61 – www. hotel-des-arts.ch – 40 rooms .* This friendly, recently renovated, modern hotel enjoys a good location near the lake and the town centre.

◌◌◌◌ **Alpes et Lac** – *2 place de la Gare* – ☎ *032 723 19 19 – www. alpesetlac.ch – 30 rooms.* This hotel is located away from the town centre but conveniently close to the station. Thanks to its dominant position, it affords unencumbered views of the town and its lake.

◌◌◌◌ **Touring au Lac** – *1 place Numa-Droz* – ☎ *032 725 55 01 – www. touring-au-lac.ch – 42 rooms.* Conveniently located next to the harbour, a stone's throw from the bustling town centre with its pedestrian streets. Try to book a room with views of the lake.

◌◌◌◌ **La Maison du Prussien** – *Gor du Vauseyon by rue de St-Nicolas*

– ☎ *032 730 54 54 – www.hotel-prussien. ch - 10 rooms.* For a complete change of scene, take a room at this 18C former brewery nestled among trees and offering large, rustic-style bedrooms named after local people. The Chambre Jean Chambrier is most unusual.

◌◌◌◌ **Beaulac** – *2 esplanade Léopold-Robert* – ☎ *032 723 11 11* – *www.beaulac.ch – 86 rooms.* Splendid location on the lake shore, near the marina. Forget about price and reserve a room overlooking the lake. There are two restaurants for your pleasure: Gourmandin and Le Colvert.

EATING OUT

One of the region's specialities is a cheese fondue known as "moitié-moitié", literally meaning half Gruyère, half Vacherin. Leave Neuchâtel and drive a few miles towards the Jura. Stop at one of the many inns dotting the countryside around Valangin, Dombresson or Vallon de St-Imier, settle down on the terrace and sample the fondue with a glass of white wine!

◌◌ **Le Jura** – *7 rue de la Treille* – ☎ *032 725 14 10 – closed Sun.* A friendly, traditional establishment with a congenial atmosphere offering bistro fare and fondues at highly affordable prices.

◌◌◌ **Au Bateau** – *Neuchâtel Harbour* – ☎ *032 724 88 00 – www.aubateau. ch - closed Mon.* If you dream of gliding along the water, then step on board this old steamboat moored along the quays. Reasonable prices, delicious meat and fish dishes and an original setting.

◌◌◌ **Le Marché** – *4 place du Marché* – ☎ *032 723 23 30 – www.hotel-dumarche.com - closed Sun.* Diners may choose between the tavern and the upstairs restaurant. Both feature a rustic decor and offer reasonable prices.

BOAT TRIPS

Boat trips on the lake run through the year, although visitors will have a greater choice of excursions between May and October. For further information, contact the Société de Navigation sur les Lacs de Neuchâtel et Morat at the port. ☎ 032 729 96 00.

NIGHTLIFE

The **Amiral Bar** of the Hôtel Beaulac features a lovely terrace looking out onto the sailing harbour. Themed evenings can be arranged and a wine exhibition is open to customers. The bar of the **Hôtel Beau-Rivage** attracts a friendly crowd and commands lovely views of the lake; there is a nightclub in the basement.

In the rue de l'Hôtel-de-Ville, the decor of the **Café Brasserie du Théâtre**, evokes the turn of the last century; it is a favourite of actors and theatre buffs.

Visitors looking for good beer and a pub-like atmosphere should try the Highlander (rue de l'Hôpital) or **Sherlock's** (rue du Faubourg-de-l'Hôpital). The **Bleu Café** (faubourg du Lac 27), popular with students, is next to the Bio cinema and offers an all-inclusive café-cinema option, which includes a snack. The **King** café (rue du Seyon 38) has live jazz several nights a week.

Night-owls should make for the **B Fly** nightclub (ruelle du Port, in the basement), which has a dynamic DJ and is particularly lively on a Thursday night.

Hôtel Du Peyrou (CZ)

This graceful building was erected in the 18C for a financier, Du Peyrou, a friend of the philosopher Jean-Jacques Rousseau. A fine entrance gate affords a view of the façade, which has pure lines and great unity of style, and gives access to a garden. The statue in the pool, *The Bather*, is the work of A Ramseyer.

Jardin Botanique (CY)

58 Chemin du Pertuis-du-Sault. Take rue de l'Hôtel-de-Ville and follow signs to the Jardin Botanique. The gardens are also signposted from the station. Bus n° 9, alighting at the Chapelle de l'Ermitage. 🕐 *Gardens and greenhouses open Apr-Sep, 9am-8pm; Oct-Mar, 9am-5pm;* 🕐 *greenhouses closed Mon.* ✺ *No charge.* ☎ *(032) 718 23 50.*

The **botanical gardens** are above the town in the wooded area of the Vallon de l'Ermitage, and includes the tropical vegetation of the greenhouses (typical of the forests of Eastern Madagascar), the rock garden, arboretum and orchard.

Centre Dürrenmatt (CY)

74 Chemin du Pertuis-du-Sault. The centre is located a little farther out of town than the Jardin Botanique. Bus n° 9, alighting at the Chapelle de l'Ermitage. 🕐 *Open Wed-Sun, 11am-5pm.* ✺*8CHF.* ☎ *(032) 720 20 60; www.cdn.ch.*

Although Swiss author Friedrich Dürrenmatt is best known as a novelist and playwright, he was also an avid artist who wanted his paintings and drawings to be accessible to the public after his death. His widow donated the villa and garden he had purchased in 1952 to the Swiss Confederation and commissioned the Ticino architect Mario Botta to design an exhibition and research centre, which involved adding an unusual slate-covered building. Part of the original villa is dedicated to the writer's theatre work (posters, manuscripts, books etc), and videos of interviews with him. The writer's striking collection of art includes ink drawings, gouaches, oil paintings, lithographs, caricatures and collages. The large room on the lower floor, lit by an impressive arch-shaped window, displays a number of paintings and drawings on the theme of the Minotaur and the Labyrinth. *The Sistine Chapel* on the same floor as the cafeteria is one of the museum's outstanding works.

Excursions

Laténium★★ (at Hauterive)

4km/2.5mi E by ① on the map, along the Bern road. ♿🕐 *Museum open daily except Mon, 10am-5pm.* 🕐 *Closed 1 Jan and 31 Dec.* 🎟 *9CHF.* ☎ *(032) 889 69 17; www.latenium.ch. Free access to the gardens.*

The Laténium retraces 50 000 years of regional history via artifacts found during archaeological digs in the canton of Neuchâtel and on the site. These digs (both on land and underwater) revealed remains of three important prehistoric periods: the Stone Age, Neolithic Age and Bronze Age. Visitors may wander through the lakeside **Parc de la Découverte** before or after the museum visit; exhibits include a lake house, piles symbolising a 6 000-year-old village, a Gallo-Roman barge, a Celtic bridge and a pool showing the level of the lake in the distant past. The modern **Musée d'Archéologie** features a permanent exhibition entitled *Yesterday… between the Mediterranean and the North Sea*. Visitors are taken back in time 100000 BC, as they make their way through the displays, many of which are interactive. The Gallo-Roman barge from Bevaix (copy) is the showpiece in the navigation section *(Room 4)*; dating back to 182 AD, it has a flat bottom made of four planks of oak. Other exhibits cover the environment ,daily life of the Celts, and the weapons, tools and jewellery from the site of **La Tène** *(Room 5),* which gave its name to the second phase of the Iron Age. Room 6, dedicated to lake dwellings, has a fine exhibition of everyday objects and a statue-menhir from Bevaix-Treytel, discovered in 1997.

Chaumont★★

8km/5mi. Take the road to Chaumont on the right (NW of the plan – AY). Leave your car at the upper Neuchâtel-Chaumont funicular station (alt 1 087m/3 576ft). To the left of and behind the station is an **observation tower** (🎟*Turnstile: 2.20CHF.* ☎ *(032) 720 06 00).* An immense **panorama** *(viewing table)* of the Bernese Alps and the Mont Blanc Massif unfolds.

▶ *It can also be reached by the* **funicular** *(Departures from La Coudre about once an hour, 9.30am-7.30pm.* 🎟*Fare there and back: 9.60CHF.* ☎ *(032) 720 06 00) from La Coudre, 3km/2mi from the centre of Neuchâtel, allow 12min.*

Papiliorama Nocturama (at Marin)

5km/3mi E by ① on the map, along the Bern road. 🕐*Open summer, 10am-6pm (Papiliorama), 10am-6pm (Nocturama); winter, 10am-5pm.* 🎟*14CHF.* ☎ *(031) 756 04 61; www.papiliorama.ch.*

The **Papiliorama** and **Nocturama** are housed in two enormous bubbles. The Papiliorama (very humid tropical heat) is planted with luxuriant tropical species, home to exotic birds and butterlies; the cooler Nocturama introduces animals from South America in a moonlit atmosphere. Unusual creatures here include the spectacled owl, the paca (a small animal that feeds on fruit and roots), the seemingly armour-clad nine-striped armadillo, the large-eyed night monkey, the dwarf cayman, a species of small crocodile, and the ocelot, a fierce carnivore also known as a tiger-cat.

Boudry

10km/6mi by S along the Yverdon road or by tramway, starting from Esplanade du Mont-Blanc.

This small medieval-looking town was the birthplace of the French revolutionary leader **Jean-Paul Marat**, editor of *L'Ami du Peuple*, murdered in his bath by Charlotte Corday in 1793. A sculpture called *Marat-L'œil* has been erected in his honour near the house where he was born. This 14m/46ft high structure in painted steel slowly revolves, creating dazzling effects of light. The renowned chocolate manufacturer **Philippe Suchard** was born at 7 rue Louis-Favre in 1797 and spent many childhood years in the house at n° 37, which is now the town hall.

The 13C-16C castle, which served alternately as a counts' residence and a prison, houses the **Musée de la Vigne et du Vin** (◔ *Open Wed-Sun, 2-6pm.* ◔ *Closed for 3 weeks after Christmas.* ▨ *3CHF.* ☎ *(032) 842 38 32)*, founded by the Compagnie des Vignolants. The wines of Neuchâtel, produced according to long-standing traditions, are made with grapes grown on a vineyard extending between Neuchâtel Lake and the Jura. The visit, which begins with a history of the wine bottle, ranging from the amphora to the wine box, provides a comprehensive review of regional wine-making from the 18C up to today. The exhibition, relying on photographs, paintings, tools and machines, explains the work of the wine-grower, defined by the four seasons and the equipment used, diseases of the vine, grape harvesting techniques and the vinification process right up to bottling.

Château de Valangin

4km/2.5mi N by ③ on the map, along the La Chaux-de-Fonds road. ◔ *Open Mar to mid-Dec, daily except Mon, 10am-noon and 2-5pm (10am-noon only Fri).* ▨*5CHF.* ☎ *(032) 857 23 83.*

This castle dates to the 12C and considerably extended under the Lords of Valangin in the 14C and 15C. Used as a prison in the 17C, it then became the property of the Neuchâtel Canton History Society at the end of the 19C. Rooms open to the public include the Salle Louis XVI (Louis XVI-style furniture); the Salle d'Armes (a fine collection of swords and sabres from the 17C-19C); the Salle des Chevaliers, where the court of the three States of Valangin used to sit (sideboards, beautiful sculpted wedding chests, Neuchâtel clocks and watches); the Salle René de Challant, named after the Lord of Valangin (17C portable notary furniture, faience stove); the Salle de Guillemette de Vergy (lace cushions and *abigans*, globe-shaped objects used by lacemakers); and the oratory (Neuchâtel lace, an important industry in the 18C, along with exhibits of clock- and watchmaking and painted canvases, also known as Indian canvases). Visitors also may tour the guardroom and the prison cell known as Farel's cell, where the French reformer is said to have been imprisoned.

LA NEUVEVILLE

BERN – POPULATION 3 131

La Neuveville is a pleasant town on the shores of Lake Biel (◔ *see BIELER SEE)* across from **Sankt Petersinsel;** its economic activity includes wine-producing, precision engineering and tourism. An old-world feeling lingers about the town with its paved streets, lanterns and five towers (remains of the fortifications), and it is an excellent base for excursions to Île St-Pierre, the three lakes (Biel, Neuchâtel and Murten) and Le Chassera. ▯ *4 rue du Marché – 2520 –* ☎ *(032) 751 49 49.*

Visitors arrive in the old town through the **Tour de Rive**, which dates from the foundation of La Neuveville (1312-18) and whose heavy oak door is adorned with the arms of the town. From Place de la Liberté, stop to admire rue de l'Hôpital to the left, where, on many of the houses, the roof projects out from the top floor; note the pulley which was used to lift objects from the street to the attic. The **Rue du Marché**★ is a long street, with two old gates at either end (Tour de Rive and Tour Rouge), serves as the main square. It is charming with, lovely Renaissance fountains with bannerets and flower-decked houses (two of which date from 1647 and 1697).

Blanche Église

East of town towards Biel, on the left. To visit, contact the Tourist office, 4 rue du Marché in La Neuveville. ☎ *(032) 751 49 49.*

This Carolingian building remodelled in the Gothic period and restored in 1915 is surrounded by 17C and 18C tombstones. There are more tombstones inside as well as a painted wooden pulpit (1536) and remains of 14C frescoes on the right of the chancel: Temptation of Christ, Christ Reviled, Entrance to Jerusalem, Adam and Eve.

NUFENENPASSSTRASSE★★

NUFENEN PASS ROAD

The road linking the Ticino to the Valais offers many spectacular views.

From Ariolo to Ulrichen *40km/25mi – about 1hr 30min*

Itinerary 3 *(* 🚗 *see SANKT-GOTTHARD-MASSIV map). The Nufenen Pass is usually closed November to May.*

From **Airolo** (alt 1 142m/3 747ft) to 8km/5mi from Nufenen, the climb up the Bedretto Valley (and from the River Ticino to its source) begins between slopes covered with fir trees. From Airolo to Fontana there are audacious examples (above and to the right) of the engineers' ingenuity when constructing the road. Then after Ossasco you can see a series of villages halfway up the slope: Bedretto is one of them. Beginning at the hamlet of All'Acqua *(cable car on the left)* the foliage becomes scarcer, the climb steeper and the hairpin curves offer a succession of views behind onto the valley's slopes. You then ascend the barren right side of the Bedretto Valley. The climb stops abruptly at the Nufenen Pass.

Passo della Novena-Nufenenpass★★

Alt 2 478m/8 130ft, you have just climbed more than 1 300m/4 265ft since Airolo. This pass offers an amazing landscape of incredible desolation. Higher up *(to the left of the restaurant)* the **view**★★ encompasses the glacier and Gries Reservoir , extending to the Upper Valais Range, the Bernese Oberland (Finsteraarhorn summit) and in the foreground the black, vertically grooved face of the Faulhorn. The downhill road on the Valais side, after a close-up view of the greyish-coloured Gries Glacier and its meltwater lake, plunges dizzily into a mineral landscape, brightened only by patches of very short grass and thistles. The glacier and the Faulhorn can still be seen.

Some 5km/3mi after the pass the view takes in the Upper Rhône Valley. The road then follows the diminished course of the River Agene, which has become the overflow of the Gries Dam and is hardly visible in its rocky bed, at the foot of the precipitous rock face of the Blashorn, on the right. The valley becomes more welcoming and is blanketed with larch as you approach the "Walser" village of **Ulrichen**, huddled around its church.

NYON

VAUD – POPULATION 15 666
ALT 410M/1 345FT

A pleasant town above Lake Geneva, Nyon was founded by Caesar under the name Colonia Julia Equestris (succeeding the Helvetian burg of Noviodunum). In the 16C Nyon was occupied by the Bernese. Examples of their style of architecture can be seen in the castle and the arcaded houses on Place du Marché. 🛈 *7 avenue Viollier – 1260 – ☎ (022) 361 62 61.*

Old Town

Walk around the Town Walls★
The walk skirts the ivy-covered walls (19C) and widens onto the Esplanade des Marronniers from where there is a pretty view of the town, the Little Lake as far as Geneva, the Salève and Mont Blanc. Roman columns add a romantic touch to the scene.

Castle
Heavily altered in the 16C, the feudal castle has five different towers, all crowned with pepper-pot roofs. From the terrace there is a nice **view** of the Rive quarter and the Little Lake *(viewing table)*.

Musée Romain
&🕐 *Open Apr-Oct, 10am-5pm; Nov-Mar, 2-5pm.* 🕐 *Closed Mon (except in Jul and Aug), 1 Jan and 25 Dec.* 👁 *6CHF (ticket gives admission to the other museums in Nyon).* ☎ *(022) 361 75 91, www.mrn.ch.*
This underground museum is marked above ground by a statue of Caesar. On the façade of the neighbouring house there is a drawing of how the Forum must have looked during the Roman era. The excavated part of this vast 1C public building (more than a third of its foundations) is the centrepiece of the museum. Around it are artifacts excavated from digs at Nyon and its environs: fragments of mosaics with simple geometric patterns or foliage motifs (including the famous Artemis mural), stone debris (capitals, military milestones), domestic objects (lamps, ceramics, crockery, coins) and a host of **amphorae** of different origins.

Quartier de Rive
A park and quays with attractive flower beds border the small sheltered yachting harbour and provide views of Lake Geneva and France on the far side. Farther along

---

Paléo Festival

For more than 20 years, Nyon has hosted a lively international music festival .Concerts are held in a large meadow near the shores of Lake Geneva, where several stages are set up for performances. All styles of music are represented: rock, jazz, blues, reggae, salsa, rap, country, techno, rai. and even classical music. Performers have included Johnny Clegg, Joe Cocker, Eddy Mitchell, Noa, Al Jarreau, Placebo, Patricia Kaas, Mc Solaar and Alan Stivell. The event attracts large crowds of locals and visitors from abroad and the atmosphere is noisy and convivial. The Prix de la Scène is a prize awarded to a young singer or group from Switzerland by an international panel made up of professional performers. During the Paléo Festival, the town of Nyon becomes a living stage, with improvised shows taking place in the streets: theatre, dance, mime, circus and magic.

on Quai des Alpes stands the 11C Tour César (Caesar's Tower). Note, high up, the Roman masque of the god Attis, consort of the Great Mother of the gods (Cybele).

Musée du Léman

 Same opening times as the Musée Romain. 6CHF (ticket gives admission to the other museums). ☎ (022) 361 09 49.

The museum is housed in an 18C hospital overlooking the harbour. The origins of Switzerland's largest lake and its flora and fauna (aquariums are home to several species of fish) are the themes of the first exhibition. The next section illustrates the various activities associated with the lake: fishing (boats, nets and tools), forestry and timber-working (barges used to transport the logs prior to the advent of the railway) as well as the history of shipping (from the early lateen-sail fishing boats, so typical of the lake, to machinery from the steamer *Helvétie II*). The first floor is dedicated to artists, both Swiss and non-Swiss, who have been drawn to Lake Geneva in the past; an area devoted to the Swiss General Naivigation Company contains a collection of models, including one of the first steamboats ever used on the lake (1823).

Excursions

Château de Prangins★★

2km/1mi NE by the road to Lausanne. Open daily except Mon, 11am-5pm. Open Whit Mon and Jeûne Fédéral public hol. Closed 1 and 2 Jan and 25 Dec. 7CHF. ☎ (022) 994 88 90.

In a landscaped garden dominating Lake Geneva, the Château de Prangins, which successively fulfilled the role of seigneurial manor, prince's residence, school and private house, currently houses a branch of the **Swiss National Museum** of Zurich. It presents the history of 18C and 19C Switzerland, focusing on its political, economic and cultural background.

Ceremonial rooms on the **ground floor** explore the theme of *The Dream of the Enlightenment*. Note the beautiful music box in the shape of a bird's cage in the living room. In Room 07 farther along, the optical instrument in the shape of a house (1781), known as "the television of the Ancien Régime", was an object of entertainment.

The **first floor** is dedicated to the period from the Revolution to the Federal State (1750-1920), a period of great upheaval. Note the **hat of liberty**, which symbolised the Swiss Republic in 1798 and took the form of William Tell's hat in the 17C. Switzerland became an urban society in the 19C; middle-class life in this period is depicted by the reconstruction of a living room (1850) and the development of transport portrayed through a collection of old bicycles and motorcycles, including several dandy-horses for children. An unusual circular shower is one of the exhibits devoted to health and hygiene. In the first-floor corridor, a striking painting by the pastor Jean-Élie Dautan entitled *Famous Swiss* appeals for unity and tolerance. Note also the small carriage known as a *char de côté*, very popular at the time, where passengers sat on the side of the carriage.

On the **top floor**, Switzerland's immigration, emigration, import and export, is explored, as is development of the country's tourist industry. The reconstruction of a storehouse for colonial foodstuffs near Seewen station (1883) is particularly worthy of note. The **cellars** are devoted to the history of the château, wine and cereals, energy, heating and light. Note the hail-cannon, much in vogue around 1900; blank shots were fired to disperse hail. The **vegetable garden** laid out in an old moat was planted in accordance with designs of the period; fruit and vegetables are grown here as they would have been in the 18C. From the garden, there are splendid views of Mont Dôle, with the Jura Mountains in the distance.

Crans

6km/4mi S of Nyon by the road to Geneva.

The château, which boasts good lines and proportions, is a fine example of the Louis XV period. The small church nearby offers a nice view of the vineyards, the lake and, in the far distance, the French mountain range.

Gingins

7km/4.5mi by the road to St-Cergue. Inaugurated at the heart of the village in 1994, the **Fondation Neumann** (🕐 *Open daily except Mon, 2pm-5pm; Sat-Sun, 10.30am-5pm.* 💰*8CHF.* ☎ *(022) 369 36 53)* presents a fine collection of Art Nouveau glasswork: around 150 pieces signed by some of the leading names from the turn of the last century (including Argy-Rousseau, Daum, Gallé, Tiffany and the Swiss native Eugène Grasset). Three times a year, temporary exhibitions are held on the subject of applied arts.

Abbaye de Bonmont

10km/6mi W by the road to Divonne. Then take the narrow road on the right. 🕐 *Open Jul-Aug, daily, 1-5pm; Sep-Oct, Mon, Sat-Sun, 1-5pm.* 🕐 *Closed most public hols and during concerts and other events.* 💰*5CHF.* ☎ *(022) 369 23 68.*

At the foot of the Vaud Jura, a few buildings remain from the former Bonmont Abbey, which became Cistercian during its construction (1131). Over the centuries, it was used as a cheese dairy and even as a garage, and consequently has not suffered too much damage. Built in the same Burgundian style as the Abbaye de Clairvaux – designed as a Latin cross, with a tripartite nave and a flat east end flanked by oblong chapels – and recently restored, the austere church nonetheless has elegant lines and boasts a fine porch enhanced by capitals with floral motifs.

OLTEN

SOLOTHURN – POPULATION 16 497

ALT 399M/1 309FT – TOWN PLAN IN THE MICHELIN GUIDE SWITZERLAND

Olten is pleasantly situated at the boundary of the Jura, on the banks of the River Aare. A wooden covered bridge (Alte Brücke), reserved for pedestrians, leads to the old town. Since the beginning of the last century the appearance of the town, which continues to spread on both sides of the Aare, has been altered by its great industrial activity: soap and cement works, food processing and the workshops of the Federal Railways. 🄸 *Klosterplatz 21 – 4600 –* ☎ *(062) 212 30 88.*

Sights

Kunstmuseum

🕐 *Open daily except Mon, 2-5pm; Sat-Sun, 11am-5pm.* 🕐 *Closed most public hols and during the summer holidays.* 💰*7CHF.* ☎ *(062) 212 86 76.*

The Fine Arts Museum possesses a fine collection of 19C and 20C paintings and sculpture, including excellent caricatures, studies and drawings by **Martin Disteli** (1802-44). This talented painter and caricaturist interpreted scenes from Swiss military history and political life, as well as fables.

Historisches Museum

🕐 *Open daily except Mon, 2-5pm; Sun, 10am-5pm.* 🕐 *Closed 1 Jan, Good Fri, Easter, Whitsun, 25 Dec.* 💰*5F* ☎ *(062) 212 89 89.*

The History Museum contains various collections relating to local art and customs, furniture and regional costumes, and also a remarkable prehistory section.

Excursions

Säli-Schlössli Panorama★

5km/3mi SE. Leave by Aarburgerstrasse and take Sälistrasse on the left. Access through the château-restaurant. ⓒ Closed Mon and Sun evening, 24 and 25 Dec and from Jan to mid-Feb. ☎ (062) 295 46 35.

The road soon starts climbing, in hairpin bends, the wooded hillside to reach the ruins of the feudal stronghold of Wartburg. From the top of the crenellated **tower** of the small neo-Gothic castle, standing amid the ruins, there is a **panorama**★ of Olten and Aarburg below, and the Aare Valley away to a horizon of green hills.

Zofingen

9km/5.5mi. Leave Olten by Aarburgerstrasse.

The old part of the town is contained within the quadrilateral formed by the alleys which have taken the place of its ramparts. The Pulvertum, a square 12C tower, is all that remains of the old fortifications. The Thut-Platz (town square) has and numerous 17C and 18C houses. The Church of St Maurice (altered), has a 17C Renaissance bell tower. To large mosaics from the Roman period *(under shelter)* can be seen as you leave the town from the south.

ORBE

VAUD – POPULATION 4 709
ALT 483M/1 585FT

Orbe, (derived from its Latin name *Urba***), terraced on a hill surrounded by the curve of the Orbe River, is a small attractive town with old-world atmosphere.**

From Place du Marché, and its fountain decorated with a banneret (1753), take the alleyway to the 15C and 16C Reformed Church (interior: side aisles with unusual keystones) and then to the terrace of the old castle from where there is a good view of Orbe and its valley. From the end of the flower-decked rue des Moulinets, a picturesque scene can be appreciated of the Roman bridge and the covered bridge.

Mosaïques d'Urba

2km/1m N of Orbe on the road to Yverdon. ⓒ Open Apr-Oct, 9am-noon and 1.30-5pm, Sat-Sun and public hols 1.30-5.30pm. ⓒ Closed 1 Nov and Easter. ⌨ 4CHF. ☎ (024) 441 13 81.

Alongside the road, four separate pavilions house Roman mosaics dating back to the early 3C. Starting from the farm nearby, the themes are: calendar of Divinities, the loveliest, consisting of polychrome medallions; pastoral scene with chariots, the most evocative; maze with lion and birds; geometric mosaic in black and white.

ORON-LE-CHÂTEL

VAUD – POPULATION 202
ALT 720M/2 362FT

This little village situated in the Haute-Braye on the left bank of the Flon, a tributary of the Broye, is dominated by the imposing mass of its fortified castle.

Castle

Guided tours (45min) Apr-Sep, Sat-Sun, 10am-noon and 2-6pm. ⊜8CHF. ☎ (021) 907 90 51.

This solid construction on a rocky promontory was built in the late 12C and early 13C. Despite many alterations, it still conveys the image of a stern, forbidding citadel. Several families have occupied the premises; an impressive display of their coats of arms is in the main hall. For 241 years the castle was the official residence of the Bernese bailiffs. The rooms on the first floor give one a good idea of how French middle-class families lived in those days. The dining hall houses some superb collections of Sèvres and Limoges porcelain, as well as pieces of Wedgwood. The library (beautiful 15C coffered ceiling) is believed to contain around 18 000 books dating from the 16C to the 19C. The visit ends with a series of tastefully decorated rooms: music room (the piano is thought to have belonged to Mozart), smoking salon decorated with wallpaper printed with hunting scenes, playroom and study for the children, tea parlour (Louis XV commode in rosewood), prior's bedroom etc.

PASSWANGSTRASSE★

PASSWANG ROAD

The harsh Lüssel Valley, along with the welcoming Birse Valley, make up the major part of this itinerary which winds between the River Aare and River Rhine.

From Oensingen to Basel *73km/45mi – about 2hr 15min*

Itinerary 6 (see Le JURA SUISSE map)

Between Oensingen and Balsthal, the road follows the bottom of the Klus or transverse valley, cutting at right-angles across the small Weissenstein Range. The Von Roll foundries pour their smoke into the corridor, keeping up the metalworking tradition of the Jura. In the valley lies **Burg Alt-Falkenstein**, unfortunately overly-restored.

Between Balsthal and the Passwang Pass, the road makes an angle at the foot of the proud ruins of the Burg of **Neu-Falkenstein**, dominated by a round tower, and enters the agricultural **Guldental** through a new – but very short – rock tunnel. The last bends in the road before the Passwang Tunnel give bird's-eye views of this secluded valley, as the Bernese Alps loom in the distance. The excursion from the Passwang Pass to the Passwang summit is recommended.

Passwanggipfel★★

Alt 1 204m/3 950ft. From the north exit of the Passwang Tunnel, 2km/1m along a narrow road with sharp gradients (close the gates behind you), plus 45min on foot there and back.

Leaving the car at the Wirtschaft Ober-Passwang café-restaurant, continue the climb on foot. On coming out of a wood, after passing through a gate, leave the road and climb, to the right, to the summit. From this point a varied **panorama**★★ extends, to the north, over the last undulations of the Basel Jura, the Plain of Alsace (note the double ribbon of the Rhine and the Kembs Canal, part of the great Alsace Canal) framed between the Vosges and the Black Forest, and to the south, to the Solothurn Jura and part of the Bernese Alps.

Between the pass and Laufen, the lonely Lüssel Valley shrinks to a narrow wooded cleft. Between Erschwill and Büsserach, the ruins of Thierstein, a massive tower flanked by a turret, stand like a sentinel. You come out in the Laufen Basin where the tilled, undulating floor lies spread before the forest ridges of the Blauen.

Between **Laufen**, a little town with fortified gates, and Aesch, the **Birstal** continues green in spite of increasing industrialisation. The keep of the Angenstein Burg, a former residence of the bishops of Basel, seems to block the last defile.

At Grellingen take the road to the east.

Seewen

On the outskirts of this charming village, huddled in a wooded basin at the foot of its white church, stands the **Musikautomaten-Museum** (*Guided tours (1hr) daily except Mon, 11am-6pm. Closed 1 Jan, Good Fri and 25 Dec. 10CHF. (061) 915 98 80*). Its galleries house a total of 800 musical mechanisms dating from the 18C to the early 20C and all in perfect working order: mechanical pianos, barrel organs, street organs, music boxes, orchestrions (imitating orchestra instruments) and especially amusing automata designed to resemble a bird, a painter, a magician.

Dornach

Built on the slopes overlooking the town and Arlesheim, the **Goetheanum** (*Unaccompanied tours 8am-10pm. Guided tours daily 2pm. 12CHF. (061) 706 42 69; www.goetheanum.ch*) cuts a striking silhouette and often surprises visitors by its sheer size and curious architecture. This gigantic concrete cathedral, in which right-angles are banished, houses the international headquarters of the Universal Anthroposophical Society and those of a Free University of Spiritual Science in which, among other activities, stages performances of classic and modern drama; including the whole of Goethe's *Faust* and the four mystery-dramas by Rudolf Steiner. The building and its annexes are designed to the very last detail in accordance with the principles of anthroposophy, whose founder **Rudolf Steiner** (1861-1925) was strongly influenced by Goethe, using the metamorphosis as a basis for his own work.

Arlesheim

The **collegiate church**★ of Arlesheim is one of the most charming examples of Baroque art in Switzerland. Built in 1680 for the episcopal principality of Basel, it was later transformed in the Rococo style (1769-71). It stands in a quiet, shaded little square bordered by the former canons' houses. The church interior, whose harmony is untarnished by any detail, is adorned with stucco discreetly picked out in pink or pale yellow, while the low vaulting bears large, misty compositions in pale colours by Joseph Appiani (1760). The road now enters the outer suburbs of Basel.

Basle★★★ – *3hr.* See BASEL.

PAYERNE★

VAUD – POPULATION 7 243
ALT 450M/1 476FT

Payerne is situated in the rich Broye Valley and boasts a remarkable abbey church, once attached to a Benedictine abbey. This abbey is believed to have been founded in the 10C by Empress Adelaide, wife of Otto the Great, first of the Holy Roman Emperors and daughter of the legendary Queen Bertha, nicknamed Bertha the Spinner, the widow of Rudolph II, King of Trans-Jura Burgundy.  *1 place Général Guisan – 1530 – (026) 660 61 61.*

Abbey Church★★

🕐 *Open daily except Mon, 10am-noon and 2-6pm (5pm Nov-Apr).* 🕐 *Closed Good Fri.* 3CHF. ☎ *(026) 662 67 04.*

The 11C church is virtually all that remains of this once large Cluniac abbey. The church fell into disuse when the Bernese introduced the Reformation into the Vaud district. It was converted into a storehouse and barracks and suffered considerable damage. Large-scale renovation has restored this Romanesque church to its former glory.

Interior – The plain nave is lit by tall windows and crowned with barrel vaulting; harmony of proportion conveys an impression of grandeur but also of severity, emphasised by sparse decoration. Remarkable capitals adorn tall windows of the chancel and transept pillars. Their crude but expressive design dates them back to the abbey's founding. Beautiful 13C frescoes can be seen in the choir, transept and narthex, including Christ at the Last Judgement, with the 24 Elders of the Apocalypse seated before him. Adjoining the church, the elegant **chapterhouse** with groined vaulting houses an exhibition on the history of the church. Note the two original bronze knockers (10C).

Museum – The museum is reached through the right arm of the transept. Permanent collections are devoted to two famous natives of the area. **Aimée Rapin** (1868-1956) was an artist born without arms who painted with her toes. Her work was presented at the Paris World Fair in 1888, when she gained widespread recognition. Her wide-ranging talent is clearly expressed in her still life works *(Fruit, The Hunt)*, portraits *(Young Girl at the Lake, Man with Pipe),* and drawings in charcoal and crayon *(Portrait of Monsieur Pierre Libaud, Woman Sitting)*. General **Antoine-Henri Jomini** (1779-1869) served under Napoleon I, becoming aide-de-camp to Marshall Ney and subsequently his Chief of Staff. After a misunderstanding with the marshall, Jomini left the French army and served under the Tsar of Russia, Alexander II. He died in Passy, near Paris, in 1869.

GORGES DU PICHOUX★

From Lake Biel to the Ajoie region (area around Porrentruy), deep gorges, pastures, fir or deciduous forests follow the road which, in the Sorne Valley, runs between the Franches Montagnes and the Delémont region.

From Biel to Porrentruy *61km/38mi – about 2hr 30min*

Itinerary 5 *(see Le JURA SUISSE map)*

Biel/Bienne★ – *1hr. See BIEL/BIENNE.*

From Biel to Sonceboz the road climbs quickly above the suburbs of Biel and halfway up the slope threads its way through the Taubenloch Gorges (Taubenlochschlucht – *lovers of deep defiles should visit these gorges preferably on foot, walking along the floor by the route described under BIEL/BIENNE: Excursions)*. The road goes up the industrialised Suze Valley *(large cement works at Reuchenette)*, narrowed by rock tunnels marking the successive ridges of the Jura.

Pierre-Pertuis

Between Sonceboz and Tavannes, the section resembles a small Alpine pass. This corridor, used since the beginning of the 3C by the Roman road from Aventicum (Avenches) to Augusta Raurica (Augst), takes its name from the l arch under which the former road passed on the Tavannes slope. The **site** is well-known throughout the region. A clearing with benches at the pass is a good place to stop.

Tavannes

The name of this prosperous, hard-working little town, situated in the Upper Birse Valley, at the foot of the rock of Pierre-Pertuis, is known for its clockmaking industry. The modern Roman Catholic church was decorated by artists of the Société St-Luc, a school of sacred art well known in Romansh Switzerland. The mosaic on the façade, representing the Ascension, is the work of Gino Severini. The countryside becomes High Jurassian and in some places the road forms an avenue bordered by fir trees.

Abbaye de Bellelay

🕐 *Open early Jan to mid-Jun and Sep-Dec, 8am-6pm; otherwise, 10am-noon and 2-6pm.* 🕐 *Closed for a week in Jun.* ⊜*5CHF.* ☎ *(032) 484 72 37.*

The **abbey church**, built in 1710 to 1714, features an imposing array of Baroque architecture in the interior, which art lovers may compare to that of Sankt Urban and Rheinau. The **interior**★ is remarkably impressive, although it lacks furnishings. The Fathers of Bellelay are believed to hold the secret of making Tête-de-Moine, or **Monk's Head**, a semi-hard cheese which cuts into appetising flakes.

After winding through wooded pastureland where the bay horses of the Franches Montagnes roam free, the road glides into the depths of the gorges cut by the Sorne.

Gorges du Pichoux★

This cutting, in which the road shares the bed of the stream, is the deepest of the *cluses,* or transverse valleys, hollowed out by the Sorne between Le Pichoux and Berlincourt. The gorges have limestone cliffs to which cling forests of fir trees.

The **climb**★ from Boécourt to the Les Rangiers Pass at first crosses the flank of an open slope planted with birch and gnarled oaks. Here you can appreciate the spaciousness of the Delémont Valley which is gracefully curved and dotted with prosperous small industrial towns. The Doubs slope is reached when the road joins the itinerary called the Jura Corniche.

Porrentruy★

👉 *The rest of the itinerary is described under WEISSENSTEINSTRASSE, in the opposite direction, starting from Porrentruy.*

PILATUS

UNTERWALDEN

The proud rock pyramid of Mount Pilatus (highest point: 2 129m/6 985ft at the Tomlishorn), a major attraction of the Swiss Alps, dominates the western basins of Lake Lucerne with its sharply defined ridges. The aerial cablecar, along a steep cliff to the top, is a marvel of modern engineering, and the view from the summit is astounding. Pilatus is both a useful landmark for the visitor to central Switzerland and a long time source of superstitious dread, as legend declared that the spirit of Pontius Pilate haunted a small lake near the summit and that anyone who approached that accursed spot would cause fearful storms.

Climb to Pilatus

From Alpnachstad, about 2hr there and back, including 1hr by rack railway (Does not operate from Nov to Apr. ☜ Fare there and back: 58CHF). Pilatus-Kulm can also be reached by cable car from Kriens, in the suburbs of Lucerne, making a round trip possible (♿ see LUZERN: Excursions).

The red cog railway, with an average gradient of 42° and maximum of 48°, is the steepest in the world for this form of traction, particularly impressive where it crosses the slopes of the Esel.

Pilatus-Kulm★★★

From the upper station, which has two mountain hotels *(Pilatus-Kulm and Bellevue)*, you will climb in a few minutes to the Esel summit (alt 2 121m/6 959ft), from where the eye follows the winding waters of Lake Lucerne, narrowed in the centre by the promontories of the Rigi and the Bürgenstock, the city of Lucerne and a command of the Swiss lowlands as far as the Black Forest and the Vosges. A walk through the gallery with openings hollowed out of the rock of the Oberhaupt is also recommended. There are hiking paths for all skill levels; if you want to climb on foot, the easiest route is from Hergiswil *(allow 5hrs)*.

We recommend visiting to Pilatus via the **Golden Round Trip:** Lucerne-Alpnachstad by lake steamer up to Pilatus-Kulm and return via Kriens-Lucerne offers the greatest variety of scenery and types of transport.

Philipp Giegel / Switzerland Tourism

Pilatus cog railway

PONTRESINA✶✶

GRAUBÜNDEN – POPULATION 1 858
ALT 1 777M/5 863FT

Pontresina is in the highest region of the Upper Engadine, at the mouth of the Bernina Valley within view of the Roseg corrie and the snowy ridges of the Piz Palü, in the heart of the Engadin still tied to Romansch traditions. Pushing up the Roseg or the Morteratsch valleys, mountaineers set out from here for magnificent glacier climbs in the Bernina Massif, especially the famous Diavolezza tour. Walkers can continue along the woodland paths of the forest of Tais (Taiswald) or climb, via a corniche from Muottas Muragl *(7km/4mi)*, the last foothills of the Piz Languard. *Kongresszentrum Rondo – 7504 – ☎ (081) 838 83 00.*

Old Town

The names of the streets and houses, some dating to the 16C, are in Romansch, which is still spoken here; the façades of many of the buildings are painted with intricate, ancient designs. There also are modern, well-appointed hotels which are more affordable than in Sankt Moritz 4km/2.5mi away. The little Romanesque chapel of Santa Maria near the 12C Spaniola Tower contains a series of mural paintings, many executedin the 15C. The series devoted to the story of Mary Magdalene will interest tourists familiar with the Golden Legend and the great Provençal traditions.

The Skiing Area

The winter season at Pontresina lasts until April. It offers long-distance excursions for skiers and sunny ski runs served by the ski lifts of Alp Languard and the Muottas Muragl funicular. The resort is also popular for **cross-country skiing**. The famous Engadine marathon, which covers a distance of 40km/25mi, is held here every year *(for further information, contact Engadin Skimarathon, CH 7504 Pontresina).*

Muottas Muragl★★

3km/2mi by the road to Samedan as far as Punt Muragl, plus about 1hr there and back, including 30min by funicular. Access from Punt Muragl and description under MUOTTAS MURAGL.

PORRENTRUY★

JURA – POPULATION 6 718
ALT 445M/1 460FT

Porrentruy, a peaceful, welcoming town in the centre of the Ajoie region, was founded 1283 by the prince-bishops of Basel. In the 16C, the city expanded and became the official residence of the rulers of the former Basel bishopric, the princes of the German-speaking Holy Roman Empire. On annexing this little district with its typical Franche-Comté character to French territory, the Revolution made Porrentruy the capital of the Mont-Terrible *département*, which included the present Jura canton and Bernese Jura as far as Biel. *5 Grand-Rue – 2900 – ☎ (032) 466 59 59.*

Old Town

The **Porte de France**, one of the few vestiges of the original ramparts, marks the entrance to the old town. Rue Pierre-Péquignat and Grand-Rue stand out thanks to three elegant 18C buildings designed by the Besançon architect Pierre-François Paris: the **Hôtel des Halles**, the former covered market; the **Hôtel de Ville** (the original stone Samaritan Fountain stands at the entrance); and the **Hôtel-Dieu**, the former hospital, which boasts a fine wrought-iron gate closing off the inner courtyard.
The town centre features many wealthy residential mansions with inner courtyards and turrets worthy of note (Grand-Rue 22) and three imposing and magnificent 16C fountains, are the work of Laurent Perroud: the Banneret Fountain, known as the Swiss Fountain (rue des Malvoisins), the Samaritan Fountain (Grand-Rue, in front of a corner house with oriel windows) and the Gilded Sphere Fountain (rue des Annonciades). The Église St-Pierre, crowned by a Comtois dome, presents a fine stained-glass window illuminating the chancel, executed by the local craftsman Jean-François Comment.

Near the pleasant botanical garden which flanks the former bishop's palace (presently a municipal college) stands the imposing Pendule de Foucauld, a clock devised by the French physicist Léon Foucault (1819-68), whose invention demonstrated the revolving movement of the earth.

Musée de l'Hôtel-Dieu

 ♿ ⏰ *Open April to mid-Nov, daily except Mon, 2-5pm.* ⏰ *Closed 1 Nov and mid-Nov to 30 Apr.* ➖*5CHF.* ☎ *(032) 466 72 72; museehoteldieu.ch).* This museum is devoted to local history features two magnificent exhibits. The first is the hospital's **pharmacy**, a fine example of 19C cabinet-making attributed to Jean-Baptiste Carraz, which skilfully combines several types of wood and presents an interesting display of pots and phials made of glass and porcelain. The second is the treasury of St Peter's Church, which contains precious objects, some dating back to the Gothic period: a 1487 crucifix used in processions, a large monstrance known as Ostensoir de Morat (1488) and a small monstrance (1493).

Château

Perched on a rocky spur, the castle's imposing silhouette rises above the Allaine Valley. Only the Tour Réfous (45m/148ft, pretty views from the top) remains of this medieval stronghold, a round tower standing near a group of buildings now housing administrative offices such as the Cantonal Law Courts. One corridor inside the Law Courts displays portraits representing prince-bishops (1575-1737) including Jacques-Christophe Blarer from Wartensee, a charismatic figure whose strong personality was to mark the history of the town. His coat of arms, a cockerel, joined with the heraldic symbol of the bishops of Basel, a crozier, features on the Tour du Coq, a tower adjoining the east façade of the castle.

Excursion

Grottes de Réclère

15km/9.5mi by the road to Besançon. 🚶 *Guided tour of the caves (1hr) Apr-Nov, 10am-noon and 1-5pm (9am-6pm Jul-Aug).* ⏰ *Closed Dec-Mar.* ➖ *9CHF (14CHF caves and park).*
These caves, located 100m/328ft underground, were discovered in 1886. Admire the fine array of stalactites and stalagmites; the latter feature "the great dome", said to be the largest in the country (13m/43ft high for 250 000 years of age). The tour may be combined with that of **Préhisto-Parc** (♿ ⏰ *Opening times same as above.* ⏰ *Closed Dec to mid-Apr.* ➖*8CHF (14CHF caves and park)* ☎ *(032) 467 61 55)*, an area of the forest filled with life-size replicas of prehistoric creatures.

BAD RAGAZ★

SANKT GALLEN – POPULATION 4 574
ALT 502M/1 647FT

Bad Ragaz, located in one of the Alpine Rhine Valley's fine settings and facing the rugged crests of the Falknis, is a leading Swiss spa. Since the 11C the resort has been known for its mineral waters, which rise at a temperature of 37°C/98°F in the Tamina Gorges below the village of Pfäfers. It is particularly recommended for circulatory troubles, rheumatism, paralysis and the after-effects of accidents. Bad Ragaz has been a midwinter ski resort since a cable car and ski lifts linked the town with the great snowfields in the Pizol district.

Excursion

Taminaschlucht★★
2hr there and back on foot by the road branching off the road to Valens on the left, SW of Bad Ragaz. 🕐 *Open May-Oct, 10am-5.30pm (5pm in May and Oct).* 🎫 *4CHF.* ☎ *(081) 302 71 61.*
These gorges are truly breathtaking. To take the waters, before they were piped, patients were lowered down on ropes to the bottom of this tremendous fissure.

RAPPERSWIL★

SANKT GALLEN – POPULATION 7 198
ALT 409M/1 342FT

The little town of Rapperswil occupies a pretty site on a short peninsula on the north shore of Lake Zurich. The upper town has kept its medieval appearance, emphasized by the imposing mass of its castle. Rapperswil is a pleasant place to stay in summer, with plenty of walks and drives around the lake and in the neighbourhood. 🏛 *Fischermarktplatz 1 – 8640 –* ☎ *(055) 220 57 57.*

Sights

Castle
A massive structure flanked by three grim-looking towers, it was built by the counts of the district in the 13C. From the outer terrace there is a fine **view** of the town below, Lake Zurich and, beyond it, the Glarus Alps and Sankt Gallen. On the opposite side, above the former ramparts and overlooking the lake, a deer park has been laid out.

Heimatmuseum
🕐 *Open Apr-Oct, Sat 2-5pm, Sun 10am-noon and 2-5pm .* 🎫 *3CHF.* ☎ *(055) 210 71 64.*
This local museum, in a 15C house, contains many relics from the Roman era and collections of weapons and works of art displayed in rooms with painted ceilings and fine period furniture.

Knie - the Swiss National Circus

In 1803 Friedrich Knie, son of Empress Maria-Theresa's personal physician, was studying medicine at Innsbruck when a chance encounter with a horsewoman from a troupe of travelling artistes changed his life. He joined them, becoming an acrobat. Later, he founded his own troupe and performed throughout Germany, Austria, Switzerland and France, gaining fame as a tightrope walker. His children and grandchildren kept up the tradition.

The Knie family became Swiss citizens in 1900; in 1919 Friedrich's cherished dream came true when the Knie Circus was founded. Today the Knies are one of the great circus families; their one-ring circus remains a family affair with the sixth generation now active. It is Switzerland's national circus, although it remains financially independent. The circus and its itinerant zoo tour March to November, giving 375 shows under the big top to capacity audiences of 3 000 in some 60 towns. Their winter quarters are in Rapperswil.

www.knie.ch

Kinderzoo

Behind the railway station. Access by Schönbodenstrasse then right on Obersee Strasse. Kids ᵔ ⏲ *Open mid-Mar to 31 Oct, daily 9am-6pm (7pm Sun and public hols).* ᴗ*10CHF.* ☎ *(055) 220 67 60, www.knieskinderzoo.ch.*
Belonging to the Knie National Circus, the zoo presents different attractions (Noah's Ark, whale aquarium and a train) as well as a limited selection of animals (zebras, camels, rhinoceroses, monkeys, parakeets) and performing dolphins.

Excursions

From Rapperswil to Pfäffikon

22km/13.5mi N. Leave Rapperswil on the road to Zurich, then bear right on the road to Winterthur; at Rüti bear left towards the motorway. After going underneath it, bear right; 300m/985ft before Bubikon turn right onto the path signposted Ritterhaus.

Ritterhaus

⏲ *Open Apr-Oct, Tue-Thur, 1-5pm, Fri 1-8pm; Sat-Sun and public hols, 10am-5pm.* ⏲ *Closed Good Fri, Easter Sun and Whit Sun.* ᴗ *8CHF.* ☎ *(055) 243 39 74.*
Founded in 1192 and rebuilt in the 15C and 16C, the Bubikon Commandery of the Order of the Hospital of St John of Jerusalem, whose outbuildings have been converted into a farm, is now used as a museum. It recounts the history of the Hospitaller Order with the aid of documents, arms, paintings. Also e visit the chapel, 16C kitchen, library and large common rooms with their *trompe-l'œil* ceilings and panelling, fireplaces, and Gothic-Renaissance furnishings.

▸ *Return to the Winterthur road.*

After skirting the Pfäffikersee, you arrive at the entrance to Pfäffikon. On the left is the tumulus of the Roman camp of Irgenhausen.

Römisches Kastell
Leave the car in the factory car park, level with the fortress, then 15min on foot there and back (pass underneath the railway line).

This small citadel (it held a maximum of 200 legionaries), set on a mound overlooking both the lake and the town, was built 285-305, part of a line of forts placed strategically to sustain an attack by the Alamans. Although the fortress walls still stand, only foundations remain of the four defensive towers on the lakeside.

RHEIN

RHINE

The Rhine is Swiss for barely a quarter of its course, for it reaches Basel after 388km/242mi. Over this relatively short distance it falls from 2 200m to 250m/7 218ft to 820ft and has the appearance of a wild and fast-flowing river.

Geographical Notes

An Alpine River
The Rhine Basin is by far the largest river basin in Swiss territory. It extends to all the Swiss cantons except those of Geneva, Valais and Ticino. With its low water in winter and its spate in summer at the melting of the snows, the Rhine is a typical Alpine river. It rises in the Grisons; its two main arms, the Vorderrhein—principal headstream of the Rhine—and the Hinterrhein—lesser headstream of the Rhine—meet at Reichenau, above Chur, and provide the power for the large-scale hydroelectric works. The courses are followed respectively by the San Bernardino and the Oberalp roads.

The river is swollen at Chur by the Plessur and farther on by the Landquart and the Tamina. It follows the **Rheinthal** cleft, which resembles Alsace by its north-south orientation, its size and its varying vegetation (maize, vines etc). It then flows into **Lake Constance** which acts as a regulator for it, as Lake Geneva does for the Rhône.

An inland sea, the Bodensee – Lake Constance, or the Bodensee, as it is known locally, is 12km/8mi wide and at the most 64km/40mi long. Though a little smaller (54 000ha/33 400 acres) than Lake Geneva, it gives an impression of sea-like immensity. At Constance, the Rhine, now limpid, leaves the main basin for the Lower Lake (Untersee), from which it escapes at Stein am Rhein.

Crossing the Jura
Between Schaffhausen and Basel the character of the river changes. Hemmed in between the slopes of the Black Forest and the Jura foothills, it forces its way among slabs of hard rock. Below Schaffhausen, where the valley narrows, the flow becomes faster and the river plunges between the rocks, forming impressive falls (👈 see SCHAFF-HAUSEN). Farther on, other rocky slabs produce rapids (*Laufen*), whose presence

Rhine-Danube Canal

Ever since Roman times, emperors, kings, engineers and visionaries dreamed of linking the Rhine and Danube rivers. Charlemagne began the great enterprise, hence the name Charlemagne's Ditch (Fossa Carolina). Bavaria's Ludwig I made another attempt, building the Ludwig Canal. However, it took until 1992 -- 12 centuries after it was begun -- that the waterway linking Europe from the north Sea to the Black Sea became a reality. The 177km/110mi canal with its hundreds of locks takes the barges up and down the 245m/800ft climb. It is truly a marvel of modern engineering. Charlemagne and Ludwig would be proud.

accounts for place names like Laufen and Laufenburg. These breaks in level make navigation impossible, but have enabled hydroelectric power from power stations on the river banks, the most recent of which is the power-dam at Rheinau.

Confluence with the Aare – The Aare makes an important contribution to the Rhine. This is the largest all-Swiss river and its basin covers two-fifths of the area of Switzerland. It flows in succession through the Brienz and Thun lakes (Brienzersee and Thunersee), waters Bern and Solothurn and receives many tributaries, the most important being the Reuss and the Limmat. The rivers meet near Koblenz, upstream from Waldshut, where the Aare has covered a greater distance than the Rhine (280km/175mi against 274km/170mi). The scene is spectacular, for the Aare brings more water than the Rhine into which it flows. From then on the Rhine becomes a great river and carries international traffic below Basel. *An extremely interesting visit to the port ofBasel is described under BASEL.*

The Picturesque Rhine

Between Lake Constance and Basel, driving along the Rhine Valley is complicated by the meandering border of the canton of Schaffhausen. Therefore do not try to follow the course of the Rhine very closely in Swiss territory. It is better to choose a few characteristic observation points for excursions:

◆ the castle, **Burg Hohenklingen**, near Stein am Rhein;
◆ the **Munot terrace**, at Schaffhausen;
◆ the **Laufener Schloss**, at the Rhine Falls (*see SCHAFFHAUSEN*);
◆ at **Laufenburg** (Swiss shore), the terrace laid out below an old tower.

Steamer Services
Steamers based at Constance, Romanshorn, Arbon and Rorschach ply the main part of Lake Constance and Lake Überlingen (in German territory). Excursion steamers also sail between Schaffhausen and Kreuslingen on the Rhine and the Lower Lake (Untersee), offering incomparable glimpses of the romantic river banks, overlooked by ruined castles, and of charming little towns like Diessenhofen and Stein am Rhein.

RHEINAU ★

ZÜRICH – POPULATION 1 338
ALT 372M/1 220FT

This little town is prettily placed in a bend of the Rhine south of the famous Rhine Falls (*for access see SCHAFFHAUSEN*). It was the seat of a Benedictine abbey (now converted into a psychiatric hospital) on an island in the river. Its abbey church is an outstanding example of Baroque art. In 1956 a large hydroelectric power station and dam were completed across the Rhine downstream of Rheinau; its reservoir stretches for 6.5km/4mi up to the Rhine Falls.

Klosterkirche
 *Open Apr, May and Oct, Tue-Sat 2-4pm, Sun and public hols 1.30-5pm; Jun-Sep, Tue-Sat 10am-noon and 1-5pm, Sun and public hols 10.30am-noon and 1-6pm.* *Closed Nov-Mar.* 3CHF. *(052) 319 31 00.*
The abbey church, with a somewhat severe façade, was rebuilt, except for its 16C south tower, at the beginning of the 18C. The **interior**★ is striking for its rich deco-

ration in the purest Baroque tradition. The nave, whose vaulting is covered with frescoes, is flanked by four chapels adorned, like the high altar, with a profusion of marble and gilding. A balustrade runs under the clerestory. The chancel, enclosed by an elaborate grille, has beautiful stalls. The organ dates back to 1715. In a small room containing the treasure, to the left of the chancel, is some fine inlaid furniture.

RHEINFELDEN★

AARGAU – POPULATION 10 335

Rheinfelden stands on the south bank of the River Rhine, separated from its German namesake by the Rheinbrücke, an arched bridge made of stone. Founded in 1130 by the Zähringen, the town is thought to be the oldest in the Aargau. It was given to the Habsburgs in 1330 by Duke Ludwig I of Bavaria and remained in their possession until 1802. ☐ Am Zähringerplatz – 4310 – ☎ (061) 833 05 25

This small town is the last stopping-place for **cruises along the Rhine** and has an attractive old centre with narrow streets, as well as a shaded riverside park with thermal baths. For a good **view** of the town, cross the bridge to the German side of the river. The discovery of salt deposits in 1844 allowed the town to develop its renowned spa. The old **n° 6 drilling tower** of Riburg saltworks – now a museum – can be seen in the thermal park (follow signs to the Kurzentrum).

The Old Town

The main street is **Marktgasse**, which runs from near the customs post by the bridge. Attractive houses with painted façades and attractive signs line the street;

Brauerei Feldschlösschen – Brewing room

J-C Saturnin/ MICHELIN

starting from the tourist office, n°s 36, 16 and 10 are particularly interesting. Also noteworthy are the painted murals in the courtyard of the **town hall** (Rathaus), recognisable by its medieval tower.

The **Fricktaler Museum** (n° 12) (🕐 *Open May-Dec, Tue and Sat-Sun, 2-5pm.* 🕐 *Closed Whit Sun and the third Sun in Sep (Bettag).* ⌀ *No charge.* ☎ *(061) 831 14 50)* is dedicated to local history and to the Saint Sebastian Brotherhood. This strange organisation has 12 members, one of whom carries a lantern, and whose members dress in black and wear long coats and tall hats. On 24 and 31 December, the Brotherhood maintains the tradition of singing canticles in front of the town's fountains in memory of the epidemic of 1541 that killed a large percentage of the population.

The nearby **Albrechtsplatz** is adorned with the Banneret Fountain. Johannmittergasse, a little farther up on the left, leads to the St-Johann chapel, which once belonged to the Knights of Malta (frescoes). A small road to the left of the chapel leads to a terrace overlooking the Rhine.

Marktgasse leads into Kupfergasse, which runs up to the Storchennestturm and a section of the ramparts. Other streets and squares with attractive façades or fountains include Geissgasse, Obertorplatz, Kapuzinergasse and Bahnhofstrasse. The Gothic-style church on Kirchplatz, **St-Martinskirche**, was heavily restored at the end of the 18C, as shown by its Baroque interior.

Brauerei Feldschlösschen

🕙 *Guided tours (1hr 30min) Mon-Fri, 9.15am-noon and 1.45-5pm. First Sat of the month 9.30am-noon.* 🕐 *Closed public hols of the Aargau canton.* ⌀ *No charge.* ☎ *(061) 833 42 58.*

Switzerland's largest **brewery** is housed in an imposing red and yellow brick building adorned with towers and ramparts. Founded in 1876, it still delivers beer to its nearest customers by horse-drawn cart. Guided tours provide insight into the production of beer; the huge copper stills and Art Deco interior of the **brewing room** are definitely worth a visit. The tour finishes with a tasting of the brewery's six different beers.

RIGGISBERG

BERN – POPULATION 2 467

As you enter the town from the north (Bern road) bear right onto the road to the Abegg Foundation; the modern buildings of this prestigious cultural venue are located on the mountainside in a verdant and peaceful setting.

Visit

Abegg-Stiftung★★

♿ 🕐 *Open Apr-Nov, 2-5.30pm.* ⌀ *5CHF.* ☎ *(031) 808 12 01.*

The institute was founded in 1961 by **Werner Abegg** for conducting scientific research in applied arts, especially textiles, and their preservation. Collections include exhibits from Europe and the Middle East dating from Antiquity to the Renaissance. In addition to its vast library boasting around 160 000 titles, there are displays of Neolithic pottery, marble pieces from the Cyclades, Iranian ceramics and gold, bronzes from Luristan, Pharoic Egyptian pieces, ivory plaquettes from the pre-Achaemenid Era and Byzantine ceramics.

The tapestry gallery houses hangings depicting Dionysos (Egypt, 4C), the goddess Artemis (4C), scenes taken from Genesis and Exodus (5C) amd fragments of *Atalanta and Meleager,* an Egyptian tapestry (3C-4C), plus Romanesque art from Italy, France (Limoges enamels), and Spain. A treasured exhibit is the chasuble of St Vital, once the property of Stiftskirche St. Peter, the abbey church in Salzburg. Gothic art includes gemeled windows from north Italy, French caskets and silverware. A painting gallery presents *Adoration of the Magi* by Fra Angelico, a triptych attributed to Van der Weyden, *Saint Thomas Aquinas* by Botticelli, *San Leonardo* by Lorenzetti and a *Virgin with Child* executed by Multscher. Also, outstanding Renaissance velvet and silk fabric, Brussels tapestries, jewellery, glasswork, silverware and sumptuous Italian vases carved in gold and rock crystal.

LE RIGI★★★

Isolated on all sides by a depression largely covered by the waters of the Lucerne, Zug and Lauerz lakes, this "island mountain", to quote the term used by German geographers for this type of feature, rears its heavy wooded shoulders, scarred by reddish escarpments, to an altitude of 1 797m/5 896ft. It has been famous for a century for its highest point, the Rigi-Kulm, on the summit of which, according to tradition, you should spend the night to see the sun rise over the Alps.

Those who like easy walks through woods and Alpine pastures, or along mountain roads, which always offer interesting views, should stay in one of the hotels scattered high on the mountainside. One of the best-situated resorts is **Rigi-Kaltbad.**

A Great Spectacle

For generations of sensitive souls the sunrise seen from the **Rigi-Kulm** was the climax of a visit to Switzerland. The splendour of the spectacle drove away memories of the harsh preliminaries, and the shivering, sleepy crowd reached a state of collective exaltation when the first rays of the sun lit up, according to Victor Hugo, that "incredible horizon", that "chaos of absurd exaggerations and frightening diminutions".

Climb to Rigi-Kulm

From Arth-Goldau or Vitznau the climb by rack railway to the Rigi-Kulm takes 35min. Another way is to take the cable car from Weggis to Rigi-Kaltbad and change there to the rack railway for the Rigi-Kulm. From Arth-Goldau, Vitznau or Weggis: ⊷ Fare there and back: 58CHF. For exact timetable, call ☎ (041) 399 87 87.

Panorama★★★
Alt 1 797m/5 896ft. From the terminus station, near which there is a large hotel, 15min on foot there and back to the signpost and the cross standing on the summit.

🕭 *For coin ranges see Legend on cover flap.*

WHERE TO STAY IN LE RIGI

⊝⊜🛏**Bergsonne** – ☎ *041 399 80 10, www.bergsonne.ch – 17 rooms –* 🕐 *open mid-Dec to mid-Mar and May-Nov.* Its ideal location above the village provides breathtaking views of the Alps and the nearby lake. Rooms are decorated with local furniture.

⊝⊜🛏 **Edelweiss** – ☎ *041 399 88 00 – 27 rooms –* 🕐 *closed mid-Mar to mid-Apr.* A blissfully quiet establishment with views of lake and mountains. The older part features rooms appointed with rustic-style furniture.

Your eye may wander from end to end of the Alps' tremendous backcloth rising between Säntis and the Bernese Alps (Jungfrau), including the Glaris and Uri Alps and the Titlis Massif. The opposite half of the horizon is less dazzling but more attractive. On this side the rounded hills of the Zurich countryside stretch into the distance, beyond the Lauerz, Zug and Lucerne lakes, to merge with the line of the Jura, the Vosges and the Black Forest.

Walk from Rigi-Kaltbad to Hinterbergen★★★

A wonderful walk *(2hr to 2hr 30min)*, easy to negotiate and clearly signposted, the perfect complement to a climb up Rigi. Get off the train at Kaltbad station (alt 1 438m/4 718ft). Follow the path to First, flanked by explanatory panels about the geology of the area. The **view**★★ widens out over Vierwaldstätter See. The route continues towards Unterstetten, wending its way through spectacularly sheer cliffs. When you catch sight of the hotel, bear left and go up the lawn for 200m/220yd, then turn right in the direction of Gletti (a steep, short climb followed by a descent). From Gletti there is a sweeping **panorama**★★★ of the whole region. To end the tour, go down to Hinterbergen, either by the direct, steep route on the right, or by the gently sloping path on the left. At the heart of the village, look out for the white house with six small windows: it is the terminus of a cable car that will take you back to Vitznau in 6min.

ROMAINMÔTIER★

VAUD – POPULATION 392
ALT 676M/2 163FT

It is impossible not to succumb to the charm of this old village nestling around a plain but graceful Romanesque church belonging to the abbey founded in the 5C by St Romanus and handed over to the monks of Cluny in the 10C. The abbey controlled seven priories, 20 parish churches, 30 villages and 50 fiefs.

Church★

🕐 *Open daily 9am-noon, 1:30pm-6pm, Sun 1:30pm-5pm. Exhibition and slide show (30min) 9am-noon and 1.30-6pm.* 💲4CHF. ☎ *(024) 453 14 65.*

Replacing two chapels from the 5C and 7C, the church was built with fine, pale Jura stone in the 11C and later modified. Its design was directly inspired by he former abbey church of Cluny, St-Pierre-le-Vieux, which preceded the great building erected in the 12C; the plan, elevation and decoration based on Lombard bands and arcading are, therefore, typically Burgundian. The transept, dominated by a central tower, and nave date from the 11C. A large, early-12C narthex is preceded by a 13C Gothic porch. Inside are 13C murals; pointed arches (13C) have replaced the original timbering, but aisles still have their semicircular vaulting. The chancel (modified in the 14C and 15C) contains priors' tombs of the 7C. The church has been Protestant since 1536. A magnificent lime tree grows behind the east end of the church. To the right of the façade, stands the former prior's house (now a tea room) dated 1605 – but going back to the 13C – with a pepperpot-roofed turret and an embossed doorway.

ROMONT

FRIBOURG – POPULATION 3 826
ALT 760M/2 736FT

The little town of Romont was built by Peter II of Savoy in the 13C, still encircled by some of its ramparts. Its occupies a picturesque site★ on a crest overlooking the valleys of the Glâne and the Glâney. ▯ 112 rue du Château – 1680 – ☏ (026) 652 31 52.

Collégiale Notre-Dame-de-l'Assomption

◷ *Open Apr-Oct, 9am-7.30pm; Nov-Mar, 9am-6.30pm.* ⬅ *Guided tour, contact the tourist office for further information* ☏ *(026) 652 31 52.*

This collegiate church is one of the finest Gothic churches in Romansh country. The original building (13C) was largely destroyed in 1434. It was immediately rebuilt and displays two aspects of the Gothic style (13C and 15C). The 15C **chancel**★ is closed by a grille and adorned with carved stalls and panelling of the same period. The church is lit by fine 14C and 15C stained-glass windows, one of which is an Annunciation and an Assumption of Burgundian origin. A modern bronze group of the Assumption (1955) dominates the modern high altar. A series of modern windows by the painter Cingria depicts the Twelve Apostles, another by the French master of stained-glass windows, Sergio de Castro, depicts characters from the Old Testament. Note the Romanesque *Virgin and Child* adorning the altar in one of the chapels on the left.

Castle

The castle dates from the 13C, as can be seen from the keep of Peter II of Savoy, but has been remodelled several times. The main gateway (16C) is surmounted by several coats of arms of Fribourg and Romont.

Since 1981, the castle has housed the **Musée Suisse du Vitrail** (◷ *Open Apr-Oct, Tue-Sun, 10am-1pm and 2-6pm; Nov-Mar, Thu-Sun, 10am-1pm and 2-5pm.* ◉*7CHF.* ☏ *(026) 652 10 95; www.vitromuseum.ch).* The museum collections include medieval stained glass and Swiss heraldic glass as well as works by non-Swiss glassmakers. The works date from the early 20C, illustrating the revival of stained glass. An audio-visual presentation recounts the making of stained glass and its history through the centuries. Temporary exhibits consist of works of art from all over the world.

SAAS FEE ✳✳

VALAIS – POPULATION 1 698
ALT 1 790M/5 873FT

Nicknamed the Pearl of the Alps, Saas Fee enjoys a magnificent **setting**★★★ offering to the newcomer sudden and dazzling contact with mountains over 4 000m/13 123ft high. The view ranges from the icy dome of the Allalinhorn to the flattened, snow-capped summit of Alphubel and the rocky group of the Mischabel (highest point: Dom – alt 4 545m/14 941ft, recognizable by its forked peak). Below, the huge Fee Glacier (Feegletscher) divides into two tongues around the rocky promontory of the Längfluh. ▯ 3906 – ☏ (027) 958 18 58

🅿 **Parking:** Cars are not permitted in Saas Fee. Park on the outskirts and walk or use electric carts within the town.

Visit

Saas Fee is a well-known mountaineering centre. For the sports enthusiast who likes ski touring it has become the terminal of the famous High Route, **Haute Route** (Chamonix – Saas Fee or more often Verbier – Saas Fee). This quiet Valais village became a fashionable resort in the 19C, thanks in part to the efforts of the abbot Johann Josef Imseng (1806-69), whose statue is in the church square. In his spare time, the abbot acted as a mountain guide, taking tourists into the mountains. He was even heralded as the "best skiier in Switzerland" in 1849, when he skied down the Saas Fee slopes to Saas Grund on wooden skis of his own construction.

The Skiing Area

The Saas Valley covers around 145km/92mi of pistes suitable for **downhill skiing**, located in a majestic setting. Beginners will find easy slopes on the edge of the resort and along the Fee Glacier, where the best snow is to be found, with gentle ski runs extending down to Längfluh. On the whole, the choice is more limited for experienced skiers, although five to six steeper slopes are available. Do not miss a visit to **Egginerjoch**. In **winter**, the cable cars of Plattjen and Längfluh serve the area; the Feldskinn cable car works in **summer** and since 1984 an underground funicular has been operating to Mittellallatin (alt 3 500m/11 483ft). There is an 11km7mi toboggan run, plus airboarding and snowtubing, and skijoring for experienced skiers (who are pulled by horses). Opportunities for **cross-country skiing** and winter hiking include more than 50km/32mi of prepared trails. The car-free village helps make Saas-Fee a favorite for families.

Saaser Museum

🕐 *Open Jun to mid-Oct, daily except Mon, 10-11.30am and 1.30-5.30pm; Dec to mid-Apr, daily except Sat-Sun, 2-5pm.* 🕐 *Closed Sun and Thu in Jun, Sep and Oct.* ⊜*4CHF.* ☎ *(027) 957 14 75.*

This former thermal establishment (1732) houses a museum devoted to life in the Saas Valley. Local traditions are explored through reconstructed interiors, farming implements, local costume and headgear, liturgical objects, minerals and photo-

Degonda/Suisse Tourisme

View of Saas Fee

graphs. Special attention is paid to the development of the spa: the growing expansion of tourism, accommodation, climbing, winter sports and the introduction of new, sophisticated equipment (compare a 1906 ski with one belonging to the Swiss champion Firmin Zurbriggen). One of the rooms presents personal mementoes of the writer Carl Zuckmayer, a one-time resident of the city of Saas.

Belvederes Accessible by Chairlift

Mittelallalin★★★
Allow half a day. 🕐 *Remember to dress warmly (trousers, jacket, sturdy mountain boots) and to bring sunglasses.*
Take the Alpin Express cable car, which affords fine sweeping views of the Saas Fee resort, travelling above an impressive stretch of ice and rock. Continue the climb up in the funicular (alt 3 500m/11 482ft). Go to the upper station of the **revolving restaurant** (the highest in the world), where you can enjoy a splendid **panorama** of the austere, awe-inspiring landscape.
For an even better view, follow the track marked out in the snow *(in summer only)* behind the restaurant. It dips over 100m/328ft and then climbs up to a rocky crag, dominating the glacier *(20min on foot there and back)*. Be sure you grip onto the handrail. To the south and west, the view encompasses the Allalinhorn (4 027m/13 211ft), the summer ski resort, the Feekopf, the Alphubel and the Dom. To the north are Saas Fee and Saas Grund lying below at the foot of the Fletschhorn and the Lagginhorn and the Bernese Oberland (Jungfrau). To the east, the long glaciers of the Hohlaub and the Allalin inch their way towards the Mattmark Dam.

Pavillon des Glaces★★
At Mittelallalin; 30min tour.
This 5 000m²/5 975sq yd cave, hollowed out of the Fee Glacier, is the highest in Europe. A total of 114 steps will take you down to 10m/33ft below the ice. It is a delightful walk in varied icy surroundings with many galleries and rooms embellished with sculptures, ice waterfalls, explanatory texts and play areas for children

Längfluh★★★
Alt 2 870m/9 416ft. 🚠*Access by the Gondelbahn Spielboden cable car, then the Luftseilbahn Längfluh cable car.*
At the heart of a mountainous cirque, Längfluh offers wonderful **views** of the crevasses and seracs of the Fee Glacier heading towards the village of Saas Fee. Note the lovely panorama of the Täschhorn. In summer, walkers may catch a glimpse of tame marmots. There is a restaurant at the site.

Plattjen★★
Alt 2 570m/8 431ft. 🚠*Access by cable car.* Five minutes walk from the cable car station, this site has superb **views**★★ of the Saas Glaciers and Mattmark Dam. Footpaths lead to the dam, as well as to the Brittanniahütte *(🕐see below)* and to Saas Almagell.

Hannig★
Alt 2 350m/7 709ft. 🚠*Access by cable car.*
Lovely **view**★ of Saas Fee, Saas Grund, Saas Almagell and the Fee Glacier to the south, with the Fletschhorn to the northeast. The main attraction of this summit is many opportunities for interesting walks. In winter, you can return to the resort on foot or by the fine **sledge piste**. In summer, Hannig is the starting-point for fascinating hiking towards **Mellig**★ and **Gebiden**★★ (alt 2 763m/9 064ft, 1hr 15min climb). Views of the Hohbalm Glacier dominated by the Nadelhorn (4 327m/14 194ft). Then 3hr 30min climb down to Saas Fee via the Bärenfälle waterfalls.

Walking Tours

Hohsaas★★★
Alt 3 098m/10 164ft. Park the car in Saas Grund (alt 1 560m/5 118ft), a small mountain resort located below Saas Fee. ⛟ Access by two cable cars. Allow 1hr 45min there and back.

As you walk, enjoy the pretty **views**★★ of the Saas Grund skiing area. The summit affords wonderful **views**★★ of Lagginhorn, the Hohlaub Glacier and Weissmies (4 023m/13 197ft), a sparkling glacier with a thick icecap. This peak is frequently used in competitions (note the roped parties of climbers in the morning). Walk up towards Geissrück (15min) for a better view of the stunning séracs. Take in the sweeping **panorama**★★★ from Mont Rose to Dürrenhorn, featuring 18 summits looming above 4 000m/13 122ft.

Egginerjoch and Britanniahütte★★★
Allow 1hr 20min.

From Felskinn (2 998m/9 840ft), the lower station of the cable car, there are pleasant walks to be had through the snow and along the glacier *(it is essential to wear sturdy mountain boots and to bring a walking stick)*. After 20min, you will reach **Egginerjoch Pass**★★ (2 989m/9 813ft), lying at the foot of the red pyramid of the Egginer. Views of Mont Rose, Dom and the Britannia refuge. Farther on, the route wends its way against a rocky and glacial backdrop, sometimes difficult to negotiate owing to poor or non-existent snow coverage, especially in late August and September *(enquire beforehand at the tourist office)*. A 40min stroll will take you to **Britanniahütte** (3 029m/9 935ft), which commands a superb **view**★★ of Lake Mattmark, flanked on the right by the lovely tongues of ice of Hohlaub, Allalin and Schwarzberg, and on the left by Stellihorn. The most arresting **panorama**★★★, encompassing the whole landscape, can be seen from a promontory on your left.

From Britanniahütte to Plattjen★★★
A 2hr 15min walk following the one described above. ☺ To be undertaken only by experienced hikers in excellent physical condition.

Go down towards the glacier, heading in the direction of the poles set up near a small lake lying directly ahead of you. Follow the yellow signs, then the red and white ones. The path is rocky and bordered by sprigs of absinthe. After walking for one hour, you will come to a crossroads. Turn left towards Plattjen. After 50m/55yd, you will skirt the rock face, aided by a handrail. The path follows a sheer cliff hollowed out of the red ferruginous rock, frequented by herds of goats and ibexes. It affords breathtaking **views**★★★ of the valley down below. After crossing a rock barrier (gneiss) clearly marked out by signs, you will reach **Plattjen**★★ (⛟ *see above*). You can return to Saas Fee on foot or by cable car.

From Plattjen to Saas Fee★★
Access: ⛟ see Plattjen above. Allow 1hr 45min.

An easy walk in an idyllic setting near Berghaus Plattjen, with a beautiful descent through the woods (larch, pine trees, Norway spruce) and rhododendrons.

From Kreuzboden to Saas Fee★★
3hr walk with a 850m/2 788ft drop in altitude as you proceed downwards.

From Kreuzboden (alt 2 397m/7 863ft), the first cable car section, take "Höhenweg" in the direction of Almagelleralp. This pretty path meandering its way across the slope is bordered by a small alpine garden (edelweiss, astragalus, gentian, juniper berry). After about 1hr, you will discover broad **views**★★ of the Saas Fee glacial cirque and Lake Mattmark. Note the impressive avalanche barrier. A little farther on, you will come across a path, which you follow, heading downwards towards Saas Grund. Leave it after 15min and choose a track on the left, marked out as

"Alpenblumen-Promenade". This somewhat steep slope, dotted with edelweiss, ends in a forest of larch trees.

Stausee Mattmark★★

Alt 2 200m/7 217ft. Drive down (by car or bus) to Saas Grund and take a narrow road for 12km/7.5mi across restful Alpine pastures and woodland. It offers beautiful **views**★★ of the Saas Fee Glaciers. Park the car at the bottom of the road. From there, walk 5min to the left end of the dam, which is 780m/2 560ft long. **View**★★ of the lake framed by four glaciers (Hohlaub, Allalin, Schwarzberg and Seewjinen), enhanced by numerous waterfalls. Glimpses can also be had of the Almagellhorn. The 1.76km²/0.67sq mi lake can hold 100 million m³/130 million cu yd of water and reaches a depth of 117m/384ft.

Monte Moropass★★

Alt 2 868m/9 408ft. 3hr 15min climb and 2hr 45min descent for experienced walkers. Skirt the Mattmark Lake along a good path until you reach the end 1hr later. Then take a narrow path which climbs steadily towards the Col de Monte Moro. After 45min, you will reach a platform within view of the pass. Continue on the right. The path is much steeper now and wends its way through rocks, which makes for a tricky and trying walk. Make sure you follow the red and white marks. From the pass, where a statue of the Virgin has been erected, there are splendid **views**★★ of the Mont Rose and its many glaciers. On the Italian side, a refuge has been built near a small lake. However, it is difficult to get to because of the steep gradient. On the Swiss side, you can admire the pretty Mattmark Lake, dominated by the Strahihorn and the Allalinhorn.

▶ *Retrace your steps to the lake, but go around it, following the opposite shore.*

Chemin Zuckmayer★

3hr 30min there and back.
This forest path is named after writer Carl Zuckmayer, who used to walk this route almost every day; quotations from his works have been engraved on stones lining the path. From Vogelweid House, where Zuckmayer once lived, the path climbs towards the Bärenfalle, then to Melchboden and the Alpenblick café (alt 2 020m/6 625ft). On the return, there is a magnificent view of Saas Fee from in front of the Hohnegg.

SACHSELN

OBWALDEN – POPULATION 3 997
ALT 472M/1 549FT

The town of Sachseln is prettily situated on the shore of Lake Sarnen and with the sacred soil of the Ranft forms a moving place of pilgrimage. Swiss Catholics affirm their attachment to their faith and their patriotic fervour by coming here to pray to St Nicholas of Flüe (🕯 *see VIERWALDSTÄTTER SEE*).

Visit

Church

The great Baroque building, supported by columns of black Melchtal marble, enshrines the relics of **St Nicholas of Flüe** on a special altar at the chancel entrance to the chancel. The remains are enclosed in a large, embossed recumbent figure (1934).

Go around the building to reach, at the foot of the detached Romanesque bell tower, the funeral chapel, where faithful come to meditate before the tombstone, carved in 1518 with the effigy of the saint. Below is the worn step of the original sepulchre.

Excursion

From Sachseln to Ranft
3km/2mi – plus 1hr 30min walk and visit. Leave Sachseln eastwards on the Flüeli road. Leave the car at the car park on the central esplanade of Flüeli.

Flüeli
The rustic character of this hamlet, where Brother Nicholas led the life of a mountain patriarch surrounded by his large family, has been preserved. The chapel (1618) can be seen on its mound from far off; it is reached by stairs and an esplanade. From the terrace there is a pleasant, open view of the Valley of Sarsen, Lake Sarnen and Pilatus on one side and the deep cleft leading into the Melchtal on the other. Besides this sanctuary, pilgrims still visit the birthplace (the oldest wooden house in Switzerland – 14C) and the family home of Nicholas.

Ranft★
Approaches are signposted on leaving Flüeli. By a steep descent *(ramp or stairs)* towards the floor of the Melchaa Valley you will first reach the hermitage-chapel. The church (17C) is decorated with painted panels recalling the life of the recluse; outstanding is a fine Gothic **Christ**★ taken from the former Sachseln church. The cell nearby – where the hermit could not stand upright – was built in 1468 by his fellow-citizens from Obwalden. Below, another chapel was built in the 16C on the spot where the Virgin appeared to Nicholas.
On returning from Flüeli bound for Lucerne, take the fork to the right towards Kerns; then cross the Melchaa on the **Hohe Brücke**★. This covered bridge was built across the torrent at a height of 100m/329ft in 1943 by Swiss Army Engineers.

SACHSELNER STRASSE

This pleasant route, lined with lovely lakes, offers a hilly road (to **Brünig Pass**) and an excursion to the famous Pilatus Mountain.

From Lucerne to Brienz *98 km/60mi – 2hr 30min*

Lucerne★★★ – *3hr.* ♾ *See LUZERN.*
To leave Lucerne quickly you should take the Stans motorway, then branch off at the Hergiswil exit. The next section, as far as Alpnachstad, runs along the lake shore. The bends in this road offer views from many different angles of the Rigi Massif, the wooded spurs of the Bürgenstock and the isolated Stanserhorn Summit.
The trip by rack railway from Alpnachstad to Pilatus is recommended.

Pilatus★★★
From Alpnachstad, about 2hr there and back, including 1hr 15min by rack railway.
♾ *For access and description see PILATUS.*
The road crosses **Sarnen** and skirts the lake of the same name.

Sachseln – ♿ *See SACHSELN.*

▶ *Turn right when you reach Giswil.*

Sörenberg

The road, while climbing up in hairpin bends to the **Glaubenbüelen Pass**, offers lovely views of Sarnen Lake and the surrounding countryside.

At the pass you discover the snowy basin of **Brienzer Rothorn**. The road then descends amid fir trees, passes the base of the Brienzer Rothorn *(on the left is the cable-car station to the mountain top)* and continues on to Sörenberg, a ski resort located in a mountainous cirque.

▶ *Return to Giswil.*

Between Giswil and Kaiserstuhl, you will get a good distant view of the Pilatus ridges rising above the shallow depression, dotted with farms and clumps of trees, partly submerged by Lake Sarnen. Upstream and in the far distance, the three snowy peaks of the Wetterhorn group appear through the Brünig Gap.

From **Lungern** to the Brünig Pass, there are pretty glimpses between the fir trees and maples of **Lake Lungern** (Lungernsee), with its curving shores. On the Bernese side of the pass the gradient becomes very steep but the excellent layout of the road and its easy bends will enable you to enjoy a wide **panorama**★ of the cleft of the Aare, hollowed out by former glaciers between the terraces of the **Hasliberg** and the Schwarzhorn foothills, from which the Wandelbach and Oltschibach cascades pour down. You may wish to stop at the point where the road is cut through the rock before tackling the last stage to Brienz.

Brienz★ – ♿ *See BRIENZ.*

SAILLON

VALAIS – POPULATION 1 503
ALT 522M/1 713FT

The village of Saillon, a wine-making centre since Roman times, sits on the banks of the River Rhône surrounded by vineyards (200ha/494 acres) and market gardens. This wide, sunny valley has an ideal climate for the cultivation of grapes, strawberries, pears, apricots and asparagus.

The Smallest Vine in the World

Planted by a group of admirers to mark the 100th anniversary of Joseph-Samuel Farinet's death, this vine is spread out over Colline Ardente. Three stocks cover an area of 1 618m²/1 933sq yd. In 1999 the Dalaï-Lama, appointed by the "Amis de Farinet" took possession of these vines, following in the foorsteps of the Abbé Pierre and Jean-Louis Barrault. Other celebrities who have symbolically tended the vine include Maurice Béjart, Peter Ustinov, Danielle Mitterand, Roger Moore, Princess Caroline of Monaco, the Lord Mayor of London, Gina Lollobrigida, Paul-Émile Victor, Auxerre football coach Guy Roux, Zinedine Zidane and Michael Schumacher. Every year, wine produced by the three stocks is blended with the best Valais vintage. One thousand bottles are made, specially labelled and sold at an auction to benefit a charity fund in memory of Farinet.

A Bit of History

The old town, with its grey rooftops clustered around the ramparts, enjoyed a strategic position of vital importance before the Rhône changed its course in this part of central Valais. An attractive group is formed by the impressive ruins of the castle and the church, with its Romanesque belfry.

A kind-hearted crook

Born near the Grand-St-Bernard in 1845, **Joseph-Samuel Farinet** was a lively character who led an eventful existence. A dedicated, self-proclaimed adventurer and forger, this Swiss Robin Hood would hand out the money he had faked to the poor and needy. Rebelling against the Establishment and forever on the run from the Swiss *gendarmes*, this kind-hearted, unorthodox figure was widely admired by the local population, who condoned his sense of justice and soon hailed him as a national hero. Hounded by the police, he was hit by a bullet and died in the Salentze Gorges, aged 35. He is buried in Saillon cemetery, at the foot of the church tower.

This outlaw is still seen by many as a benefactor who devoted his life to the poor. He remains a symbol embodying the values of freedom and mountain hospitality. His life story has inspired a ballad by the Vaud writer Charles-Ferdinand Ramuz and a film starring Jean-Louis Barrault, *Farinet et la Fausse Monnaie*.

Sights

View★

From the village, a steep path soon leads to the foot of the great tower of the castle (a former keep), from where there is a lovely view of the terraced vineyards carpeting the slopes and the alluvial plain with its orchards. The Pennine Alps can be seen like a massive wall in the distance.

Farinet's Path

45min walk. Leaving from the foot of Saillon hill, this path is dotted with 21 stained-glass works depicting human experiences, such as childhood, love, suffering and death. It wends its way through wine-growing fields to end up at the smallest registered vineyard in the world. **Farinet's Footbridge** was opened in 2001.

Spa

The spa complex opened in 1983 carries on a tradition that dates back to Roman times. The hot springs of the Salentze provide four thermal baths ranging in temperature from 28°C/82°F to 34°C/93°F; the complex also has three steam baths, two saunas, swimming pools and footbaths.

SAINT-CERGUE★

VAUD – POPULATION 1 617
ALT 1 044M/3 480FT

A high-altitude resort in the Jura long known both to the Genevese and to the French for its bracing mountain climate, St-Cergue stands at the point where the corridor of the Girvine Pass opens out within sight of the Mont-Blanc Massif and Lake Geneva. There are many belvederes near the resort from which there are good views of the forest-clad foreground and the giant of the Alps.

Visit

Those interested in botanical phenomena should go to the Borsattaz meadow, where giant pine trees, known locally as *gogants*, prosper; they are to be found only in the Jura. You reach the meadow from the Lausanne road; after 1.5km/1mi turn left into a tarred road (Route de la Prangine et du Plumet); 1.5km/1mi farther on bear right at the Carrefour des Fruitières. St-Cergue offers more than 50km/31mi of trails for **cross-country skiing** and a variety of training grounds and fairly difficult ski runs for **downhill skiing.**

Belvédère du Vieux Château★★
30min on foot there and back by a path signposted Le Vieux Château. Splendid view of Lake Geneva and the Mont Blanc.

Excursion

La Dôle★★★
Alt 1 677m/5 500ft. 21km/15mi – about 2hr 30min. Leave St-Cergue by the road to Nyon, turn right and drive on until you reach Gingins. Then take the road to the La Dôle and La Barillette.

Leave the car at the foot of La Dôle and continue on foot. Follow the path on the left, marked out in yellow. It leads to the summit, where a navigation beacon and radar station have been constructed. A vast **panorama**★★★ extends over the Alps right up to the peaks of the Valais (Matterhorn) and the Oisans (Meije). Mont Blanc looms between the two towers, with Lake Geneva in the foreground. Looking right round, you can see the Jura including Mount Tendre and the Chasseron on one side and the Valserine as far as the Reculet, on the other.

SAINT-MAURICE★

VALAIS – POPULATION 3 594
ALT 422M/1 384FT

The little town of St-Maurice, dominated to the west by the Dents du Midi and to the east by the Dent de Morcles, occupies a picturesque **site**★. Agaune (from the Celtic name *acauno*, meaning a rock) was the chief village of the Nantuates tribe. After the Roman conquest it became the capital of the present Valais under the Emperor Augustus. *1 avenue des Terreaux – 1890 – ☎ (024) 485 40 40.*

A Bit of History

The field of martyrs
At the end of the 3C a legion recruited in Africa – the Theban Legion, commanded by **Maurice** – was massacred near the town for having refused to worship the gods of Rome. In the following century a community took charge of the martyrs' tombs. The foundation of the Abbey of St-Maurice by King Sigismund of Burgundy in 515 was prompted by the desire to perpetuate the memory of Maurice and his comrades. The abbey was richly endowed from the start and it attracted many of the faithful throughout the Middle Ages. In the 9C the town took the name of its illustrious patron saint. In 1125 it welcomed the regular canons of the Order of St Augustine and on 22 September every year it still celebrates the memory of the martyrs of the Theban Legion with fervour. In the course of centuries the abbey changed and expanded;

gradually a rich treasury, consisting of gifts from pilgrims and Christian princes, was amassed. St-Maurice became one of the holy places of Christianity.

Sights

Église Abbatiale

The fine **belfry**★ is 11C and the stone spire 13C, although the abbey church itself dates only from the beginning of the 17C and has been restored (since 1949). The nave is plain. A Carolingian pulpit has been reinstalled in the recently restored outer chancel. The chancel itself is large and adorned with fine stalls. On the altar there is a fine mosaic by Maurice Denis.

Treasury★★

Guided tours (1hr) Jul and Aug at 10.30am, 2pm, 3.15pm and 4.30pm; Apr-Jun at 10.30am, 3pm and 4.30pm; Sep and Oct at 10.30am, 3pm and 4.30pm, Nov to Easter at 3pm. Closed all day Mon and the mornings of Sun and public hols. *2CHF.* ☎ (024) 486 04 04.

This is one of the richest ecclesiastical treasuries in the Christian world displaying exceptional pieces of goldsmiths' work. Pay special attention to a sardonyx vase decorated with scenes taken from Greek mythology, the Merovingian casket of Theodoric made of gold encrusted with pearls and cameos, the golden 9C ewer, said to be Charlemagne's, whose enamelwork seems to derive from the purest Oriental technique, and the reliquary of St Maurice, whose decoratives features – Christ the King, the Virgin, Angels and Apostles – probably came from an embossed and gilded altarpiece of the 12C (the medallions on the roof of the reliquary depict the story of original sin in six scenes). Two other reliquaries of the 12C and 13C, the reliquary-bust of St Candid depicted with a noble look (on the plinth, his martyrdom by beheading) and the reliquary-monstrance given by St Louis complete the priceless collection.

Fouilles de Martolet

Same admission times and charges as for the abbey treasury.

Near the belfry, at the foot of the rock overlooking the abbey, excavations have uncovered foundations of the buildings that preceded the present church from the 4C onward; their plan stands out clearly. You may see traces of a baptistery and graceful modern cloisters in the Romanesque style. It is possible to visit the catacombs, narrow underground galleries leading to the crypt and tomb of St Maurice.

Castle

Overlooking the Rhône and sheltered by the forested eastern slopes of the Dents du Midi, this small castle dates from the early 16C. The square keep and bastions were added in the 18C and now house the **Musée Cantonal d'Histoire Militaire** (Open daily except Mon, 1-6pm (5pm Oct-May). Closed 1 Jan and 25 Dec. *4CHF, no charge the first Sun in the month.* ☎ (024) 485 36 79). On display are banners, medals, arms and uniforms; another section includes models of the fortifications built along the Swiss borders during both World Wars. The dungeons house heavy artillery from the Second World War and anti-aircraft guns occupy the courtyards. On the ground floor the elegantly furnished reception room is typical of the 18C.

Grotte aux Fées

Reached by a steep uphill path starting from the level of the castle and the bridge over the Rhône at the north entrance to the town. Open daily, Jun-Sep, 9am-6pm; mid-Mar to mid-Nov, 10am-6pm. *7CHF.* ☎ (024) 485 10 45.

This grotto is formed by a natural gallery about 900m/990yd long leading to an underground lake and waterfall. From the terrace of the nearby restaurant there is a fine **view**★ of St-Maurice and the Dent de Morcles.

SAINT-URSANNE ★

JURA – POPULATION 918
ALT 494M/1 621FT

Lying away from the main roads deep in the Doubs Valley, St-Ursanne, a quaint old town that has remained unchanged since the beginning of the 19C, makes a charming place to stop when crossing the Swiss Jura (👆 see Le JURA SUISSE). It originated with the hermitage that Ursicinus, a disciple of Columba (👆 see SANKT GALLEN), set up in the 7C.

Sights

You enter the town through fortified gates surmounted by a bear carrying the symbolic crosier of the prince-bishops of Basel. An agreeable scene is presented of fountains and houses, flanked by turrets, with great brown, pointed roofs, adorned with wrought-iron signs.

View from the bridge★
From this picturesque structure, guarded by a statue of St John Nepomucene, the patron saint of bridges, there is a well-composed picture of the fortified gate, framed by the façades, of riverside houses with overhanging wooden balconies, the town roofs dominated by the church tower, the slopes of the valley and, on the crest, the scant ruins of a 14C castle.

Collegiate Church
🕐 *Open daily except Sun morning, 7.30am-7pm (8pm Jun-Oct).* ☎ *(032) 461 31 74.*
The building (restored) has a sober look. The east end and apse are Romanesque and comprise a fine, single-arched **doorway**★ adorned with statues of the Virgin and St Ursicinus. It has a pretty tympanum and capitals. Inside, the Romanesque chancel contains a Baroque canopied altar; the crypt is also Romanesque and the nave early Gothic (13C). The church has large Gothic cloisters on its north side as well as a lapidary museum containing 7C to 9C sarcophagi.

SAINTE-CROIX-LES-RASSES ★

VAUD – POPULATION 4 155
ALT 1 069M/3 507FT

The twin townships of Ste-Croix and Les Rasses lie on a sunny shoulder of the Chasseron, facing the Alps. They deserve a special place among Swiss Jura resorts for their commanding situation and their excellent tourist organisation. In winter Ste-Croix-les-Rasses is recommended for the beginners or intermediate skiers who want to enjoy themselves rather than to break records. Where cross-country skiing – the speciality of the Jura – is concerned, the resort offers more than 80km/50mi of marked trails.

A Bit of History

The Village of Sound
The history of Ste-Croix since the mid-19C is a good example of the adaptability of Swiss industry to international economic changes. Around 1850, like most small

towns in the Jura, the village was making watches. The establishment in the United States of great watch and clockmaking factories with sophisticated machine tools caused a grave crisis at Ste-Croix, which turned to the musical-box industry. But when Edison developed the phonograph, the public lost interest in little musical boxes with their tinkling notes, considered childish. Ste-Croix moved with the times and switched to making gramophones. Since then the popularity of radio has required more changes in the workshops, but today musical boxes again play an important part in local industry and Ste-Croix is still "the village of sound".

Visit

Centre International de la Mécanique d'Art

Kids ⟨⟩ *Guided tours (1hr 15min) daily except Mon in Jun at 2pm, 3.30pm and 5pm; Jan-May, Jul and Aug at 10.30am, 2pm, 3.30pm and 5pm.* ◷ *Closed 25 Dec.* 13CHF, 7CHF. ☎ (024) 454 44 77.

Step into this old music-box factory (display of disused machinery) and be transported into a wonderful, magic world where you discover the vibrant melodies coming from beautiful handmade instruments, masterpieces of acoustics and cabinetmaking. This **music box museum** gives a new lease on life to musical boxes operated by discs or cylinders (the first model dates from 1796), radio sets, phonographs, pianos, street organs, automata (clowns, acrobats, Pierrot writing to Colombine), barrel organs and bird-organs. The **Salle Guido Reuge**, named after the famous industrialist from the Jura, contains a remarkable collection of exhibits donated by his widow, presented in a superb setting portraying a magic forest.

The Resorts

Sainte-Croix lies in a pastoral basin well protected from the winds at the mouth of the wooded pass of the Covatannaz Gorges, through which a wide section of the Bernese Alps can be seen. **Les Rasses★** is an nnexe of Ste-Croix with several hotels and scattered chalets enjoying a magnificent terraced **site★★** within view of the Alps. For those interested in hiking, there are more than 200km/124mi of paths.

Excursions

Le Chasseron★★★

Alt 1 607m/5272ft. From Les Rasses, 3km/2mi – 1hr 15min by a small, winding, tarred road (there is also a chair-lift ending at Les Avattes, about 1hr walk from the summit).
Follow the road from Ste-Croix to Les Rasses, 0.5km/0.3mi beyond the Grand Hôtel des Rasses. Turn left on the Chasseron road. At the Avattes crossroads, bear right towards the Hôtel du Chasseron. On emerging from the woods, leave the car at the hotel car park.
Walk to the Hôtel du Chasseron and the summit *(signpost)* where you will see a sweeping panorama of the Alps, the Jura and Lake Neuchâtel.

L'Auberson

4km/3mi W of Ste-Croix (Pontarlier road). Turn left at the Col des Étroits.

Musée Baud

⟨⟩ *Guided tours (1hr) all year round on Sun and public hols, 10am-noon and 2-6pm, Sat 2-6pm; Jul-Sep, weekdays 2-5pm.* ◷*Closed at Christmas.* 8CHF. ☎ (024) 454 24 84; www.muséebaud.ch.

This small museum displays and keeps in working order an exceptional **collection of old musical instruments★** (Utrecht organ, barrel organ, player organ) and phonographs (note especially the ones dating from 1900, 1912 and 1920). Also exhibited and functioning are automata and animated scenes. In display cases, music boxes, mechanisms, bonbonnières, etc. can be admired.

Mont de Baulmes

Alt 1 285m/4 216ft. From Ste-Croix 4.5km/3mi – about 30min by a narrow mountain road, steep towards the end but wholly paved, plus 15min on foot there and back.

Leave Ste-Croix by the level-crossing at the railway station and continue through the hamlets of La Sagne and Culliairy. Leave the car at the Chalet-Restaurant of Mount Baulmes, and go along an avenue to the viewing table, on the edge of the precipice, for a **bird's-eye view** of the Swiss plateau, its lakes (in particular, Lake Neuchâtel) and the Alps.

SAMEDAN

GRAUBUNDEN

At the entrance to the little triangular plain where the great resorts of the Upper Engadine have found room for a golf course, aerodrome and glider field, Samedan's horizons are bounded by the high summits of the Bernina to the south: Piz Morteratsch and Piz Palü.

This old-fashioned village is dotted with houses in traditional Engadine style. Notice, in the heart of the village, the imposing double Planta House (Chesa Planta, from the name of one of the oldest families in the Grisons), which contains the **Romansch Library**, dedicated to the preservation of local language and traditions.

SAN BERNARDINO-STRASSE★★

SAN BERNADINO PASS ROAD

The San Bernardino Pass, on this great transalpine road, links Bellinzona (near Lake Maggiore) in the sunny Lower Ticino Valley to Chur, the historical capital of the Grisons, located downstream from the confluence of the Vorderrhein and Hinterrhein.

The San Bernardino Pass is usually blocked by snow from November to May. The itinerary outlined below follows the old road (blue signposts). The motorway running parallel to this itinerary is indicated on the map.

From Bellinzona to Chur *194km/120mi – allow one day*

Itinerary ② *(see GRAUBÜNDEN map)*

Bellinzona★ –   *See BELLINZONA.*

After Bellinzona the road climbs the Mesolcina Valley watered by the Moesa. On leaving Roveredo, the valley narrows and runs northwards. On the way to Soazza (alt 623m/2 044ft), look out for the last signs of typically Mediterranean farming and vegetation: plane trees, maize, vines and figs (as far as Cama).

After admiring the double **Buffalora Waterfall**, follow the old road which runs through Soazza and pass the great church. The road to the pass starts climbing.

Castello di Misox★ – 👁 See Castello di MISOX.

Beyond the village of **Mesocco**, which clusters on a ledge at the foot of its castle's ruins, the pleasant climb is resumed among grassy mounds (note the outline of the motorway and its many structures) to the **San Bernardino plateau**. This is the highest and most frequented resort in the Mesolcina Valley and it features an unusual circular church. From the village of San Bernardino to the pass, the road, after skirting the pretty Moesola Lake, follows a wayward course which leads it from level to level among fir woods and arolla pines. (👁 *For details of these conifers see Introduction: Alpine vegetation*). Eastwards, the coloured escarpments of the Pizzo Uccello appear as a rugged spur running parallel to the Pan di Zucchero (Sugar Loaf).

Passo del San Bernardino

Alt 2 065/6 775ft. The **San Bernardino Pass** is littered with rounded rocks left behind by Quaternary glaciers. Open between the Zapporthorn and the Pizzo Uccello, the pass marks the dividing line between the Moesa, southwards, a tributary of the Ticino and thus of the Pô and the Hinterrhein, northwards.

On the north side, the **Upper Inner Rhine Valley** (Hinterrhein) presents as far as Splügen a landscape which is open and pastoral but still severe.

From the approach to the Hinterrhein, the **view**★ opens out upstream towards the massif containing the sources of the Rhine. The range is also remarkable for the size of its glaciers: the great Zapportgletscher, overlooked by the flattened cone of the Rheinquellhorn, is particularly impressive.

Between Splügen and Andeer the road runs through dense woods of Norway spruce, skirts the vast Sufers Reservoir and crosses the deepest section of the Rheinwald, the Roffla Defile, which corresponds with the northward bend of the valley.

Rofflaschlucht★

🕐 *Open May-Oct, 9am-5pm; otherwise (enquire in advance), daily except Tue and Wed, 9am-6pm.* 🕐 *Closed Nov to Easter.* 🎫 *3CHF.* ☎ *(081) 661 11 97.*
The galleries, 300m/984ft long, cut out of the rock (1907-14) in this gorge through which the Rhine flows, end under an impressive waterfall, which passes just above the spectator's head. As you leave the gorge you will notice the **Bärenburg Reservoir**, another example of the engineering works on the Hinterrhein.

▶ *From Roffla, proceed to the southeast and follow directions for Innerferrera.*

Averserrhein Valley (Ferrera Valley, Avers Valley)★★

The Averserrhein, a tributary of the Hinterrhein, carves its route through a picturesque valley in the Piz Grisch and Piz Platta massifs.

Following the torrent, the road climbs through the **Ferrera Valley** within view of the rocky Piz Miez, which serves as a backdrop, and crosses the village of Ausserferrera, located in a lovely wooded site (waterfalls). After **Innerferrera**, which overlooks a large dam, the road deviates southeasterly. It follows a hilly landscape, interrupted by long tunnels (between the tunnels, a pretty waterfall is visible on the left and behind), and opens out onto the Avers Valley and its first village, **Campsut**, which is set in a basin whose sides feature fir trees, ravines and small waterfalls.

Starting at Cröt, a sudden rise in the road gives you a good view: **Avers-Cresta** (charming white church) beyond the treeline and a hanging valley on the right, closed off by the Tscheischhorn snowfields. The road ends at **Juf** (alt 2 126m/6 975ft) in a desolate site surrounded by high mountains (glaciers). Continuing down the Hinterrhein, downstream from Andeer, the road enters the agricultural Schons Basin, whose west slope is open and dotted with villages.

Avers-Cresta

Zillis

To reach the church leave the through road and follow the road marked Zur Kirche.
🚶 *Guided tours.* 🛈 *For information, call ☎ (081) 661 11 60.*

The **ceiling**★★ of Zillis Church (Kirche Sankt Martin) is one of the most valuable pieces of painting left to Switzerland by Romanesque artists. It reveals the hand of an illuminator of manuscripts in its workmanship, and is believed to date from the 12C. There are 153 square panels; those on the perimeter symbolise the Original Ocean and the Sea of the Apocalypse with waters teeming with fabulous monsters; in the corners, the Angels of the Last Judgement, portrayed with the attributes of the Four Winds. The inside panels *(follow scenes from left to right, walking backwards away from the chancel)* refer to the Life of Christ and scenes from the Life of St Martin.

Mathon

This rustic mountain village (alt 1 521m/4 990ft) is situated in a privileged **site**★ on the verdant slopes of the Piz Beverin, overlooking the Schons Basin and in view of the snowy peaks of the basin's east side. Below the church and hanging over the precipice are the ruins of a former church (1528, parts of which date from the 9C).

Via Mala★★

15min, not including the walk through the galleries.

This famous stretch of road, which for centuries has been the main obstacle to the development of traffic along the **Untere Strasse**, is divided into two gorges separated by the small, verdant Rongellen Basin. The **upstream defile**★★ – the Via Mala proper – plunges between formidable schist escarpments connected by four successive bridges. Leave the car by the pavilion at the entrance to the galleries and go towards the second bridge (upstream bridge). Now take up a position preferably on the old bridge, dating from 1739 and now restored. This spans the gorge, at the bottom of which flows the Rhine, 68m/223ft below.

To enjoy the famous view of the site of these bridges and to get as close as possible to the bed of the Rhine you can go down to the **galleries**★ (🕐 *Open May–Aug, 8am-7pm; Mar, Apr and Nov, 9am-6pm.* 🚶 *5CHF.* ☎ *(081) 651 11 34) (341 steps – 30min there and back).* The road avoids the floor of the ravine downstream and the section called the Verlorenes Loch (Lost Hole). This was considered inaccessible until a carriage road through these depths was opened in 1822. From the top of the opposite escarpment you can see the feudal ruins of Hohenrätien, a site worthy of an engraving by Gustave Doré.

Thusis

Thusis is a busy little town below the ruins of Hohenrätien (a refuge castle and a church destroyed in the 15C). The ruins are perched 200m/650ft above Via Mala at the point where this gorge opens into the Domleschg Basin.

The section between Thusis and the Rothenbrunnen Bridge runs along the bottom of the Domleschg Depression, where the Hinterrhein flows between steep sides. The steeper and more thickly wooded slopes of the Heinzenberg face the east slope – the **Domleschg** proper – dotted with villages nestling amid orchards and the ruins of feudal fortresses. Two sentinels watch over the entrance to the Domleschg Gap: upstream the Citadel of Ortenstein, and downstream Rhäzüns Castle, perched above the deeply-cut course of the Rhine.

Reichenau – ⚓ *See DISENTIS/MUSTER.*

On leaving the ravine, the road runs through the Rhine Valley opposite the rocky slopes of the Calenda, to the north. The hummocky ground in the vicinity of Domat is said to be the result of a landslide in prehistoric times.

Chur★ – ⚓ *See CHUR.*

SANKT GALLEN★★

© SANKT GALLEN – POPULATION 71 000
ALT 668M/2 201FT – TOWN PLAN IN THE MICHELIN GUIDE SWITZERLAND

Sankt Gallen – the highest town in Switzerland – nestles in the narrow Stein-ach Valley in the east of the country, 10km/6mi southeast of Lake Constance (Bodensee). The ecnomic and cultural capital of eastern Switzerland, it owes its fortune to an abbey, founded on the spot where Gallus died in 650. Sankt Gallen's Baroque cathedral and magnificent abbey library, two of UNESCO's World Heritage Sites, are situated in the old town, surrounded by typical corbelled houses with oriel (Erker) windows. 🏠 *Bahnhofplatz 1 a – 9000 – ☎ (071) 227 37 37, www.st.gallen-bodensee.ch.*

▶ **Orient Yourself:** Take the 2hr guided city tour from the tourist office (🕐 *June-Sept, Mon, Wed and Fri 2:30pm,* 🎫 *15CHF).*

🅐 **Don't Miss:** The illuminated manuscripts from the Middle Ages at the Abbey Library, St. Gallen's top tourist attraction.

🕐 **Organizing Your Time:** Allow at least two days for museums and excursions.

🄺🄸🄳🅂 **Especially for Kids:** Säntispark, a waterpark at Abtwil.

A Bit of History

The Legend of Gallus – According to legend, when Gallus arrived in the valley in 612, he tripped, fell into a bush of thorns and came face to face with a bear. The Irish monk saw the hand of God in this event and decided to found his hermitage in the valley. In 719, a monastery was founded on the site by St Otmar. This Benedictine abbey was soon to enjoy intellectual influence throughout western Europe. In the 9C, the monastery buildings proved too small and a larger building was needed; the Carolingian plans of this larger monastery are still kept in the abbey library.

Vadian and the Reformation – Joachim von Watt – known under the scholastic name of **Vadian** – a doctor and mayor of the town, introduced the Reformation to Sankt Gallen in 1524. Following the split brought about by the Reformation, the abbey experienced many upheavals; it was only in the mid-18C that it resumed its expansion with the building of the abbey church and the library. The abbey was secularised in 1805 and in 1846 it became the seat of a bishopric.

Weaving and embroidery – As long ago as the Middle Ages, workrooms in the monastery and in the town wove linen; the fabric acquired a great reputation and was exported as far as Spain and Poland. In the 18C, fine cotton fabrics and embroideries were produced throughout the canton. In 1898, 50% of the world's textile production came from Sankt Gallen, resulting in a building boom in the town; the railway station, post office and the opulent villas along St Leonhard Strasse and Multergasse all date from this period. Despite the decline in the textile industry in the 20C, a third of all textile jobs in Switzerland are still concentrated in Sankt Gallen.

Abbey Buildings★★★

Former abbey

From the Klosterhof (monastery courtyard) there is a fine general view of the former Benedictine abbey. The abbey buildings are attached to the cathedral; they now house the bishop's residence, the famous abbey library, the Cantonal Government and several schools. With that of Einsiedeln it is the most important Baroque structure in Switzerland.

Kathedrale★★ (C)

The cathedral was built from 1755 to 1767 on the site of a 14C Gothic edifice. Two elegant towers (68m/233ft) crowned with domed belfries flank the east face, which has on its pediment a low relief depicting the Coronation of the Virgin, a 1933 replica of the work by Joseph Anton Feuchtmayer.

The abbey library at Sankt Gallen

Bill Wassman / APA Publications

The exterior is plain, forming a striking contrast with the interior, an ornate masterpiece by Peter Thumb from the **Vorarlberg School** in the late-Baroque style; other examples of this style can also be seen in the Lake Constance region. In the centre of the immense structure, the **dome**★★ is richly decorated but not vulgar: the paintings on a blue background on the theme of the Eight Beatitudes are by Joseph Wannenmacher. Other murals decorate the nave and the chancel. The fine green stucco mouldings were done by Christian Wenzinger. The **chancel**★★★, enclosed by admirable grilles, is adorned with a high altar executed in the Empire style in 1810. The great stalls, of rare delicacy, and the 16 confessionals by Josef Anton Feuchtmayer form a remarkable whole.

Stiftsbibliothek★★★ (C)

🕐 *Open 10am-5pm (4pm Sun); some public hols, 10am-4pm.* 🕐*Closed mid-Nov to early Dec.* 💳 *7CHF.* ☎ *(071) 227 34 16.*

The collections of the **Abbey Library** are exhibited in a room considered to have the finest secular Rococo decor in the country, built during the same period as the cathedral (1758-67) and by the same architects. Architectural features include a parquet floor inlaid with stars in alternating light and dark wood; rich woodwork adorned with columns with gilded capitals; monochrome *(grisaille)* paintings above the eight-storey gallery; and delicate frescoes by the Gigi brothers.

The a remarkable collection of around 100 000 volumes, including over 2 000 parchments from the 8C-12C, early printed books (prior to 1500), and beautiful illuminated manuscripts from the Renaissance period. Several works are exhibited in display cabinets: note the Gospel dating from 750, the 9C Psalter decorated with miniatures depicting the story of David, and the plan of the Carolingian cloisters. A mummy from Upper Egypt (700 BC), donated in 1824 can be seen in a double sarcophagus made from sycamore at the back of the library.

Old Town★★

Around the cathedral is a picturesque quarter whose layout corresponds to that of the medieval town which once stood within the ramparts. Here are many 16C and 18C houses, sometimes with painted façades, often adorned with wrought-iron signs and carved and painted wooden **oriel windows**★, typical of the Lake Constance region. Airy, skeletal structures by Spanish architect Santiago Calatrava add avant-garde accents to the historic townscape.

On **Gallusplatz**, note the house with blue half-timbering (1606), its turret "supported" by a sculpted figure, representing a nobleman in fine dress. On **Gallusstrasse** the oriel window on south side of the **Zum Greif** or "griffon" house (second half of the 17C) depicts the struggle of Jacob with the angel from the book of Genesis. The oriel window of the **Zum Pelikan** house (Schmiedgasse 20) is decorated with symbols from the four continents – Australia had not yet been discovered – and grimacing figures. Notweorthy houses on **Spisergasse**: Nos 3, 5, 9 (**Zur Nachtigall** or "nightingale" house), 11, 13 (**Zum Bären** or "bear" house) and 19 are worthy of note, as is n° 22 (**Zum Kamel** or "camel" **house**★, c 1720), with its elaborate sculptures. Nos 25 and 30 provide further examples of this art. On **Kugelgasse**, the **Schwanen** or "swan" house (c 1690) is adorned with an aquatic decor inspired by Antiquity; the **Kugel** or "globe" house (also c 1690) in the same street is decorated with interesting images of the Earth. **Marktgasse** Nos 15, 17, 19 and 28 are particularly interesting. A statue of Joachim von Watt, also known as Vadian (1484-1551), who introduced the Reformation to Sankt Gallen, stands at the south end of the street.

Some of these buildings now house restaurants (Erststockbeisen) on the first floor, an old tradition which is the result of damp on the ground floor. These restaurants, characterised by their cosy atmosphere and wooden furnishings, serve typical regional dishes, such as *Olmat Bratwurst*, a local veal sausage.

The Upper Town

The town spreads over the nearby hills, home to several renowned universities such as the Sankt Gallen Graduate School of Economics, Business and Public Administration (Hochschule für Wirtschafts-und Sozialwissenschaften), which has more than 4 000 students.

Museums

Kunstmuseum★ (C)

🕐 *Open Tue-Fri, 10am-noon and 2-5pm (Wed to 8pm); Sat-Sun, 10am-5pm.* 🎟 *10CHF.* ☎ *(071) 242 06 71, www.kunstmuseumsg.ch.*

The **Fine Arts Museum** is housed in a Classical style building (1877) on the edge of a park. and includes German, Austrian and Swiss art from the 15C-18C, as well as several 19C and 20C paintings of rural life in the Toggenburg and Appenzell. One of the highlights of the museum is its collection of 17C Dutch art, along with French and

German works from the 19C, many of which are landscapes. Of particular interest are *Odalisque* by Corot, *Adoration of the Virgin* by Delacroix, *Garden* by Sisley, *Lake Geneva* by Courbet, *Hermitage* by Pissarro and *Palazzo Contarini* by Monet. The museum also boasts a collection of modern and contemporary art, with works by Sophie Taeuber-Arp, Klee, Picasso, Tapiès, Richard Serra, Donald Judd and Nam June Paik. A number of temporary exhibitions are also hosted here.

Naturmuseum

🕐 *Open Tue-Fri, 10am-noon and 2-5pm (8pm Wed).* 🎟10CHF. ☎ *(071) 242 06 70.*
Housed in the same building as the Fine Arts Museum, the **Natural History Museum** displays its exhibits according to themes, such as life in a drop of water, birds and mammals of the region and the relief of the Alpstein. Note the skeletons of a Plateosaurus, a Pterosaurus and an Anatosaurus (around 80 million years old).

Historisches und Völkerkundemuseum Museum (C)

🕐 *Open Tues-Fri 10am-noon and 2-5pm, Sun 10am-5pm.* 🕐 *Closed 1 Jan, Good Fri, Ascension, Easter Mon, Whit Mon, 1 Aug, 1 Nov, 24, 25 and 31 Dec.* 🎟10CHF. ☎ *(071) 242 06 42; www.hmsg.ch.*
This **History and Folklore Museum** exhibits the history and traditions of the Sankt Gallen region from the Prehistoric period to the 18C. Exhibits include a reconstruction of Sankt Gallen Abbey as it was in the Middle Ages, a fine collection of painted glass, and popular art from the Appenzell and Toggenburg regions. Other exhibits include masks and sculptures from Africa, the Pacific and Asia, Noh masks from Japan, Inuit articles, and antique Greek and Etruscan sculptures.

Textilmuseum (B)

🕐 *Open 10am-noon and 2-5pm, Sun 10am-5pm.* 🕐 *Closed Good Fri, Easter Sun, Whit Sun, 1 Aug and between Christmas and New Year.* 🎟5CHF. ☎ *(071) 222 17 44, www.textilmuseum.ch.*
The modern **Textile Museum** pays tribute to a traditional industry that brought prosperity to Sankt Gallen and eastern Switzerland for over seven centuries. Linen (15C-17C) was replaced by lace and embroidery in the 18C, and later by the growth of spinning. Each of these production processes required different skills and the industry employed mainly women – around 30 000 employees by 1790. The articles exhibited here – lace, embroidery, drawings of models, clothes, needles and thimbles – were brought together by two collectors, Léopold Iké and John Jacoby. Finished embroidered garments, historical and modern, also are displayed.

Botanischer Garten

In the suburb of Neudorf; via Rorschacher Strasse (C) then bear left onto Stephanshornstrasse. ♿ 🕐 *Open 8am-5pm. Greenhouses: 9.30am-noon and 2-5pm.* 🕐 *Closed 1 Jan and 25 Dec.* 🎟 *No charge.* ☎ *(071) 288 15 30.*
These gardens (1.5ha/3.5 acres) are home to 8 000 species from the five continents, including Chilean rhubarb, with its incredibly large leaves. A pergola stands next to a pool full of rushes and reeds and; two fine tropical greenhouses house cacti, palm trees, euphorbia, orchids and giant waterlilies.

Additional Sights

Dreilinden Hill★ (C)

Alt 738m/2 420ft. Take the Mühleggweiher automatic railway (1893), the smallest of its kind in Switzerland. Mühleggbahn station is situated in Moosbruggstrasse. Follow the small path to the right upon leaving the station.
The three pools **(Weiher)** on this hill are 200m/220yd long and were created by the monastery to supply the mills, textile workshops and canals of the town; the monks

Address Book

SHOPPING

The pedestrian streets of the old city, are the perfect setting for a shopping expedition. The main shopping streets are **Multergasse, Spisergasse, Neugasse**, and **Marktgasse**. Find genuine St. Gallen embroidery at **Boutique La Bambola** (Brühlgasse 35).

THEATRE AND MUSIC

Stadttheater – *Museumstrasse 24* – ☎ *071 242 06 06, www.theatresg.ch.*

Tonhalle – *Museumstrasse 25* – ☎ *071 242 06 32.* Classical concerts in an early-20C building, a reminder of the prosperity brought to the town by the textile industry.

Kellerbühne – *St. Georgenstrasse 3* – ☎ *071 223 39 59, www.kellerbuehne.ch*

Puppentheater (Puppet Theatre) – *Lämmlisbrunnenstrasse 34*– ☎ *071 222 60 60, www.figurentheatre-sg.ch*

🖑 *For coin ranges, see Legend on the cover flap.*

WHERE TO STAY

⊖⊜🍽 **Vadian Garni** – *Gallustrasse 36* – ☎ *071 228 18 78 – www.hotel-vadian. com* – 16 rooms – Bright, well-maintained rooms. Home-made jam for breakfast.

⊖⊜🍽🍽 **City Weissenstein** – *Davidstrasse 22* – ☎ *071 228 06 28 – www. weissenstein-st-gallen.ch* – 23 rooms – Located in a quiet neighbourhood away from the old city, offering the comfort of a modern hotel and parking facilities.

⊖⊜🍽 **Ekkehard** – *Rorschacher Strasse 50* – ☎ *071 224 04 44 – www. ekkehard.ch*– 29 rooms – ✕ 🅿 🕓 *closed 23-30 Dec.* - Close to the cathedral. Simple yet comfortable rooms.

EATING OUT

⊖⊜🍽🍽 **Gupf** - *20km/12.5mi from Sankt Gallen* – ☎ *071 877 11 10 – www. gupf.ch* - 🅿 🕓 *closed Mon and Tue in May, Sun and Mon in Jun.* Traditional cuisine and elegant decor in a restaurant commanding views of the countryside; 25,000 bottle wine cellar.

⊖⊜🍽🍽 **Alt Guggeien** – *Kesselhaldenstr 85* – ☎ *071 288 12 10* – 🕓 *closed Mon, Tue and three weeks in Jan.* A warm

welcome and delicious regional cuisine in a former farmhouse. Splendid views.

⊖⊜🍽 **Neubad** – *Bankgasse 6* – ☎ *071 222 86 83– www.restaurantneubad.ch* – 🕓 *closed Sat-Sun and 13-29 Jul.* 16C mansion serving classic local cooking. Admire the fine Gothic ceiling in the dining hall.

⊖⊜🍽🍽 **Zum Schlössli** – *Zeughausgasse 17, am Spisertor* – ☎ *071 222 12 56 – www.schloessli-sg.ch* - 🕓 *closed Sat-Sun and mid-Jul to mid-Aug.* This small 16C château is worth a visit for its frescoes, furniture, salons with vaulted ceilings and its excellent local food!

⊖⊜ **Peter und Paul** – *Kirchlistrasse 99* – ☎ *071 245 56 25, www.peterundpaul. ch* - Wonderful views of Lake Constance from its dining room.

⊖⊜ **Zum Goldenen Schäfli** – *Metzgergasse 5* – ☎ *071 223 37 37* – 🕓 *closed Sun.* This traditional restaurant is in the oldest remaining guildhall dating from the 17C. The sloping ceiling and floor add to the rustic charm. Typical Swiss dishes and friendly service.

⊖⊜🍽 **Am Gallusplatz** – *Gallustrasse 24* – ☎ *071 223 33 30* – 🕓 *closed Mon, Sat lunch, mid-Jul to early-Aug and 12-18 Oct.* Situated in the medieval district of half-timbered houses around the cathedral. Specialising in hearty roasts, good regional cuisine and a wide choice of wines. Pleasant terrace.

NIGHTLIFE

The **Pub Bar,** the piano bar of the Hôtel Einstein (Berneggstrasse) offers a cosy atmosphere, where you can sink deep into leather armchairs and enjoy a cocktail or a local beer. The **Colony Bar** (Neugasse 46) offers live music and a DJ. Near the station, order one of many draught beers at **Mr Pickwick Pub** (Poststrasse), a typical English pub, right down to the dartboard.

EVENTS

Inline one-eleven is the longest rollerblade race in Europe. The race, which takes place in August, starts in Sankt Gallen and runs for 111km/69mi, through 20 villages and two cantons before finishing back in the town.

also used to fish in them. Around the turn of the 20C, the pools were made suitable for **swimming**; in summer, they provide an idyllic setting for a cooling dip. A charming Baroque-style house (1677) can be admired near the central pool.

From the pools, a waymarked path **(Höhenweg)** winds its way through pine forests and meadows up the Dreilinden Hill. The path heads as far as **Freudenberg**a peak (alt 884m/2 899ft), from where there is a magnificent **view**★ of the old town of Sankt Gallen and, in the distance, the shimmering blue of the lake.

University of St Gallen (BU)– *Dufourstrasse 50. Take bus n° 5 from the railway station to Rotmonten. Free admission to most of the works of art.* Twenty-nine works of art by artists such as Alberto Giacometti, Jean Arp, Joan Miró, Georges Braque, Alexandre Calder and Antoni Tapiès can be admired in the buildings and grounds.

Excursions

Tierpark Peter und Paul
Kids Alt 793m/2 601ft. *3.5km/2mi N of Sankt Gallen. Leave Sankt Gallen by Müller-Friedbergstrasse (B).*
This pleasant zoological park (deer, chamois, mouflons) is situated in an open setting. Ibex from the Gran Paradiso Massif in Italy were brought here in 1911 in the first stage of their reintroduction to the Swiss Alps. At the entrance to the park, a little path to the right along the boundary fence leads to a fine **view**★ of the site of Sankt Gallen and the Alpstein Range beyond it.

Säntispark (B)
Kids *At Abtwil, 4km/2.5mi S of Sankt Gallen. Take the A 1 motorway and exit at Sankt-Gallen Winckeln.*
This **waterpark** complex has excellent facilities, including a wave machine, saltwater baths, jacuzzis, a sunbathing grotto and seven saunas.

Towards Lake Constance
12km/7.5mi to Rorschach by road n° 7.
The landscape changes as the road heads towards Lake Constance: the meadows of the Thurgau lie to the west; the Fünfländerblick and Buechberg massifs and the foothills of the Alps extend to the east. This magnificent **panorama**★ is completed by the Voralberg Alps, with Mount Pfänder near Bregenz in the distance. On the Swiss side of the lake, **Rorschach** was the main port in the Middle Ages and was highly important for the Sankt Gallen region. In the main street **(Hauptstrasse)**, several fine houses with painted and sculpted oriel windows bear witness to this period of prosperity, as does the 18C corn exchange or **Kornhaus** close to the lake. Today the port is popular with pleasure boats; in the summer, ferries ply the waters between a number of Swiss and German ports.

SANKT-GOTTHARD-MASSIV★

SANKT GOTTHARD MASSIF

This is the kernel of the Swiss Alps and the watershed which supplies the two longest rivers in western Europe. In the Sankt Gotthard Massif the two greatest longitudinal valleys, the Rhône and Rhine, and the two greatest transverse valleys, the Reuss and Ticino, of the Swiss Confederation converge at Andermatt. For the traveller, the name "Sankt Gotthard" calls to mind a road and a series of walled-in sites rather than a grand mountain landscape. Here the summits are massive, and surprisingly, rise to a uniform height: they vary around 3 000m/9 843ft.

Sankt Gotthard Road

In spite of its reputation, this is far from the oldest route in the Alps, for traffic along it could be developed only after the 13C when the terrible Schöllenen Gorges had been opened. It was, however, a vital artery for Switzerland. Without the Sankt Gotthard road the Forest cantons, and especially the canton of Uri, which held the keys to this coveted highway, would have had more difficulty in securing their emancipation from the emperor and from the Habsburgs. Today, by road or rail, the Sankt Gotthard is a first-class route for communications between German-speaking central Switzerland and Italian Switzerland. A fire in 2001 raised the question of safety in the tunnel and it was closed briefly after.

Other Roads in the Massif

The Oberalp, Lukmanier and Furka roads complete the network for circular tours, starting from Andermatt.

Driving Tours

1 Lukmanierpass Road★

From Biasca to Disentis/Mustér – about 2hr 30min. & *See ALPI TICINESI.*

2 Sankt Gotthardpass Road★

From Andermatt to Biasca – 2hr. & *See ALPI TICINESI.*

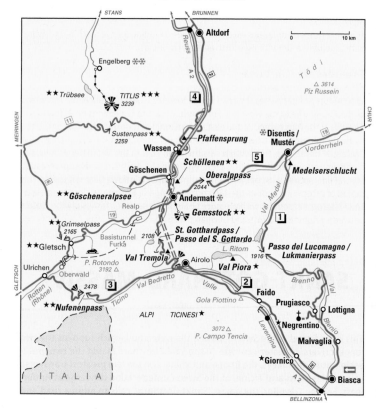

The Longest Road Tunnels

- **Sankt Gotthard (Uri, Ticino):** 16.3km/10.1mi
- **Seelisberg (Nidwalden, Uri):** 9.3km/5.7mi
- **San Bernardino (Graubünden):** 6.6km/4mi
- **Grand-St-Bernard (Valais):** 5.9km/3.6mi
- **Beichen (Solothurn/Basel-Land):** 3.2km/2mi
- **Landwasser (Graubünden):** 2.8km/1.7mi
- **Isla Bella (Ticino):** 2.4km/1.4mi
- **Binn (Valais):** 1.9km/1.2mi
- **Grancia (Ticino):** 1.7km/1mi

③ Nufenenstrasse★
From Airolo to Ulrichen – 1hr 30min. ⟳ *See NUFENENPASSSTRASSE.*

④ Schöllenenstrasse★
From Altdorf to Andermatt – 1hr 30min. ⟳ *See SCHÖLLENENSTRASSE.*

⑤ Oberalp Pass Road★
From Disentis/Mustér to Andermatt – about 1hr. ⟳ *See DISENTIS/MUSTER.*

SANKT MORITZ✳✳✳

GRAUBÜNDEN – POPULATION 5 057
ALT 1 856M/6 089FT – TOWN PLAN IN THE MICHELIN GUIDE SWITZERLAND

Living under the sign of the sun, Sankt Moritz (in Romansh, San Murezzan), is the most famous Swiss ski resort in the high mountains, a fact borne out by its slogan "Top of the World". Sankt Moritz is popular throughout the year with international visitors attracted by the resort's clear blue sky (it claims 322 sunny days a year), stunning scenery and sporting and leisure activities, including bobsleigh competitions, horse racing and even golf on the frozen lake, and a wide array of elegant boutiques, gourmet dining and world-class hotels. 🛈 *via Maistra 12 – 7500 – ☎ (081) 837 33 33, www.stmoritz.ch.*

▸ **Orient Yourself:** The heart of the village is pedestian-only Plaza da Scoula.
⌖ **Don't Miss:** Take the funicular up to Piz Nair for a memorable view over the Engadin Valley.
🕐 **Organizing Your Time:** At least two days, summer or winter, for events and excursions.

Visit

Twin Resorts
Sankt Moritz-Dorf, the main village, which has the world's oldest skiing school (1927), is grouped halfway up the slope at the foot of a leaning campanile, the only vestige of the original village. This is where you will find most of the grand hotels and luxury hotels and elegant boutiques as well as remnants of traditional Engadine architecture which are also a feature of the more typical villages of Silvaplana, Sils and Pontresina. In contrast, the mostly modern urban sprawl of **Sankt Moritz-Bad** at the lake's southwest corner may come as a surprise in such a natural setting. This

View of Sankt Moritz

is where many of the spa installations are found, offering waters rich in iron (for rheumatological, neurological, cardiological and many other disorders). Frequent shuttle busses connect the two halves of Sankt Moritz.

The Skiing Area

This is one of Switzerland's most important resorts for winter sports; it has hosted the Winter Olympics twice, in 1928 and 1948. The actual ski area, which extends over the Piz Nair Massif (alt 3 087m/10 029ft), offers opportunities for all levels, with more than 80km/50mi of downhill pistes and 23 chairlifts. The Corviglia and Piz Nair peaks offer mostly intermediate terrain on groomed runs. The Ski Engadin pass will allow you to enjoy facilities at Piz Corvatsch (3 303m/10 837ft, 65km/40mi of pistes), Diavolezza (alt 2 978m/9 755ft, 49km/30mi of pistes for more experienced skiers), Piz Lagalb (alt 2 959m/9 708ft, 29km/18mi of pistes) and Muottas Muragl (alt 2 453m/8 048ft, 8km/5mi of pistes), which form a far bigger ski area (altogether 230km/143mi of pistes). Snowboarders can enjoy numerous half-pipes and a boarder-cross at Corviglia (Piz Nair). Cross-country skiers can explore about 150km/100mi of loops throughout the whole area. Silvaplana and Pontresina are the two most popular resorts for cross-country skiing. Sankt Moritz has been the sight of the Women's Alpine World Cup downill race and the Engadin Cross-Country Marathon, held annually since 1969, in which thousands of skiers race 42km/30mi from Maloja to Zuos, running through Sils, Silvapana, Sankt Moritz and Pontresina.

In **summer,** Sankt Moritz takes becomes the ideal setting for hiking excursions through the Engadin Valley. The prettiest itineraries go past the nearby villages of Silvaplana-Surlej (🕭 *see ENGADIN)* and Pontresina (🕭 *see MUOTTAS MURAGL and BERNINASTRASSE).*

Sights

Engadiner Museum★

🕒 *Open summer, daily except Sat, 9.30am (10am Sun) to noon and 2-5pm; winter, daily except Sat, 10am-noon and 2-5pm.* 🕒 *Closed Easter, May, Nov and Christmas.* ⊜*5CHF.* ☎ *(081) 833 43 33.*

This visit is a useful preliminary to an excursion through the villages of the Engadine. With its arcaded gallery, its windows with outer embrasures, its oriel windows and its sgraffito, the building itself is built in local style. A *sulèr* leads to the rooms with their collection of furniture, mostly brought from lordly or peasant homes and decorated with carved pine woodwork. The stoves will interest experts in porcelain. The following rooms are particularly worthy of note: the **Engadine Room no II** (Zuoz house), with its elegant beamed ceiling; the luxurious **State Room no IX** (the Visconti-Venosta house at Grosio); and **State Room no VII** (a nobleman's house at Marca de Mesocco), which is simple, comfortable and full of character.

Segantini-Museum

🕐 *Open daily except Mon, 10am-noon and 2-5pm.* 🕐 *Closed May and Nov.* ⬛ *10CHF.* ☎ *(081) 833 44 54.*

This rotunda contains several works by the painter Giovanni-Segantini (1858-99), who enjoys widespread popularity in Switzerland. Note especially the symbolic **trilogy**★ *To Be – To Pass – To Become*, where details of the upper mountain landscape are illustrated.

Piz Nair★★

Alt 3 057m/10 029ft. About 45min, including 20min by funicular to Corviglia, then by cable car, and 15min on foot there and back. Cable-car: departure every 30min Jun to mid-Oct and Dec-Apr, 8am-5.30pm. ⬛*Fare there and back: 32CHF.* ☎ *(081) 836 50 50.*

From the terrace of the upper cable car station you can look down on the Upper Engadine and its lakes. Then go on foot to the highest point to enjoy the circular **panorama**★★ embracing the Bernina Summits.

Julier und Albula Pass Roads★★

Round Tour starting from Sankt Moritz

96km/59.5mi – allow 5hr. Itinerary ③ *(* 🚶 *see GRAUBÜNDEN map). Leave Sankt Moritz to the south.*

In the bends of the uphill road after Silvaplana lie, surprisingly near, the lakes of Silvaplana and Champfèr. As the road climbs to the pass,, a **panorama**★★ opens out over the Upper Engadine. It extends from the mountains overlooking the Zernez on the left to the Piz de la Margna on the right, taking in (from left to right), the Piz Vadret-Piz Muragl group, dominating Pontresina, Piz Rosatsch and Piz Corvatsch, between which the marked depression of the Fuorcla Surlej reveals the snowy Piz Bernina Summit (alt 4 049m/13 284ft) in the middle distance.

Julierpass

Alt 2 284m/7 493ft. The Latin and imperial ring of this name is enough to attract an archaeologist's attention. Two pylons, set up like milestones on either side of the road, are parts of a single column from a shrine to the pass built by the Romans. It may have served as the plinth of a statue (like the Joux column at the Little St Bernard). The road down from the pass drops 500m/1 640ft over 9km/5.5mi. The valley grows more and more desolate, but near the chalets of Mot a flourishing arolla pine with a very straight trunk stands all alone. The name **Bivio** means fork. Here the Septimer road, disused today, branches off from the Julier road at the entrance to the village, turning into a path running southwards, reaching the Septimerpass (alt 2 310m/7 788ft) before joining the Bregaglia Valley at the village of Casaccia.

Marmorera Dam

Guided tours 1 May to mid-Oct, Mon-Fri, 9am-3pm. ☎ (081) 637 68 68.
This dam (also called Talsperre), which has drowned the hamlets of Cresta and Marmorera, is unusual for having been built of earth. Over 2.7 million m³/95 million cu ft of material have been used to make a dam 400m long, 90m high and 400m thick at the base (1 312 x 230 x 1 312ft).
The essential purpose of the water storage of 60 million m³/13 200 million gallons is to feed all the hydroelectric power stations on the Julia and the Albula during the winter period of low water. The city of Zurich commissioned the works. The new reservoir blends in well with the austere landscape. During the winding descent, after the dam, three torrents, impressively full at the melting of the snows – especially the Ava de Faller – are crossed within 1km/0.5mi.

Savognin✳

Lovers of religious art may drive to the Church of St Martin, at the forest edge on the last slopes of the Piz Arlos. Leave the Julier road near the post office to go down into the valley, and after crossing the Julia on a humpback bridge take the second road to the right. This small, isolated church, tallest of three in the village, is distinguished by its classical pediment and the dazzling whiteness of its walls. The dome was decorated inside by the Milanese painter Carlo Nuvolone (1681): celestial hosts are arranged in concentric circles around the Holy Trinity and the Virgin, with a surprising effect of perspective.
Below the village of Riom, on the valley's other side, the ruined walls of the old Bishop's Castle of Raetia Ampla appear on a mound. The exit from Oberhalbstein takes you through the short defile of the Crap Ses.

Tiefencastel

This little town lies on the floor of the Albula Valley where the main road, from Chur to the Engadine by the Julier Pass, goes through the gap. Its chuch, southern in style, is the first evidence of Romansh civilization (🕭 *see GRUYÈRES)* for a traveller from Lenzerheide. Between Tiefencastel and Bergün, the Albula Valley becomes more densely forested (fir trees, larches and arolla pines), passing Alvaneu's sulphur springs on the left. It then becomes narrower and more steeply walled-in until the road is obliged to cut through rock in the **Bergüner Stein Defile**✳.

Bergün

This village, overshadowed by the triangular face of the Piz Rugnux, a spur of the Piz Ela, of which you get repeated glimpses, has several Engadine-style houses with oriel windows and window grilles, far more rustic than those of the Inn Valley.
From Bergün to Preda, while the road climbs steeply through mossy woods and fields, you will see the extraordinary contortions (loops and spiral tunnels) imposed upon the railway to gain height.
Arrival at Preda is marked by an opening-out of the mountainous horizon. The rocky Igls Dschimels Peaks and the Piz da las Blais are impressive. Between Preda and the

pass are pleasant pastures as far as the little green **Lake Palpuogna**. Higher up, beyond the Crap Alv, the road rises among rocky ledges as it skirts a marshy plateau, where numerous small cascades indicate one of the sources of the Albula. You then reach the grassy coomb marking the pass.

Albulapass

Alt 2 312m/7 585ft. The pass is usually blocked by snow Nov–June. Sse the rail-car service leaving from Tiefencastel for Samedan. The pass divides the Albula Basin to the north, a tributary of the Rhine from the Val d'Alvra, and to the south, a tributary of the Inn. Between this and La Punt, where clumps of larches reappear, you will get a quick glimpse, on the floor of the Inn Valley, of the nearby village of La Punt, dominated by the ruins of Guardaval. From La Punt to Samedan follow the flat floor of the Inn Valley until the peaks of the Bernina Massif appear through the Pontresina Gap.

Celerina – 🌢 *See CELERINA.*

▶ *From Celerina the road returns to Sankt Moritz.*

Walks

Val Suvretta da S. Murezzan★★

Go up to the Piz Nair by funicular, then by cable car. After that, allow a 3hr 30min walk, representing a 1 200m/3 937ft drop in height.
The itinerary starts with a steep descent for 50min, through arid countryside with scarce vegetation, leading to the Suvretta Pass (alt 2 615m/8 578ft). The pass commands lovely **views**★★ of the Val Suvretta da Samedan, dominated by the Piz Bever and, to the south, the Piz Julier and its glacier. Continue on the left and in 10min you will reach the **Lac Suvretta**★★, which offers a pretty view of the Bernina Massif to the south (Piz Roseg, Scerscen and Bernina).
The climb down, which becomes more and more pleasant, now follows a mountain stream, wending its way through pastures where cattle can be seen grazing. After a 1hr walk, the stream tumbles into a waterfall. Just beyond it, turn left into a steep upward path. After a short while, the path levels out, providing **views**★★ of Surlej village, the Piz Corvatsch and Lake Silvaplana. Then follow directions for Sankt Moritz-Dorf (nice overall views of the resort).

SÄNTIS★★★

Säntis, with an altitude of 2 502m/8 207ft, is the highest peak in the Alpstein Massif between Toggenburg, the Rhine Valley and Lake Constance, and the chief belvedere of eastern Switzerland. The summit with its calcareous shoulders, sometimes gently folded, sometimes sharply ridged (Wildhuser Schafberg), is one of the most easily identified in the range.

Climb to the Summit

From Schwägalp, the terminus of the roads coming from Urnäsch or Neu-St-Johann: about 1hr there and back, including 20min by cable car. Departure every 30min. 🕐 *Mid-Jun to Oct, 7.30am–6.30pm (9pm Sat–Sun); Jul and Aug, 7.30am–7pm; Nov to mid-Jun, 8.30am–5pm.* 🕐 *Does not operate the second fortnight in Jan.* ⇔*33CHF.* ☎ *(071) 365 65 65.*

From the upper station you can easily reach the summit, which is crowned by a telecommunications centre installed in 1956, and whose two restaurants and panoramic terraces have recently been renovated.

The **panorama**★★★ of the Vorarlberg Mountains, the Grisons, Glarus and Bernese Alps and the lakes of Zurich and Constance is incredibly grand. Its immensity is, however, often difficult to appreciate in full summer, especially in the middle of the day, when a heat haze obscures distant features. For a better view, go down steps to the Hôtel du Säntis, built above the wild valley of the Seealpsee (& see APPENZELL).

SCHAFFHAUSEN★

Ⓒ SCHAFFHAUSEN – POPULATION 33 461
ALT 403M/1 322FT

The old city of Schaffhausen, built on terraces on the north bank of the Rhine at the foot of the Munot Keep, is one of the most attractive towns in Switzerland because of its wonderful Renaissance and classical buildings. This is the starting-point for a visit to the Rhine Falls (Rheinfall), a traditional attraction of romantic Switzerland. 🗊 *Fronwagplatz 4 – 8200 – ☎ (052) 632 40 20, www.schaffhausen-tourismus.ch.*

A Bit of History

An Important Depot - As the Rhine Falls compelled boatmen to unload their cargoes here, merchants settled in the town and set up a depot which soon became important. By the end of the 12C Schaffhausen had become a Free Imperial City. It entered the Swiss Confederation in 1501. Nowadays, Schaffhausen depends largely on its situation as a communications junction and bridgehead. It has also become an industrial centre, drawing electric power from the river itself. Machine and electrical goods factories, spinning mills and steel works have been set up outside the old city of Schaffhausen, which has been able to keep its medieval appearance.

Sights

Old Town★
Dominated by the remains of the ramparts crowned by the **Munot**, a massive 16C keep, the old town forms a choice **belvedere**★ (Ⓞ *Open May-Oct, 8am-8pm, Nov-Apr, 9am-5pm.* 🞉 *No charge.* ☎ *(052) 632 40 20)* overlooking the town and the Rhine Valley *(to the platform of the keep: by stairs and a footbridge across the moat, now a deer park)*. The lower town contains fine houses with painted façades, often embellished with oriel windows; there are more than 170 beautiful oriels and bay windows in the quarter. The **Vordergasse**★ is one of the most typical streets, with its houses adorned with stucco and carvings and crowned with fine brown roofs, pierced by numerous dormer windows.

The Haus zum Ritter (AB A)
The Knight's House deserves special mention: the paintings adorning the façade were restored in 1938-39 by Care Roesch in the style and spirit of the original frescoes, signed by the famous Schaffhausen artist, **Tobias Stimmer**. Some of these murals, executed around 1570, can be seen in the Museum zu Allerheiligen. The themes chosen were inspired by Roman history and mythology. You also should see the

pretty fountains in Fronwagplatz and the Regierungsgebäude (A P) – Government House – a 17C building with a fine sculptured façade and a stepped gable.

Museum zu Allerheiligen★ (B M¹)

&♿ 🕐 *Open daily except Mon, 11am-5pm (8pm Thu).* 🕐 *Closed 1 Jan, Good Fri and 25 Dec. No charge when there is no exhibition, ☞9CHF other times ; guided tour by appointment.* ☎ *(052) 633 07 77.*

The museum is housed in the former Abbey of All Saints. It contains prehistoric artefacts from excavations in the region, manuscripts and early printed books, mostly 15C, which belonged to the monastery library, and works of Swiss artists from the 15C-20C. The most remarkable exhibit is an early-13C onyx, mounted on gold and inlaid with precious stones. The exhibits also include fragments of the paintings (c 1570) which originally adorned the façade of the Knight's House. These were the work of the Schaffhausen master Tobias Stimmer and they portrayed subjects from

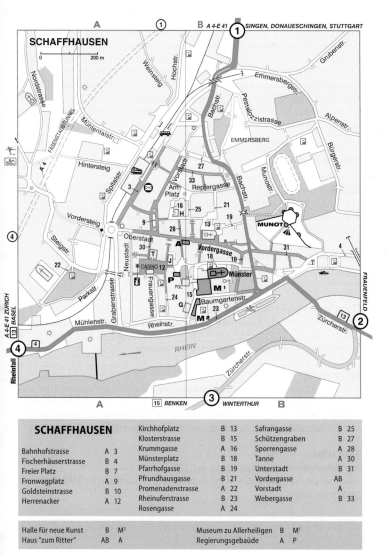

mythology and the history of Rome. A historical section retraces the city's past, whereas another gallery concentrates on natural history. Several rooms are devoted to the industries of Schaffhausen.

Münster zu Allerheiligen (B)

🕐 *Open 9am-5pm (8am-8pm summer).*

This 11C Romanesque abbey church was built with yellow ochre-coloured stone on the old basilical plan. Its interior was recently restored; tall columns support a wooden ceiling; the chancel ends in a flat east end. The cloister, abutting the south aisle of the church, has a gallery with Gothic bays and contains numerous tombstones. A bell known as Schiller's Bell, which inspired the poet's famous *Lied von der Glocke*, or *Ballad of the Bell*, is kept in a small courtyard nearby. Not far from there, a medicinal garden is planted with a wide variety of herbs and spices.

Hallen für Neue Kunst★ (B M²)

🕐 *Open Sat 3-5pm, Sun 11am-5pm.* 🕐 *Closed 25 Dec.* 📷*14CHF.* ☎ *(052) 625 25 15.*

Situated along the banks of the Rhine, this former textile factory dating back to the turn of the 20C century pays tribute to the Conceptual and Minimalist movements of the 1960s to 1980s. This temple of contemporary art, spacious and suffused with light, is laid out over an area of 5 500m²/59 200sq ft comprising four different levels; the first is set aside for temporary exhibitions. The permanent collections feature works by Mario Merz, Dan Flavin, Joseph Beuys *(Das Kapital 1970-77)*, Richard Long *(Lightning Fire Wood Circle)*, Lawrence Weiner, Bruce Nauman *(Floating Room)*, Jannis Kounellis representing Arte Povera, Carl Andre *(Cuts)*, Sol Lewitt and Robert Ryman.

Rheinfall★★

The Rhine Falls are the most powerful in Europe. The river plunges from a height of 21m/70ft. Its flow sometimes reaches 1 070m³/37 500cu ft per second (average flow, 700m³/25 000cu ft per second). The spectacle, which Goethe described as "the Source of the Ocean", is best seen in summer, at high water in July.

Scene from the north bank (Rheinfallquai)

4km/3mi by ④ and Neuhausen, where you will leave the road to Basel and follow Rheinfallstrasse.

Close views from the south bank

5km/3mi – plus 30min on foot there and back. Leave Schaffhausen by ④ on the road to Zurich, which you will then leave to turn right towards Laufen. Park the car at the entrance to Laufener Schlosses, which is now a restaurant.

Belvederes

Enter the courtyard of the castle. You will go down a staircase to the level of the falls. From the top of the staircase you will see, from a little kiosk with coloured windows, the huge mass of water below. Lower down, various platforms and gangways go very near the falls and make it possible to see them from the most varied viewpoints.

Boat trips

From Schaffhausen to Stein am Rhein: 📷*21CHF, there and back: 38CHF.*

These can take you to the rock in the middle of the falls and also ferry you from one bank to the other.

SCHÖLLENEN★★

URI

3KM/2MI N OF ANDERMATT

Between Göschenen and Andermatt the granite walls of the Reus Valley, remarkably smooth and polished, form a bottleneck. This is the legendary Schöllenen Defile which was the chief obstacle to the development of traffic on the Sankt Gotthard route until about the 13C, when a road was boldly driven through it. Modern roadworks may arouse a feeling of anticlimax in the visitor to the defile, in which case a walk along the old road is recommended.

Teufelsbrücke

In 1830, this bridge replaced one built, according to legend, at the instigation of the Devil and paid for with the soul of the first to cross it – a billy goat driven across by the crafty people of Uri. Since motor traffic is no longer permitted, the bridge is an ideal viewing spot to admire the foaming **Reuss Falls** (🔍 *best seen in sunlight around noon*). Slightly downstream, notice a cross hewn in the rocky wall of the east bank and an inscription in Cyrillic characters. It commemorates the hazardous venture of Russian General Suvarov, who, in pursuit of the French army, in 1799 came out on to the plain too late to prevent Masséna from defeating the Allies at Zurich.

SCHÖLLENENSTRASSE

SCHÖLLENEN ROAD

The itinerary, starting in the Lake Lucerne district and following the Reuss Valley, penetrates into the heart of the Sankt Gotthard Massif. Its most unusual site, the Schöllenen Defile, lies at the end of the itinerary.

From Altdorf to Andermatt *56km/35mi – about 1hr 30min*

Itinerary **4** *(🔍 see SANKT-GOTTHARD-MASSIV map). Between Altdorf and Göschenen, a motorway runs along the road we recommend.*

Altdorf – 🔍 *See ALTDORF.*

From Altdorf to Amsteg, as the valley narrows, the majestic conical Bristen Peak, rising sheer to 3 072m/10 079ft, catches the eye. The populous centre of Erstfeld marks the point where the line begins to climb the ramp to the north entrance of the Sankt Gotthard Tunnel, 600m/1 968ft higher up.

Between Amsteg and Wassen, the floor of the Reuss Valley, where the mountain section of the road begins, contains pretty shaded nooks. Bends in the road – especially before reaching Wassen, whose church can be seen directly after leaving Gurtnellen – give glimpses of the shapely pyramid of the Kleine Windgällen lying below.

Pfaffensprung

From the car park, downstream from the bridge over the Reuss, cross the road to a belvedere overlooking the Parson's Leap. The overflow of the dam built nearby forms a spectacular cascade, with beautiful iridescent effects.

Wassen

Wassen became well-known when the builders of the Sankt Gotthard railway made two successive loops in the track, partly underground, on either side of the village. Uninitiated visitors struggling to keep their sense of direction after seeing three successive views of Wassen church from different angles are a constant source of amusement to regular travellers.

From Wassen to Göschenen the bottom of the corridor is partly obstructed by landslides; among them is an enormous single rock called the Devil's Stone (Teufelsstein). Impressive road construction has been achieved on this section.

Göschenen

Göschenen is best known for its railway station at the north end of the Sankt Gotthard Tunnel (15km/9mi long, opened in 1882). It is a useful halt for tourists, who will find it pleasant to stand near the small central bridge and admire the icefield of the Upper Dammastock, which can be seen through the Göschenertal Gap.

Göscheneralpsee★★

The road that leads to this lake-reservoir offers close-up views of the Dammastock Glaciers (on the east side of the Rhône Glacier), which feed it.

The road climbs the wild, narrow Göschenen Valley, with, at the end of the ride, corniche sections along the side of superb rock faces.

Leave the car at the car park near the restaurant (alt 1 783m/5 850ft) and go to the centre of the dam's grassy crest (quite close). This dead-weight dam (capacity 9.3 million m³/204 600 million gal; 700m/2 297ft thick at base; 155m/508ft high; 540m/1 772ft length of crest) retains a reservoir-lake.

Ahead is a magnificent **landscape**★★ with the dam, cascades falling right and left and, separated by a rocky cone, gleaming glaciers below the Winterberg crests.

Schöllenen★★ – 👤 See SCHÖLLENEN.

Andermatt☼ – 👤 See ALPI TICINESI.

SCHWEIZERISCHER NATIONAL PARK

SWISS NATIONAL PARK – GRAUBÜNDEN

Situated in the heart of the Lower Engadine mountains in the eastern part of the country, Switzerland's only national park was created in 1914 by the Nature Protection League, one of the first national parks in Europe. It covers an area of 172km²/66sq mi between the Müstair Valley, the Inn Valley and the Ofen Pass, ranging in altitude from 1 400m/4 592ft to 3 200m/10 496ft. With its vast areas of untamed woodland, wild valleys and clear streams, this is the largest nature reserve in Switzerland. ☎ (081) 856 12 82, www.nationalpark.ch.

Park

🕐 Open Jun-Oct, 8.30am-6pm (10pm Tue). ✺ No charge.
The aim of the park is to protect local flora and fauna to this end visitors are required to leave their car in one of the designated car parks. Walkers must stay on marked trails. Camping, cycling, lighting of fires and picking flowers are forbidden.

Guided Tours - The national park and local tourist offices provide advice on walks and organise guided tours of the park. Some of the tours follow particular themes, such as deer-watching in the Trupchun Valley, which is especially rich in game. **Special excursions** include a visit to the park during the deer-rutting season in autumn. For further information, contact Tourismusorganisation Engadin Plaiv/ Engadin, 7524 Zuoz; ☎ 081 20 20; plaiv@spin.ch; www.engadin.ch

Nationalparkhaus

At Zernez (☾ see ZERNEZ), along route 28. ☉ *Open Jun-Oct, 8.30am-6pm (10pm Tue).* ☞*No charge.* ☎ *(081) 856 13 78.*
The National Park Centre provides information on the history of the park, as well as hosting temporary exhibitions, illustrated by video films, which introduce visitors to the protected species within its boundaries. Topoguides and a 1:45 000 scale map of the park are also available from the centre.

Walks

Access: continue along route 28, which winds its way through the Spöl Valley. Car parks at the entrance to the park. ▊ *Contact the tourist office in Zernez,* ☎ *(081) 856 13 00 or the Maison du Parc National in Zernez,* ☎ *(081) 856 13 78.*
The park is dotted with information panels in five languages, some of which are designed specifically for children, and has 80km/50mi of waymarked paths of varying lengths and difficulty (walking trails are marked with yellow signs, mountain trails that can require crossing steep or slippery sections are marked with a red stripe on a white background; alpine trails that require climbing or glacier traverse are marked by a blue stripe on a white background) . One of these starts at Ofen Pass, crosses Stabelchod Valley as far as the Margunet Pass (alt 2 328m/7 635ft) and then rejoins the Botsch Valley. Trails range from
The walks cross some magnificent scenery, especially striking from June to August, when the last snow is melting and the woods and meadows are full of flowers (edelweiss, gentian etc). Lucky visitors may even catch a glimpse of a marmot, deer, chamois, ibex or the bearded vulture, reintroduced to the park in 1991.

SCHWYZ★

ⓒ SCHWYZ – POPULATION 13 620
ALT 517M/1 696FT

This quiet little town, which prides itself on having given the Swiss Confederation both its name and its flag, occupies a majestic **site**★ at the foot of the twin Mythen peaks, between the lakes of Lucerne and Lauerz. ☾ *For the history of the original cantons, see VIERWALDSTÄTTER SEE: The Swiss national sanctuary.* **The resort of Stoos (alt 1 295m/4 249ft), built on a sunny terrace, forms its mountain annexe.** ▊ *Oberer Steisteg 14 – 6430 –* ☎ *(041) 810 19 91, www.schwyz.ch.*

Soldiers of Fortune

When foreign princes recruited mercenaries for their service from the 16C onwards, the men of Schwyz enlisted in their armies, especially in the French regiments. Their bravery and military qualities enabled many to return to their country, having made their fortunes, covered with honours and glory. They settled in their homeland and built the sumptuous homes that their descendants still own.

Sights

Bundesbriefmuseum★

🕐 *Open Tue-Fri, 9am-11.30am and 1.30-5pm; Sat-Sun, 9am (1.30pm Nov-Apr) to 5pm.*
🕐 *Closed Good Fri and 25 Dec.* 👓 *4CHF.* ☎ *(041) 819 20 64.*

A modern building, with a fresco by H Danioth on its façade, was erected (1934-36) to house the most precious original documents of the Confederation. In the great hall adorned with a fresco, *The Oath* by W Clénin, with banners of the Schwyz canton, are displayed the Pact of 1291 (Bundesbrief), the Pact of Brunnen of 1315 (Morgarten-brief), charters of freedom and pacts of alliance concerning the "XIII Cantons".

Pfarrkirche Sankt Martin

St Martin's Church has sumptuous 18C Baroque decorations. The nave is adorned with stucco and frescoes; the high altar, the altars in the side chapels, the marble **pulpit★** and baptistery are all elaborately decorated. In the transept lie the reliquaries of St Polycarb (left) and St Lazarus (right).

Rathaus

👓 *Guided tours Sat-Sun, 10am-noon and 2-5pm.* 🕐 *Closed public hols.* ☎ *(041) 811 45 05.*

Burnt down and rebuilt in the 17C, the town hall is ornamented on the outside with mural paintings (1891) recalling episodes in Swiss history. Inside are rooms with decorative woodwork and stained-glass windows.

Excursions

From Schwyz to Rigi-Scheidegg

12km/7.5mi. Leave Schwyz by the road to Zürich and at Seewen take road nº 2 towards Lucerne.

Rigi-Scheidegg★★

Leave Goldau from the south and take a narrow, winding road for 3km/2.5mi to the Station Kräbel *(also the mid-station for the rack-railway to Rigi-Kulm)* and take the cable-car to Scheidegg (🕐 *Departures every 30min from 8.10am-7.25pm.* 🕐 *Closed Apr and May.* 👓 *Fare there and back: 30CHF.* ☎ *(041) 828 18 38).*

At the top of the Rigi-Scheidegg (alt 1 665m/5 268ft) perches the small resort of the same name. Climb up the hillock behind the chapel and admire the immense **panorama★★**, similar to that of the Rigi-Kulm, but blocked to the northwest by the Rigi-Kulm's promontory.

Ibergeregg Road★

Michelin map 729 K4 – *11km/7mi. Leave Schwyz east via Rickenbachstrasse.*

Beginning at the hill's slope, after crossing Rickenbach, views open out on the left to the Mythen and on the right on part of Lake Lucerne and Lake Lauerz, separated by the Hochflue. After a magnificent stretch of corniche through woods above the deep Muotatal Valley and, in a bend in the road, there is a beautiful **view★** behind of this valley and the Lake Lucerne district. During the steep climb that follows, the snowy summits of the Glarus Alps can be seen. At the **Ibergeregg Pass** (alt 1 406m/4 613ft) admire the remarkable **views★** of the neighbouring valley.

Höllochgrotte★

15km/9mi by the Muotatal road (SE of the plan) plus 1hr tour. ♿ *See HÖLLOCH-GROTTE.*

When doing this trip you can also go to Stoos in a funicular and then to the magnificent viewpoint of the **Fronalpstock** (alt 1 922m/6 306ft).

SCUOL/SCHULS✳

GRAUBÜNDEN – POPULATION 2 134
ALT 1 244M/4 081FT

This mineral water and climatic spa, whose centres are scattered over the slopes of the widest basin in the Lower Engadine, is much appreciated for its setting of forests and rocky heights, among which the Lower Engadine Dolomites stand out against the sky. It also enjoys a dry, sheltered climate and bright sunshine.
🔳 *Stradun – 7550 – ☎ (081) 861 22 22.*

The Resorts

🚶*Walkers can avoid the main roads by using the paths linking the three resorts of Schuls, Tarasp and Vulpera.*

Scuol/Schuls✳
This village on the tilled slope of the valley has become a tourist and business centre sustained by traffic using the international Engadine-Austria route (Sankt Moritz-Landeck). At the same time, below the through road, Lower Schuls, the former nucleus of the community still stands around two paved squares built in pure Engadine style. The most imposing building is the **Chagronda House and Museum** (🕐 *Open mid-May to end Jun and in Oct, Tue-Thu, 4-6pm; Jul and Sep, Mon-Fri except Thu, 3-6pm; in winter, guided tours Tue-Thu at 5pm.* ⊚ *5CHF.* ☎ *(081) 861 22 21*), which can be recognised thanks to its two surperimposed galleries. It houses the Lower Engadine Museum.

Vulpera★★
Four hotels built on a terrace of the wooded valley side, among burgeoning flower beds, form the nucleus of the resort.

APA Publications

Schloss Tarasp

Excursions

Road to Ardez★

12km/7.5mi W by a narrow winding road.

The climb to **Ftan** will enable you to appreciate the site of Tarasp Castle. Coming down to Ardez (👌 *see ENGADIN*), the bend at the exit from the Tasna Valley and the return to the main valley provide an excellent **viewpoint**★★ overlooking the mountain setting of the Schuls Basin and Tarasp Castle.

From Tarasp to Kreuzberg

From Kurhaus Tarasp, 4km/3mi – about 30min – by a narrow, steeply winding road – plus 30min on foot there and back to the Kreuzberg. Cross the Inn River and start the climb to Vulpera; directly after the Hotel Schweizerhof turn right (hairpin bend). Leave the car at the entrance to Tarasp Fontana and take the road climbing to Tarasp-Sparsels, at the foot of the castle. At the end of Sparsels turn right along a road running into the fields within view of the cross on the grassy mound of the Kreuzberg.

Kreuzberg★

Alt 1 474m/4 835ft. From this impressive viewpoint you can admire the pretty **site**★★ of the castle and a **panorama**★ embracing the whole of the Lower Engadine with its Dolomites (Piz Lischana and Piz Pisoc) and its perched villages (Ftan and Sent).

Schloss Tarasp

Guided tours (1hr), Jun to mid-Jul, daily at 2.30pm; mid-Jul to Aug, daily at 11am, 2.30pm, 3.30pm and 4.30pm; Sep to mid-Oct, daily at 2.30pm and 3.30pm; Christmas to Easter, Tue and Thu at 4.30pm. ☜8CHF. ☎ (081) 864 93 68.

This castle remained an Austrian enclave until 1803. The fortress was restored (1907-16) and is now used at certain seasons by the Prince of Hesse-Darmstadt.

Sent

4km/2.5mi NE.

To reach Sent drive along a little road shaded by maples, traced along the flank of the ridge, within view of the Lower Engadine Dolomites and Tarasp Castle. Sent is a fine village with perfectly kept houses with Baroque gables, known as Sent gables.

SEELISBERG★

URI – POPULATION 569
ALT 845M/2 772FT

Seelisberg stands on a wooded spur dipping into Lake Lucerne within view of the Bay of Brunnen and the Schwyz Basin. It is overlooked by the twin peaks of the Mythen. As one of the exclusive summer resorts in central Switzerland, this luxurious retreat is characterised by its isolation, the majesty of its panorama and the quality of its tourist amenities. 🛈 *Im Bahnhof – 6377 – ☎ (041) 820 15 63*

Access

You can go up to Seelisberg by car, from Stans *(22km/13.5mi by a road described under STANS: Excursions)* or by **funicular**, from the Treib landing stage *(services connecting with the steamers on Lake Lucerne; duration of the climb: 8min.* 🕐 *Operates all year round, times vary according to the season. ☜5.80CHF. ☎ (041) 820 15 63).*

View from Seelisberg★★
From the public belvedere-promenade there is a view of the Fronalpstock and Lake Uri.

SEMPACH

LUZERN – POPULATION 3 183
ALT 518M/1 699FT

Founded by the Habsburgs, Sempach is built near the lake to which it gave its name; for a long time it owed its activity and prosperity to the considerable traffic on the Sankt Gotthard route (Basel-Lucerne-Milan), which now follows the opposite shore. The main street has an old-fashioned air with its Witches' Tower, its town hall (Rathaus) with a façade made cheerful by a red and white pattern, its flower-decked fountain and its houses with brown tile roofs.

A national hero
On 9 July 1386 a decisive battle took place near Sempach between the Swiss Confederates and Austrians commanded by Duke Leopold. **Arnold von Winkelried** spurred forward and grasped as many spears as he could hold in order to make a breach in the Austrian square, bristling with pikes. His heroic sacrifice secured the victory of the Confederates when Duke Leopold lost his life. A monument commemorates the events of that day, which heralded the decline of Habsburg rule in Switzerland.

Sights

Schweizerische Vogelwarte
  ♿ ⏱ *Open Apr-Sep, Tue-Sun 8am (10am Sat-Sun and public hols) to 5pm.* ⏱ *Closed Mon and Dec-Apr.* 🚾*2CHF.* ☎ *(041) 462 97 00; www.vogelwarte.ch*
The **Swiss Ornithological Centre** is devoted to local birds, as well as the survival of species and bird migration. It consists of several gardens, a number of large aviaries and a small museum presenting stuffed birds.

Kirchbühl
2km/1mi NE.
Beside the old church of Kirchbühl is a fine **view**★ of Lake Sempach and the Alps (stand in the former cemetery). A low porch roofed with tiles leads into the 13C nave. Among the damaged paintings, you will distinguish a *Last Judgement*, a *Passion* and a *Resurrection of Christ*. A 16C altarpiece adorns the chancel.

SIERRE

VALAIS – POPULATION 13 917
ALT 534M/1 752FT

Sierre is one of the sunniest cities in Switzerland. It lies in the Valais Rhône below the vineyards of the Noble Country (Noble Contrée) and at the mouth of the Val d'Anniviers. A huge landslide in prehistoric times explains the strange **site**★ of the town, in a landscape like "a gravel pit dug and turned over with a spade".

Sierre (Siders) marks the language boundary between French and German (*see Introduction: Language and religion*). 🛈 *place de la Gare – 3960 – ☎ (027) 455 85 35, www.sierre.ch.*

Several strongholds such as the Castle of the Vidômes and the Goubin Tower, perched on its rock, recall the part played by Sierre at the time of episcopal and feudal Valais. Shortly before his death in 1926, the Austrian poet **Rainer Maria Rilke** stayed in the former Château de La Cour, which now houses the town hall.

Sights

Hôtel de Ville
Formerly a manor house and a hotel, the town hall dates from the 17C and 19C. The **interior**★ is sumptuous in its decoration (elegant painted ceilings, frescoes, paintings and stained-glass windows) and yet it retains a certain intimacy. It houses a small museum: the **Musée des étains** (🕐 *Open Mon-Fri, 9-11am and 3-5pm.* 🕐 *Closed on public hols in the Valais canton.* 👁 *No charge.* ☎ *(027) 452 01 11*) Set up in the cellar, it displays approximately 180 pewter objects (tableware, utensils) from the 17C-19C.

Rue du Bourg
A small picturesque street with old houses. Note the unusual building with bartizans, known as the Château des Vidômes and the Catholic Church of St Catherine (17C-19C). Inside the church are a Baroque chancel, a carved pulpit and a lovely organ loft. At n° 30, on the ground floor, the Maison Pancrace de Courten houses the **Fondation Rainer Maria Rilke** (🕐 *Open by appointment.* 👁 *6CHF.* ☎ *(027) 456 26 46*), a tribute to the Austrian poet, who is buried nearby (👁 *see Raron, below*).

> ## The International Festival of Comics
>
> Every year, in late May and early June, the city of Sierre celebrates the joy of reading by staging a world festival devoted to comics and strip cartoons. Writers, illustrators, publishers and second-hand booksellers all gather in Sierre to attend the event. This popular festival also involves many exhibitions, street performances and concerts combining originality and humour. Children will be delighted since they, too, are included in the festivities, with a wide choice of games, quizzes, make-up workshops and drawing competitions.

Château de Villa
The **Musée Valaisan de la Vigne et du Vin** (🕐 *Open Apr- Oct, Tue-Fri, 2-5pm; Nov, Dec and Mar, Fri, Sat-Sun 2-5pm.* 🕐 *Closed in winter.* 👁 *5CHF.* ☎ *(027)456 35 25*) has been set up in one of the château outbuildings. The visit to the Wine Museum begins with a video film about traditional techniques for pressing grapes. The two following rooms are devoted to wine presses. The second one explains the work of a cellarman. The visit ends with a display of the different types of containers (bottles and labels, pewter pots, barrels) associated with the business of wine and the role it has played in society throughout the ages.

Excursions

Salgesch
A 6km/3.8mi-long **Wine Route** linking Sierre to Salgesch (**Salquenen** in French) enables you to discover part of the vineyard. The route is dotted with signposts which describe the different grape varieties (Chasselas, Pinot, Sylvaner, Malvoisie),

the quality of the soil, the various pruning methods and the long-standing tradition of *vignolage* (a day's work in the vineyard in springtime, accompanied by fife and drum music). In this quiet village, the 16C **Maison Zumofen** (🕐 *Open Apr-Oct, daily except Mon, 2-5pm; Nov, Dec and Mar, Fri-Sun, 2-5pm.* 🕐 *Closed mid-Dec to late Feb.* 🎫 *5CHF.* ☎ *(027) 456 45 25)*, easily recognisable by its double-gabled wooden roof, presents an exhibition which complements those of the **Musée Valaisan de la Vigne et du Vin** in Sierre. Several rooms enlighten visitors on the art of winemaking: soil, grape varieties, techniques and tools used in winemaking, and finally grape harvesting, conducted with the blessing of Saint Théodule, the patron saint of this noble profession.

Raron
20km/12.5mi E by road n° 9, then left onto a narrow road spanning the River Rhône.
The hamlet of Raron or Rarogne (named after an influential feudal family from the Valais) spreads at the foot of a rocky spur. The village centre features a group of pretty 16C and 17C houses made with stone and wood. A steep path leads to the top of the hill. Near the old tower, which is all that remains of the former castle, stands the 16C **Burgkirche**, clearly dominating the valley. Inside the church, a naïve fresco illustrates the Last Judgement. Note the demons, who have been portrayed in the costumes of Swiss mercenaries. The Austrian poet Rainer Maria Rilke is buried in the cemetery. At the foot of the hill, a small modern church has been carved out of the rock.

SIMPLONSTRASSE★★

SIMPLON ROAD

The Simplon road is not the boldest in the Alps – the Splügen and the Sankt Gotthard have more daring structures – but it is the noblest and most majestic. It is impossible not to succumb to the beauty of such a site★★★ as that which unfolds between the Simplon Pass (alt 2 005m/6 578ft) and Brig, on the Rhône Valley slope. This gentle winding road along the mountain flank, without sharp hairpin bends, is a model of adaptation to topography.

A Bit of History

Getting the Guns Through
As early as the 17C the Great Stockalper *(see BRIG)*, making the most of his monopolies and the position of Brig, adapted the Simplon road, used until then mainly by smugglers and mercenaries, to commercial traffic. He organised a mail service and built two hostels, which still stand at Gondo. But all this was for mule trains, not for wheeled traffic. The modern Simplon is a product of Napoleon.
After a detachment sent Italy via the Simplon had forced the passage only by perilous manoeuvres, the First Consul decided in 1800 that the road from Brig to Domodossola must be made accessible to artillery. The low altitude of the pass and its relatively scanty snowfall determined his choice, and the project received absolute priority. The undertaking was entrusted to a man from Champagne, Nicolas Céard, chief engineer of public works in the Léman *département*, who drew up plans for a road 7-8m/22-25ft wide with a maximum gradient of 10% (1 in 10). The road was officially opened to traffic in 1805, but Napoleon never had occasion to use it.

From Domodossola to Brig *65km/40mi – about 3hr*

Itinerary 2 (🚗 *see Le VALAIS map).* 😊*The Simplon Pass is sometimes blocked by snow from December to May in spite of the galleries built to keep it clear year-round.*

The really Alpine section begins at **Crevoladossola**, where you leave the warm inner plain of the Ossola, somewhat Mediterranean in character with its bushy, stony floor exposed to the meanderings of the River Toce.

From Crevoladossola to the border, the narrow Diveria Valley offers little interesting scenery. A few campaniles and the greenery of thickets of hazel, walnut and ash are not enough to make it attractive. A short distance from Crevoladossola, on the left, are the ruins of the little village of San Giovanni, razed by a landslide in 1958. The ruins increase still further the bleakness of the valley.

😊*Italian and Swiss customs control are at Paglino and Gondo respectively.*

Gondoschlucht★

The wildest section of this longvalleydefile, hemmed in by granite walls, is the confluence of the Alpienbach and the Diveria, whose falls join at the foot of a spur pierced by a road tunnel. Between Gstein (Gabi) and the pass, the road, leaving the Lagginital in the southwest where it penetrates towards the higher levels of the Weissmies (4 023m/13 199ft), climbs gradually among the Alpine pastures of the lower Simplon combe.

Above the village of Simplon the rugged appearance of the terrain still shows the devastating effects of the terrible avalanche of 1901 started by the collapse of a whole section of the Rossboden Glacier. The pile of debris can still be seen. Dominating this glacier, the Fletschhorn is the most attractive feature of the landscape. The larches thin out as you enter the upper hollow of the pass.

Simplonpass★★

Alt 2 005m/6 578ft. The road runs halfway up the side of this long, winding defile, with its uneven floor. It is overlooked from the south by the Böshorn, in the middle distance, by the snowy Fletschhorn and from the east by the greenish slabs of the Hübschhorn and the Chaltwassergletscher, coming from Mount Leone.

Of the three main features of this scene, none is more remarkable than the Alter Spittel (a former hostel built by Stockalper), which is high and flanked by a 17C tower and bell turret. The present hostel (Hospiz) was built at the same time as the road and is kept by the monks of the Great St Bernard. A stone eagle commemorates the watch kept on the frontier during the Second World War.

The **belvedere**★★ of the pass is at the highest point, that is, just before the hollow on the Valais side. Beside the Hotel Simplon-Kulm, it is possible to pick out the summits of the Bernese Alps which can seen between the Schinhorn and the Finsteraarhorn (highest point of the Bernese Alps alt 4 274m/14 022ft). A small section of the giant Aletsch Glacier can also be seen.

On the Rhône side, the road between the pass and a tunnel clings to the upper precipices of a rocky cirque laced by the icy waters of the Chaltwassergletscher which can be seen above, protected by a series of concrete galleries and roofs. Approaching the Kapfloch Pass through a gap you see the Fletschhorn, flanked on its right by the Böshorn. From the Kapfloch to Rothwald a long stretch of corniche road under larch woods finally reveals, 1 000m/3 281ft below, the town of Brig framed in the opening of the Saltine Gorges. The mountains separating the Rhône Valley from the Lötschental now unfold on the horizon: from left to right, the Bietschhorn, Briethorn, Nesthorn and Schinhorn.

Between Rothwald and Schallberg, the road detours into the **Gantertal**. On the north slope of this beautiful valley are many crooked arolla pines (🚗 *see Introduction: Alpine vegetation).* Between Schallberg and Brig the road at first overlooks the

Saltine Gorges (Saltinaschlucht), the floor of which cannot be seen. It then leaves the forest and drops to the well-tilled slopes of the Brigerberg. The towers of the Stockalper Castle and of the churches of Brig stand out behind the shining ribbon of the Rhône, often shrouded by the factory smoke of Visp.

Brig – 🕭 *See BRIG.*

SION★★

Ⓒ **VALAIS – POPULATION 27 018**
ALT 512M/1 680FT

The town of Sion is 2 000 years old. It lies in the inner Valais plain on a site★★ that can be fully appreciated when coming from Martigny or again when climbing to Savièze. The appearance of the two rocky Valère (Rhône side) and Tourbillon (mountainside) peaks, each crowned with episcopal fortresses, gives an immediate sense of history. 🚹 *place de la Planta – 1950 – ☎ (027) 322 77 27, www.sion.ch.*

🔍 **Don't Miss:** The church-fortress of Tourbillon surrounded by vineyards.

A Bit of History

The Bishopric of Sion
The bishopric of Sion was founded in the 4C, and despite rivalry with the House of Savoy, it played a key role in the religion and politics of the Middle Ages. In the early

Sion and the Valère Peak

Suisse Tourisme

11C the last King of Trans-Juran Burgundy, Rudolf III, made the bishop a temporal lord and a real sovereign prince, enjoying full royal prerogatives: dispensing justice, levying fines, minting coins and the presidency of the Diets or General Assemblies. When the Communes were emancipated, these privileges disappeared one by one. However, until 1848 the Bishop of Sion was elected jointly by the canons and the Valais Diet, and subsequently by the Grand Council until 1918. Since then, the appointment has been the sole responsibility of the Vatican.

Valère ★ (Y) *2hr 30min*

The hill of Valère, which overlooks the valley from a height of 120m/394ft, has on its summit a fortified church, the former residence of the Chapter of Sion. Leave the car on a small square, at the car park between Valère and Tourbillon, at the end of the rue des Châteaux, which goes up through the old town. You will reach the precincts and a grassy esplanade from which, looking far upstream, you may enjoy the **view**★ of the Rhône Valley. Inside the fortified area at the end of a ramp there is a terrace *(viewing table)* which affords a fine **view**★ of Sion and of the Lower Valais, looking downstream.

Église Notre-Dame-de-Valère★

🕐 *Open daily Jun-Sep, 10am-6pm; Oct-May, daily except Mon, 10am-5pm;* 🕶 *guided tours available from mid-Mar to mid-Nov, Mon to Sat at 10.15am, 11.15am, 12.15pm, 2.15pm, 3.15pm and 4.15pm, afternoons only on Sun.* 🕐 *Closed 1 Jan and 25 Dec.* 🎫 *3CHF.* ☎ *(027) 606 46 70/47 15.*

The church built on the top of the hill, has all the appearance of a fortress, with its curtain wall, battlemented tower and north wall and internal wall-walk. Building began in the early 12C and continued until the mid-13C. Magnificent 17C **stalls**★★ with panels depicting various scenes taken from the Passion adorn the chancel, which has historiated capitals dating from the Romanesque period and 16C frescoes. Note the organ-loft and organ, this is the world's oldest still-functioning organ (1390), and is played every year at the international Festival of the Old Organ.

Musée Cantonal d'Histoire★ (Y M3)

🕐 *Open daily except Mon, 11am-6pm (5pm Oct-May).* 🕐 *Closed 1 Jan and 25 Dec.* 🎫 *6CHF, no charge the first Sun in the month and 18 May.* ☎ *(027) 606 47 10.*

Originally the canon's residence, this 12C castle, the interior of which was recently renovated, houses alternate exhibitions presenting the history of the Valais area. Displays of sacred art, popular religious art (sculptures, gold and silver plate, pictures), military tradition (armour, weapons) and daily domestic life (furniture) are organised in rotation. In the large hall, enhanced by its finely sculpted fireplace and wooden beams, you can admire several painted murals (facing the fireplace) depicting the Nine Valiant Knights, three pagan heroes (Hector, Alexander and Julius Caesar), three Jewish heroes (Joshua, David and Judas Maccabeus) and three Christian heroes (Arthur, Charlemagne and Godefroy de Bouillon), seen as paragons of chivalry.

Tourbillon (Y) *1hr*

From the car park, a path leads up to the imposing ruins of a former stronghold whose crenellated walls circle the hill. During the ascent (rather steep), the **view** of Valère, its church-fortress and the surrounding hillsides planted with vines, is breathtaking. The building and the chapel were erected in the late 13C by the bishop Boniface de Challant. Although originally defensive structure, the castle became a summer residence for bishops in times of peace. Repeatedly besieged and rebuilt in the 15C, it was razed to the ground by a terrible fire in 1788. After walking through a first doorway, pierced in a ring of ramparts, one enters the enclosure of the castle, dominated by its keep. Inside the chapel, supported by ribbed vaulting ending in columns ornamented with carved capitals, a few fragments of mural paintings still remain.

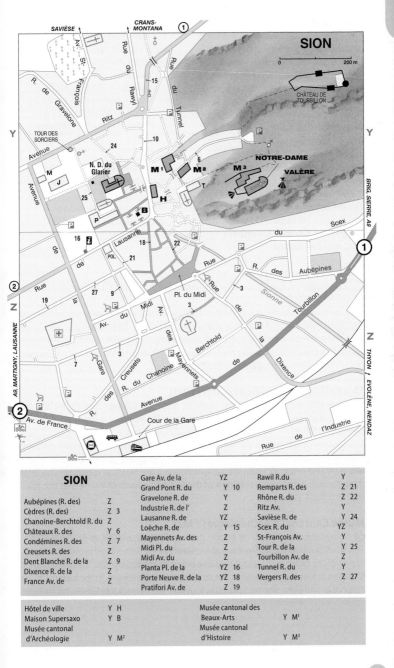

Additional Sights

🐾 *Guided tour of the town – 1-2hr, ⊜10CHF-15CHF depending on length.* 🛈 *For further information, contact the tourist office.*

Cathédrale Notre-Dame du Glarier (Y)

The 11C and 13C Romanesque **belfry**★ is adorned with Lombard arcades and ends in a graceful octagonal steeple. The ogive-vaulted nave was completed at the beginning of the 16C. The chancel contains 17C stalls and is decorated behind the high altar with a gilded wood **triptych**★ depicting the Tree of Jesse. To the northwest stands the Sorcerers' Tower (Tour des Sorciers), originally part of the medieval fortifications.

EATING OUT

⊜⊜⊜⊜ **Relais du Mont d'Orge** – *At La Muraz, NW by the road to Savièse –* ☎ *027 395 33 46 –* 🕒 *closed Sun evening, Mon and during the Christmas holidays.* This wonderful restaurant has a limited number of tables, so it is best to book ahead. In summer, meals are served on a terrace with lovely views of the valley.

Hôtel de Ville (Y H)

(🐾 *Guided tours of the town hall included in tour of the town.*) 🕒 *Mon-Fri, 8am-noon and 2-5.30pm.* 🕒 *Closed public hols.* 🛈 *For further information, contact the tourist office on* ☎ *(027) 322 85 86.*

The entrance of this 17C building is an elaborately carved wooden **door**. Roman inscriptions are exhibited in the entrance hall, one of which is Christian (377). The **Burgesses' Council Chamber**★ on the first floor has splendid woodwork and gorgeous furnishings.

Maison Supersaxo (Y B)

🕒 *Open daily except Sat-Sun, 8.30am-noon and 2-5.30pm.* 🕒 *Closed public hols.* ☎ *(027) 327 77 27.*

This sumptuous dwelling was built in 1505 by Georges Supersaxo, who wished to dazzle his rival, Cardinal Matthäus Schiner, with its luxury. The house has a very large, high **room**★ with a radially patterned woodwork ceiling with a huge rose-shaped pendant in the centre showing the Nativity of Christ. Around the room are 12 alcoves containing busts of the Magi and the Prophets.

Musée Cantonal des Beaux-Arts (Y M1)

🕒 *Open daily except Mon, 1-6pm (5pm Oct-May).* 🕒 *Closed 1 Jan, 25 Dec and following certain exhibitions. Guided tour first Thu in the month at 6.30pm.* ⊜ *5CHF, no charge first Sun in the month and 18 May.* ☎ *(027) 606 46 90.*

The Majorie and the Vidomat were formerly the residences of episcopal officers. They now house the Valais Fine Arts Museum (old prints, paintings by local artists, past and present). From the various floors of the Majorie, especially the third floor, there is a fine general **view**★ of the fortified church of Valère and the ruins of Tourbillon Castle.

Musée Cantonal d'Archéologie (Y M2)

🕒 *Same admission times as the Musée Cantonal d'Histoire.* ⊜4CHF. ☎ *(027) 606 47 00.*

This small but interesting Museum of Archaeology exhibits carved prehistoric steles, copies of the bronzes of Octodurum (the originals are displayed in the Gallo-Roman Museum at Martigny), as well as Roman and Islamic glassware. In the basement are amphorae and Gallo-Roman statuettes together with remarkable Greek and Etruscan ceramics and Neolithic vestiges: arms, jewellery, pottery and fibulae.

Excursions

Lac Souterrain de St-Léonard

6km/3.5mi by ① *on the road to Brig and then left; from the car park. Allow 10min on foot there and back.* ⊶*Closed for maintenance work.*

The lake and cave were formed by water infiltrating the gypsum bed and dissolving it little by little. The lake and cave were explored in1943 and wok was carried out so that they could receive tourists – the level of the lake is maintained by pumping (its dimensions are 300m/984ft long, 20m/65.5ft wide and 15m/49ft). The electric lighting enhances the site: the tormented relief and contrasting shades of colour (whitish gypsum, coaly schist and grey marble) of the vaulting and rocky surfaces reflect onto the lake surface.

Anzère

16km/10mi by the road to Leuk (Y 15).

This pleasant modern resort is very well equipped for both winter and summer sports. Located at 1 549m/5 082ft, its **site**★ was beautifully chosen: on the side of the Wildhorn Massif and overlooking the Liène Valley with, on the horizon, the Valais Alps extending beyond Crans-Montana.

Derborence Road★

24km/15mi. Leave Sion by S and follow road n° 9 as far as Pont-de-la-Morge.

The road climbs through vineyards and crosses the villages of Conthey, Sensine and **St-Séverin** (church with stone bell tower) where you go left. After Erde, vineyards are replaced by shrubbery; in the bend before the Aven chalets is a good view of the Rhône Valley. After St Bernard's Church (last nice view of the valley), the road goes northwards along the wild Triquent Valley, where the Lizerne runs. After the first tunnel, there is a view of the Les Diablerets blocking the combe to the north, The landscape is picturesque with snowfields here and there, pine trees, a torrent (the Lizerne, which the road crosses three times) surrounded by erratics, cascades.

The valley then opens into a grandiose **cirque**★★ of rocks, pine and larch. Bear left onto the rocky path, which ends in the Derborence Nature Reserve in a rock **corrie**★ created in the 18C, after an avalanche of the Les Diablerets.

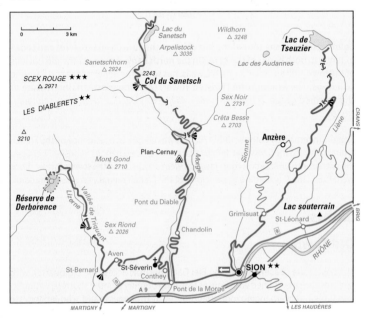

Sanetsch Pass Road★★

33km/20.5mi. Leave Sion by S and follow road n° 9 to Pont-de-la-Morge.

After crossing the Morge, the narrow road through the vineyards climbs to Chandolin, offering pleasant views of neighbouring slopes covered with vineyards and the Rhône Plain. At the Pont du Diable the corniche descends, meets up with the torrent and then enters a welcoming landscape with fir trees and a lovely cascade.

At the junction of the road to Conthey (on the left), the rocky Crêta Besse summit stands straight ahead. A steep climb (15% – 1 in 6.5) through woods ends at the chalets of Plan-Cernay.

2km/1mi farther, in front of the Zenfleuron Inn, the road crosses the Morge and in a corniche stretch passes the east slope, and after a tunnel, a **view**★ of the valley and at the opposite end onto the mountaintops (where three torrents tumble from melting glaciers). This is followed by a climb which opens, before the second tunnel, at the foot of the rocky face of the Sex Noir facing the snowy barrier of the Les Diablerets. After the last tunnel, the route continues its spectacular climb to the **Sanetsch Pass** (2 243m/7 359ft; lovely **view**★★ of the Les Diablerets preceded by the Tsanfleuron Glacier), then descends to the dam's reservoir (Sanetsch Lake) where the road ends.

Tseuzier Road★

23km/14mi. Leave Sion on the road to Crans-Montana to the north (Y).

3km/2mi after Grimisuat bear left onto the road to Ayent and at St-Romain follow the narrow but easy road signposted Barrage de Tseuzier, which climbs amid fir trees above the Liène Valley and soon offers some lovely glimpses of the valley and the terraced resort of Crans-Montana beyond (a wide **view**★, especially at the entrance to the first tunnel). At the end of the road *(restaurant)* is the small lake of Tseuzier Dam in its rocky basin.

SOLOTHURN★

Ⓒ SOLOTHURN – POPULATION 15 208
ALT 436M/1 430FT

Solothurn lies at the foot of the last ridge of the Jura (Weissenstein) and today extends to both banks of the Aare. On the north bank of the river the old nucleus of the town, still encircled by its 17C walls, has some fine Renaissance and Baroque buildings. The Krummturm (Twisted Tower) (Z) is the most striking feature of this fortified group. 🛈 *Hauptgasse 69 – 4500 – ☎ (032) 626 46 46, www.solothurn-city-ch.*

Solothurn remained Catholic until 1792 and was chosen as a residence by the French ambassadors to the Swiss Diet. Intellectual and artistic exchanges flourished between the two countries; Bourbon court fashions were adopted and the town's fortifications were built (1667) according to principles of the French military engineer Vauban.

Sights

Old Town★

The Basel Gate (**Baseltor**) and the Biel Gate (**Bieltor**) access the old quarter, with picturesque streets lined with houses featuring brightly painted shutters, wrought-iron signs and overhanging roofs. Hauptgasse, St-Urbangasse and Schmiedengasse are noteworthy. Marktplatz, the heart of the old town, is adorned with a fountain with 16C painted figures (St-Ursen-Brunnen). It is dominated by the 12C clock tower (Zeitglockenturm) (Y) whose astronomical clock face is surmounted by three figures (the King between Death and Saint Ursus, patron saint of the town).

Sankt Ursenkathedrale★ (Y)

This imposing Baroque building was designed in the Italian style (18C) by two Ticino architects, dedicated to St Ursus and St Victor, martyrs from the Theban Legion who, having escaped the massacre of Aguane (👁 *see SAINT-MAURICE*), were beheaded at Solothurn. The vast nave is supported by piers with engaged pilasters and capitals embellished with floral motifs. This decoration continues along the false gallery under the clerestory. The carved pink marble pulpit and the paintings in the chancel and at the transept crossing are the main ornamental features. Pleasant gardens are laid out behind the east end of the cathedral.

Jesuitenkirche (Y)

The Jesuits' Church (end of the 17C) features a **nave**★ consisting of three bays decorated with frescoes and stuccowork. A gallery runs along the first two bays, so that

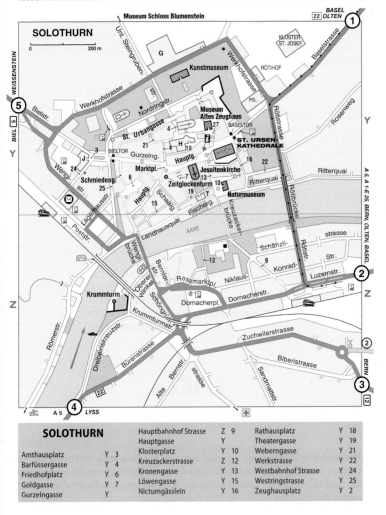

SOLOTHURN			Hauptbahnhof Strasse	Z	9	Rathausplatz	Y	18
			Hauptgasse	Y		Theatergasse	Y	19
Amthausplatz	Y	3	Klosterplatz	Y	10	Webergasse	Y	21
Barfüssergasse	Y	4	Kreuzackerstrasse	Z	12	Werkstrasse	Y	22
Friedhofplatz	Y	6	Kronengasse	Y	13	Westbahnhof Strasse	Y	24
Goldgasse	Y	7	Löwengasse	Y	15	Westringstrasse	Y	25
Gurzelngasse	Y		Nictumgässlein	Y	16	Zeughausplatz	Y	2

the third one appears to form a transept. The gigantic high altar is adorned with a great painting representing the Assumption, framed between two large green marble pillars. The double organ-loft is delicately decorated.

Museum Altes Zeughaus (Y)

🕐 *Open May-Oct, daily except Mon, 10am-noon and 2-5pm; Nov-Apr, 2-5pm; all year round Sat-Sun, 10am-noon and 2-5pm.* 🕐 *Closed 1 Jan and most Saint's day holidays.* 👓 *6CHF.* ☎ *(032) 624 35 28.*

The Arsenal Museum contains a large collection of weapons and uniforms dating from the Middle Ages up to the 20C. The second floor boasts 400 breastplates and suits of armour; the ground floor displays a German tank used in the Second World War and a collection of cannons, both old-fashioned and modern.

Kunstmuseum Solothurn (Y)

🕐 *Open daily except Mon, 11am-5pm, Sat-Sun 10am-5pm.* 🕐 *Closed 1 Jan, Good Fri, Easter, Whitsun and Christmas.* 👓 *6CHF.* ☎ *(032) 624 40 00.*

Most of the exhibitions are devoted to Swiss art from 1850 onwards. The most interesting collections are on the first floor. Alongside works by Ferdinand Hodler, Félix Vallotton, Daniel Spoerri and Cuno Amiet, all contemporary painters, note two stunning portraits executed by bygone masters. **Virgin with Strawberries**★ is a painting on wood from the Rhenish School (c 1425), remarkable for of its strong, vivid colours (blue, green, gold, crimson, ruby) and the graceful attitude of the two characters. As for the **Madonna of Solothurn**★ – the work of Holbein the Younger – it is full of majesty and shows strict composition in which gold, red and blue predominate. Visitors may also admire works by Klimt, Van Gogh, Renoir, Matisse, Picasso and Braque.

Naturmuseum (Y)

♿🕐 *Open daily except Mon, 2-5pm, Sun 10am-5pm.* 🕐 *Closed 1 Jan, Easter, Whitsun and Christmas.* ☎ *(032) 622 70 21.*

The Natural History Museum enlightens the visitor on the human race and regional fauna (alive and fossilised). The second floor contains displays on Swiss geology and mineralogy. Do not miss the fossilised tortoises from Soleure, starfish and dinosaur footprints. The basement houses temporary exhibitions.

Museum Schloss Blumenstein

Access NW of the town centre (follow directions for Schloss Blumenstein) via Untere Steingrubenstrasse (Y), the Herrenweg on the right and the Blumensteinweg on the left. 🕐 *Open Tue-Sat 2-5pm, Sun 10am-5pm.* ☎ *(032) 622 54 70.*

This large 18C building, surrounded by a small park, exhibits various collections from different periods: furniture, tapestries, sculpture (religious and cult objects), costumes, ceramics, musical instruments. On the ground floor verandah, note the lovely 16C stained-glass windows, together with a model of the town. The first floor has exhibits on the history of the town and the Solothurn canton.

SPIEZ★

BERN – POPULATION 11 928
ALT 628M/2 060FT

This charming little town on the south shore of Lake Thun at the foot of the Niesen enjoys a beautiful **site**★ best seen from a terrace at the exit from the town beside the road to Interlaken. Spiez is a pleasant summer resort and a good excursion centre. *Info-Center – 3700 – ☎ (033) 654 20 20, www.spiez.ch.*

Jerry Dennis / APA Publications

Spiez

Sights

Schloss

The medieval castle, crowned with several massive towers, stands on a spur of the Spiezberg overlooking the lake and the bay. It was built in the 12C and 13C and has since been enlarged and restored several times. From the public garden on the esplanade in front of the castle entrance, you overlook the harbour containing sailing and pleasure boats. Many chalets nestle among the greenery on the far shore. The **Castle Museum** (🕐 *Open mid-Apr to mid-Oct, Mon 2-5pm (6pm Jul to mid-Sep), Tue-Sun 10am-5pm (6pm Jul to mid-Sep).* 🎫 *5CHF.* ☎ *(033) 654 15 06)* contains mementoes of the former owners of the castle, the Erlachs and Bubenbergs, and some fine Gothic, Renaissance and Baroque inlaid furniture. The rooms are adorned with ornate woodwork and stained-glass windows. From the top of the great tower you can admire a fine **panoramic view**★★ of the lovely sites of Spiez, Lake Thun, the Niesen in the south and the Beatenberg in the east.

Alte Kirche

This Romanesque church (late 10C, now disused) near the castle was designed after the basilical plan, with three aisles and semicircular apses (fine frescoes). To the left of the chancel are the tombs of Sigismond of Erlach and Jeanne of Budenberg.

STANS

Ⓒ NIDWALDEN – POPULATION 6 744

ALT 451M/1 480FT

Stans has remained an agreeable town of purely local interest, making a good excursion centre – especially for going by funicular and cable car up to the magnificent Stanserhorn belvedere (🦶 *see below*) – or a convenient place for a stopover when the hotels in the Lucerne district are full. It was in the Diet at Stans in 1481 that **Nicholas of Flüe** (🦶 *see VIERWALDSTÄTTER SEE*) saved the still fragile structure of the young Confederation by his conciliatory intervention.
🏛 *Bahnhofplatz 34 – 6370 –* ☎ *(041) 610 88 33.*

Sights

Kirche

The large Romanesque church **belfry**★, with four tiers of arcades, towers above the main square. The spire was added in the 16C. The spacious interior, in early Baroque style, is impressive: statues adorning the nave stand out in dazzling white, whereas the chancel and aisles feature altarpieces carved in the local black marble. Below the church note the monument commemorating the sacrifice of Arnold von Winkelried at the Battle of Sempach.

Museum für Geschichte

🕐 *Open Apr-Oct, Mon-Sat, 2-5pm, Sun, 10am-noon and 2-5pm; Nov-Mar, Wed and Sat, 2-5pm, Sun, 10am-noon and 2-5pm.* 🎫 *5CHF.* ☎ *(041) 618 73 40.*

This small Museum of Local History situated at the heart of the town features a charming little chapel embellished with a 1604 altarpiece. One of the rooms evokes the Day of Horror – 9 September 1798 – when the French assault on the local mountain people caused bloodshed *(audio-visual presentation in German only).*

Excursions

Stanserhorn★★

Alt 1 898m/6 227ft. A pleasant ride in a funicular and cable car (🕐 *Operates May-Oct. Departure every 30min (every 10min at busy periods) 8.30am-5.15pm.* 🎫 *Fare there and back: 48CHF.* ☎ *(041) 618 80 40)* takes you to the upper station (the huge serrated wheels of the winch which hoisted the old funicular can be seen) from where a portion of the view *(viewing table)* seen from the top is offered. Walk to the summit *(20min there and back)* from where there is a splendid **panorama**★★ of Lake Lucerne to the north, the peaks of the Swiss Alps to the south (Titlis Glacier) and to the southwest, the summits of the Bernese Alps, including the Jungfrau Massif.

Road to Seelisberg

22km/13.5mi – about 1hr – Itinerary ② (👣 *see VIERWALDSTÄTTER SEE map).*

Start at Stans, go under the motorway to the large town of **Buochs**, located on the south bank of Lake Lucerne; continue along the lake shore via Niederdorf to the charming village of **Beckenried** *(beaches).* After St Anna and a steep climb look back and admire the silhouette of Mount Pilatus. After a pleasant wooded stretch at Emmetten, there is a lovely view to the left of the lake. The road then leads through an undulating landscape: before arriving at **Seelisberg**, there is a view, below and to the right, onto the small Seeli Lake set at the foot of the Niederbauen Chulm Cliffs.

STEIN AM RHEIN★★

SCHAFFHAUSEN – POPULATION 3 008
ALT 413M/1 355FT

The picturesque medieval town of Stein am Rhein is built on the north bank of the Rhine, close by the outflow of the Untersee, the western basin of Lake Constance. 🛈 *Oberstadt 9 – 8260 –* ☎ *(052) 741 28 35.*

Old Town★★ *45min*

Its character is apparent as you approach the bridge spanning the Rhine. On the right are half-timbered houses, whose foundations dip into the river. The Town Hall Square (Rathausplatz) and the main street (Hauptstrasse) form an exceptional picture with flower-decked fountains and oriel-windowed houses, whose fully painted façades develop the theme of each house sign: the House of the Pelican, Inn of the Sun, House of the Red Ox and the House of the White Eagle each have their own motifs.

Historische Sammlung
Housed on the second floor of the town hall (Rathaus). 👁‍🗨 *Guided tours (45min) 10-11.30am and 2-5pm.* 🕐 *Closed Sat-Sun and public hols.* 🎫 *3CHF.* ☎ *(052) 742 20 40.*
A historical collection of weapons, Delft porcelain and historiated stained-glass windows from the 16C and 17C recall the town's past.

Kloster Sankt Georgen
🕐 *Open Apr-Oct, daily except Mon, 10am-5pm.* 🕐 *Closed Good Fri.* 🎫 *3CHF.* ☎ *(052) 741 21 42.*
This former Benedictine monastery, set up at Stein in the 11C by the German Emperor Heinrich II, has kept its medieval character but has been converted into a **museum**★ (history, local art). Rooms are adorned with carved ceilings, panelling and inlaid furniture and are sometimes decorated with 16C monochrome paintings *(grisaille)*.
You will notice the monks' cells, with their fine stone paving, the bailiff's room, the cloisters and the chapterhouse. The Romanesque church, a 12C basilica with a flat ceiling and no transept, has been restored.

Excursion

Burg Hohenklingen★
2.5km/2mi N.
A steep uphill road running partly among vineyards, partly through woods, leads to Hohenklingen Castle. From the tower you will see a **panorama**★ of Stein am Rhein and its site, the Rhine, the surrounding hills and beyond them the Alps, from which the Säntis emerges.

Stein am Rhein

SURSEE

LUZERN – POPULATION 8 006
ALT 504M/1 654FT

The small old town of Sursee stands near the northwest corner of Lake Sempach. It has kept some of its old atmosphere in spite of the fires that ravaged it between the 14C and the 17C. *Banhofstrasse 45 – 6210 – ☎ (041) 921 19 45.*

Old Town

Rathaus

This fine town hall from the Late Gothic period (mid-16C) is flanked by two towers. One ends in a slender belfry, whereas the other is hexagonal and crowned by a dome. The façade with a stepped gable is pierced by many mullioned windows. The **Baseltor** or **Untertor**, the town gate, a vestige of the former ramparts, is flanked by a half-timbered house whose white façade is intersected by red beams.

Excursions

Wallfahrtskirche Mariazell

On the outskirts of town near the road to Beromünster.
Built in the 17C, this pilgrim's chapel is adorned with a ceiling decorated with naïve paintings representing Noah's Ark, the Tower of Babel and other Old Testament scenes. Near the gateway there is a **view**★ of the lake, the Alps and the Jura.

Beromünster

7.5km/5mi NE of Sursee.
This little town, near the transmitters of the Swiss National German-language Broadcasting Station, gets its name from the monastery (Münster) founded in 980 by Count Bero of Lenzburg and transformed in the 13C into a priory for lay canons.

Stiftskirche

Guided tours by appointment, Mon-Fri, 10am-5pm. ☜5CHF. ☎ (041) 930 39 82.
The collegiate church was built in the 11C and 12C but almost entirely remodelled in the Baroque style. The porch is adorned with many shields bearing the arms of former canons. The raised chancel is enclosed by a wrought-iron screen and furnished with remarkable **stalls**★ (1609). Their carved panels represent episodes in the Life of Christ. The treasury holds the reliquary of Warnebert (7C).

Schloss-Museum

Guided tours (1hr) May-Oct, Sun and public hols, 3-5pm. ☜3CHF. ☎ (041) 930 29 34/35 51.
The museum, housed in the castle's medieval tower, displays a collection of furniture, paintings, local costumes, tools and objects from Beromünster and its environs as well as a reconstruction of the Helyas Heyle print room where, in 1470, the very first book was printed in Switzerland.

SUSTENSTRASSE★★★

SUSTEN PASS ROAD

The Susten Pass road linking Wassen to Innertkirchen is a masterpiece of engineering, built between 1938 and 1945. It was the country's first great mountain road designed for motoring.

🐌 **Advice:** It is better to cancel or postpone this trip if the weather is not fair.

From Andermatt to Meiringen *62km/38mi – about 3hr 30min*

Itinerary 1 *(🐌 see BERNER OBERLAND map)*

Andermatt✳ – 🐌 *See ALPI TICINESI.*

The principal feature of the Andermatt-Wassen run, which uses the Sankt Gotthard road along the bottom of the Reuss Valley, is the steep-sided Schöllenen Defile.

Schöllenen★★ – 🐌 *See SCHÖLLENEN.*

Göschenen – 🐌 *See SCHÖLLENENSTRASSE.*

Wassen – 🐌 *See SCHÖLLENENSTRASSE.*

From Wassen to the Chapel Meien Dörfli, the Susten Pass road (Susten means public goods depot), which cuts through the rock, is at first curiously interlaced with the railway track. The latter makes a great loop, largely underground, to cross the ridge between the main Reuss Valley and the valley of the River Meienreuss (Meiental). Notice, downstream in the Reuss Valley, the isolated pyramid of the Bristen.
The road from Meien Dörfli to the pass, uphill all the way, climbs higher and higher above the Meiental, which for a long time seems to be closed by the jagged peaks of the Fünffingerstöcke (Five Fingers). As you approach the upper hairpin bends and tunnel through the crest, the final cirque appears with the symmetrical, triangular rocky faces of the Sustenspitz and the Klein Sustenhorn dominating the pass from the south. From the viewing table 700m/765yd from the east end of the tunnel it is possible to pick out the chief rocky summits of the Spannörter and Bristen groups.

Sustenpass★★
🅿 *Large car park at the west end of the tunnel (Bernese slope).*
The road reaches its highest point (2 224m/7 296ft) in the 325m/1 067ft long tunnel under the pass (alt 2 259m/7 411ft – *which can be reached on foot*). From this point on, the finest **scenery**★★★ is the 4km/2.5mi between the western entrance and the Himmelrank. This continual marvel should be taken as slowly as possible. In the foreground the huge flow of the **Steingletscher** dies away under a mass of reddish morainic deposits; the foot of the glacier reappears on the shores of a small lake, where miniature icebergs float. View the Sustenhörner group summits at the Swiss Touring Club viewing table 2km/1mi below the pass.

Himmelrank★★
🅿 *Park inside the bend.*
The road-builders named this Paradise Bend; it winds across a rocky slope formerly called Hell Upstairs by the people of Gadmental. They were more aware of the grim appearance of this section than of the **view**★★ of the verdant combe of Gadmen

and the icy Sustenhörner Summits (Sustenhorn, Gwächtenhorn). It is in the section between the Steingletscher Hotel and Gadmen that the engineers have shown the greatest audacity.

Gschletter Hairpin Bend★

P *Park inside the bend; fountain.*
This loop in steep country forms a **belvedere**★ overlooking the lower Gadmental and the majestic, ruin-like escarpments of the Gadmerflue and the Wendenstöcke. Very high up, the massive crenellated walls of the Gadmerflue and the Wendenstöcke, detached from the Titlis, stand out against the sky. Near Gadmen the valley floor shows its gentler side with maple-planted fields. Between Gadmen and Innertkirchen are two more descents: the Nessental shelf is pleasant with many walnut and fruit trees but the valley is still narrow and lonely. At the last rise before arriving in the Innertkirchen Basin, the view opens out to the snowy summits which enclose the Urbachtal, on the left of the dark and rugged crests of the Engelhörner.

Engstlenalp★

A 13km/8mi detour intended mainly for seasoned ramblers.
A few kilometres below Nessental, level with a bridge, turn right into a narrow toll road *(at 4km)* that climbs up into the forest, passing through lovely pastures where cows are put out to graze. Behind you extend splendid **views**★★ of the Bernese Oberland (Finsteraarhorn, Wetterhorn). Several walks leave from the final car park: the stunning lake, the **Engstlensee**★★ *(10min)*, then proceed to **Joch Pass**★★ by chair-lift, to **Trübsee**★★ *(second chair-lift going down)* and finally **Titlis**★★★ (*see ENGELBERG, allow a whole day*). Alternatively, you may choose to visit lakes **Tannensee**★, **Melchsee**★ and **Blausee**★ *(2hr to get there, 1hr 45min to get back)*.
Between Innertkirchen and Meiringen you follow the road to the Grimsel.

Aareschlucht★★

From the road to Meiringen, 1km/0.5mi. See MEIRINGEN: Excursions.

Meiringen★ – See MEIRINGEN.

THUN★★

BERN – POPULATION 39 854
ALT 560M/1 837FT
PLAN OF IN MICHELIN GUIDE SWITZERLAND

Thun is one of the most original towns in Switzerland, occupying an admirable **site**★★ within view of the Bernese Alps. The city was first established on an islet in the Aare where the river flows out of Lake Thun (Thunersee), and it gradually spread over the neighbouring shores at the foot of the Schlossberg, while passing from the hands of the Zähringens (*see BERN*) to those of the Kyburgs. The second dynasty having become extinct in its turn, Thun came under the control of the Gentlemen of Bern. The old quarters lie on the right bank of the Aare but the modern town with its ironworks has spread westward over the left bank.
 *Bahnhof – 3600 – ☎ (033) 225 90 90, www.thuntourismus.ch.*

Don't Miss: A cruise on Lake Thun, past castles and palaces and sun-blackened wooden chalets; excursion boats stop directly at the train station.

Address Book

WHERE TO STAY

🍽🍽🍽🍽 **Krone** –*Rathausplatz 2
– ☎ 033 227 88 88 – www.krone-thun.
ch – 27 rooms* – Conveniently located in
the heart of the old town, the recently
renovated and refurbished rooms are a
sheer feast for the eyes.

🍽🍽🍽🍽 **Arts Schloss Schadau**
– Seestrasse 45 – ☎ 033 222 25 00 – www.
*schloss-schandau.ch – ⏰ closed Mon in
Feb and Tue Nov-Apr.* This 19C château in
a sumptuous setting, a leafy park sits on
a lake, with a restaurant and a bistro for
different budgets.

Nightlife

Dancing and socialising on five levels at
Musicpark (Scheibenstrasse 49-51).

The Old Town

The bustling **Obere Hauptgasse**★ has an amusing feature: the flower-decked terraces of the houses serve as footpaths, so that one walks on the roofs of the shops
installed in the arcades at ground level. From the upper part of this street with its
broad overhanging roofs a curious covered staircase (Kirchtreppe) leads to the church
and the Zähringen Castle. Look for the city's narrowest house, only 2m/6ft wide,
at No 61. The **Rathausplatz**★ is surrounded by arcaded houses and adorned with
a flower-decked fountain. Dominated by its castle, the Rathausplatz makes a fine
picture. A covered wooden bridge (Obere Schleuse), crosses the Aare.

Schloss
Reached by the covered staircase (Kirchtreppe) mentioned above.
It rears its massive Romanesque keep – flanked by four towers – which now houses
the Schlossmuseum, at the north end of the Schlossberg.

Schlossmuseum★

⏰ Open Jun-Sep, 10am-5pm; Feb and
Mar, 1-4pm, Nov-Jan, Sunday 1-4pm.
💰6CHF. ☎ (033) 223 20 01.
The magnificent Knights' Hall contains
beautiful tapestries – one from the tent
of Charles the Bold, seized by the Confederates after the Battle of Grandson in
1476 – together with standards, breastplates, chests, ceramics (a fine collection
of old "Heimberg" pieces), archeological
artefacts, items relating to local folklore,
instruments, furniture and popular artwork evoking Thun in the 18C. Above the
Knights' Hall are special exhibits, such as
Swiss Army firearms and uniforms. From
the top floor of the tower you can reach the
four corner turrets for a **panorama**★★ of
the town, the Aare, Lake Thun and the Bernese Alps from the Stockhorn in the west
to the Niesen in the south, embracing the
Jungfrau, the Eiger and the Mönch.

Thun Castle

Jerry Dennis/ APA Publications

The Lake Shore

Jakobshübeli★★
From this hill equipped as a belvedere *(viewing table)*, there is a semicircular **panorama**★★ towards the Stockhorn and the Jungfrau.

Schadau Park
Set on the lake shore, this pleasant garden surrounding the castle offers a fine **view**★★ *(viewing table)* of the summits of the Bernese Alps, particularly the Finsteraarhorn (alt 4 274m/14 022ft), which is the highest point of this mountain group.

Wocher Panorama
🕐 *Open May–Oct, Tue–Sun, 10am–5pm (9pm Wed).* ⊕ *5CHF.* ☎ *(033) 225 84 20.*
The park is the setting for the rotunda housing Marquard Wocher's panorama portraying Thun and its environs around 1810. These pictures without boundaries were very popular towards the end of the 19C.

Excursion

Einigen
11km/6.5mi S by Frutigenstrasse.
Halfway between Thun and Spiez, the charming village of Einigen is located on the south bank of Lake Thun, across from a lovely mountain landscape. The small Romanesque church, with a brilliant roughcast façade and 15C and 16C stained-glass windows, is topped by a pinnacle turret. With the tiny cemetery surrounding it, and sloping down in terraces to the lake, the church forms a picturesque **scene**★.

THUNER SEE★★

Lake Thun 18km/11mi long, almost 4km/2.5mi wide and 217m/712ft deep, is one of the loveliest and largest sheets of water in Switzerland. Countless tourists have been captivated by its location amid green mountains and the snow-capped summit of the Jungfrau.

🚤 *Motorboat service links the different localities on the lake shore.*

From Thun to Interlaken *23km/14mi – about 1hr*

Itinerary 5 *(*⚲ *see BERNER OBERLAND map)*

Thun★★ – *1hr 30min.* ⚲ *See THUN.*

After the pretty residential suburbs of Thun, the road to Oberhofen remains within view of the summits of the Bernese Alps (Eiger-Mönch-Jungfrau and, more to the right, the three characteristic snowy ridges of the Blümlisalp). In the foreground, on the opposite shore, the Niesen pyramid and the rocky Stockhorn are prominent.

Schloss Hünegg
🕐 *Open daily mid-May to mid-Oct, 2pm–5pm, Sun 11am–5pm.* ⊕ *8CHF.* ☎ *(033) 243 19 82; www.schlosshuenegg.ch.*

Located in a wooded park which slopes down to the lake, this large edifice (1863), in spite of its size, cannot be seen from the road. The apartments (1900) have been arranged into a museum of *Jugendstil (Art Nouveau)*. One room evokie the life of the Swiss student at the time (uniforms, duelling weapons etc); works by the Bernese painter Martin Lauterburg (d 1960) are exhibited on the second floor.

Oberhofen

This 12C **castle** (🕐 *Open mid-May to mid-Oct, Tue-Sun, 11am-5pm, Mon, 2-5pm.* 🎟 *7CHF.* ☎ *(033) 243 12 35)* jutting into the waters of the lake, forms an enchanting fairytale **picture**★ *(illuminated at night)*, opposite the summits of the Bernese Alps. Enlarged and restored (17C to 19C), is now a branch of the Bernisches Historisches Museum displaying period furniture (Louis XIV, Louis XV, Empire) and collections of popular art illustrating life in the Bernese Oberland. The landscape park on the shores of the lake is one of the most pleasant features of the visit. Before leaving Oberhofen, visit the **Museum für Uhren und Mechanische Musikinstrumente** (🕐 *Open mid-May to mid-Oct, daily except Mon, 2-5pm (Sun 10am-5pm); mid-Oct to mid-May, Sun and public hols, 2-5pm.* 🎟 *6CHF.* ☎ *(033) 243 43 77)*, housed in a 16C building in a large park by the lake. The museum displays a splendid collection of watches and musical instruments spanning seven centuries.

Between Oberhofen and Merligen, there is a superb **run along the quays**★★, facing Spiez and the mouth of the Kander Valley, the best side of the lake for sun and flowers. The Blümlisalp Massif, clearly visible through this gap, now draws near.

After Merligen, the road becomes a corniche along the steep slopes of the Nase (Nose) promontory over the eastern basin of the lake, whose lonely shores form a contrast with the little Riviera you have just come through. During the descent through several tunnels, beginning 1km/0.5mi after Beatenbucht (the starting-point of the Beatenberg funicular), the view opens over the Bödeli Plain, between the wooded chains of the Harder (on the left) and the Rugen (on the right, dominated in the background by the rocky points of the Schynige Platte. This is the site of Interlaken. Before Unterseen, the road passes at the foot of the Sankt Beatus Grottoes, hidden in a impressive cliff, with a cascade tumbling down.

Sankt Beatus-Höhlen★

Allow 1hr 15min, including 1hr for the guided tour. Remember to dress warmly since the temperature is maintained between 8°C/45°F and 12°C/55°F. 👣 *Guided tour (50min) Apr-Oct, 10.30am-5pm.* 🎟 *16CHF.* ☎ *(033) 841 16 43.*

These grottoes, the longest in Switzerland, are not particularly spectacular but they make a pleasant walk. Of the 14km/8.8mi of galleries which have been excavated, only 900m/985yd are open to the public. They are reached by a steep path *(10min)* running alongside a pretty **waterfall**★. First you will come across a series of caves evoking man's life in prehistoric times. Then you enter the actual grottoes, of which the most notable features are the Domed Grotto (11m/36ft high), the Mirror Grotto (note the stalactites' reflection in the sheet of water), the Witches' Cauldron and the Snake's Grotto. You can also visit a small **museum** (Höhlenmuseum) devoted to geology and speleology, which displays several panels explaining the history of Swiss grottoes.

Interlaken★★★ – *1hr.* 👣 *See INTERLAKEN.*

VAL DE TRAVERS

The River Areuse wends through this wide lush valley where fields of crops are interspersed with attractive towns, and slopes are blanketed with firs. This valley, one of the main crossover points between France and Switzerland – the road from Pontarlier to Neuchâtel passes through – offers two pleasant walks: the Areuse Gorges and the Creux du Van Nature Reserve.

From Fleurier to Noiraigue *28km/18mi – allow 3hr*

Môtiers

This pleasant village has several well preserved 17C and 18C houses and a church, a former Gothic abbey church rebuilt in 1679. Its two small **museums** (*Guided tours (1hr) May to mid-Oct, Tue, Thu, Sat-Sun 2-5pm. 5CHF. (032) 861 35 51*) are worthy of attention: the Jean-Jacques Rousseau Museum (memorabilia) located in the house Rousseau lived in from 1762 to 1765, and the local museum set up in an 18C home with a carved façade, known locally as the Maison des Mascarons.

Mines d'Asphalte

Guided tours (1hr 30min) Apr-Oct at 10am and 2pm (Jul and Aug, additional tours at noon and 4pm); Nov-Mar, Sun at noon and 2pm. 12.50CHF. Temperature around 8°C, wear warm clothes. (032) 863 30 10.

The very first deposit of these asphalt mines was discovered in 1711 by Eirini d'Eyrinys, a Greek physician who subsequently published a book titled *Essay on Asphalt or Natural Cement*. This precious mineral, a water-resistant combination of limestone and bitumen, was exported to all corners of the world from 1830 to 1986, after which its exploitation ceased. During this period, a two million tonnes of rock were extracted, covering a distance of 100km/62mi excavations. Visitors are first shown the **Mining Museum** (geological cross-sections, diagrams explaining asphalt extraction and exploitation, photographs of miners, of early mining equipment, lumps of asphalt etc), from where you continue on foot through several galleries *(helmets and electric torches are provided)* with stops for commentary on (destruction by explosives, ventilation, supporting structures, loading, transportation), bringing to life an important chapter in the industrial and social history of the Val de Travers.

La Brévine

This small plateau has received the nickname "Swiss Siberia" because of its bitter winters: it registers the lowest temperatures in Switzerland! The ride up offers views of the Travers Valley. The plateau, surrounded by dark green fir trees squared off by walls enclosing crops and pastures (cattle, horses) and sprinkled with chalets, has as its centre La Brévine (alt 1 043m/3 422ft) at the edge of an immense combe of high pastures.

Creux du Van★★

From the Ferme Robert allow 2hr 30min there and back to walk up to the Soliat by a path to Dos d'Ane, 1km/0.5mi east of the Soliat.

This nature reserve (flora and fauna – chamois, ibexes – are protected) covering 11km^2/4sq mi, includes a typical example of a Jura blind valley crowned by a superb cirque of cliffs which open in a U-shape towards the Areuse Gorges and look down on rocks blanketed by fir trees. From its highest point, the Soliat (alt 1 463m/4 800ft), there is a magnificent **view**★★ to the south onto Neuchâtel Lake and the peaks of the Alps beyond. From paths along the top of the cliffs are pleasant views onto the verdant hills of the nature reserve and to the north onto the Jura heights.

▶ *Return to Noiraigue.*

Gorges de l'Areuse★ – *1hr 30min.* 🕯 *See Gorges de l'AREUSE.*

VALLÉE DU TRIENT★

VALAIS
ALT 476M/1 561FT

Beyond the covered bridge or the new bridge over the Drance in Martigny, a winding road heads towards Salvan (8km/5mi). The road, occasionally cut into the rock, then climbs above the Rhône Valley and enters the wild scenery of the Trient Valley, a perfect destination for mountain walkers. The valley is particularly popular with cross-country and downhill skiers during the winter season.

Gorges du Trient★★
At Vernayaz.
This mountain stream begins in the Trient glacier. It gushes through a rocky fissure 200m/656ft high and is followed by a **waymarked footpath**. A new bridge was built across the gorge in 1994. Nearby, the old **Pont du Gueuroz** (1934) is now a listed monument. The reinforced concrete bridge with its slender framework was a bold design for the time. Cross the bridge on foot for a bird's-eye view of the gorge, which is wider and wooded upstream.

Vallon de Van
The narrow road overhanging the Rhône Valley in a wild, hostile setting at a height of 800m/2 600ft provides an exciting route to Van d'en Haut. The drive back to Salvan offers some impressive views of the Vallon de Van and Martigny.

▶ *Return to Salvan, then follow the Trient Valley as far as Les Marécottes.*

Les Marécottes
A pretty mountain village with wooden chalets. A cable-car heads up to **La Creusaz** (alt 1 777m/5 800ft), from where you can enjoy a sweeping perspective of Mont Blanc and the Valais Alps. Near the village, on the right as you come down the road, the 🅺🆒 **Zoo des Marécottes** (🕐 *Open mid-May to mid-Sep, daily, 9am-nightfall; Easter hols, autumn and Christmas, 11am-nightfall; low season, use the coin ticket machine to gain entrance.* 💰 *9CHF.* ☎ *(027) 761 15 62)* is home to a wide variety of Alpine species in their natural habitat. Animals on display here include chamois, beavers, reindeer, ibexes, Valais goats and mouflons, llamas and bears.
An alpine **swimming pool** (70m/77yd long), partially heated by solar panels, is built into the rock.

Glacier du Trient★
Access: from Col de la Forclaz. Park in the car park and take the waymarked footpath from the pass (alt 1 526m/5 005ft). Follow signs to the "Glacier du Trient et Fenêtre d'Arpette".
An easy walk (1hr) through a larch wood leads to a **snack bar** with views of the glacier, which is 5km/3mi long and 500m/550yd to 900m/990yd to wide. The

WHERE TO STAY IN LES MARÉCOTTES

🛏🛏🛏🛏**Aux Mille Étoiles** – ☎ *027 761 16 66 – www.mille-etoiles. ch - 25 rooms –* 🕐*open 21 Dec-5 Apr and 10 May – 26 Oct.* A cosy chalet near the skiing pistes will welcome you during the winter season. Splendid views. Covered pool. Peace and quiet guaranteed.

path continues to the tongue of the glacier along a more difficult route which follows the right bank of the river (1hr). From here, a **glacial hike** leads up the gentle slopes of the Trient, then up the steeper strips overlooking the river. Experience of glacial hiking is essential for this section of the walk, as are crampons and ice picks; beginners wishing to tackle the walk should contact a mountain guide.

Le Châtelard
Beyond the village of Trient along the N 506 through the neighbouring valley leading to Vallorcine and Chamonix. This village is situated on the border with France. A funicular leads to the Émosson Dam *(see Barrage d'ÉMOSSON)*, offering magnificent views of the Mont Blanc Massif.

TROGEN

APPENZELL (AUSSER-RHODEN) – POPULATION 1 968
10KM/6MI SE OF SANKT GALLEN – ALT 903M/2 963FT

Trogen is built on a hill in the picturesque district of Appenzell within view of Lake Constance. It has many middle-class houses, some of which are real palaces built by rich merchants of former days.

Landsgemeindeplatz
The traditional meeting *(see Introduction: Government)* of the half-canton of Appenzell – Ausser-Rhoden – takes place every even year in the Landsgemeindeplatz; every other year, the ceremony is held at Hundwil. Among the fine houses surrounding it you will notice the Zur Krone, an inn with its overhanging roof and two superimposed gables. The many-windowed façade is ornamented with repeated patterns in which grey-blue, brown and green tones predominate.

Children's Village of Pestalozzi
1km/0.5mi S by the road to Bühler.
The houses here are reserved for war orphans from different countries. **Johann Heinrich Pestalozzi**, a citizen of Zurich (1746-1827), is honoured throughout Switzerland and abroad for his educational work and innovative teaching methods.

UTZENSTORF

BERN – POPULATION 3 626

This lovely shaded and flowered village has a small church with 16C stained-glass windows.

Schloss Landshut★
 Open mid-May to mid-Oct, Tue-Sun, 2-5pm; Sun and Whit Mon, 10am-5pm. *Closed 1 Aug and on the Federal Fast day (3rd Sun in Sep).* *7CHF.* *(032) 665 40 27.*
North of Utzenstorf, in a lovely park, stands this 17C and 18C white turretted edifice, surrounded by water (trout, ducks, swans) and pleasantly shaded by rare tree species. The château was the residence of the bailiffs of Bern until 1798. interior decor includes heavy period furnishings and huge porcelain stoves. Some rooms house the **Swiss Hunting Museum** (Schweizerisch Jagdmuseum) with trophies, decoys

and a remarkable collection of seignorial hunting arms from the 16C to 20C (knives, crossbows, pistols, guns and their accessories). Located in the attic is the **Museum of the History of Swiss Agriculture** (tools, utensils, machines).

LE VALAIS★★

WALLIS

In the mosaic of Swiss cantons, the Valais includes one of the most isolated districts of the Alps: the Upper Rhône Valley from the Furka to Lake Geneva. This wide fissure, almost completely cut off from the economic centres of German Switzerland, has been kept busy for 2 000 years by intense international traffic through the Great St Bernard and Simplon Passes. It owes its distinctive regional character to the Mediterranean clarity of its sky, the deep Catholic beliefs of its people and its impressive industrial development, which does not prevent the survival in the high valleys of the most ancient ways of life.

Here you must not expect pastoral scenes, but heroic memories evoked by such places as St-Maurice and Sion and unforgettable high mountain landscapes like those of the **lateral valleys★★★**, dotted with chalets and *raccards* or *mazots* (small barns perched on piles and used as granaries or storehouses). In these wild, uninviting regions, it is common to find wayside wooden crosses, set up to protect travellers and local residents from the dark dangers of the mountain.

The Valais Rhone

From the Glacier to the Vines

Issuing from the famous cataract of the Rhône Glacier, the great river is born at an altitude of 2 200m/7 217ft, crosses the desolate Gletschboden Basin and enters the broad Conches Valley (also known as Goms). Its volume doubles at Brig where it receives waters of the Massa flowing from the Aletsch Glacier. It then ceases to be a mountain torrent and flows onto the floor of the alluvial plain between steep rocky banks shrouded in the smoke of the factories at Visp (Viège) and Gampel.

The double obstacle created by the cone of debris of the Illgraben, cloaked in the Finges Forest (Pfynwald), and by the Sierre landslide, results in a wide break in the valley. This is where the traditional boundary between German-speaking Upper Valais and French-speaking Valais developed (👁 see Introduction: Language and religion).

A First Taste of Provence

The Central Valais between Sierre and Martigny is sheltered from winds by gigantic mountain barriers and is the driest area in Switzerland. Favoured by

Philipp Giegel/ Switzerland Tourism

Raccards. Old-fashioned Valais barn

this Mediterranean climate, the local vines (♿ *see Introduction: Food and wine*) flourish on rugged, sun-baked ridges of the slope facing south, opposite the wooded and pastoral slopes of the **mayens** (pastures where the herds wait in May for the snow to melt on the higher Alps). Valaisan peasants had to carry earth, washed down by the rain, laboriously up to the narrow terraces *(tablards)* on which their vines grew. *A route through the vineyards has been signposted between Martigny and Sierre.* As soon as river flooding could be prevented, the alluvial Rhône Plain was covered with orchards and plantations of asparagus and maize. Even strawberries are cultivated in the valleys of Bagnes and Entremont within sight of eternal snows.

From the Orchard to the Lake

At Martigny, the Rhône receives the Dranse and turns sharply north, adopting the direction of its powerful tributary. Deflected towards the last foothills of the Bernese Alps by the cone of debris from the St Barthélemy Torrent, the river passes through the rocky gateway of St-Maurice and opens out into the Lower Valais. This marshy plain, which spreads as it extends towards the shores of Lake Geneva, belongs politically to the Valais on the left shore of the lake.

The tumultuous natural phenomenon of the waters' meeting (♿ *see Lac LÉMAN*) is the last sign of this 170km/106mi long mountainous Rhône.

Life in the Valais

Valaisans and Walser

All along the Rhône Valley travellers, seeing the signs of religious unity throughout the country – the first trace, dating from 377, of the Christian conversion of Switzerland was found at Sion – might think they were in a purely Latin civilisation.

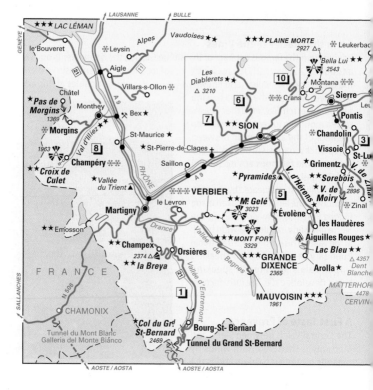

Beyond Sierre, and especially near Brig, however, they will start to hear the guttural sounds of a Germanic dialect and the name Valais yields to Wallis. The Upper Valais was invaded from the 6C onwards by Germanic peoples who probably came down from the Grimsel and pushed on as far as Sierre. Later, these restless "Walser" often infiltrated into other southern Alpine valleys, forming permanent centres of German culture in otherwise French-speaking districts, as at Davos. These hardy mountaineers, especially the Conches Valley, represented the most fiercely democratic element (Raron, Saillon), reducing the temporal rights of the prince-bishops of Sion and claims of local feudal lords by force, if necessary, found no difficulty in reconciling their ideal of independence with persecution of the French-speaking peoples of the Lower Valais.

The "Cardinal of Sion"

Matthäus Schiner, a Valaisan who combined the customary tenacity of a mountain people with a fertile mind, fired with the universalist ideas of the Renaissance, was a true product, and perpetuator, of Helvetian national character. His grand designs led the Swiss to the defeat of Marignano; this prelate is one of the great pioneers of the present Confederal system. To this period of cordial relations with the Holy See (1506) may be traced the system of recruiting still in force, by which Julius II reserved for the Swiss alone, and especially for the Valaisans of the Conches (Goms) Valley, the right to wear the picturesque uniform of the Papal Guard, designed by

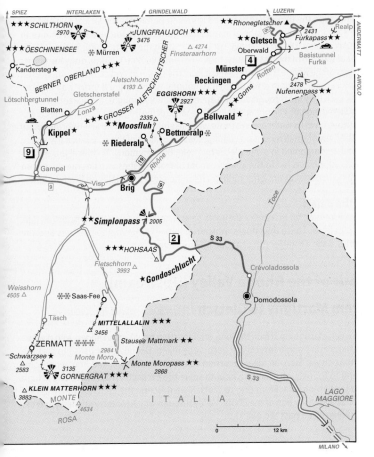

Cow Fights

Popular cow fights take place in the Valais during spring and autumn. At least 100 contestants are grouped into categories according to age and weight. The cows are usually the Herens breed, a sturdy, muscular race of cattle with curved horns and a lively, belligerent character, good for both meat and milking. The cows fight before being put out to grass or taken up to the summer pastures, or when they meet another herd. The springtime fights decide the Queen Cow who leads the herd up to the summer pastures. Heads are lowered for the clash and the locking of the horns and the struggle begins. The weaker one will retreat, often chased by the winner. Organised fights determine regional and cantonal queens; a jury awards prizes to the first six in each category. The queens then fight for the overall championship and title of Queen of Queens.

Michelangelo. The union of the Valais with the Confederation dates from 1815 (👣 see Introduction: History). Before that the country was merely allied with the XIII Cantons; then, it enjoyed the status of a protected Republic and then a French département under the name of Simplon.

The Bisses
In the middle section of the Valais (from Martigny to Brig) cultivation of tablelands overlooking the Rhône Valley caused irrigation problems. The lack of rain and torrents enclosed in the depths of inaccessible gorges gave the Valaisans a chance to display a tenacity and inventive spirit by creating the bisses. These narrow canals (207 at the turn of the last century; total length of 2 000km/1 250mi) drew the glacier waters of the Rhône tributaries almost from their sources and carried them, with an imperceptible drop in level, along the mountainsides. When a rocky wall blocked their path they ran through dizzily suspended wooden troughs, the upkeep of which required dangerous acrobatics. The maintenance of the irrigating bisse and the careful distribution of its water among those who are entitled to it, hold an important place in the lives of small mountain communities. The filling of the canals in early spring is still accompanied in some places by a religious ceremony. Technical progress in water supply has led to the abandonment of many of these rustic aqueducts, but some wooded sections offer tourists charming scenes for walks on level ground.

In the Valais
Above Verbier, for instance – they also have an ingenious way of transporting milk by pipelines. These milk ducts, which run between the Alpine pastures and the dairies, have a total length of about 220km/138mi.

Tour of the Rhone Valley (Upstream)

From Martigny to Gletsch 129km/80mi – about 1hr 30min

Between Martigny and Sion the long, straight stretches of a road edged with poplars by Napoleon's engineers do not encourage idling. Do, however, pause to visit the historic city of Sion, an ideal excursion centre. Between Sion and Brig, we recommend to tourists who have an hour to spare the excursion from Sierre to the high terrace of Montana. From Brig to Gletsch we describe the Conches Valley (👣 see GOMS), a high section of the Rhône Valley through which motorists rushing to cross the Furka often pass too quickly.

Driving Tours

Recommended itineraries
Organised according to time (longest to shortest).

1 Route du Grand-St-Bernard★★
From Martigny to the Great St Bernard Pass – about 3hr 30min. ♿ *See Route du GRAND-ST-BERNARD.*

2 Simplonstrasse★★
From Domodossola to Brig – about 3hr. ♿ *See SIMPLONPASSTRASSE.*

3 Val d'Anniviers★
From Sierre to Zinal – about 2hr 30min. ♿ *See Val d'ANNIVIERS.*

4 Goms★★
From Brig to Gletsch – about 2hr. ♿ *See GOMS.*

5 Val d'Hérens★★
From Sion to Les Haudères – about 2hr. ♿ *See Val d'HÉRENS.*

6 Sanetsch Road★★
Starting from Sion – about 1hr 30min. *See SION: Excursions.*

7 Derborence Road★
Starting from Sion – about 2hr. ♿ *See SION: Excursions.*

8 Val de Morgins★
From Monthey to Châtel – about 2hr. ♿ *See Val de MORGINS.*

9 Lötschental★
From the road fork Gampel to Kippel – about 45min. ♿ *See KIPPEL.*

10 Tseuzier Road★
Starting from Sion – about 30min. ♿ *See SION: Excursions.*

VALLORBE

VAUD – POPULATION 3 271
ALT 769M/2 530FT

Lying on the south side of the small Jurassian chain of Mount Or, the town of Vallorbe owes its activity to its varied industries (light engineering, plastic products) and especially to its frontier station, well-known to users of the Simplon line.
🛈 *Grandes Forges 11 – 1337 – ☎ (021) 843 25 83*

For the motorist coming from France, Vallorbe is a good excursion centre for charming one-day tours in the Vaud Jura (Romainmôtier, Joux Valley, Dent de Vaulion etc).

Musée du Fer et du Chemin de Fer
Kids *The Carte Trèfle (☜ 30CHF) is a ticket valid from Palm Sunday to All Saints giving access to the caves, the Iron and Railway Museum, the Parc du Mont-d'Orzaires and the Vallorbe fort. Contact the sights for further information.* ⏰ *Open Apr-Oct, daily 9.30am-*

noon and 1.30-6pm; Nov-Mar, Mon-Fri at the same times. 📞*10CHF.* ☎ *(021) 843 25 83.*
Access to the Iron and Railway Museum is through the Tourist Information Centre.

Iron Museum

Nestling on the banks of the Orbe on the former site of the Grandes Forges, this museum celebrates the history of the region's iron industry. In addition to early forges, displays include anvils, grinding-stones and other tools manufactured by the Grandes Forges, as well as modern products made through precision engineering. The energy is supplied by three paddle wheels set up outside.

Railway Museum

Vallorbe's golden age as one of the stops on the Simplon line is vividly evoked. There is a maquette of the station in 1908: plus historic railway tools and equipment, tickets, old posters and an inspector's uniform.. On the second floor, visitors can follow the adventures of their favourite train on a miniature toy circuit: *micheline*, high-speed *TGV*, regional Swiss trains.

Fort de Vallorbe

🚶 *Guided tours (1hr 30min) Jul and Aug, daily, noon-5.30pm; May-Nov, Sat-Sun and public hols at the same times.* 📞 *11CHF.* ☎ *(032) 843 25 83.*

This stronghold, carved out of the rock and facing the French border, was built shortly before the Second World War. It consists of three small forts and six heavily guarded blockhouses and watchtowers, connected by a maze of underground galleries. To your astonishment, you will discover, 30m/100ft below ground level, a machine room (air filters, production of electric current), ammunition dump, telephone exchange, barracks, dormitory, kitchen, mess, canteen, infirmary, dental surgery and operating theatre. Figurines, weapons, documents and sound effects complete this evocation of military life in the Fort de Pré-Giroud, which could house around 100 men.

Excursion

Source of the Orbe

3km/2mi – plus 30min on foot there and back. Leave Vallorbe by the road to the Joux Valley, and then take the road to the left marked Source-Grottes, sloping gently downhill. Leave your car near the power station.

Walk along a shady path and you will reach the end of the little rocky hollow where the Orbe rises: a reappearance of the waters of the Joux and Brenet lakes.

Caves

🕐 *Open Apr-Nov, 9.30am-4.30pm (5.30pm Jun, Jul and Aug).* 📞 *13CHF.* ☎ *(021) 843 25 83.*

As you come out of the 80m/263ft tunnel, there is a gallery which has been built taking in the series of pillars and delicately shaped stalactites and stalagmites. You end at the dark cave affording a view of the surging waters of the Orbe, hemmed in by curious rock walls. The **Trésor des Fées**★ (Fairies' Treasure, *Same times and charges as the caves*) is a large collection of local minerals.

VERBIER✳✳✳

VALAIS – POPULATION 2 163
ALT 1 500M/4 920FT (VERBIER RESORT)
TOWN PLAN IN THE MICHELIN GUIDE SWITZERLAND

Preceded by **Verbier-Village,** the resort of Verbier is scattered over the sunny slope of the Bagnes Valley within view of the Grand Combin and Mont-Blanc massifs, with luxurious hotels and traditional chalets in a glorious site✶. Its promimity to Geneva makes it a popular weekend retreat year-round. ⬚ *Place Centrale – 1936 – ☎ (027) 775 38 88, www.verbier.ch.*

Visit

The cirque of regular slopes converging here offers ideal topographical and climatic conditions for the great majority of present-day skiers, who find spacious and restful surroundings and considerable mechanical equipment suitable for downhill skiing. Verbier is also known to long-distance skiers as the starting-point of the High Road run, of which Zermatt or Saas-Fee is the terminus.

The Skiing Area

Verbier is the main attraction of **Les Quatre Vallées** (the Four Valleys), a huge skiing complex boasting a total of 410km/254mi of pistes and 100 chairlifts, one of the most interesting and varied Alpine ski resorts in Switzerland. A 150-person cable car and an unusual lift combining a gondola and a six-passenger chair have enhanced uphill capacity significantly. The pistes around Verbier are fairly easy (Ruinettes and Savoleyres sector) but those on Mont Fort (highest summit of the complex), the Col des Gentianes, Mont Gelé and the Plan-du-Fou Massif are recommended for experienced skiers (many steep slopes and bumpy sections). Some high-mountain itineraries are very impressive because of the austere landscape and the gradient of the slopes (Vallon d'Arbi from the Col des Mines, Mont Gelé and Mont Fort towards Tortin and its legendary bumps). The long cruiser piste from Col des Gentianes to La Chaux has fantastic views; this red piste and from Savoleyres to La Tzoumaz and from Greppon Blanc to Siviez are ideal for intermediates.

The resorts connected to Verbier (La Tzoumaz, Nendaz, Siviez, Veysonnaz, Mayens-de-l'Ours, Thyon and Les Collons) offer gentle slopes more attuned to beginners. The adventurous should take the opportunity to go paragliding in tandem with an experienced pilot-guide.

Summer activities

Summer is also very popular for many sportsi and leisure activities. On Switzerland's largest state territory (296km²/115sq mi), you can choose between **walks** covering altogether 400km/250mi: the most famous hike is the 🝮**Sentier des Chamois**✶✶ between the Mont Fort refuge and Termin Pass. Moreover, 200km/125mi of lanes have been laid out for mountain bikes, the Grand Raid Cristalp Verbier-Grimentz being the most sought after. Tourists interested in traditional Swiss architecture can visit the picturesque villages of Bruson, Fionnay and Sarreyer. Verbier also boasts facilities for hang-gliding and an 18-hole golf course. The sports centre, open all year, features an indoor and an outdoor pool and a huge skating rink. Verbier hosts one of the world's most prestigious music festivals to be held in a mountain setting.

Mont Fort✶✶✶

Alt 3 329m/1 994ft. ⬚*Access (allow 45min): by cable car from Verbier to Les Ruinettes; by shuttle (5min) or on foot (30min) up to La Chaux; by jumbo cable car to Les Gentianes,* then take another cable car up to the top. ◷ *Open Jul and Aug, 8.45am-3.30pm; Dec-Apr, 9.15am-3.30pm.* ⬤ *Fare there and back 34CHF, 10CHF on 14 and 28 Jul and 15 Aug.* ☎ *(027) 775 25 11.*

A favourite with skiers and snowboarders for long-lasting snow and ice, including in summer, Mont Fort on a clear day offers a sweeping **international panorama**★★★ *(viewing tables)* of the Alps, covering Italy (Matterhorn), France (Mont Blanc), the Valais (Mont Fort, Grand Combin) and the Bernese Oberland (Eiger).

Mont Gelé★★

Alt 3 023m/9 918ft. *Access (about 45min) via cable-car from Verbier to Les Ruinettes, then change and take another cable-car to Attelas I and change again for Attelas II (near the top).* ◷ *Operates from mid-Dec to mid-Apr only, 9.40am-12.15pm and 1-3.30 or 4pm.* ☎ *(027) 775 25 11.*

From the cross, which indicates that you are at the rocky summit of the Mont Gelé, admire the **circular view**★★: to the south Grand Combin Massif and its glaciers; to the east Mont Fort and its glaciers; to the north the peaks of Les Diablerets; to the west the Pierre d'Avoi Mountain and below, Verbier and the Entremont Valley.

VEVEY★

VAUD – POPULATION 15 502
ALT 400M/1 312FT – TOWN PLAN IN THE MICHELIN GUIDE SWITZERLAND

Vevey occupies a beautiful **site**★★ facing the Savoy Alps at the mouth of the Veveyse Valley and the foot of Mount Pèlerin, with the blue sheet of Lake Geneva and the Alps making a splendid backdrop. 🛈 *29 Grande-Place – 1800 –* ☎ *(021) 922 20 20, www.vevey.ch.*

- 🙂 **Don't Miss:** The Alimentarium (Food Museum) at Nestle's former Belle Epoque headquarters.
- ◷ **Organizing Your Time:** Allow two days for museums and a lake excursions.
- Kids **Especially for Kids:** The antique carousel along the lake front.

A Bit of History

Food and Wine

Already capital of the Lavaux vineyards, Vevey, in the 19C, became the cradle of the Swiss industry of milk and dietetic products, and also chocolate. The powerful Nestlé group has its headquarters here, together with its central laboratory and an experimental factory. Regional lore includes picturesque traditional markets *(Saturday mornings)* which are held on place du Marché in July and August.

Nestlé

This world food-processing giant was founded by **Heinrich Nestlé,** who was born in Frankfurt-am-Main in 1814 and setttled in Vevey in 1843, having first worked as a pharmacist in his home town. He had inherited a small business which manufactured fertiliser and mustard, and later, under the influence of his father-in-law, a doctor, he developed an interest in baby food. Nestlé's baby cereal, introduced in 1867 and made from milk, wheat flour and sugar, became a great success. In the previous year, the Americans George and Charles Page had turned Cham into the leading European manufacturer of condensed milk. In 1905, Nestlé and Cham merged under the name of Nestlé and Anglo-Swiss Condensed Milk Company. Other companies were later purchased by the group turning Nestlé into one of the world's leading companies.

A Distinguished Resident

Charles Spencer Chaplin was born in London in 1889 to a family of impoverished music-hall artistes. Charles and brother Sydney began performing at an early age in pantomime shows which enabled them to travel abroad. During a tour of the United States in 1913, young Charles made the acquaintance of Mack Sennett, who directed and produced burlesque movies in Hollywood. Sennett immediately offered the young man a job, which led to the birth of the **The Little Tramp** character and his legendary silhouette. With his moustache, derby hat, baggy trousers falling onto out-sized shoes, tight frock coat and cane, distinctive shuffling gait and pale features, Chaplin became highly popular and gained international acclaim.

During the 1920s, his tumultuous private life was strongly criticised by the American press; after his second divorce, authorities requested that he be expelled from the country. In 1952, during McCarthy's anti-Communist campaigns, Chaplin left America with his family and settled in Corsier-sur-Vevey. In 1975, he was knighted by Queen Elizabeth II, and on 25 December 1977, he passed away in his Swiss home. Chaplin's cinematographic career, symbolised by the colourful tramp character and his burlesque adventures, illustrates man's struggle to survive in a new world. His critical outlook on society and politics is reflected in films such as *Modern Times* (1936), a satire on the time-and-motion tyranny of mechanisation; *The Great Dictator* (his first talking movie, 1940), a parody of Fascism; *A King in New York* (1957), a virulent stand against intolerant America and its dogmatic views of Communism. *Limelight* (1952) was a moving melodrama about his boyhood days in London. From 1958 to 1962, he wrote his memoirs, which were published in 1964.

A statue of Chaplin has been erected by the city of Vevey on the shores of Lake Geneva, in front of the Alimentarium, to pay tribute to the great actor; his former home is to become the Chaplin Museum in 2008.

Sights

Église St-Martin

The present church (1530) stands on a site originally occupied by an 11C sanctuary whose walls were discovered during excavation work. The church is dominated by a large, square tower and four corner turrets. The terrace *(viewing table)* affords a sweeping **view**★ of the town, the Alps and Lake Geneva.

Musée Jenisch

♿ ⏰ *Open Mar-Oct, daily except Mon, 11am-5.30pm. The fund's permanent collections alternate with temporary exhibitions.* ⏰ *Closed Mon (except Easter Mon and Whit Mon), 25 Dec and 1 Jan.* 💳*8-15CHF (depending on exhibitions)* ☎ *(021) 921 29 50.*

Inside this 19C neo-Classical building are two museums. The ground floor houses the **Cantonal Prints Gallery**, presenting engravings by great masters of the past (Dürer, Rembrandt, Lorrain, Belletto, Corot) and by modern Swiss artists, which are shown in rotation. The **Fine Arts Museum** on the first floor displays temporary exhibitions of works by Swiss and foreign artists from the 19C and 20C.

Musée Historique du Vieux-Vevey

⏰ *Open Mar-Oct, daily except Mon, 10.30am-noon and 2-5.30pm; Nov-Feb, daily except Mon, 2-5.30pm.* ⏰ *Closed 1 Jan and 25 Dec.* 💳 *5CHF.* ☎ *(021) 921 07 22.*

This museum is housed in the castle which was once the residence of the Bernese bailiffs. It relates the history of the area and contains a fine collection of furniture from the Gothic period to the 17C, small wrought-iron objects and caskets, costumes and local mementoes. On the first floor, you may also visit the **Museum of the Wine-**

Address Book

For coin ranges, see the Legend on the cover flap.

WHERE TO STAY

Hôtel du Lac – *1 rue d'Italie* – ☎ *021 921 10 41* – *55 rooms* – A stone's throw from the harbour and the lake, this venerable hotel features comfortable rooms and a lovely terrace with a private pool giving onto the lake.

EATING OUT

Restaurant du Raisin – *3 place du Marché* – ☎ *021 921 10 28* – ○ *closed Sun and Mon.* Located opposite the market square and near the lake shore, this restaurant offers traditional bistro cuisine on the ground floor and a more sophisticated menu upstairs, with correspondingly higher prices.

La Terrasse – *Corseaux, 8 chemin du Basset* – ☎ *021 921 31 88* – ○ *closed Mon and 23 Dec-22 Jan.* Good food and reasonable prices, whether you choose the menu or à la carte. In summer, meals are served on the terrace.

Á la Montagne – *Chardonne, 21 rue du Village* – ☎ *021 921 29 30* – ○ *closed Mon, Sun, 23 Dec-7 Jan and 30 Jun-15 Jul.* A small, unassuming family inn offering an attractive menu, tasty dishes and affordable prices. Pretty terrace commanding beautiful views.

Hostellerie chez Chibrac – *Mont-Pèlerin* – ☎ *021 922 61 61* – *www.chezchibrac.ch* - ○ *closed Sun evenings, Mon and mid-Oct-1 Mar.* A homely establishment with a congenial atmosphere serving good, reasonably-priced meals.

Growers Fraternity (Confrérie des Vignerons), where models of the costumes worn at earlier wine-growers' festivals (since 1791) are kept, together with prints, records and banners used during these festivities.

Musée Suisse de l'Appareil Photographique★

99 Grande-Place. ♿○ *Open Tue-Sun, 11am-5.30pm.* ○ *Closed 25 Dec.* ⊙ *8CHF.* ☎ *(021) 925 21 40.*

The five floors of this **Swiss Camera Museum** present the history of photography, its famous inventors and its techniques through a remarkable collection of cameras dating from early models to the most recent and sophisticated devices including digital imaging. One floor is devoted to photographic equipment made in Switzerland. A renovation and expansion is scheduled in 2008.

The camera obscura in the entrance hall provides an insight into the birth of photography; one of the great early photographers was Nicéphore Niépce, born in Chalon-sur-Saône in 1765. Magic lanterns illustrate the theory of projection; the importance of photography in the army is explained via spy cameras that can be hidden in everyday objects. Another section includes the first small cameras, first flashes, Searly wiss cameras (Alpa, Escopette de Darier), famous names such as Kodak and Leica (1930-40), multi-image cameras, miniature cameras, image transmission and projection, tracing the development of photography and film industries. The "clic-clac" studio introduces children to the art of photography.

Alimentarium

Rue du Léman. ○ *Open daily except Mon, 10am-6pm.* ○ *Closed 1 Jan, 24, 25 and 31 Dec.* ⊙ *10CHF.* ☎ *(021) 924 41 11, www.alimentarium.ch.*

Since 1985 this neo-Classical mansion, formerly headquarters of the great Swiss company Nestlé, has housed the Food Museum. Exhibits are arranged by themes. *Cuisiner* (Cooking) illustrates cooking methods found around the world at different periods in history and in various ethnic and social environments. From the basic fire of prehistoric man to the modern microwave, heat is essential for cooking, as are various utensils, many of which are exhibited. *Manger* (Eating) illustrates the importance of pleasure and communication in eating, as does the art of laying a table. This section also highlights plants and animals eaten by humans, celebratory and everyday meals and how the act of eating differs by culture. The New York push-cart and snack trolley men can be considered to be the precursors of the fast-food industry, which is also explored here.

Acheter (Buying) resembles a supermarket and explores agricultural and production methods, food safety and our eating habits. *Digérer* (Digestion) is portrayed through biology, including the importance of sports. The Nestlé Room traces the history and importance of the now-global company, including advertisements and packaging dating back to 1867. There is also, of course, chocolate! There are cooking classes for adults and children (*in French only*) and a garden planted with herbs and vegetables, interspersed with picnic areas.

Excursions

Mont-Pèlerin Resort★★

Alt 810m/2 657ft. Round trip of 25km/16mi about 30min. Consult the local maps under Lac LÉMAN. Leave Vevey by the Châtel-St-Denis-Fribourg road 2.5km/2mi after having passed the road to Chardonne on your left, turn left towards Attalens, then sharp left again towards the Pèlerin or Pilgrim Mountain. Several of these roads run corniche fashion among the vines.

From a point near the arrival station of the funicular there is a wide open **view**★★ of Lake Geneva and the crest of the Vaud Alps (Dent de Jaman, Rochers de Naye, Aï Tower). The drive back through Chardonne and Chexbres is along roads with magnificent views of the Dents du Midi and the summits of the Haut-Chablais in Savoy.

La Tour-de-Peilz

2km/1mi by road n° 9 heading toward Montreux.

The castle was commissioned by the Comtes de Savoie (13C, altered in the 18C). The ramparts, moats and two corner turrets still stand. Inside the former keep is the **Musée Suisse du Jeu** (🕐 *Open daily except Mon, 2-6pm.* 🕐 *Closed 1 Jan and 25 Dec.* 🎫 *6CHF.* ☏ *(021) 944 40 50*), a collection of games from all countries and all epochs. These are split into five groups: educational games, strategic games, simulation games, games of skill and games of chance. Each section stresses the qualities required for playing and is illustrated by a series of examples. Visitors may test their own natural ability by playing, learning and even creating new games. Several exhibitions have genuine artistic appeal, as is the case with the chess figurines carved in ivory or bone.

If you bypass the castle on the left, you will come to the yachting harbour; from there you can take a pleasant walk along the shores of the lake. Opposite stands the Grammont, dominating the Swiss landscape from a height of 2 172m/6 800ft.

Blonay

4km/2.5mi E. 🅸 *29 Grande-Place, Vevey – 1800 –* ☏ *(021) 922 20 20*

The **Chemin de Fer-Musée Blonay-Chamby** (*Musée Blonay-Chamby –* ♿🕐 *Operates from May-Oct, Sat-Sun, 10am-6pm; Jul-Aug, Thu and Fri, 2-6pm.* 🎫*14 CHF including the visit to the museum.* ☏ *(021) 943 21 21*) has given new life to a railway section which opened in 1902 and closed down in 1966. Electric trams and early steam-driven trains take travellers along a steep, winding route covering a distance of 2.95km/2mi. Halfway up the hill stands the former shed. It has been converted into a museum displaying early vehicles, including a 1914 postal van, a 1904 tram from the Fribourg area and a steam engine which once linked Le Locle to Les Brenets.

VIERWALDSTÄTTER SEE★★★

Lake Lucerne is found on most maps under its German name: Vierwaldstätter See. The Lake Lucerne district offers picturesque old-fashioned villages and cities and innumerable hills and majestic mountain summits. For many visitors a town like Lucerne typifies the charm of Central Switzerland, which the road over the Brünig Pass (or Sachseln – 👁 *see SACHSELNER STRASSE*) conveniently links with the Bernese Oberland. The lake comprises three distinct sections from west to east: namely, the "lakes" of Vitznau, Gersau-Beckenried and Uri, created by a narrowing of the lake shore. The River Reuss enters Lake Lucerne to the south and leaves it at Lucerne to the north.

Its total surface area (114km²/45sq mi) makes Lake Lucerne the second largest lake within the country's boundaries after Lake Neuchâtel. The lake is overlooked by the summits of Mount Pilatus and Mount Rigi.

A Bit of History

The Cradle of Swiss Democracy – Every corner of this area has its hero, its battle-field, its commemorative chapel or its feudal ruins. Long before the Confederation existed, the **Waldstätten** (forest cantons) on the lake shores had adapted without much difficulty to a symbolic fealty when all Helvetia was owed allegiance to the Holy Roman Empire. The attachment of the district of Uri to the Empire was formally guaranteed as early as 1231, special treatment due to its strategic location on the vital Sankt Gotthard route.

The relative autonomy of the forest cantons seemed threatened when the Austrian House of Habsburg, anxious to ensure effective and profitable administration of its possessions in the region, created a corps of officials with control over in the revenues of the estates, without consulting with local authorities. These outsiders quickly became unpopular with the independent and communal farmers. The situation became critical when Rudolf I, the first of the Hapsburgs, acceded to the Imperial throne in 1273. His death opened the prospect of a dangerously confused political situation, prompting representatives of Schwyz, Uri and Unterwalden to form a permanent alliance. This mutual assistance pact did not propose disobedience to the overlords, but it staunchly rejected any administrative and judicial system imposed from outside and it is regarded by the Swiss as the founding pact of the Confederation. Its original text is carefully preserved at Schwyz, and the anniversary of its signature (1 August 1291) is celebrated as the national festival (👁 *see Calendar of Events*). The victory of Morgarten (1315) over the troops of Leopold of Austria marked the definite liberation of the three original cantons.

Dawn of liberty – However surprising such a development may have seemed to the feudal society of the time, it would not have achieved its later fame but for the legendary interpretation which, from the 15C onwards, created an incomparably more colourful and dramatic version of these events. This legend, in turn, became one of the treasures of German literature in 1804 as Schiller's **William Tell**. This version no longer described a long struggle by alternate negotiation and armed revolt but a conspiracy long matured by the representatives of the three communities, represented as victims of Bailiff Gessler's despotism, and solemnly sworn on the Field of Rütli, opposite Brunnen, by 33 spokesmen for Schwyz, Uri and Unterwalden.

After having been subjected by Gessler to the famous ordeal of the apple, the archer William Tell became the arm of justice of the conspiracy. He killed Gessler in the sunken road (Hohle Gasse) at Küssnacht, paving the way for an era of liberty. Since that time the Rütli episode has been the living source of the Swiss national tradition.

Suisse Tourisme

"Protector of the Fatherland" – The district of Unterwalden (more exactly the half-canton of Obwalden) which is crossed by the Brünig route, is proud to number among its sons the hermit **Nicholas of Flüe** (canonized in 1947), whose conciliatory intervention left an indelible mark on the Swiss patriotic temperament. Born in 1417 to prosperous peasants, Brother Nicholas (Bruder Klaus), as his fellow citizens called him, showed a keen taste for the contemplative life. After decades of family and civic duties, at the age of 50, this father of 10 children separated from his family to live the life of an ascetic in the solitude of Ranft, at the mouth of the Melchtal. Meanwhile the confederates of the eight Cantons of that time *(& see Introduction: History)* faced serious internal difficulties. Two policies were in opposition: that of the towns, governed by cautious bourgeois oligarchies, and that of the districts *(Länder)* in the mountains, which had remained faithful to the practice of direct democracy and were more open to outside views.

In 1477 the population around Lake Lucerne became agitated when they learned that Lucerne, in agreement with Zurich and Bern, had concluded a separate alliance with Fribourg and Solothurn. When Lucerne maintained the pact, in spite of the entreaties of its neighbours Uri, Schwyz and Unterwalden, the conflict became acute. In despair the parish priest of Stans went to Ranft to consult Brother Nicholas. He returned with an admirable appeal for peace. A compromise was reached in 1481.

Kunstmuseum Solothurn

William Tell by Ferdinand Hodler

Boat Trips

For seasonal visitors a boat trip around the lake, followed by a climb to one of the surrounding summits, should not be missed. Some of the lakeside sights, namely the historic Field of Rütli, can only be reached by boat.

1 North Shores★★★

From Lucerne to Altdorf *54 km/34mi – about 2hr 30min*

Luzern★★★ – *3hr.* 👣 *See LUZERN.*

Between Lucerne, Küssnacht and Weggis, the road runs through rich country planted with walnut and fruit trees, and skirts Lake Lucerne and Lake Küssnacht as it approaches the slopes of the Rigi with their reddish outcrops. Far away, to the south, the mountainous foothills of the Nidwalden (Stans-Engelberg district) succeed one another in confusion, although the Pilatus is still easily recognisable by its rugged crests.

Merlischachen
Wooden houses with pointed roofs offer some fine examples of the type of building found in central Switzerland (👣 *illustration see Introduction: Rural Architecture*).

Astridkapelle
The road follows the walls of this small chapel, erected after the tragic accident of 29 August 1935, in which Queen Astrid of Belgium was killed, when the royal car crashed into an orchard. A plain cross marks the spot where the Queen was found, now surrounded by a protective fence.

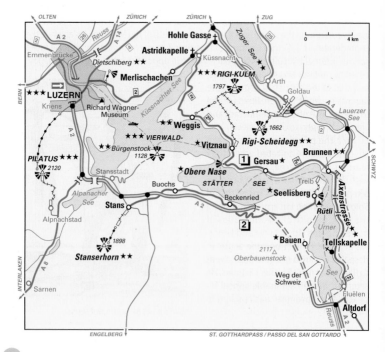

Hohle Gasse

Facilities. *From Küssnacht, 3km/2mi there and back by the road to Arth (n° 2), plus 15min on foot there and back.* Leaving your car at the Hohle Gasse Hotel, take the roughly paved sunken road (Hohle Gasse in German) steeply uphill, where according to tradition William Tell lay in wait for Gessler. The road through the woods ends at the commemorative chapel which is a place of pilgrimage for the Swiss.

Weggis★★

Weggis is the queen of the resorts situated on the shores of Lake Lucerne. It lies within view of the Pilatus and Unterwalden mountains along a promenade quay which leads to the Hertenstein Promontory. Pleasure boating and walks on the last slopes of the Rigi, planted with vines and even some almost tropical species – the warmth of the Föhn, coinciding here with a site facing due south – plus the resort's social amenities, will satisfy every visitor. From Weggis the lakeside road reveals a constantly changing landscape.

Vitznau★

Passing tourists may leave their cars for a few hours in this elegant resort, enclosed between the Rigi and the lake, to climb the Rigi-Kulm by rack railway. This was the first mountain railway built in Europe (1871).

Rigi-Kulm★★★

▶ *From Vitznau, about 3hr there and back, including 1hr 15min by rack-railway.* 👣 *See Le RIGI.*

Obere Nase★

The very pronounced bend in the road as it passes this cape is arranged as a **belvedere**★. This "Nose", thrown out by a spur of the Rigi, and the Untere Nase, an extreme outcrop of the Bürgenstock facing it, encloses a channel only 825m/2 707ft wide connecting two very different basins. Within a short distance you pass from Lake Vitznau, bounded on the south by the wooded spur of the Bürgenstock, to Lake Gersau-Beckenried, in a more open setting. The Pilatus remains a familiar landmark.

Gersau★

Lying in one of the most open **sites**★★ on the Alpine shores of the lake, the tiny Republic of Gersau – such was the status of the village between 1390 and 1817 – is now attached to the Schwyz canton. Near Brunnen the wooded Schwyz Basin, dominated by the twin Mythen Peaks, unfolds. On the right, under the arched cliffs of the Fronalpstock, the terrace of Morschach appears. You will now begin to skirt the Bay of Brunnen, followed by the Seelisberg.

Brunnen★★ – 👣 *See BRUNNEN.*

From Brunnen to Flüelen the Axenstrasse corniche overhangs the romantic **Lake Uri** (Urnersee), with its deep blue waters. Its shores are marked by places of patriotic pilgrimage recalling the birth of the Confederation (Rütli, Tellskapelle).

Axenstrasse★★

This section of road, which is one of the best-known on the Sankt Gotthard route, is also one of the busiest in the country (about 10 000 cars per day in the height of summer). It was cut last century through the cliffs which dip into Lake Uri. The section has two parts differing in character.
Between Brunnen and Sisikon the road follows a corniche facing the Seelisberg Promontory, whose wooded slopes are interrupted by the green patch of the Rütl

The Largest Lakes

◆ Lake Geneva:	580km²/224sq mi	◆ Lake Zurich:	88.5km²/34sq mi
◆ Lake Constance:	540km²/208sq mi	◆ Lake Lugano:	48km²/18.5sq mi
◆ Lake Neuchâtel:	217km²/84sq mi	◆ Lake Thun:	48km²/18.5sq mi
◆ Lake Lucerne:	114km²/44sq mi		

Field within view of the twin Uri-Rotstock peaks. The best viewpoint is on the outside of a bend above the railway; here you are exactly opposite the Rütli.

Between Sisikon and Flüelen the road has changed since a single tunnel was bored to take the place of the famous open gallery (🚗 *disused and closed to cars*) of which millions of photographs must have been taken.

Tellskapelle

From the Hotel Tellsplatte, 30min on foot there and back by a steep path.

Built on a lonely **site**★ on the shore of **Lake Uri**, this chapel commemorates one of the most dramatic episodes in the story of William Tell. As Gessler's prisoner after the ordeal of the apple, the valiant archer was thrown into a boat which was assailed by a sudden storm; the bailiff and his minions had to appeal for their captive's help. He took advantage of this to steer the boat towards the shore, leaped onto a rocky shelf and kicked the boat back into the raging waves.

Altdorf – 🕐 *See ALTDORF.*

2 Road to Seelisberg★ *22km/13.5mi – allow 1hr*

🕐 *Description see STANS: Excursions.*

Additional Sights

Pilatus★★★ – *Access and description* 🕐 *see PILATUS.*

Rigi-Scheidegg★★ – *Access from Schwyz.* 🕐 *See SCHWYZ: Excursions.*

Stans – 🕐 *See STANS.*

Stanserhorn★★ – *Access from Stans.* 🕐 *See STANS: Excursions.*

Bauen★ – *Access from Altdorf.* 🕐 *See ALTDORF: Excursion.*

VILLARS-SUR-OLLON ❄

VAUD – POPULATION 1 208
ALT 1 253M/4 111FT

Together Villars, Chesières and Arveyes form a resort perched 800m/2 625ft above the Lower Valais. It is the most highly developed mountain resort in French Switzerland and one of the most accessible for the inhabitants of the lowlands, affording a panorama of the French Alps, the Dents du Midi and the Muverans Range with Mont Blanc, the Trient Glacier and the peaks of Les Diablerets in the distance.

Address Book

STAYING IN VILLARS

🍸🍸🍸 **La Renardière** – *Route des Layeux* – ☎ 024 495 25 92 – *Fax 024 495 39 15 – 20 rooms* – 🕐 *open mid- Dec to Apr and mid-May to Oct.* Two rustic-style chalets with sparsely-furnished rooms connected by a footbridge. If you want something more luxurious, book one of the four suites. Relax in the garden, a haven of rural peace.

🍸🍸🍸🍸 **Du Golf** – *Rue Centrale* – ☎ 024 496 38 38 – *69 rooms* – 🕐 *open mid-Dec to mid-Oct.* A lovely location in a large, blissfully quiet park. Country-style rooms with a lounge area.

EATING OUT

After a long walk in the mountains, why not stop at an Alpine farm to taste home-made cheese cooked in a wood oven? Other attractions of the area include the small inns known as pintes vaudoises, where you can try the local speciality *papet aux poireaux* (a mixture of potatoes, leeks and cream), accompanied by a glass of local wine.

🍸🍸**Plambuit** – *In Plambuit, 6km/4mi N* – ☎ 024 499 33 44 – 🕐 *closed early Jan to early Feb, Wed except May-Oct, and Thu all year.* This mountain chalet with its rustic dining hall serves tasty dishes made with fresh produce bought at the local market. As there are few tables, it is advisable to book in advance.

🍸🍸🍸**Miroir d'Argentine** – *In Solalex, 8km/5mi E* – ☎ 024 498 14 46 – 🕐 *open early May to end of Oct.* This friendly establishment offers high-quality traditional cuisine. The à la carte dishes change weekly.

The Resorts

Villars

The town lies along an esplanade of parkland in an attractive rural setting dotted with low mountains. It enjoys a sunny climate and fine views of the Dents du Midi. Villar's summer facilities include a golf course, swimming pool, 300km/187mi of hiking trails and 150km/94mi of mountain-bike tracks. In winter, the skating rink and sledge piste attract large crowds. Throughout the year, Villars hosts many cultural events, namely classical music concerts.

The skiing area

The Villars-sur-Ollon skiing area is smaller than some neighboring resorts (12560km/78mi of pistes), a definite plus for families and others looking for a leisurely resort pace and a variety of novice and intermediate terrain on sunny slopes. The two main peaks (Grand Chamossaire and Croix des Chaux) are perfect for intermediates. Try the Combe d'Orsay, with its **views**★ of Leysin, and one of the many forest trails. Seasoned skiers can tackle slopes running from Croix des Chaux to La Rasse or Les Fracherets. A skiing pass now enables you to go skiing all over the Vaud Alps (🍸 *see Les ALPES VAUDOISES*), including Les Diablerets and its glacier (50km/31mi of challenging slopes, accessible by the Conches chairlift) as well as Leysin (60km/37mi of pistes) and Les Mosses (40km/25mi), which can only be reached by car. There are also 44km/27mi of cross-country trails around the resort.

Bretaye

Alt 1 806m/5 925ft. Access by rack railway.
Pretty route crossing the forest. After reaching Col de Soud, there are stunning views of Croix des Chaux and the impressive Diablerets peaks.

Grand Chamossaire

Alt 2 120m/6 955ft. Access to skiers by chairlift starting from Bretaye.
Sweeping panorama of the Vaud Alps mountain range (Leysin, Gryon, Les Diablerets) with the Valais, Mont Blanc and Dents du Midi nestling in the background.

Chesières and Arveyes

These resorts are recommended to residents who are looking for peace and quiet rather than fashionable society. The panorama from Chesières includes the Mont-Blanc Massif, between the Trient Glacier and the Aiguille Verte.

Excursions

From Villars to Pont de Nant

22km/13.5mi. Leave Villars to the south on the road to Bex.
As it dips, the road presents a plunging **view** of the wooded Gryonne Valley spanned by a concrete bridge. The La Croix de Javerne and Dent de Morcles stand straight ahead.

La Barboleusaz

Alt 1 211m/3 973ft. This winter sports resort is located in a lovely site overlooked by Les Diablerets. From here you can get to the ski fields of **Les Chaux**★ (5km/3mi by a narrow, winding road; in winter access by cable car) or to the **Solalex Refuge**★ (alt 1 466m/4 809ft) – via a small picturesque road (6km/3.5mi) following the Avançon torrent – in a cirque of Alpine pastures at the foot of Les Diablerets.

Gryon

Alt 1 114m/3 655ft. Old terraced village overlooking the Avançon Valley. The road dips rapidly, winding between fir and larch. Bear left towards Les Plans 2km/1mi before Bex. At Frenières note on the left the perched village of Gryon. After Les Plans the road climbs through woodland, running parallel to a stream.

Pont de Nant★

A lovely cirque at the base of the Grand Muveran Glaciers. An Alpine rock garden can be visited (waterlily pond; more than 2 000 kinds of Alpine or medicinal plants from all over the world).

WALENSEE

LAKE WALENSTADT

Lake Walenstadt or **Walensee** spreads its tarnished mirror beneath the gigantic rock bastions of the Churfisten, a sight remembered by travellers coming from Zurich, who pass through the Wessen-Sargans Gap on their way to the Rhine Valley, Austria and the Grisons.

Between Näfels and Murg, the road beside the lake, parallel with the railway, required large-scale engineering, including construction of six tunnels and nine stretches of road cut into the mountainside above sheer drops. It is still possible to go by the old, steep road which, as it climbs to the wooded terrace of the Kerenzerberg, affords many **bird's-eye views**★★ both westwards to the Glarus Valley of the Linth and the low alluvial plain into which the torrent flows, and eastwards to the lake and the Churfirsten.

WEISSENSTEIN★★★

SOLOTHURN

10KM/6MI NORTH OF SOLOTHURN – LOCAL MAP SEE LE JURA SUISSE

The crests of Weissenstein, standing like a rampart above the Solothurn lowland, offer one of the most impressive panoramas in the Jura.

Access

From Solothurn, 10km/6mi – allow 2hr – by ⑤, Oberdorf and then a section of mountain road of which the most difficult part can be avoided by taking the chairlift from Oberdorf station to Kurhaus Weissenstein (16min). ⏱ *Operates Apr-Oct, 8.30am (8am Sun) to 6pm; Nov-Mar, 9am (8am Sun) to 5pm.* ⏱ *Closed three weeks in spring and autumn.* ⚙ *Fare there and back: 19CHF.* ☎ *(032) 626 46 00. From Delémont, 24km/15mi by road n° 6 to Moutier, then by road n° 30 to Gansbrunnen, from where a small mountain road (for the most part not tarred) leads to the summit.*

Panorama★★★

When driving from Solothurn or Gänsbrunnen, the summit of the climb is marked by a pastoral combe. Turn into the road to the Kurhaus, which stands on the crest at an altitude of 1 287m/4 222ft.

Walk down the path more than 7km/4mi long on the road to Gänsbrunnen. Leave the car in front of the restaurant and go to the terrace *(passage to the left of the building if you do not intend taking refreshments there)*, from where the great barrier of the Alps can be seen, from the Säntis on the left to the Mont Blanc on the right. The **bird's-eye view★★★** of the Mittelland *(see Introduction: Nature)* is unequalled in the northern Jura. Bern and the Neuchâtel, Murten and Biel lakes can be distinguished in clear weather.

WEISSENSTEINSTRASSE★★

WEISSENSTEIN ROAD

This itinerary through the Jura, with many woodland and gorge sections, offers a superb panorama its final phase at Weissenstein.

From Porrentruy to Solothurn *102km/64mi – about 4hr 30min*

Itinerary 1 *(⏱ see Le JURA SUISSE map).* ⚠Between Gänsbrunnen and Oberdorf, the small Weissenstein road, usually blocked by snow December to May, is very steep on the Solothurn side (gradients up to 22% – 1 in 5 – approach the hairpin bends very carefully).

Porrentruy★ – ⏱ *See PORRENTRUY.*

After Porrentruy there is a big hump in the road to enable it to cross the Mount Terri Chain at the Les Rangiers Pass. Below the Les Malettes, just before this threshold, a steep descent through the woods leads to the **Ajoie Plateau**, which is, in fact, part of the Franche-Comté joined to Switzerland; belfries crowned in the style of the Franche-Comté can be seen here and there.

Saint-Ursanne★ – 🕐 See SAINT-URSANNE.

This hilly, nearly always wooded section is nonetheless pleasant and not too slow, but open views are rare.

▶ *Start driving towards St-Brais.*

Jura Corniche★ – 🕐 See Les FRANCHES MONTAGNES.

Road n° 6 from the pass to Delémont affords similar conditions.

Delémont – 🕐 See DELÉMONT.

From Delémont to Moutier, the Birse, whose rapid course you now follow, has hollowed out two cross valleys separated by the village of Roches. The lower cross valley is definitely industrial (the ironworks at Choindez). The upper cross valley, much narrower, cuts through the Raimeux Chain whose name it bears, and runs between great rocky walls pierced by a succession of short railway tunnels.

Chapelle de Chalières
In Moutier cemetery. Leave the town westwards on the road towards Perrefitte.
This Romanesque chapel (heavily restored), has inside its apse early 11C frescoes: on the vault is a Christ in Glory surrounded by angels, a unicorn and a griffon.

Le Weissenstein★★★
🕐 *Access and description see Le WEISSENSTEIN.*
The very hard section over the wooded Weissenstein Chain – the forest is thicker on the Solothurn side – ends at last in the lush orchards of the Mittelland, which mark the arrival at Solothurn.

Solothurn★ – 👣 See SOLOTHURN.

WENGEN✳✳

BERN
LOCAL MAP SEE INTERLAKEN: EXCURSIONS – ALT 1 275M/4 183FT

Wengen is situated at 1274m/4179ft over the valley of Lauterbrunnen on a sunny and wind-sheltered mountain terrace at the foot of the Jungfrau massif, dominated by the Jungfrau and the Eiger. One of the most fashionable and best equpped mountain resorts in the Bernese Oberland, it is popular year-round for its picturesque old-fashioned charm and car-free streets. *www.wengen-meurren.ch.*

🅿 **Parking:** Wengen is closed to cars; park in Lauterbrunnen
😊 **Don't Miss:** An excursion to the Jungraujoch

The **site★★★** of this shoulder of Alpine pastures and forests from where, after being dazzled by the Jungfrau, you can look along the Lauterbrunnen rift from a unique point of view, is a delight. It is a prefect starting point for walks, which follow well-maintained paths, regularly cleared of snow even in winter. There is 500km/310mi of signposted hiking trails. The **ski resort** has 44 modern lifts leading to more than 200km/124mi of pistes; beginner areas in the middle of the village make this an ideal destination for families. Some of the best skiing is reached by the mountain railway from the centre of town up to Kleine Scheidegg (alt 2 061m/6 762ft). From here, you can ski the famous Lauberhorn course, site of the men's downhill World Cup **Lauberhorn race**, which takes place in early January; the railway also accesses the Eigergletscher. There are 50km/32mi of groomed toboggan runs, some illuminated at night.

WERDENBERG★

BUCHS – SANKT GALLEN
ALT 451M/1 480FT

At the north end of the populous settlement of Buchs, the old village of Werdenberg, framed by deep greenery and sleepy waters, is a particularly welcome little **scene**★ in the broad Rheinthal corridor, usually more striking for its agricultural prosperity than for its picturesque quality. Leave the car either just before the promenade running along the pond, or just afterwards. You enter the tiny hamlet by a narrow alley flanked by a row of well-restored wooden arcaded houses.

The atmosphere is typical of small 17C-18C towns from the Rhine Valley, thanks to the inscriptions, dates and polychrome ornamental motifs. Between n°s 8 and 9, a passageway leads to a path circling the pond. There you face the houses of Werdenberg, closely grouped together at the foot of the Castle of Counts: note on the left the lovely painted façade of the Schlange house (note the snake, from which it takes its name, just under the roof). Retrace your steps to the alley and take the ramp leading to the castle *(access by a long staircase)*.

Schloss
🕐 *Open Apr-Oct, daily except Mon, 9.30am-5pm.* 👓*4CHF* ☎ *(081) 771 29 50*
Built and remodelled between the 13C and the 18C, the castle was converted into a residential mansion in the late 19C. The section under the eaves is devoted to the Rhine (archaeological finds, maps and plans, geology, miniature models of bridges). The top of the tower commands a lovely **view** of the Rheinthal. Before leaving, admire the collection of arms on display (rifles, revolvers, sabres, headdresses).

SCHLOSS WILDEGG★

AARGAU
5KM/3MI N OF LENZBURG

The impressive mass of **Wildegg Castle**, looming above the Aare Valley, was built in the 12C by a Count of Habsburg and enlarged and altered several times since (particularly by the Effinger family who were the owners for four centuries). It is now an outstation of the Swiss National Museum in Zurich. The castle contains fine **furniture**★ dating from the 17C - 19C. The Blue Room, the Armoury and the Library deserve special attention for the beauty of their ceilings and furnishings. From the upper storeys there is a wide view of a gently undulating landscape of fields and forests. 🕐 *Open mid-Mar to end Oct, daily except Mon, 10am-5pm.* 🕐 *Closed Good Fri.* 👓 *7CHF.* ☎ *(062) 893 10 33*

WINTERTHUR

ZÜRICH – POPULATION 88 013
ALT 439M/1 440FT
TOWN PLAN IN THE MICHELIN GUIDE SWITZERLAND

A town named Vitudurum was established here during the Roman era. At the end of Middle Ages, Winterthur made the large porcelain stoves which can still be admired in some Swiss houses. **The industrial development of the town, nowadays connected with the textile industry and mechanical engineering (railway equipment, diesel engines), has not interfered with its artistic reputation: the city boasts several museums with fine collections that show a complete record of 19C European painting. Concerts given by the Collegium Musicum, founded in 1629, always draw a large audience.** 🛈 *im Hauptbahnhof – 8400 –* ☎ *(052) 267 67 00.*

Sights

Museum Oskar Reinhart am Stadtgarten

Stadthausstrasse 6. 🕐 *Open daily except Mon, 10am-5pm (8pm Tue).* 💰*8CHF.* ☎ *(052) 267 51 72.*
Works by Swiss, German and Austrian painters from the 18C, 19C and 20C are displayed. Excellent drawings by Rudolf Wasmann, portraits of children by Anker, works by Böcklin and Koller, paintings by the German Romantics and by artists of the Munich School as well as animal studies by Jacques Laurent Agasse may be seen. The many canvases by Ferdinand Hodler (1853-1918) show the importance attached to this leader of pre-1914 Swiss painting.

Collection Oskar Reinhart "Am Römerholz"★★

Haldenstrasse 95. 🕐 *Open daily except Mon, 10am-5pm.* 🕐 *Closed 1 Jan, Good Fri, Easter Sun, Whit Sun, 1 May and 25 Dec.* 💰*8CHF.* ☎ *(052) 269 27 40.*
The art patron Oskar Reinhart, who died in 1965, bequeathed his impressive collection to the Swiss Confederation on the condition it remain in his native town. The artwork, in a house set in large grounds overlooking the town, spans five centuries including paintings by Brueghel and El Greco and drawings by Rembrandt, French works from the late 17C to the 19C with Poussin, Claude Lorraine, Watteau, Chardin and Fragonard, and sketches by Daumier. The 19C is represented by artists whose

The Day Nursery by A Anker

Stiftung O. Reinhart, Winterthur

works reflect the main contemporary trends in pictorial art, such as Corot, Delacroix, Courbet, Manet, Renoir and Cézanne, as well as Van Gogh and, closer to the present, Picasso with drawings from his Blue period.

Kunstmuseum★

🕐 *Open daily except Mon, 10am-5pm (8pm Tue).* 🕐 *Closed 1 Jan, Good Fri, Easter Sun, Whit Sun, Ascension, 1 May, St-Alban's Sunday, 1 Aug and 25 Dec.* ⛬*10CHF.* ☎ *(052) 267 51 62.*

The **Fine Arts Museum** contains works from the 16C (Cranach), 17C and 18C regional art (Graff, Mayer, Füssli) and Swiss and German painters from the 19C and 20C (Hodler, Vallotton, Giacometti, Auberjonois, Corinth and Hofer). The French Schools are represented by artists such as Renoir, Bonnard, Vuillard and Van Gogh. Part of the building is devoted to sculpture by Rodin, Maillol, Haller, Marini and Alberto Giacometti. The museum also houses the town's library and a natural history section.

Villa Flora★★

Tösstalstrasse 44. 🕐 *Open daily except Mon, 2-5pm, Sun 11am-3pm.* 🕐 *Closed 1 Jan, Good Fri, Easter, 1 May, Whitsun and 25 Dec.* ⛬*8CHF.* ☎ *(052) 212 99 66.*

The post-Impressionist works accumulated between 1907 and 1930 by Arthur and Hedy Hahnloser-Bühler are interesting in that they were acquired not through art dealers, but through their personal friends and relatives of the artists themselves. Visitors will be impressed by the high quality of the works, and the prophetic nature of the paintings, laid out in the house once occupied by these dedicated art lovers. The largest part of the collection is works by the Nabis – artists born between 1860 and 1870, who chose to rebel against academic conventions, including the Swiss Félix Vallotton *(The Barrow)*, E Vuillard *(The Game of Draughts*, with its incredible plunging perspective)—and to Pierre Bonnard *(The Fauns*, combining many different viewpoints). Fauvism—the term was first coined by art critic Louis Vauxcelles during the Salon d'Automne in 1905 – is represented by H Manguin, a close friend of the Hahnloser-Bühlers, and by Matisse. Besides the Fauves and the Nabis, of particular note is the rare series of nine paintings *(Andromède)* by Odilon Redon, dubbed "the artist of the Irrational", of which Hedy Hahnloser-Bühler had already said in 1919: "All the main components characteristic of contemporary artistic inspiration are already present in his work". Finally, note the outstanding *Portrait of the Artist* by Paul Cézanne, *The Sower* and *Night Café* by Vincent van Gogh, and many sculptures (bronzes by Bonnard, C Despiau, A Maillol, Henri Matisse, M Marini, PA Renoir, A Rodin and F Vallotton). The garden (two sculptures by Aristede Maillol) sadly is open only to groups.

Technorama

🄺🄸🄳🅂 *Technoramastrasse 1. Leave the motorway at the Oberwinterthur exit and then follow directions. You can also take bus n° 12 from the main station.* 🕐 *Open daily except Mon, 10am-5pm.* 🕐 *Closed 25 Dec.* ⛬*21CHF.* ☎ *(052) 244 08 44, www.technorama.ch.*

This attractive and amusing museum is a perfect tool to introduce young people to the world of science and technology. The permanent exhibitions of the Swiss **Science Center** can be divided into eight parts: Physics; Trains and Toys (collections of miniature trains); Energy (thermic machines); Water, Nature and Chaos (experimentation with natural phenomena); Mechanical Music (instruments and the recording of sound); Materials (processing); Textiles (spinning and weaving); Automatic Technology (analogical and digital techniques). The purpose of the visit is to operate the various machines and watch demonstrations, of which the most impressive is no doubt that of high-voltage, one of many inter-active opportunities. The "laboratory", supervised by a team of trained instructors, enables visitors to acquire scientific knowledge while having fun. The park can be used to experiment with flying machines (🕐 *open Saturdays and Sundays only).*

Excursion

Schloss Kyburg

6km/4mi S. Leave Winterthur by the Seen road. At Sennhof take the small road to the right and follow it along the Töss; after 1km/0.5mi turn left to go to Kyburg village. ⏰ *Open 10.30am-5.30pm (4.30pm in Feb, Mar, Apr and Nov).* ⏰ *Closed Mon, some public hols, Jan and Dec.* ⬛ *8CHF.* ☎ *(052) 232 46 64; www.schlosskyburg.ch*

This feudal castle was built in the 10C and 11C and passed successively from the line of the counts of Kyburg to that of the Habsburgs. In 1424 it came within the bailiwick of the town of Zurich and remained so until 1798; since 1917 the castle has belonged to the canton. Inside are remarkable collections of furniture and arms which will interest visitors with a knowledge of history and antiques. There is a good view of the surrounding countryside.

YVERDON-LES-BAINS

VAUD – POPULATION 22 981

ALT 439M/1 440FT – TOWN PLAN IN THE MICHELIN GUIDE SWITZERLAND

Yverdon-les-Bains is built at the south end of Lake Neuchâtel. It is a well-known spa because of the healing properties of its waters, which feature a high content of sulphur and magnesium and which for many centuries have sprung from a depth of 500m/1 640ft. An pleasant lakeside beach also adds to the town's attractions. ⬛ *1 avenue de la Gare – 1400 – ☎ (024) 423 62 90.*

A group of menhirs, known as the Promenade des Anglais and situated outside the town, on the road to Estavayer-le-Lac, testify to the presence of a human settlement in former times. This town was originally a Celtic settlement which later became Gallo-Roman. Of its Roman history it has kept only the remains of a *castrum* (fortified citadel), located near the local graveyard. The town hall, with its Louis XV façade, and especially the castle, are worthy of attention.

Castle

This castle dates from the 13C , built Peter II of Savoy, who captured the town in 1259 and erected this imposing fortress with its four round towers. After extensive

A Brilliant Educator

Born in Zurich in 1746, **Johann Heinrich Pestalozzi**, the son of an Italian-born surgeon and the grandson of a priest, was influenced from an early age by the educational principles of Jean-Jacques Rousseau's *Émile*, to such an extent that he devoted most of his life to educating poor children, mainly in rural areas. His theories about education are clearly presented in *Léonard et Gertrud* (1781-87). In 1804, he accepted the invitation extended by the city of Yverdon to teach deprived children. The following year, he founded an institution on the castle premises, which gained a Europe-wide reputation. In 1806, he opened an institute for girls next to the town hall, in which the teaching standards were the same as those for boys. After twenty years in Yverdon, Pestalozzi returned to the Maison de Neuhof. He died in Brugg in 1827.

His philosophy and his achievements are neatly summed up in the words which he had inscribed on the pedestal of his statue: "I myself chose to live like a beggar, so that beggars might learn to live like men."

restoration, the castle has become an important arts centre, housing the **Museé d'Yverdon-les-Bains et de sa région** (🕐 *Open Jun-Sep, 11am-5pm; Oct-May, 2-5pm.* 🕐 *Closed Mon (except Easter Mon and Whit Mon), 1 Jan and 25 Dec.* ➔*8CHF.* ☎ *(024) 425 93 10).* The collections, which take up several castle rooms, recall the history of the area since prehistoric times. Regional fauna is also represented. One room in the northeast tower presents an exhibition on the famous teacher Pestalozzi (🕭 *see TROGEN).*

Maison d'Ailleurs
🕐 *Open Wed-Fri, 2-6pm, Sat-Sun, noon-6pm.* ➔ *6CHF.* ☎ *(024) 425 64 38.*
This unique museum dedicated to science fiction, utopia and extraordinary journeys hosts temporary exhibitions of sculpture, art and design. The amusing and often disturbing exhibits are displayed on three floors.

ZERMATT✳✳✳

VALAIS – POPULATION 4 896

ALT 1 616M/5 302FT – TOWN PLAN IN THE MICHELIN GUIDE SWITZERLAND

The hooked pyramid of the **Matterhorn** (alt 4 478m/14 692ft) dominates the centre of Zermatt, situated in the Nikolaital Valley. The mountain has strongly influenced the development of this old mountain village, "discovered" a century ago by the British and launched as a resort in 1855 by the Seilers, a family of hotel-keepers. 🖹 *Bahnhofplatz – 3920 –* ☎ *(027) 966 81 00, www.zermatt.ch.*

▸ **Orient Yourself:** The main street runs the length of the village from the train station at one end to the cablecar station at the other.
🅿 **Parking:** This is a car-free village; you must park down the valley at Täsch and take the electric train the remaining 8km/5mi to the village.
🕭 **Don't Miss:** The view of the iconic Matterhorn from the Stockhorn
🕐 **Organizing Your Time:** At least two days for skiing (winter) or rambling (other seasons)
Kids **Especially for Kids:** Children under 9 travel free on all lifts and cable cars.

Zermatt is renowned as an important mountaineering centre, with a dozen peaks over 4 000m/13 120ft within easy access of the resort. It is also popular with other visitors of all nationalities and its main street is lined with luxury boutiques, hotels and souvenir shops. The resort is traffic-free, with the exception of small electric vehicles and horse-drawn carriages and sleighs. Zermatt can be reached only by rail either from Brig or Visp (Viège) where most visitors leave their cars, or from Täsch (5km/3.5mi from Zermatt), which has a large car park.

A Bit of History

Edward Whymper
In the 1860s, Edward Whymper, a young British illustrator thrilled by the mountain shapes that his publisher had asked him to draw, had been wandering over the Alps of the Valais, Savoy and Dauphiné, looking for unconquered peaks. He had already made the first ascent of the Barre des Écrins, the Aiguille Verte and the Grandes Jorasses, but he always came back to Zermatt or the Valtournanche, fascinated by the Matterhorn, which he had already vainly attempted eight times, starting from Breuil with the help of a well-known local guide, Jean-Antoine Carrel.

Competition for the summit

In 1865, changing his plan of action, Whymper decided to attack the peak along its northeast ridge – that which faces Zermatt. On 13 July the local people saw three British climbers and a guide from Chamonix – Douglas, Hudson, Hadow and Michel Croz – join Whymper and his two guides from Zermatt, the Taugwalders, father and son, and set off for the mountain. Helped by ideal weather, with no falling stones, the climbers set foot on the summit of the Matterhorn on 14 July, early in the afternoon. They scored a victory over a party of climbers led by Carrel who, unbeknown to them, had set off from Breuil to attempt to reach the summit from the Italian side, which they succeeded in doing on 17 July.

A bitter victory

Tearing themselves away from the incomprarable view of 33 peaks over 4 000m/13 120ft, the climbers began their descent. Suddenly, young Hadow, the least experienced member of the party, slipped, dragging Croz, Hudson and Douglas with him in his fall. The life-line between Douglas and the elder Taugwalder snapped. Whymper and his guides watched the frightful fall of their four companions, 1 200m/4 000ft below. An impressive celestial phenomenon, the appearance of two crosses shining in a great arc of clouds, is said to have tested the survivors' nerves once more before they regained the valley.

The skiing area

Zermatt is one of Switzerland's most extensive and most spectacular ski areas, in part for the view of the Matterhorn from several of the pistes and the opportunity to ski into Italy. The ski area is defined by three high summits with a spectacular vertical drop of 2 300m/7 546ft on the Italian side *(a separate lift pass must be purchased for Cervinia, and it should be accessed only in fine weather to prevent being stranded there unable to return to Zermatt)* and 2 200m/7 217ft on the Swiss side The 260km/162mi of gently sloping pistes are in a magnificent setting and combine high and medium altitude slopes. **Telemark** skiing, introduced from Scandinavia, is now one of the resort's specialities. The highest summit is the **Klein Matterhorn** (3 820m/12 532ft), open for both winter and summer skiing along an imposing glacier (Theodulgletscher); the slope here is groomed smooth and ideal for intermediates. Piste 20b is especially recommended for its splendid views. The **Hörnli**, too, is the starting-point for several excursions which are definitely worth a detour. The first section offers charming runs through the forest when snow coverage is sufficient.

The **Gornergrat** Massif offers easy slopes near the railway tracks. Experienced skiers will be challenged on the **Rote Nase** (3 247m/10 652ft) and the Stockhorn (3 407m/11 175ft), featuring a difference in height of 1 200m/3 936ft. Finally, the **Rothorn** (3 103m/10 180ft) provides pistes suitable for intermediate skiers, in particular those numbered 22b and 23. There are also 90km/56mi of winter hiking and snowshoeing trails (6 sign-posted trails totaling 26km/16m) and 9k/5mi of prepared trails for cross-country skiing.

The Resort

Bahnhofstrasse

The main street, from the railway station to the parish church and the lower cable car up the mountainside, is lined with fine hotels, shops and restaurants. Note the medallion dedicated to Whymper on the façade of the Monte Rosa Hotel, opened in 1855 and a favourite with British high society. Beyond the main street, the quieter district of **Old Zermatt** is dotted with typical Valais chalets and toast-coloured *mazots*. Solar-powered busses and horse-drawn sleighs are the alternative to walking.

Franziska Pfenniger / Switzerland Tourism

Zermatt nestling at the foot of the Matterhorn

Matterhorn Museum

🕐 *Open summer, 10am-noon and 4-6pm; winter, daily except Sat, 4.30-6.30pm.*
🕐 *Closed Nov to mid-Dec.* 🎫*8CHF.* ☎ *(027) 967 66 36 .*

Situated near the post office in the centre of the resort, this museum is dedicated to the first conquests of the Matterhorn, the guides and famous guests of Zermatt, and to the history of the Alps (geology, flora and fauna). An important section is devoted to Old Zermatt (reconstructions of mountain-dwellers' homes) and there is also a relief map of the Matterhorn.

Viewpoints Accessible by Chairlift

Klein Matterhorn★★★

Alt 3 886m/12 684ft. Access by three successive cable cars. Allow half a day to discover the panoramas and a whole day if you combine the visit with an excursion. In winter, it can take 2hrs to get to the summit because of the queues. The departure station, accessible by shuttle service or on foot (15min), is at the far end of Zermatt. Departures from Zermatt every 20min, 8am to around 5pm. 🎫*Fare there and back: 77CHF.* ☎ *(027) 966 64 64.*

The first section rides above the forest and a steep corridor of rubble with a view straight ahead from the mid-station of **Furi** (alt 1 865m/6 119ft) to Zermatt. This site has a number of *mazots* and inns, which are open in summer and winter. The second section rides through a mineral-like landscape within view of the Cervin before ending at **Trockener Steg** (alt 2 929m/9 610ft), where the **Theodulgletscher**★★ can be seen, its irregularly shaped pinnacles of ice in a cirque of reddish slopes streaked with cascades and topped by snowy peaks.

> *For coin ranges, see Legend on the cover flap.*

WHERE TO STAY IN ZERMATT

Hotel Jagerhof, *Steinmatte 85,* (027) 966 38 00, www.hoteljaegerhofzermatt.ch - 49 rooms - This charming chalet-style hotel is family-owned. Traditional rustic pine decor. Cosy, quiet and attentive service.

Schweizerhof Hotel, *Bahnhofstrasse 5,* (027) 966 05 55, www.summithotels.com - 95 rooms and suites - In the heart of the village, owned by the prominent Seiler family, this is a modern hotel built in old-fashioned style. Also noteworthy for its indoor pool.

EATING OUT

Le Mazot, *Hofmattstr 23, (027) 660 60 60 -* ◷ *closed Mon. and late-Apr to mid-June and late Oct.* Traditional grilled specialties and excellent service in a charming old farmhouse. Reservtions recommended.

Walliserstube, *Gryfelblatte 2 (027) 967 82 84,* ◷ *open daily -* Rustic decor, specialses in fondue: cheese, bourgignon (with meat) and chinoise (vegetables). Popular with families.

The last cable car climbs over the glacier and stops at the highest altitude station in Europe. The actual summit (3 885m/12 746ft) can be reached by a lift and several flights of steps. The 360° **panorama**★★★ is truly breathtaking. To the west loom Mont Blanc,Mont Maudit, Les Grandes Jorasses, Grand Combin, Dent d'Hérens and the iconic Matterhorn. To the north, the view encompasses Zermatt, framed on the left by the Dent Blanche, Obergabelhorn, Zinalrothorn and on the right by the Dom and the Täschhorn. In the far distance you can glimpse the Jungfrau, Mönch and Aletschhorn. The most spectacular sight is undoubtedly the long ice tongue of the Gorner (to the east) and the Breithorn (4 160m/13 644ft), Castor (4 226m/13 861ft) and Pollux (4 091m/13 421ft) summits. This wonderful circular panorama is complemented to the south by the Italian Alps, featuring Mont Viso, Grand Paradis and Grivola.

▶ *Return to Furi by cable car.*

Schwarzsee★
Alt 2 582m/8 468ft. Half a day's walk. Cable-car from Schwarzsee – Departures from Zermatt every 20min. Fare there and back: 33CHF. (027) 966 64 64.
From Furi a cable car goes up *(5min)* to the foot of the Matterhorn, which is mirrored in this small lake. A path goes around it. On its shore stands a chapel with schist roofing. The Black Lake is the starting-point for interesting walks towards Zermatt (*see below*). Return to Furi via Stafel and Zmutt.

Gornergrat★★★
Alt 3 135/10 272ft. 1hr 40min by rack railway there and back. ◷ *Open Jun-Oct, 7am-7pm, departures about every 30min.* Fare there and back: 64CHF. (027) 922 43 11/966 48 11. *Allow the whole day if you combine this trip with a walk or the ascent of the Stockhorn. Cable-car from Gornergrat to Stockhorn – Departures every 24min, summer 7.10am-7.55pm (5.55pm mid-Jun to late Oct).* Fare there and back: 67CHF. (027) 921 41 11.
The steep Gornergrat rack railway is the highest open-air railway in Europe, offering fantastic sweeping **views**★ of Zermatt. After the Riffelberg stop, where there is a very good view of the Matterhorn, you can feast your eyes on the unforgettable **Monte Rosa** (crowning summit: Dufourspitze at 4 634m/15 203ft) and its huge glaciers. Enjoy the breathtaking **panorama**★★★ of the numerous tongues of ice and the Valais. The excursion can be rounded off by the ascent first to Hohtälli (3 286m/7 499ft),

then to **Stockhorn**★★★ (3 405m/11 129ft) in two successive cable cars c 1hr there and back). Good views of Monte Rosa, Lyskam, Castor and Pollux, a glacial landscape contrasting sharply with the austere, arid setting across the valley. If you do not suffer from vertigo, walk from Gornergrat to Hohtälli, following a narrow **mountain path**★★★ for truly breathtaking views.

Rothorn★★

Alt 3 103m/10 180ft. From Zermatt by funicular (access by a long corridor) to Sunnegga, then by cable car to Blauherd and then again by cable car (20min including 5min by funicular).

The funicular climbs through a tunnel (3min) to **Sunnegga** (alt 2 285m/7 497ft), on the edge of a plateau of Alpine pastures enhanced by a small lake. Here you get your first glimpse of the Matterhorn (southwest). From **Blauherd** (alt 2 577m/8 459ft), the second mid-station, in view of a lovely fir forest (on the right), the cable car arrives on the flat, rocky summit of the Rothorn. From here the spectacular **panorama**★★, barred to the east by the Oberrothorn, stretches southwest to the Matterhorn (profile view), south onto the Findelen Glacier, west onto Zermatt and north onto the Nikolaital Valley. From the Rothorn, some of the highest footpaths in the Alps lead to the Oberrothorn (alt 3 415m/11 201ft).

Walks

There are abundant opportunities for ramblers here, with around 400km/250mi of footpaths crossing forests and Alpine pastures, dotted with picturesque villages, lakes and imposing glacial cirques.

From Schwarzsee to Zermatt★★

There is a vertical drop of 900m/2 952ft down to Zermatt or 700m/2 297ft down to Furi. Remember to wear sturdy mountain shoes. Allow at least half a day. Access to Schwarzsee by cable car and then 5min on foot.

After walking a few minutes, you reach a second, smaller lake , a fantastic **setting**★★ enhanced by reflections of the Dent Blanche to the north and the Klein Matterhorn and Breithorn to the south. Follow the path, which continues to dip steadily: it affords remarkable **views**★★ of the Matterhorn, the Zmutt and Arben glaciers, as well as the Dom and Mont Rose. After 30min walking, keep to the left-hand path then take the track on the right. This steep route brings you to Stafelalp (inn at 2 200m/7 217ft).

Majestic Peaks

A few Swiss mountains over 4 000m/13 123ft:

◆ Mount Rosa (Valais):	4 634m/15 203ft
◆ Dom (Mischabel; Valais):	4 545m/14 941ft
◆ Weisshorn (Valais):	4 505m/14 780ft
◆ Matterhorn (Valais):	4 478m/14 692ft
◆ Dent Blanche (Valais):	4 357m/14 295ft
◆ Grand Combin (Valais):	4 314m/14 153ft
◆ Finsteraarhorn (Valais):	4 274m/14 022ft
◆ Aletschhorn (Valais):	4 195m/13 763ft
◆ Breithorn (Valais):	4 165m/13 665ft
◆ Jungfrau (Bern-Valais):	4 158m/13 642ft
◆ Mânch (Bern-Valais):	4 099m/13 448ft
◆ Schreckhorn (Bern):	4 078m/13 379ft
◆ Piz Bernina (Grisons):	4 049m/13 284ft
◆ Lauteraarhorn (Bern):	4 042m/13 261ft

Then there is a steep descent following the edge of the forest. Ramblers can either walk down to the pretty village of Zmutt or continue towards Furi and then the Gorner Gorges (🕭 *see below*).

To Grünsee, Grindjisee and Leisee★★

Go up to Riffelalp (2 200m/7 217ft) by the Gornergrat rack railway. This is a very pleasant walk, which can take half a day up to a whole day depending on the route you choose. Return is by the Sunnegga funicular.

From Riffelalp, a good path *(45min)* follows the edge of a forest to the **Grünsee**★★, from where there are magnificent **views**★★ of the Matterhorn, Dent Blanche, Obergabelhorn, Zinalrothorn and the Weisshorn. Go round the lake to appreciate the reflections of glaciers in the peaceful waters. Another 45min walk brings you to **Grindjisee**★ (2 334m/7 657ft). Seasoned ramblers can complete a tour of the lakes by making a detour via **Stellisee**★, after a 200m/656ft rise in altitude (2 537m/7 322ft).

Finish the excursion at the traditional hamlet of **Eggen**, then the short but steep climb to the splendid lake of **Leisee**★ (2 200m/7 216ft). From the lake, go up to the Sunnegga *(10min)* and take the funicular for the journey back. You can also choose to return to Zermatt on foot *(1hr 15min)*, which is a pleasant walk through woodland.

Gornerschlucht

2hr on foot there and back. At the south exit from Zermatt, turn left (bridge) and follow the signposts. For information, contact Zermatt Tourist Office on ☎ (027) 966 81 00; www.zermatt.ch.

These impressive gorges are overlooked from a path cut in the sheer rock walls; far below the torrent surges on the floor of the ravine. Walk through a forest of Arolla pines and larch to the picturesque hamlet of Blatten with its chapel, its *mazots* (🕭 *illustration see Le VALAIS*) and its erratic boulders. There is a magnificent view of the Matterhorn from the charming restaurant in the hamlet.

▶ *After Zumsee take the road leading back to Zermatt.*

From Riffelberg to Zermatt★★

2hr descent with a 950m/3 117ft drop in height. You can get to this resort by taking the rack railway to Gornergrat.

Attractive route heading towards **Riffelalp** in a luxuriant alpine setting. Then proceed towards Zermatt (pretty chapel), walking through a lovely pine and larch forest. On reaching Untere Riffelalp, note the picturesque cottages used by hunters.

ZERNEZ

GRAUBÜNDEN – POPULATION 1 035
ALT 1 474M/4 836FT

This large, picturesque village overlooks the confluence of the River Spöl and River Inn. It sits on the edge of the Swiss National Park. 🖹 *Chasa Fuschina – 7530 – ☎ (081) 856 12 82.*

Ofen Pass Road★

From Zernez to the Umbrail Pass *57km/35mi – about 2hr 30min*

Itinerary 6 *(& see GRAUBÜNDEN map). The road links the Engadine with the Val Venosta in Italy.*

Schweizerischer Nationalpark – & *See SCHWEIZERISCHER NATIONALPARK.*

Ofenpass

Alt 2 149m/7 051ft. The pass separates the Val dal Spöl, to the north, from the Val Müstair, to the south, whose torrent, the Rom, is a tributary of the Adige. From the pass to Tschierv several sections of corniche afford pretty glimpses downstream, especially of the snowcapped Ortles. After Tschierv the road runs pleasantly between stretches of turf and larch woods. It owes some of its character to the Tyrolean note introduced by the domed belfries of Valchava and Fuldera.

Müstair★ – & *See MÜSTAIR.*

▶ *Return to Santa Maria.*

From Santa Maria to the Umbrail Pass the road climbs up the Muraunza Valley, whose barren appearance and limited skyline contrast with the refreshing and harmonious **scene**★ that greets you at the Alpenrösli Restaurant. From the restaurant's terrace you can look down into the Müstair Valley, a series of fields more and more narrowly bounded uphill by wooded slopes which culminate in the Ofen Pass.

ZUG★

C ZUG – POPULATION 22 366
ALT 425M/1 394FT

This charming little town is built at the northeast end of **Zuger See**★★, a charming lake nestling among gardens and orchards at the foot of the first wooded foothills of the Zugerberg. Excavations reveal that the site of Zug has been inhabited by man without interruption since the Neolithic Era. In the Middle Ages it belonged successively to the Lenzburg, Kyburg and Habsburg families before joining the Confederation in 1352. Its 13C castle has now been entirely restored. ▯ *Alpenstrasse 14 – 6300 – ☏ (041) 711 00 78, www.zug-tourismus.ch.*

Zuger See★★

The Zuger See, with a total area of 38km²/15sq mi and a depth of almost 200m/656ft, is Switzerland's sixth largest lake. It runs in a north-south direction for 14km/9mi and is divided in two by the peninsula of Kiemen. The lake, in an attractive hilly setting, is dominated by the Rigi-Kulm in the south and is very popular with visitors for its scenic beauty and many amenities.

Sights

The Quays★

From Seestrasse to Alpenquai, a promenade beside the lake offers **views**★ of the summits of central Switzerland (Rigi, Pilatus, Bürgenstock, Stanserhorn) and, in the background, of the Bernese Alps (Finsteraarhorn, Jungfrau, Blümlisalp).

Old Town★

Guided tours of the town – (1hr 30min) mid-May to Sep, every Sat at 9.50am. 5CHF. Contact the Tourist office: ☎ (041) 780 31 05.

Ruined fortifications – Powder Tower (Pulverturm), the Capuchin's Tower (Kapuzinerturm) – still mark the original nucleus of the town. The quarters known as Unter-Altstadt (Lower Old Town) and Ober-Altstadt (Upper Old Town), with their old step-gabled houses, strike a delightfully medieval note.

The **Fischmarkt** (Fish Market) has houses with painted weatherboards and overhanging balconies. The Clock Tower, **Zytturm**, features a tiled roof painted in the Zug colours (blue and white) and is crowned by a slim belfry. Under the clock face are the coats of arms of the first eight cantons of the Confederation, Zug having been the seventh canton to join the alliance.

Kolinplatz is surrounded by old houses, among them the Town House (Stadthaus), a 16C building adorned with a fine flower-decked fountain. This fountain bears the statue of the standard bearer Wolfgang Kolin, a local hero who performed brave feats to save his banner at the Battle of Arbedo (1422), when the Confederate forces, who were defending the Leventina, were defeated by the Duke of Milan's army. Kolin's son, to whom the banner had been passed, was also killed.

Sankt Oswald

Open 8am-6pm (5pm in winter). For information on guided tours, call ☎ (041) 711 00 78.

This Late Gothic church was built in the 15C and 16C. The interior, with ogive vaulting, is darkened by its massive pillars. The nave is separated from the chancel by a partition adorned with frescoes. The interior includes many statues of saints, painted and gilded wooden triptychs in the side chapels, and frescoes on the vaulting.

Excursions

Zugerberg★

Alt 988m/3 241ft. The easiest way to get to Zugerberg is to take bus n° 11 leaving from the train station in Zug (Bahnhof Metelli stop), then go to Schöneg and take the funicular. Operates all year. Departures every 30min Mon-Fri, every 15min Sat-Sun. Fare there and back: 7CHF. ☎ (041) 728 58 30.

From the summit there is a almost circular **view**★ to the northwest, of Zug and the lake, to the southwest of the Pilatus, to the south of the Uri-Rotstock and the Uri Alps, and to the east – through a gap in the fir trees – of the village of Unter-Ägeri and its lake. To the north the hills of the Mittelland can be seen rising one behind the other towards Zurich.

Zistersiengerabtei Kappel★

8km/5mi N by the road to Zürich.

The imposing silhouette of the former abbey church – buttresses, pointed roofs and slim bell tower – can be seen in the distance with its village huddled against it. It is located not far from where Zwingli was killed. Built in 13C-14C, the abbey illustrates the Early Gothic style with pure lines and elegant lancet windows. The vast nave is highlighted by stalls decorated with human or animal heads (note the bitch with her puppies). Note the remains of 14C frescoes decorating chancel walls (St Martin, Christ and Saints in medallions) and the **stained-glass windows**★.

ZUOZ★★

GRAUBÜNDEN – POPULATION 1 361
ALT 1 716M/5 561FT

Zuoz is a high-altitude resort, well equipped for a stay in summer. It has preserved a group of **Engadine houses**★★, mostly built by members of the Planta family, who played an important part in the history of the Grisons. The town is small and everything is reachable on foot.  *Via Maistra – 7524 – ☎ (081) 854 15 10.*

Sights *15min*

Hauptplatz★★

Its fountain is surmounted by the heraldic bear of the Plantas (the family arms include a severed bear's paw with the sole – *planta* – turned upwards). The square is bounded on the north by the Planta House, which consists of two distinct dwellings under one roof. This building is designed in the Engadine style (☾ *see ENGADIN*) but its unusual size and its outdoor staircase with a Rococo balustrade give it a lordly air.

> ## Gradients in Percentages
>
> On the continent gradients are usually represented as percentages. These figures will give the motorist some idea of slopes ahead.
>
> | | |
> |---|---|
> | 10% 1:10 | 14% 1:7 |
> | 18% 1:5.5 | 20% 1:5 |
> | 25% 1:4 | 30% 1:3.3 |

On the main street the Crusch Alva Inn (1570) has a gable decorated with a series of coats of arms. To the right of St Luzius, the church of the saint who converted upper Rhaetia, you will recognise the arms of the three Leagues (☾ *see Introduction*), those of the XIII Cantons of the period and finally those of the Salis (*willow – salix* in Latin), Planta and Juvalta families. Walk around the Planta House and under the arcades connecting this building with the 13C Planta Tower to the **church,** which is dominated by a slender tower and has a nave roofed with star-vaulting. The bear's paw is a recurring motif in the interior decoration. Three windows contain modern stained glass: *Hope and Charity*, were designed by the contemporary artist Augusto Giacometti; *The Three Kings*, by Gian Casty.

ZÜRICH★★★

ZURICH Ⓒ ZÜRICH – POPULATION 360 000
ALT 408M/1 339FT
TOWN PLANS IN THE MICHELIN GUIDE SWITZERLAND

Zurich is built between the wooded slopes of the Uetliberg and the Zürichberg at the point where the Limmat, emerging from Lake Zurich, merges with the Sihl. It is the most important financial, industrial and commercial centre in Switzerland and has a population of over one million, the largest of any Swiss town or city. It has a repution for being particularly receptive to contemporary trends and youth culture, and the city is much more lively at night than other towns in German-speaking Switzerland, offering a wide choice of restaurants, cinemas, nightclubs and concert halls.  *Im Bahnhof – ☎ (044) 215 40 00, www.zuerich.com.*

▶ **Orient Yourself:** Bahnhofstrasse, the city's main street, is lined by elegant shops and considered one of the world's most beautiful shopping boulevards.

🅿 **Parking:** Leave the car and use the ZurichCARD, which provides unlimited transportation on trains, buses, streetcars, ships and cableways and free entrance to 40 museums in the city and nearby; prices start at 15F.

🕑 **Don't Miss:** The Swiss National Museum (Landesmuseum) behind the main railway station.

🕓 **Organizing Your Time:** At least three days for museums, shopping and lake excursions.

Kids **Especially for Kids:** The Zoo

🕯 **Also See:** The banks of the Limmat in the Old Town, ideal for strolling.

A Bit of History

Zwingli and the Reformation – When **Ulrich Zwingli** was made parish priest of Glarus in 1506 at the age of 22, he lost no time denouncing social institutions from his pulpit, attacking the corruption of the magistracy and the practice of mercenary soldiering abroad, which he felt was weakening the nation. After two years at Einsiedeln, he was given the pastorate of the Grossmünster (cathedral) of Zurich and began to institute his most controversial religious reforms. In 1523, after a public debate at the Zurich town hall between Zwingli supporters and opponents, the Council declared itself in favour of his new ideas. Within three years Zurich had become a stronghold of the Reformation in German-speaking Switzerland. Zwingli closed monasteries, abolished pilgrimages, processions and certain sacraments and advocated the marriage of priests, setting the example himself in 1524. His authority alarmed the Catholic cantons. Lucerne, Uri, Schwyz, Unterwalden and Zug allied against Zurich and gradually excluded it from federal affairs. Another great religious debate took place at Bern in 1528. Once again Zwingli had the advantage, but war, narrowly avoided in 1529, broke out in 1531. His death that year at Kappel did not diminish the influence of his religious theories, which spread throughout German Switzerland.

Tremendous growth – Zurich still had only 17 000 inhabitants in 1800. It had to cede the title of federal capital to Bern in 1848, but six years later it became the official seat of the Federal Polytechnic School – the famous Polytechnikum. The democratic constitution it gave itself in 1869 became the model for f other cantons and even, in part, for the Federal Constitution of 1874. At the beginning of the 19C the town already extended beyond its fortifications and new buildings were mushrooming in

The Advent of the Dada Movement

The **Cabaret Voltaire** (Spiegelgasse 1 – note the commemorative plaque) was inaugurated in 1916 by poet/director Hugo Ball and wife Emmy Jennings, with friends and artists including Tristan Tzara, Marcel Janco, Jean Arp, Richard Huelsenbeck and Sophie Taeuber, to create an avant-garde movement as a reaction to established art. They decided to disrupt conventional rules by staging dance performances, reciting poems and exhibiting their paintings, an unprecedented approach to cultural life that was a resounding success. The term Dada was coined quite by accident when Ball and Huelsenbeck were trying to find a name for the cabaret singer. The word *Dada* appeared in the first issue of *Cabaret Voltaire*, a magazine published in German, English and French: it expressed the first quiverings of a moral and intellectual rebellion against the complacency of contemporary society. Although the Cabaret Voltaire had to close down after only six months of existence, the Dadaist magazine managed to survive longer.

the surrounding country. Industrial suburbs subsequently developed along the lines of communication and today Zurich is the economic capital of the Confederation.

Old Town★★

🗣 *Guided tours of the town – (2hr) with commentary in English or German from Nov-Apr, Wed and Sat at 11am; May and Jun, Sat-Sun at 11am and 3pm; Jul and Aug, Mon-Wed at 3pm and Thu-Sun at 11am and 3pm; Sep and Oct, Mon-Fri at 3pm and Sat-Sun at 11am and 3pm.* 🗐 *For further information, contact the tourist office in the railway station on ☎ (044) 215 40 00.*

West Bank of the Limmat

Bahnhofstrasse★ (EYZ)
This fine avenue planted with lime trees (1.4km/0.8mi) is the busiest street in the city. It was built along the former site of the Fröschengraben (Frogs' Moat) and leads from the central station (Hauptbahnhof) to the shore of the lake. With its banks and insurance offices, department stores and luxury boutiques, this is the most important business centre in Switzerland.

▷ *Follow the avenue as far as Paradeplatz.*

Schanzengraben (EYZ)
A detour via the Bleicherweg leads to this old moat, one of the last remains of city's old fortifications, which runs from the railway station to the lake. Panels along the moat provide information on its history.

▷ *Take Poststrasse to **Münsterhof**, a charming square that is home to the Baroque Zur Meisen building (n° 20), which houses a small museum dedicated to Swiss porcelain (⚫ see Museums).*

Fraumünster (EZ)
🕐 *Open May-Sep, daily, 9am (11am Sun) to 6pm; Mar, Apr and Oct 10am (11am Sun) to 5pm; Nov-Feb, 10am (11am Sun) to 4pm.* ☎ (044) 211 41 00.
This church replaced a convent founded in 853 by Ludwig the German and his daughters Hildegard and Bertha, who were its first abbesses. The nuns who lived here came mainly from noble families from southern Germany. Construction of the imposing church began in 1250; the façade was restored in 1911 in neo-Gothic style. The chancel is Romanesque and the nave has pointed vaulting. Note the remarkable **stained-glass windows**★; those in the north transept are by Giacometti (*The Celestial Paradise*, 1947). The five windows in the chancel (1970) and south transept (1980) are by Marc Chagall and illustrate biblical scenes. On the south side of the church, remains of the Romanesque **cloisters**★ (Kreuzgang) are ornamented with frescoes by Paul Bodmer (1920-41) representing the legend of the foundation of the abbey.

St-Peterkirche (EZ)
The origins of this church, the oldest in Zurich, date back to the 7C. The largest clock face in Europe (8.70m/28ft in diameter), built in 1534, adorns the 13C bell tower.

Weinplatz (EZ)
South of the square, adorned with a pretty fountain surmounted by a wine-grower carrying his basket, you will find, on the opposite side, some fine old houses with Flemish roofs, the town hall (Rathaus – FZ H) – a neo-Gothic building dating from 1900 – and the Wasserkirche (FZ), a recently restored 15C chapel. The cathedral (Grossmünster) dominates the whole with its two tall towers.

Address Book

GETTING AROUND

PUBLIC TRANSPORT

It is both difficult and expensive to park in the city centre. However, there is an excellent public transport network of trams, buses, metro (the S-Bahn), boats and trains, which operates downtown and to the suburbs. Unlimited day passes can be bought from the tourist office, railway station and from automatic ticket machines. Other passes combine public transport with museum entry or excursions.

BICYCLES

The city is well equipped with cycle lanes. In summer, bicycles can be borrowed free of charge (deposit and passport required) from Bahnhofstrasse near the station, Marktplatz, Oelikon and Altstetten.

SHOPPING

Bahnhofstrasse is Zurich's main shopping street. It is lined by smart boutiques with attractive window displays and is home to several **department stores,** such as Globus, Vilan, Jelmoli and Sankt Annahof. Interesting shops selling designer items, wooden toys and confectionery can be found in the **old city,** along the narrow streets surrounding Weinplatz on the left bank and in the district around Niederdorfstrasse on the right bank.

Flea market – *On Bürkliplatz,* ⏱ *Sat from May-Oct, 6am-3.30pm.*

SOUVENIRS

The long-established confectioner's **Sprüngli** (Bahnhofstrasse 21) sells all kinds of truffles and chocolates, including Luxemburgerli, a local speciality. **Schweizer Heimatwerk** (Rudolf Brun-Brücke) is part of a chain of shops selling typical Swiss souvenirs, including designer items, toys and children's clothes inspired by traditional costumes. The **Pastorini** toy shop (Weinplatz 3) in the old town specialises in wooden toys.

THEATRE AND MUSIC

Opernhaus – *Falkenstrasse 1* – ☎ *(044) 268 66 66, www.opernhaus.ch* Richard Wagner once conducted in this neo-Baroque opera house (1891).

Tonhalle – *Gotthardstrasse 5 and Claridenstrasse 7* – ☎ *(044) 206 34 34, www.tonhalle.ch* - Built in 1895, this large hall was inaugurated by Johannes Brahms.

Schauspielhaus – *Rämistrasse 34* – ☎ *(044) 258 77 77, www.schauspielhaus.ch* - This theatre (1884) is renowned for excellent music and drama programmes.

Bernhard-Theater – *Theaterplatz* – ☎ *(044) 268 66 66, www.bernhard-theater.ch*

Theater Stock – *Hirschengraben 42* – ☎ *(044) 251 22 80.*

STAYING IN ZÜRICH

Affectionately nicknamed the "little big city", Zurich can be expensive. During the high season, allow at least 160CHF for a double room, including breakfast. For the younger generation, there is a **youth hostel** at *Mutschellenstrasse 114,* ☎ *01 482 35 44.* The **Seebucht campsite** is at *Seestrasse 559, on the west bank of the lake;* ☎ *044 482 16 12.*

🕯 *For coin ranges, see the Legend on the cover flap.*

◗◗◗ **Ibis** – *Zurichstrasse 105* – ☎ *(044) 711 85 85 – www.biscayne.ch* – *73 rooms* – Situated 9km/5.6mi from the town centre. A modern and pleasant setting and reasonable prices.

◗◗◗ **Landhus** – *Katzenbachstrasse 10 – Zurich-Seebach* – ☎ *(044) 308 34 00* – *www.landhus-zuerich.ch – 28 rooms* This recently renovated hotel has English-style decor and comfortable rooms.

◗◗◗ **Leoneck** – *Leonhardstrasse 1* – ☎ *044 254 22 22 – www.leoneck.ch – 78 rooms* – This hotel features an unusual interior which revolves around the world of cows! The whole decoration, including frescoes, depict these large, friendly creatures. Conveniently located a few minutes from the old city. No parking facilities.

◗◗◗◗ **Adler** – *Rosengasse 10, am Hirschplatz* – ☎ *(044) 266 96 96 – www.hotel-adler.ch – 52 rooms* – Situated in a lively district (soundproof windows keep out the noise), an this old-fashioned hotel with a charming bohemian touch, displays works of Basel artist Heintz Hum, along with frescoes illustrating the city's main sights. Restaurant serves traditional cuisine (fondues, raclettes).

Rex – *Weinbergstrasse 92 – ☎ (044) 360 25 25 – 37 rooms* ℗ Modern, comfortable hotel near the town centre.

Alpenblick – *Bergstrasse 322, in Ütikon am See – ☎ (044) 920 47 22 –www.landhotelalpenblick.ch - 12 rooms – ⏰ closed Jan.* A rustic setting and a terrace overlooking the lake and surrounding mountains, 20min from Zurich. Peace and quiet guaranteed.

Uto Kulm – *Giusep Fry, in Ütliberg – ☎ (044) 457 66 66 – www.utokulm. ch – 55 rooms* – Perched above Zurich, this hotel has a superb view of the city below. Perfect for a restful break in the countryside.

Sorell Hotel Zürichberg – *Orellistrasse 21 – ☎ (044) 268 35 35 – www.zuerichberg.ch – 66 rooms* – Nestling in the forest not far from the lake, a few minutes from Zurich by tramway, this hotel has a terrace offering lovely city views. The combination of modern and traditional styles creates an unusual atmosphere.

EATING OUT

Zunfthaus zur Schmiden – *Marktgasse 20 – ☎ (044) 251 52 87 - www.zunfthausschmiden.ch – ⏰ closed mid-Jul to mid-Aug, public hols, and Sat-Sun.* This former blacksmiths' guildhall in the old quarter presents a fine 15C Gothic dining hall and an attractive coffered ceiling. Excellent cuisine.

Kronenhalle – *Rämistrasse 4 – ☎ (044) 262 99 00 – www.kronenhalle. com* - Typical brasserie with an artistic ambience, displaying works by contemporary painters. Charming bar and restaurant serving local fare and wide selection of wines and beers.

Haus zum Rüden – *Limmatquai 42 (1st floor) – ☎ (044) 261 95 66; www. hauszumrueden.ch – ⏰ closed Sat and Sun.* This former guildhall from the 13C features a remarkable dining room with

groined vaulting, which adds charm and atmosphere to the restaurant.

Königstuhl – *Stüssihofstatt 3 – ☎ (044) 261 76 18* –This restaurant in the old city offers a sophisticated 14C setting decorated in bright shades of red and blue.

Zunfthaus zur Zimmerleuten – *Limmatquai 40 (1st floor) – ☎ (044) 250 53 63 – www.zimmerleuten.ch – ⏰ closed public hols andmid-Jul to mid-Aug.* Charming 18C guild-house. Choose from from a rustic, cosy setting with wooden beams, a charming, light room for romantic dinners and a scenic restaurant overlooking the Limmat.

Untere Flühgass – *Zollikertstrasse 214 – ☎ (044) 381 12 15 – ⏰ closed Sat (except Nov and Dec), Sun, mid-Dec-2 Jan and mid-Jul to mid-Aug.* Rustic decor and friendly welcome.

Riesbächli – *Zollikerstrasse 157 – ☎ (044) 422 23 24 – ⏰ closed Sat (except evenings Nov-Mar), Sun, 23 Dec-2 Jan and 27 Jul-18 Aug.* Small, typical café with an impressive wine list.

Zeughauskeller – *Bahnhofstrasse 28A – ☎ (044) 211 26 90 – www. zeughauskeller.ch – ⏰ closed public hols.* Generous portions of regional cuisine served in a former 15C arms depot. Art Nouveau decor and shaded terrace in summer.

Öpfelchammere – *Rindermarkt 12 – ☎ 01 251 23 36 – ⏰ closed 24 Dec-8 Jan and mid-Jul-mid-Aug.* This is Zurich's oldest tavern, dating back to the 13C. The old-fashioned setting, medieval rafters and traditional furniture make for a delightful dining experience.

Bierhalle Kropf – *In Gassen 16 – ☎ (044) 221 18 05 – ⏰ closed Sun and public hols.* A stone's throw from the Fraumünster, this large tavern dating from 1888 has three Art Nouveau beer halls, whose ceilings are decorated with frescoes. Generous portions.

Wirtschaft zur Höhe – *Höherstrasse 73, in Zollikon, 4km/2.5mi from Zurich – ☎ (044) 391 59 59 – ⏰ closed Mon, mid-Feb and mid-Oct.* Regional dishes in a traditional Swiss farmhouse. Pleasant terrace, charming setting.

Chez Crettol, Cave valaisanne – *Florarstrasse 22, in Küsnacht, 8km/5mi from Zurich –* ☎ *044 910 03 15* – ⏱ *closed 22 Dec-7 Jan, in Jul and Aug, and Wed from Apr-Jun and Sep-Oct.* A great place for fondue and raclette!

NIGHTLIFE

The **Jules Verne bar** at the Brasserie Lipp (Uraniastrasse 9) offers a fine selection of cocktails and affords a lovely view of the city. Computer buffs can meet up and spend an evening in front of the screens of the **Internet Café** (Uraniastrasse 3) nearby.

Enjoy the cosy, intimate atmosphere of the **Hôtel Central Plaza,** not far from Bahnhofbrücke.

The old city (right bank) has many cafés and restaurants with sunny terraces.

Sample a *"déci"* (short for décilitre) of Swiss wine in the pleasant setting of the **La Barrique** (Marktgasse 17) and round off the evening by listening to some good jazz performed by the orchestra of the **Casa Bar** (Münstergasse).

The **Splendid Bar** (Rosengasse 5) is a lively piano bar favouring jazz and golden oldies by the Beatles and other groups, where clients can join in around the piano. The **Kronenhalle** (Rämistrasse), opened in 1863, is a sophisticated, luxury establishment where you can settle in a comfortable armchair and feast your eyes on paintings by Chagall, Picasso, Miró, Kandinsky, Klee and Giacometti.

The famous **Café Odéon** (Limmatquai 2) with Art Nouveau decor was once frequented by writers and famous personalities such as Thomas Mann and Lenin. Along the same quay the **Café Select** (Limmatquai 16) is a good address for billiard players. Finally, for a British ambience and a wide selection of beers, go to the **Lion's Pub** (Ötenbachgasse, left bank).

Rote Fabrik – *Seestrasse 395 –* ☎ *(044) 481 91 43, www.rotefabrik.ch . Bus 161 or 165 from Bürkliplatz.* This old factory, housing the Ziegel oh Lac bistro and a huge concert hall, is popular with Zurich's young crowd. Nightclub and concerts several times a week.

BATHS ALONG THE LIMMAT

These traditional, old-fashioned baths are situated along the banks of the Limmat.

Stadthausquai (EZ) – ☎ *(044) 211 95 92., www.badi-info.ch.* These baths, located close to Zurich's city hall, are for women only and include a solarium. Concerts and DJ-hosted events open to all are held here in the evening.

Schanzengraben (off the map by **EY**) – ☎ *(044) 211 95 94.* Also in the city centre, near the Selnaubrücke and the stock exchange, these baths are for men only.

Flussbad Oberer Letten (off the map by **EY**) – *Pier West, Lettensteg 10* – ☎ *(044) 362 92 00.* Take Limmatstrasse behind the railway station, then turn right towards Sihlquai. These baths, situated in the Letten district, are the oldest in the city. Open to men, women and children.

EVENTS

During the **Sechseläuten** spring festival, usually held on the third Monday in April, the various corporations of Zurich march through the city centre in traditional costume. The city's symbol of winter, the **Böögg**, a snowman made from cotton wool and filled with fireworks, is burned at 6pm on Sechseläutenplatz, at Bellevue.

The **Knabenschiessen**, a shooting competition for children aged between 12 and 16, is one of the oldest festivals in Zurich. It is held on the Albisgütli (last stop on tram n° 13) on the second weekend in September.

The **Züri-Fäscht**, a large fair held along the banks of the River Limmat in the old town, takes place every three years, from the end of June to the beginning of July, and includes firework displays along the lake. The next Züri-Fäscht is in 2007.

Schipfe (EZ)

This is the heart of the old town, with narrow, medieval streets running down to the Limmat. Some houses here have roof gardens. Take a detour into Augustinerstrasse, where some of the houses are adorned with oriel windows – a rare sight in Zurich.

Lindenhof (EZ)

This esplanade, shaded by 90 lime trees and adorned with a fountain, marks the summit of a hill. This strategic location guarded the crossing of the Limmat and was the site of the Celtic and Roman settlements from which Zurich sprang. Note the giant chessboard on the esplanade. From the edge of the terrace you will see the old quarters of the town rising in tiers on the east bank. The Predigerkirche stands opposite; to the right is the Grossmünster.

Jules Verne Bar Panorama (EY L)

Access from the Brasserie Lipp, Uraniastrasse 9. 🕐 *Open all year, Mon-Thu 11.30am-midnight, Fri-Sat 11.30am-1am, Sun 3pm-midnight; Jul and Aug, Mon-Thu 4pm-midnight, Fri-Sat 4pm-1am,* 🕐 *closed Sun.* ☎ *(044) 211 11 55.*
This bar commands a lovely view of the town centre.

East Bank of the Limmat

Niederdorfstrasse (FYZ)

This partially pedestrianised street crossing the Niederdorf district is particularly lively at night, with a good choice of cafés and restaurants. The street is lined with beautiful old houses that bear witness to the past wealth of Zurich's old corporations.

Grossmünster★ (FZ)

🕐 *Open daily mid-Mar to Oct, 9am-6pm; Nov to mid-Mar, 10am-5pm. Ascent of the tower: Mar-Oct, daily 9.15am-5pm; Nov-Mar, Sat-Sun, 1.30-5pm.* 👓 *2CHF for the ascent of the tower. Visit of the cloisters Mon-Fri, 9am-4.30pm.* ☎ *(044) 252 59 49.*
This impressive cathedral, erected between the 11C and the 13C, replaced a collegiate church said to have been founded by Charlemagne, and is a symbol of the Reformation for German-speaking Swiss. Zwingli preached here from 1519 until he died. Its façade is flanked by three-storey towers surmounted by wooden domes faced with metal plates. The south tower is crowned by a colossal statue (the original is in the crypt) of Charlemagne seated with a sword across his knees. The bronze doors were sculpted by Otto Münch between 1935 and 1950. The nave has pointed vaulting; the

Bill Wassman/ APA Publications

Views to Fraumünster and St-Peterkirche

raised chancel ends in a flat chevet, and a gallery runs above the aisles. Traces of frescoes may be seen in the chancel and the crypt with its characteristic triple nave. The modern stained-glass windows are by Augusto Giacometti (1932). The Romanesque **cloisters** are decorated with groin vaulting. Groups of three arcades, their rounded arches are supported by finely sculpted capitals, open onto a courtyard.

Riverside and Lakeside Walks★★

This walk starts along the banks of the Limmat, near Quaibrücke (EFZ) which links Bürkliplatz and Bellevueplatz and marks the beginning of Lake Zurich (Zürichsee). Continue the walk along the quays, along which beautifully maintained gardens are dotted with flower beds and several species of trees.

West Bank from Bürkliplatz

Bürkliplatz (EZ)
The landing-stages in Bürkliplatz are always busy with sailing and motor boats, some of which offer boat trips on the lake (*see Boat trips*). Heading farther along the **Mythenquai** the **views**★ of the lake and the Alps (with the Oberland Massif in the far distance) become more open.

Rote Fabrik (off the map by EZ)
Seestrasse 395. This old brick factory is now a popular student haunt, housing artists' studios, the Shedhalle gallery and a large concert hall (*see Address Book*).

East Bank from Bellevueplatz

▶ *Take Utoquai, then Seefeldquai. Tram n° 2 or 4, Fröhlisstrasse.*

Zürichhorn Gardens
By Utoquai (FZ).
There is an excellent **view**★ of the town from the Zürichhorn Gardens, where a mobile (*Heureka*, 1964) by the Swiss sculptor Jean Tinguely is on permanent display.

Le Corbusier Haus (off the map by FZ)
Beyond Höschgasse.
Immediately identifiable by its large white panels and bright colours, this was Le Corbusier's last work. Also known as **Heidi Weber's house**, it contains designs created by the architect.

Chinese Garden (off the map by FZ)
This park, opened in 1993, was given to Zurich by its twin town, Kunming. Hidden behind the heavy red gates – in central China red is the colour of the emperor – is a perfectly kept garden, where the theme "three friends in winter" is illustrated by pines, bamboo and winter cherry trees. Canals criss-crossed by small bridges run through the gardens, which are dotted with gingko trees and bamboo.

Museums

West Bank of the Limmat

Schweizerisches Landesmuseum★★★ (EY)
Behind the main railway station. 🕐 *Open daily except Mon, 10am-5pm.* 5CHF, *no charge last Sun in the month.* ☎ *(044) 218 65 11.*

This neo-Gothic fortress-like building (1898) houses the magnificent collections of the **Swiss National Museum,** with exhibits on all aspects of Switzerland's artistic and cultural heritage.

Ground floor - Dedicated to **archaeology.** The section from 100 000 BC to AD 800 includes a reconstruction of a mammoth and presents exhibits (tools, iron and bronze work, tombs, amphorae, jewellery etc) by topic rather than by period. Themes include land and life, raw materials and finished products, gestures and techniques, searching for food, and worship and beliefs. Of particular interest is the model of the lake village of Egolzwill (4th millennium BC). Another wing houses exhibits from the Middle Ages and the modern era: Romanesque era religious objets d'art, such as the unusual **Christ with Palms** on a donkey with wheels, and ivory tablets that once adorned Carolingian bindings. The late-Gothic period is represented by stained glass, paintings on panels (view of Zurich, 1500) and polychrome sculptures, such as the king made from walnut wood (c 1320) with slanting eyes and wavy hair, similar in style to images found in illuminated manuscripts. Note also the ceramic stove decorated with a bearded man dressed in animal skins, representing the forest (1440); the popularity of these stoves during this period was helped by the development of urban life.

A parchment (4m/13ft) decorated with 559 coats of arms and 18 banners (1340) evokes the chivalry of the 14C. Other interesting exhibits include a reconstruction of a typical Schwyz chapel (1518), with stained glass windows and ribbed vaulting; the **Mellingen council room** (1467); and three **rooms from Fraumünster abbey**, decorated in wood from top to bottom and adorned with friezes and rich metal fittings. The Renaissance style of the Reformation is represented by domestic items such as sculpted furniture and local embroidered linen (1561).

First floor – The huge gilded celestial globe with four images of Hermes symbolising the ages of man, made by the Swiss astronomer Jost Bürgi (1594), and the fine reconstructions of **interiors from 1600**, including the ceremonial room of the Werdmüller brothers, founders of the silk industry in Zurich. The 16C and 17C "stained-glass window cabinets" are decorated with coats of arms and biblical scenes. Dating from the same period, a profusion of silverware (cups, hanaps with lids etc) demonstrates the wealth of the city's corporations. Among the 17C and 18C furniture, note the wardrobe decorated with Mannerist low reliefs. The Baroque room from the "Zum langen Stadelhof" house, with its gallery of famous men, commemorates Swiss soldiers who fought for foreign armies (c 1660). Also noteworthy are ceramics from Winterthur, the leading faience city in the country.

Second and Third Floors and Basement – A collection of clothes and toys (including miniature toys) from the late 18C and early 19C. The headdress made of black silk ribbons is typical of the Zurich area and was worn around 1770. The **rural costumes** on display are particularly varied: the best known is the shepherd's costume from the Appenzell, which is red and yellow and decorated with cow motifs. Reconstructions of 19C artisan workshops (cooper, blacksmith and wheelwright). Also exhibited here is the detailed **model of the battle of Murten**, won by the Confederates against Charles the Bold in 1476.

Museum für Gestaltung Zürich

Access by Sihlquai (EY). ⏱ *Open daily Tue-Thu, 10am-8pm; Fri, Sat, Sun, 10am-5pm, poster collection Tue-Fri, 1-5pm; guided tour every Tue at 6.30pm.* 🎫 *9CHF for the hall, 7CHF for the gallery, combined ticket: 12CHF.* ☎ *(044) 446 67 67.*
Temporary exhibitions, based on themes derived from the applied arts, architecture, graphic art and industrial design from 1900 onwards, are held in these galleries. The museum also houses a collection of posters and graphic designs.

ZÜRICH

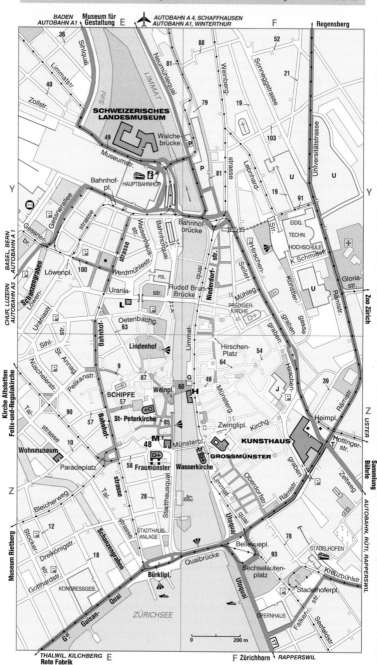

Rindermarkt	FZ 64	Strehlgasse	EZ 87	Uraniastrasse	EYZ
Stadelhoferstrasse	FZ 78	Sumatrastrasse	FY 88	Usteristrasse	EY 100
Stampfenbachplatz	FY 79	Talacker	EZ 90	Weinbergfussweg	FY 103
Stampfenbachstrasse	EFY 81	Tannenstrasse	FY 91		
Storchengasse	EZ 85	Theaterstrasse	FZ 93		

Haus "Zur Meisen"	EZ M¹	Panorama Bar Jules Verne EY	L	Rathaus	FZ H

Zunfthaus "Zur Meisen" (EZ M¹)

Between Münsterhof and Limmat.

This corporate building dates from 1757 and is adorned with a fine wrought-iron balcony. It contains the collections of 18C ceramics (faience and porcelain) belonging to the Schweizerisches Landesmuseum *(see above).* The ceramics are displayed in two Rococo-style rooms on the first floor. Originally, faience was imported from towns such as Strasbourg and Lunéville, but eventually workshops were opened in Zurich and Nyon. Most of the pieces exhibited here are decorated with chinoiserie, although several wild boar hunting scenes are also depicted. A fine dinner service dating from 1775 is decorated with a profusion of chubby cherubs.

Wohnmuseum (EZ)

Open daily except Mon, 10.30am-5pm. Closed some public hols. 8CHF. (044) 211 17 16.

This museum is located in two adjoining houses (late 17C – heavily restored). It presents on three floors *(lift)* many examples of furniture, stoves and utensils etc covering the mid-17C to the mid-19C. In the basement is a collection of dolls created by a local artist in the 1920s.

Rietbergmuseum★★

Gablerstasse 15. Access by Bleicherweg (off the map by EZ). Open daily except Mon, 10am-5pm (8pm Wed). Closed most public hols. 6CHF (permanent collections), 12CHF (temporary exhibitions). (044) 206 31 31.

This museum is set up in the former Wesendonck and Rieter Villas in the middle of a park and in view of the lake. It contains the valuable collections formed by Baron von der Heydt: statues from India, Cambodia, Java, China, Africa and the South Sea Islands. The collections of Japanese prints by Willy Boller and Julius Mueller, works of art from the Near East, Tibet and pre-Columbian America, paintings from the Far East, a collection of Swiss masks and some Flemish and Armenian carpets complete the exhibition.

East Bank of the Limmat

Kunsthaus★★ (FZ)

Open daily except Mon, 10am-5pm (9pm Tue-Thu). Closed some public hols. 16CHF (permanent collections), no charge Wed for temporary exhibitions. (044) 253 84 84.

The **Fine Arts Museum** gives a prominent place to modern painting. There are also displays of sculpture from the early French and German Middle Ages and Swiss and German primitives of the 15C.

On the first floor are the most representative canvases of Ferdinand Hodler, considered to be the leading Swiss painter of the early 20C, and pictures by Vallotton, Böcklin, Anker, Auberjonois and Barraud. The French School is represented by works by Delacroix, Toulouse-Lautrec, Cézanne, Renoir, Degas, Matisse, Utrillo, Léger, Braque and Picasso. One room contains 14 works by Marc Chagall. The museum also houses the largest collection outside Scandinavia of the work of Edvard Munch, as well as Dada works by Man Ray and Hans Arp. Finally the Alberto Giacometti Foundation has on view a considerable collection of the artist's works (1901-66).

Sammlung Bührle★★

Access by Zeltweg (FZ). 🕐 *Open Tue, Wed, Fri and Sun 2-5pm.* 🕐 *Closed most public hols.* ➔9CHF. ☎ *(044) 422 00 86.*

This villa, set in the lovely southeast suburb, houses one of the most important private art collections in Switzerland: works of art (paintings and sculpture) collected by Emil Bührle between 1934 and 1956. A fervent admirer of Claude Monet, this German industrialist, who moved to Zurich in 1924, succeeded in barely 20 years in bringing together a superb collection of some 300 paintings, mainly 19C French works.

Ground floor – Four rooms are devoted to works from the 16C to the 19C: the landing and the Dutch Gallery present Hals *(Portrait of a Man)*, Rembrandt, Van Ruysdael *(View of Rhenen)* and Teniers; works on display in the Louis XVI Salon include paintings by Boucher, Degas *(Portrait of Mme Camus*, flanked by two sketches), Fragonard and Ingres *(Portrait of M. Devillers)*; the Venetian Salon exhibits works by Canaletto (two variations on the Grand Canal taken from a series of six), Goya *(Procession in Valencia)*, El Greco and Tiepolo *(Diane Bathing)*.

The Pink Salon and the Music Chamber contain important Impresssionist works: *Sunflowers on an Armchair* by Gauguin, *The Road to Versailles at Louveciennes* by Pissarro or Manet's *The Swallows*, painted at Berck-sur-Mer in 1873. The charming portrait *Little Irène* was painted by Renoir just before he broke loose from the Impressionist movement. *The Poppies near Vétheuil* is a lovely landscape by Monet where the characters, rendered by quick, soft strokes, seem to merge into the background. *Messalina* by Toulouse-Lautrec was to influence the Fauves by its luminous colour. Note the fine series of three portraits by Cézanne, including *The Boy in the Red Waistcoat* and his nostalgic gaze. Finally, the dazzling *Chestnut Tree in Blossom*, reflecting the influence of Japanese art, painted by Vincent van Gogh during one of his rare bouts of optimism.

Staircase and First Floor – Seven Delacroix paintings *(Self-Portrait)* and canvases by Courbet and Dufy laid out along the first flight of steps are followed by another series by Chagall, Picasso, Rouault and a *Recumbent Nude* by Modigliani. The landing is devoted to the 20C with Cubist works by Braque *(The Violinist)*, Picasso and Gris, and several Fauvist pictures by Derain, Marquet, Matisse (note the change in technique between *The Pont St-Michel in Paris* and *Still Life*, executed five years later) and Vlaminck *(Barges on the Seine near Le Pecq)*. The Courbet Gallery shows Realist works such as *Free Performance* by Daumier and *Portrait of A Sisley* by Renoir. An adjoining room set aside for Renoir also features the splendid *Garden at Giverny* by Monet and *Sailing Boats* by Boudin. In the Manet Gallery are *La Sultane*, *Pond with Water-Lilies* and *Waterloo Bridge* by Monet, alongside one of the 22 original bronzes of *The Dancer* by Degas. The last three rooms concentrate on Vincent van Gogh *(Self-Portrait* and *The Sower)*, Sisley *(Summer in Bougival)* and Bonnard *(Portrait of Ambroise Vollard,* clearly a tribute to Cézanne). Also of interest are *The Offering* by Gauguin (painted on the Marquise Islands shortly before he died), *The Milliners* by Paul Signac and *Salon Natanson* (the meeting-place of the Nabis) signed by E Vuillard. The Gothic Gallery (note two landscapes by Patenier) and the second floor house a set of fine religious sculptures (12C-16C).

Additional Sights

Felix-und-Regulakirche★

Access by Talacker, west of the plan (EZ). 🕐 *Open Mon-Fri, 9-11.30am and 1.30-4.30pm.* ☎ *(044) 405 29 79.*

This modern church is dedicated to St Felix and St Regula, siblings who, according to tradition, suffered martyrdom at Zurich, beheaded on the orders of Decius. The tall bell tower is detached from the rest of the building. The interior is unusual: the oblong church, shaped like an almond, is roofed with a barely curved vault supported by sloping pillars. Stained-glass windows near the vault are modern.

Mühlerama

Access by Kreuzbühlstrasse, east of the plan (FZ). 🕐 *Open Tue-Sat, 10am-5pm; Sun, 1.30-6pm.* 👛 *7CHF.* ☎ *(044) 422 76 60; www.muehlerama.ch.*

This Belle Époque-style flour mill, built in 1913 on the foundations of an old brewery, was in operation until 1983 and now houses a museum with functioning milling machines, allowing visitors to learn about the production of flour. Sections within the exhibition cover the development of milling techniques, from crushing grain by foot to the use of watermills; the role of the miller in history; bread in popular culture; and the themes of abundance and famine. The ramp which was once used to roll down sacks of flour is now a slide for children. Flour can be bought from the museum, which produces 60t a year. The building also contains a restaurant, theatre, gallery, workshops and several small shops.

Zoo Zürich★

Kids *Access by Gloriastrasse (FY).* ♿🕐 *Open 9am-6pm (5pm Nov-Feb).* 👛 *22CHF.* ☎ *(044) 254 25 05/25 31; www.zoo.ch*

Nicely laid out at Zürichberg, in a very pretty, leafy setting, this zoo houses more than 2 000 animals. Giant tortoises, an otter and a beaver can be seen playing in the water and on land. Just as fascinating are the monkeys and the elephants' bath *(around 10am)*. A board at the main entrance announces the zoo's recent births.

Botanischer Garten

Access by Kreuzbühlstrasse, east of the plan (FZ)

The botanical gardens comprise three huge plexiglass domes and are planted with tropical forest vegetation, as well as species from the Alps and the Mediterranean.

Ref. Kirche von Zürich-Altstetten

Access by Talacker, west of the plan (EZ).

This modern church is dominated by a tall, graceful, open-work square tower. The nave is asymmetrical and lit by high windows on one side.

Boat Trips on Lake Zurich

ℹ️ *Information from the tourist office or at the main landing-stage at Bürkliplatz, near Bellevue (EZ). Tram nᵒˢ 2, 5, 8, 9 and 11 run to the landing-stage. Boat trips from March to October. Trips last from 1hr to 5hr; meals are served on board from Apr-Oct. To reserve, call ☎ (044) 487 13 13.*

Boat trips run along the Limmat *(1hr 30min),* from the Schweizerisches Landesmuseum as far as the Zürichhorn. Large boats operate trips on the lake, including a short trip *(1hr 30min),* stopping at Erlenbach and Thalwil, and a longer half-day excursion on a steamboat, stopping at Rapperswil *(see RAPPERSWIL)* and Schmerikon, at the other end of the lake.

Excursions

Uetliberg and Felsenegg★★

Access by train: 20min on line nᵒ 10 from Zurich station, platform 2; departures every 30min. 👛 *14.40CHF. A map is available from the tourist office.*

The **Uetliberg** (alt 871m/2 856ft) is a favourite day trip for locals. The railway journey is mainly through woods. From the arrival station (no cars), there is a fine view of the snowy summits of the Alps. Take the steep path to the nearby terrace of the Gmüetliberg restaurant *(viewing table)*.

You can go to the top of the belvedere tower *(167 steps)* for a sweeping **panorama**★★ of the whole Zurich district, the Limmat Valley, Lake Zurich and the Alpine range – from Säntis in the east to the Jungfrau and Les Diablerets in the southwest. The ridges of the Jura and the Vosges are faintly visible to the west and northwest on the horizon. From here, it is possible to follow the ridge to Felsenegg (alt 804m/2 637ft; a walk of approximately 1hr 45min). A "planet path" (Planetenweg) features models of the planets on a scale of 1:1 billion. At Felsenegg, a cable car climbs to Adliswil *(return to Zurich by train, line n° 4)*.

Albis Pass Road★

53km/33mi. Leave Zurich southwest via Gessnerallee (EY) and then road n° 4.

The road follows the Sihl Valley between the slopes of Uetliberg *(right)* and Lake Zurich (left), in front of which stretches the motorway and a string of towns. At Adliswil leave road n° 4 and bear right on the road to Albis which crosses the Sihl Forest.

Wildpark Langenberg

This wildlife park (European species) extends on either side of the road (mostly on the left side) north of Langnau am Albis on a couple of acres of forest and rocky hillocks: deer, chamois, marmots, wild boar can be seen. The road climbs to the Albis Pass (alt 791m/2 596ft) from where magnificent views extend over the undulating countryside; then it descends between Lake Turler and the Albis Mountain before turning left in the direction of Hausen at the foot of the Albishorn.

Former Abbey of Kappel★ – *See ZUG: Excursions.*

▶ *From Kappel descend to the left and bear left again to pick up road n° 4 to Hirzel, then bear right towards Schönenberg.*

Some time after Hütten, there is a stretch of corniche *(2km/1mi)* which overlooks the widest part of Lake Zurich. The road then rises as far as Feusisberg in charming countryside enhanced by glimpses of the lake; during the downhill stretch the two wooded islets of the lake can be seen.

After a winding section of road through woods, there is a plunging **view**★ which reveals both sections of the lake (Obersee on the right) which the Rapperswil causeway divides.

Rapperswil★ – *See RAPPERSWIL.*

Alpamare at Pfäffikon

34km/21mi SE by the A 3; take the Seedamm Center exit. ◷ *Open 10am (9am Sat-Sun and public hols) to 12am (midnight Fri and Sat).* ◿34CHF *(37CHF Sat-Sun and public hols) for 4hr, (31CHF Sat-Sun and public hols).* ☎ *(055) 415 15 19.*

Situated on the south bank of Lake Zurich, this water park has the longest water slide in Europe (261m/287yd), with fast-running water and a number of rapids. Other facilities include hot (36°C/97°F) and cold pools, a swimming pool with a wave machine, jacuzzis, a sauna and a solarium.

Regensberg

*Alt 617m/2 024ft. 17km/10mi. Leave Zurich by Universitätstrasse (**FY**) and then turn left immediately into the road to Dielsdorf. Turn left in the village to take a little road to Regensberg.*

Regensberg, a small vine-growing village with a perfectly preserved atmosphere and old, half-timbered houses standing one beside the other all around its single

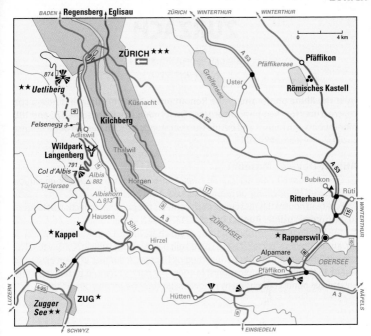

square, is a charming and picturesque place to stop. There is an extensive **view** of the vineyards and the local countryside from the Romanesque watchtower.

From Zurich to Eglisau

▶ *23km/14mi. Leave Zurich by Universitätstrasse (**FY**) and road n° 4. 5km/3mi after Kloten at the north exit of Seeb-Winkel, bear left on a small road which leads (0.5km/0.3mi) to the Roman ruins.*

Römischer Gutshof Seeb

In a pleasant site, with wide views *(viewing tables)* of the plain and neighbouring heights, are scattered the remains of a farm dating to the 1C which was enlarged until the 3C and then destroyed and abandoned. The foundations of the west wing of the villa are under shelter. The pile of bricks of the hypocaust and part of the baths, an attractive black and white mosaic, a model of the farm and a display case of pottery (found here) are exhibited. Outside, the remains of the watertower can be seen as well as a kiln and a piscina with a central well (6m/19.5ft deep).

Eglisau

This picturesque old town near the German border, is located in a charming **site**★, terraced amid trees and vines on the north bank of the Rhine. Above the domed church (transformed 18C) a shaded belvedere-terrace, with a bronze statue of a young woman, offers a lovely view of the river.

Kilchberg

*7km/4mi. Leave Zurich by General Guisan-Quai (**EZ**).*
Road n° 3 runs along the west shore of the lake to Kilchberg, a suburb of Zurich. Swiss poet Conrad Ferdinand Meyer (1825-98) and German writer Thomas Mann (1875-1955) spent their last days in this area and are buried in the small cemetery.

ZURZACH

AARGAU – POPULATION 3 859
ALT 339M/1 129FT

Near the Rhine on the site of the Roman town, Tenedo, Zurzach is now a spa centre (cures for rheumatic disorders). On its main street are some 17C and 18C monuments and houses and beside the river stands a 19C château. ▯ *Quellenstrasse 1 – 8437 – ☎ (056) 249 24 00.*

August-Deusser-Museum

♿ ◷ *Open daily 1-6pm.* ◷ *Closed 1 Jan, Easter Thu, Fri and Sat, 24 Dec and in Jan and Jul.* ⊚*6CHF, no charge on preview days.* ☎ *(056) 249 20 50.*

The château houses this museum, which contains the personal collection belonging to the Germain painter **August Deusser** (1870-1942) as well as his own works of art. On the first floor are furnishings (some of which are in the Louis XVI style), works of art, an 18C Chinese low relief and a carved gilt bed made for Ludwig II of Bavaria. The second floor presents works bequeathed by Deusser. A number of them evoke the war of 1870 and seem Impressionist in style. The park, enhanced by fine trees and an artificial pond, contains many modern sculptures by Johann Ulrich Steiger.

INDEX

INDEX

INDEX

INDEX

INDEX

INDEX

INDEX

ACCOMMODATIONS

RESTAURANTS

INDEX

MAPS AND PLANS

LIST OF MAPS

COMPANION PUBLICATIONS

MICHELIN MAP 729 SUISSE

- a practical map on a scale of 1:400 000 which includes an index of towns and shows the major roads subject to snow cover.

MICHELIN ATLAS EUROPE

- Main road atlas with a full index. 1:1 000 000 scale map of Western Europe and 1:1 000 000 scale map of Eastern Europe. 74 town and city plans.
- 1136 Small Spiral
- 1129 Large Spiral
- 1135 Paperback
- 1133 Hardback

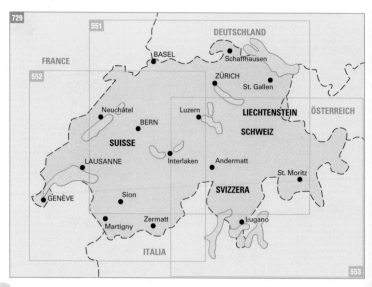

Legend

	Sight	Seaside Resort	Winter Sports Resort	Spa
Highly recommended	★★★	≋≋≋	❋❋❋	⊹⊹⊹
Recommended	★★	≋≋	❋❋	⊹⊹
Interesting	★	≋	❋	⊹

Tourism

◉⇨	Sightseeing route with departure point indicated	AZ B	Map co-ordinates locating sights
🛆🛆🛆	Ecclesiastical building	🛈	Tourist information
🔲 🛆	Synagogue – Mosque	⚊ ⋰	Historic house, castle – Ruins
▢	Building (with main entrance)	⌣ ☼	Dam – Factory or power station
■	Statue, small building	☆ ⋒	Fort – Cave
✝	Wayside cross	⊓	Prehistoric site
◎	Fountain	▼ ₩	Viewing table – View
●━■━▪━	Fortified walls – Tower – Gate	▲	Miscellaneous sight

Recreation

🏇	Racecourse	🚶	Waymarked footpath
⛸	Skating rink	◈	Outdoor leisure park/centre
≋ ▦	Outdoor, indoor swimming pool	🐎	Theme/Amusement park
⛵	Marina, moorings	🦌	Wildlife/Safari park, zoo
⛺	Mountain refuge hut	✹	Gardens, park, arboretum
▫━▪━▫	Overhead cable-car	◉	Aviary, bird sanctuary
🚂	Tourist or steam railway		

Additional symbols

═ ═	Motorway (unclassified)	⊗ ◎	Post office – Telephone centre
❶ ❶	Junction: complete, limited	✉	Covered market
⊏━━	Pedestrian street	⁕✕⁕	Barracks
ⲭ═══ⲭ	Unsuitable for traffic, street subject to restrictions	△	Swing bridge
▦▦ ┄┄	Steps – Footpath	⌣ ✕	Quarry – Mine
🚆 🚌	Railway – Coach station	⬛ ⬜	Ferry (river and lake crossings)
▫┼┼┼┼▫	Funicular – Rack-railway	⛴	Ferry services: Passengers and cars
━•━ ⦿	Tram – Metro, underground	⛴	Foot passengers only
Bert (R.)…	Main shopping street	③	Access route number common to MICHELIN maps and town plans

Abbreviations and special symbols

Ⓒ	Capital of a "Canton" (Kantonshauptort)	P	Offices of cantonal authorities (Kantonale Verwaltung)
G	Local police station (Kantonspolizei)	POL.	Police (Stadtpolizei)
H	Town hall (Rathaus)	T	Theatre (Theater)
J	Law courts (Justizpalast)	U	University (Universität)
M	Museum (Museum)	🅿	Park and Ride